PLUTARCH'S *SERTORIUS*

Plutarch's *Sertorius*

A HISTORICAL COMMENTARY

C. F. Konrad

The University of North Carolina Press

Chapel Hill and London

© 1994 The University of North Carolina Press
All rights reserved

The paper in this book meets the guidelines for permanence
and durability of the Committee on Production Guidelines
for Book Longevity of the Council on Library Resources.

Library of Congress Cataloging-in-Publication Data
Konrad, Christoph F.
Plutarch's Sertorius : a historical commentary /
by C. F. Konrad.
p. cm.
Includes a reproduction of the Greek text of Sertorius from
Plutarchi vitae parallelae, vol. 2, fasc. 1, edited by K. Ziegler
and published: Leipzig : B. G. Teubner, 1964.
Includes bibliographical references and index.
ISBN 978-1-4696-1378-9 (pbk.)
1. Plutarch. Sertorius.   2. Sertorius, d. 72 B.C.
3. Generals—Rome—Biography.   4. Rome—History—
Revolt of Sertorius, 82–72 B.C.   5. Spain—History—
Roman period, 218 B.C.–414 A.D.   I. Plutarch.
Sertorius. 1994. II. Title.
DG260.S4K66 1994
937'.05'092—dc20
[B]   93-36131
                  CIP

Greek text of the *Sertorius* is reproduced with permission
of B. G. Teubner Verlagsgesellschaft, Stuttgart and Leipzig,
from: *Plutarchi vitae parallelae*, vol. 2, fasc. 1, edited by
Cl. Lindskog and K. Ziegler, second edition by K. Ziegler,
Leipzig, 1964.

O. L. W.
manibus
sacrum

CONTENTS

Preface ix

Abbreviations xi

A Note on Nomenclature xvii

Maps xx

INTRODUCTION xxv

1. Plutarch xxv
   1. Life xxv
   2. The *Parallel Lives* xxvi
2. The *Sertorius* xxx
   1. Purpose xxx
   2. *Sertorius* and *Eumenes* xxxi
   3. Structure of the *Sertorius* xxxiii
   4. Rhetorical Elements xxxv
   5. Historical Method xxxix
3. Sertorius: Sources and Tradition xli
   1. The First Generation xli
   2. Sallust xliv
   3. Diodoros xlv
   4. Authors of the Late First Century B.C. xlv
   5. Livy and the Livian Tradition xlvi
   6. Velleius Paterculus xlix
   7. Memnon xlix
   8. Florus xlix
   9. Appian li
   10. Granius Licinianus lii
   11. *Exempla* and *Memorabilia* lii
   12. Oral Tradition liii
   13. Plutarch liii

SERTORIUS 3

Comparison of Sertorius and Eumenes 27

COMMENTARY 31

Appendix: A Chronology of Sertorius' Life 221

Bibliography 223

Index 245

PREFACE

Commentaries on Plutarch's *Lives* are in vogue, as a glance at the past decade's production will confirm. No excuses are to be offered for one on the *Sertorius*. Leopold's annotated edition appeared two centuries ago, and Stenten's comments (1969), in Dutch, are rather limited in scope and depth. Yet despite the great revival of Plutarchean studies, *Sertorius* has received scant attention from students of the Chaironeian. Not because of a dearth of material on the life's subject, for interest in the historical Sertorius continues at a lively pace—to wit, for instance, Gabba's magisterial contributions in his work on Appian, or the consequences of the Social War; Scardigli's numerous studies clarifying problems in Sertorius' career; or Spann's recent biography, a long-desired corrective to Schulten's fundamental and charmingly hagiographic treatment. The cause must be seen in the life itself: brief and austere, it can offer but little to scholars accustomed to feast on the riches of *Antony, Perikles, Themistokles,* or *Alexander.* Temptation to dismiss it as a mere byproduct of that grand project, the *Parallel Lives,* easily rises and easily prevails. On closer inspection, however, the *Sertorius* emerges as one of the biographer's more carefully crafted, indeed controlled, compositions. The resulting portrait of the hero shows Plutarch at his manipulative best, and teaches the historian who must use him for his principal source a somber lesson: few things are what they seem, and the biographer's oblique hints and silent moments deserve our dedicated scrutiny. Bosworth's trenchant little study has just shown the same to be true, fittingly enough, of the life's counterpart, the *Eumenes*. The pair warrants exploration.

My debts in this endeavor are manifold. Ernst Badian, Erich Gruen, and C. B. R. Pelling critically and with diligence read the entire manuscript. Their comments have been of immeasurable help; if I have not in every instance followed their advice, it must be marked up to my stubbornness. At any event, errors herein are my own. Henry Boren read, to my great benefit, an embryonic version of the commentary when it was a doctoral dissertation many years past. Barbara Scardigli received me with the kindest hospitality in Florence, enabled me to inspect the premier manuscript, Laurentianus conventuum suppressorum 206, in its home, and most graciously let me peruse her unfinished draft of a *Sertorius* commentary abandoned, sadly, some twenty years ago; I fear these pages do not do enough justice to her immense erudition. Special gratitude must be expressed to Philip Stadter: as a teacher and as a scholar, he has opened my eyes not only to Plutarch but to historiography itself; if this book helps illuminate, in a small way, the biographer's art it is due to his example and instruction. What I owe to Jerzy Linderski is beyond evaluation.

Many colleagues, teachers, and friends have given of their time to listen, encourage, or discuss with me problems, large and small, that surround the subject. I must single out T. R. S. Broughton, W. M. Calder III, Pedro Barceló, P. T. Keyser, Mark Possanza, N. K. Rauh, Robert Renehan, Klaus Rosen, and Walter Schmitthenner. Others whose help and unfailing friendship is gratefully acknowledged include Lisa Carson, George Garrett, F. V. Hickson, Borimir Jordan, J. T. Kirby, D. G. Martinez, Tadeusz Maslowski, Elizabeth Meyer, Timothy Moore, R. M. Smith, and W. J. Tatum. Thanks also, and not the least, to the staff of the Interlibrary Loan Office in Norlin Library at the University of Colorado, Boulder, who with admirable patience and tenacity located innumerable materials for me to use.

A good part of the research for this commentary, in Spain, Italy, and Vienna, was carried out with the aid of a grant from the University of Colorado Council on Research and Creative Work. Hermann Harrauer, Director of the Österreichische Nationalbibliothek Papyrus Collection, made inspection of the Vienna fragment of Sallust's *Histories* not only possible but a most pleasant experience. Silvio Panciera generously imparted some of his expertise concerning the Pompeius-Strabo bronze from Asculum. V. Alonso Troncoso in Madrid and F. J. Fernández Nieto in València were of invaluable help in arranging my autopsy of presumptive Sertorian battlefields and making materials difficult of access available. Scholars in the Peninsula to whom I am indebted for suggestions include J. M. Blázquez Martínez, G. Chic García, A. J. Domínguez Monedero, L. A. García Moreno, and J. Remesal Rodríguez.

Thanks to the very kind permission of the B. G. Teubner Verlagsgesellschaft, Stuttgart and Leipzig, the text of the *Sertorius* in Konrat Ziegler's edition is reproduced in this volume. Translations, unless indicated otherwise, are my own.

Publication of this book was greatly assisted by a generous grant from the Committee on University Scholarly Publications of the University of Colorado. The University of North Carolina Press and its staff, in particular my copyeditor, Laura Oaks, have been of exemplary help and patience. For that I am deeply grateful.

ABBREVIATIONS

The following abbreviations of reference works and frequently cited material are used in the Commentary. Periodicals are abbreviated according to the system of *L'année philologique,* with the customary modifications. Authors listed in the Bibliography with no more than one title are usually cited by name only; where there are two or more titles, citations contain the author's name and a short title or a brief journal reference. *RE* numbers have been added to names in the prosopographical notes of the commentary. Chapter and section numbers for Plutarch's *Lives* correspond to the Teubner edition. Comparisons of the *Lives* are usually identified only by the life they follow; both the separate and consecutive chapter numbers are given: e.g., *Eum. Synkr.* 1(20).2 = Comparison *Sert.–Eum.* 1(*Eum.* 20).2. Unless noted otherwise, citations of Appian refer to book 1 of the *Civil Wars.*

ANRW	*Aufstieg und Niedergang der römischen Welt: Geschichte und Kultur Roms im Spiegel der neueren Forschung.* 1972–. Edited by H. Temporini and W. Haase. Berlin and New York.
Badian, FC	Badian, E. 1958. *Foreign Clientelae (264–70 B.C.).* Oxford.
Bennett, *Cinna*	Bennett, H. 1923. *Cinna and His Times: A Critical and Interpretative Study of Roman History During the Period 87–84 B.C.* Menasha, Wis.
Bennett, "Death"	Bennett, W. H. 1961. "The Death of Sertorius and the Coin." *Historia* 10:459–72.
C	Clark, A. C. 1907. *Q. Asconii Pediani orationum Ciceronis quinque enarratio.* Oxford.
Carney, *Marius*	Carney, T. F. 1961. *A Biography of C. Marius.* Proceedings of the African Classical Associations, Supplement 1. Assen.

Cichorius, *RS*	Cichorius, C. 1922. *Römische Studien*. Leipzig.
CIL	*Corpus Inscriptionum Latinarum*. 1863–. Berlin.
Cr	Criniti, N. 1981. *Grani Liciniani reliquiae*. Leipzig.
Crawford, *CMRR*	Crawford, M. H. 1985. *Coinage and Money under the Roman Republic: Italy and the Mediterranean Economy*. Berkeley and Los Angeles.
Crawford, *RRC*	Crawford, M. H. 1974. *Roman Republican Coinage*. 2 vols. London and New York.
E-K	Edelstein, L., and I. G. Kidd. 1972. *Posidonius*. Vol. 1, *The Fragments*. 2d ed., 1989. Cambridge.
Fernández-Galiano, "Nombre"	Fernández-Galiano, M. 1973. "Sobre el nombre de Sigüenza." *EClás* 17:291–302.
FGrHist	Jacoby, F. 1923–58. *Die Fragmente der griechischen Historiker*. 3 vols. in 15. Berlin and Leiden.
Gabba, *App BC 1*	Gabba, E. 1958. *Appiani Bellorum civilium liber primus: Introduzione, testo critico e commento con traduzione e indici*. Firenze.
Gabba, *Appiano*	Gabba, E. 1956. *Appiano e la storia delle guerre civili*. Firenze.
Geiger, "Choice"	Geiger, J. 1981. "Plutarch's Parallel Lives: The Choice of Heroes." *Hermes* 109:85–104.
Geiger, *Nepos*	Geiger, J. 1985. *Cornelius Nepos and Ancient Political Biography*. Stuttgart.
GL	Keil, H. 1857–80. *Grammatici Latini*. 8 vols. Leipzig.
Grueber, *CRRBM*	Grueber, H. A. 1910. *Coins of the Roman Republic in the British Museum*. 3 vols. London.

HLL	*Handbuch der lateinischen Literatur der Antike.* Vol. 5, *Restauration und Erneuerung: Die lateinische Literatur von 284 bis 374 n. Chr.* 1989. Edited by R. Herzog. München.
HRR	Peter, H. 1906–14. *Historicorum Romanorum reliquiae.* 2 vols. (vol.1, 2d ed.). Leipzig.
IDélos	*Inscriptions de Délos.* 1929–37. Edited by F. Durrbach, P. Roussel, and M. Launey. Vols. 2–4. Paris.
IG	*Inscriptiones Graecae.* 1873–. Berlin.
ILLRP	Degrassi, A. 1957–63. *Inscriptiones Latinae liberae rei publicae.* 2 vols. Firenze.
ILS	Dessau, H. 1892–1916. *Inscriptiones Latinae selectae.* 3 vols. Berlin.
Inscr. Ital.	*Inscriptiones Italiae.* Vol. 13.1, *Fasti consulares et triumphales.* 1947. Edited by A. Degrassi. Roma.
Jones, *Plutarch*	Jones, C. P. 1971. *Plutarch and Rome.* Oxford.
JSEAM	*Memorias de la Junta Superior de Excavaciones y Antigüedades.* Madrid.
Katz, "Sertorius"	Katz, B. R. 1981 [1984]. "Sertorius, Caesar, and Sallust." *AAntHung* 29:285–313 = *Helios* 11 (1984) 9–46.
Keaveney, *Sulla*	Keaveney, A. 1982. *Sulla: The Last Republican.* London and Canberra.
K-G	Kühner, R., and B. Gerth. 1898–1904. *Ausführliche Grammatik der griechischen Sprache.* Teil 2, *Satzlehre.* 3d ed. 2 vols. Hannover and Leipzig.
KP	*Der Kleine Pauly: Lexikon der Antike.* 1964–75. Edited by K. Ziegler, W. Sontheimer, and H. Gärtner. München.
La Penna, "*Historiae*"	La Penna, A. 1963. "Le *Historiae* di Sallustio e l'interpretazione della crisi repubblicana." *Athenaeum* 41:201–74.

LEW	Walde, A., and J. Hofmann. 1954. *Lateinisches etymologisches Wörterbuch*. 3d ed. 2 vols. Heidelberg.
LSJ	Liddell, H. G., R. Scott, and H. S. Jones. 1940. *A Greek-English Lexicon*. 9th ed. Oxford. Supplement 1968.
Malitz, *Historien*	Malitz, J. 1983. *Die Historien des Poseidonios*. München.
Maurenbrecher	Maurenbrecher, B. 1891–93. *C. Sallusti Crispi Historiarum reliquiae*. Fasciculus 1, *Prolegomena*. Fasciculus 2, *Fragmenta*. Leipzig.
Mommsen, *RG*	Mommsen, Th. 1912–17. *Römische Geschichte*. 11th ed. 5 vols. Berlin.
Mommsen, *RMW*	Mommsen, Th. 1860. *Geschichte des römischen Münzwesens*. Berlin.
Mommsen, *StR*	Mommsen, Th. 1887–88. *Römisches Staatsrecht*. 3 vols. (vols. 1–2, 3d ed.). Leipzig.
MRR	Broughton, T. R. S. 1951–52. *The Magistrates of the Roman Republic*. Vols. 1–2. New York. Vol. 3, *Supplement*. Atlanta, 1986.
Perl, "Sallust"	Perl, G. 1963. "Zu Sallust Hist. II 93." *WZRostock* 12:269–73.
RE	*Paulys Realencyclopädie der classischen Altertumswissenschaft*. 1893–1980. Edited by G. Wissowa, W. Kroll, K. Mittelhaus, and K. Ziegler. Stuttgart.
Scardigli, "Vita"	Scardigli, B. ca. 1970. "Plutarco: La vita di Sertorio." Typescript draft of an abandoned commentary project.
Schulten	Schulten, A. 1926. *Sertorius*. Leipzig.
Schulten, *FHA*	Schulten, A., and P. Bosch Gimpera, eds. 1922–40. *Fontes Hispaniae Antiquae*. 5 vols. Barcelona.
Spann	Spann, P. O. 1987. *Quintus Sertorius and the Legacy of Sulla*. Fayetteville, Ark.

Spann, diss.	Spann, P. O. 1976. *Quintus Sertorius: Citizen, Soldier, Exile*. Diss. Univ. of Texas, Austin.
Spann, "Isles"	Spann, P.O. 1977. "Sallust, Plutarch, and the 'Isles of the Blest.'" *Terrae Incognitae* 9:75–80.
St	Stangl, T. 1912. *Ciceronis orationum scholiastae*. Wien.
StudNon	*Studi Noniani*. Pubblicazioni dell'Istituto di Filologia Classica e Medievale dell'Università di Genova, Facoltà di Lettere. Genova.
Th	Theiler, W. 1982. *Poseidonios: Die Fragmente*. 2 vols. Berlin.
Untermann, *MLH*	Untermann, J. 1975–. *Monumenta linguarum Hispanicarum*. Wiesbaden.
Wardman, *Lives*	Wardman, A. E. 1974. *Plutarch's Lives*. London.
Wiseman, *New Men*	Wiseman, T. P. 1971. *New Men in the Roman Senate, 139 B.C.–A.D. 14*. Oxford.
Wiseman, *Roman Spain*	Wiseman, F. J. 1956. *Roman Spain: An Introduction to the Roman Antiquities of Spain and Portugal*. London.
W-M	Weissenborn, W., and H. J. Müller. 1880–81. *Titi Livi ab urbe condita libri*. Vol. 10, *Libri XLIII–XLV, Periochae et Fragmenta*. 2d ed. Berlin.
Z	Zorzetti, N. 1982. *Iulii Exuperantii opusculum*. Leipzig.
Ziegler	Ziegler, K., and C. Lindskog. 1964. *Plutarchi Vitae parallelae*. Vol. 2.1, *Phokion–Cato Minor, Dion–Brutus, Aemilius–Timoleon, Sertorius–Eumenes*. 2d ed. Leipzig.
Ziegler, *Plutarchos*	Ziegler, K. 1949. *Plutarchos von Chaironeia*. 2d ed., 1964 (separatum of *RE* 21.1 [1951] 636–962). Stuttgart.

A NOTE ON NOMENCLATURE

The terms "Hispanian" and "Hispanians" in this work denote collectively the indigenous (i.e., non-Punic, non-Greek, non-Roman) population of the Iberian Peninsula in antiquity, without distinguishing between its individual cultures such as Iberian, Celtic, or Celtiberian. "Iberian" and "Iberians" (other than in the standard expression "Iberian Peninsula") will be used only with reference to the Iberian civilization proper (see Commentary, 6.7: Peoples of the Peninsula).

Modern Spanish place-names herein are identified, as is customary, by town and province, except for capitals of homonymous provinces. To ease location on more recent maps, the name of the respective autonomous region is usually added, e.g., Botorrita, Zaragoza Prov., Aragón. Provinces used to be named uniformly after their capitals; where that is no longer the case, the name of the capital is added in parentheses in the list below, though not in the text. Place-names in the regions of the Baleares, Catalonia, and València are mostly given in their Catalan forms; where these differ from the Castilian version, the latter is added below in square brackets: e.g., Lleida [Lérida].

Regions and Their Provinces

Andalucía (Andalusia)
  Almería
  Cádiz
  Córdoba
  Granada
  Jaén
  Huelva
  Málaga
  Sevilla

Aragón
  Huesca
  Teruel
  Zaragoza

Asturias (*Principado de Asturias*)
  Asturias (Oviedo)

Baleares (Balearic Isles)
  Baleares (Palma)

Canarias (Canary Islands)
  Las Palmas de Gran Canaria
  Santa Cruz de Tenerife

Cantabria
  Cantabria (Santander)

Castilla–La Mancha (New Castile and La Mancha)
  Albacete
  Ciudad Real
  Cuenca
  Guadalajara
  Toledo

Castilla y León (Old Castile and León)
  Ávila
  Burgos
  León
  Palencia
  Salamanca
  Segovia
  Soria
  Valladolid
  Zamora

Catalunya (Catalonia)
  Barcelona
  Girona [Gerona]
  Lleida [Lérida]
  Tarragona

Extremadura
  Badajoz
  Cáceres

Galicia
  La Coruña
  Lugo
  Orense
  Pontevedra

La Rioja
  La Rioja (Logroño)

Madrid (*Comunidad de Madrid*)
  Madrid

Murcia (*Región de Murcia*)
 Murcia

Navarra (*Comunidad Foral de Navarra*)
 Navarra (Pamplona)

País Valencià (*Comunitat Valenciana*)
 Alacant [Alicante]
 Castelló [Castellón] de la Plana
 València [Valencia]

País Vasco (Basque Country)
 Alava (Vitoria)
 Guipúzcoa (San Sebastián)
 Vizcaya (Bilbao)

Map 1.
The Iberian Peninsula in the Early First Century B.C.

Map 2.
Spain and Portugal

INTRODUCTION

1. Plutarch

1. Life

Plutarch hailed from a family of wealthy and well-established landowners in the Boiotian town of Chaironeia, where he was born probably not long before A.D. 45. His higher education—in Athens—was excellent, and he soon achieved a remarkable degree of accomplishment in the areas of mathematics and rhetoric. By 66 or 67 he had become a student of the Platonist Ammonios, whose influence directed Plutarch toward his lifelong intellectual pursuit and commitment, the philosophy of Plato and the Academy.[1]

He traveled widely, to Asia, Egypt, and Italy; nothing indicates, however, that he saw the western provinces of the Empire, Gaul, Spain, or Africa. On several occasions he visited Rome; it is a reasonable assumption that he did so on official business, representing concerns of Chaironeia or other Greek cities. The first of these visits surely falls in the reign of Vespasian, and there is evidence of his being in Rome in A.D. 88–89 and 92–93.[2] The circle of his Roman friends was large and influential. L. Mestrius Florus, the consular who unsuccessfully sought to correct Vespasian's vulgar Latin, frequently appears in the *Table Talk* as host or dialogue partner. It was Florus who had sponsored Plutarch (or perhaps already his father) in obtaining Roman citizenship; hence the philosopher's formal name, L. Mestrius Plutarchus.[3] To the brothers C. Avidius Nigrinus and T. Avidius Quietus Plutarch dedicated his *On Brotherly Love*, to Quietus alone the treatise *On Divine Vengeance*. Both, it seems, had been Proconsuls of Achaea, and Quietus (a friend of Nero's great opponent, the Stoic T. Clodius Thrasea Paetus) succeeded to a suffect consulship in A.D. 93. His son was to be Consul (*suff.*) in 111 and eventually Proconsul of Asia—the most prestigious senatorial post, next to Africa—in 125/6, and his nephew, Avidius Nigrinus the younger, became a trusted lieutenant of Trajan: Consul Suffect in 110, *legatus pro praetore* of Achaea soon afterwards (and very likely known personally to Plutarch), commander in chief of Dacia by

---

1. On Plutarch's life and education see in detail Ziegler, *Plutarchos* 4–60; Jones, *Plutarch* 8–64; Russell, *Plutarch* 1–17.
2. Jones, *Plutarch* 21–25.
3. Ziegler, *Plutarchos* 51; Jones, *Plutarch* 22, 48–49; cf. Suet. *Vesp.* 22 on Florus.

117, and one of the four consulars executed in 118.⁴ Pride of place among the philosopher's Roman friends, however, must go to Q. Sosius Senecio, Trajan's marshal in the Dacian Wars, twice Consul Ordinary (99, 107), and possibly himself a Greek from the Near East. To him Plutarch dedicated *On Progress in Virtue, Table Talk,* and the *Parallel Lives.* It probably was Sosius who prevailed on Trajan to bestow the *ornamenta consularia,* a rare honor, on Plutarch, and the suggestion has been voiced that he may also have introduced him to the later Emperor Hadrian.⁵ In 119, at any event, Plutarch was named Caesar's Procurator in Achaea—a sinecure no doubt signifying the high esteem he was held in by the residents of the Palatine.

The last three decades of his life saw Plutarch mostly in Chaironeia and Delphi, where he served as one of the two priests of Apollo. He spent his time writing, with occasional trips to Athens (where, too, he held citizenship): her libraries were indispensable for his studies. But he did not shun civic service in his hometown, or as a Boiotian delegate to the Amphiktyonic Council. At his home, a lively circle of friends and pupils formed what amounted to a small philosophical school. He died about A.D. 120.⁶

2. The *Parallel Lives*

Of Plutarch's vast literary output perhaps one-third survives. Writings on philosophy, ethics, education, politics, religion, psychology, science, literature, and rhetoric, collectively known as the *Moralia,* constitute about three-fifths of his extant work.⁷ Biography accounts for the rest: twenty-two pairs of *Parallel Lives,* plus the independent lives of Aratos, Artaxerxes, Galba, and Otho. The last two are part of a series, *Lives of the Caesars,* composed earlier in his literary career.⁸ Yet they already show the approach Plutarch brought to bear on the *Parallel Lives.* His outlook is moral, not political. His interest is not in the fall of states and rise of empires, the tactics of battle, or the chronology of events. It is in the character of men. Their deeds and little doings, their behavior in good fortune and bad, could reveal their nature. From their virtues and vices, their right choices as well as their mistakes, present and future generations can learn, and better themselves.⁹ Presenting his heroes in pairs enhances the didactic effect. Similar virtues, or sometimes sim-

---

4. Jones, *Plutarch* 51–54.
5. Jones, *Plutarch* 54–57; cf. Ziegler, *Plutarchos* 52–53.
6. Ziegler, *Plutarchos* 23–29; Jones, "Chronology" 63–66.
7. See list and discussion in Ziegler, *Plutarchos* 60–66. On the *Moralia* see also Russell, *Plutarch* 42–99.
8. Between A.D. 77 and 96, more or less: Jones, "Chronology" 71; see also *Plutarch* 72–80. Geiger, *Historia* 24 (1975) 444–51, suggests the reign of Nerva, A.D. 96–98.
9. The locus classicus is *Aem.* 1.1–5, and illuminating statements can be found in *Per.* 1–2; *Nik.* 1.1–5; *Eum.* 9.1–2; *Alex.* 1; *Dtr.* 1.4–7. Plutarch's purpose in writing the *Lives* has seen extensive discussion: Jones, *Plutarch* 103–9; Wardman, *Lives* 18–37; Russell, *Plutarch* 100–116; Frost, *Themistocles* 53–55; Pelling, *Antony* 10–18; Stadter, *Pericles* xxiv–xxvii; cf. Stadter, *Methods* 11.

ilar weaknesses, determine his choice of individuals in each pair, but their differences, variations, and contrasts are what bring life to abstract qualities.[10]

The *Parallel Lives* were probably written after A.D. 96; the first consulship of Sosius Senecio, their addressee, in 99 offers an attractive starting point.[11] Their precise order of composition remains unknown, but enough has been learned to establish a relative chronology in general terms. *Demosthenes–Cicero* was the fifth pair composed (*Dem.* 3.1), *Perikles–Fabius* the tenth (*Per.* 2.5), *Dion–Brutus* the twelfth (*Dion* 2.7). The lost *Epameinondas–Scipio* surely formed the first of the twenty-three pairs,[12] and a general consensus has emerged regarding the relative position of I–X:[13]

   I. *Epameinondas–Scipio*
  II. *Pelopidas–Marcellus*
 III. *Kimon–Lucullus*
  IV. *Philopoimen–Flamininus*
   V. *Demosthenes–Cicero*
  VI. *Lykourgos–Numa*
 VII. *Theseus–Romulus*
VIII. *Themistokles–Camillus*
  IX. *Lysander–Sulla*
   X. *Perikles–Fabius*

The order of the remaining thirteen syzygies is far more doubtful, although help can be invoked from several angles. Cross-references taken together with Plutarch's apparent practice of simultaneously preparing a series of related lives provide some tenuous guidance, to be followed with great caution.[14] The comparative rarity of references in the *Moralia* to most of his Hellenistic heroes (Agis, Demetrios, Eumenes, Kleomenes, Pyrrhos) as well as to their Roman counterparts (the Gracchi, Antony, Sertorius, Marius) offers a more promising cue, suggesting a late date of composition for these pairs.[15] Topical similarities connecting certain lives may be another significant indicator of closeness in sequence.[16]

Dion–Brutus, Aemilius–Timoleon, Alexander–Caesar, and *Agesilaos–Pompey* are agreed to have appeared in close succession, whereas *Brutus, Caesar, Pompey, Cato Minor, Antony,* and possibly *Crassus* were probably prepared

---

10. Stadter, *Pericles* xxvii; cf. Erbse, passim; Wardman, *Lives* 234–44; Pelling, "Synkrisis."
11. Jones, "Chronology" 70.
12. Ziegler, *Plutarchos* 259–60.
13. Stadter, *Pericles* xxviii–xxix; cf. his "Searching" 358–59. The studies of Stoltz, Jones ("Chronology"), and van der Valk are fundamental.
14. Geiger, "Munatius Rufus" 61 n. 47, succinctly points out the dangers of blindly accepting Stoltz's conclusions as regards the reliability of cross-references; cf. also Pelling, "Method" 81. For simultaneous preparation see Pelling, "Method" 74–83, elaborating and improving upon a view first put forward by Mewaldt.
15. Geiger, "Choice" 89–94.
16. Frazier 70–75; Stadter, "Paradoxical Paradigms" 48–50.

as a single research project.[17] Stadter has recently shown how pairs VIII–X, *Themistokles–Camillus, Lysander–Sulla,* and *Perikles–Fabius,* constitute a unit exploring "common themes of ambition, political strife, and power." Ambition, though flawed, leads the first pair to become the saviors of their cities; even rejected and in exile, Themistokles and Camillus remain loyal to Athens and Rome. Ambition also drives Lysander and Sulla, but boundless and lethal, with devastating repercussions for Sparta and Rome. The heroes of the third pair combine ambition with self-control (*praotēs*), justice (*dikaiosynē*), and noble-mindedness (*megalophrosynē*), qualities of character that enable them to protect their cities from enemies abroad as well as against civil strife within.[18] Just as the theme of the statesman's relation to his city can be traced back to VI–VII, *Lykourgos–Numa* and *Theseus–Romulus,* the lawgivers and founders, so it can be seen to continue, especially as developed in *Perikles–Fabius,* with *Solon–Poplicola* and *Dion–Brutus* (securely attested as pair XII): all four of them just and wise leaders whose ambition is tempered by philosophy and strength of character. Caesar and Alexander stand in brutal contrast. *Agesilaos–Pompey* pursues the theme with a new twist: outstanding military commanders, yet ineffective statesmen at home.[19]

Aemilius–Timoleon is a study in *tychē*, the vicissitudes of which are explored, in varying degrees, in virtually all the later lives: the pair almost reads as an introduction to a new section of biographies. Personal rectitude suggests a theme unifying it with *Aristeides–Cato Maior* and *Phokion–Cato Minor.* Another common denominator of most lives from XII (*Dion–Brutus*) onward is failure as a statesman or general. The biographer can be sympathetic where he recognizes steadfast principle (*Phokion–Cato Minor*), good intentions (*Agis/Kleomenes–Gracchi*), or good men struck down by bad luck (*Sertorius–Eumenes*); he is critical where failure combines with less lofty characteristics, as in *Nikias–Crassus, Pyrrhos–Marius,* or *Demetrios–Antony.* The latter resumes a didactic approach first taken in *Lysander–Sulla,* presenting vice as a deterrent rather than displaying virtue as an example to be emulated.[20]

The heroes of *Agis/Kleomenes–Gracchi, Sertorius–Eumenes,* and *Coriolanus–Alkibiades* all end up in conflict with the established order of their respective political environments: the first set well-meaning and driven by honor and shame, the second fighting (partly) against their will and for survival, the third acting in self-centered arrogance. As with pairs VIII–X, the common theme strongly suggests a compositional unit. Agis, the Gracchi, Sertorius, and

---

17. Jones, "Chronology" 66–68; Pelling, "Method" 74–83. Hillard's questioning the theory (p. 21) carries little persuasion, but the doubts voiced about the *Crassus* are serious; as suggested below, that life is thematically much closer to *Pyrrhos–Marius, Sertorius–Eumenes,* and *Agis/Kleomenes–Gracchi* than to Pelling's group of Late Republican lives.

18. Stadter, "Paradoxical Paradigms" 48–50. For thematical connections among pairs I–IV and VI–VII see Stadter, *Pericles* xxviii.

19. Cf. Stadter, "Paradoxical Paradigms" 54 n. 38, on *Agesilaos–Pompey.*

20. Cf. Stadter, "Paradoxical Paradigms" 50–51.

Coriolanus are men raised by their mothers; Alkibiades, too, grew up without a father. All except Agis and the Gracchi spend a historically significant part of their careers in exile, as leaders of nations not their own—characteristics that extend a bridge to *Demetrios–Antony,* which may be credited with a similarly pivotal function among the later lives as enjoyed by *Perikles–Fabius* among the earlier ones. In both *Sertorius* (the Isles of the Blest, 8.2–9.1) and *Antony* (the Timoneion, 69.3–7), Plutarch exhibits an interest in yet another facet of human nature: escapism in the face of defeat. *Sertorius–Eumenes* is probably later than *Demetrios–Antony*: Demetrios' efforts to save Eumenes, reported in *Eum.* 18.6, go untold in *Dtr.* 3–4 despite those chapters' emphasis on the hero's kindness and fairness.[21] With due caution, the following sequence of the later lives may be suggested:

XI. *Solon–Poplicola*
XII. *Dion–Brutus*
XIII. *Alexander–Caesar*
XIV. *Agesilaos–Pompey*
XV. *Aemilius–Timoleon*
XVI. *Aristeides–Cato Maior*
XVII. *Phokion–Cato Minor*
XVIII. *Demetrios–Antony*
XIX. *Agis/Kleomenes–Ti./C. Gracchus*[22]
XX. *Sertorius–Eumenes*
XXI. *Coriolanus–Alkibiades*
XXII. *Nikias–Crassus*
XXIII. *Pyrrhos–Marius*[23]

It appears that during his later years Plutarch became attracted to darker, more complex, and less fortunate characters. *Sertorius–Eumenes* properly belongs in that last group of lives.

---

21. Pelling, "Method" 83 n. 68. A late date of the *Sertorius* is also argued by Scardigli, "Considerazioni" 33–41; cf. Stadter, "Searching" 358 n. 6.

22. The elaborate introduction to this syzygy, esp. *Agis* 2.7–8 with its insistence that the Gracchi were well-intentioned and noble men led astray by circumstances, evidently prepares the reader for a new kind of hero, as seen by van der Valk 317–18. His claim, of course, that *Demetrios–Antony* therefore must be later, lest readers mistake vice and corruption also for the theme of *Agis/Kleomenes–Gracchi,* turns the matter on its head: Plutarch's introduction is designed to forestall just such a misunderstanding.

23. The cross-references between *Alkibiades* (13.9) and *Nikias* (11.2) indicate simultaneous preparation (Mewaldt 573; Jones, "Chronology" 68), and Plutarch's less than admiring attitude toward Nikias and Crassus, men felled by poor judgment and ambition exceeding their abilities, betrays a thematic affinity not only with pairs XVIII–XXI but even more with *Pyrrhos–Marius.* Van der Valk (316–17, 330–35) argues persuasively in favor of *Pyrrhos–Marius* as the last pair completed and *Coriolanus–Alkibiades* as anterior to *Nikias–Crassus.*

2. The *Sertorius*

1. Purpose

Moral improvement was the aim of the *Parallel Lives*; the study of illustrious men's characters was to furnish the means. The reader must not look for a comprehensive historical narrative, political analysis, or even a complete listing of all available biographical data. Plutarch can be rather selective, and what he chooses to tell us is meant to illustrate the pedagogical themes of each life. That is true of the *Sertorius* in perhaps a higher degree than most other lives.

How do good men hold up under the strain of an adverse fate? Plutarch had raised the issue in *Aemilius–Timoleon*; here he explores it in a very different setting. Both Sertorius and Eumenes are possessed of excellent qualities: self-restraint, loyalty, clemency; the equals in military skill of the greatest captains, and their betters in resourcefulness. But no man controls his fate, and Fate can be cruel and unjust. No skill or talent known is capable of preventing betrayal (*Sert.* 1.9–12). When luck and friends forsake him, Sertorius, of good character but lacking the moral underpinning of philosophy, becomes savage and cruel (10.5–7). Eumenes through clever talk tries to save his life, thus losing his dignity (*Eum.* 17.5–11, 18.7–9). Good qualities alone are not always enough to steel a person against adversity. Even good character needs to be schooled. There is a reason why Brutus and the younger Cato did not end like Eumenes and Sertorius.

The pair thus presents a cautionary tale, like *Demetrios–Antony* or *Coriolanus–Alkibiades*. Yet Plutarch is filled with genuine admiration for Sertorius, and unlike in the other two syzygies, his emphasis here is not on deterrence. If *tychē* alone can destroy men of good character and talent, the reader must be convinced that the hero came to grief through no fault of his own. Hence no critical treatment; rather, as often in Plutarch though more so than usual, the hero's flaws are downplayed or go unmentioned altogether.[24] Where faults are too severe to be suppressed, they are calmly presented and explained carefully, so as to avoid damage to the overall portrait. Nor is the biographer content with merely being protective. His picture of Sertorius consistently exhibits traits of the ideal ruler-sage of the Cynic and Stoic tradition: responsibly watching over those entrusted to his care (at Castulo, 3.5–10), preferring guile and ruses over brute force (e.g., Castulo; the relief of Langobriga, 13.7–9; the caves of the Characitani, 17; or the two camps at Lauro, 18.5–10), persuasive rather than imperious (the parable of the two horses, 16), and adept at manipulating religious beliefs to further his efforts as ruler

---

24. Cf. Stadter, "Searching" 358, with reference to the *Themistokles*. Plutarch's own principles of how the biographer should treat his subject's shortcomings are set forth in *Kim.* 2.3–5.

and military leader (the white doe, 11.3–12.1; 20).[25] After such preparation, the sad fate that befalls the hero touches the reader all the more deeply.

This, then, is what Plutarch wants to achieve in the *Sertorius*: to show that his hero was a man of excellent qualities who put them to the best possible use; to prove that his ruin was due to sheer bad fortune; to refute those who portrayed Sertorius as innately base and vicious, an adventurer without roots and loyalty toward Rome; and to warn the reader that a good character not properly grounded in a rational decision to be good may be corrupted by adversity.

2. *Sertorius* and *Eumenes*

The *Lives* were meant to be read in pairs; Plutarch employs similarity as well as contrast to achieve his didactic goal.[26] As the formal comparison (*synkrisis*) at the end of a pair tends to concentrate on differences between the characters, so the introduction tends to emphasize qualities they have in common. But the body of each life also contains comparisons, usually frequent, with its counterpart: implicit rather than outspoken, they are often more subtle and telling than the formal kind.

Sertorius is paired with Eumenes of Kardia, the Greek secretary of state to two Macedonian kings, Philip II and Alexander III. After the latter's death in 323 B.C., Eumenes was propelled into the ensuing epic struggle for power over a disintegrating empire. Though of little previous military experience, he quickly demonstrated a natural talent for leadership and the arts of war, and for a number of years was able to maintain an independent position in Asia Minor. Betrayal at the hands of some of his Macedonian officers and troops brought about his downfall in 316: they surrendered him to his archenemy, Antigonos Monophthalmos, who had him put to death.

In the introduction to the *Sertorius,* Plutarch explains his choice of heroes by setting out their similarities. Both were commanders of superior craft and cunning, far from their own home and kind, leaders of foreigners. Both suffered a cruel and unjust fate: to be betrayed by the very men they had led to victory (1.11–12). The *synkrisis* at the end of the *Eumenes* at first presents the usual artificialities of contrast, then moves on to more substantial observations. Sertorius' lifelong military training equipped him with an excellent background for his struggle in Spain; Eumenes became a general overnight, and successfully so. Eumenes faced rivals and internal opposition continuously, Sertorius only briefly toward the end of his life (*Synkr.* 1[20].6–9).

---

25. The Cynic-Stoic elements in Plutarch's Sertorius are well developed by García Moreno, "Paradoxography," esp. 143–52. Despite some exaggeration and too ready an acceptance of Sallust, rather than Plutarch himself, as the origin of those Sertorian traits, that study offers a salutary check to those who—like the present writer—tend toward what García would dismiss as a "positivist" approach.

26. Erbse, *Hermes* 84 (1956) 398–424, and Stadter, *GRBS* 16 (1975) 77–85, provide fundamental studies of Plutarch's comparative method.

On those counts Eumenes is to be admired more, but as Plutarch turns to the subject of the heroes' character, Sertorius is seen as desiring peace (ἡσυχία) and equanimity (πραότης); he fought out of necessity, to secure his survival, since his enemies would not leave him alone. Eumenes, on the other hand, was enamored of war and victory (φιλοπόλεμος καὶ φιλόνικος); he had the opportunity to live safely and in peace but preferred to be a contender for supreme power, and for that reason was constantly in danger (2[21].1–3). Thus Eumenes willingly waged war for the sake of leadership, whereas Sertorius assumed command reluctantly when others made war on him. The war-lover (φιλοπόλεμος) sacrifices safety to ambition (φιλονεξία); the true master of the art (πολεμικός) fights to ensure his safety (2[21].4–5). Viewed from that angle, Sertorius gains in stature, while his counterpart faces even harsher criticism in the final section of the Comparison (2[21].6–8). Sertorius was assassinated, suspecting no evil: a sign of his good nature (ἐπιείκεια). Eumenes was arrested while trying to flee: a mark of weakness (ἀσθένεια). Sertorius' death put no blemish on his life, but Eumenes, unable to escape, wished to continue to live after his capture, and thus is revealed as one who could neither avoid catastrophe nor face death with dignity. Instead "with his entreaties and begging he made his enemy, who seemed to have power merely over his body, also master of his soul."

Such strictures at first come as a surprise. In the narrative itself, Plutarch does not mention any attempt by Eumenes to flee (at 16.5 the latter merely considers the option without acting on it), and neither the formal address to his Macedonian troops (17.6–11) nor the brief exchange with the guard posted over him (18.7–9), though clearly designed to evoke sympathy, contains an actual plea that his life be spared.[27] Yet we must not forget Plutarch's opening portrait of Eumenes: instead of the glowing brights usually reserved for that occasion, the subject is painted as a man given to petty bickering (2.1–3), attached to material wealth (2.4–6), a liar (2.4–6) and dissembler (2.9–3.1). Money and material possessions loom large throughout the life (e.g., 3.11, 5.5, 8.9–10, 13.2); on one occasion Eumenes secures his safety through financial transactions (13.12–13). Contrast Sertorius' frugality (e.g., 13.2–3). Even Eumenes' end is triggered by greed, and not without a certain irony: when his army baggage is captured by the enemy, the officers of the Argyraspides trade him to Antigonos in exchange for its return (16.9–17.2); yet on an earlier occasion, Eumenes had consciously passed up an opportunity to seize Antigonos' train (9.6–12).

Sertorius–Eumenes is one of only three *Parallel Lives* that puts the Roman before the Greek. Certainly the proem, with its lengthy tongue-in-cheek disquisition on historical coincidence culminating in one-eyed generals, could not have been prefixed to *Eumenes*. But such levity aside, there is no doubt that Plutarch's attraction and attention from the beginning was focused on Ser-

---

27. Such discrepancies between the Comparison and the life itself occur in other pairs, too: see Russell, "Coriolanus" 21; Pelling, *Antony* 20.

torius; the proem admits as much (1.8–11). *Eumenes*, if anything, is even more austere a life than the *Sertorius*,[28] and no amount of fleshing out could add to the Kardian's career the fairytale elements and high drama the biographer found present in his sources—friendly and hostile alike—for Sertorius. Getting one's tent burned down in a practical joke gone awry (*Eum.* 2.5–6) hardly matches a heroic swim across the Rhône in grabbing the reader's attention, and assassination far surpasses death by casual execution (*Eum.* 19.1). The "Tent of Alexander" (*Eum.* 13.5–8), clearly intended as a parallel,[29] cannot help but pale in narrative charm against the white doe of Sertorius. Plutarch here as always is keenly aware of the need to capture and maintain the reader's interest; treating Eumenes first would have required a very different kind of life, one perhaps beyond even the master raconteur's ability to tell.

It would be wrong, however, to see in Eumenes merely a darker foil enabling Sertorius to shine the more brightly. The Roman, it is true, displays heroic qualities from the start (3–4), but his character cannot withstand the blows of fate (10.5–7, 25.6), and Plutarch allows us brief glimpses of Sertorius' ruthlessness early on (e.g., 3.7, 3.10, 5.6–7, 18.11)—albeit so carefully shielded that the casual reader may easily miss them. Sertorius is always excellent, until his fall; Eumenes, who first appears as a self-important, greedy schemer, rises in adversity (9.1–5). He never loses his composure when it really matters (his silly agitation in 2.1–3 is thus put in perspective): facing the most fearsome of Alexander's marshals (6.3–7), in the thick of battle (7.7–13), during negotiations (10.3–8, 12.1–4), under siege (11); he even issues receipts for horses requisitioned (8.5). Sertorius' great crime is his slaughter of hostages (25.6; cf. 10.7). Eumenes releases his (12.5), and although he knows full well that his officers are plotting against him he refrains from violent measures (16.1–4). When in the end he abases himself, he is the only one to suffer. Sertorius, his character ruined along with his fortunes, lashes out against innocents.[30]

3. Structure of the *Sertorius*

The *Sertorius* is among the shortest of the *Parallel Lives*, about twenty-five Teubner pages in length; only *Eumenes*, *Agis*, and each of the *Gracchi* are shorter. The narrative is austere, stripped to the bare essentials of Plutarch's purpose. For grand drama lavishly painted on a wide canvas, for the lively anecdotes he usually is so fond of, we must look elsewhere. The brevity is not due to a lack of information, or lack of interest in the subject. Some important events in Sertorius' life he had dealt with at length in earlier biographies: part of the Cimbrian Wars, the Social War, Sulla's March on Rome, and the Civil

---

28. Cf. Bosworth's excellent study, esp. 56–59.
29. Cf. Bosworth 62.
30. Plutarch strikes a similar note in the Comparison of *Demetrios–Antony*, 4(91).6. On the way *Sertorius–Eumenes* complement each other see also Pelling, *Antony* 23–26.

War (83–82 B.C.) in the *Sulla*, the Third Mithradatic War in the *Lucullus*, and the rise of Pompeius in the *Pompey*. Plutarch was not afraid to repeat himself. Yet his purpose in the *Sertorius* demanded a concise and concentrated approach. He wished to present a leader so ingenious, so brave, so resourceful and resilient, so generous and just as to seem well-nigh unconquerable. Only thus could his ultimate failure credibly be ascribed to Fate alone, could his moral decline be reported yet its extent minimized without loss of didactic effect. Everything extraneous to that goal, no matter how interesting biographically, was to be excised, and anything pertinent but reflecting negatively on the hero's character had to be set out in a place and fashion least likely to be detrimental.

The resulting narrative follows chronological lines more closely than most of the *Lives*, though it contains two substantial eidological segments.[31] An outline might look like this:

1. Sertorius' formation and early career (chs. 2–6)
    2, family and upbringing
    3.1–4, first military exploits
    3.5–10, first proof of leadership
    4.1–6, first political experience and setback
    4.6–6.4, civil war: Sertorius' foresight and moderation
    6.5–9, first independent command: moderation in Spain
2. First period of adversity (7–9)
    7.1–8.1, first military defeat: Sertorius at the low point of his fortunes
    8.2–9.1, Blessed Isles excursus: desire for peace
    9.2–11, in Africa: resilience. End of first chronological section.
3. Sertorius as leader at the height of success (eidological section, 10–17):
    10, overview of character qualities: defense against charge of "cruel by nature"
    11.1–12.1, *apatē, praotēs*; psychological leadership (the white doe)
    12.2–7, military genius: in general terms, against Roman forces; summary of early years of the Sertorian War
    13.1–6, physical qualities, guerrilla warfare; first contrast with Metellus
    13.7–12, military genius: specific example, with Hispanian forces
    14, admired as leader by Hispanians; Sertorius' policy toward them
    15, admired as leader by Romans; introduction of Perperna
    16, *apatē*, psychological leadership (the two horses)
    17, a stratagem: military cunning. Transition to second chronological section.
4. Victory and defeat (18–21)
    18.1–4, introduction of Pompeius: his fame and military reputation

---

31. See Weizsäcker 66–67.

18.5–10, defeat of Pompeius at Lauro: Sertorius' most brilliant exploit

18.11, moderation in treatment of Lauro

19, the Sucro: Sertorius' heroic battle-management; but forced to retreat: first sign of failure

20, psychological leadership in time of trouble (return of the white doe)

21.1–3, defeat at Segontia

21.4–9, resilience: recovery through guerrilla warfare. End of second chronological section.

5. Sertorius the Roman (22–24)

22.1–4, decadence of Sertorius' enemies: Metellus excursus

22.5–6, *megalophrosynē*: his *Romanitas* demonstrated by treatment of fellow Romans in Spain

22.7–8, *philopatria*: his desire for a peaceful return to Rome

22.9–12, *megalophrosynē*: grief over death of mother as proof of his gentle nature and fundamental reluctance to engage in this war

23, *Romanitas*: negotiations with Mithradates; Sertorius protecting Roman interests in Asia

24, treaty with Mithradates, moderation of Sertorian government in Asia; Sertorius at the height of his renown.

6. Betrayal and end (25–27)

25.1–4, grievances of Perperna and others; their mistreatment of Hispanians leads to

25.5–6, Hispanian defections and Sertorius' *metabolē* of character

26, the plotters; assassination

27, fate of the murderers.

4. Rhetorical Elements

Apart from the noteworthy exceptions (*Demetrios–Antony, Coriolanus–Alkibiades, Pyrrhos–Marius*) Plutarch generally took care to present his subjects in a positive light. Yet rarely does he go to such lengths in attempting to protect the hero as he does in the *Sertorius*. The need to shield Sertorius from all criticism derives from the syzygy's moral purpose: to show that good nature and excellence of ability are no proof against adverse fate and may crack under the strain of undeserved misfortune. Hence the hero must be as perfect as possible, lest the reader suspect his catastrophe might be attributable to his own shortcomings. In the case of Sertorius, Plutarch faced a formidable obstacle: much—not all—of the historiographical tradition known to him and his readers portrayed Sertorius in not so pleasant a light. The charges leveled against him were essentially these: (1) Sertorius was a traitor who abandoned his Roman heritage when he led natives of Spain against Rome and allied himself with her most implacable foe; and (2) he was a cruel and savage despot who in his later years slaughtered the guilty and the innocent alike. Wherever possible, the reader had to be convinced of the falsehood of such accusations. Where Plutarch could neither deny nor refute them—as in the matter of Sertorius' behavior during the final years—his explanation of the nature and cause of the change in character would serve to complete the didactic goal of the life. The reader does well to keep in mind that persuasion is a fundamental tool of Plutarch's biographical method.[32]

First impressions tend to last, and Plutarch selects accordingly. The swim in the Rhône and the espionage adventure among the German hordes (3.1–4)—achievements literally too good to be true as told—introduce Sertorius as a young man of heroic qualities. His leadership skills are demonstrated on several levels and compared favorably to those of other Romans of his generation (3.5–4.5). When despite all his merits Sertorius fails to become elected Tribune because of Sulla's machinations, we feel the injustice of it and understand how the experience might leave him with a lasting hatred of Sulla (4.6). Never mind that Plutarch will not say what had caused Sulla's opposition, or precisely what form it took.

The life contains several large biographical gaps; the most frustrating for us are the ones during the time Rome had her first taste of civil war, the years 88 to 82 B.C. Sertorius played a prominent part in those events, and plenty of information was available to Plutarch: the gaps are no accident. In the context of the siege of Rome and the ensuing political murders in 87, we learn, in one and one-half Teubner pages, only three hard facts regarding Sertorius' participation. He opposed cooperation with Marius (5.1–5), he refrained from taking personal vengeance (5.6), and he took action against Marius' slave bands when they got out of hand (5.7). That selection duly shows him in a most favorable light; embarrassing questions—Plutarch himself, after all, is anything but sympathetic to Marius and Cinna—are forestalled by a lengthy and studied explanation of how Sertorius came to join ranks with Cinna rather than Octavius (4.7–9). The first half of chapter 6 is a masterly summary of Sulla's civil war, 83–82 B.C.: without going into details it perfectly captures the chaotic conditions, incompetence, and treachery that made Sulla's victory possible. Sertorius' foresight in opposing negotiations stands in stark contrast to noble inertia (6.1–3), yet his mysterious capture of Suessa—an act that served Sulla with a pretext for ruining all prospects of a peaceful settlement— goes unmentioned. Instead Sertorius is described in glowing terms as the very model of a humane governor in Spain (6.7–9), along with a reminder of the rapacity and brutality more typically displayed by Roman officials in the provinces.

In chapters 7–9 we find Sertorius, expelled from Spain, at the low point of his career. A lesser man might have given up, or turned to outlawry and brigandage. Not so Plutarch's hero. His interest in the Blessed Isles, easily taken to reveal a streak of escapism in his character, is interpreted as yet another

---

32. Stadter, *Pericles* xxxviii–xliv, offers an excellent discussion of Plutarch's rhetorical approach. This section owes much to it.

sign of his desire for peace and abhorrence of civil strife (8.2–9.1). The subsequent intervention in Mauretania promptly demonstrates his resilience.

Thus the reader has been carefully prepared for chapter 10. We are not surprised to learn that the Lusitani invite Sertorius to become their leader on account of his reputation, not only for military prowess but for justice and clemency (10.1). The summary of his skills and character traits that follows (10.2–4) is borne out by everything we have read so far. Only when we are as well disposed toward the hero as we ever will be does Plutarch alert us, cautiously, to the fact that there were problems in the final years. Yet he just vaguely alludes to the precise nature of Sertorius' worst lapse ("the act committed against the hostages") and hastens to set forth a psychological explanation lest the reader conclude that the hero was, after all, cruel and violent throughout. The *tychē* that abandoned him, and his false friends who wronged him: those are the true causes of his moral decline (10.5–7). When later Plutarch feels compelled to mention the burning of Lauro (18.11), his report of the incident is coupled with the assertion that Sertorius acted not in anger or out of cruelty but upon purely rational and strategic concerns.

The long central section (chs. 11–17) reinforces our admiring view of the hero. He leads through winning the minds (11.2–12.1) and hearts (14) of the Hispanians; in describing the School at Osca, Plutarch avoids any hint at the hostages' eventual fate (14.3–4). When faced with a lapse of discipline, Sertorius has no need to resort to punishment or bribery (as will Eumenes, 8.9–12 and 13.12–13): persuasion does the trick (16). He easily bests his Roman adversaries, as a general (12.2–7, 13.7–12) and as a human being (13.1–6). When Perperna, with a large army, arrives intent on waging war against the Senate's forces independently, his own troops force him to accept Sertorius as overall commander: such is the hero's reputation for "saving himself and others" (15).[33]

Chapters 18–21 give splendid examples of Sertorius' military leadership and resourcefulness against Pompeius Magnus, the greatest Roman commander of the age; yet they also prepare us, almost imperceptibly, to accept the hero's ultimate failure. From victory at Lauro (18) we move to a draw at the Sucro (19), and on to defeat at Segontia (21.1–4, puncturing the sweeping claim at 19.1 that only his lieutenants suffered routs, and never he in person). Again, however, Sertorius' resilience prevails (21.4–9), or so it seems. We learn nothing further about the war in Spain, for the story of success is over.[34]

Sertorius ended as a victim of assassins who were convinced he had abandoned the ways of a Roman and become a tyrant. Those were serious charges requiring a well-crafted rebuttal, set forth in chapters 22–24. Plutarch begins by resuming a rhetorical device first explored in chapter 13: a character sketch of the hero's opponent, Metellus, that paragon of nobility and champion of

---

33. On this aspect see Plácido 103.
34. On similar examples of glossing over the hero's defeats in *Eumenes* see Bosworth 78–79.

the Sullan settlement. Unable to overcome Sertorius in open warfare, Metellus resorts to bribes and treachery, while indulging himself in all sorts of degenerate luxury (21.1–4): we suddenly realize that it was not old age alone (13.1, 18.1) that kept him from vanquishing his adversary. Any tales of Sertorius' succumbing to debauchery in his later years will now lose significance and credibility. Perperna and his comrades may claim that Sertorius showed nothing but contempt for his Roman followers while extending preferential treatment to the Hispanians (25). Having already read the rest of chapter 22, we will find that hard to believe: for who could be more in step with Roman tradition, be it in matters of government, patriotism, or love of family? Any lingering doubts as to the hero's loyalties are dispelled in chapters 23 and 24, detailing his negotiations and alliance with Mithradates. We learn that his fellow senators—that is, Perperna and the other assassins-to-be—are the ones willing to sell out on the question of the province of Asia: Sertorius alone insists on upholding Rome's honor and the indivisibility of her empire (23.5–7). Once his deputy takes charge of the province and begins to govern it according to Sertorius' principles, the East experiences the same outpouring of goodwill toward Sertorius, and, ultimately, toward Roman rule as did Spain (24.4–5).

Hence the reader is not inclined to give much credence to the grievances aired by the hero's detractors, as presented in chapter 25. But Fate is not fair. Perperna and the other malcontents find a way to alienate the Hispanians from their leader; defections mount, and Sertorius, feeling betrayed and facing defeat, loses control of himself. With that, he furnishes the pretext for his removal. His deterioration of character from benevolence to cruelty is not denied, just as earlier instances of ruthlessness (at Castulo, in Rome, at Lauro) did not go unmentioned. But moral responsibility is shifted to those who envy and detest him, and who themselves are wanting in virtue throughout. As always, Plutarch is too honest to lie outright, or even to suppress unpleasant facts altogether. Instead, his *Sertorius* is a magisterial exercise in the art of making the ominous sound innocuous.

Regarding the assassination itself, *Caesar* may serve for illumination. There we find a huge portrait of the Dictator-turned-tyrant (56–61), followed by a character sketch of Brutus (62) that leaves no doubt about his honorable motives. Numerous portents warn of the impending blow of fate (63), and Caesar has several close brushes with survival (64–65). The killing is told in rambling detail, with "it is also said" and "some also report" added liberally to the main storyline (66).

By comparison, the scene in the *Sertorius* is a masterpiece of narrative economy and concentration. The first half of chapter 26 centers on the conspirators' machinations. Perperna's associates are revealed to be an even sorrier lot than we would already expect after chapter 25: pederastic jealousy and pompous bragging threaten to unravel the entire plot, thus propelling Perperna into action. There are no portents announcing the leader's doom, no last chances to heed a warning and be safe. The setting of the actual murder is as sordid as the motive: a drunken banquet, with one final assurance that Sertorius was not given to debauchery and convivial abandon. The plotters' fate is ignominious (27), as befits their character. Perperna dies attempting to buy his life: Schulten's "der elende Mensch" ("that miserable wretch") sums it up neatly. Fate and the moral depravity of those he had saved and led to victory have destroyed the hero.

5. Historical Method

Plutarch's historical methods have been studied, in depth and conclusively, by a long line of scholars.[35] Extensive repetition is tedious and unnecessary. A brief review of what must be kept in mind when reading the *Lives* as sources of historical knowledge will suffice.

Plutarch read widely, and he had access to virtually all existing works of literature and reference. But working from papyrus scrolls made scholarly writing a cumbersome undertaking, far more so than working from books in codex form. The roll required both hands for perusal, and as chapter, section, or line numbering was largely unknown, speedy location of any given item was difficult. As for note taking, Plutarch did employ it to some degree, but here, too, technical limitations stood in the way of effectiveness. Notecards in the modern sense were unavailable, though wax tablets might be employed in a similar way. Most note taking, however, would be done on a papyrus roll, and excerpts consequently appeared in the order in which the material was encountered in the scholar's reading. Rearrangement according to different topical criteria faced formidable obstacles. Not notes and constant cross-checking, but extensive preliminary reading of sources, "handle to handle," and reliance on memory were Plutarch's chief instruments of research and writing.[36]

The biographical purpose determines Plutarch's presentation of the material. A chronological framework contains each life, but chronology is not so important as to dictate rigidly the internal arrangement. While Plutarch distinguishes major stages in an individual's career, subject matter and especially questions of character exercise the greatest influence over his grouping of events and facts. Chronological precision was not his aim, and must not be expected.[37]

Where full detail is not required by or helpful for his biographical purpose, Plutarch likes to abridge or rearrange his material. In a seminal study, Pelling has identified the main techniques through which the biographer achieves that objective.[38]

---

35. Fundamental are Theander, *Plutarch und die Geschichte*; Gomme 54–84; Stadter, *Methods* passim, and *Pericles* xliv–lii; Hamilton, *Alexander* xxxvii–xlix; Jones, *Plutarch* 81–109; Pelling, "Method" and "Adaptation," passim, and *Antony* 31–36; Frost, *Themistocles* 40–59.
36. Pelling, *Antony* 31–33; Stadter, *Pericles* xlv–xlvii.
37. See Russell, *Plutarch* 115.
38. Pelling, "Adaptation," summarized in what follows.

Conflation. Several events of a similar nature may be reshaped into a single one. Take, e.g., Pelling's most striking example, the three debates in the Senate on the fate of the Catilinarians. *Caes.* 7.7 gives the impression that there was only a single session, in the course of which the conspirators were unmasked and sentenced. Yet in *Cic.* 19.1–4 and 20.4–21.5, Plutarch clearly knew of at least two separate meetings, and *Crass.* 13.3 may indicate his being aware also of the third. For the purpose of the *Caesar*, the hero's role in those debates was all that mattered: hence only the third meeting, on 5 December.[39] In the *Sertorius*, the two separations of the Roman armies in Spain during the winters of 76/5 and 75/4 B.C. have been conflated into one (21.8), with dire results in modern attempts to establish a chronology of the Sertorian War.

Compression. Events distant in time but related in cause or theme may be represented as following immediately or closely upon each other.[40] Examples in the *Sertorius* are 12.3–5, where events covering a period of more than three years—summer 80 (Sertorius' return from Africa) to fall 77 (Pompey's arrival in Spain)—are paraphrased in rapid succession without indication of the time elapsed, and 21.4–8, where Pompey's letter to Rome (end of 75) seems to be not much later than the siege of Clunia (end of 76).

Displacement. An item may be shifted from its proper position in the sequence of events so as to arrange the material in a more logical or pleasing manner, or to create a different emphasis and greater dramatic effect than could be achieved by a strictly chronological narrative.[41] Thus the establishment of the Sertorian "Senate" (22.5) is mentioned only after the military events of the war down to the end of 75 (21.9) have been dealt with, although it should be dated to 77 (or perhaps 76; see Commentary, 22.5n.). The treaty with Mithradates is reported still later (23–24); yet it belongs in 76 or 75. Plutarch in these passages is emphasizing the *Romanitas* of Sertorius, and the conclusion of the alliance is represented as the height of the hero's career.

Suppression. Besides chronological distortion the biographer achieves narrative emphasis, concentration, or simply economy by reducing the role of a secondary—though historically important—character, or dropping him altogether.[42] Sertorius' principal lieutenant, L. Hirtuleius (see Commentary, 12.4n.), is referred to only once, in passing and without being named. Yet his importance is amply attested by the other sources. His defeat at Italica at the hands of Metellus was of strategic consequence; Plutarch never mentions it. At Lauro a sizable part of Pompey's army was destroyed (see Commentary,

---

39. For another illuminating example—Plutarch's treatment in the *Crassus, Cato Minor,* and *Pompey* of the two different laws assigning or extending the provinces of Pompeius, Crassus, and Caesar in 55 B.C.—see Pelling, "Adaptation" 127. Cf. also Russell, "Coriolanus" 23–27.
40. Pelling, "Adaptation" 127–28.
41. Pelling, "Adaptation" 128–29.
42. Pelling, "Method" 77.

18.9–10: Battle of Lauro), but neither of the protagonists, Sertorius and Pompeius, took part in the fighting. Plutarch does not record the incident. The battle of Segontia (21.1–3), a day-long affair fought in three separate engagements, is reduced to a climactic struggle between Sertorius and Metellus: it was only this part of the battle that led to Sertorius' only defeat in the field. Pompey's presence is merely implied (by mentioning the death of his Quaestor), Perperna's role ignored.[43]

Transfer. Acts of one character may be attributed to another: e.g., Caesar's inflammatory address to his troops on the eve of the Civil War is reported correctly in *Caes.* 31.3, but ascribed to Antonius and Cassius in *Ant.* 5.10.[44] There is no demonstrable instance of this device in the *Sertorius*.

Condensation and rearrangement of his material are not the only features of Plutarch's technique. When his sources give but meager information on a matter of interest to him, he is not above creating illuminating detail, or explanatory context.[45] The scene between Cinna and Sertorius (5.1–4) is a good example: the bare facts are credible enough, but the elaborate dialogue looks like the biographer's own work. At 24.4 M. Marius enters towns in Roman Asia ahead of the King of Pontos: probably the terms of the treaty stipulated such a procedure, but it is unlikely that Marius and Mithradates ever entered any town in the province together. Caution must be exercised, though. Metellus' victory celebrations (21.2–3) might easily be suspected to be another instance of fabricated detail, if we had not Sallust *Hist.* 2.70, of which they are a faithful rendering, almost verbatim.

Lastly, the reader of the *Sertorius* no less than of the other lives is advised to heed the "general principles for reading Plutarch" laid down by Frost and Stadter.[46] They are ignored at great peril.

3. Sertorius: Sources and Tradition

1. The First Generation

No contemporary records of the life and deeds of Quintus Sertorius have survived. However, several contemporary authors—contemporary in the sense that they were adults for the better part of his career—are known or can be surmised to have written about him.

a. *L. Cornelius Sulla.* The pervasive influence exercised by the dictator's memoirs over the way the history of his age was to be written, down to the present

---

43. For similar suppression of major fighting in the *Eumenes* see Bosworth 58, 76–79.
44. Pelling, "Adaptation" 129, 139–40.
45. Pelling, "Adaptation" 129–31; cf. Stadter's remarks (*Methods* 138–39): "Such small bits of gratuitous information are the stock in trade of the storyteller who wishes to add charm to his anecdote and is not tied to a written text." See also Carney, *JHS* 80 (1960) 28–29; Russell, "Coriolanus" 23–25.
46. Frost, *Themistocles* 55–59; Stadter, *Pericles* li–lii.

day, is well known.⁴⁷ In Plutarch it can be felt throughout the *Sulla,* the *Marius,* and in the early chapters of the *Pompey.*⁴⁸ Surely in Sulla's depiction of events from 87 to 82 B.C., Sertorius played a part, and not a flattering one. Nothing survives that could be safely identified; however, the guess seems not too adventurous that Appian's account of Sertorius' role in the Civil War of 83–82 ultimately goes back to Sulla.

b. *L. Cornelius Sisenna.* In no fewer than twenty-three books, Sisenna offered an exhaustive treatment of the Social and Civil War, 91–82 B.C. It quickly became the standard history, in Latin, of that unhappy decade. A contemporary and an active politician (Praetor in 78, hence born no later than 118), Sisenna could avail himself of abundant and independent information, but the shadow of Sulla's memoirs nonetheless seems to have loomed large over his history. Sallust mixed praise of thoroughness with criticism of political subservience to the Sullan point of view (*Iug.* 95.2, *parum libero ore locutus*). A sympathetic treatment of Sertorius is not to be expected, though like Sulla's memoirs, Sisenna's work did not cover the main period of his career, that is, the war in Spain.

c. *Poseidonios of Apameia.* The greatest scientific mind of the age was imbued with a keen interest in history, and often approached it from angles unusual in ancient historiography. His *Histories,* in at least forty-nine books (probably fifty-two), were designed to continue the universal history of Polybios, from the destruction of Carthage in 146 to the sack of Athens in 86. They dealt at length with Rome's wars in Spain, the Cimbrian invasions, and the beginnings of violent civil strife in Italy from the Social War to the death of Marius.⁴⁹ It is a tantalizing question whether Poseidonios also furnished material for Sertorius' later career.

No fully confident answer is possible. Scholars are largely agreed that the *Histories* terminated with Sulla's capture of Athens in 86 B.C.⁵⁰ Hence coverage of the Sertorian War in that work seems a priori improbable. It would, however, have been an obvious component of Poseidonios' *History of Pompey*—if such a work ever did exist, and there are serious doubts.⁵¹ Yet a con-

---

47. For a plausible assessment of the work's structure see Lewis, *Athenaeum* 79 (1991) 509–19.
48. Valgiglio's study, "L'autobiografia," is fundamental.
49. Malitz, *Historien* 96–134, 198–228, 394–408.
50. See, e.g., Jacoby, *FGrHist* II C 156; Malitz, *Historien* 70–74. Important dissenters are Strasburger 44 and Momigliano, *H&T* 11 (1972) 280, 17 (1978) 15, who would let the work reach down to 63 or at least 70. Ruschenbusch, *Hermes* 121 (1993) 70–76, argues for 88.
51. The sole testimony is Strabo 11.1.6 (Poseid. *FGrHist* 87 T 11 = F 79 E-K = F 47 Th): . . . καὶ τὴν ἱστορίαν συνέγραψε τὴν περὶ αὐτόν. Reference to a monograph about Pompeius has been doubted by Jacoby (II C 157, 162) and denied by Theiler (2:59–60, following Schwartz, *Philologus* 86 [1931] 391 n. 22). Malitz, *Historien* 72–73, is undecided but skeptical; K. Reinhardt, *RE* 22.1 (1953) 638, maintains its existence. Kidd, *Posidonius* 2:331–33, in a sober discussion shows that, while doubts must remain, "the Greek strongly favors a reference to Pompey."

siderable amount of Poseidonian thought appears to be preserved in other areas of the history of the 70s and 60s B.C., as narrated in the surviving sources. The treatment of the pirates in Strabo, Plutarch's *Pompey,* and Appian offers perhaps the most striking example, and it is difficult to reject the conclusion that Poseidonios covered much of the two decades after Sulla, at least as far as Pompey's career was concerned (which would include the Sertorian War).[52] Whether he did so in a separate history of Pompeius, or continued the *Histories* down to about 63, or employed in the *Histories* a number of anticipatory excursuses that went beyond the general terminal point in 86 B.C.[53] cannot be said.

d. *M. Terentius Varro.* That scholarly and prolific author wrote at length about the Sertorian War on at least one occasion, his autobiographical *legationum libri III;* perhaps also in the logistoricus *Pius aut de pace* and in the three books *De Pompeio.* His knowledge of the war was firsthand, as one of Pompey's Legates (*RR* 3.12.7; cf. Sall. *Hist.* 2.69). A friendly treatment of Sertorius naturally must not be presumed, but absolutely nothing is known that would permit us to postulate substantial distortion.[54] Varro's was the fundamental account in Latin, and if Poseidonios did not furnish one of his own (see above, 3.1.c), the ultimate source of all later narratives. No doubt Sallust was heavily indebted to him for facts if not interpretation, though the notion that he criticized Varro as being "credulous about rumors" rests on a misunderstanding of his Latin.[55]

e. *M. Tullius Cicero.* As a young man, Cicero had known Sertorius (or at least heard him speak) in the 80s; he mentions him as a talented though less than polished orator (*Brut.* 180). There are vague and scattered references to the Sertorian War, but not to the man himself, in the speeches.[56] The earliest ones,

52. Strasburger 42–44, 49–51. For a fuller discussion see below, section 3.13.

53. A possibility entertained (for the case of Sertorius) though not endorsed by Malitz, *Historien* 100 n. 37. To the present writer it seems the most attractive solution, especially in view of the near certainty of a similar excursus dealing with M. Claudius Marcellus: see Malitz, 361–64.

54. That the *Pius aut de pace* contained an attack on certain moralizing and "censorious" elements in Sallust's *Histories* (Gell. 17.18) obviously says nothing about Varro's own historiographical tendency.

55. Sall. *Hist.* 2.69, *haec postquam Varro maius in more rumorem audivit,* evidently belongs in a narrative context: i.e., Varro, while serving under Pompeius in Spain, had been told (*postquam audivit*) an exaggerated version of some incident (cf. Tac. *Ann.* 3.44.1, *at Romae non Treveros modo et Aeduos, sed quattuor et sexaginta Galliarum civitates descivisse, adsumptos in societatem Germanos, dubias Hispanias, cuncta, ut mos famae, in maius credita*). Maurenbrecher (ad loc.) and Cichorius, *RS* 193, of course, saw the matter correctly. Surprisingly, Syme, *Sallust* 206, mistook the fragment as a comment by Sallust, referring to Varro's account. Syme's error was uncritically absorbed by Spann, 215 n. 4, and made the basis of far-reaching speculations by Katz, *Maia* 33 (1981) 111, 120. In a similar vein, though no more convincing, McGushin, 224, makes the fragment refer to *Hist.* 2.70.

56. 2*Verr.* 1.87, 5.72, 5.146–47, 5.151–55; *Imp. Cn. Pomp.* 9, 21, 46; *Mur.* 32; *De leg. agr.* 2.83.

in the Verrines, fall several years after Sertorius' death, and Cicero's reticence permits no guess as to how he felt about the man.

2. Sallust

Some 530 fragments of Sallust's *Histories* survive. The work, probably unfinished at the time of his death in 34 B.C., treated in five books the years from Sulla's dictatorship to Pompey's Mithradatic command. The first three books, with almost 400 fragments extant, contained the Sertorian War from its inception in 82 to Perperna's death in 73 or 72; well over a hundred fragments attest to the prominent position Sertorius occupied in this part of the work. A late (fourth century?), brief, and muddled epitome extracted by one Iulius Exuperantius covers the same time span and offers occasionally useful, often tantalizing glimpses of the lost original.[57]

Sallust's sympathy for Sertorius is evident. Both were Sabines, both New Men, and in an introductory sketch the historian openly accuses earlier writers of downplaying Sertorius' achievements: *multaque tum ductu eius peracta primo per ignobilitatem, deinde per invidiam scriptorum incelebrata sunt* (1.88). Among such earlier writers we may readily suspect Sisenna, Varro, and probably Poseidonios, all of whom can be surmised to have served as Sallust's sources. He set out to rectify their misrepresentations, a task he apparently accomplished rather well. For not only was he eventually to furnish Plutarch with most of the material for this life, but quite possibly the biographer was prompted to write it by his readings in Sallust to begin with.[58]

Yet caution is advised. We must not imagine Sallust's treatment of Sertorius an uncritical eulogy, idealized though it probably was. It is dangerous to impute to Sallust Plutarch's criteria of judgment or biographical purpose merely because much, perhaps all, of the life's factual framework along with its favorable view of the hero is derived from the historian.[59] Sallust may have toned down somewhat the change from benign to tyrannical in Sertorius' character, but nothing indicates that his account of the last years differed substantially from that of the other sources as far as the plain facts are concerned. Plutarch did his best to make Sertorius appear without moral blemish, yet would not see fit to deny or altogether suppress reports of the hero's cruelty. If Sallust had given him evidence to the contrary, one should think he would have put

---

57. Standard editions of Exuperantius by G. Landgraf and C. Weyman, "Die Epitome des Iulius Exuperantius," *Archiv für Lateinische Lexicographie* 12 (1902) 561–78, and N. Zorzetti (Leipzig 1982). The latter's attempt, however, at claiming Exuperantius for the Livian tradition (xiv–xx) remains quite unconvincing. On the year of Sallust's death see G. Perl, *Klio* 48 (1967).

58. First suggested by Peter, *Quellen* 62. Plutarch drew heavily on the *Histories* for *Lucullus, Sulla, Pompey,* and *Crassus,* all except perhaps the last earlier than the *Sertorius.* But see below, sections 3.4.c and 3.13, on Cornelius Nepos.

59. A warning sounded by Büchner, *Sallust* 163, not heeded enough by García Moreno, "Paradoxography" 141–52. See also Syme's salutary remarks, *Sallust* 205.

it to good use. Which is not to say that Sallust agreed with an interpretation that saw in Sertorius little more than a *hostis populi Romani*.⁶⁰

3. Diodoros of Sicily

Diodoros' universal history in forty books reached to the outbreak of Caesar's Gallic War⁶¹ and apparently was written in the 30s B.C., roughly contemporaneous with Sallust's *Histories*. The Sertorian War was dealt with at some length; a sizable Byzantine excerpt (fr. 37.22a) describing Sertorius' final years and assassination survives. It is not a sympathetic picture, though we cannot know how Diodoros portrayed Sertorius in his better years. That he had access to sources unavailable to Sallust is improbable. He relied on Poseidonios where possible; if indeed the latter wrote about Sertorius, the Diodoros excerpt is likely to reflect his views.⁶²

4. Authors of the Late First Century B.C.

a. *C. Sulpicius Galba*. The grandfather of the later emperor wrote a history of Rome, from the beginnings (it seems) to his own time. Orosius 5.23.6 (= HRR F 2), presumably via Livy, cites a detail from the Sertorian War. If Peter (HRR 2:lviii) correctly dated Galba's birth about 75 B.C., the work was probably not yet available to Sallust.

b. *Tanusius Geminus*. Tanusius wrote a history of undetermined scope; it included Sertorius' sojourn in Africa during 81/80 (Strabo 17.3.8 = HRR F 1) and Caesar's operations in Gaul in 55 B.C. (*Caes.* 22.4 = HRR F 3) and hence was not completed prior to the second half of the century. It is impossible to say whether the work would have been ready for Sallust's perusal.

c. *Cornelius Nepos*. This friend of Cicero, Atticus, and Catullus may justly be called the father of Latin biography. Nepos' earlier writings include a three-volume chronological handbook of important events in world history, a collection of *exempla*, and probably a geographical work. His most significant contribution came late in life: sixteen or more books *De viris illustribus*, composed in the late 40s and 30s B.C. The series was arranged in pairs, one book of Greek individuals facing one of Romans, and apparently dealt mostly with men of intellectual achievement—orators, philosophers, writers. But a later pair offered lives of Greek/foreign and Roman generals, respectively; the Greek book is the only fully extant volume of Nepos' entire work. It was first published some time prior to the death of Atticus in 32 B.C., though the version preserved constitutes a second edition dating to a later year. The lives are plain and short, typically six to eight pages in an Oxford Classical Text.⁶³

---

60. Büchner's thesis, 263–68, rightly castigated by Spann, 156–57.
61. On the terminal point see Fornara, CP 87 (1992) 387–88.
62. García Moreno, "Paradoxography" 136–37, takes derivation from the Rhodian for certain.
63. See Geiger, *Nepos* 66–104.

Inclusion of Sertorius among the Roman generals cannot be postulated, of course; but it would seem wise not to rule it out.

d. *Strabon of Amaseia.* Strabo's *Historika Hypomnēmata*, intended to continue Polybios, treated the history of the Greek and Roman world from 146 B.C. to the end of the Civil Wars, in at least thirty-nine books. The work apparently was completed around 25 B.C., half a century before the final redaction of the author's *Geography*. Repeated mention of Sertorius in the latter work suggests that Strabo treated the Sertorian War at some length in his *Histories*.

5. Livy and the Livian Tradition

a. *Livy.* T. Livius of Patavium in his epic history gave plenty of attention to Sertorius: though the books in question are lost, the fourth-century book-by-book summaries known as the *Periochae*[64] still attest to the character's major role in books 79–80 (the siege of Rome, 87 B.C.), 90–94, and 96 (the Sertorian War). Livy is often thought to be the chief exponent of a tradition virulently hostile toward Sertorius, depicting him as "basically malignant."[65] The surviving evidence does little to support such an extreme view. A long fragment (22 W-M) of book 91 depicts Sertorius as a competent commander, without adding hostile touches.[66] His treatment of Contrebia (lines 1–14), surrendering after a long and bitter siege, is characterized as rather mild and fully within traditional Roman practice: *obsidibus acceptis pecuniae modicam exegit summam armaque omnia ademit;* free deserters are to be handed over alive, whether to be punished (as would be customary) or pardoned remains untold; runaway slaves are to be killed by the townspeople themselves. His words and actions at the subsequent *conventus sociorum* (lines 15–35) are simply those of a Roman promagistrate, albeit at war with the ruling faction in Rome, not those of an Iberianized robber baron bent on destroying the Roman order.[67] Sertorius' *Romanitas* was emphasized, not denied by Livy.

That, of course, does not imply general approval and political sympathies along Plutarch's or Sallust's lines. Sertorius' shift toward arbitrariness and cruelty was told at length in book 92; but in all the sources at Livy's disposal, Sallust included, those facts were undisputed, and unlike Plutarch and Sallust, he had no reason to mitigate their impact by way of excuse or psychological interpretation. The last reference to Sertorius in the *Periochae* (book 96) sug-

---

64. On their date see Bessone, "Tradizione" 1259 n. 137, and P. L. Schmidt, *HLL* 5:192.

65. Spann, xi; cf. Stahl, 21–22; Schulten, 13–15; García Moreno, "Paradoxography" 141.

66. Ogilvie's postumous edition of the fragment, *PCPS* 30 (1984) 116–25, offers an improved text in a number of instances, though without crucial significance for matters Sertorian.

67. Spann, 59–62 and diss. 164, saw this clearly enough, yet failed to take it into consideration when he dismissed Livy as strictly anti-Sertorian.

gests Livy found him worthy of an obituary impressive enough to catch the epitomizer's eye: *magnus dux et adversus duos imperatores, Pompeium et Metellum, ⟨saepe par⟩ vel frequentius victor, ad ultimum et saevus et prodigus.* According to the Elder Seneca (*Suas.* 6.21), Livy granted an obituary to all *magni viri*. His treatment of Sertorius surely was not idealized, but it must not be imagined as replete with malicious distortion either: rather, the story was of a great Roman whose life went all wrong. As some scholars saw long ago, Livy's account differed from Sallust's in tone and judgment, not in substance or fact.[68]

b. *The "Lost Epitome" and the* Periochae. This is not the place to venture into the old and ongoing dispute concerning the transmission of Livian material in excerpted or abbreviated form in antiquity. What can be considered certain is the existence of two strands of epitomizing works, one chronographic in nature and chiefly represented by the Oxyrhynchos Epitome, Iulius Obsequens, and Cassiodorus, the other of a narrative orientation as surviving in the *Periochae*, Ampelius, Eutropius, and Orosius, with Valerius Maximus and Florus as early cousins.[69] Direct descent of each group from the full text of Livy is certainly arguable,[70] but the nineteenth-century belief in an earlier epitome, similar in character to the *Periochae* but considerably more extensive, as the ultimate purveyor of Livian material to those authors has been persuasively restated, with important modifications, by Luigi Bessone.[71] Compiled in the first century, probably as early as the age of Tiberius, this "Lost Epitome" would have served as the Livian source of the chronographic branch as well as Valerius Maximus and Orosius.[72] A certain amount of extraneous material, more pervasive in some (Florus, Ampelius, Eutropius) than in others (the *Periochae*, Orosius), is common to all representatives of the Livian tradition. Individual differences make it unlikely that these non-Livian accretions can simply be traced back to the first-century Epitome; by the same token, the level of agreement is too high for the intrusions to be attributable to each author's discretion. Hence Bessone postulates, cautiously yet persuasively, the existence of a later compilation, drawn from the "Tiberian" one but augmented with material from other sources and no longer taking account of Livy's book divisions. This Second Epitome should be seen as the Livian source of Florus and, mostly through that author, Ampelius and Eutropius; knowledge of Florus also accounts for the occasional "contamination" in Oro-

---

68. Bieńkowski, "De fontibus" 95, 107; Treves 128–29; cf. Syme, *Sallust* 206.
69. Schmidt, *Obsequens* 22–64, excepting, however, Valerius Maximus and Florus.
70. So chiefly Schmidt, whose reconstruction goes as follows, simplified. A late third-century Livy chronicle ("ein korrekteres Exemplar der Oxyrhynchos-Chronik"), based directly on Livy, is the source of Obsequens, Cassiodorus, and the extant Oxyrhynchos Epitome; likewise the *Periochae* are derived immediately and independently from Livy and furnished the Livian material found in Eutropius and Orosius (*Obsequens* 64–65; *HLL* 5:190–93, 204).
71. Bessone, "Tradizione" passim, and "*Periochae*" 50–55.
72. Bessone, "Tradizione" 1238 n. 33a, 1248–52, 1259–62.

sius—generally a straight follower of the original Epitome.[73] The *Periochae* exhibit some vulgate material, though rather less than Orosius, and like the third-century Livy Chronicle are essentially drawn from the First Epitome, if not from Livy's complete text itself.[74]

c. *Eutropius.* The *Breviarium ab urbe condita,* commissioned by the Emperor Valens (A.D. 364–378), summarizes in ten sections ("books") Roman history down to the death of Jovian in A.D. 364. In accordance with its purpose, the treatment is brief and cursory, a total of about seventy Teubner pages. The Sertorian War (6.1.2–3) occupies ten lines. Eutropius drew the Republican part of his breviary from Livy, or rather a Livy epitome, supplemented with a biographical source;[75] his matter-of-fact account is of little help in establishing Livy's own attitude toward Sertorius. Plutarch, though, would have agreed with Eutropius' opening comment: *Sertorius, qui partium Marianarum fuerat, timens fortunam ceterorum, qui interempti erant, ad bellum commovit Hispanias* (cf. *Synkr.* 2[21].2–5).

d. *Orosius.* Paulus Orosius of Bracara Augusta was presbyter in Spain until A.D. 414, when, fleeing the Visigothic invasion, he moved to Africa where he became a pupil and associate of Saint Augustine. His *Historiae adversum paganos,* in seven books *ab orbe condito* (1.1.14) to A.D. 417, are the first attempt to write a universal history from a Christian point of view. The work aims at contrasting the cruelty and violence of the pagan world against the peace and happiness of the new age; hence we find a constant emphasis on internecine warfare, civil strife, and massacres, and a penchant for gargantuan casualty figures. Orosius' account of Rome's Republican period was based on Livy; as in the case of Eutropius there is strong reason to think that he worked from an epitome rather than the complete text.[76]

Next to Plutarch and Appian, Orosius offers the most complete coherent account of the Sertorian War (5.23.2–15); in addition, he gives some details regarding Sertorius' participation in the siege of Rome in 87 (5.19.9–10). Sertorius is castigated as *civilis belli incentor*; his chief characteristic is *audacia*: so at 5.20.11, where it compares favorably, however, to *potentia Cinnae, crudelitas Marii,* and *insania Fimbriae,* or 5.23.2, *vir dolo atque audacia*

---

73. Bessone, "Tradizione" 1253–62. The compilation would have to be dated prior to Florus, i.e., no later than the early second century (cf. below, section 3.8). One wonders, though—partly along the lines of Schmidt, *HLL* 5:191—whether this second epitomizer might not be more economically identified with Florus himself. On Ampelius' Livian material, derived in part though not entirely from Florus, see Bessone, 1238 n. 35 (Florus plus epitome), and Schmidt, 177 (Florus plus a biographical collection).

74. Bessone, "Tradizione" 1238, 1259, 1263; cf. Schmidt, *HLL* 5:191–92, firmly in favor of a direct excerpt.

75. So Schmidt, *HLL* 5:203–4, inclined to identify the epitome with our *Periochae*. But overlaps of Eutropius with Florus and Ampelius, i.e., Bessone's Second Epitome tradition, are too strong to make that derivation plausible; see Bessone, "Tradizione" 1262–63.

76. C. Zangemeister, ed., *Pauli Orosii Historiarum adversum paganos libri VII* (Wien 1882) xxv–xxvi, and cf. above, 3.5.b.

potens. In a group with Lepidus, Scipio, Brutus, Carbo, Domitius, and Perperna, Sertorius stands out as *omnium atrocissimus* (5.24.16), but the context suggests the epithet was determined by the severity of the war rather than personal characteristics. His turn toward cruelty and despotism in the later years, prominent in Livy (*Per.* 92), goes unmentioned; instead the sack of Lauro is held up as an example of savagery (5.23.7). Plutarch's labored excusation (18.11) would seem to support such a view. Overall, Orosius treats Sertorius neither admiringly nor as a bloodthirsty monster in the mold of Marius or Sulla. As he is not kindly disposed in general toward the warlords of the Heathen Age, the negative elements in his picture of Sertorius must be assumed to reflect his own views and purpose at least as much as they reflect Livy's. Even the idealized Sertorius of Sallust and Plutarch would have found but little favor in Orosius' eyes.

e. *De viris illustribus*. This anonymous compilation offers brief biographical summaries of eighty-six individuals important in Roman history, from Proca to Kleopatra. It dates probably from the first half of the fourth century and ultimately would seem based on Livy through the use of intermediary sources, such as an epitome and Florus, or on a biographical source such as Nepos and Hyginus.[77] Sertorius does not rate a separate entry but finds brief mention under Metellus Pius (chapter 63) and Pompeius Magnus (chapter 77).

6. Velleius Paterculus

Velleius' history, finished in A.D. 30, probably contained a brief section on the Sertorian War. Unfortunately a lacuna has deprived us of all but its end (2.29.5–30.1). Livy appears to be the most likely source for this part of Velleius' work.[78]

7. Memnon of Herakleia

Memnon's history of Herakleia on Pontos, written, it seems, in the first century A.D., survives in part through summaries of books 9–16, compiled by Photios. The work is naturally not concerned with Sertorius, but it contains valuable information regarding the treaty with Mithradates. Memnon's authorities for the early first century B.C. were mostly local histories of Herakleia; his work thus stands outside the general source tradition as far as Sertorius is concerned.[79]

8. L. Annaeus Florus

This mysterious author, whose very name remains in doubt, compiled, probably in the reign of Hadrian, a survey of all of Rome's wars from Romulus to

---

77. Schmidt, *HLL* 5: 187–90, with copious literature; cf. also above, 3.5.b, and Bessone, "Tradizione" 1257–63.
78. Bieńkowski, "De fontibus" 91; Stahl 18–19.
79. Jacoby, *FGrHist* III b *Kommentar* 267–71.

Augustus.[80] The title imposed on the work in the manuscripts and traditionally retained by editors, *Epitoma de Tito Livio*, is, though ancient, not the author's own; it is also apt to mislead in a twofold manner. The two books do not constitute an excerpt from or an abbreviation of a larger work: they are a list of wars, both external and civil, independently arranged by Florus according to chronology, geography, and subject matter.[81] Nor is the material all drawn from Livy: there are traces of Cato, Caesar, Lucan, and—of greatest importance for our purpose—Sallust.[82] Florus' accounts of both the Jugurthine War (1.36) and the Catilinarian affair (2.12) are evidently based on Sallust, and the rather hostile treatment of Sulla (in the sections *bellum civile Marianum sive Sullanum*, 2.9, and *bellum civile sub Lepido*, 2.11) suggests either Sallustian influence or a less than friendly portrait of the dictator at the pen of Livy. (On the evidence of Orosius and the *Periochae* one may suspect the latter to be true in any case.)

Regarding Sertorius (2.10), Florus, to say the least, is not unsympathetic. *Bellum Sertorianum quid amplius quam Sullanae proscriptionis hereditas fuit?* (2.10.1) opens the section; next, Sertorius is introduced as *exul et profugus feralis illius tabulae* (2.10.2): Sulla's brutality rather than Sertorius himself must be held morally responsible for this war. The characterization continues: *vir summae quidem sed calamitosae virtutis*. Not that enemies of the Roman People are routinely credited with *virtus* in adversary historiography. Four times Florus refers to Sertorius as a *Romanus dux:* thrice verbatim (2.10.1, 3, 8), once implicitly in his concluding remark, *victores duces externum id magis quam civile bellum videri voluerunt, ut triumpharent* (2.10.9)— hardly a flattering comment on Metellus and Pompeius. Emphasis on Sertorius the *Romanus dux* agrees with Livy (see above, 3.5.a) as well as Sallust and Plutarch. Florus' portrait is critical, yet far from hostile slander; admiring where proper, yet not a eulogy; approving of the man and leader, though not of his actions' consequences.

Highly rhetorical like the rest of his work, Florus' account of the Sertorian War is of little value as regards historical fact. Its significance lies in the judgment and sentiment exhibited. If drawn from Livy, the latter's portrait of Sertorius was a far cry from the venomous bias so often postulated. If based on Sallust, it confirms the view (see above, 3.2) that his presentation was considerably less idealized than that of Plutarch. On balance, Livy seems slightly more probable: Florus' treatment of the Hirtulei brothers as a unit[83] corresponds rather too closely to Orosius 5.23.12 and *De viris illustribus* 63.2.

---

80. The correct name may well be P. Annius Florus, as transmitted for the probably identical author of the dialogue *Vergilius orator an poeta*. See Baldwin's stimulating study, 134–37, on name and identity, and 149–42, on the date: perhaps as late as Antoninus Pius.

81. Jal, *Florus: Oeuvres* xxi–xxix, cii–cxiv. See also Bessone, "Tradizione" 1235 n. 24 and 1258 n. 133, in favor of an epitome as Florus' Livian source; on the title see Baldwin 138–39, correcting Jal xxii–xxiii.

82. Jal, *Florus* xxix–xxxii, with earlier literature.

83. Jal at 2.10.7 adopts B's *Hirtuleius* and consequently emends *his* to *hoc*. That rests on the mistaken belief that there was only one Hirtuleius; see Commentary, 12.4n.

9. Appianos of Alexandria

Of Appian's *Roman History* in twenty-four books, composed between roughly A.D. 150 and 163, the five subtitled *Emphylia,* "Civil Wars," offer a continuous narrative from 133 to 36 B.C. That in itself lends them unique status in what survives of Roman historiography. Appian's weaknesses and frequent lack of care with facts are well known, but to dismiss his work as "sensationalist"[84] is both to misunderstand it and deprive ourselves of a difficult and often frustrating yet nonetheless valuable source for the history of the Late Republic.

Book 1 of the *Civil Wars* covers events from Tiberius Gracchus to Pompey's and Crassus' first consulship in 70 B.C. Appian's sources have been the subject of much dispute; for the period 88–73 B.C., relevant to Sertorius, claims range from Varro to Sallust to Timagenes to Livy.[85] Detailed studies by Ensslin and Gabba have shown the Patavian to be one of the most likely candidates, though Hahn rightly insists that Appian used a variety of authorities.[86] Appian's arrangement of the material closely parallels the *Periochae,* and in the Sertorian War (*BC* 1.108.505–115.538) in particular it exhibits certain features that strongly point to his using not the original text of Livy but a fairly detailed epitome.[87] Thus the exact year-by-year account is atypical for Appian: clearly he did not cull it from Livy but conveniently found it in a summary listing events under the Consuls of each year, along the format of the Oxyrhynchos Epitome. The odd and maddeningly confused synchronism at 1.111 (with reference to 75/4 B.C.) bears a suggestive resemblance to the one given by Eutropius (6.1.1) and Orosius (5.23.1) under 78 B.C.; both authors are strong suspects when it comes to identifying users of an epitome.[88] Appian's substitution of Metellus for Afranius in the Sucro battle (110.513) is unsurprising if he was working from a source that failed to mention Afranius on that occasion; it is out of the question that Livy himself was responsible. Appian's entire understanding of grand strategy during the war is extremely schematic and patently wrong. He imagines Pompeius and Metellus to have operated together throughout the war when in fact they did so only briefly, though decisively, in 76–75. He is quite unaware of their provincial assignments—

---

84. Thus Spann, xi.
85. Varro: Stahl 31. Sallust: Bieńkowski, "De fontibus" 101–2; Maurenbrecher, *Prolegomena* 32–35. Timagenes: Schulten 15 n. 65 (following a suggestion of A. Klotz, *Cäsarstudien* 84 n. 4). One may add E. Schwartz, *RE* 2.1 (1895) 216–37, who thought Appian's source in the *Civil Wars* to be the work "eines sehr geschickt erzählenden, staatsrechtlich raisonierenden und fälschenden, emsigen und gewissenlosen Ausläufers der republikanischen Annalistik unter Augustus oder Tiberius" (235).
86. Ensslin, *Klio* 20 (1926) 415–65; Gabba, *Appiano* 89–101; Hahn, "Appian und seine Quellen."
87. I.e., most likely Bessone's First Epitome: cf. "Tradizione" 1235 n. 23.
88. Gabba, *Appiano* 100–101; see, however, Hahn, "Appian und seine Quellen" 251–60. On the basis of an unusual cluster of Olympiad dates in *BC* 1 (84.379, 99.463, 111.517), Hahn makes a strong argument in favor of a Greek source for Appian's narrative of the Sullan period.

Metellus in Farther Spain, Pompeius in Hither—and each year envisages them launching their campaign from the Pyrenees, just as he makes Sertorius and Perperna launch theirs from Lusitania. There are in fact no grounds whatsoever to believe Sertorius ever returned to Lusitania after his conquest of Hither Spain in 78–77; virtually all attested fighting involving his presence thereafter took place in the latter. Appian is frequently careless, but such sweeping misconceptions are difficult to account for if he read Livy—or any other full-scale narrative—in the original.

His portrait of Sertorius is the least favorable of the ones that survive. The "Senate" in Spain is gathered in deliberate mockery of the one in Rome (108.507), the white doe is indicative of Sertorius' own rather than the natives' superstition (110.514), and the leader's deterioration is displayed in full color: despotic savagery amidst women and wine (113.526–27). How much of this animus should be attributed to Livy directly rather than to Appian himself? The evidence found in other representatives of the Livian tradition—the *Periochae,* Orosius, and probably Florus—suggests the Patavian took a less inimical attitude while essentially reporting the same salient facts.

10. Granius Licinianus

The palimpsest fragments of Granius Licinianus' historical compendium are a sobering reminder of how much detailed knowledge about the early first century B.C. has been irrecoverably lost. The work, probably dating to the Antonine period, covered Roman history from early times to Caesar's death, perhaps in forty books. Fragments of book 35 contain a thorough yet tantalizingly lacunose account of the siege of Rome in 87. Granius' sources remain in question, though a Livian substratum, while not certain, appears likely.[89]

11. *Exempla* and *Memorabilia*

Bits and pieces of information concerning Sertorius are recorded by various collectors of *exempla* and *memorabilia*. The most important of these is Sex. Iulius Frontinus (*cos. II* A.D. 98, *III* 100), whose *Strategemata* contain numerous episodes from the Sertorian War; of particular interest are his detailed accounts of the battles of Lauro (2.5.31) and Italica (2.1.2, 2.3.5). Valerius Maximus reports the stories of the white fawn (1.2.4 *Epit. Par.*), the two horses (7.3.6), Metellus' victory celebrations (9.1.5), and the otherwise unrecorded fact that Sertorius had a wife (9.15.3). None of the other authors of this genre provides anything not known through the major sources, though Aulus Gellius' story of the white doe (15.22) may preserve traces of Sallust (see Commentary, 11.2–4, 20.1nn.). Pliny the Elder (*NH* 8.117) and Polyainos (*Strat.* 8.22) mention only the doe.

---

89. N. Criniti, *Grani Liciniani reliquiae* p. v; cf. Scardigli, *Grani Liciniani reliquiae* 3–10.

12. Oral Tradition

We must assume that besides historical writings, personal informants such as contemporaries and surviving eyewitnesses—on both sides—of the Sertorian War were available to the early chroniclers of Sertorius, that is, Poseidonios (?), Varro (himself a participant), Sallust, Diodoros, perhaps also Tanusius and Galba. That Poseidonios—provided he did write on that subject—and Sallust would have made use of such sources seems as likely as that Diodoros did not. Certainly the Characitani episode in Plutarch (chapter 17) and the details of Sertorius' assassination (26.7–11), along with the exact seating arrangements preserved by Sallust (*Hist.* 3.83), carry the ring of autopsy.

13. Plutarch

Sallust's *Histories* were the principal source for the *Sertorius*. That much is beyond dispute; the numerous fragments with close verbal parallels in the life speak for themselves. Compare, for instance, *Sert.* 3.5, 4.1–4, and *Hist.* 1.88; *Sert.* 4.5 and *Hist.* 1.89; *Sert.* 7.6–7 and *Hist.* 1.98–99; *Sert.* 8.2–9.1 and *Hist.* 1.100–103; *Sert.* 14.6 and *Hist.* 1.126; *Sert.* 21.2 and *Hist.* 2.67; *Sert.* 22.2–4 and *Hist.* 2.70; *Sert.* 23.2 and *Hist.* 2.78. No need, either, to assume that Plutarch did not read Sallust in the original but knew him only through some mysterious intermediary source or a Greek translation.[90] His Latin, though less than perfect in his own judgment (*Dem.* 2.2–4), was surely serviceable for his purpose: inadequate to appreciate the finer points of style, especially in oratory, but good enough to follow a historical narrative.[91] Absent evidence to the contrary we must accept that he read for himself the Latin authors he cites,[92] and that occasional misunderstandings are his own.

The sources he used besides Sallust are far less certain; in that respect as in others Plutarch is rather reticent in this life. He read widely and must be expected to supplement Sallust whenever it served his purpose. Works he had

---

90. An early second-century translation of the *Histories*, attested in the Suda (Z 73 Adler), is occasionally invoked in support of the view that Plutarch read virtually no Latin—most recently by García Moreno, "Paradoxography" 142. Since precise dates of publication are known for neither the *Sertorius* nor that translation, no argument can be based on the latter; any certain belief that it was available to Plutarch is mere illusion. Note, too, that Sallust very likely served as a source already in *Lucullus* (11.6, 33.3; cf. *Hist.* 3.42, 5.10) and *Sulla* (*Synkr.* 3[41].3; cf. *Hist.* 1.61), lives composed long before the *Sertorius* and probably not much after A.D. 100 (see above, section 1.2).

91. On Plutarch's knowledge of Latin see, e.g., Peter, *Quellen* 61; Russell, *Plutarch* 54; Valgiglio, "L'autobiografia" 246–51; and La Penna, "Cesare" 221–22. Ziegler, *Plutarchos* 224, 289–90, takes too limited a view. Plutarch's probable employment of "research assistants" fluent in Latin is emphasized by Jones, *Plutarch* 81–87.

92. Evidence to the contrary occasionally appears: see Valgiglio, "Aspetti," regarding Plutarch's knowledge of Cicero's writings—often at second hand, though Valgiglio at times too readily postulates an intermediary source. But as he points out (299), Cicero was an unusual case, quoted or paraphrased innumerable times in subsequent biographical and historical literature. In Plutarch's eyes, the need for autopsy would have been much diminished.

consulted when preparing other lives would provide an ample reservoir of information, even if tapped only via memory—a research tool whose importance is often underrated.[93] Concerning possible informants of Plutarch besides Sallust, some speculation, cautious and duly advertised as such, may be ventured briefly.

There is no trace in the *Sertorius* of Sulla's memoirs, despite Plutarch's abundant familiarity with that work. As regards Varro, Plutarch knew some of his works quite well,[94] but direct use for the *Sertorius* cannot be shown. Nothing indicates he knew Sisenna's history, or ever used Diodoros.

More problematic, and of far greater significance, is Poseidonios. Plutarch drew heavily on the Rhodian for the relevant parts of the *Marius* (11–27, 41–45).[95] The *Sertorius*, though probably earlier, like *Marius* belongs to the last group of lives written (see above, 1.2), and a case has been made for Poseidonios as Plutarch's source in the early chapters.[96] Whether the same can be true of subsequent parts of the life depends on how one answers the question, did Poseidonios offer a narrative of the Sertorian War? An affirmative view has already been suggested, with due caution, on general grounds (above, 3.1.c). Indeed, some elements in Plutarch's narrative contain an unmistakable Poseidonian flavor. The Castulo episode (3.5–10) with its emphasis on Roman misconduct and brutality toward a provincial population is an obvious case, but as it falls into Sertorius' early years it has no bearing on the question of Poseidonian material later on. It is a different matter with Plutarch's emphasis on Sertorius' humane and unusual treatment of provincial subjects (6.7–9, 24.5)—a topic dear to Poseidonios.[97] The discussion of meteorological phenomena in the excursus on the Blessed Isles (8.2–5) and the Characitani episode (17.5–11) hints at a like origin. Metellus' extravaganza at Corduba (22.2–3) presumably comes from Sallust (*Hist.* 2.70), but it would be perfectly at home in Poseidonios, another example of τρυφή; one wonders whether Sallust himself here drew on the Rhodian. Outside the *Sertorius*, attention has recently been called to elements of a strongly Poseidonian character in the corresponding chapters of *Pompey* (17–20).[98]

Finally, the question of character deterioration. Poseidonios held that man's emotional urges must be brought under the control of rational faculties (δύναμις λογιστική), through a process of ethical instruction and education. Where the irrational forces have not been properly contained by the rational,

---

93. See Frost's salutary warning (*Themistocles* 42–45) against imposing upon Plutarch a modern historian's way of using his sources—constantly "consulting material or notes as he writes."

94. Ziegler, *Plutarchos* 223–24, 290.

95. Other citations of Poseidonios in the *Lives*: *Fab.* 19.4; *Brut.* 1.7–8; *Marc.* 1.1, 9.7, 20.11; *Mar.* 1.2; *Pomp.* 42.10.

96. Scardigli, "Considerazioni" 42–54.

97. See esp. Strasburger 41, 51–52. For Plutarch's own interest in that subject see Pelling, "Roman Politics" 179—but where did the biographer find relevant information? Not in many accounts written by Romans, it is safe to say.

98. García Moreno, "Paradoxography" 138–39.

favorable circumstances—wealth or poverty, power or oppression, the loss of external restraining factors—may enable a character's existing negative dispositions to become dominant; hence human evil such as indulgence in luxury and wallowing in cruelty.[99] Those are precisely the issues Plutarch addresses in chapter 10. Having stressed Sertorius' moderation in exercising power (10.4), he allows (10.5) that his behavior late in life may easily lead to the conclusion (δοκεῖ) that his natural disposition (φύσις) was not gentle but tending toward cruelty (ὠμότης) and vengefulness (βαρυθυμία) instead, inclinations previously restrained with reasoned calculation (λογισμῷ) due to the necessity of circumstances (διὰ τὴν ἀνάγκην). In other words, when no further advantage was to be gained from acting nobly, external restraints fell by the wayside, and the natural negative disposition of Sertorius' character gained the upper hand. That explanation is consistent with Poseidonios' views; Plutarch, however, is not satisfied. He agrees that true excellence of virtue (ἀρετή) must be grounded in an unalterable, rational decision to be good, but he rejects the notion that deterioration of behavior (ἦθος) necessarily implies a natural disposition towards evil: he considers it possible that a character wholly good by nature yet lacking the reinforcement of rational ethical schooling may actually be destroyed under the blows of undeserved fate, and exhibit immoral behavior inconsistent with its natural goodness (10.7). So it happened with Sertorius (10.8). Did the charge that Sertorius was cruel by nature originate with Poseidonios?

Regarding authors of the later first century B.C., Galba's history was known to Plutarch through Iuba (*Rom.* 17.5 = HRR F 1) but does not seem to have been consulted directly. Certain parallels between Strabo 17.3.8 (= Tanusius Geminus HRR F 1) and *Sert.* 9.10 allow for the possibility that Plutarch used Tanusius for parts of the *Sertorius* as well as the *Caesar* (22.4 = HRR F 3). Strabo's *History* was well known to Plutarch;[100] if he did not read Tanusius Geminus himself, Strabo surely was his intermediary. On the other hand, Plutarch seems not to have used the latter's *Geography*.[101]

Whether Cornelius Nepos' book on Roman generals contained a life of Sertorius is impossible to say. What is certain is Plutarch's knowledge of Nepos and use of the work for some of his Roman lives (*Luc.* 43.2 = HRR F 10; *Marc.* 30.5; *Synkr.* 1[31].8 = F 7 and 6; *Ti. Grac.* 21.3 = F 9). A strong and plausible case has recently been made for the view that Nepos' book on Roman generals served Plutarch, not so much as a major source but rather as a guide in determining which Romans were worthy of inclusion in the *Parallel Lives*.[102] Although a Nepotian *Sertorius* is not needed to explain Plutarch's

---

99. F 31–34, 169, 186 E-K; see also Bringmann's excellent study, esp. 37–39.

100. Cf. *Luc.* 28.8 = *FGrHist* 91 F 9; *Caes.* 63.3 = F 19; *Sulla* 26.4 = F 8.

101. Thus Peter, *HRR* 2:lxv, taking Strabo for granted as the direct source. But see Theander, "Plutarch und die Geschichte" 54–66, and Geiger, *Nepos* 59–60, demolishing once fondly entertained notions—not persuasively revived by Delvaux, *LEC* 56 (1988)—of Plutarch's heavy dependency on *Mittelquellen*.

102. Geiger, "Choice" 92–99, *Nepos* 58–62, 104–7, 117–20, and *ICS* 13.2 (1988) 245–50.

choice—Sallust's elaborate portrait was surely capable of triggering his interest by itself—the existence of such a biography deserves serious consideration as it may have offered information on Sertorius' early career that was absent from Sallust.

Plutarch's knowledge and use of Livy is not generally doubted, but the Patavian's influence on the Late Republican lives remains shadowy.[103] In the *Sertorius* it may be sought in the early chapters, in narratives such as the hero's Cimbrian exploits or Social and Civil War activities. But on the former occasion, Poseidonios is just as likely, if not more so; on the latter, Plutarch remains too vague even to permit informed speculation.

The foregoing survey does not bristle with confidence at revealing Plutarch's authorities, Sallust excepted. But with no other such sources as were available to him extant, to go any further would be to cross the line dividing conjecture from fantasy and self-delusion. Stadter's advice very much needs heeding here.[104] We would know little about Quintus Sertorius but for Plutarch's biography, and even the ability to pinpoint all of his sources would ultimately leave us none the wiser. If in reading the *Sertorius* we keep reminding ourselves that historical completeness, factual accuracy, and documentation of sources were not Plutarch's principal concerns, we will be able to see this *Life* for what it was meant to be: the character study of a gifted yet imperfect man struggling against an unkind fate, to no avail.

103. See Pelling, "Method" 88.
104. Stadter, *Pericles* lii: "It is wise to resist the temptation to name lost writers as Plutarch's sources for specific passages, and especially to interpret Plutarch on the basis of their supposed bias or reliability. This is a game with few rewards and many pitfalls."

SERTORIUS

CONSPECTVS SIGLORVM

Λ = L cum apographis **H A D** Iunt.
   L = cod. Laurentianus conv. suppr. 206 saec. X
   H = cod. Parisinus 1678 saec. XI
   A = cod. Parisinus 1671 a. 1296
   D = cod. Parisinus 1674 saec. XIII/XIV
  Iunt. = editio Iuntina anni 1517
K = cod. Marcianus Venetus 386 saec. XI
P = cod. Palatinus Heidelbergensis 168 saec. XI
Q = **C B M V**^{b} aut omnes aut plures
   C = cod. Parisinus 1673 saec. XIII/XIV
   B = cod. Parisinus 1672 saec. XIII/XIV
   M = cod. Monacensis 85 saec. XII
   V^b = cod. Vindobonensis 60 saec. XII
Z = **F F**^{a}**M**^{b}
   F = cod. Parisinus 1677 saec. XIV
   F^a = cod. Parisinus 1676 saec. XIV
   M^b = cod. Marcianus Venetus 385 saec. XIV/XV

NOTAE

Am.	= Amyot	Rei.	= Reiske
Anon.	= Anonymus	Ri.	= Richards
Br.	= Bryan	Sch.	= Schaefer
Cob.	= Cobet	Sint.	= Sintenis
Cor.	= Coraes	Sol.	= Solanus
Emp.	= Emperius	Vulc.	= Vulcobius
Ha.	= Hartman	Wil.	= von Wilamowitz-Moellendorff
Herw.	= van Herwerden	Xy.	= Xylander
Li.	= Lindskog	Zie.	= Ziegler
Mu.	= Muret		

1. Θαυμαστὸν μὲν ἴσως οὐκ ἔστιν, ἐν ἀπείρῳ τῷ χρόνῳ τῆς τύχης ἄλλοτ᾽ ἄλλως ῥεούσης, ἐπὶ ταὐτὰ συμπτώματα πολλάκις καταφέρεσθαι τὸ αὐτόματον. εἴτε γὰρ οὐκ ἔστι τῶν ὑποκειμένων ὡρισμένον τὸ πλῆθος, ἄφθονον ἔχει τῆς τῶν ἀποτελουμένων ὁμοιότητος χορηγὸν ἡ τύχη τὴν τῆς ὕλης ἀπειρίαν· εἴτ᾽ ἔκ τινων ὡρισμένων ἀριθμῷ συμπλέκεται τὰ πράγματα, πολλάκις ἀνάγκη ταὐτὰ γίνεσθαι, διὰ τῶν αὐτῶν περαινόμενα. ἐπεὶ δ᾽ ἀγαπῶντες ἔνιοι τὰ τοιαῦτα συνάγουσιν ἱστορίᾳ καὶ ἀκοῇ τῶν κατὰ τύχην γεγονότων ὅσα λογισμοῦ καὶ προνοίας ἔργοις ἔοικεν — οἷον ὅτι δυεῖν Ἄττεων γενομένων ἐμφανῶν, τοῦ μὲν Σύρου, τοῦ δ᾽ Ἀρκάδος, ἑκάτερος ὑπὸ συὸς ἀπώλετο, δυεῖν δ᾽ Ἀκταιώνων ὁ μὲν ὑπὸ τῶν κυνῶν, ὁ δ᾽ ὑπὸ τῶν ἐραστῶν διεσπάσθη· δυεῖν δὲ Σκιπιώνων ὑφ᾽ οὗ μὲν ἐνικήθησαν Καρχηδόνιοι πρότερον, ὑφ᾽ οὗ δ᾽ ὕστερον ἄρδην ἀνῃρέθησαν· ἑάλω δὲ τὸ Ἴλιον ὑφ᾽ Ἡρακλέους διὰ τὰς Λαομέδοντος ἵππους, καὶ ὑπ᾽ Ἀγαμέμνονος διὰ τοῦ δουρείου προσαγορευθέντος ἵππου, τρίτον δ᾽ ὑπὸ Χαριδήμου, ταῖς πύλαις ἵππου τινὸς ἐμπεσόντος ἀποκλεῖσαι ταχὺ τῶν Ἰλιέων μὴ δυνηθέντων· δυεῖν δ᾽ ὁμωνύμων τοῖς εὐωδεστάτοις φυτοῖς πόλεων, Ἴου καὶ Σμύρνης, τὸν ποιητὴν Ὅμηρον ἐν ᾗ μὲν γενέσθαι λέγουσιν, ἐν ᾗ δ᾽ ἀποθανεῖν —, φέρε καὶ τοῦτο προσθῶμεν αὐτοῖς, ὅτι καὶ τῶν στρατηγῶν οἱ πολεμικώτατοι καὶ πλεῖστα δόλῳ κατεργασάμενοι μετὰ δεινότητος ἑτερόφθαλμοι γεγόνασι· Φίλιππος, Ἀντίγονος, Ἀννίβας, ⟨καὶ⟩ περὶ οὗ τόδε τὸ

Codices: Λ (= L cum apographis A Iunt.); K; P; Q (= CBMV^b aut omnes aut plures); Z (= F^a M^b)

Cf. B. Maurenbrecher, Sall. hist. fgg. I, p. 27—32. Ad. Schulten, Sertorius, 1926. K. Ziegler Mus. Rhen. 83, 1934, 1 sq. ‖ 11 mor. 772 e. f. schol. Ap. Rh. 4, 1212. Max. Tyr. 18, 1 ‖ 15 Demosth. 23, 154. Aen. tact. 24, 3—8. Polyaen 3, 14

[ΛΚPQZ] 2.3 ἄλλοτε ἄλλως τῆς τύχης Q ‖ 2 ἄλλωι P ‖ 4 ὡρισμένων P ‖ 5 ἔχειν P² ‖ τῆς om. K ‖ ἀποτελουμένων] ἀποκειμένων Q ‖ τὴν om. K ‖ 6 ἀπειρίαν L¹: εὐπορίαν KPQL² editt., cf. Zie. l. c. 1 ‖ ἀριθμῶν: corr. Mu. ‖ ἐμπλέκεται: corr. Cor. ‖ 9 ἔργον L¹ ‖ 11 ὤλετο K ‖ ἀκτεώνων L¹ ἀκταιόνων QK ‖ 12 σκηπιώνων PQL² ‖ 13 ἀνῃρ. ἄρδ. P ‖ 15 δουρίου L¹Q ‖ 17 δυοῖν hic Λ ‖ 20 πλείστῳ Q ‖ 21 καὶ add. Rei.

9 σύγγραμμα, Σερτώριος· ὃν Φιλίππου μὲν ἄν τις ἀποφαίνοιτο σωφρονέστερον περὶ [τὰς] γυναῖκας, Ἀντιγόνου δὲ πιστότερον περὶ φίλους, Ἀννίβου δ'
e ἡμερώτερον πρὸς πολεμίους, λειπόμενον δὲ συνέσει μὲν οὐδενὸς τούτων,
10 τύχῃ δὲ πάντων· ᾗ πολὺ τῶν ἐμφανῶν πολεμίων χαλεπωτέρᾳ περὶ πάντα χρησάμενος, ἐπανίσωσεν ἑαυτὸν ἐμπειρίᾳ μὲν τῇ Μετέλλου, τόλμῃ δὲ τῇ Πομπηΐου, τύχῃ δὲ τῇ Σύλλα, δυνάμει δὲ τῇ Ῥωμαίων φυγὰς καὶ βαρβάρων ἔπηλυς ἄρχων ἀντιταξάμενος.

11 Τούτῳ δὴ μάλιστα τῶν Ἑλλήνων τὸν Καρδιανὸν ὁμοιοῦμεν Εὐμενῆ· ἀμφότεροι γὰρ ἀρχικοὶ καὶ σὺν δόλῳ πολεμικοί, καὶ τῆς μὲν αὑτῶν ἀποξενωθέντες, ἡγησάμενοι δ' ἀλλοδαπῶν, τύχῃ δὲ χρησάμενοι βιαίῳ καὶ
12 ἀδίκῳ περὶ τὴν τελευτήν· ἐπιβουλευθέντες γὰρ ἀμφότεροι, μεθ' ὧν τοὺς πολεμίους ἐνίκων, ὑπὸ τούτων ἀνῃρέθησαν.

2. Κοΐντῳ Σερτωρίῳ γένος ἦν οὐκ ἀσημότατον ἐν πόλει Νουρσίᾳ τῆς Σαβίνων· τραφεὶς δὲ κοσμίως ὑπὸ μητρὶ χήρᾳ πατρὸς ὀρφανός, ὑπερφυῶς
2 δοκεῖ φιλομήτωρ γενέσθαι· ὄνομα τῆς μητρὸς Ῥαῖαν λέγουσιν. ἤσκητο μὲν οὖν καὶ περὶ δίκας ἱκανῶς καί τινα καὶ δύναμιν ἐν τῇ πόλει μειράκιον ὢν ἀπὸ τοῦ λέγειν ἔσχεν· αἱ δὲ περὶ τὰ στρατιωτικὰ λαμπρότητες αὐτοῦ καὶ κατορθώσεις ἐνταῦθα τὴν φιλοτιμίαν μετέστησαν.

3. Πρῶτον μὲν οὖν Κίμβρων καὶ Τευτόνων ἐμβεβληκότων εἰς Γαλατίαν στρατευόμενος ὑπὸ Καιπίωνι, κακῶς ἀγωνισαμένων τῶν Ῥωμαίων καὶ τροπῆς γενομένης, ἀποβεβληκὼς τὸν ἵππον καὶ κατατετρωμένος τὸ σῶμα τὸν Ῥοδανὸν διεπέρασεν, αὐτῷ τε τῷ θώρακι καὶ θυρεῷ πρὸς ἐναντίον ῥεῦμα πολὺ νηχόμενος· οὕτω τὸ σῶμα ῥωμαλέον ἦν αὐτῷ καὶ διάπονον
2 τῇ ἀσκήσει. δεύτερον δὲ τῶν αὐτῶν ἐπερχομένων μυριάσι πολλαῖς καὶ δειναῖς ἀπειλαῖς, ὥστε καὶ τὸ μένειν ἄνδρα Ῥωμαῖον ἐν τάξει τότε καὶ πείθεσθαι τῷ στρατηγῷ μέγ' ἔργον εἶναι, Μάριος μὲν ἡγεῖτο, Σερτώριος δὲ
3 κατασκοπὴν ὑπέστη τῶν πολεμίων. ἐσθῆτι δὲ Κελτικῇ σκευασάμενος καὶ τὰ κοινότατα τῆς διαλέκτου πρὸς ἔντευξιν ἐπὶ καιροῦ παραλαβών, ἀναμεί-

13 c. 2 Sall. hist. 1, 88 Maur. Cic. Brut. 180 ‖ 17 cf. Sall. hist. 1, 87 M. ‖ 19 c. 3, 1 Amm. Marc. 24, 6, 7. Val. Max. Nepot. 21, 3

[ΛKPQ] 2 τὰς del. Zie. | περὶ] πρὸς Rei. ‖ 4 πολλοὶ P | πάντων L¹P¹ ‖ 6 τῇ¹] τοῦ Q ‖ 8 Εὐμένη Cor. al. ‖ 13 Κοΐντῳ] καίτοι P | οὐκ del. Leopold ἄσημον Ri. οὐ τῶν ἀσημοτάτων Zie. | Νουρσίᾳ Xy.: νούσσοις ΛK νόσσοις P νούσοις Q | τῆς] τῇ Q ‖ 15 ῥαίαν L²: ῥάον L¹ ῥέαν mg. L³ et cet., cf. W. Schulze. lat. Eigennamen 217 ‖ 17 ὃν K ‖ 19 ἐκβεβληκότων Q ‖ 20 Καιπίωνι Xy.: σκηπίωνι vel σκιπίωνι | ῥωμαϊκῶν L¹K ‖ 22 τε aut del. aut lac. post νηχόμενος stat. Zie. ‖ 25 πείθεσθαι K: τὸ πείθεσθαι (τῷ π. L¹) ‖ 28 περιλαβὼν K

γνυται τοῖς βαρβάροις, καὶ τὰ μὲν ἰδών, τὰ δ' ἀκοῇ πυθόμενος τῶν ἐπειγόντων, ἐπανῆλθε πρὸς Μάριον. τότε μὲν οὖν ἀριστείων ἔτυχεν· ἐν δὲ τῇ
λοιπῇ στρατείᾳ πολλὰ καὶ συνέσεως ἔργα καὶ τόλμης ἀποδειξάμενος, εἰς
ὄνομα καὶ πίστιν ὑπὸ τοῦ στρατηγοῦ προήχθη.

Μετὰ δὲ τὸν Κίμβρων καὶ Τευτόνων πόλεμον ἐκπεμφθεὶς ὑπὸ Δειδίῳ
στρατηγῷ χιλίαρχος ἐπ' Ἰβηρίας, ἐν τῇ πόλει Κάστλωνι παρεχείμαζε τῆς
Κελτιβήρων. ἐπεὶ δὲ τῶν στρατιωτῶν ἐν ἀφθόνοις ὑβριζόντων καὶ τὰ πολλὰ
μεθυόντων καταφρονήσαντες οἱ βάρβαροι μετεπέμψαντο νυκτὸς ἐπικου-
ρίαν παρὰ τῶν ἀστυγειτόνων Ἰστουργίνων, καὶ κατ' οἰκίας ἐπιόντες ἔκτει-
νον αὐτούς, ὑπεκδὺς ὁ Σερτώριος μετ' ὀλίγων καὶ τοὺς ἐκπίπτοντας
συναγαγών, κύκλῳ τὴν πόλιν περιῆλθε· καὶ καθ' ἃς οἱ βάρβαροι πύλας ἔλα-
θον παρεισπεσόντες, ἀνεῳγμένας εὑρών, οὐ ταὐτὸν ἐκείνοις ἔπαθεν, ἀλλὰ
φρουρὰς ἐπιστήσας καὶ καταλαβὼν πανταχόθεν τὴν πόλιν, ἔκτεινε τοὺς ἐν
ἡλικίᾳ πάντας. ὡς δ' ἀνῃρέθησαν, ἐκέλευσε τοὺς στρατιώτας πάντας τὰ
μὲν αὑτῶν ὅπλα καὶ τὴν ἐσθῆτα καταθέσθαι, τοῖς δὲ τῶν βαρβάρων ἐν-
σκευασαμένους ἕπεσθαι πρὸς τὴν πόλιν ἐκείνην, ἐξ ἧς ἀπεστάλησαν οἱ
νύκτωρ ἐπιπεσόντες αὐτοῖς. ψευσάμενος δὲ τῇ τῶν ὅπλων ὄψει τοὺς βαρβάρους, τάς τε πύλας ἀνεῳγμένας εὗρε, καὶ πλῆθος ἀνθρώπων ἔλαβεν οἰομέ-
νων ἀπαντᾶν εὖ πεπραχόσι φίλοις καὶ πολίταις. διὸ πλεῖστοι μὲν ὑπὸ τῶν
Ῥωμαίων ἐσφάττοντο περὶ τὰς πύλας, οἱ δὲ λοιποὶ παραδόντες ἑαυτοὺς
ἐπράθησαν.

4. Ἐκ τούτου Σερτώριος ἐν τῇ Ἰβηρίᾳ διεβοήθη, καὶ ὅτε πρῶτον ἐπανῆκεν εἰς Ῥώμην, ταμίας ἀποδείκνυται τῆς περὶ Πάδον Γαλατίας ἐν δέοντι.
τοῦ γὰρ Μαρσικοῦ πολέμου συνισταμένου, στρατιώτας τε προσταχθὲν
αὐτῷ καταλέγειν καὶ ὅπλα ποιεῖσθαι, σπουδὴν καὶ τάχος προσθεὶς τῷ
ἔργῳ παρὰ τὴν τῶν ἄλλων νέων βραδυτῆτα καὶ μαλακίαν ἀνδρὸς ἐμπρά-
κτως βιωσομένου δόξαν ἔσχεν. οὐ μὴν ὑφήκατο τῆς στρατιωτικῆς τόλμης
εἰς ἀξίωμα προεληλυθὼς ἡγεμόνος, ἀλλὰ καὶ χειρὸς ἀποδεικνύμενος ἔργα

---

5 Sall. hist. 1, 88 M. App. 1b. 99, 431 sq.; Plin. n. h. 22, 12 huc refert Schulten
31 || 24 c. 4, 2—5 Sall. hist. 1, 88 M.

[ΑΚΡQ] 3 ἐπιδειξάμενος C et s. s. B || 6 Κάτλωνι Q (Καστλῶνι Sint.) || 9 Ἰστουρ-
γίνων Zie. l. c. 2.: γυρισοιωῶν ΑΚQ γουρισυνῶν P γυρισηνῶν C Ὠρισίων Sol.
Ὠριτανῶν Sint. cl. Steph. Byz. s. v. Ὠρισία; cf. Schulten 31, 173 | περιϊόντες Li.
recte ut vid. || 14 πάντας² del. Sint. || 15.16 σκευασαμένους Q || 18 ἔλαβεν ⟨ἐκχυ-
θὲν⟩ Rei. || 22 ἔν ⟨τε⟩ Zie., cf. v. 24 || 23 Ῥώμην] τὴν πόλιν K | ἐν δέοντι] 'in tem-
pore' recte interpr. Cruser., errat Schulten 31, 176 || 24 τε del. Zie. | προσταχθὲν K:
προσταχθέντας C προσαχθέντας LPQ προσαχθὲν V^b || 27 ὑφήκετο: corr. Steph. ||
28 προελθὼν PC | ἐπιδεικνύμενος: em. Herw.

θαυμαστὰ καὶ τὸ σῶμα τοῖς ἀγῶσιν ἀφειδῶς ἐπιδιδούς, τῶν ὄψεων ἀπ-
4 έβαλε τὴν ἑτέραν ἐκκοπεῖσαν. ἐπὶ τούτῳ δὲ καὶ καλλωπιζόμενος ἀεὶ διε-
f τέλει· τοὺς μὲν γὰρ ἄλλους οὐκ ἀεὶ τὰ μαρτύρια τῶν ἀριστείων περιφέρειν,
ἀλλὰ καὶ ἀποτίθεσθαι, στρεπτὰ καὶ δόρατα καὶ στεφάνους, αὑτῷ δὲ τῆς
ἀνδραγαθίας παραμένειν τὰ γνωρίσματα, τοὺς αὐτοὺς ἔχοντι τῆς ἀρετῆς 5
5 ἅμα καὶ τῆς συμφορᾶς θεατάς. ἀπέδωκε δὲ καὶ ὁ δῆμος αὐτῷ τιμὴν πρέ-
πουσαν. εἰσελθόντα γὰρ εἰς θέατρον ἐδέξαντό τε κρότῳ καὶ κατευφήμη-
σαν, ὧν οὐδὲ τοῖς πάνυ προήκουσιν ἡλικίᾳ τε καὶ δόξῃ τυχεῖν ἦν ῥᾴδιον.
a.883 6 Δημαρχίαν μέντοι μετιών, Σύλλα καταστασιάσαντος αὐτόν, ἐξέπεσε·
570 διὸ καὶ δοκεῖ γενέσθαι μισοσύλλας. ἐπεὶ δὲ Μάριος μὲν ὑπὸ Σύλλα κρατη- 10
a.87 7 θεὶς ἔφευγε, Σύλλας δὲ Μιθριδάτῃ πολεμήσων ἀπῆρε, τῶν δ' ὑπάτων
Ὀκτάβιος μὲν ἐπὶ τῆς Σύλλα προαιρέσεως ἔμενε, Κίννας δὲ νεωτερίζων
ὑποφερομένην ἀνεκαλεῖτο τὴν Μαρίου στάσιν, τούτῳ προσένειμεν αὑτὸν
ὁ Σερτώριος, ἄλλως τε καὶ τὸν Ὀκτάβιον ὁρῶν αὐτὸν μὲν ἀμβλύτερον 380Z¹
8 ὄντα, τοῖς δὲ Μαρίου φίλοις ἀπιστοῦντα. γενομένης δὲ τοῖς ὑπάτοις ἐν 15
ἀγορᾷ μάχης μεγάλης, Ὀκτάβιος μὲν ἐκράτησε, Κίννας δὲ καὶ Σερτώριος
9 οὐ πολλῷ τῶν μυρίων ἐλάττους ἀποβαλόντες ἔφυγον, καὶ τῶν περὶ τὴν
b Ἰταλίαν ἔτι διεσπαρμένων στρατοπέδων προσαγ⟨αγ⟩όμενοι τὰ πλεῖστα
πειθοῖ, ταχὺ κατέστησαν ἀξιόμαχοι τοῖς περὶ τὸν Ὀκτάβιον.
5. Μαρίου δὲ καταπλεύσαντος ἐκ Λιβύης καὶ τῷ Κίννᾳ προστιθέντος 20
ἑαυτὸν ὡς ἰδιώτην ὑπάτῳ, τοῖς μὲν ἄλλοις ἐδόκει δέχεσθαι, Σερτώριος
δ' ἀπηγόρευεν, εἴτε τὸν Κίνναν ἧττον οἰόμενος ἑαυτῷ προσέξειν ἀνδρὸς
ἡγεμονικωτέρου παρόντος, εἴτε τὴν βαρύτητα τοῦ Μαρίου δεδοικώς, μὴ 928
πάντα τὰ πράγματα συγχέῃ, θυμῷ μέτρον οὐκ ἔχοντι πέρα δίκης ἐν τῷ
2 κρατεῖν προερχομένως. ἔλεγεν οὖν μικρὸν εἶναι τὸ ὑπολειπόμενον ἔργον 25
c αὐτοῖς ἤδη κρατοῦσι, δεξαμένων δὲ τὸν Μάριον, τὸ σύμπαν οἴσεσθαι τῆς
δόξης ἐκεῖνον καὶ τῆς δυνάμεως, χαλεπὸν ὄντα πρὸς κοινωνίαν ἀρχῆς καὶ
3 ἄπιστον. εἰπόντος δὲ τοῦ Κίννα, ταῦτα μὲν ὀρθῶς ὑπολογίζεσθαι τὸν

6 c. 4, 5 Sall. hist. 1, 89 M. || 15 Plut. Mar. 41, 1. 2. App. civ. 1, 64, 287 sq.
Flor. 2, 9, 9. 10 | 20 c. 5 Plut. Mar. c. 41, 3—44 et ibi l. l.

[ΛKPQ] 1 τὸ om. Q || 2 καὶ om. P || 3 ἀριστείων ΛKP || 4 τρεπτὰ P || 5 ἔχοντα Q ||
6 τιμὴν ⟨τὴν⟩ Zie. || 7 ἐδέξαντο K: ἐδέξατο L¹ ἐξεδέξατο PQ L² ἐξεδέξαντο B Steph. |
κατευφήμησεν Mu. editt. κατευφήμισαν C Sol. || 8 προσήκουσιν L¹P¹Q || 13 τοῦτο Q ||
14 ὀκταβίου υἱὸν P | μὲν αὐτὸν Λ || 15 γενομένοις LV^b || 17 ἐλάττους τῶν μυρίων:
trp. Benseler | καίτοι τῶν Br. || 18 προσαγόμενοι: em. Sch. || 21 ἑαυτὸν om. P |
ἰδιώτης P || 22 ἀπηγόρευσεν KQ || 25 προσερχόμενος: em. Mu., qui et προσχρώμε-
νος | ἀπολειπόμενον: em. Cor. | ἔργον ante εἶναι pon. Q || 26 οἴεσθαι L¹Q

Σερτώριον, αἰδεῖσθαι δὲ καὶ διαπορεῖν ὅπως ἀπώσεται τὸν Μάριον, αὐτὸς
ἐπὶ κοινωνίᾳ πραγμάτων κεκληκώς, ὑπολαβὼν ὁ Σερτώριος εἶπεν· „ἀλλ᾽
ἐγὼ μὲν αὐτὸν ἀφ᾽ ἑαυτοῦ Μάριον ἥκειν νομίζων εἰς Ἰταλίαν τὸ συμφέρον ἐσκόπουν, σοὶ δὲ τὴν ἀρχὴν οὐδὲ βουλεύεσθαι καλῶς εἶχεν ἥκοντος
ὃν αὐτὸς ἐλθεῖν ἠξίωσας, ἀλλὰ χρῆσθαι καὶ δέχεσθαι, τῆς πίστεως
μηδενὶ λογισμῷ χώραν διδούσης." οὕτως μεταπέμπεται τὸν Μάριον
Κίννας, καὶ τριχῇ τῆς δυνάμεως διανεμηθείσης, ἦρχον οἱ τρεῖς. διαπο-
λεμηθέντος δὲ τοῦ πολέμου, καὶ τῶν περὶ τὸν Κίνναν καὶ Μάριον
ἐμφορουμένων ὕβρεώς τε καὶ πικρίας ἁπάσης, ὥστε χρυσὸν ἀποδεῖξαι
Ῥωμαίοις τὰ τοῦ πολέμου κακά, Σερτώριος λέγεται μόνος οὔτ᾽ ἀποκτεῖναί
τινα πρὸς ὀργὴν οὔτ᾽ ἐνυβρίσαι κρατῶν, ἀλλὰ καὶ τῷ Μαρίῳ δυσχεραίνειν,
καὶ τὸν Κίνναν ἐντυγχάνων ἰδίᾳ καὶ δεόμενος μετριώτερον ποιεῖν. τέλος δὲ
τῶν δούλων, οὓς Μάριος συμμάχους μὲν ἐν τῷ πολέμῳ, δορυφόρους δὲ τῆς
τυραννίδος ἔχων ἰσχυροὺς καὶ πλουσίους ἐποίησε, τὰ μὲν ἐκείνου διδόντος
καὶ κελεύοντος, τὰ δὲ καὶ ἰδίᾳ παρανομούντων εἰς τοὺς δεσπότας, σφαττόν-
των μὲν αὐτούς, ταῖς δὲ δεσποίναις πλησιαζόντων, καὶ βιαζομένων τοὺς
παῖδας, οὐκ ἀνασχετὰ ποιούμενος ὁ Σερτώριος ἅπαντας ἐν ταὐτῷ στρατοπεδεύοντας κατηκόντισεν, οὐκ ἐλάττους τετρακισχιλίων ὄντας.

6. Ἐπεὶ δὲ Μάριος μὲν ἐτελεύτησε καὶ Κίννας ἀνῃρέθη μικρὸν ὕστερον,
ὁ δὲ νεανίας Μάριος ἄκοντος αὐτοῦ παρὰ τοὺς νόμους ὑπατείαν ἔλαβε,
Κάρβωνες δὲ καὶ Νωρβανοὶ καὶ Σκιπίωνες ἐπιόντι Σύλλᾳ κακῶς ἐπολέμουν, καὶ τὰ μὲν ἀνανδρίᾳ καὶ μαλακίᾳ τῶν στρατηγῶν ἐφθείρετο, τὰ
δ᾽ οἱ προδιδόντες ἀπώλλυσαν, ἔργον δ᾽ οὐδὲν ἦν αὐτοῦ παρόντος τοῖς πράγ-
μασι μοχθηρῶς ὑποφερομένοις διὰ τὸ χεῖρον φρονεῖν τοὺς μᾶλλον δυναμένους, τέλος δὲ Σύλλας Σκιπίωνι παραστρατοπεδεύσας καὶ φιλοφρονούμενος, ὡς εἰρήνης ἐσομένης, διέφθειρε τὸ στράτευμα, καὶ ταῦτα προλέγων
Σκιπίωνι καὶ διδάσκων Σερτώριος οὐκ ἔπεισε, παντάπασιν ἀπογνοὺς τὴν
πόλιν ὥρμησεν εἰς Ἰβηρίαν, ὡς, εἰ φθάσει τὴν ἐκεῖ κρατυνάμενος ἀρχήν,
καταφυγὴ τοῖς πταίουσιν ἐνταῦθα τῶν φίλων ἐσόμενος. χειμῶσι δὲ χαλε-
ποῖς χρησάμενος ἐν χωρίοις ὀρεινοῖς, ὑπὸ βαρβάρων ἐπράττετο τέλη καὶ

---

10 Sall. hist. 1, 90 M. || 19 c. 6, 1–3 Plut. Mar. 45. 46. Sulla 27. 28 et ibi l. l. ||
28 App. b. c. 1, 86, 392. 108, 505. 506

[*Λ*KPQ] 2 κοινωνίαν Q || 3 μὲν om. P | αὐτὸν om. Q || 13 μάρ. μὲν συμμ. ἐν τ.
π. P μάρ. μὲν ἐν τ. π. συμμ. C || 14 πλουσίους (Am.) Cor.: πολλοὺς || 15 καὶ² om. P |
ἰδίᾳ Latte: βίᾳ || 17 στρατοπ. ἐν ταυτῷ K || 20 δὲ om. L¹ || 21 σκηπίωνες L²Q et
postea || 22 ἐφθείροντο Q || 25 στρατοπεδεύσας K || 27 ἔπειθε: em. Sch. || 28 φθάσοι Q

6 μισθοὺς τοῦ παρελθεῖν τὴν ὁδόν. ἀγανακτούντων δὲ τῶν σὺν αὐτῷ καὶ δεινολογουμένων, εἰ Ῥωμαίων ἀνθύπατος τέλη καταβαλεῖ βαρβάροις ὀλέθροις, μικρὰ φροντίσας τοῦ δοκοῦντος αἰσχροῦ καὶ καιρὸν ὠνεῖσθαι φήσας, οὗ σπανιώτερον οὐδὲν ἀνδρὶ μεγάλων ἐφιεμένῳ, τοὺς μὲν βαρβάρους ἐθε-
7 ράπευσε χρήμασι, τὴν δ᾽ Ἰβηρίαν ἐπειχθεὶς κατέσχε. παραλαβὼν δ᾽ ἔθνη, πλήθεσι μὲν καὶ ἡλικίαις ἀκμάζοντα, πλεονεξίᾳ δὲ καὶ ὕβρει τῶν πεμπομένων ἑκάστοτε στρατηγῶν πρὸς ὅλην κακῶς διακείμενα τὴν ἡγεμονίαν, ἀνελάμβανεν ὁμιλίᾳ τε τοὺς δυνατοὺς καὶ φόρων ἀνέσει τοὺς πολλούς.
8 μάλιστα δὲ τῶν ἐπισταθμῶν ἀπαλλάξας ἠγαπήθη· τοὺς γὰρ στρατιώτας ἠνάγκαζεν ἐν τοῖς προαστίοις χειμάδια πήγνυσθαι, πρῶτος αὐτὸς οὕτω
9 κατασκηνῶν. οὐ μὴν ἐπὶ τῇ τῶν βαρβάρων εὐνοίᾳ τὸ πᾶν ἐποιήσατο, Ῥωμαίων δὲ τῶν αὐτόθι μετοικούντων τοὺς ἐν ἡλικίᾳ καθοπλίσας, μηχανάς τε παντοδαπὰς καὶ ναυπηγίας τριήρων ὑποβαλόμενος, διὰ χειρὸς εἶχε τὰς πόλεις, ἥμερος μὲν ὢν ἐν ταῖς εἰρηνικαῖς χρείαις, φοβερὸς δὲ τῇ παρασκευῇ [κατὰ] τῶν πολεμικῶν φαινόμενος.

7. Ὡς δὲ Σύλλαν μὲν ἐπυνθάνετο τῆς Ῥώμης κρατεῖν, ἔρρειν δὲ τὴν Μαρίου καὶ Κάρβωνος στάσιν, αὐτίκα προσδοκῶν στρατιὰν διαπολεμήσουσαν αὐτῷ μεθ᾽ ἡγεμόνος ἀφίξεσθαι, φράγνυται τὰ Πυρηναῖα ὄρη διὰ
2 Λιουίου Σαλινάτορος, ἑξακισχιλίους ὁπλίτας ἔχοντος. καὶ μετ᾽ οὐ πολὺ Γάϊος Ἄννιος ἐκπεμφθεὶς ὑπὸ Σύλλα καὶ τὸν Λίουιον ἀπρόσμαχον ὁρῶν, ἐν
3 ἀπόρῳ καθῆστο παρὰ ταῖς ὑπωρείαις. Καλπουρνίου δέ τινος ἐπίκλησιν Λαναρίου δολοφονήσαντος τὸν Λίουιον καὶ τῶν στρατιωτῶν τὰ ἄκρα τῆς Πυρήνης ἐκλιπόντων, ὑπερβαλὼν Ἄννιος ἐπῄει χειρὶ μεγάλῃ, τοὺς ἐμπο-
4 δὼν ἀνιστάς. Σερτώριος δ᾽ οὐκ ὢν ἀξιόμαχος, μετὰ τρισχιλίων εἰς Καρχηδόνα τὴν νέαν καταφυγὼν κἀκεῖθεν ἐπιβὰς τῶν νεῶν καὶ διαπεράσας τὸ
5 πέλαγος, Λιβύῃ κατὰ τὴν Μαυρουσίαν προσέσχεν. ἀφυλάκτοις δὲ τοῖς στρατιώταις ὑδρευομένοις τῶν βαρβάρων ἐπιπεσόντων, συχνοὺς ἀποβαλὼν

8 Sall. hist. 1, 93. 94 M. ‖ 19 c. 7, 2. 3 Sall. hist. 1, 95—97 M.

[ΛΚPQ] 2 καταβάλῃ L¹K καταβάλει L², sed mg. εῖ ‖ 4 οὐδὲν om. P ‖ ἐθεράπευε P ‖ 5 ἔσχεν corr. in παρέσχεν P ‖ 6 πλήθεσι Zie.: πλήθει | ἡλικίαις Benseler: ἡλικίᾳ ‖ 8 ἐλάμβανεν Q | τε] δὲ Κ ‖ 9 ἐπισταθμίων KPQ ‖ 10 προαστείοις: em. Zie. | οὕτως LPQ ‖ 12 δὲ om. PQ | κατοικούντων Sch. ‖ 13 ὑποβαλόμενος K Steph.: ὑποβαλλόμενος | χειρῶν Λ ‖ 15 κατὰ del. Rei. | πολεμικῶν ΛPQ: πολεμίων K Steph. editt. ‖ 16 αἴρειν Q ‖ 17 προσδοκῶν] πολεμῶν L¹ | στρατείαν L¹ Steph. ‖ 18 πυριναῖα KQ ‖ 19 Λιουίου Holzapfel et Cichorius, Röm. Stud. 256: ἰουλίου, item v. 20. 22 | σαλινάτωρος L² | μετ᾽] τ᾽ L¹ ‖ 21 καθίστατο KQ | ὑπωρίαις L¹ ‖ 23 πυρίνης L¹K | ἐκλειπόντων P | ὑπερβάλλων L¹PQ

αὖθις εἰς Ἰβηρίαν ἀπέπλει, καὶ ταύτης μὲν ἀποκρούεται, Κιλισσῶν δὲ
λῃστρίδων αὐτῷ προσγενομένων, Πιτυούσσῃ νήσῳ προσέβαλε καὶ ἀπέβη
τὴν παρ' Ἀννίου φρουρὰν βιασάμενος. Ἄννιος δὲ μετ' οὐ πολὺ παρῆν ναυσί
τε πολλαῖς καὶ πεντακισχιλίοις ὁπλίταις· πρὸς ὃν ἐπεχείρησε μὲν διαναυμαχεῖν, καίπερ ἐλαφροῖς καὶ πρὸς τάχος, οὐ πρὸς ἀλκήν, πεποιημένοις
σκάφεσι χρώμενος, ζεφύρῳ δὲ λαμπρῷ τοῦ πελάγους ἀνισταμένου καὶ τὰ
πολλὰ τῶν τοῦ Σερτωρίου πλοίων ὑπὸ κουφότητος πλάγια ταῖς ῥαχίαις
περιβάλλοντος, αὐτὸς ὀλίγαις ναυσί, τῆς μὲν θαλάσσης ὑπὸ τοῦ χειμῶνος
εἰργόμενος, τῆς δὲ γῆς ὑπὸ τῶν πολεμίων, ἡμέρας δέκα σαλεύων πρὸς
ἐναντίον κῦμα καὶ κλύδωνα τραχὺν ἐπιπόνως διεκαρτέρησεν.

8. Ἐνδόντος δὲ τοῦ πνεύματος, φερόμενος νήσοις τισὶν ἐναυλίζεται σπο-
ράσιν ἀνύδροις, κἀκεῖθεν ἄρας καὶ διεκβαλὼν τὸν Γαδειραῖον πορθμόν, ἐν
δεξιᾷ τοῖς ἐκτὸς ἐπιβάλλει τῆς Ἰβηρίας, μικρὸν ὑπὲρ τῶν τοῦ Βαίτιος ἐκβολῶν, ὃς εἰς τὴν Ἀτλαντικὴν ἐκφερόμενος θάλατταν ὄνομα τῇ περὶ αὐτὸν
Ἰβηρίᾳ παρέσχεν.

Ἐνταῦθα ναῦταί τινες ἐντυγχάνουσιν αὐτῷ, νέον ἐκ τῶν Ἀτλαντικῶν νήσων ἀναπεπλευκότες, αἳ δύο μέν εἰσι, λεπτῷ παντάπασι πορθμῷ διαιρούμεναι, μυρίους δ' ἀπέχουσαι Λιβύης σταδίους, καὶ ὀνομάζονται Μακάρων.
ὄμβροις δὲ χρώμεναι μετρίοις σπανίως, τὰ δὲ πλεῖστα πνεύμασι μαλακοῖς
καὶ δροσοβόλοις, οὐ μόνον ἀροῦν καὶ φυτεύειν παρέχουσιν ἀγαθὴν καὶ
πίονα χώραν, ἀλλὰ καὶ καρπὸν αὐτοφυῆ φέρουσιν, ἀποχρῶντα πλήθει καὶ
γλυκύτητι βόσκειν ἄνευ πόνων καὶ πραγματείας σχολάζοντα δῆμον. ἀὴρ
δ' ἄλυπος ὡρῶν τε κράσει καὶ μεταβολῆς μετριότητι κατέχει τὰς νήσους.
οἱ μὲν γὰρ ἐνθένδε τῆς γῆς ἀποπνέοντες ἔξω βορέαι καὶ ἀπηλιῶται διὰ
μῆκος ἐκπεσόντες εἰς τόπον ἀχανῆ διασπείρονται καὶ προαπολείπουσι,
πελάγιοι δὲ περιρρέοντες ἀργέσται καὶ ζέφυροι, βληχροὺς μὲν ὑετοὺς καὶ
σποράδας ἐκ θαλάττης ἐπάγοντες, τὰ δὲ πολλὰ νοτεραῖς αἰθρίαις ἐπιψύχον-

---

3 c. 7, 6. 7 Sall. hist. 1, 98. 99 M. ‖ 16 c. 8, 2—9, 1 Sall. hist. 1, 100—103 M.
Flor. 2, 10, 2. Diod. 5, 19. 20. π. θαυμ. ἀκουσμ. 84. cf. Plin. n. h. 6, 202—205

[ΛΚPQ] 2 προσγινομένων L¹PQ | πιτυούσῃ em. Cor. (πητυούση νήσσω L¹) ‖
7 πελάγια P ‖ 10 διεκαρτέρησεν ΚP: διεκράτησεν ΛQ ‖ 11 φερόμενος om. K | πρὸς
σποράσιν Q ‖ 12 τὸν] τῶν L¹ | γαδειραίων L¹P ‖ 16 c. 8, 2—9, 1 hab. Phot. bibl.
396sq. | νέον om. Phot. νέων L¹ νεῶν PQ ‖ 17 ἐκπεπλευκότες K ‖ 18 ἀπέχουσι
Phot. ‖ 19 σπανίους P | δὲ² om. Phot. | πνεύματα P ‖ 20 καταπνεόμεναι ante οὐ
add. B Photii, quod si verum, transponendum ante μαλακοῖς | ἔχουσιν Q ‖ 21 φέ-
ρουσαν Emp. ‖ 24 μὲν om. Phot. ‖ 25 προσαπολείπουσι Κ ‖ 26 ἀβληχροὺς Q ‖
27 νοτεραῖς om. P | αἰθρίαις] διορίαις L¹

a. 81 5 τες, ἡσυχῇ τρέφουσιν· ὥστε μέχρι τῶν βαρβάρων διῖχθαι πίστιν ἰσχυράν, αὐτόθι τὸ Ἠλύσιον εἶναι πεδίον καὶ τὴν τῶν εὐδαιμόνων οἴκησιν, ἣν Ὅμηρος ὕμνησε (Od. 4, 563 sqq.).

9. Ταῦθ᾽ ὁ Σερτώριος ἀκούσας ἔρωτα θαυμαστὸν ἔσχεν οἰκῆσαι τὰς νήσους καὶ ζῆν ἐν ἡσυχίᾳ, τυραννίδος ἀπαλλαγεὶς καὶ πολέμων ἀπαύστων. 5
2 αἰσθόμενοι δ᾽ οἱ Κίλικες, οὐδὲν εἰρήνης δεόμενοι καὶ σχολῆς, ἀλλὰ πλούτου καὶ λαφύρων, εἰς Λιβύην ἀπέπλευσαν, Ἄσκαλιν τὸν Ἴφθα κατάξοντες 96S
c 3 ἐπὶ τὴν Μαυρουσίων βασιλείαν. οὐ μὴν ἀπέκαμεν ὁ Σερτώριος, ἀλλὰ τοῖς πρὸς τὸν Ἄσκαλιν διαπολεμοῦσιν ἔγνω βοηθεῖν, ὡς οἱ σὺν αὐτῷ καινήν τινα λαβόντες ἐλπίδων ἀρχὴν καὶ πράξεων ἑτέρων ὑπόθεσιν, μὴ διαλυθεῖεν 10
4 ὑπὸ τῆς ἀπορίας. ἀσμένοις δὲ τοῖς Μαυρουσίοις ἀφικόμενος, εἴχετο ⟨τοῦ⟩
5 ἔργου, καὶ καταμαχεσάμενος τὸν Ἄσκαλιν ἐπολιόρκει. Σύλλα δὲ Πακκιανὸν ἐκπέμψαντος βοηθῆσαι τοῖς περὶ τὸν Ἄσκαλιν μετὰ δυνάμεως, συμβα- 386 Z¹
λὼν ὁ Σερτώριος τὸν μὲν Πακκιανὸν ἀπέκτεινε, τὴν δὲ στρατιὰν κρατήσας προσηγάγετο, καὶ τὴν Τίγγιν, εἰς ἣν ὁ Ἄσκαλις συνέφυγε μετὰ τῶν ἀδελ- 15
6 φῶν, ἐξεπολιόρκησεν. ἐνταῦθα τὸν Ἀνταῖον οἱ Λίβυες ἱστοροῦσι κεῖσθαι,
d καὶ τὸν τάφον αὐτοῦ Σερτώριος διέσκαψε, τοῖς βαρβάροις ἀπιστῶν διὰ
7 μέγεθος. ἐντυχὼν δὲ τῷ σώματι, πηχῶν ἑξήκοντα μῆκος ὥς φασι, κατεπλάγη, καὶ σφάγιον ἐντεμὼν συνέχωσε τὸ μνῆμα καὶ τὴν περὶ αὐτοῦ τιμὴν
8 τε καὶ φήμην συνηύξησε. Τιγγῖται δὲ μυθολογοῦσιν Ἀνταίου τελευτήσαν- 20
τος τὴν γυναῖκα Τίγγην Ἡρακλεῖ συνελθεῖν, Σόφακα δ᾽ ἐξ αὐτῶν γενόμενον βασιλεῦσαι τῆς χώρας καὶ πόλιν ἐπώνυμον τῆς μητρὸς ἀποδεῖξαι·
9 Σόφακος δὲ παῖδα γενέσθαι Διόδωρον, ᾧ πολλὰ τῶν Λιβυκῶν ἐθνῶν ὑπ-
e ήκουσεν, Ἑλληνικὸν ἔχοντι στράτευμα τῶν αὐτόθι κατῳκισμένων ὑφ᾽
10 Ἡρακλέους Ὀλβιανῶν καὶ Μυκηναίων. ἀλλὰ ταῦτα μὲν ἀνακείσθω τῇ 25

16 Strab. 17, 829. Mela 3, 106. Plin. n. h. 5, 2 (Lucan. 4, 589 sqq.)

[ΛΚPQ] 1 τρέφουσιν] βρέχουσιν Emp. | διῆχθαι Q Phot. | 4 οἰκήσας L¹ οἰκίσαι Cor. ‖ 5 ἀπαύστων L¹KQ Phot.: ἁπάντων PL² ‖ 6 πλούτων Q ‖ 7 ἀπεπέρασαν P | ἄσκαλιν P et C corr.: ἀσκάλιον hic et v. 9 cet., sed infra ἄσκαλιν omnes | κατάξαντες PQ ‖ 11 τοῦ add. Zie. ‖ 12 ἔργων P | ἐπολιόρκει – 13 ἄσκαλιν om. L¹, in mg. add. L² | πακκιανὸν Q: πακκιακὸν ΛΚ παμηίακον P; sed v. 14 πακκιανὸν Q πακκιακὸν ΛΚ πακκιακον P; cf. Crass. 32, 2, ubi eadem discrepantia in codd. ‖ 13 βαλὼν Q συλλαβὼν C ‖ 15 καὶ τὴν δὲ L¹Q | Τίγγιν Xy.: τιγέννην L τίγεννιν KQ ἀετίγεννιν P (quod ortum ex δὲ τίγεννιν) | συνέφευγε Q ‖ 18 τῷ del. Rei. ‖ 19 πλάγιον Q | αὐτόν Sch. ‖ 20 ηὔξησε Q | τιγεννῖται (vel -νῖται): em. Cor. Τιγγιτανοί Leopold ‖ 21 τιγγίην Κ et ante ras. L τιγίην Q | σώφακα constanter C | ἐξ αὐτῶν] inc. Z (= Fᵃ Mᵇ), cf. Ziegler, Überlieferungsgesch. 63 sqq.

Ἰόβα (FGrH 275 T 10) χάριτι, τοῦ πάντων ἱστορικωτάτου βασιλέων·
ἐκείνου γὰρ ἱστοροῦσι τοὺς προγόνους Διοδώρου καὶ Σόφακος ἀπογόνους
εἶναι. Σερτώριος δὲ πάντων ἐγκρατὴς γενόμενος, τοὺς δεηθέντας αὐτοῦ 11
καὶ πιστεύσαντας οὐκ ἠδίκησεν, ἀλλὰ καὶ χρήματα καὶ πόλεις καὶ τὴν
5 ἀρχὴν ἀπέδωκεν αὐτοῖς, ὅσα καλῶς εἶχε δεξάμενος διδόντων.

10. Ἐντεῦθεν ὅποι χρὴ τραπέσθαι βουλευόμενον ἐκάλουν Λυσιτανοὶ a. 80
πρέσβεις πέμψαντες ἐφ' ἡγεμονίᾳ, πάντως μὲν ἄρχοντος ἀξίωμα μέγα καὶ
ἐμπειρίαν ἔχοντος δεόμενοι πρὸς τὸν ἀπὸ Ῥωμαίων φόβον, ἐκείνῳ δὲ f
πιστεύοντες αὐτοὺς μόνῳ, καὶ πυνθανόμενοι παρὰ τῶν συγγεγονότων τὸ
10 ἦθος αὐτοῦ. λέγεται γὰρ ὁ Σερτώριος οὔθ' ὑφ' ἡδονῆς οὔθ' ὑπὸ δέους 2
εὐάλωτος γενέσθαι, φύσει τ' ἀνέκπληκτος [ὢν] παρὰ τὰ δεινά, καὶ μέτριος
εὐτυχίαν ἐνεγκεῖν, καὶ πρὸς μὲν εὐθυμαχίαν οὐδενὸς ἀτολμότερος τῶν καθ' 3
ἑαυτὸν ἡγεμόνων, ὅσα δὲ κλωπείας ἐν πολέμοις ἔργα καὶ πλεονεξίας
περὶ τόπους ἐχυροὺς καὶ διαβάσεις τάχους δεομένας ἀπάτης τε καὶ ψευδῶν
15 ἐν δέοντι, σοφιστὴς δεινότατος. ἐν δὲ ταῖς τιμαῖς τῶν ἀνδραγαθημάτων 4 573
δαψιλὴς φαινόμενος, περὶ τὰς τιμωρίας ἐμετρίαζε τῶν ἁμαρτημάτων. καί- 5
τοι δοκεῖ περὶ τὸν ἔσχατον αὐτοῦ βίον ὠμότητος καὶ βαρυθυμίας τὸ περὶ
τοὺς ὁμήρους πραχθὲν ἔργον ἐπιδεῖξαι τὴν φύσιν οὐκ οὖσαν ἥμερον, ἀλλ'
ἐπαμπεχομένην λογισμῷ διὰ τὴν ἀνάγκην. ἐμοὶ δ' ἀρετὴν μὲν εἰλικρινῆ 6
20 καὶ κατὰ λόγον συνεστῶσαν οὐκ ἄν ποτε δοκεῖ τύχη τις ἐκστῆσαι πρὸς
τοὐναντίον· ἄλλως δὲ προαιρέσεις καὶ φύσεις χρηστὰς ὑπὸ συμφορῶν μεγάλων παρ' ἀξίαν κακωθείσας οὐκ ἀδύνατον τῷ δαίμονι συμμεταβαλεῖν τὸ
ἦθος. ὃ καὶ Σερτώριον οἶμαι παθεῖν, ἤδη τῆς τύχης αὐτὸν ἐπιλειπούσης ἐκ- 7 b
τραχυνόμενον ὑπὸ τῶν πραγμάτων γινομένων πονηρῶν πρὸς τοὺς ἀδικοῦντας.
25 **11.** Οὐ μὴν ἀλλὰ τότε γε τῶν Λυσιτανῶν καλούντων, ἀπῆρεν ἐκ Λιβύης.

25 Sall. hist. 1, 104 M.

[ΛΚΡQΖ] 6 ὅπῃ Q ‖ 7 ἡγεμόνι Ζ | παντὸς ΡΖC ‖ 8 ἑλόντος L¹PQZ | ἀπὸ τῶν
ΚC | δὲ om. Q ‖ 9 καὶ del. Cor. | συγγενῶν in exar. in συγγενότων corr. L¹, γο s. s.
m. 2 ‖ 10 c. 10, 2—7 hab. Phot. p. 397a | γὰρ Ζ: δὲ cet. (om. Phot.) ‖ 11 τ' Phot.:
δὲ | ὢν om. Phot. (εἶναι vel ἦν Cor.) | παρὰ] περὶ Q ‖ 12 ἐνεγκ. εὐτ. Phot. | καὶ
πρὸς μὲν om. Phot. pergens οὐδενὸς μέντοι οὐδὲ πρὸς εὐθυμ. ἀτολμ. ‖ 13 αὐτὸν Ζ |
κλωπίας L¹ κλοπείας KQZ Phot. | πολέμῳ L¹K | intellige ἔργα κλωπείας ... καὶ
πλεονεξίας ... ἀπάτης τε καὶ ψ. ‖ 14 ὀχυροὺς K Steph. Phot. | τε om. Z | ψεύ-
δους C ‖ 17 δοκεῖ ⟨τισι⟩ Zie. | τε καὶ βαρύτητος Phot. ‖ 18 ἔρημον Sint. Ri. ‖
19 ἀπεχομένην vel ἐπεχ. Phot. | μὲν om. ΡΖ ‖ 20 δοκεῖ P Phot. et ante corr. L:
δοκῇ QZ et ex corr. L δοκεῖ ἦ K | τις om. K | ἐκστῆναι L¹ ‖ 22 παρ'] κατ' Q |
κακοθήσας corr. ex κακοθείσας m. 1 P κακοθείσας K κακοηθείας Z ‖ 23 ὑπολι-
πούσης Z ἐπιλιπούσης KC et Photii A ‖ 24 γινόμενον πονηρὸν em. Cor. ‖ 25 τότε
γε τῶν KPQ τότε τῶν vel τό γε τῶν Z τόγε L¹ τότε γε L²

19 BT Plut. vit. II 1 ed. Ziegler [1674]

$a.\overset{80}{_2}$ καὶ τούτους ⟨τε⟩ συνέταττεν εὐθὺς αὐτοκράτωρ στρατηγὸς ⟨ἀποδειχθείς⟩, καὶ τὴν ἐγγὺς Ἰβηρίαν ὑπήκοον ἐποιεῖτο, τῶν πλείστων ἑκουσίως προστιθεμένων, μάλιστα μὲν διὰ τὸ πρᾷον αὐτοῦ καὶ δραστήριον· ἔστι δ' ἃ
3 καὶ σοφιστικῶς αὐτὸς εἰς ἀπάτην καὶ κήλησιν ἐμηχανᾶτο. καὶ πρῶτόν 988 γε πάντων τὸ περὶ τὴν ἔλαφον. ἦν δὲ τοιόνδε· ⟨Λυ⟩σιτανὸς ἀνὴρ δημότης 5
c τῶν ἐπὶ χώρας βιούντων ἐλάφῳ νεοτόκῳ φευγούσῃ κυνηγέτας ἐπιτυχών, αὐτῆς μὲν ἀπελείφθη, τὴν δὲ νεβρὸν ἐκπλαγεὶς τῇ καινότητι τῆς χρόας,
4 λευκὴ γὰρ ἦν πᾶσα, λαμβάνει διώξας. κατὰ τύχην δὲ Σερτωρίου τοῖς τόποις ἐναυλισαμένου, καὶ πᾶν ὅ τις ἐξ ἄγρας ἢ γεωργίας ἥκοι κομίζων δῶρον ἀσμένως δεχομένου, καὶ φιλοφρόνως ἀμειβομένου τοὺς θεραπεύον- 10
5 τας, ἐγχειρίζει φέρων αὐτῷ τὴν νεβρόν. ὁ δὲ δεξάμενος, αὐτίκα μὲν ἥσθη μετρίως, χρόνῳ δὲ ποιησάμενος τιθασὸν οὕτω καὶ φιλάνθρωπον, ὥστε καὶ καλοῦντος ἀκούειν καὶ βαδίζοντί ποι παρακολουθεῖν, ὄχλου τε καὶ
d 6 θορύβου παντὸς ἀνέχεσθαι στρατιωτικοῦ, κατὰ μικρὸν ἐξεθείαζε φάσκων 380Z¹ Ἀρτέμιδος δῶρον τὴν ἔλαφον εἶναι, καὶ πολλὰ τῶν ἀδήλων ἐπεφήμιζεν 15 αὐτῷ δηλοῦν, γινώσκων εὐάλωτον εἰς δεισιδαιμονίαν εἶναι φύσει τὸ
7 βαρβαρικόν. ὁ δὲ καὶ προσετεχνᾶτο τοιάδε· γνοὺς γὰρ ἂν κρύφα τοὺς πολεμίους ἐμβεβληκότας ποι τῆς ὑπ' αὐτὸν χώρας ἢ πόλιν ἀφιστάντας, προσεποιεῖτο τὴν ἔλαφον αὐτῷ κατὰ τοὺς ὕπνους διειλέχθαι, κελεύουσαν
8 ἐν ἑτοίμῳ τὰς δυνάμεις ἔχειν. αὖθις δὲ νίκην τινὰ τῶν ἑαυτοῦ στρατηγῶν 20 ἀκούσας, τὸν μὲν ἄγγελον ἔκρυπτε, τὴν δ' ἔλαφον ἐστεφανωμένην ἐπ' εὐαγγελίοις προῆγεν, εὐθυμεῖσθαι παρακαλῶν καὶ τοῖς θεοῖς θύειν, ὡς ἀγαθόν τι πευσομένους.

c 12. Οὕτως δὲ χειροήθεις ποιησάμενος αὐτούς, ἐχρῆτο πρὸς ἅπαντα μετριωτέροις, οὐχ ὑπ' ἀνδρὸς ἀλλοδαποῦ λογισμῶν, ἀλλ' ὑπὸ θεοῦ στρα- 25 τηγεῖσθαι πειθομένοις, ἅμα καὶ τῶν πραγμάτων ἐπιμαρτυρούντων τῷ
2 παρὰ λόγον τὴν δύναμιν αὐξάνεσθαι. δισχιλίοις γὰρ ἑξακοσίοις, οὓς ὠνόμαζε Ῥωμαίους, συμμείκτοις δ' ἑπτακοσίοις Λιβύων εἰς Λυσιτανίαν

4 c. 11, 3—8 App. b. c. 1, 110, 514. Polyaen. 8, 22. Val. Max. 1, 2, 4. Plin. n. h. 8, 117. Frontin. strat. 1, 11, 13. Gell. 15, 22, 3—5; cf. c. 20 ‖ 27 Sall. hist. 1, 104—107 M.

[ΑΚΡQΖ] 1 τε add. Zie. | ἀποδειχθείς add. Zie. l. c. 5 ‖ 2 προτιθεμένων ΑΡΖ ‖ 5 τοιοῦτον Κ | σπάνος: em. Zie. l. c. 5 ‖ 6 ἐλάφων ΡΖ ‖ 7 νευρὸν Ζ ‖ 9 ἐπαυλισαμένου Q | ὅστις ΚΡΖ | κομίζων ἥκοι Κ κομίζοι omisso ἥκοι C (ἥκοι ex οἴκοι corr. L) ‖ 12 τιθασσὸν QZ ‖ 13 ὑπακούειν Cob. ‖ 16 αὐτῷ δηλοῦν om. L¹KQ | γινώσκων ΑΚQ: ἔστι δὲ ΡΖ, unde γινώσκων ⟨ὡς⟩ ἔστιν εὐάλ. Zie., nisi praestat γιν. εὐάλωτον ⟨ὄν⟩ | εἶναι hab. ΑΚ om. ΡQΖ ‖ 17 ὁ δὲ] ὅθεν Zie. | καὶ om. Q ‖ 18 ὑπ' αὐτὸν] αὐτῶν Q | ἀμφιστάντας Rei. ‖ 26 πειθομένοις Mᵇ (Anon.): πειθομένους αὐτῷ συνδιαβᾶσι πελταστὰς τετρακισχιλίους Λυσιτανῶν καὶ ἱππεῖς ἑπτα- κοσίους προσλαβών, ἐπολέμει τέτταρσι Ῥωμαίων στρατηγοῖς, ὑφ' οἷς ἦσαν πεζῶν μὲν δώδεκα μυριάδες, ἱππεῖς δ' ἑξακισχίλιοι, τοξόται δὲ καὶ σφενδονῆται δισχίλιοι, πόλεις δ' ἀναρίθμητοι τὸ πλῆθος, αὐτὸς εἴκοσι τὰς πάσας ἐν ἀρχῇ κεκτημένος. ἀλλ' ὅμως ἀσθενὴς οὕτω καὶ μικρὸς ἀρξάμενος, οὐ μόνον ἐθνῶν ἐκράτησε μεγάλων καὶ πόλεις εἷλε πολλάς, ἀλλὰ καὶ τῶν ἀντιστρατήγων Κότταν μὲν ἐν τῷ περὶ τὴν Μελλαρίαν πορθμῷ κατεναυμάχησε, Φουφίδιον δὲ τὸν ἄρχοντα τῆς Βαιτικῆς περὶ τὸν Βαῖτιν ἐτρέψατο, δισχιλίους ἀποκτείνας Ῥωμαίων, Δομίτιον δὲ Καλουῖνον ἀνθύπατον ὄντα τῆς ἑτέρας Ἰβηρίας διὰ τοῦ ταμίου κατ- αγωνισάμενος, καὶ Θωρ[άν]ιον, ἄλλον ἡγεμόνα τῶν ὑπὸ Μετέλλου πεμ- φθέντων, μετὰ δυνάμεως ἀνεῖλεν, αὐτόν τε τὸν Μέτελλον, ἄνδρα Ῥωμαίων ἐν τοῖς τότε μέγιστον καὶ δοκιμώτατον, οὐκ ὀλίγοις σφάλμασι περιβαλὼν εἰς τοσαύτην ἀπορίαν κατέστησεν, ὥστε Λεύκιον μὲν Μάλλιον ἐκ τῆς περὶ Ναρβῶνα Γαλατίας ἐλθεῖν αὐτῷ βοηθόν, Πομπήϊον δὲ Μᾶγνον ἐκ Ῥώμης κατὰ τάχος ἀποσταλῆναι μετὰ δυνάμεως. οὐ γὰρ εἶχεν ὁ Μέτελ- λος ὅ τι χρήσαιτο, προσπολεμῶν ἀνδρὶ τολμητῇ, πάσης ἐξαναδυομένῳ φανερᾶς μάχης, πᾶσαν δὲ μεταβαλλομένῳ μεταβολὴν εὐσταλείᾳ καὶ κου- φότητι τῆς Ἰβηρικῆς στρατιᾶς, αὐτὸς ὁπλιτικῶν καὶ νομίμων ἀσκητὴς γεγονὼς ἀγώνων καὶ στρατηγὸς ἐμβριθοῦς καὶ μονίμου φάλαγγος, ὥσα- σθαι μὲν εἰς χεῖρας ἐλθεῖν τοὺς πολεμίους καὶ καταβαλεῖν ἄριστα γεγυμ- νασμένης, ὀρειβατεῖν δὲ καὶ συνηρτῆσθαι διώξεσι καὶ φυγαῖς ἀπαύστοις ἀνθρώπων ὑπηνεμίων καὶ λιμὸν ἀνέχεσθαι καὶ δίαιταν ἄπυρον καὶ ἄσκη- νον ὥσπερ ἐκεῖνοι μὴ δυναμένης.

13. Ἔτι δ' αὐτὸς μὲν ἤδη πρεσβύτερος ἦν, καί τι καὶ πρὸς ἀνειμένην

---

8 Sall. hist. 1, 108. 109 M. ‖ 9—12 Sall. hist. 1, 111 M. Liv. per. 90. Flor. 2, 10, 6. 7. Oros. 5, 23, 2—4 Eutrop. 6, 1; cf. Cic. de fin. 2, 63 ‖ 12 c. 12, 5—13, 1 Plut. Pomp. 17, 2. 18, 2. Sall. hist. 2, 70 M. Val. Max. 9, 1, 5

[ΛΚΡQΜᵇ] 2 στρατηγοῖς] desinit Fᵃ, cf. ad p. 264,21 ‖ 4 πόλις L¹P ‖ 6 μόνων L ‖ 8 Φουφίδιον Ruhnken: πουφίδιον ‖ 9 δομήτιον L¹K δομέτιον L² ‖ 10 Καλουῖνον Sint.¹ app.: καλούσιον PQMᵇ κλούσιον K Steph. καὶ λούσιον Λ Λεύκιον Am. Xy. Sint.² Καλουίσιον Rei. Sint.¹ text. ‖ 11 καὶ del. Sch. ‖ Θώριον Zie. cl. Flor. et Cic.: θωράνιον codd. (θράνιον K Steph.); cf. Münzer RE VI A 332. 346 ‖ 12 μετὰ δυνά- μεως coniungebant cum πεμφθέντων ‖ ῥωμαίων Mᵇ: ῥωμαῖον ‖ 14 Μάλλιον Sol.: λόλλιον vel λόλιον codd. ‖ 18 μάχης] τύχης K ‖ εὐσταλία Λ ‖ 19 πολιτικῶν PCMᵇ ὁπολιτικῶν L ‖ μονίμου] στασίμου Zie. cl. Pomp. ‖ 22 ὀριβατεῖν L¹KP ‖ συνειθίσθαι Rei. ‖ 23 ἄπυρον] ἄπορον L¹ ἄσπορον K ‖ 25 καί τοι καὶ Mᵇ

ἤδη καὶ τρυφερὰν δίαιταν ἐκ πολλῶν ἀγώνων καὶ μεγάλων ἐνδεδωκώς, 100 s
τῷ δὲ Σερτωρίῳ συνειστήκει πνεύματος ἀκμαίου γέμοντι καὶ κατεσκευα-
2 σμένον ἔχοντι θαυμασίως τὸ σῶμα ῥώμῃ καὶ τάχει καὶ λιτότητι. μέθης
μὲν γὰρ οὐδὲ ῥᾳθυμῶν ἥπτετο, πόνους δὲ μεγάλους καὶ μακρὰς ὁδοιπορίας
καὶ συνεχεῖς ἀγρυπνίας ὀλίγοις εἴθιστο καὶ φαύλοις ἀρκούμενος σιτίοις 5
διαφέρειν· πλάνοις δὲ χρώμενος ἀεὶ καὶ κυνηγεσίοις ὁπότε σχολάζοι,
πάσης διεκδύσεως φεύγοντι καὶ διώκοντι κυκλώσεως ἀβάτων τε καὶ
3 βασίμων τόπων ἐμπειρίαν προσειλήφει. διὸ τῷ μὲν εἰργομένῳ μάχης ὅσα
d νικώμενοι πάσχουσιν ἄνθρωποι βλάπτεσθαι συνέβαινεν, ὁ δὲ τῷ φεύγειν
4 εἶχε τὰ τῶν διωκόντων. καὶ γὰρ ὑδρείας ἀπέκοπτε, καὶ σιτολογίας εἶργε, 10
καὶ προϊόντι μὲν ἐκποδὼν ἦν, ἐκίνει δ᾽ ἱδρυνθέντα, πολιορκοῦντι δ᾽ ἄλλους
5 ἐπιφαινόμενος ἀντεπολιόρκει ταῖς τῶν ἀναγκαίων ἀπορίαις, ὥστε τοὺς
στρατιώτας ἀπαγορεύειν, καὶ τοῦ Σερτωρίου μονομαχῆσαι προκαλουμένου
τὸν Μέτελλον, βοᾶν καὶ κελεύειν μάχεσθαι στρατηγὸν στρατηγῷ καὶ
Ῥωμαίῳ Ῥωμαῖον, ἀναδυόμενον δὲ χλευάζειν. ὁ δὲ τούτων μὲν εὖ ποιῶν 15
6 κατεγέλα· στρατηγοῦ γὰρ ὥς ἔφη Θεόφραστος (fg. 140 Wimmer) δεῖ θάνα-
e 7 τον ἀποθνῄσκειν τὸν στρατηγόν, οὐ πελταστοῦ τοῦ τυχόντος. ὁρῶν δὲ τοὺς 392 Z¹
a.79/8 Λαγγοβρίγας οὐ μικρὰ τῷ Σερτωρίῳ συλλαμβανομένους, δίψῃ δ᾽ ὄντας
εὐαλώτους (ἓν γὰρ ἦν αὐτοῖς φρέαρ ἐν τῇ πόλει, τῶν δ᾽ ἐν τοῖς προαστίοις
καὶ παρὰ τὰ τείχη ναμάτων ὁ πολιορκῶν ἐπικρατεῖν ἔμελλεν), ἧκεν ἐπὶ τὴν 20
πόλιν ὡς ἡμέραις δυσὶ συναιρήσων τὴν πολιορκίαν ὕδατος οὐκ ὄντος· διὸ
καὶ πένθ᾽ ἡμερῶν ἐπιφέρεσθαι σιτία μόνον προείρητο τοῖς στρατιώταις.
8 ὁ Σερτώριος δ᾽ ὀξέως βοηθήσας, ἐκέλευσε δισχιλίους ἀσκοὺς ὕδατος ἐμ-
9 πλῆσαι, καθ᾽ ἕκαστον ἀσκὸν ἀργύριον συχνὸν τάξας, καὶ πολλῶν μὲν Ἰβή-
f ρων, πολλῶν δὲ Μαυρουσίων ὑφισταμένων τὸ ἔργον, ἐπιλεξάμενος ἄνδρας 101 s
εὐρώστους ἅμα καὶ ποδώκεις ἔπεμψε διὰ τῆς ὀρεινῆς, κελεύσας, ὅταν 25
παραδῶσι τοὺς ἀσκοὺς τοῖς ἐν τῇ πόλει, τὸν ἄχρηστον ὑπεξαγαγεῖν
10 ὄχλον, ὅπως ἐξαρκῇ τοῖς ἀμυνομένοις τὸ ποτόν. ἐκπύστου δὲ τούτου γενομένου πρὸς τὸν Μέτελλον, ἤχθετο μὲν ἤδη τὰ ἐπιτήδεια τῶν στρατιω-
575 τῶν ὑπαναλωκότων, ἐξέπεμψε δ᾽ ἐπὶ σιτολογίαν Ἀκυῖνον ἑξακισχιλίων 30

16 cf. Plut. Sulla 42, 4. Pel. 2. Marc. 33 || 30 Sall. hist. 1, 120. 121 M.

[ΑΚΡQΜᵇ] 4 μὲν om. Q || 5 ἀγρυπνίαις ΡΜᵇ || 7 κυκλήσεως ΡΜᵇ | τε om. Κ ||
8 τόπων om. Κ || 11 ἐκποδὼν C: ἐν ποδῶν L ἐμποδὼν cet. | ἱδρυθέντα ΡQ || 15 ῥω-
μαίον ῥωμαίῳ: trp. Zie. || 18 λαγγοβρίτας: em. Zie. cl. Plin. n. h. 3, 26 Mela 3, 7 |
δίψει ΚQ || 19 ἦν γὰρ ἐν Μᵇ | προαστείοις em. Zie. || 21 αἱρήσων L¹ || 22 προείρη-
ται L¹Q || 23 δ᾽ om. Q || 27 τοῖς] τοὺς Q om. Μᵇ || 30 edebant Ἀκυῖνον; Aquilium
Aretinus Xy., unde Ἀκυΐλλιον Mu. Anon.

ἡγούμενον. αἰσθόμενος δ' ὁ Σερτώριος καὶ προλοχίσας τὴν ὁδόν, ἐπαν- 11
ερχομένῳ τῷ Ἀκυΐνῳ τρισχιλίους ἄνδρας ἔκ τινος συσκίου χαράδρας
ἐπανίστησιν, αὐτὸς δὲ κατὰ στόμα προσβαλὼν τρέπεται, καὶ τοὺς μὲν
διαφθείρει, τοὺς δὲ λαμβάνει ζῶντας. Ἀκυΐνον δὲ μετὰ τῶν ὅπλων καὶ 12
τὸν ἵππον ἀποβεβληκότα δεξάμενος Μέτελλος αἰσχρῶς ἀπῄει, πολλὰ
χλευαζόμενος ὑπὸ τῶν Ἰβήρων.

14. Ἔκ τε δὴ τούτων θαυμαζόμενος ἠγαπᾶτο παρὰ τοῖς βαρβάροις ὁ
Σερτώριος, καὶ ὅτι Ῥωμαϊκοῖς ὁπλισμοῖς καὶ τάξεσι καὶ συνθήμασιν
ἀφαιρῶν τὸ μανικὸν καὶ θηριῶδες αὐτῶν τῆς ἀλκῆς ἀντὶ λῃστηρίου b
μεγάλου στρατὸν ἐποιεῖτο τὴν δύναμιν. ἔτι δ' ἀργύρῳ χρώμενος ἀφει- 2
δῶς καὶ χρυσῷ κράνη τε κατεκόσμει καὶ θυρεοὺς αὐτῶν διεποίκιλλε, καὶ
χλαμύσιν ἀνθιναῖς καὶ χιτῶσι χρῆσθαι διδάσκων, καὶ χορηγῶν εἰς
ταῦτα καὶ συμφιλοκαλῶν, ἐδημαγώγει. μάλιστα δ' εἷλεν αὐτοὺς τὰ τῶν 3
παίδων· τοὺς γὰρ εὐγενεστάτους ἀπὸ τῶν ἐθνῶν συναγαγὼν εἰς Ὄσκαν
πόλιν μεγάλην, διδασκάλους ἐπιστήσας Ἑλληνικῶν τε καὶ Ῥωμαϊκῶν
μαθημάτων, ἔργῳ μὲν ἐξωμηρεύσατο, λόγῳ δ' ἐπαίδευεν, ὡς ἀνδράσι
γενομένοις πολιτείας τε μεταδώσων καὶ ἀρχῆς. οἱ δὲ πατέρες ἥδοντο 4
θαυμαστῶς, τοὺς παῖδας ἐν περιπορφύροις ὁρῶντες μάλα κοσμίως φοι- c
τῶντας εἰς τὰ διδασκαλεῖα, καὶ τὸν Σερτώριον ὑπὲρ αὐτῶν μισθοὺς τελοῦν-
τα, καὶ πολλάκις ἀποδείξεις λαμβάνοντα, καὶ γέρα τοῖς ἀξίοις νέμοντα,
καὶ τὰ χρυσᾶ περιδέραια δωρούμενον ἃ Ῥωμαῖοι βούλλας καλοῦσιν.
ἔθους δ' ὄντος Ἰβηρικοῦ τοὺς περὶ τὸν ἄρχοντα τεταγμένους συναπο- 5
θνῄσκειν αὐτῷ πεσόντι, καὶ τοῦτο τῶν ἐκεῖ βαρβάρων κατάσπεισιν ὀνομα-
ζόντων, τοῖς μὲν ἄλλοις ἡγεμόσιν ὀλίγοι τῶν ὑπασπιστῶν καὶ τῶν ἑταί-
ρων, Σερτωρίῳ δὲ πολλαὶ μυριάδες ἀνθρώπων κατεσπεικότων ἑαυτοὺς
ἠκολούθουν. λέγεται δὲ πρός τινι πόλει τροπῆς γενομένης καὶ τῶν πολε- 6 d
μίων ἐπικειμένων, τοὺς Ἴβηρας ἀμελήσαντας αὐτῶν τὸν Σερτώριον
σῴζειν καὶ τοῖς ὤμοις ἐπαραμένους ἄλλους ὑπὲρ ἄλλων ἀνακουφίσαι πρὸς
τὰ τείχη, γενομένου δ' ἐν ἀσφαλεῖ τοῦ ἄρχοντος, οὕτω τραπέσθαι πρὸς
φυγὴν ἕκαστον αὐτῶν.

22 Sall. hist. 1, 125 M. Cass. Dio 53, 20, 2 || 26 Sall. hist. 1, 126 M.

[ΔΚΡQΜ^b] 1 προλοχήσας QM^b || 3 ἀνίστησιν C ὑπανίστησιν Zie. | βαλὼν Q ||
5 τῶν ἵππων P || 16 ἐπαίδευσεν MM^b || 18 φοιτῶντες P || 20 ἀποδόξης PM^b συνδεί-
ξεις Mu. ἐπιδείξεις Rei., sed mor. 736 d. 737 b cft. Sint. | ἀναξίοις K || 21 περι-
δέρεα L¹ περιδέρρεα P | βούλας L¹Q || 24 ἑτέρων PM^b || 27 κειμένων Q || 28 ὑπὲρ
Emp.: πρὸ codd. (πρὸς M^b); cf. Sall. l. l. || 29 τραπέσθαι K: τρέπεσθαι

15. Οὐ μόνον δὲ τοῖς Ἴβηρσιν ἦν ποθεινός, ἀλλὰ καὶ τοῖς ἐξ Ἰταλίας στρατευομένοις. Περπέννα γοῦν Οὐέντωνος ἀπὸ τῆς αὐτῆς Σερτωρίῳ στάσεως εἰς Ἰβηρίαν παραγενομένου μετὰ χρημάτων πολλῶν καὶ μεγάλης δυνάμεως, ἰδίᾳ δὲ καθ' ἑαυτὸν ἐγνωκότος πολεμεῖν πρὸς τὸν Μέτελλον, ἐδυσχέραινον οἱ στρατιῶται, καὶ πολὺς ἦν τοῦ Σερτωρίου λόγος ἐν τῷ στρατοπέδῳ, τὸν Περπένναν ἀνιῶν, εὐγενείᾳ καὶ πλούτῳ τετυφωμένον. οὐ μὴν ἀλλ' ἐπεὶ Πομπήιος ἠγγέλλετο τὴν Πυρήνην ὑπερβάλλων, ἀναλαβόντες οἱ στρατιῶται τὰ ὅπλα καὶ τὰ σημεῖα τῶν τάξεων ἀναρπάσαντες κατεβόησαν τοῦ Περπέννα, κελεύοντες ὡς τὸν Σερτώριον ἄγειν αὐτούς· εἰ δὲ μή, καταλιπόντες ἐκεῖνον ἠπείλουν αὐτοὶ βαδιεῖσθαι πρὸς ἄνδρα σῴζεσθαι καὶ σῴζειν δυνάμενον. συγχωρήσας δ' ⟨οὖν⟩ ὁ Περπέννας ἤγαγεν αὐτοὺς καὶ συνέμειξε τῷ Σερτωρίῳ, πεντήκοντα καὶ τρεῖς ἔχων σπείρας.

16. Σερτώριος δέ, τῶν ἐντὸς Ἴβηρος αὐτῷ ποταμοῦ πάντων ὁμοῦ τι προστιθεμένων, πλήθει μὲν ἦν μέγας· ἐπέρρεον γὰρ ἀεὶ καὶ συνεφέροντο πανταχόθεν πρὸς αὐτόν· ἀταξίᾳ δὲ βαρβαρικῇ καὶ θρασύτητι ταραττόμενος, ἐπιχειρεῖν τοῖς πολεμίοις βοώντων καὶ τὴν τριβὴν δυσανασχετούντων, ἐπειρᾶτο παραμυθεῖσθαι διὰ λόγων. ὡς δ' ἑώρα χαλεπαίνοντας καὶ βιαζομένους ἀκαίρως, προήκατο καὶ περιεῖδε συμπλεκομένους τοῖς πολεμίοις, ἐν οἷς οὐ παντελῶς συντριβέντας, ἀλλὰ πληγὰς λαβόντας ἤλπιζε πρὸς τὰ λοιπὰ κατηκόους μᾶλλον ἕξειν. ὧν δ' εἴκαζε γενομένων, ἐπιβοηθήσας ἀνέλαβέ τε φεύγοντας αὐτοὺς καὶ κατέστησεν ἀσφαλῶς εἰς τὸ στρατόπεδον. βουλόμενος δὲ καὶ τὴν ἀθυμίαν ἀφελεῖν, μεθ' ἡμέρας ὀλίγας πάνδημον ἐκκλησίαν ἀθροίσας ἵππους εἰσήγαγε δύο, τὸν μὲν ἀσθενῆ τελέως καὶ πρεσβύτερον ἤδη, τὸν δ' ἕτερον εὐμεγέθη μὲν αὐτὸν καὶ ἰσχυρόν, θαυμαστὴν δὲ πυκνότητι καὶ κάλλει τριχῶν οὐρὰν ἔχοντα. παρειστήκει δὲ τῷ μὲν ἀσθενεῖ μέγας ἀνὴρ καὶ ῥωμαλέος, τῷ δ' ἰσχυρῷ μικρὸς ἕτερος καὶ τὴν ὄψιν εὐκαταφρόνητος. σημείου δὲ δοθέντος αὐτοῖς, ὁ μὲν ἰσχυρὸς ἀμφοτέραις ταῖς χερσὶ τοῦ ἵππου τὴν κέρκον ὡς ἀπορρήξων

---

2 Exup. 7 || 14 Liv. per. 91 || 16 Frontin. strat. 1, 10, 2 Suda s. v. ἀποκινδυνεύοντες || 23 Val. Max. 7, 3, 6 Plin. ep. 3, 9, 11 Frontin. strat. 1, 10, 1 = 4, 7, 6

[ΔΚΡQΜ^b] 2 περπένα QM^b et postea, semel hoc loco P || 7 ἠγάλλετο L¹ | πυρίνην L¹K || 10 καταλειπόντες, sed ε del., L || 11 δ' ⟨οὖν⟩ Zie. (οὖν pro δ' Rei.) || 12 ἤγεν PM^b || 14 τι om. KP || 15 προστεθειμένων Cor. προσθεμένων Zie. || 16 ἀξία L¹Q | παραταττόμενος L¹ || 18 λόγου Q || 19 προσήκατο Q | περιεῖδε PM^b: περιιδεῖν L¹ περιδεῖν L²Q περιιδὼν K || 20 ἐν] ἐφ' Sol. ὑφ' ὧν Zie. || 21 μᾶλλον κατηκόους Q

εἷλκε βίᾳ πρὸς αὐτόν, ὁ δ' ἀσθενὴς τοῦ ἰσχυροῦ κατὰ μίαν τῶν τριχῶν ἐξέτιλλεν. ἐπεὶ δ' ὁ μὲν οὐκ ὀλίγα πράγματα μάτην ἑαυτῷ καὶ πολὺν 8 γέλωτα τοῖς θεωμένοις παρασχὼν ἀπεῖπεν, ὁ δ' ἀσθενὴς ἀκαρεὶ καὶ σὺν οὐδενὶ πόνῳ ψιλὴν τριχῶν ἀπέδειξε τὴν οὐράν, ἀναστὰς ὁ Σερτώριος 9 „ὁρᾶτ'" εἶπεν „ἄνδρες σύμμαχοι τὴν ἐπιμονὴν ἀνυσιμωτέραν τῆς βίας οὖσαν καὶ πολλὰ τῶν ἀθρόως ἀλήπτων ἐνδιδόντα τῷ κατὰ μικρόν. ἄμα- 10 χον γὰρ τὸ ἐνδελεχές, ᾧ πᾶσαν ἐπιὼν ὁ χρόνος ⟨ἀν⟩αιρεῖ καὶ κατεργά-ζεται δύναμιν, εὐμενὴς ὢν σύμμαχος τοῖς δεχομένοις λογισμῷ τὸν καιρὸν αὐτοῦ, τοῖς δ' ἀκαίρως ἐπειγομένοις πολεμιώτατος." τοιαῦτα μὲν ὁ Σερ- 11 τώριος ἑκάστοτε πλέκων παραμύθια τοῖς βαρβάροις, διεπαιδαγώγει τὸν καιρόν.

17. Οὐδενὸς δ' ἧττον αὐτοῦ τῶν πολεμικῶν ἔργων ἐθαυμάσθη τὸ περὶ τοὺς λεγομένους Χαρακιτανούς. εἰσὶ δὲ δῆμος ὑπὲρ τὸν Ταγώνιον ποτα- 2 μόν, οὐκ ἄστεσιν οὐδὲ κώμαις ἐνοικοῦντες, ἀλλὰ λόφος ἐστὶν εὐμεγέθης καὶ ὑψηλός, ἄντρα καὶ κοιλώματα πετρῶν βλέποντα πρὸς βορέαν περιέχων. ἡ δ' ὑποκειμένη πᾶσα χώρα πηλὸν ἀργιλώδη καὶ γῆν ὑπὸ χαυνότητος 3 εὔθρυπτον ἀναδίδωσιν, οὔτε τοὺς ἐπιβαίνοντας ἀνέχεσθαι καρτεράν, καὶ μικρὸν ἁψαμένων ὥσπερ ἄσβεστον ἢ τέφραν ἐπὶ πολὺ διαχεομένην. τῶν 4 οὖν βαρβάρων, ὁσάκις φόβῳ πολέμου καταδύντες εἰς τὰ σπήλαια καὶ τὴν λείαν εἴσω συναγαγόντες ἀτρεμοῖεν, ὄντων ἀλήπτων ὑπὸ βίας, τὸν δὲ Σερτώριον τότε διακεκριμένον ἀπὸ τοῦ Μετέλλου καὶ καταστρατοπεδεύσαντα παρὰ τὸν λόφον ὑπερφρονούντων ὡς κεκρατημένον, εἴθ' ὑπ' ὀργῆς ἐκεῖνος, εἴτε [τὸ] μὴ δοκεῖν φεύγειν βουλόμενος, ἅμ' ἡμέρᾳ προσελάσας κατεσκέπτετο τὸν τόπον. οὐδαμόθεν δὲ προσβολὴν ἔχον- 5 τος, ἄλλως [δ'] ἀλύων καὶ κεναῖς χρώμενος ἀπειλαῖς, ὁρᾷ τῆς γῆς ἐκείνης κονιορτὸν ἄνω πολὺν ὑπὸ πνεύματος ἐπ' αὐτοὺς φερόμενον. τέτραπται 6 μὲν γὰρ ὡς ἔφην τὰ σπήλαια πρὸς βορέαν, ὁ δ' ἀπὸ τῆς ἄρκτου ῥέων ἄνεμος, ὃν Καικίαν ἔνιοι καλοῦσιν, ἐπέχει μάλιστα καὶ πλεῖστός ἐστι τῶν ἐκεῖ πνευμάτων, ἐξ ὑγρῶν πεδίων καὶ νιφοβόλων συμφυσώμενος ὀρῶν· τότε δὲ καὶ θέρους ἀκμάζοντος ἰσχύων καὶ τρεφόμενος τῇ τῶν 7

[ΑΚPQM^b] 3 ἀκαρεὶ L²P²M^b: ἀκαρῆ L¹P¹Q ἀκαρι K ǁ 4 πόνῳ Aldina: χρόνῳ ǁ 6 τῶι ΑΚQ: τὸ PM^b om. B ǁ 7 αἴρει L¹KPM^b: suppl. Zie. ǁ 9 αὐτοῦ del. Zie. ǁ 10 ⟨πρὸς⟩ τὸν κ. Rei. τὸν κ. del. Sch. ǁ 13 χαρακιτιανοὺς PM^b | Τάγον Mu. Xy. ǁ 21 διακεκλεμμένον Rei. ǁ 23 τὸ del. C Cor. (τῷ K καὶ Rei.) ǁ 24 ἔχων L¹ ǁ 25 δ' del. Rei. | καιναῖς PM^b ǁ 26 ἄνω om. Q | ὑπὸ τοῦ πν. K | ἐπ'] ὑπ' L¹K ǁ 27 μὲν om. Q et supra add. P | ῥέων] πνέων Herw. ǁ 28 ὃν om. Q Sint. | κεκίαν L¹P¹ | πλεῖστον Q ǁ 29 συμφυσόμενος PM^b

ὑπαρκτίων ἀνέσει πάγων, ἥδιστος ἐπέπνει καὶ κατεῖχεν αὐτούς τε καὶ
8 βοτὰ δι' ἡμέρας ἀναψύχων. ταῦτα δὴ συλλογιζόμενος ὁ Σερτώριος καὶ
f παρὰ τῶν ἐγχωρίων ἀκούων, ἐκέλευσε τοὺς στρατιώτας τῆς ἀραιᾶς καὶ
τεφρώδους γῆς ἐκείνης ἀποσπῶντας καὶ παραφέροντας καταντικρὺ τοῦ
λόφου θῖνα ποιεῖν, ἣν οἱ βάρβαροι χώματος ἐπ' αὐτοὺς εἶναι κατασκευὴν 105 S
9 ὑπονοοῦντες ἐχλεύαζον. τότε μὲν οὖν ἐργασαμένους τοὺς στρατιώτας ἄχρι 6
νυκτὸς ἀπήγαγεν· ἅμα δ' ἡμέρᾳ πρῶτον μὲν αὔρα μαλακὴ προαπέπνει,
διακινοῦσα τῆς συμπεφορημένης γῆς τὸ λειότατον, ὥσπερ ἄχνην σκιδνά-
10 μενον· ἔπειτα σοβαροῦ τοῦ Καικίου πρὸς τὸν ἥλιον ἐκχεομένου καὶ τῶν
577 λόφων κονιωμένων, ἐπιστάντες οἱ στρατιῶται τόν τε χοῦν ἀνέτρεπον διὰ 10
βάθους καὶ τὸν πηλὸν ἔκοπτον, ἔνιοι δὲ καὶ τοὺς ἵππους ἄνω καὶ κάτω δι-
εξήλασαν, ἀνιστάντες τὸ χαύνωμα καὶ τῇ πνοῇ μετέωρον παραδιδόντες.
11 ἡ δ' ὑπολαμβάνουσα πᾶν τὸ θρυπτόμενον καὶ κινούμενον ἄνω προσέβαλλε
12 τοῖς οἰκήμασι τῶν βαρβάρων, κατὰ θύρας δεχομένοις τὸν Καικίαν. οἱ δ',
ἅτε δὴ τῶν σπηλαίων μίαν ἐκείνην ἀναπνοὴν ἐχόντων, ᾗ τὸ πνεῦμα προσ- 15
έπιπτε, ταχὺ μὲν ἀπεσκοτοῦντο τὰς ὄψεις, ταχὺ δ' ἀνεπίμπλαντο πνιγώδους
13 ἄσθματος, τραχὺν ἀέρα καὶ πολλῇ κόνει συμπεφυρμένον ἕλκοντες. ὅθεν 398 Z¹
b ἡμέρας δύο μόλις ἀνασχόμενοι, τῇ τρίτῃ παρέδωκαν ἑαυτούς, οὐ τοσοῦτον
Σερτωρίῳ δυνάμεως ὅσον δόξης προσθέντες, ὡς τὰ δι' ὅπλων ἀνάλωτα
σοφίᾳ κατεργασαμένῳ. 20

18. Μέχρι μὲν οὖν τοῖς περὶ Μέτελλον ἐπολέμει, τὰ πλεῖστα κατευτυ-
χεῖν ἐδόκει, γήρᾳ καὶ φυσικῇ βραδυτῆτι τοῦ Μετέλλου πρὸς ἄνδρα τολμη-
τὴν καὶ λῃστρικῆς μᾶλλον ἢ στρατιωτικῆς ἡγούμενον δυνάμεως οὐκ
a. 76 2 ἀναφέροντος· ἐπεὶ δὲ καὶ Πομπηΐῳ τὴν Πυρήνην ὑπερβαλόντι παραστρατοπεδεύσας, καὶ πᾶσαν ἅμα μὲν διδοὺς ἅμα δὲ λαμβάνων στρατηγικῶν παλαι- 25
c σμάτων πεῖραν, ἀντιτεχνώμενός τε καὶ φυλαττόμενος πλεῖον εἶχε, κομιδῇ
διεβοήθη μέχρι Ῥώμης ὡς δεινότατος ὢν πόλεμον μεταχειρίσασθαι τῶν
3 τότε στρατηγῶν. οὐ γάρ τοι μικρὸν ἦν τὸ Πομπηΐου κλέος, ἀλλ' ἤνθει 106 S
τότε μάλιστα πρὸς δόξαν ἐκ τῶν περὶ Σύλλαν ἀνδραγαθημάτων, ἐφ' οἷς

29 Plut. Pomp. 13, 7. 14 et ibi l. l.

[*Λ*KPQM^b] 1 ἀπαρκτίων K || 3 ἐκέλευε Q | τῆς γὰρ ἀρ. PM^b || 4 ἐκείνης γῆς Q |
ἀποσμῶντας Rei. || 7 προσανέπνει K προεπέπνει Rei. προσεπέπνει Cor. || 9 καικία
PM^b || 9.10 τῶν λόφων KCM^bL²: τὸν λόφων L¹ τὸν λόφον PQ || 10 κονιώμενον P¹ ||
11 πηλὸν PQM^b: σπίλον K σπηλόν, sed σ del., L || 16 ἀνεσκοτοῦντο P ἀνεσκο-
ποῦντο M^b | ἀνεπίπλαντο L¹ || 17 συμπεφυρμένον L²: συμπεφορημένον L¹KPQM^b ||
19 ἀναλώματα PM^b || 24 ἀναφέρετος L¹P ἀναφαίρετος M^b | πυρίνην L¹K | ὑπερβάλ-
λοντι *Λ*Q || 26 πλέον Q || 28 τοι Cor.: τι codd. (om. P)

καὶ Μᾶγνος ὑπ' αὐτοῦ, τουτέστι Μέγας, ἐπωνομάσθη, τιμῶν τε θριαμ- βικῶν οὔπω γενειῶν ἔτυχεν. ὅθεν καὶ πολλαὶ τῶν ὑπὸ Σερτωρίῳ πόλεων ἀποβλέψασαι πρὸς αὐτὸν ὁρμὴν μεταβολῆς ἔσχον, εἶτ' ἐπαύσαντο, τοῦ περὶ Λαύρωνα πάθους παρὰ πᾶσαν ἐλπίδα συμβάντος. Σερτωρίου γὰρ πολιορ- κοῦντος αὐτούς, ἧκε Πομπήϊος πανστρατιᾷ βοηθήσων· εἶθ' ὁ μὲν λόφον εὖ δοκοῦντα πεφυκέναι κατὰ τῆς πόλεως προληψόμενος, ὁ δὲ τοῦτο κωλύσων ἠπείγετο. τοῦ δὲ Σερτωρίου φθάσαντος, ἐπιστήσας τὸν στρατὸν ὁ Πομπήϊος ἔχαιρε τῇ συντυχίᾳ, νομίζων ἐν μέσῳ τῆς πόλεως καὶ τῆς αὐτοῦ στρατιᾶς ἀπειλῆφθαι τὸν Σερτώριον, καὶ πρὸς τοὺς Λαυρωνίτας εἰσέπεμψε, θαρρεῖν κελεύων καὶ καθῆσθαι περὶ τὰ τείχη, θεωμένους πολιορκούμενον Σερτώ- ριον. ἐκεῖνος δ' ἀκούσας ἐγέλασε, καὶ τὸν Σύλλα μαθητὴν (οὕτω γὰρ τὸν Πομπήϊον ἐπισκώπτων προσηγόρευεν) αὐτὸς ἔφη διδάξειν, ὅτι δεῖ τὸν στρα- τηγὸν κατόπιν μᾶλλον ἢ κατὰ πρόσωπον βλέπειν. ταῦτα δὲ λέγων ἅμα τοῖς πολιορκουμένοις ἐπεδείκνυεν ἑξακισχιλίους ὁπλίτας, ὑπ' αὐτοῦ καταλελειμ- μένους ἐπὶ τοῦ προτέρου χάρακος, ὅθεν ὁρμηθεὶς κατειλήφει τὸν λόφον, ὅπως ἐπὶ σφᾶς τρεπομένῳ τῷ Πομπηΐῳ κατὰ νώτου προσπέσοιεν. ὃ δὴ καὶ Πομπήϊος ὀψὲ μάλα συμφρονήσας, ἐπιχειρεῖν μὲν οὐκ ἐθάρρει κύκλω- σιν δεδοικώς, ἀπολιπεῖν δ' ᾐσχύνετο κινδυνεύοντας ἀνθρώπους, παρὼν δὲ καὶ καθήμενος ἠναγκάζετο ⟨περι⟩ορᾶν ἀπολλυμένους· ἀπέγνωσαν γὰρ αὐτοὺς οἱ βάρβαροι καὶ τῷ Σερτωρίῳ παρέδωκαν. ὁ δὲ τῶν μὲν σωμάτων ἐφείσατο καὶ πάντας ἀφῆκε, τὴν δὲ πόλιν κατέπρησεν, οὐχ ὑπ' ὀργῆς οὐδ' ὠμότητος, ἐλάχιστα γὰρ δοκεῖ θυμῷ χαρίσασθαι τῶν στρατηγῶν οὗτος ἀνήρ, ἀλλ' ἐπ' αἰσχύνῃ καὶ κατηφείᾳ τῶν τεθαυμακότων Πομπήϊον, ἵν' ᾖ λόγος ἐν τοῖς βαρβάροις, ὅτι παρὼν ἐγγὺς καὶ μονονοὺ θερμαινόμενος τῷ πυρὶ τῶν συμμάχων, οὐ προσήμυνεν.

19. Ἧτται μὲν οὖν τῷ Σερτωρίῳ πλείονες συνέβαινον, αὐτὸν μὲν ἀήτ- τητον ἀεὶ φυλάττοντι καὶ τοὺς καθ' αὑτόν, θραυομένῳ δὲ περὶ τοὺς ἄλλους ἡγεμόνας· ἐκ δ' ὧν ἐπηνωρθοῦτο τὰς ἥττας, μᾶλλον ἐθαυμάζετο νικώντων

2 Plut. Pomp. 18, 1 || 3 Plut. Pomp. 18, 4 Sall. hist. 2, 29 M. App. b. c. 1, 109, 510 Flor. 2, 10, 7 Oros. 5, 23, 6. 7 cf. Frontin. strat. 2, 5, 31

[ΛΚΡQΖ] 3 εἶτ'] inc. Fᵃ, cf. ad p. 267, 2 || 4 παρὰ om. Z || 9 ἀπολειφθῆναι Z || 9 καὶ – 10 Σερτώριον om. PZ || 11 ἐκεῖνο Z || 12 προσηγόρευσεν KZ || 14 κατακε- κλιμένους Z || 16 περιπέσοιεν K || 17 μάλιστα KZ || 18 ἀπολειπεῖν ante corr. LP | οὐκ ᾐσχύνετο Z || 19 ⟨καθ' ἡσυχίαν⟩ καθήμενος Zie. καθ. ⟨ἄλλως⟩ Latte | ⟨περι⟩- ορᾶν Zie. (ἐπεῖδε Pomp. ἐφορῶντος App.) || 20 αὐτοὺς om. Z || 23 ἀνὴρ Sch.: ἀνὴρ | ἀλλ' om. PZ | ἐπ' om. Q || 26 οὖν om. Q || 27 ἀεὶ διαφυλάττοντι M

a. 75 τῶν ἀντιστρατήγων, οἷον ἐν τῇ περὶ Σούκρωνι μάχῃ πρὸς Πομπήϊον, καὶ
3 πάλιν ἐν τῇ περὶ Σεγουντίαν πρός τε τοῦτον ὁμοῦ καὶ Μέτελλον. ἡ μὲν οὖν
περὶ Σούκρωνι μάχη λέγεται γενέσθαι τοῦ Πομπηΐου κατεπείξαντος, ὡς
4 μὴ μετάσχοι τῆς νίκης Μέτελλος. ὁ δὲ Σερτώριος ἐβούλετο μὲν τῷ Πομ
πηΐῳ πρὶν ἐπελθεῖν τὸν Μέτελλον διαγωνίσασθαι, παραγαγὼν δ' ἑσπέ- 5
b ρας ἤδη συνέβαλεν, οἰόμενος ξένοις οὖσι καὶ ἀπείροις τῶν χωρίων τοῖς
5 πολεμίοις τὸ σκότος ἔσεσθαι καὶ φεύγουσιν ἐμπόδιον καὶ διώκουσι. γενο
μένης δὲ τῆς μάχης ἐν χερσίν, ἔτυχε μὲν οὐ πρὸς Πομπήϊον αὐτός, ἀλλὰ
πρὸς Ἀφράνιον ἐν ἀρχῇ συνεστηκώς, ἔχοντα τὸ ἀριστερόν, αὐτὸς ἐπὶ τοῦ
6 δεξιοῦ τεταγμένος. ἀκούσας δὲ τῷ Πομπηΐῳ τοὺς συνεστῶτας ὑποχωρεῖν 10
ἐγκειμένῳ καὶ κρατεῖσθαι, τὸ μὲν δεξιὸν ἐπ' ἄλλοις ἐποιήσατο στρατη
7 γοῖς, πρὸς δ' ἐκεῖνο τὸ νικώμενον αὐτὸς ἐβοηθρόμει. καὶ τοὺς μὲν ἤδη
τρεπομένους, τοὺς δ' ἔτι μένοντας ἐν τάξει συναγαγὼν καὶ ἀναθαρρύνας,
ἐξ ὑπαρχῆς ἐνέβαλε τῷ Πομπηΐῳ διώκοντι καὶ φυγὴν ἐποιήσατο πολλήν·
c 8 ὅτε καὶ Πομπήϊος ἐγγὺς ἐλθὼν ἀποθανεῖν καὶ τραυματισθείς, παραλόγως 15
διέφυγεν. οἱ γὰρ μετὰ Σερτωρίου Λίβυες ὡς ἔλαβον αὐτοῦ τὸν ἵππον χρυσῷ
κεκοσμημένον καὶ φαλάρων ἀνάπλεων πολυτελῶν, ἐν τῷ διανέμεσθαι καὶ
9 διαφέρεσθαι πρὸς ἀλλήλους προήκαντο τὴν δίωξιν. Ἀφράνιος δὲ τοὺς ἀνθ- 108 S
εστῶτας πρὸς αὐτὸν ἅμα τῷ Σερτώριον ἀπελθεῖν ἐπὶ θάτερα βοηθοῦντα   401 Z¹
τρεψάμενος, εἰς τὸ στρατόπεδον κατήραξε, καὶ συνεισπεσὼν ἐπόρθει 20
σκότους ὄντος ἤδη, μήτε τὴν Πομπηΐου φυγὴν εἰδώς, μήτε τοὺς στρατιώ
10 τας τῆς ἁρπαγῆς ἐπισχεῖν δυνάμενος. ἐν τούτῳ δὲ Σερτώριος ἀνέστρεψε,
d τὸ καθ' αὑτὸν νενικηκώς, καὶ τοῖς Ἀφρανίου δι' ἀταξίαν ταρασσομένοις
11 ἐπιπεσών, πολλοὺς διέφθειρε. πρωὶ δ' αὖθις ἐξοπλισθεὶς ἐπὶ μάχην κατέ
βαινεν, εἶτα Μέτελλον αἰσθόμενος ἐγγὺς εἶναι, λύσας τὴν τάξιν ἀνέζευξεν, 25
εἰπών· „ἀλλ' ἔγωγε τὸν παῖδα τοῦτον, εἰ μὴ παρῆν ἡ γραῦς ἐκείνη, πλη
γαῖς ἂν νουθετήσας εἰς Ῥώμην ἀπεστάλκειν."
20. Ἠθύμει δὲ δεινῶς διὰ τὸ μηδαμοῦ φανερὰν τὴν ἔλαφον ἐκείνην
εἶναι· μηχανῆς γὰρ ἐπὶ τοὺς βαρβάρους ἐστέρητο θαυμαστῆς, τότε δὴ

2 Plut. Pomp. 19, 1—6 Sall. hist. 2, 60—63. 98, 6 M. Cic. p. Balb. 5 Liv. per. 92
Flor. 2, 10, 7 Oros. 5, 23, 11 App. b. c. 1, 110, 512 sq. || **26** Plut. Pomp. 18, 1 ||
28 c. 20 Gell. 15, 22, 6—9 App. b. c. 1, 110, 514

[*ΛΚPQZ*] 1 et 3 *Σούκρωνα* Mu. Anon. || **2** *Σεγουντίαν* Zie.: *τουττίαν ΛQ σουν
τίαν* PZ (*καὶ πάλιν* — **3** *μάχη* om. K) *Τουρίαν* Aretinus Sint. *Duriam* Xy. | *τε τοῦ
τον*] *τὸν* Z || **3** *μάχη*] desin. Z, cf. ad p. 264, 21 || **7** *ἐμποδὼν* K || **16** *σερτώριον* L¹ P ||
18 *φέρεσθαι* Q | *προσήκαντο* P || **20** *κατήρραξεν* LK || **21** *ἤδη ὄντος*: trp. Sint. (*ὄν
τος* om. K) || **22** *ἀνέστρεψε* C: *ἀνέστρεφε* || **24** *πρωΐ* — *κατέβαινεν* om. Q || **26** *παρῆν* om. P

μάλιστα παραμυθίας δεομένους. εἶτα μέντοι νυκτὸς ἄλλως πλανώμενοί
τινες ἐπιτυγχάνουσιν αὐτῇ, καὶ γνωρίσαντες ἀπὸ τῆς χρόας λαμβάνουσιν.
ἀκούσας δ' ὁ Σερτώριος, ἐκείνοις μὲν ὡμολόγησεν, ἂν μηδενὶ φράσωσι,
χρήματα πολλὰ δώσειν, ἀποκρύψας δὲ τὴν ἔλαφον καὶ διαλιπὼν ὀλίγας
ἡμέρας, προῄει μάλα φαιδρὸς ὡς ἀπ' ὄψεως ἐπὶ τὸ βῆμα, διηγούμενος τοῖς
ἡγεμόσι τῶν Ἰβήρων, ὡς ἀγαθόν τι μέγα τοῦ θεοῦ προμηνύοντος αὐτῷ
κατὰ τοὺς ὕπνους· εἶτ' ἀναβὰς ἐπὶ τὸ βῆμα τοῖς ἐντυγχάνουσιν ἐχρημάτιζεν. ἡ δ' ἔλαφος ὑπὸ τῶν φυλαττόντων αὐτὴν ἐγγὺς ἀφεθεῖσα καὶ κατι-
δοῦσα τὸν Σερτώριον, ἐχώρει δρόμῳ περιχαρὴς πρὸς τὸ βῆμα, καὶ παρα-
στᾶσα τὴν κεφαλὴν ἐπέθηκε τοῖς γόνασιν αὐτοῦ, καὶ τῷ στόματι τῆς δε-
ξιᾶς ἔψαυεν, εἰθισμένη καὶ πρότερον τοῦτο ποιεῖν. ἀντιφιλοφρονουμένου δὲ
τοῦ Σερτωρίου πιθανῶς, καί τι καὶ δακρύσαντος, ἔκπληξις εἶχε τοὺς παρόν-
τας τὸ πρῶτον, εἶτα κρότῳ καὶ βοῇ τὸν Σερτώριον ὡς δαιμόνιον ἄνδρα καὶ
θεοῖς φίλον οἴκαδε προπέμψαντες, ἐν εὐθυμίαις καὶ χρησταῖς ἐλπίσιν ἦσαν.

21. Ἐν δὲ τοῖς τῶν Σεγουντίνων πεδίοις εἰς τὰς ἐσχάτας ἀπορίας κατα-
κεκλεικὼς τοὺς πολεμίους, ἠναγκάσθη συμβαλεῖν αὐτοῖς καταβαίνουσιν
ἐφ' ἁρπαγὴν καὶ σιτολογίαν. ἠγωνίσθη δὲ λαμπρῶς παρ' ἀμφοτέρων, καὶ
Μέμμιος μὲν ὁ τῶν ὑπὸ Πομπηίῳ στρατηγῶν ἡγεμονικώτατος ἐν τῷ
καρτερωτάτῳ τῆς μάχης ἔπεσεν, ἐκράτει δὲ Σερτώριος καὶ φόνῳ πολλῷ
τῶν ἔτι συνεστώτων ἐωθεῖτο πρὸς αὐτὸν τὸν Μέτελλον. ὁ δὲ παρ' ἡλι-
κίαν ὑποστὰς καὶ περιφανῶς ἀγωνιζόμενος, παίεται δόρατι. τοῦτο τοὺς
μὲν ἰδόντας τῶν Ῥωμαίων, τοὺς δ' ἀκούσαντας, αἰδὼς ἔσχεν ἐγκαταλιπεῖν
τὸν ἡγεμόνα, καὶ θυμὸς ἅμα πρὸς τοὺς πολεμίους παρέστη. προθέμενοι
δὲ τοὺς θυρεοὺς καὶ συνεξενεγκόντες εὐρώστως, ἐξωθοῦσι τοὺς Ἴβηρας·
καὶ γενομένης οὕτω παλιντρόπου τῆς νίκης, ὁ Σερτώριος ἐκείνοις τε φυγὰς
ἀδεεῖς μηχανώμενος, καὶ τεχνάζων ἑτέραν αὐτῷ δύναμιν συνελθεῖν ἐφ'
ἡσυχίας, εἰς πόλιν ὀρεινὴν καὶ καρτερὰν ἀναφυγὼν ἐφράγνυτο τὰ τείχη καὶ
τὰς πύλας ὠχυροῦτο, πάντα μᾶλλον ἢ πολιορκίαν ὑπομένειν διανοούμενος,

---

15 c. 21, 1—8 Sall. hist. 2, 64—68 M. Cic. p. Balb. 5 Liv. per. 92 Frontin. strat. 2, 13, 3 App. b. c. 1, 110, 515 Oros. 5, 23, 12

[ΑΚΡQ] 5 φαιδρὸς ὡς V^b: φαιδρὸς ΑΚΡ φαιδρῶς Q ∥ 6 ἰβήρων L¹ΚΡQ: βαρβάρων L² et editt. ∣ προμην. αὐτ. τοῦ θεοῦ Κ ∥ 12 πειθανῶς L¹Ρ ∣ ἐπιδακρύσαντος
Rei. ∥ 15 σαγουντίνων Barocc. 114 et multi editt. ∣ εἰς τὰς] ἐκστὰς L¹ ἐστὰς Ρ ∣
19 καρτερικωτάτῳ Q ∥ 20 ἐξεωθεῖτο Q ∣ τὸν add. Κ Steph. ∣ καὶ παρ' ΚΡQ ∥ 21 ἀγω-
νισάμενος Cor. ∥ 22 ἐγκαταλειπεῖν L¹ ∥ 24 δὲ om. Α ∣ τοὺς θεοὺς Ρ ∣ εὐρώστους Ρ ∥
25.26 φυγάδας ἀδεεῖς ἐμηχανήσατο Q ∥ 26 εἰσελθεῖν Q ∥ 28 διαμένειν ὑπονοούμενος Q

20*

5 ἀλλ' ἐξηπάτα τοὺς πολεμίους. ἐκείνῳ γὰρ προσκαθεζόμενοι καὶ τὸ χωρίον οὐ χαλεπῶς λήψεσθαι προσδοκῶντες, τούς τε φεύγοντας τῶν βαρβάρων προΐεντο, καὶ τῆς ἀθροιζομένης αὖθις τῷ Σερτωρίῳ δυνάμεως ἠμέλησαν.
6 ἠθροίζετο δὲ πέμψαντος ἡγεμόνας ἐπὶ τὰς πόλεις αὐτοῦ καὶ κελεύοντος,
c 7 ὅταν ἤδη πολλοὺς ἔχωσιν, ἄγγελον ἀποστεῖλαι πρὸς αὐτόν. ἐπεὶ δ' ἀπέστειλαν, σὺν οὐδενὶ πόνῳ διεκπαισάμενος τοὺς πολεμίους, συνέμειξε τοῖς ἑαυτοῦ, καὶ πάλιν ἐπῄει πολὺς γεγονώς, καὶ περιέκοπτεν αὐτῶν τὴν μὲν ἀπὸ τῆς γῆς εὐπορίαν ἐνέδραις καὶ κυκλώσεσι καὶ τῷ πανταχόσε φοιτᾶν ὀξὺς ἐπιών, τὴν δ' ἐκ θαλάττης λῃστρικοῖς σκάφεσι κατέχων τὴν παραλίαν,
8 ὥστ' ἠναγκάσθησαν οἱ στρατηγοὶ διαλυθέντες, ὁ μὲν εἰς Γαλατίαν ἀπελθεῖν, Πομπήϊος δὲ περὶ Βακκαίους διαχειμάσαι μοχθηρῶς ὑπ' ἀχρηματίας,
d γράφων πρὸς τὴν σύγκλητον ὡς ἀπάξει τὸν στρατόν, εἰ μὴ πέμποιεν ἀργύριον αὐτῷ· καταναλωκέναι γὰρ ἤδη τὰ αὑτοῦ, προπολεμῶν τῆς Ἰταλίας.
9 καὶ πολὺς ἦν [οὗτος] ἐν Ῥώμῃ λόγος, ὡς Πομπηΐου πρότερος εἰς Ἰταλίαν ἀφίξοιτο Σερτώριος· εἰς τοσοῦτον τοὺς πρώτους καὶ δυνατωτάτους τῶν τότε στρατηγῶν ἡ Σερτωρίου δεινότης κατέστησεν.

22. Ἐδήλωσε δὲ καὶ Μέτελλος ἐκπεπληγμένος τὸν ἄνδρα καὶ μέγαν ἡγούμενος· ἐπεκήρυξε γάρ, εἴ τις αὐτὸν ἀνέλοι Ῥωμαῖος, ἑκατὸν ἀργυρίου τάλαντα δώσειν καὶ πλέθρα δισμύρια γῆς, εἰ δὲ φυγάς, κάθοδον εἰς Ῥώμην, ὡς ἀπογνώσει φανερᾶς ἀμύνης ὠνούμενος τὸν ἄνδρα διὰ προδοσίας.
e 2 ἔτι δὲ νικήσας ποτὲ μάχῃ τὸν Σερτώριον οὕτως ἐπήρθη καὶ τὴν εὐτυχίαν ἠγάπησεν, ὥστ' αὐτοκράτωρ ἀναγορευθῆναι, θυσίαις δ' αὐτὸν αἱ πόλεις
3 ἐπιφοιτῶντα καὶ βωμοῖς ἐδέχοντο. λέγεται δὲ καὶ στεφάνων ἀναδέσεις προσίεσθαι καὶ δείπνων σοβαρωτέρων ὑποδοχάς, ἐν οἷς ἐσθῆτα θριαμβικὴν ἔχων ἔπινε, καὶ Νῖκαι πεποιημέναι δι' ὀργάνων ἐπιδρόμων χρύσεα τρόπαια καὶ στεφάνους διαφέρουσαι κατήγοντο, καὶ χοροὶ παίδων καὶ γυναι-
4 κῶν ἐπινικίους ὕμνους ᾖδον εἰς αὐτόν. ἐφ' οἷς εἰκότως ἦν καταγέλαστος, εἰ δραπέτην Σύλλα καὶ λείψανον τῆς Κάρβωνος φυγῆς ἀποκαλῶν τὸν Σερτώ-
f ριον, οὕτω κεχαύνωται καὶ περιχαρὴς γέγονεν ὑποχωρήσαντος αὐτοῦ περιγενόμενος.

7 Plut. Pomp. 19, 10. 11 Sall. hist. 2, 88—90 M. ‖ 11 Plut. Pomp. 20, 1 Luc. 5, 3 Sall. hist. 2, 47, 6. 93—98 M. ‖ 22 Sall. hist. 2, 70 M. Val. Max. 9, 1, 5

[ΔKPQ] 4 αὐτοῦ om. P | 6 διεκπεσάμενος L¹P | τοῖς om. Q | 8 καὶ τὸ L¹K ‖ 9 τὴν δ' ἐκ Zie.: τὰς δ' ἐκ L¹KQ τὰ δ' ἐκ cet. | παρέχων Q ‖ 10 οἱ μὲν P ‖ 11 διαχειμάσας L¹ ‖ 12 ἀπάξοι KPQ et fort. L¹: ἀπάξει cet. (εἰς Ἰταλίαν ἀπάξοι Luc.) | πέμποι Q ‖ 13 αὐτῷ Λ: om. K αὐτοῦ P αὐτὸν Q ‖ 14 οὗτος ἦν λόγος ἐν ῥώμῃ C | οὗτος del. Zie. | πρότερον K ‖ 20 ἐξωνούμενος Latte ‖ 22 θυσίαι L¹ ‖ 24 προίεσθαι P

Μεγαλοφροσύνης δὲ τοῦ Σερτωρίου πρῶτον μὲν τὸ τοὺς φεύγοντας ἀπὸ Ῥώμης βουλευτὰς καὶ παρ' αὐτῷ διατρίβοντας σύγκλητον ἀναγορεῦσαι, ταμίας τε καὶ στρατηγοὺς ἐξ ἐκείνων ἀποδεικνύναι, καὶ πάντα τοῖς πατρίοις νόμοις τὰ τοιαῦτα κοσμεῖν· ἔπειτα τὸ χρώμενον ὅπλοις καὶ χρήμασι καὶ πόλεσι ταῖς Ἰβήρων μηδ' ἄχρι λόγου τῆς ἄκρας ἐξουσίας ὑφίεσθαι πρὸς αὐτούς, Ῥωμαίους δὲ καθιστάναι στρατηγοὺς καὶ ἄρχοντας αὐτῶν, ὡς Ῥωμαίοις ἀνακτώμενον τὴν ἐλευθερίαν, οὐκ ἐκείνους αὔξοντα κατὰ Ῥωμαίων. καὶ γὰρ ἦν ἀνὴρ φιλόπατρις καὶ πολὺν ἔχων ἵμερον τοῦ κατελθεῖν· ἀλλὰ δυσπραγῶν μὲν ἠνδραγάθει, καὶ ταπεινὸν μὲν οὐδὲν ἔπραττε πρὸς τοὺς πολεμίους, ἐν δὲ ταῖς νίκαις διεπέμπετο πρὸς Μέτελλον καὶ πρὸς Πομπήϊον, ἕτοιμος ὢν τὰ ὅπλα καταθέσθαι καὶ βιοῦν ἰδιώτης καθόδου τυχών· μᾶλλον γὰρ ἐθέλειν ἀσημότατος ἐν Ῥώμῃ πολίτης ἢ φεύγων τὴν ἑαυτοῦ πάντων ὁμοῦ τῶν ἄλλων αὐτοκράτωρ ἀναγορεύεσθαι. λέγεται δ' οὐχ ἥκιστα τῆς πατρίδος ἐπιθυμεῖν διὰ τὴν μητέρα, τραφεὶς ὀρφανὸς ὑπ' αὐτῇ καὶ τὸ σύμπαν ἀνακείμενος ἐκείνῃ. καλούντων δὲ τῶν περὶ τὴν Ἰβηρίαν φίλων αὐτὸν ἐφ' ἡγεμονίᾳ, πυθόμενος τὴν τελευτὴν τῆς μητρὸς ὀλίγον ἐδέησεν ὑπὸ λύπης προέσθαι τὸν βίον. ἑπτὰ γὰρ ἡμέρας οὔτε σύνθημα δοὺς οὔτ' ὀφθείς τινι τῶν φίλων ἔκειτο, καὶ μόλις οἱ συστράτηγοι καὶ ἰσότιμοι τὴν σκηνὴν περιστάντες ἠνάγκασαν αὐτὸν προελθόντα τοῖς στρατιώταις ἐντυχεῖν καὶ τῶν πραγμάτων εὖ φερομένων ἀντιλαμβάνεσθαι. διὸ καὶ πολλοῖς ἔδοξεν ἥμερος ἀνὴρ φύσει γεγονὼς καὶ πρὸς ἡσυχίαν ἔχων ἐπιεικῶς, † δι' αἰτίας παρὰ γνώμην ταῖς στρατηγικαῖς ἀρχαῖς χρῆσθαι, καὶ μὴ τυγχάνων ἀδείας, ἀλλὰ συνελαυνόμενος ὑπὸ τῶν ἐχθρῶν εἰς τὰ ὅπλα, φρουρὰν ἀναγκαίαν τοῦ σώματος περιβάλλεσθαι τὸν πόλεμον.

23. Ἦν δὲ καὶ τὰ πρὸς Μιθριδάτην αὐτοῦ πολιτεύματα μεγαλοφροσύνης. ἐπεὶ γὰρ ἐκ τοῦ κατὰ Σύλλαν σφάλματος ὁ Μιθριδάτης ὥσπερ εἰς πάλαισμα δεύτερον ἀνιστάμενος αὖθις ἐπεχείρησε τῇ Ἀσίᾳ, μέγα δ' ἤδη τὸ Σερτωρίου κλέος ἐφοίτα πανταχόσε, καὶ τῶν περὶ αὐτοῦ λόγων ὥσπερ

---

1 App. b. c. 1, 108, 507 Mithr. 68, 286 ǁ 13 cf. c. 2, 1 ǁ 25 c. 23. 24 App. Mithr. 68, 287 sq. Sall. hist. 2, 78. 79. 93 M. Cic. de imp. 46

[ΛΚΡQ] 1 μεγαλοφροσύνη L¹ | φυγόντας PQ ǁ 3 ἀποδειχθῆναι L¹ ǁ 4 χρώμενος P ǁ 7 ἀνακτώμενος KQ ǁ 9 μὲν² om. Q ǁ 11 καταθέσθαι τὰ ὅπλα Q ǁ 18 οἱ ἰσότιμοι K ὁμότιμοι Λ ǁ 20 ⟨οὐκ⟩ εὖ Br. ǁ 22 δι' αἰτίας om. L¹ δι' αἰτίας ⟨τινας⟩ 'or an epithet' Ri. δι' ἀπ⟨ορ⟩ίας Latte ἡσύχιον . . . δίαιταν Emp. | παρὰ γνώμην om. P | ἀρεταῖς κεχρῆσθαι Rei. χρήσασθαι Cor. ǁ 24 περιβαλέσθαι K P ǁ 25 αὐτοῦ – 26 Μιθριδάτης om. L¹ ǁ 28 τὸν . . . λόγον PQ et λόγον etiam L¹

φορτίων ξενικῶν οἱ πλέοντες ἀπὸ τῆς ἑσπέρας ἀναπεπλήκεσαν τὸν Πόντον,
3 ὥρμητο διαπρεσβεύεσθαι πρὸς αὐτόν, ἐπηρμένος μάλιστα ταῖς τῶν κολάκων ἀλαζονείαις, οἳ τὸν μὲν Σερτώριον Ἀννίβᾳ, τὸν δὲ Μιθριδάτην Πύρρῳ παρεικάζοντες, οὐκ ἂν ἔφασαν Ῥωμαίους πρὸς τηλικαύτας ὁμοῦ φύσεις τε καὶ δυνάμεις ἐπιχειρουμένους διχόθεν ἀντισχεῖν, τοῦ δεινοτάτου στρατη- 5
4 γοῦ τῷ μεγίστῳ τῶν βασιλέων προσγενομένου. πέμπει δὴ πρέσβεις ὁ Μιθριδάτης εἰς Ἰβηρίαν, γράμματα Σερτωρίῳ καὶ λόγους κομίζοντας, δι' ὧν αὐτὸς μὲν ἐπηγγέλλετο χρήματα καὶ ναῦς παρέξειν εἰς τὸν πόλεμον, ὑπ' ἐκείνου δ' ἠξίου τὴν Ἀσίαν αὐτῷ βεβαιοῦσθαι πᾶσαν, ἧς ὑπεχώρησε
5 Ῥωμαίοις κατὰ τὰς πρὸς Σύλλαν γενομένας συνθήκας. ἀθροίσαντος δὲ 10 τοῦ Σερτωρίου βουλήν, ἣν σύγκλητον ὠνόμαζε, καὶ τῶν ἄλλων δέχεσθαι τὰς προκλήσεις καὶ ἀγαπᾶν κελευόντων – ὄνομα γὰρ καὶ γράμμα κενὸν αἰτουμένους περὶ τῶν οὐκ ὄντων ἐπ' αὐτοῖς, ἀντὶ τούτων λαμβάνειν ὧν μάλιστα
6 δεόμενοι τυγχάνουσιν –, οὐκ ἠνέσχετο [ὁ] Σερτώριος, ἀλλὰ Βιθυνίαν μὲν ἔφη καὶ Καππαδοκίαν λαμβάνοντι Μιθριδάτῃ μὴ φθονεῖν, ἔθνη βασιλευό- 15 μενα καὶ μηδὲν προσήκοντα Ῥωμαίοις· ἣν δὲ τῷ δικαιοτάτῳ τρόπῳ Ῥωμαίων κεκτημένων ἐπαρχίαν ἀφελόμενος καὶ κατασχών, πολεμῶν μὲν ἐξέπεσεν ὑπὸ Φιμβρίου, σπενδόμενος δὲ πρὸς Σύλλαν ἀφῆκε, ταύτην οὐκ
7 ἔφη περιόψεσθαι πάλιν ὑπ' ἐκείνῳ γενομένην· δεῖν γὰρ αὔξεσθαι τὴν πόλιν ὑπ' αὐτοῦ κρατοῦντος, οὐκ ἐλαττώσει τῶν ἐκείνης κρατεῖν αὐτόν· γενναίῳ γὰρ ἀνδρὶ μετὰ τοῦ καλοῦ νικᾶν αἱρετόν, αἰσχρῶς δ' οὐδὲ σῴζεσθαι. 21

24. Ταῦτ' ἀπαγγελθέντα Μιθριδάτης διὰ θάμβους ἐποιεῖτο, καὶ λέγε-
2 ται μὲν εἰπεῖν πρὸς τοὺς φίλους· ,,τί δῆτα προστάξει Σερτώριος ἐν Παλατίῳ καθεζόμενος, εἰ νῦν εἰς τὴν Ἀτλαντικὴν ἐξεωσμένος θάλασσαν ὅρους
3 ἡμῶν τῇ βασιλείᾳ τίθησι καὶ πειρωμένοις Ἀσίας ἀπειλεῖ πόλεμον;" οὐ 25 μὴν ἀλλὰ γίνονταί γε συνθῆκαι καὶ ὅρκοι, Καππαδοκίαν καὶ Βιθυνίαν ἔχειν Μιθριδάτην, Σερτωρίου στρατηγὸν αὐτῷ καὶ στρατιώτας πέμποντος, Σερτώριον δὲ παρὰ Μιθριδάτου λαβεῖν τρισχίλια τάλαντα καὶ τεσσα-
4 ράκοντα ναῦς. πέμπεται δὲ καὶ στρατηγὸς εἰς Ἀσίαν ὑπὸ Σερτωρίου τῶν ἀπὸ βουλῆς πεφευγότων πρὸς αὐτὸν Μᾶρκος Μάριος, ᾧ συνεξελὼν τινας 30 πόλεις τῶν Ἀσιάδων ὁ Μιθριδάτης εἰσελαύνοντι μετὰ ῥάβδων καὶ

3 cf. App. b. c. 1, 112, 522

[ΛΚΡQ] 1 ἀναπεπλήκασι Q ‖ 6 δή] δὲ Q ‖ 7 καὶ λόγους] καταλόγους P ‖ 8 πόλεμον – 10 κατὰ om. Q ‖ 11 τοῦ K: om. cet. ‖ 13 λαμβάνει P ‖ 14 ὁ del. Sint. ‖ 20 κρατεῖν] κρατῶν L¹Q ‖ 24 καθεζόμενος om. P ‖ 30 ᾧ] ὡς P πελέκεων αὐτὸς εἵπετο, δευτέραν τάξιν καὶ σχῆμα θεραπεύοντος ἑκουσίως ἀνειληφώς. ὁ δὲ τὰς μὲν ἠλευθέρου, ταῖς δ' ἀτέλειαν γράφων χάριτι Σερτωρίου κατήγγελλεν, ὥστε τὴν Ἀσίαν αὖθις ἐνοχλουμένην μὲν ὑπὸ τῶν τελωνῶν, βαρυνομένην δὲ ταῖς πλεονεξίαις καὶ ὑπερηφανίαις τῶν ἐπισκήνων, ἀναπτερωθῆναι πρὸς τὴν ἐλπίδα καὶ ποθεῖν τὴν προσδοκωμένην μεταβολὴν τῆς ἡγεμονίας.

25. Ἐν δ' Ἰβηρίᾳ τῶν περὶ Σερτώριον συγκλητικῶν καὶ ἰσοτίμων, ὡς πρῶτον εἰς ἀντίπαλον ἐλπίδα κατέστησαν ἐπανέντος τοῦ φόβου, φθόνος ἥπτετο καὶ ζῆλος ἀνόητος τῆς ἐκείνου δυνάμεως. ἐνῆγε δὲ Περπέννας, δι' εὐγένειαν ἐπαιρόμενος φρονήματι κενῷ πρὸς τὴν ἡγεμονίαν, καὶ λόγους μοχθηροὺς διεδίδου κρύφα τοῖς ἐπιτηδείοις· „τίς ἄρα πονηρὸς ἡμᾶς ὑπολαβὼν ἐκ κακῶν εἰς χείρονα φέρει δαίμων, οἳ Σύλλᾳ μὲν ὁμοῦ τι συμπάσης ἄρχοντι γῆς καὶ θαλάττης ποιεῖν τὸ προσταττόμενον οὐκ ἠξιοῦμεν οἴκοι μένοντες, δεῦρο δὲ φθάσαντες ὡς ἐλεύθεροι βιωσόμενοι δουλεύομεν ἑκουσίως, τὴν Σερτωρίου δορυφοροῦντες φυγήν, ὄνομα χλευαζόμενον ὑπὸ τῶν ἀκουόντων, σύγκλητος, ὄντες, ὕβρεις δὲ καὶ προστάγματα καὶ πόνους οὐκ ἐλάττονας Ἰβήρων καὶ Λυσιτανῶν ὑπομένοντες;" τοιούτων ἀναπιμπλάμενοι λόγων οἱ πολλοὶ φανερῶς μὲν οὐκ ἀφίσταντο, δεδοικότες αὐτοῦ τὴν δύναμιν, κρύφα δὲ τάς τε πράξεις ἐλυμαίνοντο καὶ τοὺς βαρβάρους ἐκάκουν, κολάζοντες πικρῶς καὶ δασμολογοῦντες ὡς Σερτωρίου κελεύοντος. ἐξ ὧν ἀποστάσεις ἐγίνοντο καὶ ταραχαὶ περὶ τὰς πόλεις. οἱ δὲ πεμπόμενοι ταῦτα θεραπεύειν καὶ ἀποπραΰνειν ἐπανήρχοντο πλείονας ἐξειργασμένοι πολέμους καὶ τὰς ὑπαρχούσας ηὐξηκότες ἀπειθείας, ὥστε τὸν Σερτώριον ἐκ τῆς προτέρας ἐπιεικείας καὶ πρᾳότητος μεταβαλόντα περὶ τοὺς ἐν Ὄσκῃ τρεφομένους παρανομῆσαι παῖδας τῶν Ἰβήρων, τοὺς μὲν ἀνελόντα, τοὺς δ' ἀποδόμενον.

26. Ὁ δ' οὖν Περπέννας πλείονας ἐνωμότους ἔχων πρὸς τὴν ἐπίθεσιν, προσάγεται καὶ Μάλλιον, ἕνα τῶν ἐφ' ἡγεμονίας. οὗτος ἐρῶν τινος τῶν ἐν ὥρᾳ μειρακίου καὶ φιλοφρονούμενος πρὸς αὐτό, φράζει τὴν ἐπιβουλήν, κελεύων ἀμελήσαντα τῶν ἄλλων ἐραστῶν αὐτῷ μόνῳ προσέχειν, ὡς ἐντὸς

7 c. 25 App. b. c. 1, 112, 520—522 Diod. 37, 22a Liv. per. 96 ‖ 27 c. 26 App. b. c. 1, 113, 527 sq. Diod. 37, 22a Strab. 3, 161 Sall. hist. 3, 81—83 M. Liv. per. 96 Vell. 2, 30, 1 Oros. 5, 23, 13 Amm. Marc. 26, 9, 9

[ΛΚPQ] 3 κατήγγειλεν Q | τῶν om. Κ ‖ 5 ἀναπτερωθῆναι Κ: ἀναπτοηθῆναι ‖ 8 φόνου P ‖ 9 περπένας Q et postea ‖ 11 τοὺς ἐπιτηδείους P | ὑμᾶς ΛPC ‖ 13 πραττόμενον P ‖ 14 φθάσαντες Zie.: φθαρέντες ‖ 16 δὲ] τὲ Κ ‖ 18 ἀφίστανται L¹ ‖ 19 δὲ om. P ‖ 22 καὶ ἀποπραΰνειν om. L¹ ἐπιπραΰνειν Sch. ‖ 23 ἀπειθίας L¹ ‖ 24 ἐπιεικείας καὶ om. Q ἐπιεικίας L ‖ 27 γ' οὖν Κ | ἔχων ἐνωμότους Κ ἡμερῶν ὀλίγων μεγάλῳ γενησομένῳ. τὸ δὲ μειράκιον ἑτέρῳ τινὶ τῶν ἐραστῶν Αὐφιδίῳ μᾶλλον προσπεπονθὸς ἐκφέρει τὸν λόγον. ἀκούσας δ' ὁ Αὐφίδιος ἐξεπλάγη· καὶ γὰρ αὐτὸς μετεῖχε τῆς ἐπὶ Σερτώριον συνωμοσίας, οὐ μέντοι τὸν Μάλλιον ἐγίνωσκε μετέχοντα. Περπένναν δὲ καὶ Γραικῖνον καί τινας ἄλλους ὧν αὐτὸς ᾔδει συνωμοτῶν ὀνομάζοντος τοῦ μειρακίου, διαταραχθεὶς πρὸς ἐκεῖνον μὲν ἐξεφλαύριζε τὸν λόγον καὶ παρεκάλει τοῦ Μαλλίου καταφρονεῖν ὡς κενοῦ καὶ ἀλαζόνος, αὐτὸς δὲ πρὸς τὸν Περπένναν πορευθεὶς καὶ φράσας τὴν ὀξύτητα τοῦ καιροῦ καὶ τὸν κίνδυνον, ἐκέλευσεν ἐπιχειρεῖν. οἱ δ' ἐπείθοντο, καὶ παρασκευάσαντες ἄνθρωπον γράμματα κομίζοντα τῷ Σερτωρίῳ προσήγαγον· ἐδήλου δὲ τὰ γράμματα νίκην τινὸς τῶν ὑπ' αὐτῷ στρατηγῶν καὶ φόνον πολὺν τῶν πολεμίων. ἐφ' οἷς τοῦ Σερτωρίου περιχαροῦς ὄντος καὶ θύοντος εὐαγγέλια, Περπέννας ἑστιᾶσιν αὐτῷ καὶ τοῖς παροῦσι φίλοις (οὗτοι δ' ἦσαν ἐκ τῆς συνωμοσίας) ἐπηγγέλλετο, καὶ πολλὰ λιπαρήσας ἔπεισεν ἐλθεῖν. ἀεὶ μὲν οὖν τὰ μετὰ Σερτωρίου δεῖπνα πολλὴν εἶχεν αἰδῶ καὶ κόσμον, οὔθ' ὁρᾶν τι τῶν αἰσχρῶν οὔτ' ἀκούειν ὑπομένοντος, ἀλλὰ καὶ τοὺς συμπίνοντας εὐτάκτοις καὶ ἀνυβρίστοις παιδιαῖς χρῆσθαι καὶ φιλοφροσύναις ἐθίζοντος· τότε δὲ τοῦ πότου μεσοῦντος ἀρχὴν ἀψιμαχίας ζητοῦντες, ἀναφανδὸν ἀκολάστοις ἐχρῶντο ῥήμασι, καὶ πολλὰ προσποιούμενοι μεθύειν ἠσέλγαινον ὡς παροξυνοῦντες ἐκεῖνον. ὁ δ' εἴτε δυσχεραίνων τὴν ἀκοσμίαν, εἴτε τὴν διάνοιαν αὐτῶν τῇ θρασύτητι τῆς λαλιᾶς καὶ τῇ παρὰ τὸ εἰωθὸς ὀλιγωρίᾳ συμφρονήσας, μετέβαλε τὸ σχῆμα τῆς κλίσεως, ὕπτιον ἀνεὶς ἑαυτὸν ὡς οὔτε προσέχων οὔτε κατακούων. ἐπεὶ δ' ὁ Περπέννας φιάλην τινὰ λαβὼν ἀκράτου καὶ μεταξὺ πίνων ἀφῆκεν ἐκ τῶν χειρῶν καὶ ψόφον ἐποίησεν, ὅπερ ἦν αὐτοῖς σύμβολον, Ἀντώνιος ὑπερκατακείμενος παίει τῷ ξίφει τὸν Σερτώριον. ἀναστρέψαντος δὲ πρὸς τὴν πληγὴν ἐκείνου καὶ συνεξανισταμένου, περιπεσὼν εἰς τὸ στῆθος κατέλαβε τὰς χεῖρας ἀμφοτέρας, ὥστε μηδ' ἀμυνόμενον πολλῶν παιόντων ἀποθανεῖν.

27. Οἱ μὲν οὖν πλεῖστοι τῶν Ἰβήρων εὐθὺς ᾤχοντο καὶ παρέδωκαν

29 c. 27 Plut. Pomp. 20, 3—8 App. b. c. 1, 114, 529—115, 538 Sall. hist. 3, 84. 85 M. Frontin. strat. 2, 5, 32 Amm. Marc. 26, 9, 9

[*Δ*KPQ] 2 ἀφιδίῳ Q et mox || 3 καὶ γὰρ καὶ C || 4 *Γραικῖνον* Zie. cl. Frontin. 2, 5, 31 (ubi *Graecinium*): γρακῖνον *Δ*K editt. γραβῖνον P γρακίναν Q || 6 ἐξεφαύλιζε P || 8 ἐκέλευεν PQ || 9 διαχειρεῖν Q || 10 κομίζοντα om. L¹ | ἐδίδου P || 14 ἔπεισεν ἐλθεῖν] εἰσελθεῖν Q || 16 συμπίνοντας K: πισυνόντας P συνόντας *Δ*Q | ἀνύβρις L¹ ἀνύβροις K || 21 θρασύτητι Emp.: βραδυτῆτι || 22 κλίσεως Sol.: κλησίας P κλισίας cet. | οὔτε Sch.: οὐδὲ || 23 καὶ del. Emp.

ἑαυτοὺς ἐπιπρεσβευσάμενοι τοῖς περὶ Πομπήϊον καὶ Μέτελλον· τοὺς δὲ
συμμείναντας ὁ Περπέννας ἀναλαβὼν ἐπεχείρει τι πράττειν. χρησάμενος
δὲ ταῖς Σερτωρίου παρασκευαῖς ὅσον ἐνασχημονῆσαι καὶ φανερὸς γενέσθαι
μήτ' ἄρχειν μήτ' ἄρχεσθαι πεφυκώς, Πομπηΐῳ συνέβαλε, καὶ ταχὺ συν-
τριβεὶς ὑπ' αὐτοῦ καὶ γενόμενος αἰχμάλωτος, οὐδὲ τὴν ἐσχάτην ὑπέμεινε
συμφορὰν ἡγεμονικῶς, ἀλλὰ τῶν Σερτωρίου γραμμάτων κύριος γεγονώς,
ὑπισχνεῖτο Πομπηΐῳ δείξειν ὑπατικῶν ἀνδρῶν καὶ μέγιστον ἐν Ῥώμῃ
δυναμένων αὐτογράφους ἐπιστολάς, καλούντων Σερτώριον εἰς Ἰταλίαν, ὡς
πολλῶν ποθούντων τὰ παρόντα κινῆσαι καὶ μεταβαλεῖν τὴν πολιτείαν.
ἔργον οὖν ὁ Πομπήϊος οὐ νέας φρενός, ἀλλ' εὖ μάλα βεβηκυίας καὶ κατηρ-
τυμένης ἐργασάμενος, μεγάλων ἀπήλλαξε τὴν Ῥώμην φόβων καὶ νεωτε-
ρισμῶν. τὰς μὲν γὰρ ἐπιστολὰς ἐκείνας καὶ τὰ γράμματα τοῦ Σερτωρίου
συναγαγὼν ἅπαντα κατέκαυσεν, οὔτ' ἀναγνοὺς οὔτ' ἐάσας ἕτερον, αὐτὸν
δὲ τὸν Περπένναν κατὰ τάχος ἀνεῖλε, φοβηθεὶς μὴ τῶν ὀνομάτων ἐξενεχ-
θέντων πρός τινας ἀποστάσεις καὶ ταραχαὶ γένωνται· τῶν δὲ τῷ Περπέννᾳ
συνομοσαμένων οἱ μὲν ἐπὶ Πομπήϊον ἀναχθέντες διεφθάρησαν, οἱ δὲ φεύγοντες εἰς Λιβύην ὑπὸ Μαυρουσίων κατηκοντίσθησαν, διέφυγε δ' οὐδεὶς
πλὴν Αὐφίδιος [ὁ τοῦ Μαλλίου ἀντεραστής]· οὗτος δ' ἢ λαθὼν ἢ παραμε-
ληθεὶς ἔν τινι βαρβάρῳ κώμῃ πενόμενος καὶ μισούμενος κατεγήρασεν.

Comparison of Sertorius and Eumenes

20 (1). Ταῦτ' ἔστιν ἃ περὶ Εὐμενοῦς καὶ Σερτωρίου μνήμης ἄξια παρει-
λήφαμεν. ἐν δὲ τῇ συγκρίσει κοινὸν μὲν ἀμφοτέροις ὑπάρχει τὸ ξένους καὶ
ἀλλοδαποὺς καὶ φυγάδας ὄντας ἐθνῶν τε παντοδαπῶν καὶ στρατευμάτων
μαχίμων τε καὶ μεγάλων δυνάμεων ἡγουμένους διατελεῖν· ἴδιον δὲ Σερτωρίῳ μὲν τὸ παρὰ πάντων τῶν συμμάχων δεδομένην ἔχειν διὰ τὸ ἀξίωμα τὴν
ἀρχήν, Εὐμενεῖ δὲ τὸ πολλῶν διαφερομένων περὶ τῆς ἡγεμονίας πρὸς αὐτὸν
ἐκ τῶν πράξεων λαμβάνειν τὸ πρωτεῖον· τῷ μὲν γὰρ ἄρχεσθαι βουλόμενοι
δικαίως εἴποντο, τῷ δ' ἄρχειν μὴ δυνάμενοι πρὸς τὸ συμφέρον ὑπήκουον.
καὶ γὰρ ὁ μὲν Ἰβήρων καὶ Λυσιτανῶν Ῥωμαῖος, ὁ δὲ Χερρονησίτης Μα-
κεδόνων ἦρχεν, ὧν οἱ μὲν ἔκπαλαι Ῥωμαίοις ἐδούλευον, οἱ δὲ τότε πάντας ἀνθρώπους ἐδουλοῦντο. καὶ Σερτώριος μὲν ἀπὸ βουλῆς καὶ στρατηγίας

[ΑΚPQ] 3 ταῖς] τοῦ K || 4 προσέβαλε ΑQ || 7 μεγίστων P || 13 ἀναγν. ⟨αὐτὸς⟩
οὔτ', deinde [αὐτὸν] τὸν δὲ (Naber) Zie.; αὐτὸν δὲ om. Q || 15 πρός τινας om. Q
τινα L¹ | [ἀπο]στάσεις Zie. || 16 φυγόντες Zie. || 17 δ' om. Q || 18 ἀφίδιος Q | ὁ τοῦ
Μ. ἀντεραστής propt. hiat. suspecta hab. Sint., del. Zie. ||
23 τε del. Sint. δυνάμεων del.
Bekker ἐθνῶν τε παντ. καὶ μαχίμων στρατευμάτων τε μεγάλων καὶ δυνάμεων Zie. ||
25 εὐμενῆ L¹ | ἡγεμονείας L¹ || 26 τῶι μὲν γὰρ K: καὶ τῶι μὲν γὰρ L¹P καὶ τῷ
μὲν L² τῷ μὲν Q || 27 τῷ] τὸ L¹

θαυμαζόμενος, Εὐμενὴς δὲ διὰ τὴν γραμματείαν καταφρονούμενος, ἐφ' ἡγεμονίαν προῆλθεν. οὐ μόνον τοίνυν ἐλάττοσι πρὸς τὴν ἀρχὴν ἀφορμαῖς, ἀλλὰ καὶ μείζοσι πρὸς τὴν αὔξησιν ἐχρήσατο κωλύμασιν Εὐμενής. καὶ γὰρ ἄντικρυς τοὺς ἐνισταμένους καὶ κρύφα τοὺς ἐπιβουλεύοντας εἶχε πολλούς, οὐχ ὥσπερ τῷ ἑτέρῳ φανερῶς μὲν οὐδείς, λάθρα δ' ὕστερον καὶ ὀλίγοι τῶν συμμάχων ἐπανέστησαν. διὸ τῷ μὲν ἦν πέρας τοῦ κινδυνεύειν τὸ νικᾶν τοὺς πολεμίους, τῷ δ' ἐκ τοῦ νικᾶν ὁ κίνδυνος ὑπὸ τῶν φθονούντων.

21 (2). Τὰ μὲν οὖν κατὰ τὴν στρατηγίαν ἐφάμιλλα καὶ παράλληλα· τῷ δ' ἄλλῳ τρόπῳ φιλοπόλεμος μὲν ὁ Εὐμενὴς καὶ φιλόνικος, ἡσυχίας δὲ καὶ πραότητος οἰκεῖος ὁ Σερτώριος. ὁ μὲν γάρ, ἀσφαλῶς καὶ μετὰ τιμῆς βιοῦν ἐξὸν ἐκποδὼν γενομένῳ, τοῖς πρώτοις μαχόμενος καὶ κινδυνεύων διετέλεσε, τῷ δ' οὐδὲν δεομένῳ πραγμάτων ὑπὲρ αὐτῆς τῆς τοῦ σώματος ἀσφαλείας πρὸς οὐκ ἐῶντας εἰρήνην ἄγειν ἦν ὁ πόλεμος. Εὐμενεῖ μὲν γὰρ Ἀντίγονος ἐκστάντι τῶν ὑπὲρ τοῦ πρωτεύειν ἀγώνων ἡδέως ἂν ἐχρῆτο, τὴν μετ' αὐτὸν ἀγαπῶντι τάξιν· Σερτωρίῳ δ' οἱ περὶ Πομπήϊον οὐδὲ ζῆν ἀπραγμόνως ἐπέτρεπον. διὸ τῷ μὲν ἑκοντὶ συνέβαινε πολεμεῖν ἐπ' ἀρχῇ, τῷ δ' ἀκουσίως ἄρχειν διὰ τὸ πολεμεῖσθαι. φιλοπόλεμος μὲν οὖν ὁ τῆς ἀσφαλείας τὴν πλεονεξίαν προτιμῶν, πολεμικὸς δ' ὁ τῷ πολέμῳ κτώμενος τὴν ἀσφάλειαν. καὶ μὴν ἀποθανεῖν γε συνέβη τῷ μὲν οὐ προαισθομένῳ, τῷ δὲ καὶ προσδεχομένῳ τὴν τελευτήν· ὧν τὸ μὲν ἐπιεικείας, φίλοις γὰρ ἐδόκει πιστεύειν, τὸ δ' ἀσθενείας, βουλόμενος γὰρ φυγεῖν συνελήφθη. καὶ τοῦ μὲν οὐ κατῄσχυνε τὸν βίον ὁ θάνατος, πάσχοντος ὑπὸ τῶν συμμάχων ἃ τῶν πολεμίων αὐτὸν οὐδεὶς ἐποίησεν· ὁ δὲ φεύγειν μὲν πρὸ αἰχμαλωσίας μὴ δυνηθείς, ζῆν δὲ μετ' αἰχμαλωσίαν βουληθείς, οὔτ' ἐφυλάξατο καλῶς τὴν τελευτὴν οὔθ' ὑπέμεινεν, ἀλλὰ προσλιπαρῶν καὶ δεόμενος, τοῦ σώματος μόνον κρατεῖν δοκοῦντα τὸν πολέμιον καὶ τῆς ψυχῆς αὐτοῦ κύριον ἐποίησεν.

[ΛΚPQ] 2 τοίνυν Rei.: ταῖς νῦν ‖ 3 καὶ om. PQ ‖ 6 ὀλίγοις L¹ | τῷ] τὸ L¹ ‖ 7 ὑπὸ] ἀπὸ Rei. ‖ 9 στρατηγίαν Rei.: στρατείαν ‖ 12 γενόμενος: corr. Mu. | τοῖς πρώτοις cum γενομένῳ coniung. Sint. | μαχομένοις K ‖ 16 τὸν πομπήϊον PC ‖ 17 ἀκοντὶ Q ἑκουσίως C | ἐπ' Rei.: ἐν ‖ 18 ἑκουσίως KM | φιλοπόλεμος — 20 ἀσφάλειαν hab. Phot. p. 396b ‖ 20 θανεῖν Λ ‖ 21 ἐπιεικίας L ‖ 24 τῶν μὲν πολεμίων L¹P | αὐτὸς Q ‖ 25 αἰχμαλωσίας L¹ ‖ 27 δοκοῦντας K | αὐτῆς Sol.

COMMENTARY

1

The proem shows us the biographer in one of his lighter moods. Given the infinity of time, the recurrence of historical events in the same or a similar fashion is hardly surprising; such coincidence is only to be expected (1.1–2). There are of course those who would attribute a rational purpose and deeper significance to it—and in an almost Herodotean manner, P. proceeds to enumerate some popular examples (1.3–7) and cheekily offers a novel one of his own: one-eyed warlords. Sertorius, in P.'s judgment, ranks among the foremost four of great, shrewd, resourceful commanders, and a peculiarity he shares with the other three—Philip, Antigonos, and Hannibal—is the loss of an eye (1.8). It is a purely external feature, as the biographer hastens to point out, lest anyone take his little lecture on *tychē* repeating herself too seriously. In terms of character, the four have little in common (1.9). While the series of one-eyed generals makes a fine example of historical coincidence, such is not P.'s concern in the pair of lives following. Rather, the discourse on coincidence serves to capture the reader's interest (compare, e.g., the discussion of Roman proper names in *Mar.* 1): a particularly advisable approach, perhaps, in the case of Sertorius—among the subjects of the *Lives* arguably the one least known to a Greek audience. (For an excellent discussion of the literary functions of P.'s proems see Stadter, "Proems.")

As with the other *Parallel Lives*, the proem introduces the entire pair, *Eumenes* as well as *Sertorius*. Which is not to say that its first and longest point—a wealth of recurring coincidences in myth and history—applies equally to both: Eumenes has no place in the gallery of one-eyed men. That is not unusual: the body of the proem of *Nikias–Crassus,* for instance, relates only to Nikias, that of *Kimon–Lucullus* only to Lucullus. Eumenes has other things in common with Sertorius, qualities more important than external features: skilled in command, wily and warlike, far away from home, a leader of peoples other than his own, and suffering a cruel and unjust fate (1.11–12). *Tychē* rather than *to automaton* (1.1) governs human events. *Sertorius–Eumenes* study how good men bear up under an adverse fate.

1.5

δυεῖν δὲ Σκιπιώνων: P. Cornelius (336) Scipio Africanus, Consul in 205 and 194; Censor in 199; ended the Second Punic War with the defeat of Hannibal near Zama in 202. P. Cornelius (335) Scipio Africanus Aemilianus, Consul in 147 and 134; Censor in 142; destroyed Carthage in 146.

1.8

οἱ πολεμικώτατοι . . . ἑτερόφθαλμοι: One-eyedness is associated not with military skill as such, but with craft and cunning (δόλος, δεινότης) paired with military skill. P. does not mean to say that his one-eyed four were the greatest commanders of all time; they are merely the ones who most successfully combined shrewdness and martial prowess. P.'s choice, however, may have been influenced by factors other than his military judgment. Both Philip and Antigonos played decisive parts, though of a rather different nature, in Eumenes' life, and although P. himself never makes the point, the Hispanians saw in Sertorius a reincarnation of Hannibal (Appian 112.522)—a notion one suspects Sertorius was only too willing to cultivate (see 9.1, 12.1nn.).

Philip II (Philippos 7): ca. 382–336 B.C., King of Macedon 360/59[356]-336. Father of Alexander III the Great. He lost his right eye during the siege of Methone in 355/4 (Diodor. 16.34.5; Strabo 7 fr. 22 and 8.6.15; Iustin. 7.6.14).

Antigonos (I) Monophthalmos, also called Kyklops (Antigonos 3): ca. 380–301 B.C. After Alexander's death (323) Satrap of Phrygia, Lykia, and Pamphylia, he soon became a major contestant in the Successor Wars. Named Strategos of Asia in 321 or 320 (on the date, see below, 1.11n.) at the conference of Triparadeisos, there followed his conquest of the western parts of Alexander's Asian empire (320–311) and the execution of Eumenes of Kardia (316; cf. below, 1.11). He subsequently intervened in Greece ("liberation" of Athens by his son, Demetrios [I] Poliorketes, 307) and captured Cyprus. After Demetrios' naval victory over Ptolemaios of Egypt near Salamis (Cyprus), Antigonos assumed the title of King (307/6); his opponents (chiefly Ptolemaios, Seleukos, Lysimachos, and Kassandros) followed suit. From 306 to 301 he saw further warfare in Egypt, the Aegean, and Asia Minor; he was defeated and killed in the battle of Ipsos in 301. On what occasion he lost an eye seems to have escaped record, though Billows, 27–28, strongly argues that the ἑτερόφθαλμος of *Alex.* 70.4–6 (cf. *De Alex. fort.* 339B–D; *Apophth. reg.* 181A) is really Antigonos rather than Antigenes. If so, the wound would have been incurred during the siege of Perinthos in 340/339. From Plin. *NH* 35.90 it is certain that Antigonos was not merely blind in one eye but suffered an actual loss, as his being grouped with Philip, Hannibal, and Sertorius would indicate anyway. Cf. also Polyb. 5.67.6; Plut. *De liber. educ.* 11B–C; *Quaest. conv.* 633D; Aelian *VH* 12.43; Macrob. 7.3.12.

Hannibal (8): son of Hamilqar Barqa ("Thunderbolt"), ca. 247–183 B.C. He lost an eye in 217 due to an infection contracted during the march across the swamps of the Arno river (Polyb. 3.79.12; Nepos 23.4.3, the right eye; Livy 22.2.11). No mention here of (C.?) Iulius Civilis, the one-eyed originator of the Batavian revolt of A.D. 69–70. Indeed P. had no reason to count him among history's outstanding commanders, but Tacitus notes (*Hist.* 4.13.2) that Civilis liked being compared to two of P.'s masters in the art of war: *Sertorium se aut Annibalem ferens simili oris dehonestamento*.

Σερτώριος: On the loss of his eye see 4.3. Noting that the Germanic war god Wotan (or Nordic, Odin) was one-eyed, wily, and treacherous besides being endowed with shamanic qualities such as the ability to change shape and appear in disguise, T. W. Africa (528–38) suggested that Wotan's one-eyed as-

Commentary 1.9

pect may have been derived, via Civilis (cf. preceding note) from Hannibal and Sertorius. Against that see Moeller (402–5), convincingly showing that one-eyedness, along with lameness or loss of an arm, had always been closely associated with warrior gods, magic, and shamanism in both Germanic (Wotan/Odin) and Celtic (Lug, Cúchulainn) religion and myth: rather than supplying Wotan's one-eyed aspect, Hannibal, Sertorius, and Civilis were able to exploit their disfigurement as a divine attribute in their dealings with Celto-Hispanians, Celtiberians, Gauls, and Germans. (See also below, 8–9, 11, 12.1nn.) As both Africa and Moeller point out, the one-eyed warlord has lost nothing of his mystique in modern times: witness Horatio Nelson, Mikhail Kutuzov, or Moshe Dayan.

1.9

λειπόμενον ... πάντων: The hero shares none of the faults so typical of the other *heterophthalmoi*, and none of their good luck. When he eventually fails, we will know it is not due to a flaw in his character.

1.10

Sertorius was pitted against the three foremost Roman generals of his time and proved their equal; he faced the military resources of Rome as a stranger leading barbarians and almost prevailed. Well aware of Sertorius' relative obscurity, P. makes sure the reader stays interested: clearly, the hero's achievements must have been significant.

1.11

Eumenes (4) of Kardia: 362/1–316 B.C. Secretary of state (ἀρχιγραμματεύς) of Philip II and Alexander the Great; after Alexander's death (323) Satrap of Paphlagonia and Kappadokia. He defeated Krateros in 321 or 320, but after the death of his protector Perdikkas in the same year he was outlawed by the Macedonian army assembly at Triparadeisos. Since 320 or 319 (the chronology is in dispute, depending on the year of Triparadeisos: 320 according to R. M. Errington, *JHS* 90 [1970] 75–77, or—traditional—321, most recently defended by Bosworth, 75–78) Strategos of Asia by appointment of the new regent, Polyperchon. Fighting with varying success against Antigonos Monophthalmos (see above, 1.8), he was handed over to the latter by his own troops in 316 and executed.

2

Chapter 2 contains all we learn about Sertorius' origins and upbringing. The terse style and the scarcity of information stand in stark contrast to the corresponding parts in other Roman lives, particularly those belonging to the Late Republic; only *Mar.* 3.1 is equally brief. P. may have been unable to find out more. Scardigli, "Considerazioni" 46–54, is inclined toward Poseidonios as the source for chapters 2–3, and rejects a hypothetical earlier biography from which P. might have drawn. Recently Geiger has forcefully argued in favor of believing that P. used Cornelius Nepos for guidance in the selection of Romans for his *Parallel Lives* (see Introduction 3.13). If indeed Nepos wrote a *Sertorius*, P. would not stop at guidance if that source offered information not available elsewhere. Given the format of Nepos' biographies, details about Sertorius' youth would be scant, but the content of chapter 2, and perhaps 3.1 or even 3.1–4, might conceivably have been found there. Yet we should not hastily rule out Sallust: while the narrative of chapter 3 is unlikely to come from the *Histories*, chapter 2 makes a perfect fit in front of *Hist*. 1.88.

2.1

Κοΐντῳ Σερτωρίῳ: On the name see Schulze 230, 332–41, though the Etruscan origin postulated there is not certain. The name is rare and occurs mainly in central Italy.

γένος ἦν οὐκ ἀσημότατον: Sertorius almost certainly was an *eques Romanus* prior to becoming a senator. Nicolet lists him among the *equites certi* (*L'ordre équestre* 2:1022 no. 324), pointing out that the phrase *nostri ordinis* (Cic. *Brut*. 180) with reference to Sertorius merely signifies, as elsewhere in Cicero, current senatorial rank regardless of ancestry. The somewhat unusual superlative in γένος οὐκ ἀσημότατον has led Richards, *CQ* 4 (1910) 17, to suggest ἄσημον; Ziegler in his apparatus criticus entertained οὐ τῶν ἀσημοτάτων. It may be simply an attempt to render a Latin phrase such as *domi nobilis*. Leopold wanted to delete οὐκ, but the general impression created by chapters 2–4 is not one of obscure origin.

Nursia: now Norcia, a city in the Sabine country (Plin. *NH* 3.107); received *civitas sine suffragio* in 290 and full citizenship in 268 B.C. (Vell. 1.14.6, 8). It was enrolled in the Tribus Quirina; Festus (262 Lindsay) lists it as a *praefectura*. See further Nissen, *Italische Landeskunde* 2.1:467–68; H. Philipp, *RE* 17.2 (1937) 1489–90; Stenten 61–62. The town was the birthplace of Vespasian's mother, Vespasia Polla (Suet. *Vesp*. 1.3); a local inscription has recently been identified as pertaining to her father, Vespasius Pollio (Alföldy, *ZPE* 77 [1989] 155–80). There is no epigraphical evidence for Republican Sertorii at Norcia, but an inscription found there in 1975, apparently dating from the Imperial period, now attests a freedman and freedwoman of a Q. Sertorius: *Q. Sertorius Q. [l.] | Eutichus | Sertoria Q. l. | Antiopa*; see Cordella and Criniti, *Iscrizioni latine di Norcia e dintorni* 63–64. (The notice in *AE* 1983 no. 292 incorrectly lists the inscription as dating from the first century B.C. and misprints the freedwoman's name as *Antiope*.) Nursia remained staunchly Republican during the civil wars of the Triumviral period and suffered heavily under the wrath of Octavian (Suet. *Aug*. 12; Dio 48.13.6).

τῆς Σαβίνων: The Sabine country was known for its harsh and cold climate, and its people had a reputation for being hardy, brave, devout, and old-

Commentary 2.2

fashioned: e.g., Cic. *Vat.* 36; Dion. Hal. 2.49.5; Strabo 5.4.12; Hor. *Epist.* 2.1.25; Livy 1.18.4; Ovid *Amor.* 2.4.15; Plin. *NH* 3.108. Elsewhere (*Rom.* 16.1) P. is aware of those Sabine characteristics; here he makes no comment, although they would seem to be pertinent to his portrayal of the hero.

τραφεὶς δὲ . . . ὀρφανός: cf. *Cor.* 1.2 and *Ti. Grac.* 1.5–7, two other instances of Plutarchean heroes raised by their mothers. P. may have wanted to show how in Roman society widowed mothers were able to educate their children as they saw fit, and with good results; the contrast to *Alk.* 1.1–3, with its list of guardians and pedagogues, is striking. One wonders, though, whether P. had another coincidence in mind: the five subjects of his lives who ended in conflict with their city or its established order—Coriolanus, Alkibiades, the Gracchi, Sertorius—all had lost their fathers at an early age.

ὑπερφυῶς δοκεῖ φιλομήτωρ γενέσθαι: Stenten's diagnosis (p. 63), on the basis of this passage and 22.9–11, of a "strongly developed Oedipal complex" is somewhat rash.

'Ραῖαν: thus Ziegler, and Flacelière and Chambry, following L² rather than the other codices' ῥέαν (L¹: ῥᾶον). Schulten (27) preferred to write "Rea," but Sertorius' mother's name is surely the feminine form of the gentilicium Raius; Schulze, 217; Weiss s.v. "Rea Silvia," *RE* 1A.1 (1914) 343; cf. also *CIL* I² 363 = *ILLRP* 631 (Norba), 1701 = 692 (Venusia); *ILLRP* 235, 736 (Minturnae). Katz, "Sertorius" 287, unaware of the epigraphical evidence and hence mistaking 'Ραῖα for a mere spelling variant of Rhea, engages in quite unwarranted divagations on the name's "formidable mythological antecedents."

2.2

καί τινα καὶ δύναμιν . . . ἔσχεν: Cicero gave his first public speech at age twenty-five (*Pro Quinctio*, in 81), L. Licinius Crassus (*cos.* 95, born in 140: Cic. *Brut.* 161; Sumner, *Orators* 94–96) at age twenty-one when prosecuting C. Papirius Carbo (*cos.* 120) in 119. Q. Hortensius (*cos.* 69) was nineteen at the time of his first appearance (Cic. *Brut.* 229). No comparison with such giants of Roman oratory is implied by P., however. The sentence is to be understood in contrast with the one following (ἤσκητο μὲν . . . αἱ δέ); together they explain why Sertorius did not pursue what might have been a promising career as a speaker. Nor is too much made of his oratorical achievement: ἱκανός ("sufficient") and καί τι καὶ ("even some degree of . . .") indicate a solid but hardly stellar performance as an orator. That view is confirmed by Cic. *Brut.* 180, attesting talent and intelligence combined with lack of formal training and polish: *sed omnium oratorum sive rabularum, qui et plane indocti et inurbani aut rustici etiam fuerunt, quos quidem ego cognoverim, solutissimum in dicendo et acutissimum iudico nostri ordinis Q. Sertorium.* Not Sertorius' level of forensic speaking, but his doing so at an early age, is significant.

ἐν τῇ πόλει: Rome or Nursia? Spann (3–7), Katz ("Notes" 45), and Rijkhoek

(40–42) take it as referring to Rome, as do Kaltwasser, Doehner, Perrin, and Ziegler in their translations; Stenten (63) is undecided ("te Rome of Nursia"). Schulten (27), Wiseman (*New Men* 87), and Flacelière and Chambry assume that Sertorius gained his first forensic successes in Nursia, which is more plausible for the following reasons.

(a) When the context permits absolutely no ambiguity, P. indeed uses ἐν τῇ πόλει as the equivalent of Latin *in urbe*: "in the City," the City being the one on which the general narrative is centered. That may be Rome (e.g., *Cic.* 9.2; *Flam.* 3.3; *Caes.* 7.6), or Athens (e.g., *Thes.* 27.1; *Dtr.* 27.1), or Sparta (*Ages.* 3.1), or Sikyon (*Arat.* 2.3, 7.2), or Syrakuse (*Dion* 27.3), or Chaironeia (*Kim.* 1.7). But whenever ἐν τῇ πόλει (or τὴν πόλιν, etc.) appears after a city has been mentioned in the same or a closely preceding sentence, the phrase invariably refers to that city, not to any different one: so in *Popl.* 22.2–3; *Luc.* 29.3–4; *Fab.* 3.1; *Dion* 26.5; *Tim.* 28.10; *Marc.* 20.11; *Caes.* 27.1–5; *Pyr.* 10.7. On the evidence of P.'s usage, the town in question ought to be Nursia.

(b) P. in this chapter is concerned with the hero's upbringing and education, which were largely supervised by his mother. The item must be given its full weight: as with Cornelia and the Gracchi (*Ti. Grac.* 1.6–7), Raia's character-forming influence did not stop in the boy's childhood years but extended well into his teens. P.'s story offers no basis for conjecturing that Sertorius left Nursia to take up residence in Rome before he entered the army.

(c) To assume that all future senators of municipal origin received their higher education in Rome is dangerous; C. Marius proves otherwise (*Mar.* 3.1, and see Carney, *Marius* 10–12). Those who would use Cicero as the paradigm move on treacherous ground. Cicero's father owned a house in Rome (*Cic.* 8.6; cf. Cic. *Q. fr.* 2.3.7) and was well enough acquainted with L. Crassus (*cos.* 95) and Q. Mucius Scaevola Augur (*cos.* 117)—the foremost speaker, respectively, and the foremost jurist of their time—to entrust his sons' education to them. He clearly intended the boys to become senators themselves. Indeed young Cicero's Roman connections were so strong that in his life (contrast the other three *novi* of the collection: Cato, Marius, and Sertorius) P. gives not a hint of his municipal origin. We cannot postulate a similar fortune for the young Sertorius (as Spann, 2–7, is inclined to do). On the contrary, we are told (below, 2.2) that only his early military exploits turned his interests toward a military career—which in a Roman context means a political, that is, a senatorial career. In other words, in his late teens Sertorius was still contented with the life his father had led: a Roman Knight and local magnate in Nursia. Even in a small country town, that would involve the usual duties of patronage, forensic business being among the more important ones (cf., e.g., *Cat. Mai.* 3.2).

(d) Cicero (*Brut.* 180, see preceding note) numbers Sertorius among the "ranters" (*rabulae*), speakers *qui nec habiti sint oratores neque fuerint* (181). At the same time he attests to Sertorius' natural talent, characterizing him as *solutissimus in dicendo et acutissimus*. Spann himself wonders whether Nursia rather than Rome might have "produced his accent and speaking style"

(177 n. 18). Certainly that is the correct explanation. The coarse and rustic manner of speech witnessed by Cicero when he heard the mature Sertorius (not before the late 90s: Cicero himself would hardly have been knowledgeable enough, and Sertorius was in Spain for most of that decade) would be difficult to explain in a man of great oratorical ability who had not only received his schooling, rhetorical and otherwise, in Rome but also achieved early recognition there as a speaker. Rijkhoek (44–50) argues that some orators undoubtedly raised in Rome affected a rustic manner of speech (L. Aurelius Cotta *tr. pl.* 103, Cic. *Brut.* 137, 259; P. Sulpicius *tr. pl.* 88, Cic. *De orat.* 3.46), and that C. Scribonius Curio (*cos.* 76) could be characterized as completely uneducated yet an effective speaker (Cic. *Brut.* 213, *neminem ex his quidem, qui aliquo in numero fuerunt, honestarum artium tam indoctum, tam rudem*; cf. *Brut.* 210, 214–20). True enough; but the point is that it did not occur to Cicero to deny these men the label *orator* and classify them instead under *rabulae*. The case of Q. Valerius Soranus, mistakenly adduced by Rijkhoek (49) as another example of rustic speech among Romans from the City, clinches the argument: a Latin from Sora, esteemed among Allied and Latin *oratores* and highly educated, yet immediately given away by his accent (Cic. *Brut.* 169; *De orat.* 3.43–45). His rhetorical training (and, as evident from the *Brutus* passage, most of his later practice) took place in his hometown.

μειράκιον ὤν: in P., usually a young man around the age of twenty, give or take—more likely give—a few years: e.g., *Alk.* 7.3; *Cic.* 44.1; *Caes.* 1.3; *C. Grac.* 1.2; *Pomp.* 3.1. The term, unfortunately, is not a reliable guide to someone's age. Marius (born ca. 157) is so called while serving at Numantia (*Mar.* 3.5) at age twenty-three to twenty-five; the elder Cato both at seventeen and twenty-five (*Cat. Mai.* 1.7, 2.3); Philopoimen at thirty (*Phil.* 6.13). P. clearly knew their correct age (*Mar.* 33.2, 41.6, 45.12; *Cat. Mai.* 15.5; *Phil.* 5.1). Brutus, born 85/4, is termed *meirakion* with reference to the year 58 (*Brut.* 3.1) when about twenty-seven; Lucullus when about the same age, ca. 91 B.C. (*Luc.* 1.2; for the date see Badian, "Non-Trials" 301–4); P. Clodius Pulcher (*Cic.* 28.2) at the time of the Bona Dea scandal in 62, when he was thirty-one (born 93; see Sumner, *Orators* 136). P. may have thought them younger than they actually were: Clodius is characterized as μήπω γενειῶν, and in *Brut.* 5.2 Caesar's affair with Brutus' mother, Servilia, is said to have been at the height of passion when Brutus was born. Yet elsewhere (*Brut.* 5.3–4; cf. *Cat. Min.* 24.1–3) P. knows quite well that the relationship was flourishing in the 60s. Octavian in 43 is stated even to be "not yet fully a *meirakion*, but in his twentieth year" (*Brut.* 27.3, ὑπατείαν ἔλαβεν οὔπω πάνυ μειράκιον ὤν, ἀλλ' εἰκοστὸν ἄγων ἔτος), whereas in *Arat.* 46.2, οὔπω πάνυ μειράκιον denotes Philip V at age sixteen or seventeen. Clearly P.'s usage is quite elastic. Unless the biographer specifically states a person's precise age—and then not always—his labeling someone (rather) young or (rather) old must be treated with great caution: see also Frost's salutary remarks, *Themistocles* 70–71 (and cf. below, 13.1n.). One may observe that Latin shows similar (if not greater) flexibility in the meaning of *adulescens*: see Badian, "Non-Trials" 302–5, and cf. Konrad, *Klio* 66 (1984) 152–54.

P. likes to comment on his subjects' rhetorical and intellectual background before proceeding with the portrayal of their political and military career (e.g., *Them.* 2.1–4; *Kim.* 4.5; *Luc.* 1.2–8; *Per.* 4.1–6.1; *Cat. Min.* 4.3–4; *Marc.* 1.3; *Ti. Grac.* 2), and his observations need not pertain exclusively to the time before the hero's first military service. Thus the elder Cato's forensic training and practice described in *Cat. Mai.* 1.5–7 must in large part belong in the time during and after his military service, which he started at age seventeen (1.8). Indeed it has been argued by Katz ("Notes" 44–49, where he missed the Cato parallel) and Rijkhoek (40–41) that the events of 3.1–4 (Sertorius' early military service) should be understood as contemporaneous with, or even subsequent to, his forensic appearances in 2.2: Sertorius could have spent each year partly in the field, partly in Rome. That view is difficult to sustain. The very emphasis (μὲν . . . δέ) on the contrast between Sertorius' gaining forensic recognition while still a *meirakion* and the change of outlook and priorities effected by his early military exploits suggests that his pursuit of oratory came first in time: for P., Sertorius did not choose one of two options presenting themselves simultaneously, but abandoned one career for another. When P. calls his subject a *meirakion* it is usually in connection with what he considers the hero's first noteworthy achievement or activity, mostly of a public nature. The young Cato (*Cat. Mai.* 1.7) is so termed when receiving wounds in battle, and first military exploits are indeed the most frequent context (*Cor.* 3.1; *Alk.* 7.3; *Aem.* 15.4; *Brut.* 3.1; *Phil.* 6.13; *Pyr.* 4.4; *Pomp.* 3.1), followed closely by political success (*Alk.* 13.1; *Brut.* 27.3; *Agis* 7.1; *Arat.* 4.1, 6.5, 15.3). Theseus the *meirakion* lifts the stone (6.2), Phokion (4.2) and Kleomenes (2[23].2) receive philosophical instruction important for their later development. Occasionally the context may be negative: Gaius Gracchus seems not to want a political career (1[22].2), Kimon (4.4) and Clodius (*Cic.* 28.2) in their early years as adults are notorious rather than noteworthy. Only twice besides *Sert.* 2.2 is the *meirakion* found to excel in forensic speaking: in the case of Lucullus (1.2) possibly, in Caesar's certainly (1.3), the event comes before the first military service. Clearly P. saw in Sertorius' performance at Arausio (3.1) a noteworthy achievement: had it been his first, the qualifying μειράκιον ὤν would have been applied there, not at 2.2. Precisely because it was unusual to earn forensic recognition so early in life, in the *municipia* no less than in Rome (Quintilian *Inst.* 12.6.1 has heard of *praetextati* but gives no names; only temerity would conjecture Sertorius as one of them), P. needed to make the point: as so often elsewhere (esp. *Luc.* 1.2; *Caes.* 1.3; *Mar.* 8.6; *Brut.* 27.3), μειράκιον ὤν emphasizes the exceptional character of the situation.

Sertorius' Date of Birth

No birthdate is recorded for Sertorius. Seeing that Sertorius had joined the army by 105 B.C. (below, 3.1n.), Schulten took 122 for the *terminus ante quem*, as the minimum age required for military service was seventeen (apparently enforced since 123/2 B.C.: *C. Grac.* 5.1). Subsequently 123/2 became the canonical date (thus recently, e.g., Sumner, *Orators* 108; Nicolet, *L'ordre équestre* 2:1022, writes 127, apparently following Schulten, 38 n. 199, on the conjectural date of Sertorius' praetorship, 87 B.C.). The first dissenter was Spann. Giving full weight to the meaning of μειράκιον ὤν in 2.2, he argued that gaining even limited recognition as a speaker would have been difficult to achieve by age seventeen, and suggested that Sertorius did not start his military service until he was about twenty, and hence was born no later than 126/5 (158–59; cf. diss. 2–3). Less elaborately, García Mora has argued that Sertorius indeed joined the army at age seventeen, but two or three years before the battle of Arausio (*Studia Historica* 7 [1989] 88–90). The attempt by Katz, "Notes" 44–49, to read *Sert.* 2.2 and 3.1–4 as parallel events in order to salvage the "traditional" date founders upon close inspection of the role played by the term *meirakion* in P.'s lives (see 2.2n., above); the "tradition," after all, is entirely modern. Spann's proposal, on the other hand, has much in its favor. Ample evidence exists of Roman *equites* and nobles starting their military careers at an age considerably later than seventeen. Marius was twenty-three when he joined Scipio's army at Numantia (*Mar.* 3.2, πρώτην δὲ στρατείαν στρατευσάμενος). P.'s explicit statement, seemingly contradicted by Sall. *Iug.* 63.3, *ubi primum aetas militiae patiens fuit, stipendiis faciundis . . . sese exercuit*, has been rejected or at least doubted by some (e.g., Chantraine, 65–67; Paul, 168–70), unnecessarily: for the correct interpretation see Carney, *Marius* 11 nn. 62–63, and Badian, *DUJ* 25 (1963–64) 143–44. Caesar first served in 81/80 (Suet. *DJ* 2; cf. *MRR* 2:76), at the age of nineteen or twenty-one—depending on the year of his birth (Sumner's argument in favor of 102, *Orators* 134–37, is still convincing). That Metellus Pius could be found, *annos natus circiter viginti*, on his father's staff in Numidia in 108 (Sall. *Iug.* 64.4; cf. Plut. *Mar.* 8.6) was surely no coincidence: most likely he had waited with his military service until Metellus Numidicus' consulship (not hazardous to predict). At age twenty, Cato the Younger had not yet seen military service, as follows from *Cat. Min.* 3.9; probably the campaign against Spartacus in 72, with his half-brother Caepio as military Tribune, was his first: at age twenty-two or twenty-three (*Cat. Min.* 8.1). Given those parallels, a birthdate ca. 126/5 for Sertorius agrees more easily with P.'s account than a later one.

αἱ δὲ περὶ τὰ στρατιωτικὰ λαμπρότητες αὐτοῦ καὶ κατορθώσεις . . . μετέστησαν: generally and properly taken as referring to the events of chapter 3. Katz ("Notes" 45–48), however, maintains that Sertorius' participation in the battle of Arausio (3.1) could not be called a "brilliant success" and that his first military feat deserving such an epithet was his spy mission under Marius (3.2–4). Accordingly, he thinks that "the phrase 'τὰ στρατιωτικὰ λαμπρότητες' [*sic*] appears to refer to the deed under Caepio, . . . while 'αἱ . . . κατορθώσεις' appears to refer to his spy mission under Marius" (45 n.

6). That is sorely to misunderstand the grammar. Concerning the remainder of Katz's argument, it does not matter so much whether Arausio was an unqualified military success for Sertorius in our eyes, but whether P. could regard it as λαμπρότης or κατόρθωσις. Katz would not deny that it was a "fine show of youthful endurance" (46), and as such it has entered the annals of history, to be retold as late as Ammianus Marcellinus (24.6.7; cf. Nepotian. *Epit. Val. Max.* 21.3). If, moreover, P. was "reading into Sertorius' life his own belief that oratory is a pursuit of the second rank," as Katz suggests, that scholar's line of reasoning defeats itself, for then even a very limited exploit would be good enough for P. to postulate a change of his hero's mind.

3

Three carefully chosen episodes introduce the reader to important aspects of the hero's physical, mental, and moral constitution. Sertorius' bravery at Arausio (3.1) shows him as strong and enduring, not merely in body but also of will: this man does not give up, will not surrender. In the scouting mission (3.2–3), he proves his courage and readiness to undergo danger, and P. gives us a first glimpse of Sertorius' most characteristic trait: a masterful reliance on disguise, decoys, and deception. The hero easily and willingly adapts to an alien environment; that will come handy later in Spain. Strength, courage, and cleverness make a great warrior, but not yet a leader of men: the Castulo incident (3.5–10), described in lavish detail and at greater length than the other two episodes together, dispels any doubts we might hold in that respect. Yet besides level-headed resourcefulness and leadership, it hints at something else. The hero can be utterly ruthless when confronted with opposition.

3.1

πρῶτον μέν: contrasted by δεύτερον δὲ in 3.2; hence here not an adverb accompanying στρατευόμενος (as in the translations of Kaltwasser and Floerke, Stenten, Ziegler, and Flacelière and Chambry), but introducing the first of two connected events: "primum quum in Galliam Cimbri et Teutones irrupissent . . . (2) Deinde iis cum multis millibus reversis . . ." (Doehner), or: "To begin with, when the Cimbri and Teutones invaded Gaul . . . (2) In the next place, when the same enemies were coming up . . ." (Perrin). Cf. Katz, "Notes" 45.

Κίμβρων καὶ Τευτόνων ἐμβεβληκότων εἰς Γαλατίαν: The home of the Cimbri, Teutoni, and Ambrones (a third tribe usually mentioned in conjunction with the Teutoni), while not known for certain, is generally held to have been at least since ca. 200 B.C. in Jutland; they may have originated in Norway (Demougeot 921–22). By the last quarter of the second century they were migrating south, fighting unsuccessfully with the Boii in Bohemia and encountering the Scordisci along the middle Danube (Strabo 7.2.2). They then turned westward and in 113 invaded the Alps after defeating a Roman army

Commentary 3.1   41

under the Consul Cn. Papirius Carbo at Noreia in Noricum (Appian *Celt.*
13; cf. Strabo 5.1.8, 7.2.2.; Livy *Per.* 63). By 111 they seem to have reached
Switzerland, where they were joined by two cantons of the Helvetii, the Tigurini and Toygeni (or Tougeni, Strabo 7.2.2, Τωυγένους; on their possibly
being confused with the Teutoni by either Strabo or Poseidonios see Malitz,
Historien 219 n. 151; Kidd, *Posidonius* 2:932), and continued towards Gaul.
There in 109 or 108 they defeated another Roman force under M. Iunius
Silanus after their request for land had been refused (Livy *Per.* 65; Ascon. 68,
80 C; Flor. 1.38.2–4); in 107, the Consul L. Cassius Longinus fell in battle
against the Tigurini, and his army was sent under the yoke (Caes. *BG* 1.7.4,
1.12.5–7; Appian *Celt.* 1.8; Oros. 5.15.23–24). The invaders' movements
about Gaul in the years 109–105 are not known in detail; the attribution by
all sources of Cassius' defeat to the Tigurini alone suggests that the various
tribes or peoples did not always stay and operate together. Except for the far
North, where the Belgae offered successful resistance, Gaul suffered heavily
during those years (Caes. *BG* 2.4.2, 7.77.12–14; cf. Malitz, *Historien* 220).

P.'s account of the Cimbrian invasion is limited to the bare minimum here
(as in *Sulla* 4.5): only the hero's personal involvement matters. This contrasts
starkly with the detail offered in the *Marius* (11–27), much of which is evidently taken from Poseidonios (Malitz, *Historien* 208–9, 224–28; Kidd,
Posidonius 2:930). P. does not always tell everything he knows (cf. Stadter,
Pericles 351), and the *Sertorius* is one of his least discursive lives.

στρατευόμενος ὑπὸ Καιπίωνι: P. does not identify this as the hero's first
campaign (as sometimes he does: *Cat. Mai.* 1.8; *Cor.* 3.1; *Dtr.* 5.2; *Mar.* 3.2),
but the πρώτη στρατεία is a frequent feature of the *Lives,* and usually evident
from the context (e.g., *Cam.* 2.1; *Alk.* 7.3; *Marc.* 1.5–2.3; *Ant.* 4.1; *Pomp.*
3.1). Probably Sertorius joined Caepio's army already in 106, when the Consul took command in Transalpine Gaul, rather than only in 105 (Spann, 159);
indeed an obscure detail known about his part in the battle of Arausio suggests he was not a first-year *tiro* on that occasion (see below).

Q. Servilius (49) Caepio: ca. 150–95 B.C. As Praetor in 109 and Proconsul
108/7 he governed Hispania Ulterior and defeated the Lusitani; he triumphed
in 107. The *lex Servilia* passed under his consulship in 106 returned control
of the juries at least in part to Senators (Cic. *De orat.* 2.199–200; *Inv.* 1.92;
Livy 66 W-M ex Cassiod. *Chron.*; Obseq. 41; Val. Max. 6.9.13; Tac. *Ann.*
12.60). As Consul in Gallia Transalpina he defeated the Tectosages and captured Tolosa, whose temple treasure mysteriously disappeared on its way to
Rome; Caepio was suspected of having had a hand in the affair (Strabo 4.1.13;
Gell. 3.9.7; Dio fr. 90; Iustin. 32.3.9–11; Oros. 5.15.25; Auct. *De vir. ill.*
73.5). Proconsul in 105, he was chiefly responsible for the disaster at Arausio
by refusing to cooperate with the Consul Cn. Mallius Maximus; upon his
return to Rome he suffered *abrogatio imperii* (Livy *Per.* 67). In 104 he lost
his seat in the Senate (Ascon. 78 C), and in 103 was tried and convicted for
the loss of his army; he died in exile in Smyrna (Cic. *Balb.* 28; *De orat.* 2.197–

98; Auct. *Ad Herenn.* 1.24; Strabo 4.1.13; Val. Max. 4.7.3; [Gran. Lic.] 33.24 Cr).

κακῶς ... γενομένης: The disastrous defeat of two Roman armies, considered the worst since Cannae, at Arausio (now Orange) in southern Gaul occurred on 6 October 105 B.C. (*Cam.* 19.11; *Luc.* 27.8–9; *Imperat. apophth.* 203A; Gran. Lic. 33.16 Cr). The sources do not permit a detailed reconstruction of the battle, but the following appears reasonably certain. After destroying an advance corps under M. Aurelius Scaurus (*cos. suff.* 108), apparently a Legate of the Consul Mallius (see preceding note), the Cimbri, Teutoni, and various other tribes of the invaders marched south along the Rhône against the armies of Mallius and Caepio. Bickering between Consul and Proconsul prevented any effective coordination on the Roman side, and the barbarians' peace overtures, coupled with a request for land and grain, were dismissed out of hand. Two separate battles followed on the same day, each Roman army being annihilated in turn: first Caepio's, it seems, then that of Mallius (Livy *Per.* 67; Gran. Lic. 33.1–17 Cr, the best surviving account; Dio fr. 91; Oros. 5.16.1–7; brief mentions: Sall. *Iug.* 114.1; Vell. 2.12.2; Tac. *Germ.* 37.4; Plut. *Mar.* 16.9, 19.3; Flor. 1.38.4; Appian *Illyr.* 4.10; Veget. 3.10; Eutrop. 5.1.1).

ἀποβεβληκὼς τὸν ἵππον: As an *eques Romanus*, Sertorius properly served on horseback. Young men of equestrian or senatorial families usually were members of the *cohors amicorum*, the "general staff" of the commander in chief, and were commonly known as *contubernales* (see Cichorius, "Offizierskorps" passim; Tullio, "Cohors"; Harmand 383–86, 455–59). We may postulate the same for Sertorius. Personal connections seem to have played a large part in their decision under whom to serve (the locus classicus is Caes. *BG* 1.39.2), and Spann (4, 11–12) plausibly suggests that the Sertorii of Nursia may have had ties to the Servilii Caepiones. A little-known note in the *Scholia Bernensia* on Vergil's *Georgics* (first published by Mommsen, *RhM* 16 [1861] 451 = *Ges. Schriften* 7 [1909] 507) adds an intriguing detail. Under the lemma *vellere signa* (G. 4.108) the scholiast writes: *mos enim fuerat bellantium ut signa figerent eaque moverent profecturi. Si facile vellentium manus sequerentur, prospera pugna ostendebatur, si cum conatu, tum exitium significabant, ut in historia: Sertorius effodit signa, pugnavit et victus est, vix ipse ut evaderet, Rhodanum transnatavit.* Noting that the scholion pertains to the battle of Arausio, Mommsen concluded: "Sertorius muss danach die erwähnte Niederlage als Befehlshaber erlitten haben, da auf sein Geheiss die widerstrebenden Feldzeichen aus dem Boden gerissen wurden." *Befehlshaber* is probably putting Sertorius in too exalted a position: orders to move the signa and commence battle surely were the prerogative of the commanding general, in this case, Caepio, and *Sertorius effodit signa* should be taken quite literally. (Making too much of the plural *signa*, Rijkhoek, 58–59, 65–68, would not only assign to Sertorius the responsibility for giving that order but even have him face criminal prosecution subsequently.) If Sertorius had to dig out recalcitrant standards, he must have been responsible for them, and since he fought on horseback, he cannot have been the standard bearer of an infantry unit. The most likely explanation is that he served as *signifer* of a cavalry troop (*turma*), or, less probably, as *vexillarius* of a larger cavalry force (on the distinction see Mayer, 33–37; Speidel 38–40, 51–52). There is evidence that the *contubernales,* or a select number of them, went into combat as a *turma* under the general's personal command: *Marius ... cum turma sua, quam ex fortissumis magis quam familiarissumis paraverat, ... modo laborantibus suis succurrere, modo hostis ... invadere* (Sall. *Iug.* 98.1). Provided the scholion's account is reliable and not merely a confusion with some other defeat of Sertorius, one may conclude that at Arausio he served as the standard bearer of Caepio's personal troop. If so, the scholion supports the view that Sertorius had joined Caepio's army already in 106: *signiferi* were usually men of some experience, not raw recruits (Speidel 51).

τὸν ʽΡοδανὸν διεπέρασεν ... νηχόμενος: a feat still remembered in late antiquity: *et miratur historia Rhodanum arma et loricam retinente Sertorio transnatatum* (Ammian. 24.6.7, on the occasion of Julian's crossing the Tigris in A.D. 363; cf. Nepotian. *Epit. Val. Max.* 21.3 and Landolfus Sagax, *Hist. Misc.* 4.29, with a spear stuck in Sertorius' eye). Resemblance to the tale of Horatius Cocles, another one-eyed warrior (Polyb. 6.55; Dion. Hal. *Ant. Rom.* 5.23.2–24.3; Livy 2.10; Plut. *Popl.* 16.6–8), is obvious and invites skepticism. In fact, Polybios has Horatius drown; likewise perish the soldiers who seek to escape the massacre at the Trasumenian Lake by trying to swim across it in full armor (3.84.9). Polybios clearly thought swimming in body armor impossible; we must assume he knew what he was talking about (see also Frost, *Themistocles* 157). If indeed Sertorius was wearing chain mail (see following note), that element of the story at least should be discounted. On the other hand, certain Germanic—especially Batavian—cavalry units of the Imperial period were famous for their ability to swim across rivers with armor, weapons, horses, and other equipment (Tac. *Agr.* 18.4; *Hist.* 4.12.3; *Ann.* 2.8.3; Dio 60.20.2–6; *CIL* III 3676 = *ILS* 2558; cf. Dio 69.9.6); their horses may have been of help, of course (though at least the soldier of *ILS* 2558 and those of Dio 60.20.2–6 do not seem to have been so assisted), and their protective armament was probably light and largely nonmetallic. Julian's troops used their shields for buoyancy (Ammian. 24.6.7), and Sertorius could have done the same.

Doubts notwithstanding, a wholesale invention of the story is improbable. Its earliest source that can be conjectured with some probability is Poseidonios (Scardigli, "Considerazioni" 52), who had no incentive to make up such a tale about Sertorius. Sallust may have mentioned the event in his sketch of Sertorius' early life that preceded the surviving fragment 1.88 (cf. the sketch of Marius' career, *Iug.* 63.3–6), but there is no evidence to support Katz's notion ("Sertorius" 290; cf. "Notes" 46 n. 9) that the historian heavily emphasized the episode, modeling it after Caesar's swim to safety at Alexandria (*BAlex* 21.2–3; Plut. *Caes.* 49.7–8; Suet. *DJ* 64): a brief sentence is all we may legitimately expect. One would assume Livy to have told the story (Maurenbrecher, *Prolegomena* 29; Scardigli, "Considerazioni" 52), as he would not lightly pass over an example of individual bravery at a time of universal disaster, regardless of the hero's less desirable development later on. But the Livian tradition—especially Orosius 5.16.1-7 in a rather lengthy account—is oddly silent; whether Valerius Maximus and Ammianus found the tale in Sallust or in Livy is anybody's guess.

θώρακι: By Polybios' time Roman cavalry had adopted the use of body armor (6.25.3-4). Chain-mail is attested for legionary cavalry in the first century B.C. (Harmand, 82, 88; cf. 64 n. 72), though Sertorius, *eques Romanus*, may have worn a more elaborate cuirass (cf. Harmand 401-2). If, however, he really made it across the river in his armor, we must assume a leather or linen corselet, perhaps with a (light) pectoral or metal studs. Swimming in full metal armor was clearly impossible: see preceding note.

θυρεῷ: probably a smallish round shield (*parma equestris*), though Harmand is inclined toward a somewhat larger oblong or oval version (88, 401 n. 591, 404).

3.2

δεύτερον δὲ . . . ἐπερχομένων: Even after their victory at Arausio in 105 the barbarian invaders showed no intention of advancing toward Italy. They spent the winter in southern Gaul; in 104 the Cimbri (though not the others) crossed the Pyrenees and invaded Spain, only to be soon driven out by the Celtiberians. Late in 104 or early in 103 they were back in Gaul, where they rejoined the Teutoni and others in the region of the Veliocasses on the lower Seine (Livy *Per.* 67; Plut. *Mar.* 14.1, 9-10; cf. Caes. *BG* 2.4.2-9). The year 103 was spent in futile attempts to enter and plunder the northeast of Gaul. In spring or summer of 102, at last, with the ability of central and southern Gaul to support the migrant peoples exhausted, they decided to invade Italy. The Cimbri and Tigurini were to cross the central Alps and enter Italy through the valley of the Adige, while the Teutoni and Ambrones moved south along the Rhône valley so as to reach Italy from the west (*Mar.* 15.5-6; Flor. 1.38.18). Both Consuls of 102 were sent to counter the threat. Marius, commander in chief in Gaul since 104, took up a heavily fortified position at the confluence of Rhône and Isère, near Valence, thus blocking the access to the Graian Alps and the Little St. Bernard or Mont Cenis passes and forcing the Teutoni to take the southerly route along the Ligurian coast (*Mar.* 15.1, 15.7, 18.1-2; Oros. 5.16.9; on Marius' strategy and location—Rhône-Isère rather than Rhône-Durance—see Donnadieu, 283-85, still the most convincing study, *pace* Demougeot). As the Teutoni and Ambrones together appear to have been considerably more numerous than the Cimbri, Miltner's argument (290-98) that they originally intended to take separate routes to Italy—the Ambrones and the mysterious Toygeni (see 3.1n.) through Liguria all along, the Teutoni, however, across the Graian Alps—has something in its favor, the author's chauvinistic (not to call them worse) overtones notwithstanding; trekking separately would certainly ease their supply situation. (On the numbers of the invaders, see Demougeot 931 n. 106.) In two successive battles near Aquae Sextiae (Aix-en-Provence) Marius annihilated both Ambrones and Teutoni late in 102 (*Mar.* 18.3–21.8; cf. Livy *Per.* 68; Vell. 2.12.4). Meanwhile his colleague, Q. Lutatius Catulus, failed disastrously against the Cimbri, who advanced across the Brenner pass and down the Val d'Adige (see below). By the spring of 101 the barbarians controlled most of the country north of the Po and east of Cremona, but in the summer, they were routed and destroyed by the joint armies of Marius and Catulus at Vercellae (probably not Vercelli but an area near Ferrara, as argued by Zennari).

δειναῖς ἀπειλαῖς: cf. *Mar.* 15.6 and 16.5, of the Teutoni and Ambrones, and 24.4–6, of the Cimbri.

ὥστε . . . εἶναι: Marius followed a careful regimen of getting his troops accustomed to the sight and sound of the barbarians, i.e., Teutoni and Ambrones, while he was encamped at the Rhône-Isère juncture (*Mar.* 16.3–5). Against the Cimbri on the other side of the Alps, Catulus first watched his cavalry routed and ignominiously put to flight in the Adige valley near Tridentum (Val. Max. 5.8.4; cf. Frontin. *Strat.* 4.1.13); then, unable to bring his panic-stricken forces under control, he gave up his position at the narrows of the Adige (the Chiuse Veronesi), thereby opening northern Italy to the invaders (*Mar.* 23.4–7; cf. Livy *Per.* 68; Plin. *NH* 22.11). If P. here has any specific incidents in mind (the notice reads more like a general comment on the situation), the tribulations of Catulus are surely among them. Hence the passage cannot be used to pinpoint Sertorius' reconnaissance mission (3.3) to the weeks or days immediately preceding the battle of Aquae Sextiae (as Spann, 14, and Rijkhoek, 74–75, would like to do).

Μάριος μὲν ἡγεῖτο: C. Marius (14), ca. 157–86 B.C. Consul in 107, 104–100, and 86. In command in Gaul since 104, he restored the troops' morale and combat readiness, aided considerably by the lull in the fighting between 104 and 102. P. is as brief as possible, withholding all background information on Sertorius' commander in chief. There is no good reason to doubt that Sertorius' service with the army in Gaul continued without interruption. Rijkhoek's attempt (62–76) at reconstructing an intervening two-year sojourn in Rome, 104–103 B.C., is based entirely on farfetched speculations about Sertorius' supposed attachment to various factional groups among the nobility and his hypothetical involvement in their political infighting.

κατασκοπήν: P.'s terminology makes no distinction between military units carrying out tactical reconnaissance (cf. *Fab.* 12.1; *Crass.* 23.2; *Marc.* 29.8–11), usually called *exploratores* in Latin (e.g., Caes. *BG* 1.12.2, 2.17.1, 7.44.3), and individual scouts or spies engaged in intelligence gathering missions such as here and perhaps *Eum.* 9.9, in Latin usually *speculatores* (Caes.

BG 2.11.2–3, apparently distinguishing the two; 5.49.8; *BC* 3.66.1, 67.1; [Caes.] *BAfr* 35.2–4; *BHisp* 13.3). Harmand (137–41) offers a survey of Roman military reconnaissance and intelligence practices.

3.3

If Arausio illustrated the hero's strength and endurance, the *kataskopē* shows his courage and cleverness along with a fondness for disguise. The episode has been attributed to the weeks before the battle of Aquae Sextiae in 102 (Schulten, 29; Spann, 14–17), and Spann in particular made a strong case in favor of placing it at the time when Marius was encamped at the Rhône and Isère. But the Romans seem to have had reason to expect, in the fall of 104, another attack for the spring of the following year (*Mar.* 14.9–10), and in 102 they apparently were well informed about the invaders' aims and intended routes (*Mar.* 15.1, 15.5, 23.2; clearly Catulus was not caught by surprise when the Cimbri appeared in the Val d'Adige: cf. Lewis, *Hermes* 102 [1974] 95). Sertorius' mission may have been connected with that sort of intelligence rather than with Marius' maneuverings in the weeks before Aquae Sextiae. If Marius wanted to find out about the barbarians' intended movements he had to do so early each year, before they got under way: by the time the Teutoni reached his fortifications at the Rhône and Isère, he must have known their plans for quite a while, and there was little in the way of strategic intelligence Sertorius could gather at this late point. Given the vagueness of P.'s account, Sertorius' mission is as likely to have taken place in fall 104 as in fall 102, or at any time in between.

ἐσθῆτι ... Κελτικῇ: chiefly trousers and long-sleeved coats; see Strabo 4.4.3 for a full description (cf. also Polyb. 2.28.7; Plut. *Otho* 6.6).

τὰ κοινότατα τῆς διαλέκτου ... παραλαβών: Sertorius had been serving in Gaul now for several years and may have acquired some basic Gaulish through contacts with Gallic auxiliaries, or with dignitaries frequenting the headquarters of the Roman commander in chief. It is now generally agreed that Poseidonios, P.'s principal source for the Cimbrian Wars, was not fully aware of the ethnic differences between Celts and Germans and thought the Cimbri and the other invading tribes to be Celtic peoples (Malitz, *Historien* 198–210; Kidd, *Posidonius* 2:323–26). Conceivably P.'s account here is merely a reflection of Poseidonios, and Sertorius really dressed as a German. But elsewhere P. clearly knows Cimbri, Teutoni, and Ambrones as Germans, different from Celtic Gauls (*Mar.* 11.3–5, 15.6). Hence Spann thought that Sertorius limited his scouting to one of several Celtic groups that had joined the German invaders along the way. (The Helvetian Tigurini and Toygeni are known to have done so, but the Tigurini certainly, the Toygeni possibly, were not present at the Rhône–Isère; see above, 3.1–2nn.) It is, however, quite improbable that Sertorius, with just a smattering—τὰ κοινότατα—of their language, should have attempted to pass for a member of one of the migrant peoples, Celtic or Germanic: he would not have survived the first encounter with a native speaker. Passing for a Gaul among Germans would have been an entirely different matter. The migrant peoples did not live in fortified, closely guarded camps, and despite their reputation for plunder and pillage, there must have occurred frequent peaceful contacts with the Gallic population, in particular traders and craftsmen. Those could provide an effective cover. Presumably many of the Germans had acquired a smattering of Gaulish themselves over the years, but few would be able to identify Sertorius' accent as that of a Roman.

τὰ μὲν ἰδών, τὰ δ'ἀκοῇ πυθόμενος: How much he could have overheard from "random conversations" while "riding casually about the camp" (Spann, 16) is debatable. Of the Germans' own language he was presumably ignorant, and even if there were groups of Celts among the invaders his limited command of Gaulish would hardly permit that sort of analysis. Masquerading as a Gaul on nonmartial business, Sertorius may have been able to ask a few seemingly innocuous questions (and as Spann notes, the invaders were probably not very much concerned about secrecy). This entire touch of detail, however, looks like P.'s own embellishment rather than factual information. *Opsis* and *akoē* are, of course, Herodotean means of inquiry.

τῶν ἐπειγόντων: In the closest known parallel case, [Caes.] *BAfr* 35, Metellus Scipio was looking for quite specific information: what preparations, if any, had Caesar made against an elephant attack? P.'s vagueness here should caution us against attributing too much military significance to the episode; it is related chiefly to illustrate the hero's character. If Sertorius undertook the mission before the campaign of Aquae Sextiae, he will have wanted to know the barbarians' next moves; if during the standoff at the Rhône–Isère, most likely such items as the number of warriors or the horde's speed of march (Spann, 16).

3.4

ἐν ... τῇ λοιπῇ στρατείᾳ: surely Sertorius participated in the battles of both Aquae Sextiae (102 B.C.) and Vercellae (101).

συνέσεως ἔργα καὶ τόλμης: A sharp and quick mind is one of the most typical and important assets of a military leader: thus Fabius Maximus the Cunctator is characterized as ὁ πλεῖστον ἔχων ἀξίωμα ... συνέσεως (*Marc.* 9.4), and Themistokles (*Kim.* 5.1), Philip II, Antigonos, Hannibal, and Eumenes all share that quality (*Sert.* 1.9; *Eum.* 16.1). Often it is paired with daring (τόλμα) and manly bravery (ἀνδρεία), e.g., *Kim.* 5.1; *Luc.* 2.1, 36.5; *Crass.* 8.3, 21.6–9 (of Spartacus and the Surenas, respectively: the subject of that life lacks both); *Alk.* 35.3; *Tim.* 3.5; *Phil.* 7.9. *Synesis* is not limited to humans: observe Poros' elephant, *Alex.* 60.13.

εἰς ὄνομα καὶ πίστιν ... προήχθη: lit. "he was advanced by the general to a position of renown and trust" (i.e., holding the general's trust), not "he was advanced by his general to positions of honour and trust" (Perrin's translation). The point is that Sertorius became well known to Marius and entered into his *fides*: "nomen apud imperatorem fidemque sibi paravit" (Doehner).

3.5

μετὰ δὲ τὸν ... πόλεμον: Some two or three years intervened between the battle of Vercellae in the summer of 101 and Sertorius' departure for Spain in 98, but P. gives no hint of that. Whatever Sertorius did during those years—his whereabouts remain unknown—it evidently was of no consequence for P.'s purpose in this chapter. If he continued to serve in the military (Spann, 18, discusses some possible postings) he accomplished nothing noteworthy.

ἐκπεμφθείς: probably in 98 rather than 97. To judge from Obsequens 47 (*Hispani pluribus proeliis devicti*), Didius started his Spanish campaign during his consulship.

T. Didius (5) T. f. Sex. n.: cf. Badian, "Consuls" 404–5. Ca. 140–89 B.C. As Tribune of the Plebs in 103 he attempted to prevent the prosecution of Q. Servilius Caepio (Cic. *De orat.* 2.197; see above, 3.1n.). Praetor no later than 101 and governor (*pro consule?*) of Macedonia until 100 or 99; for subduing the Scordisci he was awarded a triumph. As Consul in 98 he took command of Hispania Citerior, where he successfully and ruthlessly fought until 93 (Livy *Per.* 70; Obseq. 47–48; Frontin. *Strat.* 2.10.1; Appian *Iber.* 99.431–100.436); second triumph in that year. Legate during the Social War under the Consul L. Iulius Caesar in 90 (Cic. *Font.* 43; Appian 40.179) and under Sulla in 89; he captured Herculaneum (Vell. 2.16.2) but apparently was killed in battle on 11 June 89 (Ovid *Fasti* 6.567).

στρατηγῷ: Didius was Consul in 98 and Proconsul from 97 to 93. Στρατηγὸς as a term for Roman officials means principally "commander, general, commander in chief, governor"; the meaning "Praetor" is secondary and should be employed in translation only when there is independent evidence that the official in question actually was holding that magistracy at the time (cf. Mason, 155–63). P.'s own usage conforms to that pattern: e.g., just above in 3.2, the word is used simply for "general," and the *stratēgos* of 3.4 is the Consul Marius. But P. may not have known (or cared to find out) Didius' precise rank, and Flacelière and Chambry are perhaps right to suggest that στρατηγῷ here renders a more generic term or phrase in a Latin source, such as *imperator/imperante*: cf. Sall. *Hist.* 1.88, *magna gloria in Hispania tribunus militum T. Didio imperante ... fuit*.

χιλίαρχος: Sertorius was an elected Military Tribune (on the correct title, *tribunus militum legionibus quattuor primis aliqua earum*, as opposed to the colloquial *tribunus militum a populo factus*, see Mommsen, StR 2³:576–78; for a different interpretation of *a populo* see Nicolet, MEFR 79 [1967] 29–

76), as ἐκπεμφθεὶς ὑπὸ Δειδίῳ . . . ἐπ' Ἰβηρίας makes clear: "having been posted to Spain under Didius" (Kaltwasser and Perrin mistranslate *"by Didius"*) must imply that someone other than the Consul was responsible for the appointment. (I owe this observation to E. Badian.) *Cat. Min.* 9.1, ἀποδειχθεὶς δὲ χιλίαρχος, εἰς Μακεδονίαν ἐπέμπετο πρὸς Ῥούβριον τὸν στρατηγὸν, is a more explicit parallel. Nor is an elective tribunate as improbable as Spann (19) thought (the confused argument of García Mora, *Florentia Iliberritana* 1 [1990], contributes little). Marius, a man of comparable social standing, was an elected Tribune (Sall. *Iug.* 63.4). Carney (*Marius* 17), Nicolet ("Armée" 136–38), and Wiseman (*New Men* 143–47) all have shown that for young *nobiles* and *novi* alike wishing to enter upon a political career, the elective tribunate was the office of choice if they had a distinguished military record; it offered an opportunity to run for public office before attaining the minimum requirements for the quaestorship. Despite the assertions of Mommsen (*StR* 1³:511) and others (e.g., Harmand, 354 and n. 222), there is no reason to assume that the Polybian (6.19.1) requirements of previous service (five years for junior, ten for senior elected Tribunes) were no longer in effect at this time (see Fraccaro, "I 'decem stipendia,'" esp. 475–94). Cn. Plancius (*aed. cur.* 55 or 54) became Military Tribune in 62—surely of the elected kind, after seven years or more as a *miles* and *contubernalis* (he did his first service under A. Manlius Torquatus, before 68 B.C.: see Cic. *Planc.* 27-28; Broughton, *MRR* 2:133, 177). Among the elected Tribunes of 69 were at least three Senators (Cic. *1Verr.* 30): one, Cn. Tremellius, already a quaestorian and of recorded military experience (*MRR* 2:122, 3:208, *pace* Nicolet, *L'ordre équestre* 2:1050), the other two either likewise quaestorians or adlected by Sulla a decade earlier. Whichever the case, all three must have been men in their early thirties, unlikely to have waited for this office so long if it was conveniently available after a mere year or two in the army. Sertorius certainly would have fulfilled the five years' requirement.

Ἰβηρίας: Didius' province was Hispania Citerior (*Acta Tr.* = *Inscr. Ital.* XIII 1:84–5, *de Celtibereis*; cf. Livy *Per.* 70).

Κάστλωνι: Castulo, Iber. *Kaśt(i)lo,* sited on the heights stretching from the Casa de la Muela to the Torreón de Santa Eufemia on the northern bank of the Río Guadalimar (a tributary of the Guadalquivir), ca. six kilometers south of Linares (Jaén Prov., Andalucía). The town was famous for its silver and lead mines and had served as winter quarters for Roman troops as early as the Second Punic War (Livy 24.41.7, 28.20.8–12; Appian *Iber.* 16.61); later it marked the boundary between Hispania Citerior and Ulterior. Excavations conducted since 1970 have so far resulted in five volumes of reports (*Cástulo I–V,* Madrid 1974–85), edited by J. M. Blázquez (vols. 1, 3–5), R. Olmos (vol. 2), et. al. See also E. Hübner, *RE* 3.2 (1899) 1778–80; and, on the location, Spranger, *Historia* 7 (1958) 95–112; R. Contreras, in *Cástulo I* 12–18; on the name, Untermann, *MLH* 1:325–28; Correa, *Habis* 14 (1983) 107–113. A convenient summary of the town's history and social and economic development is offered by Blázquez, "Die Stadt Cástulo (Hispanien) in der römischen Kaiserzeit."

Κελτιβήρων: In fact, Castulo was a town of the Oretani and therefore Iberian, not Celtiberian, as is evident from the language used on coins and inscriptions (Hübner, *RE* 3.2 [1899] 1778; Schulten, 30 n. 172; Untermann, *MLH* 1:80, 325–28). See also below, 6.7: Peoples of the Peninsula.

3.6–10

The Castulo episode completes P.'s introduction to the hero's character by demonstrating his qualities as a leader and reinforcing the impression, created previously, of swift reaction, resolute daring, and resourcefulness. When he extricates himself and his troops from a seemingly hopeless predicament Sertorius acts clear-headedly and decisively, in a manner reminiscent of Hannibal (e.g., *Fab.* 6.4–10, though P. does not draw the parallel). As in the scouting episode, disguise is a major element of the story. Yet the events at Castulo illustrate the character not only of Sertorius but of Roman rule in Spain. The Roman soldiers terrorizing the native population, the massacre of adult males once Sertorius regains control of Castulo, and the cold brutality shown in the punishment of its neighbors follow a long line of atrocities. L. Licinius Lucullus (*cos.* 151), Ser. Sulpicius Galba (*cos.* 144), and Sertorius' own commander in chief, Didius, were models of treachery and savagery (see Appian *Iber.* 51–53, 59–60, 99–100); Scipio Aemilianus' treatment of the town of Lutia during the Numantine War (ibid. 94.409–411) bears an eerie resemblance to what happened at Castulo. P. could have downplayed those aspects and hidden the fact that it was the Roman troops' behavior that drove the Iberians to their desperate uprising. He chose not to, and neither did his source: which is why Poseidonios is a strong candidate (cf. Strasburger, 51–52, and above, Introduction 3.1.c and 3.13). Finally, while emphasizing Sertorius' positive qualities, the episode offers a glimpse of a darker side in his character. He gave the orders to kill and enslave. Years later, when he returned to Spain (6.7–9), he behaved quite differently, and his (for a Roman governor) uncharacteristically humane approach won him the hearts of the native population. Gratuitous cruelty surely was not his mark. Yet cruelty there was in the end, and it is foreshadowed at Castulo: when he kills or sells the hostages at Osca (10.5, 25.6), cold brutality becomes manifest again. The hero can be ruthless when thwarted, savage when cornered. Those aspects of his character, attested by the eminently sympathetic biographer, must be kept in mind when judging the credibility of similar reports of ruthlessness in other, less favorably disposed sources (see below, 25.6n.): we lightly dismiss them at our peril. P. does not like to dwell on the streak of cruelty in Sertorius, but he is too honest to suppress it altogether.

3.6

στρατιωτῶν: When spending the winter in camp, Roman practice generally was to keep legions together rather than have cohorts camp individually or in

Commentary 3.9

small groups. Obviously that was not feasible when troops were to be quartered in allied or subject towns, most of which would be too small to offer space and provisions for an entire legion. But Castulo was fairly large and wealthy, and the force quartered there may have numbered several cohorts. It is not certain, though likely, that Sertorius was the officer in charge.

ὑβριζόντων ... μεθυόντων: Excessive drinking and wanton acts directed at the civilian population were not unheard-of patterns of behavior among Roman troops quartered in provincial towns: e.g., Sall. *Iug.* 66.2–67.2; Plut. *Kim.* 1.3. If Sertorius was in command, he failed to restrain his men; P. may not have wished to stress that point.

'Ιστουργίνων: thus Ziegler's emendation ("Plutarchstudien" 2–3); the mss. have γυρισοινῶν ΛΚQ: γουρισυνῶν P: γυρισηνῶν C. But Schulten's objection (31 n. 173) to earlier emendations (Solanus' Ὠρισίων, Sintenis' Ὠριτανῶν)—too great a distance from Castulo for help to be sought and sent within a single night—applies to Isturgi (near Andújar, Jaén Prov.) as well, over 40 kilometers west of Castulo, at least eight hours' walk each way. A better identification was put forward in 1860 by Manuel de Góngora y Martínez in his *Colección de antigüedades de las provincias de Jaén y Granada*. (Reprinted under the title "Viaje literario por las provincias de Jaén y Granada," *Revista Don Lope de Sosa* 28 [Jaén, 1915], pp. 35 ff.; cited by Spranger, *Historia* 7 [1958] 100 n. 3, and Contreras, in: *Cástulo I* 30 n. 56. I have been unable to see the original.) Considerable ruins of an ancient settlement exist at Guiribaile, a small mountain between the Guadalimar and its tributary, the Guadalén, ca. 15 kilometers northeast of Castulo. Certainly that location would fit the circumstances of P.'s story. If Guiribaile preserves part of its ancient name, Ci-/Girisia or Cu-/Gurisia should come close, and Γ(ο)υρισηνῶν or Γ(ο)υρισινῶν may be what P. wrote. Given the evidence, however, all emendation here is illusory: a dagger is called for.

ὑπεκδὺς ... συναγαγών: Sertorius first made his way out of the town with a small number of men, then rounded up the rest of those who had managed to escape. It must have been a sizable group, since they easily regained control of the town. The Roman troops that escaped did so, it seems, with their arms and in fairly good order.

3.9

τάς τε πύλας ἀνεῳγμένας εὗρε: The counterattack surely did not take place during the night, as the "Gyrisinoi" would not expect their men to return while it was still dark. On the other hand, Sertorius could not afford to wait too long, lest news of the massacre at Castulo arrive first and warn the neighboring town. Arriving in the twilight of dawn would provide the best cover for his ruse.

4.1–6

Having established the hero's qualities as a soldier and officer, P. proceeds to show him in the Social War: in a position of high command requiring the ability to organize, and acquitting himself splendidly—better than most of his generation, *nobiles* no doubt (sections 1–2). Again there are acts of personal bravery, unspecified this time, though with visible effects in the form of facial disfigurement, and a not un-Roman pride in such proofs of valor (3–4). Public recognition follows (5), and although the quaestorship really marked the beginning of a political career, P. prefers to treat Sertorius' failed attempt at the tribunate as his first political experience (6). Thus the narrative of Sertorius' early life with its heavy emphasis on his military background comes to an end: from 4.7 all through chapter 6, we will be introduced to the hero in politics.

4.1

ἐκ τούτου ... διεβοήθη: Schulten's notion (p. 31) that Sertorius was awarded the *corona graminea* for saving his unit at Castulo has been refuted by Scardigli, "A proposito" 174–77.

ὅτε πρῶτον ἐπανῆκεν ... ἀποδείκνυται: Didius celebrated his second triumph on 10 June 93 B.C. (*Acta Tr.* = *Inscr. Ital.* XIII 1:84–85) and presumably had returned to Rome in the first half of that year. The natural assumption is that Sertorius returned with him and subsequently was elected Quaestor—in 91 (τοῦ γὰρ Μαρσικοῦ πολέμου συνισταμένου) for 90, according to the standard view (Broughton, *MRR* 2:27; Gabba, *App BC 1* 184; Scardigli, "Problemi" 230; Katz, "Notes" 53–56). But recently Spann (161–62) suggested that Sertorius continued to serve in Spain for another year under Didius' successor, C. Valerius Flaccus (*cos.* 93), and returned to Rome only in 92 to be elected Quaestor for 91—otherwise, P.'s statement that he was elected "as soon as he returned" would be incorrect (similarly Sumner, *Orators* 108). Spann argues further that *Sert.* 4.2 describes the situation obtaining during Sertorius' quaestorship, and since the Social War broke out in late 91, he must have been in office that year. What P. says is as follows: "Sertorius, as soon as he returned to Rome, was made Quaestor in Cisalpine Gaul, and at the right time: for with the Marsic War breaking out, it being his task to levy troops and have arms manufactured, he ...." Return to Rome; election to the quaestorship; beginning of the war; procurement of men and arms: P. presents these items as closely connected in time and fact. Were they really, or is the biographer compressing events (see Introduction 2.5) to heighten the dramatic impact?

Hostilities erupted toward the end of 91 (late October; see 4.2n.). Despite mounting tensions through much of the year, Rome clearly was caught unprepared for the magnitude of the revolt; but the onset of winter prevented full-scale war until the following spring. There is neither evidence nor reason to think that the Quaestor in Cisalpine Gaul—whoever he was—spent the

Commentary 4.1

better part of 91 raising troops and procuring equipment: any such activity must fall in the autumn and winter months of 91/90. By the same token, there is neither evidence nor reason to think that Sertorius spent most of the first year of the war collecting men and material in Gaul; certainly P. nowhere suggests that. On the contrary, serving in that capacity all through 90 would have drastically curtailed Sertorius' opportunity to excel in combat, the war being largely over by the end of 89—and excel he did, as both P. and Sallust (*Hist.* 1.88) emphasize. One may further ask, with Spann, whether a Quaestor of Sertorius' military credentials would not rather have been assigned, *extra sortem,* to one of the Consuls in 90. A Quaestor's year began on 5 December; if Sertorius was Quaestor in 91, he would have been spending the last month or two of his term with military procurement as described in 4.2, plus another month, perhaps, until his successor arrived. That is sufficient to account for P.'s description. To insist on his connecting these events with Sertorius' election rather than the last months in office would be unwise: election to the quaestorship was a major step in the hero's career, not to be passed over, but dwelling on a largely uneventful year in Gaul would spoil the effect of the scenery painted here.

On balance, then, 91 should be accepted (without subscribing to Perrin's misinterpretation of συνισταμένου as "threatening"; cf. below, 4.2n.) as the more likely year of Sertorius' quaestorship. No need, however, for Spann's postulating an additional year in Spain. If Sertorius returned with Didius in 93, he could theoretically run in the same year, for 92. Evidently he did not; that much is established by his activities during the beginnings of the Social War. But a successful candidacy required careful preparation, and time, in particular for a New Man: Sertorius' waiting until 92, for a quaestorship in 91, would be unsurprising—as would be P.'s writing ὅτε πρῶτον ἐπανῆκεν to describe that situation. Even if P. knew and cared about the precise dates involved (by no means a safe assumption; cf. Katz, "Notes" 54), he is unlikely to have considered one year's delay significant enough to warrant mention or explanation. The entire passage is concerned with emphasizing the hero's speedy advance on the road of *gloria.* An extra year in Spain, requested, due to his experience and reputation, by the new commander (so Spann, 161), might have been worth the mention; a year's canvassing in Rome was not.

ταμίας ... Γαλατίας: The usual view (e.g., Mommsen, *StR* 2³:570–72) that Cisalpine Gaul was one of the *provinciae* of the four so-called *quaestores classici,* who exercised various administrative functions in Ostia and other parts of Italy, has been refuted by Harris, *CQ* 26 (1976); he suggests that Sertorius served either as a regular provincial Quaestor under the command of a Praetor in 91 or 90, or was himself in charge of Gaul as *quaestor pro praetore.* The second suggestion is attractive, the first not without problems: it is P.'s consistent practice to note under whose command his heroes served in subordinate positions (*Cat. Mai.* 3.6; *Caes.* 5.6; *Ti. Grac.* 5.1; *C. Grac.* 1[22].4; *Sulla* 3.1—Quaestors all; *Luc.* 2.1; *Cat. Min.* 8.1, 9.1; *Ant.* 3.1; *Mar.* 3.2,

7.1; *Sulla* 4.1–3); the sole exception is Cicero as Quaestor in Sicily, where the Praetor's presence is merely—though clearly—implied (*Cic.* 6.1–2). In that instance as well as here, it seems rather unlikely that P.'s sources failed him. In a modified form, however, Harris's thesis may work. Badian showed long ago that C. Coelius Caldus, *cos.* 94, was probably in charge of Gaul on both sides of the Alps when he defeated the Salluvii in 90 B.C., and may still have been so in 87 ("Governors" 12–13 = *Studies* 90–92). More recently Ebel advanced reasons to believe that prior to the 70s the *provincia Gallia* tended to reach from Cisalpina to the Rhône, whereas southern Gaul from the Rhône to the Pyrenees usually was treated as part of Hither Spain (*Phoenix* 29 [1975]; I am not convinced by Hackl, *Historia* 37 [1988] 253–56). If those views are correct, we may conclude that Sertorius was allocated Coelius and Gaul as his quaestorian province, and entrusted by his commander with the administration of Cisalpina—for all practical purposes on his own, while the Consul was fighting in Transalpina. That scenario could explain P.'s silence regarding Sertorius' superior.

τῆς περὶ Πάδον Γαλατίας: thus also *Cras.* 9.10; *Caes.* 20.1, 25.1; cf. *Brut.* 19.5, τὴν περὶ τὸν Ἠριδανὸν Γ. Usually P. prefers ἡ ἐντὸς Ἄλπεων Γ. (e.g., *Luc.* 5.2; *Pomp.* 16.3; *Brut.* 6.10).

ἐν δέοντι: "at the right time" (cf. Doehner, "opportuno tempore"). Schulten (31 n. 176) mistakes it as referring to election *suo anno*.

4.2

Μαρσικοῦ πολέμου: the Social War, 90–88 B.C. Likewise *Luc.* 1.7, 1.8, 2.1; *Cic.* 3.2; but συμμαχικὸς πόλεμος, *Mar.* 32.5; *Sulla* 6.2, 16, 17. *Bellum Marsicum* is the earliest Latin appellation (Sulla *HRR* F 10; Cic. *Leg. agr.* 2.90; *Phil.* 8.31; *Div.* 1.99, 2.54, 2.59; Sall. *Hist.* 1.88; cf. Diod. 37.2.1; Strabo 5.4.2; Suet. *Aug.* 23.2), and with *Bellum Italicum* the most common one in Republican times (e.g., Cic. *Cluent.* 21; *Leg. agr.* 2.80; *Arch.* 8, and generally in the speeches). Authors of the Imperial period prefer *bellum sociale*: e.g., Plin. *NH* 2.99; Frontin. *Strat.* 1.5.17, 2.4.16. For a full discussion see Domaszewski, "Bellum Marsicum" 1–10.

συνισταμένου: M. Livius Drusus *tr. pl.* 91, whose assassination triggered the war (Appian 36.164), was still alive when his most important ally, L. Licinius Crassus *cos.* 95, died on 19 September (Cic. *De orat.* 3.2–6). The collapse of Drusus' support in the Senate and the repeal of his legislation (Cic. *Dom.* 41; *Leg.* 2.31; Ascon. 68–69 C; Diod. 37.10.5), though swift, must have taken some time, and his murder will not have occurred before the middle of October (Gabba, *App BC I* 123). The massacre of Romans at Asculum (Appian 38.170–174) and the open outbreak of hostilities may be dated to the end of October, perhaps later (Broughton, *MRR* 2:24 n. 4, entertains the possibility that the Asculum incident happened "very early in 90"). Major field operations did not start until the spring of 90 (cf. Kiene 191–206). To translate "when the war was threatening" (Perrin; cf. Stenten, "want toen de Marsische oorlog dreigde") seems not quite accurate. From Sertorius' activities described in the following clause it is clear that P. meant to say "at the outbreak of the war" (cf. Doehner, "Marsico enim bello commisso"; and see Katz, "Notes" 55 n. 24).

στρατιώτας τε ... ποιεῖσθαι: cf. Sall. *Hist.* 1.88, *magno usui bello Marsico paratu militum et armorum fuit.* Cisalpine Gaul was the most important recruiting area for legionary troops during the Late Republic (Chilver, 8, 112). Gabba (*App BC 1* 130) suggests that Sertorius may have levied mostly Roman citizens in Cisalpina, but many of the numerous Gallic forces fighting for Rome were probably also raised by him (*CIL* I² 864; Appian 41.188 and perhaps 50.219–20, if Gabba's suggestion that the Gauls mentioned here may have been deserters from the Roman side is accepted).

σπουδὴν ... μαλακίαν: details not offered by Sall. *Hist.* 1.88. They might be P.'s own embellishment, but the sentiment is eminently Sallustian (no doubt the *neoi* are not just any young men, but *nobiles*). For the biographer Sertorius' administrative talent, his ability to organize and improvise, are important: such qualities would be essential for success in Spain (6.7–9; 13.7–10; 14.1; 21.4–9).

4.3

εἰς ἀξίωμα προεληλυθὼς ἡγεμόνος: cf. Sall. *Hist.* 1.88, ... *multaque tum ductu eius peracta.* Ἡγεμών in P. may correspond to Latin *dux* but has a wider range. Occasionally it designates a commanding general (7.1) or fellow generals of the same social standing, serving with rather than under a supreme commander (e.g., *Cat. Min.* 54.7; *Brut.* 34.2; perhaps also *Sert.* 19.1). Usually the term refers to senior but still subordinate officers (e.g., *Aem.* 17.12; *Sert.* 12.4; *Marc.* 19.1; *Mar.* 16.3; *Sulla* 23.2); sometimes it seems to comprise everyone between commander in chief and common soldiers (*Aem.* 20.9; *Brut.* 5.1, 41.4). In our case P.'s choice of word was probably influenced by Sallust's *ductu eius*: which is equally vague, though it might just hint at an independent command or assignment (if *Hist.* 2.98.2—Pompey's *ductu meo*—could be pressed). An ex-Quaestor, Sertorius could have been appointed as someone's Legate, but service as a Prefect or, again, Military Tribune cannot be ruled out. Since Gaul saw no fighting during the Social War, Sertorius probably moved to the Italian theater soon after the expiration of his quaestorship, in the spring of 90.

Sertorius in the Social War

Schulten (32) suggested that during the Social War Sertorius fought under T. Didius in the South (cf. Cic. *Font.* 43; Ovid *Fasti* 6.567–68; Vell. 2.16.2; Appian 40.179); both Katz ("Notes" 57, while stressing our ignorance) and Rijkhoek (103–4) favor that view. Unfortunately, its underlying assumption that Sertorius was an old family client of the Didii and hence, by extension, a follower of the Metellan *factio* (most extensively argued by Rijkhoek, 34–36) becomes groundless—though, of course, not demonstrably wrong—once it is realized that Sertorius had been elected to the military tribunate of 98, not appointed by Didius (above, 3.5n.).

Spann (22) argued for a command first under Q. Servilius Caepio (*pr.* by 91; cf. Livy *Per.* 73; Appian 40.179) and Marius in 90; then, in 89, successively under the Consuls L. Porcius Cato and Cn. Pompeius Strabo, all in central and northern Italy (for sources, see Broughton, *MRR* 2:32). There is indeed reason to believe that Sertorius served under Strabo in 89. Strabo's general staff, as of 17 November 89, is known almost in full from the famous bronze tablet discovered in 1908/10 (*Decretum Cn. Pompei Strabonis de civitate equitibus Hispanis danda in castris apud Asculum a. d. XIV k. Dec.*, *CIL* VI 37045 = I² 709; Cichorius, "Offizierskorps" 131; Criniti, *L'epigrafe* 16–26). Three of the men listed there are later found as officers under Sertorius in Spain: Q. Hirtuleius (*RE* 4) L. f., the brother of Sertorius' principal lieutenant, L. Hirtuleius (see 12.4n.; Cichorius 167, no. 34); L. Insteius (*RE* 2), presumably a brother of the *praefectus equitum* C. Insteius (*RE* 1; cf. Livy 91 fr. 22.14, 75 W-M; Cichorius 167, no. 40); and C. Tarquitius (*RE* 8) L. f., commander of a cavalry brigade in the battle of Lauro (see 18.9–10: Battle of Lauro; 26.6n.; Cichorius 167, no. 37). The presence of three later *Sertoriani* on Strabo's staff is likely to be more than a mere coincidence; already Cichorius (168) and Schulten (37) assumed that these went over to Sertorius during the siege of Rome in 87. We may still be able to pinpoint the occasion.

In the *Pompey* (3.1–5) P. tells the story of L. Terentius, a *contubernalis* in Pompeius Strabo's army at the time of the siege, who along with others was "bribed" by Cinna to assassinate the Proconsul along with his son, the later Pompeius Magnus, and bring the entire army over to the Marian side. The attempt misfired, and in the end only some eight hundred men changed sides. Two years before that incident, one L. Terentius (*RE* 24) A. f. is found as a member of Pompeius' *consilium* at Asculum in 89 (Cichorius 160–61, no. 26); and the basic veracity of P.'s story cannot be doubted. Now we know that Pompeius' army was encamped near the Porta Collina (Appian 67.304), the main northern gate of Rome, and that of the four Cinno-Marian army corps, only the one commanded by Sertorius was positioned on the east bank of the Tiber and to the north of the City, thus facing Pompeius (Appian 67.307; cf. Bennett, *Cinna* 13). Hence even if some of them eventually joined one of the other Marian leaders, the eight hundred defectors naturally would first have gone to the camp of Sertorius. No doubt the later *Sertoriani* (and Terentius, who seems to have survived his failed coup) were among them. Sertorius' camp would also have functioned as a base for the various emissaries conducting negotiations between Cinna and Pompeius Strabo (Gran. Lic. 35.16, 33 Cr).

Perhaps those pieces make a picture. The choice of Sertorius rather than Cinna as the commander of the corps facing Pompeius, despite Cinna's willingness to negotiate, makes eminent sense if of the two it was Sertorius who was thought to have a better chance at effecting a change of allegiance in Strabo or, failing such, of bringing over his army or at least creating internal trouble by corrupting officers and men. Some money may have been involved, as P. alleges, but the major motivation to switch sides would have come, as always in Rome's civil wars, from personal influence and connections. If a rather junior player such as Sertorius could be expected to deal with Pompeius Strabo in the fashion outlined, the most likely explanation would seem that he was well and recently acquainted with his staff and soldiers. Only the Social War could have given him that opportunity.

4.3–4

χειρὸς ἀποδεικνύμενος ἔργα θαυμαστὰ . . . θεατάς: cf. Sall. *Hist.* 1.88 = Gell. 2.27.2, *multaque tum ductu eius peracta prima per ignobilitatem, deinde per invidiam scriptorum incelebrata sunt: quae vivos facie sua ostentabat aliquot adversis cicatricibus et effosso oculo. neque illis anxius, quin ille dehonestamento corporis maxime laetabatur, quia reliqua gloriosius retinebat.* P. here so closely follows Sallust that one is tempted, with L. D. Reynolds's new Oxford Classical Text (1991), to adopt Linker's emendation *multaque tum ductu eius ⟨manu⟩que peracta* rather than Maurenbrecher's deletion *eius[que]*. (Hertz's ⟨*iussu*⟩*que*, followed by P. K. Marshall in his Oxford Classical Text [1990] of Gellius, is no improvement.)

4.4

στρεπτὰ καὶ δόρατα καὶ στεφάνους: a detail not found in the *Histories* fragment. P. was perfectly capable of adding it on his own, but Caviglia (156–57) argues that it goes back to Sallust all the same. In the *Bellum Iugurthinum* (85.29–30), the historian has Marius strike a very similar note: *Non possum fidei causa imagines neque triumphos aut consulatus maiorum meorum ostentare, at, si res postulet, <u>hastas, vexillum, phaleras</u>, alia militaria dona, praeterea cicatrices adverso corpore. hae sunt meae imagines, haec nobilitas, non hereditate relicta, ut illa illis, sed quae ego meis plurimis laboribus et periculis quaesivi.* P. knew that passage (*Mar.* 9.2), and *hastas vexillum phaleras* may have suggested the tricolon στρεπτὰ καὶ δόρατα καὶ στεφάνους, the last item perhaps substituting for *vexillum*, a term for which the Greeks had no real equivalent, as Caviglia points out. Στρεπτά, though, properly are *torques* (necklaces) rather than *phalerae* (disks), and P. may have confused the two (Scardigli, "Vita").

4.5

Cf. Sall. *Hist.* 1.89, *et ei voce magna vehementer gratulabantur.*

4.6

δημαρχίαν μέντοι μετιών: Sertorius' candidacy is usually dated to 88, for the tribunate of 87 (Schulten 32; Scardigli, "Problemi" 229–37; Sumner, *Orators* 108). Spann (162–64) made an attractive case for dating it to 89, taking P.'s ἐπεὶ δὲ in 4.7 as indicating that Sulla's March on Rome took place after Sertorius' *repulsa,* and arguing that the tribunician elections in 88 were probably held after the March on Rome (cf. Scardigli, "Problemi" 235–36). Too much should not be made of ἐπεὶ δέ, however; P. at that point is not providing a narrative but a compressed list of events or, better, circumstances and causes that cumulatively result in Sertorius' decision to join Cinna. At least in part, Spann's other arguments can also be met: see Katz, "Notes" 58–62. Without knowing more about the circumstances, both years must remain a possibility. P. was not concerned with the date. The failure at the polls, in stark contrast (μέντοι) to the hero's popularity with the urban crowds, marks the end of the early period of his life, the beginning of his political career and education, and his first bout with unkind fate.

Senatorial rank is attested for Sertorius by Cicero *Brut.* 180 and Appian 65.295, the latter with reference to 87 B.C. Evidently Sertorius was enrolled in the Senate by the Censors of 89.

Σύλλα καταστασιάσαντος αὐτόν: In P. καταστασιάζω denotes successful personal political agitation against an opponent (e.g., *Them.* 5.7, 11.1; *Cic.* 45.4; *Cat. Min.* 29.5; *Dion* 37.6; *Brut.* 22.3); the emphasis is less on the circumstances than on the result: severe damage or defeat (e.g., *Per.* 9.5; *Phil.* 13.8, 15.11), sometimes exile (*Caes.* 14.17). Only once (*Mar.* 28.7) is actual violence involved. (See also Stadter, *Pericles* 117–18.) Perrin's translation "Sulla formed a party against him" is far off the mark and should never have misled Spann (24) into being "certain that [P.] refers to the political juggernaut represented by the Metellan *factio."*

What caused Sulla's enmity is unknown, and probably beyond recovery. Katz, "Studies" 511–12 and "Notes" 61–62, suggested "personal incompatibility"—the haughty Patrician versus the New Man—combined with an unusual degree of alienation, on the part of Sertorius, by Sulla's March on Rome, and aggravated by the death in 89 of T. Didius (see 3.5n.), a staunch supporter of the *factio* and, in Katz's view, Sertorius' most important backer since the early 90s. Spann (24–25) thought of a personal quarrel, triggered perhaps by professional envy when both Sulla and Sertorius served under Marius in Gaul in 104–103; on the political side, he adduced Sertorius' connection with the Servilii Caepiones: once at the center of the Metellan *factio,* by 92 the younger Caepio (see Sumner, *Orators* 117) had broken with the *boni* and allied himself with Marius. Rijkhoek (120–23), like Katz viewing Sertorius as associated with the *factio*, entertains the possibility that he supported the abortive consular candidacy of C. Iulius Caesar Strabo (in 89 for 88). Strabo's attempt has been seen, with some plausibility, as having the backing of part of the *factio* and being directed against Sulla's candidacy (so

Katz, *RhM* 120 [1977] 45–63; Keaveney, *Latomus* 38 [1979] 451–60). Caesar's bid was derailed by the Tribune P. Sulpicius, then still closely tied to Sulla and the bulk of the *boni* (Badian, *FC* 230–31); but if Sertorius was thought to favor Strabo, opposition from Sulla at the time of the tribunician elections—probably late in 89, due to the war, but earlier than the consular ones—would be natural. (By implication, Rijkhoek's thesis places the *repulsa* in 89.) All three scholars deny, rightly, a major role of Sertorius in the subsequent activities of Marius and Sulpicius in 88: otherwise he would surely have been among those outlawed by Sulla. P. represents Sertorius' decision to side with Cinna in 87 as the result of deliberation and a careful weighing of the political situation (4.7), and later indicates (5.1–6.1) that his relations with Marius, both father and son, were strained, at least in 87 and 83/2. On the other hand, in 4.7 P. implicitly seems to consider Sertorius among Marius' friends, and there is evidence, admittedly tenuous, that points to Marian associations of his at the time of the Social War (see above, 4.3: Sertorius in the Social War). Possibly Sertorius had ties to both sides of the power struggle. If there were more solid grounds (above, 4.3) for assuming an association with the Metellan *factio*, Rijkhoek's suggestion would be appealing; as it stands, the Caepionic-Marian angle favored by Spann has at least as good a claim. Perhaps in the heated political atmosphere of late 89 or 88, his connections with Marius, no matter how weak, were enough to prompt Sulla's opposition (an explanation entertained by Spann).

διὸ καὶ δοκεῖ γενέσθαι μισοσύλλας: For the biographer, this is a matter of interpretation (δοκεῖ) and does not indicate surprise at Sulla's opposition on Sertorius' part (as Spann 25 believes). P. has a habit of ascribing the cause of his heroes' political rivalries and enmities to a single event or situation of a personal nature early in their career: see, e.g., Themistokles and Aristeides (*Them.* 3.2; *Arist.* 2.3), Lucullus and Pompeius (*Luc.* 4.5), Sulla and Caesar (*Caes.* 1.2), Marius and Sulla (*Mar.* 10.7–9; cf. *Sulla* 3.8–9).

4.6–9: Tribune of the Plebs?

P.'s report (4.6) of the *repulsa* suffered in 89 or 88 when running for the tribunate is the last notice, in any source, with explicit regard to Sertorius' *cursus honorum*. Spann (33) recently revived Bennett's suggestion (*Cinna* 65 n. 18) that he eventually became Tribune of the Plebs in 86. There is no evidence for that, nor does it seem likely on circumstantial grounds. In 88 or 87, a tribunate would have given Sertorius the opportunity to prove himself politically, preferably by pursuing the interests of influential groups or ambitious men of the Senate, and thus to accumulate political and personal credit for future advancement. By the end of 87, during and after the siege of Rome, he had proved himself both capable and reliable, and his massacre of the slave bands must have done more for his popularity than any tribunate could do. Yet while we have no reason to assume that he was Tribune in 86, there is just enough circumstantial evidence to consider a tribunate in 87. Sertorius' activity in the latter year raises four major questions.

(a) If merely a *privatus*, why was it so important for him to choose between Cinna and Octavius early in 87, before the onset of civil strife (below, 4.7)? The Tribunes of that year were evidently involved in the political debates from the beginning (as follows from Appian 64.290).

(b) In what capacity was Sertorius present with Cinna on the *dies Octavianus* (below, 4.8n.)? A majority of Tribunes vetoed Cinna's bill (Appian 64.290), but one should think those who supported it were likewise at hand.

(c) Who were the six Tribunes that fled the City along with Cinna? (Although the numeral is corrupt in both Livy *Per.* 79 and Gran. Lic. 35.2 Cr, the restoration *sex* is virtually certain.) Scholars rightly think that Appian 65.295 refers to the same occasion (Gabba, *App BC 1* 183–84) when he names "the other [*sic*] Gaius Marius" (i.e., M. Marius Gratidianus), C. Milonius, and Sertorius as fleeing from Rome to Cinna (cf. 4.8n.). Of the three, Gratidianus almost certainly was Tribune in that year (*Comm. Bern. in Lucan.* 2.173 = p. 62 Usener; a tribunate in 86, entertained by Broughton, *MRR* 3:140, is quite hypothetical). The same is generally thought of Milonius (*MRR* 2:47; Gabba, *App BC 1* 184; Katz, "Studies" 502 n. 18, has doubts). Why not Sertorius, too? If his *repulsa* falls in 89—in itself as likely as 88 (see above, 4.6n.)—there is no a priori obstacle to his succeeding on a second attempt, in 88 for 87.

(d) How was it that Sertorius, supposedly a *privatus* and very junior Senator of quaestorian rank, ended up being one of the four major commanders in the siege of Rome (below, 5.5n.)? His association with Cinna was rather recent, and his political connections to Marius were tenuous at best; moreover, he had opposed joining forces with Marius, and Cinna had overruled him. His military expertise may be cited, but the point ought not to be pressed. Nothing suggests that Carbo owed his command to martial prowess: he was a *praetorius* (possibly with *imperium*: below, 6.1n.) and next to Cinna and Marius clearly the senior Senator among the group. Neither Milonius nor Gratidianus are known as *viri militares*, yet both held important commands during the siege (Gran. Lic. 35.11, 19 Cr on Milonius, and 35.28 with Appian 67.308 on Gratidianus; cf. *MRR* 2:50). As Tribunes of the Plebs, they were probably the highest-ranking incumbent magistrates next to Cinna; no Praetors or Aediles of 87 are known to have joined his forces. (M. Iunius Brutus *pr.* 88 had returned from exile in Spain [Gran. Lic. 35.7 Cr], but his whereabouts and activities thereafter are unknown.)

Undeniably, each of those points may be explained individually without resorting to a reconstruction that would make Sertorius a Tribune in 87. Collectively, however, they point in that direction. Arguments to the contrary can be met as follows.

(e) "The *repulsa* more likely belongs in 88, as Sertorius, fresh from the Social War, would not have had time to pursue a candidacy in 89." That point needs to be raised; but surely we must not assume that all (or even most) of the successful candidates in 89 had spent the better part of the year safely in Rome, nurturing their political careers while others fought. The war certainly did nothing to impede Sulla's candidacy, even though hostilities had not yet fully ceased in his area of command, southern Italy. In the current debate the case for either year, 89 as well as 88, remains replete with unverifiable assumptions and conjectures (cf. above, 4.6n.). No further argumentation can be based on the presumed year of Sertorius' failed candidacy.

(f) "Though the *repulsa* may be dated to 89, it is inconceivable that Sertorius could have secured his election in 88." If the tribunician elections in 88 were held before Sulla's March on Rome (as argued, e.g., by Gabba, *App BC 1* 181) there is no reason to insist that Sertorius could not possibly have succeeded in a repeat attempt; after all, Sulla's previous opposition, whatever form it had taken, did not yet carry the force of divine prohibition. If the elections took place after the coup (the view of, e.g., Scardigli, "Problemi" 235–36; Katz, "Studies" 498–513), it is manifest that a considerable number of eventual supporters of Cinna were successful. P. explicitly testifies to a public backlash against Sulla at the polls (*Sulla* 10.4–8), and while his examples are not specifically concerned with the tribunician elections, the partisan breakdown of the college of 87 is assurance enough that they constituted no exception. One of the Tribunes elected, M. Vergilius (*sive* Verginius), promptly launched legal proceedings against Sulla. Sertorius would not look out of place in that company.

(g) "If Sertorius had been successful in a second attempt, P. would have told us." P.'s silence certainly might be considered odd, but it is hardly inexplicable. As a general rule, attempts to guess what he would have mentioned had it happened are fraught with danger; any such divination must proceed not from our historical curiosity but from P.'s biographical purpose. Perhaps the most celebrated *repulsa* in the lives, that of Sulla (5.1–5), is instructive. The causes of his defeat are set out at length, and P. emphasizes the ease with which Sulla secured the praetorship in the following year, after the requisite bribes. But note the context: the splendid and unencumbered progress of Sulla the Fortunate from Quaestor to Consul is the theme of chapters 3–6. Not so in the *Sertorius*. The *repulsa* of 4.6 marks his first stroke of undeserved bad luck, his first encounter with an unjust fate. Throughout 4.6–6.4 his career and doings in the civil war years 87–82 are deliberately obscured and minimized, his relations with the Cinno-Marian leaders depicted as strained and distant. Altogether P. creates the impression that contemporaries treated Sertorius' qualities with neglect and contempt during that period. Only the command in Spain was to permit the hero, at last, to display his excellence to the fullest. P.'s narrative purpose entirely explains why he chose not to mention Sertorius' praetorship, attained in those very years (below, 6.1–4: Sertorius' Praetorship). It would likewise explain his passing over a successful repeat candidacy for the tribunate in 88.

On balance, I am inclined to think that Sertorius indeed was Tribune of the Plebs in 87, perhaps styling himself *tribunus plebis pro praetore* during the siege, in the manner of M. Antonius (in 49; Cic. *Att.* 10.8A). By implication that would date his *repulsa* to 89, not 88. The conjectural nature of this reconstruction, however, cannot be stressed enough.

4.7

ἐπεὶ δὲ Μάριος μὲν . . . ἔφευγε, Σύλλας δὲ . . . ἀπῆρε: In two sentences P. covers a period of roughly half a year, from Sulla's coup in the summer or early fall of 88 to his departure from Italy in the spring of 87. All detail is suppressed; even a momentous event such as a Consul of the Roman People leading his army against the State in order to settle a political dispute colored by personal rivalry is alluded to only in the vaguest terms. P. reported those events at length elsewhere (*Mar.* 35; *Sulla* 8–9), though a horror of redundancy did not cause their omission here. Sertorius was not directly involved (if involved at all), and while ultimately of importance for his career, the coup of 88 in P.'s eyes produced no actions suitable to his portrait of the hero.

Μάριος . . . ἔφευγε: After Sulla's troops occupied the City a terrified Senate declared Marius, Sulpicius, and ten others *hostes publici* (Livy *Per.* 77; Val. Max. 3.8.5; Plut. *Sulla* 10.1–2; Appian 60.271), a vote later confirmed by the Tribal Assembly (Vell. 2.19.1; Plut. *Mar.* 43.3–4): see Pais 67–72, and Bauman, *Athenaeum* 51 (1973) 270–93. Marius' adventurous escape to Africa is narrated at length in *Mar.* 35.8–40.12 and Appian 61.272–62.280.

Mithradates VI Eupator Dionysos (Mithridates 12): 132–63 B.C.; King of Pontos ca. 120–63. The name is Mithridates in the literary sources, but Mithradates (Iran. *Mithra-data*, "Mithras-given") in the royal coins and inscriptions. The more authoritative form is adopted herein. Reinach's *Mithradates Eupator* remains the standard study of the reign; an important recent contribution is McGing's *Foreign Policy of Mithridates VI*. The immediate cause of the First Mithradatic War (89–85 B.C.) was the King's invasion of Bithynia in 89, triggered by a Roman-instigated Bithynian attack on his realm, and followed in the spring of 88 by his conquest of the Roman province of Asia. A massacre of tens of thousands of Roman and Italic residents accompanied that liberation (Appian *Mithr.* 11–23; cf. Plut. *Sulla* 24.7; Dio fr. 101.1). On the outbreak of the war and the role of certain Roman senators in provoking it see Badian, *AJAH* 1 (1976); Glew, *Athenaeum* 55 (1977); and McGing, *Foreign Policy* 78–88.

Cn. Octavius (20) Cn. (?) f.: ca. 130–87 B.C.; Consul in 87. Commonly thought to be a son of Gnaeus *cos.* 128, and a brother of Lucius *cos.* 75; M. Octavius (father of Gnaeus *cos.* 76), the famous Tribune and opponent of Tiberius Gracchus in 133, would have been his uncle: see Sumner's stemma, *Orators* 115. Another brother, Marcus, as Tribune in an undetermined year between 99 and 87, carried a *lex frumentaria* limiting the grain dole established by Gaius Gracchus (Cic. *Off.* 2.72; cf. Sumner, 115). However, that genealogy rests on the identification of the Consul of 87 with the στρατηγὸς

Cn. Octavius Cn. f. of *IDélos* IV 1:1782. Badian recently has advanced new arguments in favor of attributing that inscription to the Consul of 128 instead ("Consuls" 405–7; cf. "Governors" 18 n. 162 = *Studies* 104 n. 168), and would identify the Consul of 87, rather than Octavius Ruso *q.* 105, with the Cn. Octavius Q. f., second Legate of Pompeius Strabo at Asculum; the Consul of 87 thus would have no known ties to the family so active in optimate politics. While his family and political antecedents must remain in question (he lost a bid for the aedileship: Cic. *Planc.* 51), his stance in 87 leaves no doubt that he belonged to the more extreme elements among the optimates.

L. Cornelius (106) **Cinna**: Consul 87–84 B.C.; presumably a son of the Consul of 127. He "bursts onto the stage of Roman history with no prior warning from our sources" (Gruen, *Criminal Courts* 229): a successful command as a praetorian Legate in the Social War (Cic. *Font.* 43) is all we know about his early career. He is usually thought to have served under Pompeius Strabo (Bennett, *Cinna* 1; *MRR* 2:36), but given his attested fighting against the Marsi in 89 (Livy *Per.* 76), he probably was a Legate of the other Consul, L. Porcius Cato, killed in battle against that same enemy (Cichorius, "Offizierskorps" 140–41; cf. Livy *Per.* 75; Appian 50.217). Cato's army apparently contained plenty of Marian sympathizers (Oros. 5.18.24; cf. Dio fr. 100), which does not prove that Cinna was one of them. But his election in 88 went much against Sulla's wishes, and P. labels him "a man from the opposite faction" (ἀπὸ τῆς ἐναντίας στάσεως, *Sulla* 10.6): not so much, it seems, an old ally of Marius as the newly emerging leader of those who disapproved of Sulla's coup (cf. Katz, "Studies" 523, 534–38).

νεωτερίζων ... στάσιν: Cinna's bill, if passed, would have distributed the new citizens enfranchised under the *lex Iulia* of 90 and the *lex Plautia Papiria* of 89 among all thirty-five Tribes, rather than limiting them to eight as prescribed by (apparently) the *lex Iulia*. An identical measure had been part of the program of P. Sulpicius in 88 (Cic. *Phil.* 8.6; Livy *Per.* 77; Vell. 2.20.2; Appian 55.242, 64.287; Exuper. 4.2–8 = 23–24 Z), and a recall of Marius and other exiles may have been planned (Appian 64.287, with Gabba's note; cf. Auct. *De vir. ill.* 69.2). P. shows no interest in the substance of Cinna's policy; his account of Sulpicius' legislation is similarly vague (*Mar.* 34.1, 35.1–3), not to say distorted (*Sulla* 8.1–5). Only measures directly affecting the hero (the Mithradatic command in the case of Marius and Sulla) or apt to characterize some other figure (Sulpicius' "selling" Roman citizenship, or hypocritically limiting the amount of debts a Senator could have) are of concern to him.

τὸν Ὀκτάβιον ὁρῶν αὐτὸν μὲν ἀμβλύτερον ὄντα: cf. Dio fr. 102.5, Ὀκτάουιος φύσει βραδὺς ἦν πρὸς τὰ πολιτικά.

τοῖς δὲ Μαρίου φίλοις ἀπιστοῦντα: The reasoning is presented as that of Sertorius himself (ὁρῶν). In view of the subsequent attempts to dissociate him from the actions of Marius father and son (5.1–6.1), P.'s explanation here of the hero's choice may not be his own but that of his source, somewhat carelessly incorporated. If Sertorius did not consider himself a friend of Marius at this time, his ties to such apparently were close enough to guide his decision.

4.8

γενομένης δὲ ... μάχης μεγάλης: Appian 63.289–92 gives the only detailed account. On voting day Cinna's supporters (mostly new citizens), armed with daggers, had succeeded in occupying the Forum; a large number of opponents, likewise armed, gathered at the house of Octavius. When the bill was vetoed, apparently by several Tribunes, the newly enfranchised started a riot which rapidly turned against the Tribunes opposed. On learning about those developments, Octavius, with a densely packed throng of followers, marched down the Sacra Via into the east end of the Forum and quickly cleared the area around the temple of Castor and Pollux, where Cinna presumably had been holding the assembly. (On the *rostra* of the *aedes Castorum* and their use in legislative *comitia* see Taylor, *Roman Voting Assemblies* 25–28.) Apparently that was what Octavius had wanted to accomplish; but his men exceeded their orders and attacked the new citizens now crowded into the western part of the Forum. From the ensuing melee the *Octaviani* emerged victorious, pursuing the defeated into distant parts of the City.

οὐ πολλῷ τῶν μυρίων ἐλάττους ἀποβαλόντες: no doubt exaggerated. But the bloodshed was considerable: Cicero twice (*Cat.* 3.24; *Sest.* 77) makes reference to the battle in the Forum as having claimed more lives than any other riot within memory. He probably had witnessed it himself.

Κίννας δὲ καὶ Σερτώριος ... ἔφυγον: Octavius' men did not assault Cinna personally during the fight in the Forum: at least that appears to be the meaning of Appian's τὸν Κίνναν ἐκτρεπόμενος (64.292; cf. Gabba' comments). But after attempts to rally his supporters had failed, the Consul, it seems, was forcibly driven out of town: *Cn. Octavius consul armis expulit ex urbe conlegam*, says Cicero (*Cat.* 3.24)—not a pro-Cinnan source, and surely preferable to Appian's palliating version (65.293–94) that has Cinna leave on his own accord. P. implies that Sertorius had been present with Cinna on the day of the massacre; whether they left the City together is less certain. Appian in his detailed narrative may be correct in stating that Sertorius and other Senators did not join up with Cinna until some time later, when the Consul was already gathering financial and military support from the newly enfranchised towns of Latium and southern Italy (65.294–95). Hence it may have been only after the Senate backed Octavius in depriving Cinna of his consulship and replacing him with L. Cornelius Merula, the Flamen Dialis (65.296; cf. Vell. 2.20.3; Plut. *Mar.* 41.2), that Cinna's closest adherents, including Sertorius, decided their position in Rome had become untenable. For a fuller discussion see Katz, "Studies" 500–504, and *RhM* 122 (1979) 162–66.

4.9

τῶν ... στρατοπέδων ... τὰ πλεῖστα πειθοῖ: The only army won over by Cinna in this fashion was the one at Nola in Campania under Ap. Claudius Pulcher, *cos.* 79 (Livy *Per.* 79; Vell. 2.20.4; Appian 65.298–66.301).

ταχὺ κατέστησαν ἀξιόμαχοι: vast numbers of Italians, newly enfranchised, were ready and willing to serve in Cinna's army; Velleius' figure (2.20.4) of more than three hundred cohorts seems not so exaggerated if it is understood that most of these were small local units of volunteers. Italian towns provided supplies and funds, and more Romans of standing left the City to join Cinna, thus adding respect and political support (Appian 66.302).

τοῖς περὶ τὸν 'Οκτάβιον: "Octavius and his forces," though perhaps simply "Octavius." For this use of οἱ περί with the accusative of a proper name, see K-G 1:269–71; LSJ s.v. περί, C.2; and especially Radt, *ZPE* 38 (1980). Cf. also below, 5.6n., 18.1, 27.1. Octavius had set about repairing the walls and readying the City for a siege (Appian 66.303); he also levied troops, presumably in Rome and the vicinity, and sent as far as Cisalpine Gaul for additional forces, but he clearly did not feel strong enough to take the offensive against Cinna. Pompeius Strabo, Proconsul in Picenum, was ordered back to Rome with his army; he complied and took up a position near the Porta Collina. After arriving at Rome, Cinna's forces initially seem to have been encamped not far from Strabo's (Appian 66.303–67.304).

5

As in the previous chapter, P. studiously avoids all but the most rudimentary narrative of the historical context; the focus is exclusively on Sertorius. Yet even so he is remarkably selective: we are given not a hint of the considerable military role played by the hero in the siege of 87. Similarly, we learn nothing about his career under the Cinnan regime between 86 and 83, and his actions in the Civil War of 83/2 are referred to only in the vaguest manner (6.1–3). All of that was amply documented, as the other sources make clear; Sallust himself gave a fairly detailed account of the period from 87 to 82, not omitting Sertorius: e.g., *Hist.* 1.91–92; Exuper. 7.4–8.11 = 43–50 Z. (The matter has been abundantly demonstrated: see La Penna, "*Historiae*" 207–211, 220–25; "Ricostruzione" 11–12; Rawson, *CQ* 37 [1987] 163–80; and cf. Konrad, *AHB* 2 [1988] 12–15.) The reason for P.'s reticence becomes evident once we look at what he does tell us. As much as possible, the hero is to be isolated from the unsavory company of the vengeful Marius and the unedifying business of civil war. That view of Sertorius as a rare example of moderation in the internecine strife of the 80s goes back to Sallust: *inter arma civilia aequi bonique famas petit* (1.90; it is hard to imagine anyone but Sertorius as the subject). The other sources show no such distinction between Sertorius and the other Cinno-Marian leaders; clearly P. here based his account on the *Histories* (cf. La Penna, "*Historiae*" 220–25; Scardigli, "Considerazioni" 43–46).

5.1–5: Cinna's Invitation to Marius

Katz ("Siege" 335 n. 28 and "Notes" 62) voiced doubts about the historicity of the entire story (although he would allow for a kernel of truth behind it: "Studies" 511 n. 45). Scardigli, "Considerazioni" 38, 44–45, 53–54, strongly argued that the passage was mostly Plutarchean embellishment of a few bare facts known to the author. Yet it may provide the key for solving an apparent contradiction in our sources. The majority of these state or imply that Cinna "recalled" Marius from exile: Vell. 2.20.5, *C. Marium . . . de exilio revocavit*; Livy Per. 79, *arcessito C. Mario ex Africa*; Auct. De vir. ill. 67.6, *mox Cinnana dominatione revocatus*; Schol. Gronov. 286.8 St, *misit ad Marium in Africa*. Against this, P. describes Marius as leaving Africa on his own initiative (*Mar.* 41.3–4) and offering his support to Cinna (41.5–6, τούτῳ [sc. Κίννᾳ] προσνέμειν ἑαυτὸν ἔγνω . . . [6] ἔπεμψεν οὖν ἐπαγγελλόμενος ὡς ὑπάτῳ πάντα ποιήσειν τὰ προστασσόμενα). So does Appian (ἐς Κίνναν διῆλθεν ἀσμένως αὐτὸν ἐπὶ κοινωνίᾳ τῶν παρόντων δεχόμενον, 67.306). In the *Sertorius*, P. seems to have it both ways. At 5.1, Marius clearly is offering his support on his own initiative, but at 5.3, Cinna claims to have invited him; again at 5.5, Marius is sent for (οὕτως μεταπέμπεται τὸν Μάριον Κίννας), rather than received: strange, if Marius had already been invited by Cinna at an earlier point. Thus the sources that report Marius' entrance in the civil war in some detail, P. and Appian, ascribe the initiative to him; those dealing with the matter in only a summary fashion, including the entire Livian tradition, ascribe it to Cinna. Naturally, the discrepancy may simply be due to divergent traditions. But a closer look at the story suggests otherwise.

Marius offers his support, and all are in favor of it, except Sertorius (5.1). "All" means that Cinna submitted the matter to his *consilium*—good Roman practice, it may be noted, and unlikely to be invented by P. Sertorius' objections carry weight, as Cinna is compelled to admit (5.3). Only then the Consul informs his staff that he himself had asked Marius to join them (αὐτὸς . . . κεκληκώς): information obviously contrary to what his officers had known hitherto (5.4, ἀλλ' ἐγὼ μὲν αὐτὸν ἀφ' ἑαυτοῦ Μάριον ἥκειν . . . ἐσκόπουν). Why should Cinna have kept such an invitation a secret until then? If in fact he had not issued an invitation previously, the story makes perfect sense. When Marius offered himself and his sizable force, Cinna was determined to accept. Running into opposition, he resorted to "prior invitation," and Sertorius was in no position to call the Consul's bluff. Once Cinna had "revealed" the facts of the matter, further debate would indeed have been pointless. That Cinna's lie should become a fact in the much abbreviated accounts of Velleius and Livy's epitomizers (who tend to emphasize Cinna's role in the civil war of 87, rather than Marius') need not surprise. As told by P., the story is not at all implausible. Which is not to say that he did not embellish what he found in Sallust: surely a much briefer account, without direct discourse.

P.'s elaborate story sets the stage for his subsequent attempt at distancing the hero from the atrocities of civil war, in particular those committed by Marius (5.6–7). It illustrates Sertorius' persuasive powers—invented or not, the logic of the situation implies that Cinna's *consilium* was on the verge of being swayed by his arguments. In casting Sertorius in the role of the wise counselor whose advice is spurned, with dire consequences, the incident also foreshadows the disastrous events of 83, when those ignoring his warnings will find themselves the victims of their refusal to listen (6.1–3). P.'s fascination with the *topos* of the unheeded warner puts Sertorius in interesting company: e.g., Fabius Maximus (9–10), Alkibiades (36.6–37.1), Cato the Younger (58.7–13), and Brutus (22.4–6).

5.1

Μαρίου δὲ καταπλεύσαντος ἐκ Λιβύης: Marius had not been well received by the governor of Africa and spent most of his exile on the island of Cercina (now Kerkennah), just north of the Syrtis Minor (*Mar.* 40). Upon learning of the outbreak of civil war in Italy in 87, he sailed with a force of about 1,000 (including a number of African horsemen) to Etruria, where he landed at Telamon. Within a short time, he recruited an army of some 6,000 men, mostly from Etrurian peasants, shepherds, and freed slaves, and commanded a fleet of forty ships (*Mar.* 41.1–4; Appian 67.305–6; Gran. Lic. 35.6–8 Cr; Flor. 2.9.11; Auct. *De vir. ill.* 67.6). For a detailed account see Carney, *Marius* 57–62 and *G&R* 8 (1961).

προστιθέντος ἑαυτόν: see above, 5.1–5: Cinna's Invitation.

ὡς ἰδιώτην: Marius was *privatus* in 87, since the *leges Sulpiciae*, one of which gave Marius *imperium* (no doubt *pro consule*) for the war against Mithradates, had been abrogated by Sulla: Appian 59.268; cf. Cic. *Phil.* 8.7. (Of course, even without abrogation Marius would have been *privatus cum imperio*, but P. is not thinking of that technicality.) Cinna recognized him as Proconsul and even sent him lictors; Marius declined both (*Mar.* 42.6) and later demanded formal legislation to recall him from exile (*Mar.* 43.3; cf. Vell. 2.21.6; Appian 70.323–24). His insistence on constitutional niceties is well pointed out by Carney, *Marius* 62 (with nn. 273–74).

ὑπάτῳ: While not contesting the legality of Sulla's *acta* that made him a *hostis publicus*, Marius pointedly ignored the Senate's having Cinna removed from office (cf. *Mar.* 41.6).

τοῖς μὲν ἄλλοις ἐδόκει δέχεσθαι: Authority and responsibility rested solely with the holder of *imperium*, but it was customary to decide all matters of importance *de consilii sententia* (Mommsen, *StR* 1³:307, 311).

εἴτε ... προερχόμενος: Sertorius' real grounds for opposing collaboration with Marius are beyond recovery. Of the explanations P. offers, the first at least is a reasonable conjecture: Sertorius was the only one of Cinna's followers who is known to have had significant military experience, and the arrival of Marius was bound to diminish his own importance. That sort of jealousy would not at all be un-Roman. As Scardigli, "Considerazioni" 45, has pointed out, P.'s Cinna is easily influenced (cf. 5.3, 6), and the motive ascribed to Sertorius fits that characteristic. But it throws a somewhat unflattering light on the hero's character. Whether P. found that explanation already in Sallust (not averse to critical remarks directed at individuals he generally favors) or thought of it himself, we cannot say; he certainly was not so protective of Sertorius as to ignore an obvious part of human nature. The second motive suggested by P. illustrates Sertorius' farsightedness and abhorrence of personal revenge in civil strife: he is dedicated to the common good alone. It may all be true, of course, but neither Sallust nor P. could have known it for a fact. The actual arguments put in Sertorius' mouth (5.2) ignore it altogether.

5.2

μικρὸν . . . κρατοῦσι: such was clearly not the case; on the contrary, the *Cinnani* had been making little headway until Marius effectively assumed control of operations (cf. below, 5.2–6: The Siege of Rome). *Pace* Katz, "Siege" 335 n. 28, this does not render P.'s story doubtful: misrepresentation and exaggeration are common elements of persuasion, easily added by the biographer to flesh out the facts.

δεξαμένων δὲ τὸν Μάριον . . . ἄπιστον: Whatever Sertorius' true motives, his reasoning as presented here addresses only the first of the concerns suggested in 5.1 (τὸν Κίνναν ἧττον οἰόμενος ἑαυτῷ προσέξειν ἀνδρὸς ἡγεμονικωτέρου παρόντος), suitably clad, of course, in an appeal to Cinna's and the other leaders' self-interest.

5.3

αὐτὸς . . . κεκληκώς: see above, 5.1–5: Cinna's Invitation.

5.5

μεταπέμπεται: a somewhat puzzling expression at this point, if Cinna had indeed sent an invitation to Marius earlier.

τριχῇ . . . τρεῖς: Livy *Per.* 79–80; Appian 67.307; Flor. 2.9.13; and Gran. Lic. 35.9 Cr all present Carbo (below, 6.1n.), in addition to Marius, Cinna, and Sertorius, as one of the principal commanders, but from Appian it is clear that Carbo's troops operated jointly with Cinna's, and no independent actions of Carbo are reported. As far as deployment during the siege of Rome is concerned, there were indeed only three corps (Bennett, *Cinna* 13): Marius, Cinna and Carbo, and Sertorius. Not that ἦρχον οἱ τρεῖς is the result of strategic insight: for the biographer, there was simply no reason to mention Carbo in this context.

5.5–6: The Siege of Rome

The fullest account of the civil war of 87 is Appian 66.303–70.324. Diodoros 38/39.1–3 and Granius Licinianus 35.1–50 Cr add important detail. For other sources see *MRR* 2:45–53. Bennett, *Cinna* 9–23; Gelzer, *APAW 1941* 14:17–20 = *Kleine Schriften* 2:121–25; Carney, *Marius* 61–63; Bulst, "Cinnanum Tempus" 307–18; and Katz, "Siege" 62–64, are the most important modern studies of the siege. Cf. also Gabba's commentary on Appian and Scardigli's on Granius. Only a brief summary of events can be given here.

After joining forces with Marius, the combined armies took up new positions to place the City under siege: Marius to the south, Cinna and Carbo on the west bank of the Tiber (probably in the *ager Vaticanus*: Bennett, *Cinna* 13). Sertorius remained in their original camp north of Rome, facing the army of Pompeius Strabo near the Porta Collina. Pompeius had been secretly negotiating with Cinna in the hope of securing a second consulship for 86; when the deal fell through—either upon Cinna's arrangement with Marius (Katz, "Siege" 331–32) or soon thereafter—he launched an attack on Sertorius which resulted in a draw (Gran. Lic. 35.16 Cr; Oros. 5.19.10–11). Whether the failed assassination of Pompeius (*Pomp.* 3) should be dated before or after that battle remains uncertain; though his move may well have been prompted by the attempt on his life. Meanwhile both Marius and Sertorius had bridged the Tiber and were preventing all food supplies from reaching the City by way of the river. Aided by treachery, Marius captured Ostia. But a subsequent general assault on the Ianiculum ended in defeat. Some of Sertorius' troops, though not Sertorius himself, took part in that battle (*Mar.* 42.1–4; Appian 67.307–68.312; Gran. Lic. 35.13–20 Cr). No further details of his involvement in the siege are known.

Having failed to capture the Ianiculum and breach the City's defenses (see Bennett, *Cinna* 18–19, on the battle's topographical significance), the Cinno-Marians decided to reduce Rome by starvation. With Ostia already taken, Marius now systematically attacked and captured the towns of Latium—Antium, Aricia, Lanuvium, and others—that served as outlying grain storage centers and had kept Rome supplied with provisions even after the Tiber communications had been severed (Appian 69.313–14). An epidemic disease claimed thousands of lives in the City and its defending armies, and the death of Pompeius Strabo removed the ablest (though not the most reliable) of their commanders. (No need here to decide whether Pompeius died struck by lightning, or of the plague, or both; for the latest—unsatisfactory—discussion of that old question see Watkins, *RhM* 131 [1988].) When Metellus Pius, recalled earlier from Samnium, prepared to engage the enemy his troops nearly fraternized, while Octavius' army demanded to be put under Metellus' command. The latter refused, but realizing that further military resistance had become hopeless he persuaded the Senate to open negotiations with Cinna, much against Octavius' wishes. Yet when Cinna insisted on being recognized as Consul, the Senate's emissaries were not prepared to do so (Diodor. 38/39.1; Plut. *Mar.* 42.5–6; Appian 69.315–17; Gran. Lic. 35.46–50 Cr). In the meantime, famine and despair caused widespread desertion both of soldiers and civilians. Metellus eventually took it upon himself to recognize Cinna as Consul; Octavius reacted with acrimonious reproaches, prompting Metellus to abandon the City and leave Italy. The Senate, seeing no alternative, resolved to resume negotiations, and Merula cooperated by abdicating his consulship. Cinna was formally reinstated, and an agreement to surrender the City was reached (Diodor. 38/39.2–3; Livy *Per.* 80; Plut. *Mar.* 42.6–43.2; Appian 69.317–70.323). Cinna refused to give a general guarantee that there would be no reprisals and further bloodshed, and only promised for his own person that he would not order anyone's death "willingly," i.e., without further provocation. He did, however, indicate that Octavius would be spared provided he kept out of public sight (Appian 70.320–22; cf. 71.326).

5.6

τῶν ... ἁπάσης: According to Diodor. 38/39.4, after the City surrendered, Cinna and Marius convened a meeting of their senior followers in which it was agreed to put to death the most prominent of their adversaries, ostensibly so that the new regime would not have to face an immediate challenge by men of *auctoritas*. A likely procedure: as was the case in the triumviral proscriptions forty-four years later, such a conference would ensure that close friends who happened to be one's allies' personal enemies would survive, or at least not be killed without a trade-off. The first victim was Octavius, who had not agreed to the surrender and continued with a pointed show of resistance by withdrawing to the Ianiculum with a few remaining troops (Appian 71.326, rightly emphasized by Bulst, 315): he was cut down by a squadron of Cinna's cavalry (cf. *Mar.* 42.7–9). P. Licinius Crassus *cos.* 97 had commanded part of the army defending Rome; he committed suicide while one of his sons was killed (Cic. *De orat.* 3.10; *Sest.* 48; Ascon. 23, 25 C; Liv. *Per.* 80). M. Antonius *cos.* 99, C. Caesar Strabo, and his brother, L. Caesar *cos.* 90, suffered death as disloyal former friends of Marius (Cic. *De orat.* 3.10; *Brut.* 307; Ascon. 25 C; Plut. *Mar.* 44.1–7; *Ant.* 1.1; Appian 72.332–35; see also Badian, "Caepio" 323, 332–42 = *Studies* 38, 47–57, and specifically on Antonius, *Chiron* 14 [1984] 121–26, 138–47). Against Q. Lutatius Catulus *cos.* 102 and L. Cornelius Merula, Flamen Dialis and Consul Suffect in 87, legal proceedings were launched; both ended by their own hand (Cic. *De orat.* 3.9; Diodor. 38/39.4.2–3; Plut. *Mar.* 44.8; Appian 74.341–42). All in all, the names of fourteen victims are known, and Bulst (314) persuasively argued that the total of politically motivated executions was probably not much higher. For detailed discussion of the killings see Bennett, *Cinna* 24–40; Carney, *Marius* 65–68; Keaveney, "Sullani" 114–17.

τῶν περὶ τὸν Κίνναν καὶ Μάριον: i.e., Cinna and Marius: see above, 4.9n. P. is decidedly more critical of Cinna here than in the *Marius*, where his share in the responsibility for the murders is alluded to rather obliquely (Κίννας . . . ἀμβλὺς ἦν καὶ μεστὸς ἤδη τοῦ φονεύειν, 43.7). But Sertorius' intervention with Cinna (λέγεται . . . τὸν Κίνναν ἐντυγχάνων ἰδίᾳ καὶ δεόμενος μετριώτερον ποιεῖν) would carry little significance were the Consul depicted as the relatively harmless bystander of the *Marius*.

Σερτώριος . . . κρατῶν: cf. Sall. *Hist*. 1.90, *inter arma civilia aequi bonique famas petit*. Sertorius' moderation need not be doubted. It is difficult to see upon whom he should have revenged himself; Sulla (the only *inimicus* we can surmise) was out of town. Yet Sertorius was undoubtedly present at the meeting of Cinno-Marian leaders that authorized the executions (Diodoros 38/39.4.1; cf. preceding notes). P.'s passing over the conference in silence may indicate that Sertorius, while not taking personal vengeance, supported the joint decision and choice of victims. To say he killed no one πρὸς ὀργὴν is not to say he killed no one at all: cf. below, 9.11n., 11.2n.

τῷ Μαρίῳ δυσχεραίνειν: The wholesale slaughter of private citizens and their families at the hands of armed bands of slaves (5.7) had certainly not been sanctioned at the leaders' meeting. After the ordeal of the siege, it must have wiped out whatever sympathies were left for the new regime. Sertorius might well be angry. But as 4.8 and 5.1–2 indicate, the ill feeling between him and Marius seems to date back long before the siege of Rome.

5.7: The Slave Bands Massacre

On this see especially Carney, *Marius* 63–66; Sartori, passim; Corbellini, *Aevum* 50 (1976) 154–56. The least problematic aspect of the event is Sertorius' part in it. Appian (74.343–44) and Orosius (5.19.24) attribute responsibility to Cinna, P. in the *Marius* (44.10) to Cinna and Sertorius, here to Sertorius alone. Sertorius was not powerful enough to take a measure of such magnitude without the Consul's permission, but the biographer here again is stressing what the hero did, without concern for the political powers behind it. (On his habit of assigning to the hero what was done in conjunction with others, see Introduction 2.5.) Bennett's conclusion (*Cinna* 30 n. 31) that "Cinna made the decision and Sertorius gave it effect" stands.

Less clear are the precise circumstances of the massacre and the identity and allegiance of the slaves. The sources (*Sert.* 5.7; *Mar.* 43.4–5, 44.10; Appian 74.343–44; Oros. 5.19.19, 24) agree that bands of fugitive slaves went on a killing and pillaging spree throughout the City; Appian and P. specify atrocities committed in particular against former masters. According to Appian, these slaves had left the City during the siege and joined Cinna in response to his edict (69.316) promising freedom to all slaves that went over to his side; Cinna ordered the massacre after repeatedly trying, without success, to stop the rampage. Marius is never mentioned in that context. According to Orosius, the slaves were brought into the City by Marius. In P. the rampage was the work of armed bands picked by Marius out of the mass of fugitives; they served as his bodyguard and were called "Bardyaei" (*Mar.*; on the name, see following note). Since they turned especially against their former masters, they must have been fugitives from the City. A few observations can be made.

(a) Considerable numbers of slaves joined the attackers during the siege; many of them used the moment of victory to settle old grudges against their masters.

(b) The Bardyaei were a select troop with a name (or nickname), and trusted by Marius. Contrary to the impression given by P., they cannot have been recruited from City slaves: Cinna's edict came too late in the siege to make the formation of such a body likely. Their origins should be sought in the *ergastula* of Etruria that were opened by Marius before he joined Cinna (Auct. *De vir. ill.* 67.6; Schol. Gronov. 286.9 St; cf. Plut. *Mar.* 41.3, ἐκήρυττε δούλοις ἐλευθερίαν; see also Harmand 460).

(c) The execution of the slaves was intended to restore order throughout the City. It is therefore improbable that only the Bardyaei, as an easily identifiable body, were killed (as Bennett, *Cinna* 30 n. 29, and Carney, *Marius* 66, think).

(d) According to P. (*Mar.*) and Appian, the slaves were cut down at night in their sleep; P. (*Mar., Sert.*) specifies "in their camp." Orosius has them killed in the Forum, where they had been called *quasi stipendii causa*. There need be no contradiction here. Slaves going on a rampage were not likely to return to military quarters (and discipline) out of town at dusk. Marius' private force had to be available at all times in the City; the natural place for them to bivouac would be the Forum. If the terror was to be stopped throughout Rome, it was necessary first to gather the looters in one place. The Forum would be an obvious choice. The *fugitivi* from the City who had joined the Cinno-Marian armies during the siege presumably had not yet received any pay. A pretext for requiring all those wanting to receive their pay to be in the Forum the night before payday would not be hard to find. Sertorius had firsthand experience at such practices: when his commanding general in Spain, T. Didius (see above, 3.5n.), massacred an entire Celtiberian tribe, precisely such a pretext was used to get the Hispanians into the Roman camp where they could be slaughtered at ease (Appian *Iber.* 100.434–36). One may also compare the identical ruse employed by the *magister utriusque militiae per Orientem*, Iulius, in A.D. 378: *Gothos ... universos ... uno eodem die mandavit occidi exspectatione promissi stipendii securos ad suburbana productos* (Ammian. 31.16.8).

δούλων: cf. *Mar.* 43.4, 44.9, where they are called "Bardyaei." The meaning of the name remains unknown, despite various speculations. Schulten, *FHA* 4:145, wanted to identify the Bardyaei with the northern Hispanian tribe of the Varduli (cf. *RE* 8A.1 [1955] 373); *contra*, rightly, Rodríguez Adrados,

Emerita 14 (1946) 195. Kühne, *StudClas* 4 (1962) 196 n. 1, suggested Africans and Greeks, which does not help to explain the name. The Illyrian tribal name Ardiaioi (cf. Tomaschek, *RE* 2.1 [1895] 615) or Vardaei (cf. Saria, *RE* 8A.1 [1955] 365) comes closest to the form given in P., but it seems improbable that Marius' special force was entirely composed of Illyrians (cf. Harmand 460; Sartori 165–67). Bennett's explanation may come nearest the truth (*Cinna* 23): calling attention to a somewhat enigmatic reference to a *bardaicus calceus* in Juvenal (16.13; cf. Martial 4.4.5), he suggested that the Bardyaei were called so because of their distinctive (Illyrian?) footgear, worn by all of Marius' slave bands regardless of national origin (Bennett would render the name as "Spiked Boots"). See also Keaveney, *Philologus* 128 (1984) 138–39.

οὓς Μάριος . . . ἐποίησε: Clearly, P. writes under the impression that only Marius' private army was involved in these events. As argued above (The Slave Bands Massacre), this is not very probable. Συμμάχους . . . ἐν τῷ πολέμῳ itself reflects the fact that the Bardyaei had already been formed by Marius as a body before the siege of Rome, and therefore were not slaves from the City.

τὰ δὲ καὶ ἰδίᾳ . . . παῖδας: cf. *Mar.* 44.9–10; Appian 74.343; without specifying revenge against former masters, Oros. 5.19.24.

στρατοπεδεύοντας: perhaps in the Forum, as Oros. 5.19.24 reports.

κατηκόντισεν: According to Appian 74.344, the troops employed were auxiliaries from Gaul: perhaps recruited by Sertorius in the winter of 91/90, at the onset of the Social War (4.1)?

οὐκ ἐλάττους τετρακισχιλίων: 8,000, according to Orosius (5.19.24).

6.1–4

On the Cinno-Marian rule in Rome (87–83 B.C.) and the Sullan Civil War (83–82) see Linden, passim; Pozzi, *AAT* 49 (1913–14) 641–79; Bennett, *Cinna* 25–69; Badian, "Waiting"; Bulst, passim; Gabba, *ANRW* I.1 (1972) 765–805; Keaveney, "Sullani." For sources see *MRR* 2:45–74.

One long sentence—eleven Teubner lines—takes us from the death of Marius in January 86 to Sertorius' departure for Spain four years later. As in the Social War (4.2) and after the surrender of Rome (5.6), the hero's behavior stands out against the established leaders of the State. The election to the consulship, *contra leges annales,* of the younger Marius opens a cycle of military ineffectualness and treachery at the end of which no hope is left of saving the Republic, and Sertorius' only choice is to abandon Italy and create overseas a safe refuge for Cinno-Marian survivors. The section thus marks the end of Sertorius' political career in Rome and leads up to his arrival in the place of his destiny: Spain.

Sertorius' Praetorship

It is universally assumed that Sertorius was Praetor no later than 83, since his being sent as governor to Spain would seem to require at least that magisterial rank. Indeed 83 has become the canonical date (e.g., Wehrmann 29; Broughton, *MRR* 2:63; Wiseman, *New Men* 260 no. 394; Sumner, *Orators* 108; Katz, "Notes" 63–65; Boren, *CW* 83 [1989–90] 239; Rijkhoek 159–63). Dissenters are few: Stahl (37) thought an earlier year possible, Schulten (38 n. 199) suggested 87, "weil er damals eine leitende Stellung hatte." But only Spann (33, 164) has made a detailed case in favor of an earlier date, 85 or 84 B.C.

First, it must be noted that a praetorship for Sertorius is nearly certain—but only nearly. For the possibility remains that he was sent to Spain as *privatus cum imperio*, like Scipio before and Pompeius after him. Marius' Eastern command under the *lex Sulpicia* in 88 had taken the same form. There is no evidence that the Cinno-Marian leaders resorted to such extraordinary measures after 87, but they conveniently ignored the *leges annales* when they saw to the election of the younger Marius to the consulship (6.1n.). What makes a special command unlikely is the absence of any hint to that effect in our sources as well as the simple fact that Sertorius, born no later than 123/2 and probably earlier (above, 2.2: Date of Birth), by 83 had reached the minimum age of forty required for the praetorship. While we know of tensions between him and the Marii, father and son (5.1–5: Cinna's Invitation; 6.1nn.), nothing ever warranted Schulten's assumption (38) that the leaders of the *factio* relegated him to political obscurity after their victory in 87. We must look for neither special advancement nor retardation. A *novus homo* could reasonably expect to reach the praetorship (on his average chances see Wiseman, *New Men* 162–63); given Sertorius' performance in 87 and his close association with Cinna, evidenced best in the slave bands massacre (5.7nn.), it is difficult to see how the leaders of the *factio* could have prevented him from reaching the office *suo anno* even if they had wanted to do so.

From Exuperantius (8.1–11 = 49–50 Z) it is evident that Sertorius was dispatched to Spain sometime during the winter 83/2. That would agree with his being Praetor in 83, with duties in the City, followed by a provincial promagistracy in 82. Yet Appian, eschewing details given by Exuperantius and simply placing Sertorius' departure after the events at Suessa (probably in July or August 83; see below, 6.3nn.), twice states specifically that Sertorius had been picked to govern Spain a considerable time before he left: ἐκ πολλοῦ στρατηγεῖν ἐρημένος Ἰβηρίας μετὰ τὴν Συέσσης κατάληψιν ἔφευγεν ἐς τὴν Ἰβηρίαν (86.392; cf. 108.505). That implies, obviously, that Sertorius was given Spain no later than at the sortition of praetorian provinces at the beginning of the year. Spann (164) rightly points out that Appian's statement "says nothing about when Sertorius was praetor," but rashly dismisses it as incorrect. Far from contradicting each other, Appian's and Exuperantius' accounts are complementary, as Spann would have realized had he consid-

Commentary 6.1-4   75

ered Appian's second reference to the matter: ᾕρητο μὲν Ἰβηρίας ἄρχειν, Κάρβωνι δ' ἐπὶ Σύλλα συμμαχῶν Σύεσσαν πόλιν ἐν σπονδαῖς κατέλαβε καὶ φεύγων ἐπὶ τὴν στρατηγίαν ᾤχετο (108.505). Appian's explanation is lucid and makes sense. Sertorius had been assigned Spain as his province, but instead of going there he helped Carbo against Sulla: in other words, the Civil War intervened and prevented him from going to his province as planned. That eventually he went there at all may indeed be due as much to political infighting among the *factio* (so Exuperantius) as to strategical considerations (below, 6.4: Mission to Spain). When considered in the entire context of Appian's narrative of the Civil War, his comments on Sertorius' provincial assignment render 83 highly improbable as the year of his praetorship.

The province had been assigned ἐκ πολλοῦ, "a long time," before the Suessa incident in the summer of 83. How long a time, that is the question. That Appian bothers to mention it at all, twice, is suggestive: clearly he—or at any event his source—thought the delay significant and unusual. Now the supporters of 83 must base their view, by implication (no one has ever spelled it out, to my knowledge), on the following set of assumptions: when the provinces for the Praetors of 83 were allocated in January (no later, it is to be hoped, though we cannot be certain), the political and military situation made it feasible and desirable that Sertorius go to Spain, but Sulla's landing at Brundisium a few months later (probably in May; see Linden 33; Gabba, *App BC 1* 221) dramatically altered that picture, and Sertorius decided or was advised to stay in Italy until the crisis should pass. A logical interpretation, impeccable in principle—yet utterly improbable within the supposed time frame, i.e., January 83 and thereafter. For Appian informs us beyond any doubt (and Badian has shown Appian's account here to be both reliable and uncontaminated by source material critical of Sulla: "Waiting" 57–60 = *Studies* 224–30) that Sulla's return in arms had been on the horizon since late 85 (the famous letter to the Senate, 77.350–52) and certain since the death of Cinna early in 84: upon learning of it, Sulla immediately broke off negotiations (79.362–63; see Badian's comments, "Waiting" 59 = *Studies* 228). Civil war now had become inevitable. Summer and fall 84 found Sulla back in Greece, recruiting auxiliary forces and getting ready for the invasion of Italy. As soon as weather conditions permitted early in 83, his fleet sailed from Peiraieus to Patrai and from there to Dyrrachium, where it met with his army, which had marched through Thessaly and Macedonia (Appian 79.363–64; cf. Plut. *Sulla* 26.1–27.1).

The Consuls, Cinna and Carbo, had launched preliminary military preparations already in the winter of 85/4 (Appian 76.348, 77.354). Cinna's entire Liburnian campaign in the spring of 84 was designed to create an army capable of facing Sulla's in a year's time, should that become necessary. No one, of course, expected Sulla to be back before the end of 84: it was a long way from Ephesos to Italy, and the Proconsul was not in too much of a hurry (see Badian, "Waiting"). But since the spring of 84, "they had all been waiting for Sulla."

Here, then, is the situation that precisely fits Appian's account of Sertorius' provincial assignment. In the winter of 85/4, Sertorius could still be scheduled to go on an overseas command; by the spring of 84, the dramatic change of circumstances had occurred that explains his remaining in Italy. With Cinna's death the regime had lost not only its political leader but also an experienced and capable commander (a fact rightly emphasized by Badian), and civil war had become predictable. Sertorius now was needed in Italy. Indeed Appian (108.505) has Sertorius help Carbo against Sulla, whereas the only specific actions he reports of Sertorius are associated with Scipio, the Consul of 83 (85.384–85). Yet he is well aware that Carbo in 83 was neither Consul nor operating together with Scipio (86.390–91), just as he is aware of Carbo's position as the head of the Cinno-Marians after Cinna's death. Κάρβωνι δ' ἐπὶ Σύλλᾳ συμμαχῶν may be one of Appian's many careless mistakes, but his entire narrative of the years in question suggests otherwise: for him there existed a connection between Carbo on the one hand and Sertorius' remaining in Italy on the other, contrary to his provincial assignment. All of it points to 85/4 rather than 83 as the time those decisions were made.

Thus upon closer inspection, 85 and 84 emerge as far more likely years for Sertorius' praetorship than 83. On balance, the evidence favors 85. As Badian saw long ago ("Governors" 2 = *Studies* 73), the Late Republican practice of keeping Praetors in Rome during most of their year of office and only subsequently sending them on provincial commands, with their *imperium* prorogued, was not so much a Sullan innovation but rather was essentially in place by the 90s B.C. (Not that the practice was always rigidly observed, before or after Sulla, but as a general rule it stands firm enough.) That view is corroborated by more recent studies in the development of the *quaestiones perpetuae*, at least five of which—*de repetundis, de maiestate, de ambitu, de peculatu, de veneficiis*, plus a separate one, it seems, *de parricidiis*—can be shown to have existed by the mid-80s (Gruen, *Criminal Courts* 258–64). Even if two *quaestiones* were occasionally placed under a single Praetor (or the murder courts, as was the custom later, under aedilician *iudices quaestionis*), the number of Praetors able to leave for their provinces long before the end of the year must have been small, there being only four of them besides the Urban and the Peregrine. Given those observations, we may reconstruct the case of Sertorius. Most probably he was Praetor in 85, with duties in the City. Either late in that year or early in 84 he was designated to take command of Spain as a promagistrate, but the political crisis triggered by Sulla's threatening return and the death of Cinna in the spring of 84 caused him to stay in Italy, presumably with the approval, if not at the request, of Carbo and other leaders of the *factio*. No doubt his *imperium* was prorogued for 83 as well as 84.

6.1

ἐπεὶ δὲ . . . μικρὸν ὕστερον: Marius died on 13 January 86 B.C., barely two weeks into his seventh consulship (Livy *Per.* 80). Cinna was killed in his fourth consulship, in the spring of 84, at Ancona by mutinous troops refusing to go to Illyricum, where he had planned to wage a summer campaign in order to get his army into fighting shape: Sulla was expected to return from the East later in the year, or early in 83 (Liv. *Per.* 83; Vell. 2.24.5; Plut. *Pomp.* 5; Appian 77.354–78.357; Auct. *De vir. ill.* 69.4; on Cinna's plans and the political background see Badian, "Waiting" 58–59 = *Studies* 226–28). The temporal compression—μικρὸν ὕστερον equals two years and a couple of months, and the next sentence takes us down another two years, to 82 B.C.— is vintage Plutarch. He is not merely indifferent to chronological precision (Marius' election belongs at the very end of the sequence of events enumerated in 6.1–4); he has chosen not to tell us anything about Sertorius' life in the intervening years, instead guiding the reader along to the next item as swiftly as possible. It is artfully done, conveying the pervasive sense of confusion, chaos, and despair of Sulla's Civil War as well as key information: with Marius and Cinna, the two most significant characters in Sertorius' early career as told by P. are gone. In their place follows a rapid succession of nonentities that overshadow the hero despite his superior ability and succeed in ruining the Cinno-Marian war effort against Sulla. The latter, mentioned hitherto only briefly and in passing (4.6–7), now grows into Sertorius' principal adversary, and remains so through chapter 9.

ὁ δὲ νεανίας Μάριος: C. Marius (15), 109/8–82 B.C. Son of C. (14) *cos.* 107, 104–100, 86. He was outlawed by Sulla along with his father in 88 and fled to Africa; presumably he served under his father during the events of 87. Consul in 82. As commander in chief of the southern army he was badly beaten by Sulla near Sacriportus but escaped to Praeneste, where he committed suicide late in 82 after Sulla's final victory at the Porta Collina.

ἄκοντος αὐτοῦ . . . ὑπατείαν ἔλαβε: The younger Marius was elected Consul for 82 (with Cn. Papirius Carbo *cos.* 85, 84) at the age of twenty-six or twenty-seven (*annos natus XXVI*, Vell. 2.26.1; ἑπτὰ καὶ εἴκοσιν ἔτη γεγονώς, Appian 87.394; *XXVII*, Auct. *De vir. ill.* 68.1; *ante annos XX* in Livy *Per.* 86 should be emended to either *XXVII* [Appian; *De vir. ill.*] or *XXX*). This was clearly an attempt to rally the Italians by appealing to the great general's memory (see Badian, *FC* 243–45; Bulst 326). It also was an outright violation of the *leges annales*, which since 180 B.C. had required a minimum age of forty-three for the consulship (for a detailed study of pre-Sullan requirements see Astin, *The Lex Annalis before Sulla*).

Sertorius opposed the election of Marius not merely because it was illegal, although that embarrassing fact undoubtedly permitted him to be outspoken without drawing too much attention to his own ambitions. Exuperantius' epitome shows that Sallust presented the matter in considerable detail (8.1– 5 = 49 Z; cf. below, 6.4): *tunc Sertorius de Marii potestate securus Romam venit et omnium coepit accusare segnitiem et[iam] ex multis promptissimis factis Syllae industriam virtutemque laudare, cui nisi [pariter] obviam iretur, actum iam ac debellatum foret* (cf. Sall. *Hist.* 1.92, *cui nisi pariter obviam iretur*; and see Caviglia 158–59). In other words, Sertorius challenged the military competence of the Consuls-designate, and for good reason. Neither Carbo nor Marius had distinguished themselves hitherto in warfare, and their performance in 82 was to confirm the worst fears. Yet if he thought Marius and Carbo unfit for command, what alternative did he have in mind? Gabba, *App BC 1* 229, laconically stated: "È probabile che alla carica aspirasse Sertorio." That, indeed, is the most likely explanation. Of all the Cinno-Marian leaders', Sertorius' military record was the most distinguished by far, and he certainly did not doubt his ability to direct a major war. Having been Praetor in 85 (so it seems: see above, 6.1–4: Sertorius' Praetorship), he was eligible for the consulship under the *leges annales*.

Cn. Papirius (38) Carbo: ca. 129/8–82 B.C. Tribune of the Plebs in 92, Praetor probably in 89 or 88 (*MRR* 2:33). Virtually nothing is known about his political background prior to his becoming one of Cinna's principal collaborators. He is usually thought to have been Cinna's Legate during the siege of Rome, but if he is indeed the Carbo who held command in Lucania in 89 or 88 (Flor. 2.6.13), he may still have been with *imperium* (*pro praetore* or even *pro consule*) in 87. Consul in 85 and 84 with Cinna, in 82 with C. Marius the son; leader of the ruling faction after Cinna's death in 84. During the Civil War of 83/2 Carbo commanded in the north of Italy (*Pomp.* 6.3–6; Appian 86.390, with Gabba's comments, and 87.394–92.425). Late in 82 he abandoned Italy and fled to Africa; returning soon afterwards to Sicily to organize resistance on the island, he was captured and put to death by Pompeius (cf. *Pomp.* 10.4–6).

C. Norbanus (5): a New Man and probably a new citizen (though most likely not from Norba: Badian, "Caepio" 334–35 = *Studies* 49–50; Wiseman, *New Men* 245 nos. 278–79); born no later than 129/8, presumably much earlier. As Tribune in 103 he prosecuted, together with Saturninus, Q. Servilius Caepio for the loss of his army at Arausio (above, 3.1nn.). Quaestor of M. Antonius probably in 101 in Cilicia (thus Badian, "Silence," improving, persuasively, on Münzer's thesis, *Hermes* 67 [1932] 225–27), though a case can be made for 99, when Antonius was Consul (Gruen, *CP* 61 [1966] 105–7; Broughton, *MRR* 3:149). Probably in 95 he was tried *de maiestate* by P. Sulpicius (*tr. pl.* 88) for sundry acts of violence committed during the trial of Caepio eight years earlier; Antonius defended him successfully (Cic. *De orat.* 2.107, 124, 197–203; for the trial's political significance see Badian, "Caepio" passim). Praetor probably in 90 or 89, and governor of Sicily until 86/5; during the Social War he skillfully kept the island as well as Regium safe from Italian attacks (Diodor. 37.13–14; cf. Cic. *2 Verr.* 3.117, 5.8; on the dates, Badian, "Governors" 9 = *Studies* 85–86). Consul in 83 with L. Scipio (see following note); defeated by Sulla in Campania, he was forced to retreat to Capua. Unlike his colleague, however, Norbanus refused to negotiate with Sulla and kept his army intact (Livy *Per.* 85; Vell. 2.25.2–4; Plut. *Sulla* 27.8–11; Appian 82.373–86.389). In 82 he held a command in Cisalpine Gaul and suffered defeat at the hands of Metellus Pius (below, 12.5n.) near Faventia. Among the first to be proscribed by Sulla, he fled to Rhodes, where he chose to end his own life rather than face extradition (Appian 91.418–22; cf. Livy *Per.* 89; Oros. 5.20.7, 21.3).

L. Cornelius (338) **Scipio Asiaticus**: great-grandson of the victor of Magnesia. Praetor in 86, Proconsul of Macedonia 85–84, successfully fighting Illyrian tribes. Consul in 83 with C. Norbanus (see preceding note). His election despite an apparent lack of Marian credentials carried significance: not so much as a "concession to the moderate coalition" (thus Frier 600) as by signaling that men of Rome's noblest families, unburdened by factional motives, recognized Sulla for what he was and were determined to stop him. In addition, Scipio had military experience. Yet twice his armies deserted him: first in the encounter with Sulla at Teanum (below, 6.3n.), and again when he marched against young Pompey in Picenum (*Pomp.* 7.5). His activities in 82 are not known. Proscribed by Sulla, he escaped to Massilia, where he was still alive in the late 70s or early 60s (Cic. *Sest.* 6–7; cf. Schol. Bob. 126.18–22 St).

ἐπιόντι Σύλλᾳ κακῶς ἐπολέμουν: Only Norbanus encountered Sulla in battle prior to Sertorius' departure for Spain; Scipio and Carbo suffered defeats at the hands of Pompeius, though that of Carbo may belong in 82, later in which year he fought Sulla to a draw at Clusium and along with Norbanus was routed by Metellus at Faventia (see preceding notes). P.'s suggestion of general military disaster better fits 82, the year that saw the vast majority of Marian defeats. Historical accuracy is sacrificed to highlight the contrast between Sertorius' unappreciated qualities as a leader and the incompetence of those in supreme command, and to emphasize his alienation from the heads of the *factio*.

6.2

τὰ μὲν ἀνανδρίᾳ ... τὰ δ' οἱ προδιδόντες ἀπώλλυσαν: Appian's detailed narrative of the Civil War hardly supports the charge of sloth and cowardice, certainly not for 82, when there was bitter and continuous fighting all over Italy. Still, the second half of 83, after the events in Campania, shows the government's inactivity vis-à-vis Sulla and its inability to suppress Pompey's insurrection in Picenum. The accusation at least of a lack of effort goes back to Sallust, who more directly put it into Sertorius' mouth, as is clear from Exuperantius 8.1–5 = 49 Z (quoted above, 6.1n.). Treason is another matter. Plenty of leading figures joined the winning side in good time, but few (perhaps only the notorious Cethegus: Appian 80.369) can be shown to have done so before the beginning of 82, by which time Sertorius was leaving Italy. P. hardly would have Pompey's activities in mind here, nor can he be thinking of the *stratēgoi* just mentioned: rather, the traitors will be the likes of Q. Lucretius Afella (Vell. 2.27.6; cf. Appian 88.402), P. Albinovanus (Appian 91.420–21), the ever-so-well-adjusted L. Marcius Philippus (Livy *Per.* 86), or

C. Verres (Cic. 2 *Verr.* 1.34–38), all of whom switched sides during 82. The anachronism serves to underscore the hero's position apart from the rest of the Cinno-Marians.

ἔργον δ'οὐδὲν ... δυναμένους: see below, 6.4n.

6.3

τέλος δέ: P. has rearranged the sequence of events here; Scipio's abortive peace talks with Sulla took place in the summer of 83 (Linden 37–38), long before Marius' election to the consulship (6.1n.). As in Cinna's invitation to Marius (above, 5.1–5n.), Sertorius is cast in the role of the warner whose advice goes unheeded, with disastrous consequences for the *res publica*. But this time, there are personal consequences as well. For P., Scipio's failure marks the turning point of the hero's life: Sertorius leaves Italy, never to return, and embarks on the adventurous career that earned him a place in the *Lives*. In choosing the events at Teanum (see following note) as the point and cause of Sertorius' departure, rather than his bickering with Carbo and the younger Marius (as Sallust apparently had seen it: above, 6.2n.), the biographer creates a send-off both more dramatic and more dignified.

Σύλλας ... διέφθειρε τὸ στράτευμα: The best reconstruction of the opening moves of the Civil War is still Pozzi, followed here. Sulla landed at Brundisium in the spring of 83; marching on the Via Appia he reached Campania in the summer and near Mount Tifata defeated Norbanus, who retreated to Capua (above, 6.1n.). Meanwhile the second consular army under Scipio and Sertorius (*pro consule,* see above, 6.1–4: Praetorship, with 6.6n., below; the exact nature of his command or function in Scipio's army remains unknown, but see 6.4n.) was approaching Teanum Sidicinum (ca. 30 kilometers northwest of Capua) on the Via Latina from the north; with Norbanus' army still intact and in his rear, Sulla now was caught in the middle and unable to advance towards Rome safely on either road. With twenty cohorts, he proceeded to Cales (ca. 18 kilometers northwest of Capua, ca. 12 kilometers south of Teanum) and offered to negotiate with Scipio. The latter agreed, and Sulla sent hostages to guarantee a cessation of hostilities for the duration of the talks; then both commanders met between Cales and Teanum, each accompanied by two advisors (Cic. *Phil.* 12.27, giving the location; Appian 85.383–84, with number of participants). The issues discussed are known from Cicero: *de auctoritate senatus, de suffragiis populi, de iure civitatis leges inter se et condiciones contulerunt.* On what followed accounts diverge.

According to the *Periochae* (85), the negotiations failed, Sulla sent soldiers into Scipio's camp to corrupt his troops, and the Consul's army went over to Sulla as soon as he drew near with his own. In P. (*Sulla* 28.1–5), the rebellious Proconsul's desire to negotiate was insincere from the start—a view supported at least in part by Cicero (*Phil.* 13.2, *pacem cum Scipione Sulla sive faciebat sive simulabat*) and Appian (85.383)—and merely designed to give him time and opportunity to stir up trouble in Scipio's camp. He saw to it that the talks dragged on under various pretexts, while his soldiers fraternized with those of Scipio and eventually won them over. When he approached Scipio's camp with his twenty cohorts, the consular army (forty cohorts, i.e., four legions) deserted to him.

Appian's account (85.383–86.388) is different and far more dramatic. Sulla and Scipio reached an agreement (85.384 and 95.441; see Gabba, *App BC* 1 224, 254), but the Consul wished to submit the matter to his colleague and dispatched Sertorius to inform Norbanus in Capua of the talks. The armistice was to continue until Norbanus' response arrived. On his way, Sertorius seized the town of Suessa Aurunca, which had sided with Sulla (85.385; cf. *CIL* I² 720 = X 4751 = *ILS* 870). Sulla protested, and Scipio, "either because he had been in the know, or because he was at a loss how to respond in the face of Sertorius' strange act," returned Sulla's hostages. His army held "the Consuls" responsible for the capture of Suessa and the unasked-for return of the hostages (evidently, Sertorius was considered to have broken the armistice, Scipio to have renounced it formally), and immediately opened secret communications with Sulla: they would switch sides if he drew near. And so it happened. Diodoros (38/39.16) attributes the desertion to bribery, others (Vell. 2.25.2–3; Flor. 2.9.19) add nothing. All sources agree that Scipio was taken alive, and let go unharmed; Velleius alone specifies the same of Sertorius (disbelieved by Spann, 36, for insufficient reasons; Scipio was not the "bungler" Spann makes him out to be, and Sulla had no reason as of yet to be in awe of Sertorius' military prowess). Sulla subsequently treated that day as the *terminus post quem* in deciding eligibility for inclusion among the proscribed, explaining, after his final victory at the Colline Gate, that he considered the agreement worked out with Scipio valid and binding, and that the Consul's reneging on it marked, in his eyes, the beginning of the Civil War (Appian 95.441; cf. Frier 601). On what actually happened at Suessa, and P.'s silence regarding it, see below.

ταῦτα προλέγων . . . οὐκ ἔπεισε: This is the extent to which P. will acknowledge Sertorius' involvement in the Civil War in general, and in the events that made a negotiated settlement impossible in particular. His passing over the Suessa incident need not surprise, at first glance, in the *Sertorius,* as even P. would have found it difficult to present it as an example of the hero's moderation (though elsewhere he chose not to suppress acts far more reprehensible: 10.5, 25.6). What gives one pause is the episode's absence in the *Sulla,* studded elsewhere with choice specimens from the dictator's memoirs. There Sulla prevails through clear-cut treachery, with no wrongdoing on the part of his opponents (otherwise treated with little sympathy throughout that life). It may be argued that P. is emphasizing the ἀνὴρ πολύτροπος, a frequent theme in the *Sulla* (the famous fox-and-lion comparison ends the chapter). Yet a troubling discrepancy to Appian—as faithful a transcript of Sullas's memoirs as we shall ever have—and agreement with Livy remains: in P. as in Livy, it is Sulla who deliberately corrupts the Consul's army; in (Sulla–)Appian, Scipio's soldiers desert wholly on their own initiative, and nothing stronger is admitted of Sulla's part in these events than his expectation of such an outcome (86.383, 386). We have also seen how Cicero, a contemporary of those events, was less than convinced of Sulla's sincerity (*Phil.* 13.2, see preceding note). Did there exist a tradition prior to Livy that knew of Sulla's succeeding through deceit and bribery, but not of Sertorius and Suessa? Or that at least would not draw a connection between Sertorius' action and the failure to reach a peaceful settlement?

Conveniently, a pertinent fragment of Sallust's *Histories* survives: *cuius adversa voluntate colloquio militibus permisso corruptio facta paucorum et exercitus Sullae datus est* (1.91). Its attribution to what happened between Cales and Teanum is not in doubt, and it evidently agrees with both Livy and P., except for one small though significant detail. In the *Sertorius* P. makes it look as if the hero objected to negotiations with Sulla as such, whereas in Sallust, Sertorius' opposition is directed, sensibly enough, against permitting the troops to fraternize. It is also evident that the Sallust fragment was not part of a narrative of the Civil War but belongs to a retrospective passage centered on Sertorius, quite possibly continuing the long introduction of Sertorius that survives in 1.88. Hence its report is necessarily abbreviated, and yet the wording makes it difficult to imagine Sallust describing, here or elsewhere, the Suessa incident in a light resembling Appian's, if mentioning it at all. As for the defection of Scipio's army, in Sallust it was clearly Sulla's work. Exuperantius' summary concurs: *vetante Sertorio colloquia consules permiserunt inter suum et Syllae exercitum, et facta proditio est omnisque exercitus Syllae traditur* (7.13–15 = 45 Z). It would seem thus that P.'s silence on Suessa is due not merely to an attempt to protect Sertorius but at least as much to his choice of sources: in this instance, he followed not Sulla but others. The question remains, what actually happened? Appian's version of an agreement reached but not kept has the backing of Cicero (*Phil.* 12.27, *non tenuit omnino conloquium illud fidem*), yet while the latter is careful not to say which side he thought failed to keep faith, he strongly imparts his doubts that Sulla was sincere to begin with (*Phil.* 13.2). Despite the other sources' silence, it appears improbable that Sulla in his memoirs invented the Suessa affair out of whole cloth. Which is not to say that as told by Appian we read the truth, and the whole truth.

The Suessa Incident

Suessa Aurunca lies about 16 kilometers west of Teanum, a little more than halfway along the road to Minturnae; from Minturnae to Capua the distance on the Via Appia is about 50 kilometers to the southeast. As Gabba observed (*App BC* 1 224), Sertorius did not take the direct route from Teanum to Capua, ca. 30 kilometers on the Via Latina, but instead a detour that more than doubled the distance. Surely the reason was not that Sulla's forces controlled the Via Latina south of Cales: they also kept Capua itself under siege (*Sulla* 27.10), and since Sulla had evidently agreed to give Sertorius free access to Norbanus, he logically must have agreed to grant him safe passage all the way. Next, seizing (καταλαβών) Suessa must have involved military backup at the very least, if not outright use of force: evidently Sertorius left Scipio's camp with a sizable military escort. The capture of Suessa had been one of his objectives from the outset (correctly emphasized by Rijkhoek, 172–74).

Scholars have variously tried to explain Sertorius' action. Some saw a military reason: e.g., Pozzi (658, essentially followed by Gabba) thought that Sulla's control of Suessa posed a threat to Scipio's right flank. But with part of Sulla's army blocking Scipio's advance at Cales, and the remainder needed to prevent Norbanus from breaking out of Capua, Sulla surely lacked the strength to build up a third front around Suessa. Out of the question, for identical reasons, is Rijkhoek's notion (174–75) that Scipio needed to secure Suessa in order to carry out a strategic withdrawal, Sulla somehow having cut off his retreat to Teanum. Others have sought political motives: thus Schulten (38–39), admiringly if ineptly likening the deed to Yorck's arrangement at Tauroggen, was certain that Sertorius deliberately violated the truce in order to force a breakup of the "dangerous" peace talks. Spann (36–37) was non-committal, but on an earlier occasion (diss. 44) pointed out that Sertorius had reason to fear he might be the price of a compromise between Sulla and the Cinno-Marian regime. A tempting interpretation, yet based on the common erroneous assumption that Sertorius opposed all negotiations with Sulla; as we have seen (Sall. *Hist.* 1.91 and Exuper. 7.13–15 = 45 Z), he only voiced objections against permitting the troops to fraternize. P.'s διέφθειρε τὸ στράτευμα, καὶ ταῦτα προλέγων . . . καὶ διδάσκων Σερτώριος, while easily mistaken for general opposition, is clearly based on nothing more than what we find in Sallust—which is not to say, of course, that Sertorius agreed with the result of the talks. But he had been a member of the negotiating team, as can be concluded from Cic. *Phil.* 12.27, *cum alter nobilitatis florem, alter belli socios adhibuisset*: the preceding details of Pompeius Strabo's meeting, *me praesente*, with Vettius Scato in 89 as well as the entire context—should they negotiate with Antony or not?—makes it clear that *adhibuisset* refers to the actual participants of the talks, not merely to political supporters in general. Of either group as characterized, Metellus Pius and Sertorius were the most prominent representatives. (Spann, 35–36, missing the significance of Cicero's remark, is more tentative: "Sertorius . . . almost certainly . . . , and . . . likely . . . Metellus." The latter's presence is virtually assured by Appian 85.383.) Surely Sertorius was an odd choice to inform Norbanus about the talks if indeed he disapproved of their outcome (correctly Rijkhoek 171–72, against Keaveney, *Sulla* 133).

The answer to a different question may hold the key. When exactly did Suessa declare itself in favor of Sulla? If it had done so before the start of the talks, Sertorius was unquestionably violating the truce. If, however, the town changed its allegiance only after the armistice had taken effect—say, just as

Sertorius was preparing to leave for Capua—the government could view such an act as a violation on the part of Suessa, all the more if Sulla, tacitly or openly, welcomed the defection. If that was the case, Sertorius might legitimately think of himself as merely restoring the frontline to where it had been when the cessation of hostilities had been agreed upon. Long ago Pozzi, without arguing the matter, assumed as much. He was probably right. Cicero questioned Sulla's sincerity, as should we. The primary object of the talks was not a negotiated settlement but a chance to undermine Scipio's hold on his army: so the later sources are quite in agreement, even Appian. Sulla protested, though his complaint hardly had standing: no matter, for by this time he had sufficient reason to believe the Consul's army would not fight. But in making an issue out of Suessa, Sulla gave proof to Scipio that he was not really interested in a peaceful end to the conflict, short of unconditional surrender. The Consul returned the hostages. Sulla naturally made the most of that supposed breach of truce and agreement. As he lied in his memoirs about whose soldiers took the first steps in arranging the defection of Scipio's army, so he gave full weight to the Suessa incident, taking care merely to omit at what point in time the town changed sides. But not all were fooled: Sallust, Diodoros, probably Livy, and no doubt others—P. among them—realized that the loss of the Consul's army was not caused by the seizure of Suessa. The biographer's silence gives eloquent testimony to his acumen in evaluating his sources. Moderns, as often, have been more gullible.

6.4

παντάπασιν ... Ἰβηρίαν: Again P. compresses events. After the disaster at Teanum, Sertorius went north to Etruria to conduct new levies, which eventually comprised forty cohorts (Exuper. 7.15–27 = 46–48 Z). While they were clearly meant to replace the troops lost in Campania (and indeed were partly the same, having returned to the government's standards after soon becoming disillusioned with Sulla: ibid.), several hints in Appian and Exuperantius suggest that part of what is known as Scipio's army may actually have been under Sertorius' own command, and that some of the new levies were intended for himself. According to Appian (85.386), Scipio's army blamed "the Consuls" for the breakdown of negotiations with Sulla: but Norbanus had no part in those proceedings. Might "the Consuls" be shorthand, imprecisely, for "the Consul (Scipio) and the Proconsul (Sertorius)"? At Exuper. 7.11 = 44 Z, Sertorius is counted among the *duces* chosen to command in the war against Sulla (*dux* tends to denote an independent commander rather than a subordinate: cf. Livy 4.20.6, *nec ducem novimus nisi cuius auspicio bellum geritur*); after Teanum, Sertorius is *destitutus atque omnium copiarum nudatus auxilio*, which description serves to introduce his going to Etruria, and the narrative concludes with the following comment: *nam et multi milites qui se venienti Syllae tradiderant frustrati omnibus ad priorum ducum castra reverterunt, quae ante prodiderant*. Exuperantius at least seems to have been under the impression that Sertorius was one of those *priores duces*.

While Sertorius was in Etruria, Carbo (for the third time) and the younger Marius were elected Consuls (Exuper. 8.1–11 = 49–50 Z). It appears that already prior to his departure for Etruria, Sertorius had voiced his opposition to the candidacy (and predictable election) of Marius (ἄκοντος αὐτοῦ . . . ὑπατείαν ἔλαβε, 6.1). Upon his return to Rome, he accused the leadership of inertia and incompetence, predicting swift and certain defeat unless a more aggressive strategy was adopted (Exuper. ibid.; cf. 6.1n.). His candid criticism of the conduct of the war did little to endear him to the new Consuls and other leaders of the *factio*.

Sertorius' Mission to Spain

Since 93/2, Hither Spain and (probably) Farther Spain had been governed by C. Valerius Flaccus *cos.* 93; the evidence is fairly conclusive that by 86/5, he had also assumed command of Transalpine Gaul (for a detailed exposition see Badian, "Governors" 10–15 = *Studies* 88–96). His cousin L. Valerius Flaccus had been Marius' colleague in the latter's sixth consulship in 100 B.C. ("attendant rather than colleague," as Rutilius Rufus saw it: *Mar.* 28.8), Censor in 97 with M. Antonius (then still a friend of Marius), and one of Marius' most loyal supporters throughout; in 86, the Censors elected under the Cinno-Marian regime made him *princeps senatus*. Gaius' own brother Lucius was the unfortunate Suffect Consul of 86. There are no grounds for thinking that Gaius at first differed greatly in his attitude toward the regime. Certainly the escape to Gaul of M. Caecilius Cornutus, one of the intended victims of Cinna and Marius in 87 (*Mar.* 43.10), cannot be construed to indicate that Flaccus was prepared to give aid and comfort to enemies of the regime (as would Keaveney, "Sullani" 130–31, in a somewhat desperate attempt to locate supporters of Sulla prior to 83). We simply do not know what reasons prompted Cornutus' choice of refuge—if he had a choice; after all, Gaul was close to Italy, and accessible by land. M. Licinius Crassus, another prominent fugitive, surely would not have felt compelled to go into hiding in Spain for nearly a year, eight months of it in a cave (ca. spring 85–spring 84, until after Cinna's death: *Crass.* 4.1–6.1), had Flaccus been willing to receive him with open arms.

L. Flaccus, the Consul of 86, was murdered probably early in 85 at the hands of one of his officers, C. Flavius Fimbria (below, 23.6n.; cf. *MRR* 2:53–59, 3:212), at Nikomedeia in Bithynia. His homonymous son (later to be Praetor in that *annus mirabilis,* 63) had accompanied him to the East, no doubt on his first military tour of duty; he now found it prudent to leave and eventually joined the army of his uncle, C. Flaccus, in Gaul (Schol. Bob. 96.3–11 St; cf. Cic. *Flacc.* 63, 100). To interpret that as his "taking refuge" seems hardly warranted; at least *ex hoc aetatis gradu se ad exercitum C. Flacci patrui contulit* does not suggest flight and exile. That the younger Flaccus should speedily remove himself from Fimbria's reach is natural enough, but his very return to western Europe indicates no break with his family's loyalty to the ruling clique in Rome: had it been otherwise, he might have found Sulla's headquarters considerably more convenient to approach. (Keaveney, "Sullani" 131, stands the matter on its head in concluding that Flaccus was "not compelled to take refuge with Sulla . . . because [he] could find a haven with [C.] Flaccus.")

Yet by the time the younger Flaccus reached his uncle's camp—not before summer 85, to judge from the distance to be travelled and a likely stopover in Rome—the loyalty of both would seem to have come under serious strain. The Senate had taken no action, no matter how symbolic, against Fimbria: the Consul's assassin was tacitly at least, if not even formally, recognized as commander *pro praetore* of what had been the army of Gaius' brother (Lintott, *Historia* 20 [1971] 701). By the end of 85 the *princeps senatus*, L. Flaccus cos. 100, had taken the lead in advocating negotiations with Sulla (Livy *Per.* 83; cf. Badian, "Waiting" 58 = *Studies* 226). It should not surprise if during the winter of 85/4 the leaders of the *factio* concluded that at least part of the only significant military forces west of Italy had better be put in more reliable hands.

Hence the original decision to send Sertorius to Spain. Badian saw that connection long ago ("Governors" 15 = *Studies* 96), and Frier (597) went a step farther in suggesting that Flaccus, prompted by his cousin the *princeps senatus*, had already sided with Sulla. Both scholars, influenced by the "traditional" date of Sertorius' praetorship, were thinking of winter 83/2; though already Badian had noted that the government had reason to doubt Flaccus' loyalty since his brother's "unavenged death early in 85." Clearly the evidence better agrees with the crisis of late 85–early 84 than with a later date (above, 6.1–4: Sertorius' Praetorship).

Yet surely Sertorius was not to relieve Flaccus *tout court,* in all three of his provincial commands: the government could ill afford to alienate the man even further when he had shown no actual sign of disaffection (cf. Rijkhoek 182–84). The challenge was to neutralize his military importance without giving him grounds for rebellion. To send him a successor for both Spains, where he had been holding command for eight or nine years by the spring of 84, was a reasonable measure by any standard. Nor could it be construed as a vote of no confidence as long as he was left in charge of Gaul and, what is more significant, of his army there. As Flaccus' main activity and personal presence had already shifted from Spain to Transalpina since 86/5 (*MRR* 2:58; Badian, "Governors" 11, 15–16 = *Studies* 89, 95–97), Sertorius' Hispanian assignment could be presented as relief, long overdue, from an anomalous burden, while at the same time Flaccus' confirmation in the command of Gaul expressed the Senate's continuing trust in him. A face-saving solution, and strategically sound. Flaccus' army would be locked between those of Spain and Italy, all safely in the hands of loyalists. Should he actually side with Sulla, his military effectiveness in an upcoming war would be quite limited, as indeed it turned out to be the case after Sertorius' arrival in Spain two years later. We may be confident that during 82 Flaccus was watching events to his rear, beyond the Pyrenees, as closely as he was watching events beyond the Alps. Only after the *Sullani* had established control of Cisalpine Gaul did he become free to make his move.

By late 83 relations between Sertorius and the Marian leaders had deteriorated to a point where cooperation in Italy was no longer feasible. At the same time, concerns about Flaccus' loyalty must have become ever more urgent in view of the war's inauspicious first season. Sertorius, at long last, proceeded to his *provincia,* no doubt by mutual agreement: his opponents got rid of a frustrated and embittered know-it-all-better, and Sertorius could be trusted to secure the important Hispanian for the government while keeping a close watch on his neighbor in Transalpine Gaul. He left Italy late in 83 or early in 82.

ὡς ... ἐσόμενος: If P. was aware of the political and strategic considerations behind Sertorius' mission to Spain (see preceding note), he ignored them. Thus the decision to leave becomes all the hero's own, which probably it was not (though Schulten's and Spann's contention that it amounted to a dismissal by Carbo et al. overstates the case), and once more exemplifies his farsightedness and superior judgment. The motive of wanting to secure a haven for Cinno-Marian refugees need not be entirely anachronistic, however: Spain had sheltered fugitives of various political color throughout the 80s (Gran. Lic. 35.7 Cr; Plut. *Crass.* 4–5), and Sertorius was pessimistic about the outcome of the war in Italy.

6.5

ἐν χωρίοις ὀρεινοῖς: generally assumed to indicate the Pyrenees, but the Alps are just as likely: during the Triumviral period, the Salassi (in the vicinity of what eventually became Augusta Praetoria, now Aosta) repeatedly exacted payment from Roman forces trying to cross (Strabo 4.6.7). If the Pyrenees are meant, Padró and Piedrafita (*Latomus* 46 [1987] 359) may be right in suggesting that Sertorius did not follow the coastal road via the relatively low Col du Perthus (elev. 290 m) but crossed the mountains farther east in the vicinity of Andorra, e.g., via the Col de la Perche (elev. 1,610 meters): the tribes exacting a toll then would have been the Cerretani, in the Catalonian districts of Cerdanya and Alt Urgell. Conceivably C. Flaccus in Gaul was blocking the coastal pass (Padró and Piedrafita 159).

6.6

ἀνθύπατος: The title Proconsul is now independently attested by several sling bullets: a pair found in Huelva Province, Andalucía, is inscribed *Q Sertori | pro. cos.* (see Chic García, "Q. Sertorius, procónsul," 171–73); another pair, from the vicinity of Pamplona, Navarra, reads *Q Sertor | pro cos* on one side, *pietas* on the other (F. Beltrán Lloris, "'Pietas'" 212–15); cf. also *Q. Sert. | pro cos.* on a bullet from Huesca Province, Aragón (A. Domínguez, M. A. Magallon, and P. Casado, *Carta arqueológica de España: Huesca*, Zaragoza, 1984 [*non vidi*] 160). Schulten's comments (38 n. 198), followed by Flacelière and Chambry (19 n. 1) and, unfortunately, Chic, are a model of muddle-headedness: "Plut. Sert. 6 nennt ihn ungenau ἀνθύπατος . . . , wie denn auch sonst die spanischen Proprätoren oft als Prokonsuln bezeichnet werden." Of course P. is perfectly accurate. A promagistrate's designation derived from the terms of his appointment: *pro consule* (with "consular" *imperium* and twelve lictors) if he was to go "instead of a Consul," *pro praetore* (with "praetorian" *imperium* and six lictors) if "instead of a Praetor." The magisterial rank last attained in Rome—Consul or Praetor—was irrelevant in that respect; Propraetor after all does not mean ex-Praetor, and *pro praetore* is not synonymous with *vir praetorius*. The same holds for the consular variants. (The reminder, sadly, still seems necessary.) As has long been known, the promagistrates governing Spain as a rule served *pro consule*, whether they had held the consulship or not: Mommsen, *StR* 2^3:647–48. (The terminological monstrosity of a *propraetor pro consule*, admitted by McDonald, *JRS* 43 [1953] 144, is impossible and, not surprisingly, unattested.)

βαρβάροις ὀλέθροις: the adjective only here, *Eum.* 18.2, and *Artax.* 14.9 (= Ktesias *FGrHist* 688 F 26, though hardly a verbatim quotation). The strongly contemptuous ring is picked up, with devastating effect, in the *Eumenes* passage: see Bosworth 64–65.

καιρὸν . . . ἐφιεμένῳ: The emphasis on hurrying corresponds to 6.4, εἰ φθάσει τὴν ἐκεῖ κρατυνάμενος ἀρχήν. If Sertorius had little faith in Carbo's and Marius' ability to handle Sulla, he would naturally want as much time as possible to create a defensible position in Spain. But τάχος is one of the hero's qualities repeatedly stressed by P.: e.g., 3.8 (quick reaction and counterattack at Castulo), 4.2 (σπουδὴ and τάχος in levying troops for the Social War), 12.7–13.5 (comparison with Metellus' methodical slowness), 18.5–6 (beating Pompeius in a race for control of an important hill); cf. also *Pomp.* 19.6–7. In 218 B.C., Hannibal had used bribes and presents to accelerate his march across southern Gaul from the Pyrenees to the Rhône (Polyb. 3.41.7; Livy 21.23.1, 24.4–5, 26.6), and P. may have been aware of that precedent.

τὴν δ''Ἰβηρίαν . . . κατέσχε: On the basis of Exuper. 8.9 = 50 Z, *misere in citeriorem Hispaniam*, most authors assume that Sertorius' province was Hither Spain (e.g., Mommsen, *RG* 2:324; Maurenbrecher, *Prolegomena* 21; Stahl 37; Schulten 39; Broughton, *MRR* 2:63; Spann 39 with n. 68). But Badian has demonstrated a staggering scarcity of governors throughout the empire during the 80s B.C. and convincingly argued ("Governors" 11, 15; cf. "Waiting" 59 = *Studies* 88, 96, 229) that Sertorius was in charge of both Hither and Farther Spain. The last governor that can be conjectured for Ulterior is P. Cornelius Scipio Nasica in 93 B.C.: Obseq. 51; see *MRR* 2:16 n.

2 for the correct interpretation. (Sumner's doubts [*Orators* 74] that the man was governor are excessive—Obsequens frequently misdates events to the preceding consular year: so at 57, 63–66.) Nothing is known about his further career, and given the fact that C. Valerius Flaccus stayed in command of Citerior for an entire decade beginning in 93, with Gallia Transalpina added by 85 (Badian, "Governors" 11–12 = *Studies* 88–90), it is at least conceivable that Nasica likewise had to remain through the 80s. Sertorius does not seem to have set foot into the Farther Province during the brief period of his official governorship; naturally no conclusions can be drawn from that. On the other hand, Badian's view may find support in Livy 91 fr. 22.32–33 W-M, *quantum Hispaniae provinciae interesset suas partes superiores esse,* which suggests that Sertorius held the *provincia Hispania* as a whole. C. Annius, who drove Sertorius from Spain in 82/1, surely was in charge of both provinces (below, 7.2n.). As regards Exuperantius, his wording cannot be taken to limit Sertorius to the Nearer Province. There is a suspicious congruence between 6.7, πρὸς ὅλην κακῶς διακείμενα τὴν ἡγεμονίαν, Exuper. 8.8–9 = 50 Z, *sive ut feroci provinciae cuius infidelitatem timebant idoneam praeponerent ducem misere in citeriorem Hispaniam,* and Sall. *Hist.* 1.85, *ardebat omnis Hispania citerior.* (Maurenbrecher assigned that fragment to the year 77, just before Pompey's dispatch to Spain: possible but not very likely, since by then all Spain was "burning.") If Hither Spain was in a state of near revolt in 83/2, the new commander, even if sent for both provinces, would obviously have to deal with it first and foremost.

According to Appian (86.392, 108.506; cf. *Iber.* 101.438–39), the previous governors, in order to curry favor with Sulla, refused to hand Spain over to Sertorius; he expelled them in short order and continued to fight valiantly with Metellus, sent against him by Sulla. Attempts to identify those "previous commanders" have caused much needless headache, most recently to Spann (41). The truth was seen by Gabba long ago (*App BC 1* 228): Appian is patently unaware of any of the events related to Sertorius in the years 82–80, such as his governorship of Spain, his expulsion by Annius, his adventures in Africa, and return from there. (Noted by Stahl, 30, who failed to see the consequences.) In fact, Appian manifestly writes as if Metellus was dispatched immediately after the victory at the Colline Gate in late 82, even before Sulla became Dictator (97.450; cf. 98.459–61)—fully two years earlier than his actual departure. Gabba's conclusion is inescapable: the "previous governors" of Appian in reality are the ones who tried to prevent Sertorius' return from Africa in 80 B.C. (on which see below, 12.1–5). Since P. gives no indication that Sertorius overcame resistance when he first entered Spain, it is safe to say that he encountered none.

6.7

ἔθνη: the best surveys of the Iberian Peninsula in antiquity are Schulten, *Geografía,* and Tovar, *Landeskunde.* Keay (8–28) and Curchin (*Roman Spain* 3–

23) offer concise and helpful introductions. On linguistic aspects, the studies of Gómez-Moreno, Schmoll, Tovar (*Estudios* and *Ancient Languages*), and Untermann are fundamental; the latter's "Althispanische Sprachen" (with extensive bibliography) and Anderson's *Ancient Languages* are convenient recent surveys of the evidence. Villaronga, *Numismatica* 63–76, provides a useful introduction to the various indigenous systems of writing. A brief summary here will suffice.

The Peoples of the Iberian Peninsula

The Hispanian (i.e., non-Roman, non-Greek, and non-Punic) population of the Iberian Peninsula may be classified, crudely, into two major groups, Celtic and non-Indo-European. The latter constitute the earliest known civilizations of the Peninsula. The evidence of place names, inscribed texts, and personal names shows Celtic predominant in the North and West, non-Indo-European in the East and South. A linguistic demarcation line based on place names (Celtic *-briga, seg-*, and non-Indo-European *il(t)ir-/iler-, il(t)ur-*) runs southeast along the upper Ebro River from modern Bilbao in the Basque Country to the confluence of Ebro and Jalón near Zaragoza, then curves southward through lower Aragón into La Mancha, across the headwaters of the Júcar, and continues in a southwesterly direction through southern New Castile and northern Andalusia to the mouth of the Guadiana, at the border of Spain and Portugal (see the maps of Untermann, "Althispanische Sprachen" 792 and 808, and Anderson, 89).

The best known representative of what may be called, with some hesitation, indigenous Hispanian civilizations is the culture of the East Coast, of uncertain origin; its people, and they alone, are properly termed Iberian. Their language was non-Indo-European, agglutinative in structure rather than inflected. The Iberian script, developed during the fifth and fourth centuries from the Greek and Phoenician systems of writing, and combining alphabetic with syllabic elements, is attested through most of the area where the Iberian language was spoken. In the East—Aragón, Catalonia, and the País Valencià, as well as Languedoc in France—the script shows greater Greek influence in lettering and direction of writing. In a southern (and possibly older) variant—encountered in eastern Andalusia (provinces of Málaga, Jaén, Granada, and Almería), Murcia, and Albacete Province in Castilla–La Mancha—Phoenician elements, such as writing from right to left, are prevalent, but whereas scholars are in general agreement as to the interpretation of the eastern Iberian, or Levantine, alphabet-syllabary, the phonetic value of some southern characters remains in doubt. The overall evidence, however, makes it fairly certain that the language rendered by the southern variant was the same as that of the Levantine script, i.e., Iberian.

Inscriptions from southern Portugal (Algarve and Alentejo) and, in smaller number, western Andalusia (provinces of Huelva, Sevilla, Córdoba, and Cádiz)—known as Turdetania in Roman times—and Extremadura reveal another system of writing, variously labeled Southern Lusitanian or Tartessian, with characters closely related to Iberian, in particular its southern variant, but of greatly disputed phonetic value. The evidence, scant as it is, points to a separate language, rich in vowels, neither Indo-European nor related to any other known one. Some scholars (e.g., Gómez-Moreno, *Escritura*, passim) are inclined to consider, under the name Bastulo-Turdetan, both Southern Lusitanian and Southern Iberian as the early and intermediate stages, respectively, of one and the same script (not language), out of which the Iberian culture to the east eventually developed the Iberian/Levantine system. Current opinion, however, favors the view that Southern Lusitanian is later rather than earlier than the oldest examples of Iberian script and constitutes a local variant developed separately, quite likely by retreating remnants (such as the Conii in Algarve) of the Tartessian civilization (thus, tentatively, Untermann, "Althispanische Sprachen" 806–9) that once—until the sixth or early fifth century—flourished in the Southwest of the Peninsula. Frequent place names ending in *-ip(p)o* and *-uba* are found in southern Portugal and western Andalusia, but not on the East Coast, that is, the area of Iberian script and speech proper; since Southern Lusitanian writing is found only within that southwestern onomastic area, it is reasonable to postulate the existence of a distinct Southwest Iberian culture. That notion finds strong support in the art and architecture of the Southwest, and scholars insist with increasing frequency (thus, e.g., most recently Curchin, *Roman Spain* 19) that the ancient culture and language of southern Portugal and western Andalusia not be labeled, indiscriminately, "Iberian," but might better be termed "Tartessian" or "Tartesso-Iberian." Both the eastern and southwestern cultures shared a high level of urbanization and artistic achievement, and commerce-oriented economy, with extensive production and use of coinage. As in the respective scripts, Greek and Phoenician influence is manifest in art and architecture—Greek mainly on the East Coast, Phoenician in the South; but there is considerable overlap.

An entirely different system of writing, known as Libyo-Phoenician, was employed in the southwestern corner of Andalusia (southern Cádiz Province) after the Iberian script had been adopted in the Southeast. Whether it represents the survival of a more ancient script or a late, local development of Phoenician is impossible to say; it appears exclusively on coins, none earlier, apparently, than the second century. The script rendered a language of unknown identity, perhaps Iberian, perhaps Libyan, perhaps Phoenician; the scarcity of evidence barely permits speculation. The Phoenician towns of the Atlantic and Mediterranean coast (such as Gades, Malaca, Sexi, or Abdera) and the Greek settlements in Catalonia (Emporion and Rhode) wrote, naturally enough, in their native alphabets.

There remains the question of Basque. The intractable problem of its origins and relations (if any) cannot be addressed here, and scholarly opinions on the subject do not even remotely approach agreement. Today the Basque language is spoken in the northern quarter of Navarra, the provinces of Vizcaya, Guipúzcoa, and (partly) Alava in the Basque Country, and the departments of

Pyrénées Atlantiques and Hautes-Pyrénées in France; the area was larger in the Middle Ages, when it encompassed most of Navarra and Alava. In Roman times a people known as the Vascones inhabited Navarra and the southern part of Alava. From their name the modern words "Basque" and (Spanish) "Vasco" sprang clearly enough, but though that derivation makes it an attractive conjecture that the Vascones in fact spoke Basque, or an early form thereof, it is far from being proof. Basque speakers, at any event, call their language "Euskera": if that term has an antecedent in an ancient name it should be sought in that of the Ausci, a people attested on the northern foothills of the Pyrenees, in Aquitania. Little indigenous epigraphy, mostly late and employing the Latin alphabet, survives from the extreme Northeast. The onomastic evidence shows a considerable degree of resemblance between ancient Iberian and modern Basque—e.g., place names ending in Basque -*berri* or -*urri(s)*—mostly between the upper/middle Ebro and the Pyrenees (i.e., Navarra, La Rioja, and Aragón). It suggests a fair amount of linguistic interaction, such as borrowing, but not necessarily a genetic relation. The once fashionable view of Basque as the direct and sole surviving descendant of ancient Iberian has largely been abandoned in favor of an independent language, at home in pre-Roman times in and beyond the Pyrenees, spoken probably among the Vascones, possibly along the northern coast of the Peninsula, and almost certainly related to the indigenous language of Aquitania. (For detailed discussion see Tovar, most recently in *Landeskunde* 3:49–59; Untermann, "Althispanische Sprachen" 811–12; and Anderson, 103–30.)

In the early first century B.C., some twelve or fourteen peoples can be seen as the major carriers of Iberian civilization. The coastal areas of Catalonia were occupied by the Indicetes (Girona Prov.) and the Laietani (in the Vallès district, Barcelona Prov.), the latter famous for producing ancient Spain's most prized wines. Farther south along the coast lived the Cessetani (Tarragona Prov.), Ilercaones (Castelló Prov.), and Contestani (Alacant Province and part of Murcia). Situated between the latter two, the Edetani controlled not only the coastal plain from Saguntum to Dianium (Denia) but also the inland of the modern province of València, along the Júcar and Turia rivers. Their territory may have extended to the north well into southern Aragón (Teruel Prov.), perhaps as far as Salluia/Salduba (later Caesaraugusta, now Zaragoza; on the Iberian name see Schmoll, *Glotta* 35 [1956] 304–5), in close proximity to the Celtiberian cities (more on which below) southwest of the Ebro River; an argument can be made, however, to identify the population of that area as a different people, named Sedetani (for the distinction of Sedetani and Edetani see Untermann, "Reitermünzen" 114 n. 113; Tovar, *Landeskunde* 3:33–34, is hesitant). The southernmost extension of Iberian civilization was marked by the territories of the Bastetani (provinces of Almería and Granada, Andalucía) and the Oretani (provinces of Jaén and Corduba).

The left side of the central Ebro Valley was held by the great federation of the Ilergetes, centered on the cities of Ilerda (Lleida, Catalunya) and Osca (Huesca, Aragón). Between the plains of the Ebro and the foothills of the

Pyrenees, the northern parts of the Huesca and Lleida provinces were ruled by the warlike Lacetani or Iacetani. (Both forms occur, but never in one and the same author, and it is fairly evident from Strabo 3.4.9–10, Pliny *NH* 3.22–24, and Ptolemy *Geogr.* 2.6.71 that they refer to a single people; the case made by Barbieri, passim, and Tovar, *Landeskunde* 3:35–37, 48–49, in favor of two distinct identities, falls short of persuasion.) Adjacent to the east lived the Ausetani (in the Osona district, northen Barcelona and western Girona provinces). The southern slopes of the Pyrenees were home to the Cerretani, chiefly in the districts of Cerdanya and Alt Urgell (Catalunya).

From about the tenth to the sixth century, Celtic peoples crossed the Pyrenees and settled in the north and west of the Peninsula. As with Hispanians who spoke non-Indo-European languages, several Celtic cultural zones are to be distinguished. Celts who settled along the upper courses of the Ebro, Duero, Tajo, and Júcar rivers, and in the valley of the Jalón, adopted numerous features of the more developed Iberian civilization to the east and south, such as a relatively high degree of urbanization, the Iberian script, and a sophisticated system of coinage, while retaining their Celtic language, social and religious organization, and customs of warfare. The resulting culture has been known since antiquity as "Celtiberian," an appellation properly limited to it, though at times (then and now) applied indiscriminately to all the Hispano-Celtic peoples, or ignorantly to Hispanians in general. (Confusion is easily prompted by the habit of some ancient geographers, beginning with Polybios and continued by Strabo, of employing "Celtiberians" in the restrictive sense while at the same time making "Celtiberia" designate the entire central highlands, the vast plateau known as the Meseta: see Schulten, *Hermes* 46 [1911] 574–76.) The Celtiberians, who mark the most advanced level of civilization among Celts in the Peninsula, fiercely resisted the Roman conquest. Southern Celtiberia (corresponding to the modern region of Madrid, the provinces of Guadalajara, Cuenca, and eastern Toledo in Castilla–La Mancha, and southwestern Zaragoza Province in Aragón) was dominated by three smallish though warlike tribes, the Belli, Titti, and Lusones, collectively referred to simply as the "Celtiberi"; their principal cities were Bilbilis, Contrebia Belaisca, and Segobriga. In northern Celtiberia, the far-flung and powerful federation of the Arevaci held sway over the upper Duero, inhabiting Soria, southern Burgos, northeastern Segovia (all provinces in Castilla y León), and northern Guadalajara (Castilla–La Mancha). Uxama Argaela, Segontia Lanka, Termes, Clunia, Segovia, and Segontia-on-Henares (Sigüenza, Guadalajara Prov.) were their leading towns in the early first century, and Numantia had been in that number until its destruction in 133. Farther north the Berones inhabited what is now La Rioja; although not Celtiberians in the strict sense, they belong to the same cultural zone (see, e.g., coins attributable to Tritium Magallum, now Tricio, near Nájera: Untermann, "Reitermünzen" 143 n. 171; Tovar, *Landeskunde* 3:366). Vareia (near Logroño) is attested as their principal city. The Autricones—in Vizcaya, northern Burgos, and southwestern Alava—may be regarded as the northernmost carriers of Celtiberian civilization, at least if coins with the legend *auta* can be assigned to them (Untermann, "Reitermünzen" 143–44, tentatively).

The ethnographic scene is far more obscure in the west and the far north of the Peninsula. Celts who settled there were for the most part not in close contact with the civilizations of the Northeast and South and adopted none of their advanced features; they struck no coins and made no use of the Iberian script. The study of language and culture in these parts is largely reduced to onomastic observations; what exiguous epigraphic texts exist are limited to Lusitania, late, and written in the Latin alphabet. Still, the evidence has resulted in general acceptance now of the view that the Lusitani (inhabiting, by the early first century, central Portugal and the western half of Spanish Extremadura between the Duero and the Guadiana) were Celts, or rather a mix of Celts and non-Indo-European indigenous peoples, and that they spoke a Celtic language or dialect distinct from Celtiberian, and probably older (see below, 10.1n.). Closely related were the peoples of the Northwest, the Callaeci (a number of small tribes in Galicia and northern Portugal between the Minho and Douro rivers) and the Astures (in Asturia and León). As in Lusitania though perhaps more so, the names of places, persons, and deities there point to a blending of Celtic and pre-Indo-European elements. Within the Hispano-Celtic area, that indigenous substratum appears to have been preserved longest, both linguistically and culturally, among the Cantabri, inhabiting Cantabria and northern Palencia Province, and the Varduli, in Guipúzcoa and northern Alava, País Vasco (see Tovar, *Landeskunde* 3:59–60, 64–71, 103–9, 115–26; Anderson 92).

The center of the Peninsula was populated by three extensive tribal confederations. The Vaccaei occupied the plains of the middle Duero (provinces of Palencia, Segovia, and Valladolid, all in Castilla y León), the Vettones the southwestern part of the central highlands between Duero and Tajo (provinces of Zamora, Salamanca, and Ávila, in Castilla y León). Between Tajo and Guadiana, the territory of the Carpetani (southern Madrid region, provinces of Toledo and Ciudad Real in Castilla–La Mancha, and eastern Extremadura) marked the southern limits of contiguous Celtic settlement; pockets of Celts could be found, however, in Andalusia and southern Portugal. To judge from the onomastic evidence, the Vettones belong to the Lusitanian sphere. The Vaccaei and Carpetani show closer affinity to the Celtiberians than to Lusitania, but their thinly scattered towns and chiefly pastoral-agricultural way of life set them sufficiently apart from their neighbors to the east.

πλεονεξίᾳ ... τῶν πεμπομένων ἑκάστοτε στρατηγῶν ... ἡγεμονίαν: The *stratēgoi* are governors in general, not specifically "Praetors" (as Flacelière and Chambry translate; cf. above, 3.5n.). Rapacity and brutality had long been a hallmark of Roman commanders in Spain, the most egregious examples being L. Licinius Lucullus and Ser. Sulpicius Galba in 151/50 (Appian *Iber.* 51–55, 59–60), T. Didius and C. Flaccus in the 90s (*Iber.* 99–100), and C. Iulius Caesar in 61 (*Caes.* 11–12). The theme of exploitation and abuse of power by Roman officials recurs frequently in P. (see Jones, *Plutarch* 100, and Pelling, "Roman Politics" 179); his unusually keen awareness of the prevailing standard may have contributed to his fascination with Sertorius, exceptional in that regard as in others.

6.8

μάλιστα ... ἠγαπήθη: At Castulo (3.5–10) Sertorius had seen ample evidence of the hardships and degradation imposed on the native population by the Roman practice of billeting troops. The same incident would also have taught him that billeting could be dangerous to Roman forces, and that they might be safer in their own winter camps. As with other measures designed to win the trust and goodwill of the Hispanians, an element of the Roman imperialist's self-interest was present. P. is silent on the question—not without bearing on the events to follow—how popular those orders were with Sertorius' troops.

πρῶτος ... κατασκηνῶν: Elsewhere (*Mar.* 7.3–6; cf. *Caes.* 17.1–3; *Ant.* 4.4) P. explains at length how the willingness to share one's soldiers' hardships is a mark of a leader of men. Sallust's Marius expresses a similar sentiment (*Iug.* 85.33–35), and its presence here with Sertorius can hardly surprise. On the commonplace see Pelling, *Antony* 124–25.

6.9

Ῥωμαίων δὲ ... μετοικούντων: On Roman and Italic settlers in Spain (the so-called *Hispanienses*) during the early first century B.C. see Wilson 9–18, 22–34, 40–42, and Brunt, *Manpower* 159–233. Both studies show that their number in the time of Sertorius was rather small. The center of Roman and Italic presence was the Baetica (i.e., Hispania Ulterior), with three major cities. Italica was founded with ailing veterans by Scipio Africanus in 206 B.C. as a *vicus civium Romanorum* (Appian *Iber.* 38.153; *CIL* II 1119); by Caesar's time it had become a *municipium* ([Caes.] *BAlex* 52.4). Carteia was established by *senatus consultum* in 171 as a *colonia Latina* (Livy 38.3.1–4) for descendants of Roman soldiers and Iberian concubines; native Carteians were also permitted to enroll. The next colony (presumably Latin) in Spain was Corduba, founded probably in 169/8 B.C. by M. Claudius Marcellus; but here too Iberians were enrolled (Polyb. 35.2.2; Strabo 3.2.1; cf. Vell. 1.15.4, 2.7.7; see Knapp, *Córdoba* 10–14, and for a rather radical re-dating to 26/5 B.C., Canto, *Latomus* 50 [1991]). On the East Coast, Carthago Nova and Tarraco, although not constituted as Roman settlements, no doubt had a sizable Romano-Italic population due to their long history as bases for Roman operations in Spain. Both cities served as residence of the governor of Citerior (Strabo 3.4.20). The remains of a Roman town next to the ancient Greek city of Emporion have recently been dated to ca. 113 B.C. (J. Aquilué et al., *El forum Romà d'Empúries*, Barcelona 1984 [*non vidi*], cited in Keay 50–52;

see also Ruiz de Arbulo 476–79, 487); in Late Republican or Augustan days, both towns were amalgamated into a single *municipium*, Emporiae (Untermann, "Reitermünzen" 100; Brunt, *Manpower* 603–4; Ruiz de Arbulo 484–87). Valentia was founded in or about 138 B.C. for Roman veterans of the Viriatic War, probably as a Latin colony (so Wiegels in his exhaustive study, *Chiron* 4 [1974]). In 123, Palma and Pollentia were established on Mallorca, the largest of the Balearic Isles, with 3,000 Roman settlers from Spain (Strabo 3.5.1). Brunt estimates the number of Romans settled in Spain by 49 B.C. at ca. 30,000 (*Manpower* 232); obviously there were fewer a generation earlier.

Hispanienses and Sertorius

In his great study of the Social War and its aftermath, Emilio Gabba argued at length ("Guerra sociale" 284–313) that the Sertorian War was not merely a continuation of Sulla's Civil War (as Treves saw it, surely correctly) but even more so of the Social War: supposedly much of Sertorius' support in Spain came from *Hispanienses* who were of Italic rather than Roman ancestry and only too eager to renew the struggle against the She-Wolf. While fully aware that Sertorius enjoyed virtually no support among the *Hispanienses* of the Baetica, Gabba pointed to a considerable degree of Romanization in the Ebro Valley, a Sertorian stronghold, and to Valentia and Tarraco as places that sided with his insurrection. Gabba explained the discrepancy between pro-Sertorian sentiment in the Northeast and lack of it in the South by claiming Oscan origins, and hence a traditional and deeply rooted hatred of Rome, for the *Hispanienses* of the Ebro Valley and the East Coast ("Guerra sociale" 292–306). Gabba's interpretation, in particular his assumption that the bulk of Sertorius' and Perperna's Roman forces (cf. below, 15.5n.) were recruited locally among the *Hispanienses*, has been refuted in large part by Spann (169–74; curiously Scardigli in her review of Spann's book, 431, faults him for ignoring Gabba's views); suffice it here to address a few points only.

Valentia was taken by Pompeius in 76 (*Pomp.* 18.9; cf. Sall. *Hist.* 2.98.6), Tarraco remained in Sertorian hands until the very end (Strabo 3.4.10). As we do not know how and when Sertorius gained those towns' allegiance in the first place, we cannot say whether they supported him of their own volition or under duress: conclusions as to their anti-Roman attitude hence are tenuous. (One might argue, though, that Tarraco had ample opportunity to side with Pompeius once he had arrived in Spain: but what if it was taken by the Sertorians only later in the war?) A fair degree of Romanization among the Iberian and Celtiberian population of the Ebro Valley is a generally accepted fact (Keay 55) for the early to mid–first century, but Gabba fails to show how that implies an abundance of Romano-Italic settlers or settlements, what he calls "una vera e propria colonizzazione." Certainly Graccurris (Alfaro, La Rioja, on the upper Ebro), founded by Ti. Gracchus in 178 (Livy *Per.* 41; cf. Festus 86.5 Lindsay), was not a Roman town—as Gabba would have it (291, 295)—but entirely Iberian (Brunt, *Manpower* 215; Wiegels, *Chiron* 4 [1974]

169). As for the Oscan aspect, lastly, Gabba is surprisingly vague. From the admittedly meager epigraphical evidence on Republican Spain, he adduces some seventeen names of Etruscan, Oscan, or other Italic origin (297–98), and no one will deny the presence in Spain of a substantial element "dell'Italia centro-meridionale"; Gabba himself admits that Oscan names abound wherever Romano-Italic commercial interests were active, be it Sicily or the East (296). But thirteen names of those seventeen occur in Italica, Carteia, and Carthago Nova, places he knows full well were never Sertorian (304). Only four hail from Valentia: hardly a ringing endorsement of his view. One suspects—though Gabba cautiously allows for some distance (295)—at the bottom of all that the problematic thesis of Menéndez Pidal (*Orígenes* 303–6, 461) that Oscan-Umbrian immigration heavily influenced the linguistic development of the Ebro region and even gave the Ilergetan (Strabo 3.4.10)—i.e., Iberian (cf. above, 6.7: Peoples)—city of Osca its name. Yet the numismatic evidence of Osca permits such a development, if at all, only for the period beginning with the Sertorian War, not prior to it (below, 14.3n.). The Oscan-Italic aspect of Sertorius' struggle looks very much like a modern myth.

What then about Valentia and Tarraco? As Spann (170) has shown, Sertorius found no support whatsoever in northeastern Spain in 82/1: once Annius succeeded in turning Salinator's position at the Pyrenees (below, 7.2–4), Sertorius' hold on the province collapsed overnight. The situation was different after his return from Africa. In Ulterior Metellus Pius, while unable to crush the uprising, proved quite successful in protecting the core of his province, i.e., the Baetica, from enemy inroads between 80 and 77. But effectively no Roman army operated in Citerior during those years, and by 78/7 Sertorius had established his virtual control over the Hither Province (below, 12.4–5nn.). With no Roman forces to protect them, the Romans (and unenfranchised Italics, if any: Brunt, *Manpower* 206–7; cf. Sherwin-White, *Citizenship* 150–52) of the East Coast, especially Valentia and Tarraco, would have found it prudent (and safer) to join Sertorius rather than challenge him. Spann (170) is quite right to emphasize that. By the time Pompeius arrived in late 77, the other side's hold on those cities may have been too firmly established to be cast off by their inhabitants.

τοὺς ... καθοπλίσας, μηχανάς τε ... ὑποβαλόμενος: Pointing out that καθοπλίζω merely means "to equip with arms," Spann (43) denied any attempt at recruiting *Hispanienses* and took the passage as referring to precautionary measures against a possible native revolt. But the building of warships makes little sense unless an attack from the sea (i.e., Italy) was expected, and the entire context, from P.'s announcement (6.4) that Sertorius aimed at creating a refuge for Cinno-Marian survivors to his subsequent narrative (ch. 7) of Annius' invasion, makes it evident that the biographer was thinking of defensive preparations against the *Sullani*. How exactly one ought to envision the arming of Roman residents without subjecting them to military discipline Spann does not say (he cites no parallels); if Sertorius could not rely on their political allegiance (as Spann correctly sees it), to put them in the unsupervised possession of military equipment was surely more dangerous than drafting them. (Not every single one, of course: P. implies no such totality.)

Yet clearly there was a Hispanian angle to all that. P. alludes to a considerable degree of native unrest at the time of Sertorius' arrival (6.6n.), confirmed by Exuperantius: *sed ubi in provinciam venit, ita strenue sociorum animos iam deficientes atque alia cupientes in favorem partium suarum modeste tuendo atque blandiendo perduxit* (8.11–14 = 51 Z). But where the biographer sees primarily Hispanian disaffection with rapacious Roman governors, Sallust (hence Exuperantius) evidently recognized more immediate political concerns: Rome's Hispanian allies were contemplating, understandably, a switch to what might turn out to be the winning side in the Civil War. By addressing their grievances immediately and instituting a reformed way of Roman rule, Sertorius delivered what the *Sullani* might not even be willing to promise. Years later he would still stress the benefits Spain derived from being governed by his faction rather than the post-Sullan oligarchy: *convocatis deinde omnium populorum legationibus et civitatium . . . ad reliqua belli cohortatus est paucis edoctos quantum Hispaniae provinciae interesset suas partes superiores esse* (Livy 91 fr. 22.28–33 W-M, winter 77/6 B.C.).

ἥμερος μὲν ὤν . . . φοβερὸς δὲ . . . φαινόμενος: clearly from Sallust, *modicoque et eleganti imperio percarus fuit* (*Hist.* 1.94—it could refer to Lucullus, but for Exuperantius: *ut et carus esset et tamen ab omnibus timeretur*, 8.13–14 = 51 Z). On Reiske's deletion of κατὰ see Ziegler, "Plutarchstudien" 3–4.

7.1

ὡς δὲ . . . στάσιν: Sulla's final victory came on 1 November 82, in the Battle at the Porta Collina (Vell. 2.27.1, with the date), but the outcome of the war had been decided long before. The younger Marius suffered his disastrous defeat at Sacriportus early in the spring, and Sulla took control of Rome no later than April (Livy *Per.* 87; Vell. 2.26.1; Plut. *Sulla* 28.7–15; Appian 87.397–89.408; on the chronology see Linden 40–53, generally convincing). By the middle of summer, Metellus Pius and Pompeius had conquered the Ager Gallicus, and the great battles in Etruria (Clusium) and Umbria (Spoletium) had established Sullan control of central Italy; worse, they had effectively broken the back and morale of the government's armies: henceforth, desertion became rampant (Appian 87.394–96, 88.401, 89.408–90.415; cf. Livy *Per.* 88). Not much later (August), if later at all, Metellus and M. Lucullus eliminated the government's last forces in Cisalpine Gaul at Faventia and Fidentia, respectively, and the entire region declared its allegiance for Sulla. Carbo and Norbanus abandoned Italy soon afterward (Appian 91.418–92.425).

Given those developments, it seems likely that Sertorius knew the situation to be hopeless by midsummer 82. The first List of Proscription was published soon after the Colline Gate, probably on 3 November (Livy *Per.* 88; Plut. *Sulla*

31.1–5; Appian 95.441–42; for the date see Hinard, *Proscriptions* 104–10). Sertorius' name appeared on it (Oros. 5.21.3; cf. Livy *Per.* 90; Val. Max. 7.3.6; Flor. 2.10.2; Schol. Gronov. 317.6 St), his qualifications being impeccable: τοὺς στρατηγοὺς ἢ ταμίας ἢ χιλιάρχους ἢ ὅσοι τι συνέπραξαν ἄλλοι τοῖς πολεμίοις, μεθ' ἣν ἡμέραν Σκιπίων ὁ ὕπατος οὐκ ἐνέμεινε τοῖς πρὸς αὐτὸν ὡμολογημένοις, μετελεύσεσθαι κατὰ κράτος, so Sulla had announced (Appian 95.441). News of the proscriptions would have reached Spain early in 81 if not sooner.

(L.?) **Livius** (31) **Salinator**: cf. Broughton, *MRR* 2:79 n. 5. The gentilicium is ἰουλίου in the codices, but Cichorius, *RS* 256, showed conclusively that *Livius* is often confused with *Iulius* in Greek manuscripts; as there is no known instance of the cognomen Salinator in the *gens Iulia*, his emendation of the name to Livius ought to be retained. (Spann, 47, 172–74 seems unaware of Cichorius' note and writes *Iulius*; Ziegler, and Flacelière and Chambry, adopt the emendation.) Salinator's praenomen may have been Lucius, if he is identical with the moneyer of that name ca. 84 (Crawford, *RRC* no. 355). The notion that he was "one of the Quaestors" who accompanied Sertorius to Spain in 82 (Gabba, "Guerra sociale" 306) has little in support: the only such Quaestor on record is L. Hirtuleius (below, 12.4n.), and the only other Quaestor attested as serving under Sertorius, in the year 76, is M. Marius (below, 24.4n.). If Sertorius had two Quaestors in 82 (conceivable, as he was in charge of both provinces, but far from certain), Marius will have the better claim.

ἑξακισχιλίους ὁπλίτας ἔχοντος: probably one legion (cf. Brunt, *Manpower* 470). Whether it actually numbered 6,000 is questionable: P. routinely writes "6,000 troops" when his source(s) simply state(s) "one legion." For a discussion see below, 12.2n.; cf. also 13.10.

7.2

μετ' οὐ πολὺ ... ἐκπεμφθείς: Annius is generally thought to have reached the Pyrenees in the spring of 81 (e.g., Bieńkowski, "Chronologie" 138, 144; Schulten 45; cf. *MRR* 2:77). Claiming that Spain was not "Sulla's primary concern in the winter of 82–81" and that the dictator could not "afford to send out a 'large force' to deal with Sertorius" until after Pompey's return from Sicily and Africa, Spann (45–47) dates Annius' departure from Italy to late March, his arrival at the Pyrenees to May or June. But Pompeius was dispatched to Sicily soon after the Battle of the Colline Gate, probably in November 82 (Appian 92.426–93.428 implies he was still in Italy, though not at Rome, on 1 November, whereas Val. Max. 6.2.8, 9.13.2, implies that Carbo was put to death by Pompeius in Sicily while still Consul, i.e., by 29 December: Keaveney, *AC* 51 [1982] 122). His army consisted of six legions (*Pomp.* 11.3), leaving at least seventeen to be employed elsewhere. (This assumes that Pompey's legions were among the twenty-three eventually granted land in

Italy: Appian 100.470.) No shortage of troops ready and willing to go on soldiering can plausibly be postulated (for more on which see Keaveney, *CS* 19 [1982] 538–43). Spain was important, and there is no reason why Sertorius should have ranked low on Sulla's list of priorities. Most likely Annius was sent to Spain very early in 81, quite possibly still in 82.

C. Annius (9) T. f. T. n.: son and grandson of the Consuls of 128 and 153; the cognomen Luscus is unattested and improbable (Badian, *BICS* Suppl. 51 [1988] 6 n. 4). He is styled Proconsul on his coins (*RRC* no. 366), but his career remaines a mystery. Unless like Pompeius in Africa he was a *privatus cum imperio,* he must have held a praetorship with his *imperium* prorogued through 81; Broughton suggests 83 or 82 (*MRR* 3:15). He would then have sided with Sulla in a timely fashion, and been entrusted with an independent command (cf. L. Marcius Philippus *cos.* 91, conquering Sardinia for Sulla early in 82: Livy *Per.* 86). But a praetorship in 83/2 would put his birth ca. 125, rather late in his father's life. (Parallels could be adduced, though: see Badian, "Consuls" 401–2.) The problem may be circumvented by making him the grandson of the Consul of 128, a possibility entertained by Badian (*BICS*). Yet Annius is just as likely to have been Praetor between 90 and 87, and to have spent the years of *"Cinnae dominatio"* away from Italy, as did Metellus Pius (*pr.* 89), Appius Claudius (*pr.* 89 or 88), and L. Licinius Murena (*pr.* 88 or 87: *MRR* 2:40, 3:123). Like them (and Sulla), he could have regarded his *imperium* to be continuous no matter how the government in Rome saw it. Annius' identification with the Prefect of four Ligurian cohorts in 108 (Sall. *Iug.* 77.4) is entirely uncertain, there being a number of C. Annii attested for that period (*MRR* 2:529–30). The Military Tribune T. Annius T. f. Ouf(entina) of Pompeius Strabo's *consilium* at Asculum in 89 (Cichorius, "Offizierskorps" 128 no. 12), however, may be the Proconsul's nephew (or younger brother, if the Consul of 128 was Gaius' grandfather). As the general scarcity of provincial governors so characteristic of the 80s hardly came to an end immediately after Sulla's victory, Annius probably held both Spains (Badian, "Governors" 11 = *Studies* 88, and already Mommsen, *RMW* 600); but if only one, it was certainly Citerior (Schulten 45 n. 231). Despite his successful recovery of Spain for the Sullan regime, that command in 81 marks the end of his career, perhaps of his life: he disappears from history.

7.3

(P.) Calpurnius (49) Lanarius: The praenomen is based on his identification—reasonable but not certain—with a person mentioned in Cic. *Off.* 3.66 (cf. Val. Max. 8.2.1) involved in a lawsuit during the 90s (F. Miltner, *RE* 22.1 [1953] 166). He may be related to the moneyer P. Calp(urnius), ca. 133 B.C. (*RRC* no. 247), who may be identical with the Calpurnius *vir praetorius* of Pliny *NH* 3.21 (for other possibilities see Syme, "Missing Senators" 57–58 = *Roman Papers* 1:277). Whether Calpurnius Lanarius was an officer of Sertorius or of Annius is much disputed: see following note. P.'s phrasing (ἐπίκλησιν) follows Sallust verbatim: *Calpurnius cognomento Lanarius* (*Hist.* 1.95).

δολοφονήσαντος τὸν Λίουιον: Exactly what happened remains unclear, except that P.'s source told of treachery and murder (δολοφονέω thus always: *Tim.* 16.5–6; *Phil.* 15.3; *Arat.* 3.4; *Pomp.* 20.2, of Sertorius' assassination; *Parall. Gr. et Rom.* 315B; *Amat. narr.* 773B); the natural conclusion is to see in Calpurnius an officer of Salinator who had decided to throw in his lot with the *Sullani* and proceeded to assassinate his commander. Yet based on two Sallust fragments (1.96, *Salinator in agmine occiditur*, and 1.97, *paucos saltum insidentis*), Schulten (45) conjectured the matter a bit differently: misled by Calpurnius into believing that Annius was trying to cross the Pyrenees by another pass, Salinator abandoned his original position and on the march was ambushed and killed. Accepting Schulten's reconstruction, Syme ("Missing Senators" 58–59 = *Roman Papers* 1:278) went a step further and roundly declared that P. misunderstood his Latin source: no treachery at all was involved, and Calpurnius was an officer of Annius (so also *MRR* 2:78) who employed "some Thermopylean flank movement" to dislodge and eliminate Salinator.

No such drastic rewriting of P.'s account is justified. For one, *Hist.* 1.97 ought to be removed from the discussion as Maurenbrecher assigned it to the Salinator incident on tenuous grounds: it may equally well—not to say better—pertain to the events narrated in 13.10–12, where an ambush is actually attested. Next, *in agmine occiditur*: while implying that Salinator's forces were on the move, it does not preclude assassination by one (or several) of his men, nor is it suggestive of "a tactical manoeuvre or ruse," as McGushin (164) would have it. As for P. here misunderstanding Sallust's Latin, that pretext for substituting one's own ideas, however unfounded in the evidence of the sources, is as gratuitous as it is convenient. Spann (47–48) rightly exercised caution.

τῶν στρατιωτῶν . . . ἐκλιπόντων: evidently not an orderly retreat; cf. below, Ἄννιος . . . τοὺς ἐμποδὼν ἀνιστάς.

ὑπερβαλὼν . . . χειρὶ μεγάλῃ: certainly with no less than two legions, but the governor of Transalpina in 78 had three at his disposal (Oros. 5.23.4; cf. Broughton, *MRR* 2:87, and see below, 13.5n.). If both Sertorius and Annius were in charge of all of Spain (above, 6.6 and 7.2nn.), the latter had to be ready to face a force of perhaps several legions (see below, 7.4n.). After Sulla's victory in Italy, there was an abundance of troops available; three or four legions seem a good estimate of Annius' force.

7.4

Σερτώριος δ' οὐκ ὢν ἀξιόμαχος: It appears that once Annius had crossed the Pyrenees, Sertorius was left in no position to fight in the field. Spann (48) theorizes that he "must have joined the retreating soldiers with part of his

Spanish forces and attempted to regroup and oppose the enemy at some strategic point." But any "Spanish," i.e., Celtiberian (ibid.) forces or allies of Sertorius at that time are highly conjectural at best. He was to leave Spain from New Carthage far to the south, which may suggest that he never was as far north as the Pyrenees or even the Ebro: otherwise, we must ask why he did not embark at Barcino, Tarraco, or Valentia. Those places, of course, may have sided with Annius. All that can be said is that Sertorius was quickly forced to retreat to Cartagena.

μετὰ τρισχιλίων: Whether these were remnants of Salinator's corps (so Spann, 48) or additional forces (Schulten 44) cannot be established. Probably Sertorius had brought some troops with him from Italy (though Appian 108.506, στρατὸν ἔχων ἐκ τῆς Ἰταλίας αὐτῆς, proves nothing, as it refers really to his return from Africa: above, 6.6n.), and we must allow for the possibility that the usual garrison of two legions may still have been present in either province (see Smith, *Service in the Post-Marian Roman Army* 14, 21; and cf. Brunt, *Manpower* 434). Thus the forces under Sertorius' command may be estimated at anywhere from one legion fresh out of Italy (Spann 40) to four or more, albeit severely depleted, since the only supplements sent to Spain in the 80s would have come with Sertorius.

εἰς Καρχηδόνα τὴν νέαν: On Carthago Nova (Cartagena, Murcia) see E. Hübner, *RE* 3.2 (1899) 1620–26. Founded by Hasdrubal the Barqid ca. 228/7 B.C. and in Roman hands since Scipio's brilliant assault in 209, the town controlled some of the richest silver mines in the ancient world and served, with Tarraco, as a principal residence of the Roman commander in Hither Spain (Strabo 3.2.10, 3.4.20).

7.5

κατὰ τὴν Μαυρουσίαν: Mauretania, i.e., Northwest Africa. The Muluccha River marked its eastern boundary with Numidia (Sall. *Iug.* 19.7). Μαυρουσία (so always in P.: *Mar.* 41.3; below, 9.2, 9.4, 13.9, 27.6) may be an earlier form of the name; cf. Coelius Antipater, *HRR* F 55, *Maurusii;* Polyb. 3.33.15, Μαυρούσιοι.

αὖθις . . . ἀποκρούεται: No details are known. Spann (48) suggests that Sertorius attempted "some sort of attack" on one of the coastal cities, "such as Malaca" (Málaga, Andalucía). Evidently, Sertorius was not yet willing to admit defeat.

Κιλισσῶν δὲ . . . προσγενομένων: Piracy had been endemic to the coast of Kilikia from times immemorial, and the effective end of Seleukid control over the area in the second century had resulted in its steady growth. Despite Roman intervention beginning with the establishment of a military *provincia Cilicia* in 102 (*MRR* 1:568; cf. Badian, "Silence" 170 n. 40), the early decades of the first century saw a rapid expansion of Kilikian piratical activity throughout the entire Mediterranean, along with the development of a rather complex military organization, including proper squadrons and admirals. During the First Mithradatic War (89–85 B.C.), the Pontic King was able to use the pirates as a virtual extension of his own naval forces. Participation was by no means limited to the native peoples of southeastern Anatolia, but Kilikia remained the organization's operational center, and the literary sources habitually talk about "Kilikian pirates" without distinguishing on a regional or ethnic basis. For ancient accounts see *Pomp.* 24; Appian *Mithr.* 92–93 and cf. 63.262; Dio 36.20.1–23.3; useful modern surveys are offered by Ormerod, *Piracy* 190–247; Maróti, *Altertum* 7 (1961) 32–41 and *Ricerche Barbagallo* 1:481–93.

Πιτυούσσῃ νήσῳ προσέβαλε: The Pityussians are the southernmost of the Balearic Isles, Ebusus (Eivissa [Ibiza]) and Ophiussa (Formentera). Sertorius evidently sailed to the larger one, Ebusus; Ophiussa was uninhabited (Strabo 3.5.1; cf. Schulten 47 n. 237). The Roman conquest of the Baleares in 123 B.C. had been prompted at least in part by piratical activity centered there (see Morgan, *CSCA* 2 [1969]; Prieto Arciniega, *Habis* 18–19 [1987–88], adds nothing). Spann (48–49) persuasively suggests that Annius, in establishing a garrison on Ebusus (see following note), had eliminated a pirate base there, and that the Kilikians had been looking for Sertorius to enlist his help in their attempt to recover the island.

ἀπέβη τὴν . . . φρουρὰν βιασάμενος: an indication that Annius took his duties seriously. The Pityussae offered an advantageous base of operations not only to pirates but also to Sertorius, and the garrison may have been established with that eventuality in mind. Since Annius had had time to do so, Sertorius' capture of Ebusus will belong to the summer or fall of 81 (cf. below, 7.6n.). P.'s narrative is moving very rapidly.

7.6

ναυσί τε πολλαῖς: Whether Annius brought a fleet with him to Spain is unknown; in any case, most of the ships built by Sertorius in 82 (6.9) would have fallen into his hands.

πεντακισχιλίοις ὁπλίταις: probably one legion (so Brunt, *Manpower* 471), though P. does not normally convert "one legion" into "5,000 men" (below, 12.2n.): he may have found the figure in Sallust.

πρὸς ὃν ἐπεχείρησε μὲν διαναυμαχεῖν: Annius' forces were superior at sea, but even more so on land (cf. 7.4). If Sertorius allowed him to disembark his army, he was as good as lost. A naval engagement entailed a chance, if not of victory, then at least of escape. ("At the very least, he might simply run for it": Spann 49.)

ζεφύρῳ δὲ λαμπρῷ τοῦ πελάγους ἀνισταμένου: a mistral, i.e., a vehement wind from the northwest, common in the Gulf of Valencia during the winter months (Schulten 48 n. 238; Casson, *Ships* 272): the events seem to be datable to late 81.

τὰ πολλὰ ... περιβάλλοντος: "causing most of Sertorius' vessels to founder sideways amidst the reefs, because of their light build." In heavy weather the safest course is normally to heave to, i.e., back the sail(s) against the wind so as to make no headway. The consequence will be considerable drift backwards, all the more rapidly in the case of a lightly built ship with a shallow draft (cf. above, ἐλαφροῖς καὶ πρὸς τάχος ... πεποιημένοις σκάφεσι χρώμενος). Close to a leeward coast such a situation is apt to be lethal. Barely more promising, unfortunately, is the alternative, apparently chosen by many of Sertorius' captains: to run before the sea, i.e., taking the wind abaft, in the hope of making a suitable port or clearing the land, since the ship, before the wind, will retain some steerageway and be able to hold a course. To execute the necessary turn the vessel will have to wear round with the wind, a risky maneuver under the circumstances as it requires plenty of sea room. The oncoming wind has reduced the boat's speed through the water, thereby diminishing its ability to respond to the rudder quickly; as a result it will turn slowly. The slower the turn, the more dangerous: as the vessel broaches to, i.e., comes to lie parallel to the trough of the waves, it loses steerageway, and—apart from being in imminent danger of capsizing—will be blown sideways in the direction of the storm until it completes its turn—off a leeward coast, again, a situation apt to be lethal. Unable to keep heading into the storm and lacking the necessary sea room to wear round safely, those of Sertorius' ships closest to the shore were caught helplessly with their beam to the sea (πλάγια) and shattered on the rocks. Others—as a relevant detail preserved from Sallust indicates—while already far enough onto the open sea to evade the reefs, nonetheless did not escape capsizing: *earum aliae paululum progressae nimio simul et incerto onere, cum pavor corpora agitaverat, deprimebantur* (*Hist.* 1.98). The boats were crowded, hence topheavy, besides having a shallow draft—a deadly combination in heavy weather. Evidently the bulk of Sertorius' fleet had not yet progressed very far when the mistral struck; Spann (49) may be right in placing the incident in or near the Bay of San Antonio Abad, between Cap Nunó and the Isla Conejera on the west coast of Eivissa. Caution is advised, however, with regard to the scope of Sertorius' losses. Taking τὰ πολλὰ τῶν ... πλοίων literally, Spann thinks that "more than half of his ships" were destroyed; but 9.1–5 shows that Sertorius had a sizable force left, even without his Kilikian allies.

7.7

αὐτὸς ... πολεμίων: closely following Sallust, *cum Sertorius neque erumpere tam levi copia navibus ...* (*Hist.* 1.99). Maurenbrecher took *navibus* as instrumental with *erumpere*, Caviglia (160–61) in a separative sense (i.e., *cum neque levi copia militum in terram escendere posset*). P.'s description would seem to support the latter: Sertorius was kept from the open sea by the storm, not a shortage of ships, and from making it back to land because Annius' troops already had secured the shore. (McGushin, 165, follows Maurenbrecher, with no indication of knowing Caviglia's study.) But again, the biographer withholds information a historian would consider crucial. Evidently the expected battle (ἐπεχείρησε μὲν διαναυμαχεῖν, 7.6) did not take place: were Annius' ships simply blown into port (Spann 49) by the same northwester that partly sank Sertorius' vessels, partly prevented them from getting away safely?

8.1

νήσοις . . . ἀνύδροις: identified by Schulten (48) with the small islands in the Gulf of Alicante, such as El Peñón (off Benidorm), Isla Plana (off Santa Pola), or Isla Grosa (north of Cabo de Palos, near Cartagena). But the storm would have driven Sertorius south, toward the African coast, and P.'s wording may indicate that these islands were closer to the Straits than to Eivissa. One should consider islands along the coast of North Africa, e.g., the Chafarinas or the Farallones off Morocco.

τὸν Γαδειραῖον πορθμόν: the Straits of Gibraltar.

ἐν δεξιᾷ . . . τῆς Ἰβηρίας: Sailing north after passing the Straits, he reached the Atlantic coast of Spain.

μικρὸν ὑπὲρ τῶν τοῦ Βαίτιος ἐκβολῶν: Schulten suggests that Sertorius landed at Onuba (Huelva, Andalucía), "the first port north of the Baitis." While ὑπὲρ here probably means "above" = "north" rather than "upstream," one may doubt whether Sertorius could freely sail into any harbor town of the Roman province. A landfall on an uninhabited stretch of coast is more likely.

Two mouths of the Baetis (Río Guadalquivir) are attested by Strabo 3.1.9, 2.11; cf. Paus. 6.19; Ptol. 2.4.4. In earlier times there were four (Avien. *Ora mar.* 286–90); today only the easternmost arm still exists, emptying into the sea at Sanlúcar de Barrameda (Cádiz Prov., Andalucía).

ὅς . . . ὄνομα . . . παρέσχεν: not, of course, in Republican times; P. reflects the provincial arrangements of his own day, as established by Augustus. *Hispania Baetica* is the old Ulterior, minus the districts west and north of the Anas (Río Guadiana); essentially it corresponds to the modern region of Andalucía and the province of Badajoz (southern Extremadura). Augustus' newly created province *Lusitania* comprised all the territory between the Anas and Durius (Duero) rivers west of Toletum (Toledo, Castilla–La Mancha), roughly corresponding to modern Portugal, northern Extremadura (Cáceres Prov.), and southwestern Old Castile (provinces of Salamanca and Ávila). The rest of the Peninsula formed the province of *Hispania Citerior sive Tarraconensis*.

8.2

ναῦταί τινες ἐτυγχάνουσιν αὐτῷ: perhaps not the whole truth. The sailors returning from the Atlantic would presumably be headed for a major port, either Gades (Cádiz) or Hispalis (Sevilla); that they should happen to make their landfall just where Sertorius had gone ashore awhile earlier stretches coincidence a bit far. His Kilikian friends were still with him (as follows from 9.2): presumably they were practicing their trade—Sertorius, after all, needed to support himself and his men—and thus encountered, i.e., intercepted the sailors.

τῶν Ἀτλαντικῶν νήσων ... Μακάρων: Pliny *NH* 6.199–205 gives a summary of what was known in his time (and P.'s, presumably) about the islands off the Atlantic coast of Africa. Identification is difficult, however. Cerne (6.199) may reasonably be identified with Herne Island (23° 45' N, near the coast of Western Sahara: see W. H. Schoff, in Oikonomides, *Hanno the Carthaginian: Periplus* 46), and the Gorgades (6.200) with either the Bissagos Group (Arquipélago dos Bijagós, off Guinea-Bissau) or Sherbro Island (off Sierra Leone). But only Pliny's description (6.203–5) of the Fortunate Isles as explored by King Iuba II of Mauretania (see below, 9.10n.) leaves no doubt: these six islands are the Canaries (Islas Canarias).

That does not, alas, settle the question of P.'s and Sertorius' Isles of the Blest. Evidently Sallust told the same story: *quas duas insulas propinquas inter se et decem ⟨milia⟩ stadium procul a Gadibus sitas constabat suopte ingenio alimenta mortalibus gignere* (*Hist.* 1.100; cf. 101–3). Yet the fragment does not permit us to tell whether Sallust continued with a full description such as 8.3–4, and there are troubling discrepancies as regards P. Λεπτῷ παντάπασι πορθμῷ διαιρούμεναι is decidedly more specific than *propinquas inter se*, and Gades is not the same as Λιβύη. That may simply be due to carelessness on P.'s part (so Schulten 49–50), but J. Morr (67 n. 96) long ago adduced good reason to believe that the biographer here was not merely excerpting Sallust but used a different (though probably common) source for the details on the Isles: likely enough Poseidonios. Indeed Spann recently argued in favor of P.'s account being the one following Poseidonios more accurately ("Isles," passim), and proposed to identify the Blessed Isles with the easternmost of the Canaries, Lanzarote and Fuerteventura.

Yet Iuba's Fortunate Isles are six, whereas both P. and Sallust know only two. Moreover, P.'s careful description does not well fit the Canaries. His Blessed Isles are characterized by perfect Oceanic climate, since they are located far from any shore and the effects of continental winds, especially those from the north and east: their prevailing winds come from the west and northwest, i.e., from the sea (8.4). Spann's contention ("Isles" 76) that P.'s "10,000 stades from Libya" means not "from the nearest point on the African coast"—the distance between the eastern Canaries and the coast is only ca. 100 kilometers—but "from the area around Tangier" is quite untenable. P.'s source clearly and specifically placed the islands in the expanse of the Atlantic (cf. Müller, *Erdkunde* 6). Nor do the prevailing wind patterns agree with the Canaries, where north and east winds (i.e., the continental βορέαι and ἀφελιῶται of 8.4) dominate (Müller, 6; Spann, "Isles" 75 n. 4, cites that study but takes no account of the wind patterns outlined in it). Spann's claim ("Isles" 77) that Lanzarote and Fuerteventura were truly paradisiacal as late as the sixteenth century, hence also in antiquity, was refuted by Müller long ago (*Erdkunde* 6, 13–17, 29–30). Their continental climate could never approximate the even and moderate temperatures year-round specified by P., and their description in Pliny (6.203–4: Lanzarote appears to be Iuba's *Ombrion,* Fuerteventura his *Capraria*) has nothing idyllic about it. (See also Fernández-Armesto, *Canary Islands* 2, on fifteenth- and sixteenth-century conditions: "Lanzarote and Fuerteventura, with their scant rainfall, low reliefs, and sandy, stony soil, could only sustain in this period a life that was at best precarious and poor.") Spann finally postulates Poseidonios as the common source not only of Sallust and P. but of Strabo as well (. . . Μακάρων τινὰς νήσους . . . ἃς καὶ νῦν δεικνυμένας ἴσμεν οὐ πολὺ τῶν ἄποθεν τῶν ἄκρων τῆς Μαυρουσίας τῶν ἀντικειμένων τοῖς Γαδείροις, 3.2.13). Obviously Strabo knew those Blessed Isles to be near the African coast, which agrees with the Canaries but not with the isles of P.: Morr (67) was rightly skeptical about ascribing Poseidonian origins to the Strabo passage.

Now P.'s description perfectly fits, as is well known, Madeira: the moderate climate all year, the prevailing winds from the west, northwest, and south, the location far (600 kilometers) from the African coast. The story of the discovery of Madeira by Phoenician seafarers was told by Timaios (*FGrHist* 566 F 164 = Diodor. 5.19–20; cf. [Arist.] *MA* 836B30–837A6). Thus most scholars have been inclined to see the Blessed Isles of Poseidonios, Sallust, and P. in the two largest islands of the Madeira Archipelago, Madeira and Porto Santo (Müller, *Erdkunde* 5–8, with the essential argumentation; cf. C. T. Fischer, *RE* 7.1 [1910] 42–43; Schulten 49–50). Müller also showed how in the later first century B.C. that appellation shifted to the Canaries: first to Tenerife and Gran Canaria (almost certainly the *Fortunatae* of Statius Sebosus, Plin. *NH* 6.202), then with Iuba's exploration to the entire archipelago (*Erdkunde* 21–29). Müller's findings have recently been affirmed, with additional evidence and detailed refutation of Spann's view, by Keyser (112–26).

μυρίους . . . σταδίους: The true distance is considerably less for both Madeira and the Canaries. Madeira is ca. 1,100 kilometers = ca. 6,000 stades from Cádiz, roughly the same from northwest Mauretania. (The nearest point on the African coast is Essaouria, Morocco, at ca. 650 kilometers = ca. 3,600 stades distance; but other than in the case of the Canaries it seems doubtful whether the ancients were able to determine that.) Lanzarote is likewise ca. 1,100 kilometers = 6,000 stades from Gades, but merely 120 kilometers = 660 stades from Cape Juby (Morocco); Fuerteventura is even closer to the continent: both islands could have come within sight of a coasting vessel (Keyser 118). The discrepancy should not surprise. Lacking reliable means of measuring speed and distance at sea, ancient mariners apparently assumed as a prevailing rule of thumb that a ship would travel 1,000 stades in a day and a night with a favorable wind, correspondingly less when winds were unfavorable (Casson, *Ships* 281–91, esp. 288 n. 83).

8.4

ἀὴρ ... τρέφουσιν: The careful attention paid to the role of the winds in shaping the islands' climate has a strong Poseidonian flavor: Morr 67 n. 96.

8.5

αὐτόθι ... ὕμνησε: cf. Sall. *Hist.* 1.101, *secundum philosophos elysium est insulae fortunatae, quas ait Sallustius inclitas esse Homeri carminibus* (Servius *In Aeneid.* 5.735). Homer's Elysium is a land ἐς πείρατα γαίης, on the shores of the Okeanos, with a mild climate and soft breezes of the Zephyr (*Od.* 4.563–68); the notion of μακάρων νῆσοι παρ' Ὠκεανὸν βαθυδίνην first occurs in Hesiod (*Erga* 168), and its earliest attestation in Latin literature is found in Plautus (*Trin.* 549). Far from having spread from the Greeks to the barbarians, however, the motif of a land of the dead situated in the Far West is much older than Homer, and quite common among Indo-European peoples (nor limited to them: see G. Bibby, *Looking for Dilmun,* New York, 1969, on the Sumerian tale of Dilmun, Isle of the Blest in the Persian Gulf). Wagenvoort has shown how widespread was the belief that the souls of the dead traveled westward to a land or island(s) beyond or in the Ocean ("Journey," passim), and has called attention to the related notion, prevalent in regions located on a western coast, that people cannot die except at low tide: their souls must be able to cross the sea (116–17; cf. Plin. *NH* 2.220; Philostr. *Vita Apollon.* 5.2). In western Europe those beliefs are attested in particular for the Germanic and Celtic peoples (Wagenvoort, "Journey" 116 and "Nehalennia" 273–92; *Mnemosyne* 24 [1971] 273–92; cf. Prokop. *Goth.* 4.48); T. W. Africa (534 n. 65) points to the Isle of Avalon, Tirnan Oc (the Land of Youth), and Mag Mell (the Field of Happiness)—all Celtic Islands of the Blest in the Atlantic. Spain was the last segment in the "Heraklean Way," the "road" traveled by the souls of the dead, under the guidance of Herakles, from Greece via Italy and southern Gaul to the Isles of the Blest in the western Ocean (Wagenvoort, "Journey" 114–15, 153–54, and "Inscription," surely offering the correct interpretation of [Arist.] *MA* 837A7–11 and *IG* XIV 2462; cf. also DeWitt 59–61, on Hannibal's exploiting Heraklean associations with his march on Italy). The Celts and Celto-Hispanians of northern and western Spain will not have greatly differed in their beliefs. For the Northwest there is evidence: six "Islands of the Gods" *quas aliqui Fortunatas appellavere* were said to lie in the Atlantic off the Promunturium Arrotrebarum or Nerium (between Cabo de Finisterre and La Coruña in Galicia: Plin. *NH* 4.119; cf. 4.111 and Strabo 3.3.5; see also Schulten, *Geografía* 378), and the river Limia/Limaea (Río Limia) in northern Lusitania was variously known as Lethe (Strabo 3.3.4–5; Appian *Iber*. 71.301, 72.304) or Oblivio (Sall. *Hist*. 3.44; Livy *Per*. 55; Plin. *NH* 4.112, 115), of evident association with the land of the dead (cf. Wagenvoort, "Journey" 130–31). In southern Lusitania, one may add the island sacred to Herakles off Onuba (Huelva): Strabo 3.5.5.

9.1: Sertorius and the Blessed Isles

P. reports similarly fantastic plans of Kleopatra after the disaster at Actium, and dwells at length on Antony's seclusion in his "Timoneion" in the harbor of Alexandria (*Ant*. 69.3–7; cf. Pelling, *Antony* 289–90). Lucullus' withdrawal into private life is likewise attributed to political defeat and disappointment (*Luc*. 38.2–3). Note, however, the peculiar twist here: what is decadent resignation in the case of Lucullus and escapist withdrawal in that of Antony becomes an admirable wish for peace and weariness of civil war, mingled with an irrepressible will to survive, in the person of Sertorius.

Treves (133) doubted that the historical Sertorius ever thought of sailing to the Isles of the Blest, and La Penna ("*Historiae*" 230) suspected Sallust of injecting some of his own "soul weary and disgusted with politics" into that tale. In his attempt to establish Sallust's Sertorius as a largely fictional character, a composite of Caesar, Alexander, and Odysseus, Katz likewise would see here a "Sallustian literary creation" somehow related to Odysseus' *Nekyia* ("Sertorius" 300–301; cf. "Notes" 66 n. 62). García Moreno, in a similar vein, considers the story a fictional design by Sallust to enhance his portrait of Sertorius as the ideal Cynic-Stoic ruler-hero, and condemns "positivist" attempts at locating the Isles ("Paradoxography" 142–48). Yet such dismissal is rash.

The prevalence of Celtic beliefs in islands of the dead situated in the western Ocean (above, 8.5n.) must not be seen in isolation. Both T. W. Africa (533–34) and Moeller (402–7) have demonstrated how deeply Sertorius was possessed of the characteristics associated in Celtic and Germanic mythology with shamanic war leaders: one-eyedness (see 1.8n.), the ability to change shape (i.e., using a disguise: 3.3), and his divine messenger the white fawn (below, 11.3–8nn.). Indeed P. attests how the Celto-Hispanian Lusitani perceived Sertorius as a godlike leader (12.1, οὐχ ὑπ' ἀνδρὸς ἀλλοδαποῦ λογισμῶν, ἀλλ' ὑπὸ θεοῦ στρατηγεῖσθαι πειθομένοις). A century and a half earlier, another one-eyed warrior from a distant land had with divine guidance led Celtiberians and Gauls across the Alps and on to victory, using various disguises to keep Celtic chieftains in check (Livy 21.22.5–9, and esp. Polybios 3.47.8–48.12, 78.1–4, labeling the wigs, with the true rationalist's incomprehension, a Φοινικικὸν στρατήγημα): in years to come, his Celtiberian troops were to call Sertorius a Hannibal returned (Appian 112.522). García Moreno does well to stress the Heraklean-Odyssean traits in the literary tradition about Sertorius ("Paradoxography" 146–48), traits equally characteristic of Hannibal: but past masters of politics and leadership in war at all times have availed themselves of myth, superstition, prejudice, or folklore—in short, of whatever in a people's cultural tradition might serve their purpose. All propaganda is ultimately based on that. When we read about Mussolini announcing the restoration of the *Impero,* Marshal Stalin proclaiming a new Great Patriotic War (and, in anticipation—briefly suspended—thereof, putting his indelible stamp on the production of *Aleksandr Nevskii*), or MacArthur referring to himself in the third person, we recognize the intended historical allusions: yet few would see in such reports mere fiction, tailored to suit some literary model. When Rommel commits suicide at the Führer's orders, we are looking at reality, not the reworking of a Tacitean *topos* in twentieth-century historiography. The mythical elements surrounding the person of Sertorius were deliberately cultivated, not by Sallust or P., but by the man himself.

Sertorius spoke some Gaulish (above, 3.3) and clearly had used his years as a Military Tribune in Spain to learn more about the natives: the ease and skill with which he was to exercise his leadership (see the numerous examples in chapters 11 through 17) indicates a more than superficial understanding of Hispanian, and particularly Celto-Hispanian, culture. When he learned of the real islands in the Atlantic, he could hardly have failed to realize their significance in the context of Celtic beliefs. At the moment, that insight would not have begotten any practical results, his small force consisting largely of Romans. But when he returned to Spain to become the leader of the Celto-Hispanian Lusitani (below, 10.1n.), any prior association with the Isles of the Blest would be a valuable addition to his shamanic attributes: though he had not actually been there, he possessed the knowledge of where the Isles could be found (cf. T. W. Africa 534, and in greater depth Moeller 408). Herakles and Hermes, the Germanic Odin, and probably the Celtic Lug all were psychopomps, guides of the dead on their way to Elysium; so was, among Celtic and Germanic peoples, the stag (below, 12.1n.). In the light of 11.3–8, it is difficult to believe that Sertorius was not aware of such associations (consider especially γιγνώσκων εὐάλωτον εἰς δεισιδαιμονίαν εἶναι φύσει τὸ βαρβαρικόν); it is even more difficult to believe that they were created by the literary artistry of Sallust, who—unlike Poseidonios—is not known for taking an interest in matters Celto-Germanic, or knowledge thereof. Concerning matters Hispanian, "there is no trace of any comprehensive excursus on Spain" in the *Histories,* Syme perceptively remarked (*Sallust* 194). There may be a reason for that.

Sertorius' interest in the Isles of the Blest appears, then, to have been genuine, if for reasons quite different from those ascribed to him by the philosophically minded (or the poets, if Horace *Epod.* 16.41–66 indeed alludes to him). Nor was the story first spread by Sallust: Sertorius himself had the most to gain from its circulation, and surely saw to that.

9.2

Ἀσκαλιν ... βασιλείαν: Askalis apparently was a local dynast (*regulus*) in western Mauretania; Sulla's support for him (9.5) would suggest that he was a loyal vassal or ally of the dictator's old friend, King Bocchus I, and of Bocchus' son Bogud (cf. Oros. 5.21.14). For a full discussion see Scardigli, "Problemi" 246–51, with earlier literature cited there. Askalis' opponents remain unknown; nothing supports Scardigli's assumption that Askalis had been overthrown by a popular revolt.

9.3

οὐ μὴν ἀπέκαμεν ὁ Σερτώριος: The implied claim that it was the pirates' departure that forced Sertorius to abandon his expedition to the Blessed Isles is patently false. He did not depend on them for transportation, having ships of his own (7.4; correctly Spann 51, against Schulten 52). The true reason can be found below: ὡς ... ἀπορίας.

ἀλλὰ ... βοηθεῖν: If indeed Askalis was a friend of Bocchus and Bogud, hence of Sulla, the decision to fight against him makes perfect sense, even if it entailed battling former friends.

ὡς ... ἀπορίας: That Sertorius should have abandoned any plans to sail to the Blessed Isles once the opportunity to intervene in Mauretania offered itself is hardly astonishing. A permanent settlement on the islands (οἰκῆσαι τὰς νήσους, 9.1) had probably never been on his mind; without a sufficient number of female settlers it would have been impractical. It would have meant leaving the *orbis Romanus*—something we are told (22.7–8) to be quite out of character. Nor would it have guaranteed his safety: if Sertorius was able to find out about the Isles, so was Sulla's government in Rome, if determined enough to hunt down the proscribed. (It probably was not, but Sertorius may have seen matters differently at the time.) His troops were his insurance. An intervention in Africa would keep them together and in fighting shape; success, moreover, would provide him with a foothold on the fringe of the Roman world, a foothold that in time could be developed into a bastion not easily taken by his enemies (cf. Spann 53). P.'s explanation here shows the levelheaded, calculating, risk-taking soldier we encountered in chapters 3 to 6; surely it is correct.

9.4

ἀσμένοις ... ἀφικόμενος: The Mauretanian adventure is generally dated to 81 B.C. (Scardigli, "Problemi" 248–49); Bieńkowski ("Chronologie" 145) and Spann (51) would set Sertorius' arrival in midsummer. But the "battle" off the Pityussae seems to have occurred in the second half of that year (above, 7.5–6nn.), and the sailors returning from the Atlantic Isles would not have done so in midwinter, nor would Sertorius have entertained going there at such a time. He probably went to Africa in the spring of 80 (so Stahl 43), though fall 81 cannot be ruled out.

τὸν Ἀσκαλιν ἐπολιόρκει: in Tingis (below, 9.5).

9.5

Παχχιανόν: thus all editors, following the reading of Q (= Paris. 1673 and related codd. BMV^b). But Λ (= Laur. conv. suppr. 206 and apographa) and K (Marcian. Venet.) read παχχιαχόν, and P (Palat. Heidelberg.) has παμηίαχον here, παχχιαχὸν in the next sentence. Ziegler himself (*Vitae* 2.1:viii) judged the Q tradition largely useless, the Laurentian with PK outstanding: "*antiquissimi et purissimi* (id est interpolatione plerumque carentes)." Clearly the same name occurs in *Crass.* 4.2 and 32.2, with the same confusion in the mss.: σπαρχιάχου N (Matritensis N 55): παχιαχοῦ Y (Vatic. Gr. 138 [= U] and Paris. 1671 [= A]): παχιανοῦ S(eitenstettensis) at 4.2; παχχιαχός N: παχχιανός SY at 32.2. Münzer long ago saw the correct answer (*RE* 18.2 [1942] 2061–62). A certain L. Vibius Paciaecus was an active partisan of Caesar during the war in Farther Spain in 45 B.C.; the author of the *BHisp* calls him *hominem eius provinciae notum et non parum scientem* (3.4). The same individual kept his correspondents in Rome informed about the movements of Cn. Pompeius the son (Cic. *Att.* 12.2.1 [pacietus codd.]; *Fam.* 6.18.2: *Paciaeci*). The Οὐίβιος Παχιαχὸς or Παχιανὸς of *Crass.* 4.2, who sheltered young M. Crassus during the *dominatio Cinnae*, was a substantial landowner in Hispania Ulterior with long-standing connections to Crassus (4.1); Münzer convincingly identified him as the father of the Caesarian. Two (or more?) Paciaeci at an unknown time were involved in a blood feud with some local *tyrannus* in Spain (Val. Max. 5.4. ext. 3; reference kindly provided by E. Badian). The evidence of the Plutarch mss. points to Pac(c)iaecus rather than Pac(c)ianus, at any event, and in the text of the *Sertorius*, Παχχιαχὸν should be restored—or even Παχχιαϊχόν, though none of the manuscript readings preserves the diphthong of the Latin name form. It is safe to see in Sertorius' opponent a Vibius Pac(c)iaecus, either Crassus' friend or another member of the family.

μετὰ δυνάμεως: a small force evidently, since Sertorius even after incorporating its survivors among his own troops had well under 3,000 men (12.2). Presumably Pacciaecus attacked from Spain, not the Roman province of Africa (Spann 51). Whether his mission was prompted by Sertorius' intervention (so Spann) or merely intended to back up Askalis against his internal enemies, without prior knowledge of Sertorius' involvement, cannot be determined.

συμβαλών: "engaging the enemy"; cf. 19.4, 27.3; *Arist.* 14.6; *Flam.* 8.3.

τὸν μὲν Παχχιανὸν ἀπέκτεινε, τὴν δὲ . . . προσηγάγετο: The narrative sequence suggests that Pacciaecus was killed in battle, whereupon his defeated troops joined Sertorius, and no doubt that is the effect intended. P. does use (ἀπο)κτείνω for combat casualties (over one hundred occurrences in the *Lives*), but nearly as often—some seventy times—the word denotes a deliberate killing outside of battle: either murder/assassination (about thirty instances, e.g., *Eum.* 8.11; *Alex.* 55.3; *Pyr.* 5.14; *Pomp.* 5.3) or execution (some forty instances, e.g., *Mar.* 38.3; *Crass.* 10.4; *Ages.* 32.9; *Ant.* 82.1). Nine times among the latter group, individuals taken prisoner or who had surrendered are put to death after the fighting: the young men of Castulo (3.7), deserters in two other cases (*Cat. Mai.* 11.2; *Marc.* 14.2), the rest enemy leaders: *Luc.* 12.2; *Nik.* 28.2; *Eum.* 19.1; *Phil.* 19.3; *Caes.* 53.7; *Pomp.* 20.3. One suspects the same happened to Pacciaecus; the biographer might not wish to stress the fact that Sertorius had him executed after the battle, and yet avoid an outright lie.

Τίγγιν: Tangier (Tandja, Morocco). The town became a Roman colony in 38 B.C. (Dio 48.45), and eventually the capital of the province Mauretania Tingitana. There is, however, a slight chance that the town in question here was not Tingis but Lix, considerably farther south: see following note.

9.6

τὸν τάφον ... μέγεθος: Presumably one of the Libyan royal tombs in the shape of an enormous conical earth mound, in some cases reaching 60 meters in diameter (Schulten 53 with n. 265; cf. Strabo 17.3.8; Mela 3.10.106; Pliny *NH* 5.2–3). The "Tomb of Antaios" actually was not near Tingis but at Lix (Λίγξ, Lixos: Strabo, Pliny ibid.), the modern Larache (El-Araïsh, Morocco), on the Atlantic coast ca. 75 kilometers southwest of Tangier. P.'s ἐνταῦθα is either used rather loosely, or the biographer has confused the two towns—which could easily happen if he was following a Greek source that mentioned Lix in an oblique case (e.g., πρὸς τῇ Λιγγί). There is no merit in the suggestion that P. deliberately transferred the location from Lix to Tingis so as to create a closer connection between Sertorius and Iuba, or, more precisely, the latter's Heraklean ancestry (García Moreno, "Paradoxography" 146): Iuba was no more closely associated with Tingis than with Lix, the King's residence and cultural center being Caesarea (Cherchel, Algeria; cf. Pliny *NH* 5.20). Note that Strabo himself earlier seems to have confused Lix and Tingis (17.3.2, though at 17.3.6 he distinguishes the two).

9.7

πηχῶν ἑξήκοντα μῆκος ὥς φασι: cf. Strabo 17.3.8, καὶ Τανύσιος δὲ ὁ τῶν Ῥωμαίων συγγραφεὺς οὐκ ἀπέχεται τῆς τερατολογίας τῆς περὶ τὴν Μαυρουσίαν· πρὸς γὰρ τῇ Λυγγὶ Ἀνταίου μνῆμα ἱστορεῖν καὶ σκελετὸν πηχῶν ἑξήκοντα, ὃν Σερτώριον γυμνῶσαι καὶ πάλιν ἐπιβαλεῖν γῆν (= Tanusius Geminus *HRR* F 1). Sixty cubits convert to 26.6 meters; the length of the body was probably calculated on the basis of the mound's dimensions (Schulten 53).

κατεπλάγη ... συνηύξησε: Unless the mound contained the bones of some antediluvian animal, Sertorius of course did not find a sixty-cubit skeleton. But the incident illustrates his skill at manipulating native beliefs and traditions to his own advantage: having first expressed skepticism, he now pretended to be fully convinced. Hence the sacrifice and revival of the cult; as "the One Who Had Seen the Bones of Antaios," Sertorius' standing among the Mauretanians of these parts would have been much enhanced. (Note also the "Heraclean resonances" of the visit: García Moreno, "Paradoxography" 148.) After all, he might have to spend his future there (cf. Schulten 53: "[er] mag an die Begründung einer mauretanischen Herrschaft gedacht haben").

9.8–10: Tingitanian Genealogy

This and the Isles of the Blest (8.2–5) are the only true excursuses in the *Sertorius*. Together they serve to separate Sertorius' preliminary, Roman career from the heroic struggle in Spain that won him fame and literary immortality. The fairy-tale character especially of the Blessed Isles, together with P.'s mythological discursiveness in the Tingis episode, suspends the rather rapid action of this life; the romantic, even idyllic picture of the Far West sketched here offers a beckoning contrast to the "hardheaded world of Rome and Italy, rather as P. develops Alexandria and the East in *Antony*" (thus C. B. R. Pelling's appealing suggestion). The reader almost wishes for Sertorius to sail to the far-off Isles, or at least stay in Mauretania. When the time comes to emphasize his *Romanitas* (22.5–8, 23), we will remember that he did not succumb to those escapist temptations.

Yet while the description of the Blessed Isles is directly connected with the hero's desire to visit them, no such relevance is apparent regarding the descendants of Herakles and Tinge. P. felt that too, and hurried to add 9.10: perhaps all the explanation we need, though one suspects that the excursus also helps mask the unenviable fate of Askalis (9.11n.).

9.8

'Ανταίου ... τὴν γυναῖκα Τίγγην Ἡρακλεῖ συνελθεῖν: thus the local Mauretanian version (Τιγγῖται δὲ μυθολογοῦσιν) of the myth. It runs counter to the pattern of Herakles' begetting sons with his opponents' daughters, not widows, and a Kyrenaian tradition indeed tells of a daughter of Antaios (Pind. *Pyth*. 9.103–23; cf. Jacoby, *FGrHist* I a *Kommentar* 414). But already Pherekydes knows of the wife, named Iphinoë (*FGrHist* 3 F 76, συνῆλθε τῇ γυναικὶ αὐτοῦ Ἰφινόῃ καὶ ἐγέννησε τὸν Παλαίμονα), and the same relationship is implied by the catalogue of Herakles' sons, [Apollod.] *Bibl*. 2.7.8, Αὐτονόης τῆς Πειρέως Παλαίμων.

9.8–9

Σόφακα ... Διόδωρον: so again the local tradition; Greek versions name Herakles' son Palaimon. An interesting variant of the Tingitanian tradition, current by the early first century B.C., was told by the Jewish writer Kleodemos Malchos as preserved through Alexander Polyhistor (*FGrHist* 273 F 102; on Alexander's date, fl. 80–50 B.C., see Jacoby, III a *Kommentar* 248). After killing Antaios, Herakles married the daughter (nameless) of his companion Iaphras son of Abraham, and begat Diodoros, who begat Sophon. The names of Herakles' descendants are inverted, and no connection is made between their mother and Antaios, but the similarities point to the same origin as P.'s story. (I am indebted to Erich Gruen for the reference to Kleodemos' version.)

9.10

Iuba II of Mauretania: ca. 50 B.C.–A.D. 23/4. Son of Iuba I of Numidia; after Caesar's victory at Thapsus in 46 taken to Rome and paraded in the Dictator's triumph, then raised in the Julian household (*Caes.* 55.3; Appian *BC* 2.101.418). He received Roman citizenship (C. Iulius Iuba) probably through Octavian (Braund 45), and ca. 25 B.C. was installed as King of Mauretania (Dio 53.26.1–2; cf. Strabo 6.4.2, 17.3.7). Ca. 20 B.C. he married Kleopatra Selene, the only surviving child of M. Antonius and the great Queen (*Ant.* 87.2). Of his extensive writings, nine works in some fifty volumes are known, with about one hundred fragments preserved. Jacoby judged him essentially a compiler (*FGrHist* III a *Kommentar* 317–22).

P.'s appreciation of Iuba's learned writings is evident: μακαριωτάτην ἁλοῦς ἅλωσιν, ⟨ὡς⟩ ἐκ βαρβάρου καὶ Νομάδος Ἑλλήνων (!) τοῖς πολυμαθεστάτοις ἐνάριθμιος γενέσθαι συγγραφεῦσι (*Caes.* 55.3; cf. *Ant.* 87.2). He cites him frequently (*Rom.* 14.7, 15.4, 17.5; *Marc.* 31.8; *Numa* 7.11, 13.9; *Sulla* 16.15; *De soll. an.* 972B–C; *Aet. Rom.* 264C–D; 269B–C; 278E; 282D–E; 285D). Of course 9.8–10 is not a citation (García Moreno, "Paradoxography" 145, inexplicably thinks P. "himself declared" Iuba here to be his source) but "a family tree custom-tailored by some court historiographer with little imagination": Jacoby, *FGrHist* III a *Kommentar* 323.

9.11

τοὺς δεηθέντας αὐτοῦ . . . οὐκ ἠδίκησεν, ἀλλὰ . . . αὐτοῖς: vague, and deliberately so, it seems. Note that we learn nothing about what happened to Askalis and his brothers, last mentioned at 9.5. (Schulten, 52, unaccountably thought they were the ones reinstated: but clearly those who had "begged his help and put their trust in him" are the ones he had decided to support in their war with Askalis, 9.3.) If Askalis survived the capture of Tingis, it was probably not for long, though Sertorius need not directly have ordered his death: handing him over to his enemies would have been quite enough. The entire paragraph is strongly reminiscent of 5.6 (cf. also 11.2n.), with the same somewhat strained emphasis on the hero's moderation when in a position of unrestrained power. He committed no abuses against his friends; what he did to his opponents we are not told.

10.1

Λυσιτανοί: The Lusitani represent the westernmost carriers of Celtic language and civilization in the Peninsula. They descended from Indo-European invaders who mingled with the non-Indo-European indigenous population in the early first millennium B.C. Celtic elements are predominant in Lusitanian personal, divine, and topographical nomenclature, and what is known about their society, religion, and manner of warfare resembles in part the Celtiberians. The Lusitani appear more closely linked, however, to the peoples of the far Northwest (Callaeci and Astures), with indigenous elements more prominent than in Celtiberia. The presence of Indo-European but non-Celtic (or pre-Celtic) material in the linguistic evidence led earlier scholars to believe in a prior wave of migrant peoples, eventually settling in Lusitania, who spoke not a Celtic but nevertheless an Indo-European language, Ligurian and Illyrian being the principal candidates (see, e.g., Tovar, *Ancient Languages* 91–126). More recent research, however, favors the view that the language of the western Peninsula was Celtic except in the South, albeit of a different and probably earlier strain than the Celtiberian (Faust 199–206; Anderson 90–97; and see above, 6.7: Peoples).

Originally inhabiting the land between the Durius (Douro/Duero) and Tagus (Tejo/Tajo) rivers in present-day Portugal, the Lusitani had expanded south to the Anas (Guadiana) by the middle of the second century B.C. They are described as brave and warlike, with a penchant for hit-and-run tactics, and brigandage seems to have been their way of life (Diodor. 5.34.4–7 = Poseid. *FGrHist* 87 F 117 = F 89 Th; cf. Strabo 3.3.5–6). Human sacrifice reportedly was common (Strabo 3.3.6–7). The Lusitani were subdued between 138 and 136 by D. Iunius Brutus Callaicus, *cos.* 138 (Livy *Per.* 55, 56; Appian *Iber.* 71.301–73.310). But uprisings are recorded in 105, 102/1, and 99 B.C. (Appian *Iber.* 100.433; Obseq. 42, 44a, 46), and one may doubt whether the effective control of the Roman governor of Ulterior extended beyond the Tejo River, if that far. See also Chic García, *Gades* 5 (1980) 15–25.

ἐκάλουν ... ἐφ' ἡγεμονία: not to be misunderstood as an agreement on the part of Sertorius to lead the Lusitani in a war of liberation against Rome—though P.'s phrasing here (unlike 22.5–8) is apt to create that impression; cf. below, 11.2n. Sertorius never ceased to consider himself the Roman Proconsul of Spain, as is evident from both 22.5–8 and Livy 91 fr. 22 W-M, esp. lines 15–35 (hardly an apologetic source); cf. also the evidence of the lead *glandes* (above, 6.6n.). The Lusitani for their part were surely aware (as were their Roman advisers: see following note) of the political background separating Sertorius and numerous other Romans from the current regime. They offered to recognize him as the legitimate Proconsul and agreed to fight, as auxiliaries normally would, under his command. Sertorius in turn promised to keep Sulla's appointees at bay, and to protect the Lusitani from the usual depredations of Roman provincial government, just as he had done in mostly the Hither Province during his brief undisputed tenure in 82. See Spann's excellent discussion, 58–62.

πρὸς τὸν ἀπὸ Ῥωμαίων φόβον: The cause of this fear is nowhere stated. If the Lusitani—as argued below—had sheltered officers of Sertorius and other Marian refugees left stranded in Spain by his hasty departure in 81 (7.4), the

Commentary 10.2–7

new governor of Ulterior, L. Fufidius (below, 12.4n.) may have been preparing a punitive expedition in 80 (cf. Bieńkowski, "Chronologie" 145).

πυνθανόμενοι ... αὐτοῦ: Together with 22.10, καλούντων δὲ τῶν περὶ τὴν Ἰβηρίαν φίλων αὐτὸν ἐφ' ἡγεμονίᾳ, this passage strongly suggests that the Lusitanian offer to make Sertorius their leader was actually brought about by Roman refugees in Lusitania: members of his staff who had been unable to leave the Peninsula along with him in 81, and other Marians that had come to Spain during the last months of the Civil War. In the *Sertorius*, P. never uses φίλοι except for fellow Romans and social equals (1.9, 4.7, 6.4, 26.6; *Synkr.* 2.6; cf. 24.1). The Hispanians are termed Ἴβηρες (14.6, 20.3, 22.6, 25.3, 25.6, 27.1), Λυσιτανοί (10.1, 11.1, 25.3), or simply βάρβαροι (6.5–6, 6.9, 14.1, 16.1, 16.11, 20.1, 25.4). Their leaders are called ἡγεμόνες (20.3) and ἄνδρες σύμμαχοι (16.9). For a full discussion see Konrad, "Friends" 524–27. Clearly πυνθανόμενοι κτλ. explains why the Lusitani would trust Sertorius alone (ἐκείνῳ δὲ πιστεύοντες αὐτοὺς μόνῳ), and the καί is awkward. With Coraës, Sintenis, and Flacelière and Chambry, it is best deleted.

10.2–7

Having assured us that it was the hero's character (rather than his military reputation) that prompted the Lusitani to make their offer, P. proceeds with a lengthy disquisition on Sertorius' ἦθος. Such digressions on character, habits, and qualities are not infrequent; they usually mark a major turn in the hero's life (e.g., *Luc.* 29.6, 33.1–4, 36.5–7; *Crass.* 6.5–7.8; *Tim.* 6.1–7.1; *Caes.* 15–17; *Dtr.* 19.4–20.5; *Mar.* 7.2–6, 28.1–7, 34.5–7; *Sulla* 6.3–17, 30.5–6; and see Pelling, *Antony* 123). Thus 13.1–6 leads up to the culmination of Sertorius' career, his virtual control of Spain until the arrival of Pompeius, with Metellus reduced to utter helplessness. Similarly 22.5–12 marks the transition from events in Spain to what may be called Sertorius' foreign policy, and prepares the reader for P.'s presentation of Perperna's grievances (ch. 25) as malicious and baseless: the end is drawing near. Here in chapter 10, the digression introduces Sertorius' final return to Spain that propelled him on the path of glory and disaster; at the same time it serves to protect the hero's reputation as much as could be done short of completely suppressing the truth.

10.2

λέγεται: not an attempt by P. to distance himself from such a view: he clearly endorses it (cf. 5.6).

οὔθ' ... γενέσθαι: more specifically 1.9, abstinence regarding women; 13.2, abstinence from drink and unneeded sleep and food; 26.7, the decent and very proper manner of his dinner parties. A rather different view was current concerning the hero's last years: γυναιξὶ καὶ κώμοις καὶ πότοις σχολάζων· ὅθεν ἡττᾶτο συνεχῶς (Appian 113.526; cf. Livy *Per.* 96, *ad ultimum et sae-*

vus et prodigus). No doubt P. was aware of it; the contradiction of the flaws listed in Appian is too obvious to be a coincidence. Yet P. did not dare give his rebuttal in the same context, the years after 75, when Sertorius' star was sinking and military success failed him (below, 21.7–8, 25.1nn.): for by that time, his character did undergo a change for the worse, as the biographer well knew (10.5–7). Evidently even the most pro-Sertorian of his sources offered no material that would have permitted him to mention and roundly deny the sort of thing exhibited by sources less favorably disposed. (Their attitude most clearly survives in Appian.) But P. could make the best of it by stressing the lack of bad qualities and abundance of good ones when that was still true; hence the choice to make this chapter the main line of defense, and to adopt in chapters 22 and 25 a different approach that carefully avoided discussing the hero's character at a time when it showed signs of deterioration.

The characterization of Sertorius' qualities as a leader here as well as in 10.3–4 and 13.2 is strikingly similar to Diodoros' portrait of Viriatus, the great Lusitanian warrior-chief of the second century: "He was universally judged the most warlike fighter in battle, and the ablest commander when it came to recognizing in advance the best course of action. Most importantly, through all his years as a leader he was loved by his troops like no other.... He was sober, with little need for sleep, and ready to face any trouble and danger; he never succumbed to any pleasure" (33.21a = Poseid. F 120 Th; cf. 33.1.1–4 = F 96a Th, and see below, 13.2n.). Diodoros' description very probably derives from Poseidonios (Malitz, *Historien* 121; cf. Edelstein and Kidd, *Posidonius* I²: xx n. 3), whose original account would have been known to P. (see Introduction 3.1.c, 3.1.13). The biographer could hardly fail to observe the historical parallel between the native Lusitanian guerrilla leader and his Roman reincarnation, but to draw it explicitly by mentioning Viriatus would diminish the hero's unique stature. To let Poseidonios inspire his characterization of Sertorius was another matter.

φύσει τ' ἀνέκπληκτος [ὢν] παρὰ τὰ δεινά: cf. *Mar.* 28.2, τὸ παρὰ τὰς μάχας ἀνέκπληκτον.

10.3

πρὸς μὲν εὐθυμαχίαν ... ἡγεμόνων: LSJ gloss εὐθυμαχία as "fair fight," citing this passage; the noun occurs only here in P. and hardly elsewhere in classical Greek literature. In Pindar *Ol.* 7.15, εὐθυμάχας (Dor.) means "fighting openly" rather than "fairly," and the contrast in our passage with the subsequent κλωπείας ἐν πολέμοις ἔργα ... ἀπάτης τε καὶ ψευδῶν demands the same meaning. The reference is to open, pitched battles, as opposed to ambushes, ruses, and maneuvering. P. is exaggerating, though: to judge from his own account (not contradicted by other evidence), the only open battle in which Sertorius engaged without hesitation was the one at the Sucro (19.3–4); at Segontia he clearly would have preferred to avoid a fight (21.1). The sober assessment in 12.6 is no doubt correct: πάσης ἐξαναδυονέμῳ φανερᾶς μάχης.

ὅσα δὲ κλωπείας ἐν πολέμοις ἔργα καὶ πλεονεξίας περὶ τόπους ἐχυροὺς καὶ διαβάσεις τάχους δεομένας ἀπάτης τε καὶ ψευδῶν ἐν δέοντι, σοφιστὴς δεινότατος: "whenever the military situation called for acts of stealth and seizing the advantage, be it in occupying a strong position or effecting a crossing that required rapid action, he proved himself an awe-inspiring master of ruses and deceit applied at the right moment." This translation (cf. also Kaltwasser's) follows Leopold's punctuation, placing the comma after δεομένας rather than δέοντι. Perrin ("where speed, deceit, and, if necessary, falsehood are required"), Ziegler ("... Stellungswechsel ..., die Schnelligkeit, List und Täuschung im rechten Augenblick erforderten"), and Flacelière and Chambry ("bref pour tout ce qui exige de la rapidité, de la ruse, des tromperies") obscure the close connection of ἀπάτης τε καὶ ψευδῶν ("both ... and") by making τε point backward to τάχους instead of forward to καί (the usual meaning), thus creating an even tricolon. But a general's mastery of craft and cunning is important to the biographer (cf. δόλος, 1.8), and stressing it separately does not exclude mastery of τάχος, obviously. Δεινότατος, of course, might simply be "of the highest degree," but in this martial context the literal translation seems more appealing. Whether ἐν δέοντι should be rendered "as needed" (Perrin) or "at the right moment" (Ziegler, Flacelière and Chambry) is a matter of taste: the point is Sertorius' ability to come up with a solution to any critical situation.

10.4

ἐν δὲ ταῖς τιμαῖς ... δαψιλὴς φαινόμενος: like Viriatus, Diodor. 33.1.5 = Poseid. F 96b Th.

περὶ τὰς τιμωρίας ἐμετρίαζε τῶν ἁμαρτημάτων: again the hero's moderation is emphasized, as in 1.9 and 5.6. At least one lapse from his usual clemency is reported by Appian 109.511 (below, 18.11n.).

10.5

ὠμότητος καὶ βαρυθυμίας τὸ ... ἔργον: the slaughter of the hostages at Osca; see below, 14.3–5, 25.6. Ὠμότης is characteristic of, e.g., the brigands populating the Isthmos (Thes. 6.4), the Parthians and their King (Crass. 26.7, 33.7), Marius and his son (Crass. 4.2; Mar. 46.7), Metellus Scipio and Iuba of Numidia (Cat. Min. 58.1), Alexander of Pherai (Pel. 29.5–8, with copious illustration), Philip V of Macedon (Arat. 54.2), or Aristion of Athens (Sulla 13.2). It is also exhibited, atypically though, in the Athenian treatment of Samos (Per. 28.2) and Fabius' butchery of the Bruttians at Tarentum (Fab. 22.5). Stadter's translation: "savagery, brutal cruelty" (Pericles 258) perfectly renders the sense. With regard to Sertorius' behavior, P. for once is not mincing words: ὠμότης puts the hero in a league with the worst.

Βαρυθυμία is comparatively rare; sometimes "depression" (*Alex.* 70.6; *Mar.* 40.8). Here the meaning is "bitterness, vengefulness," as in *Pyr.* 26.19 (ὑπ' ὀργῆς καὶ βαρυθυμίας) and *De def. orac.* 417D (ὀργὰς καὶ βαρυθυμίας ἀφοσιούμενοι . . . ἀλαστόρων: in a discussion of human sacrifice). In all instances, the associations are anything but pleasant. Spann's attempt (133–34) to deny a "reign of terror" in Sertorius' last years completely ignores the significance of P.'s choice of words.

τὴν φύσιν . . . διὰ τὴν ἀνάγκην: Although qualifying this explanation in his subsequent discussion (10.6), P. endorses it in the case of Philip V of Macedon (*Arat.* 51.4).

10.6: The Character of Sertorius

What follows is based on the fundamental studies of Dihle (*Studien zur griechischen Biographie* 60–103; *Entstehung der historischen Biographie* 46–53) and the excellent discussion of Gill, *CQ* 33 (1983) 409–87. See also Russell, "Reading" 144–47; Wardman, *Lives* 132–35; Pelling, *ICS* 13.2 (1988) 257–74; and Swain, *Phoenix* 43 (1989) 62–68.

(a) A person's natural disposition (φύσις) is essentially fixed and immutable. It is most easily recognizable in a man's youth, before moral or immoral patterns of behavior have been instilled or developed (Dihle, *Studien* 61–63, 84).

(b) *Physis*, however, is of relatively little interest to the biographer; like a good plot of land that is not properly cultivated, the best nature will produce much evil along with good if it lacks moral schooling (*Cor.* 1.3). Hence P.'s concern is chiefly with the developed adult character (ἦθος), the sum of moral/immoral patterns of behavior resulting from a person's actions (πράξεις) and reactions to fortune experienced (πάθη) over the course of a lifetime. While not immutable, ἤθη become more strongly rooted as the same behavioral patterns are followed consistently (Dihle, *Studien* 73–83; *Entstehung* 51–53). Yet P. was uncomfortable with the thought of a man's developed adult character changing suddenly for the worse; on the three occasions where such a thing nevertheless occurred (here and *Sulla* 30.6) or seemed to occur (*Arat.* 51.4), he felt he owed the reader an explanation.

(c) Genuine excellence of character (ἀρετὴ εἰλικρινής) is founded on rational decision and will (κατὰ λόγον συνεστῶσα); hence it is "virtually unthinkable that someone who had made a rational decision to be a good person should then deliberately choose to become bad" (Gill 479–80, with important observations on P.'s belief in *aretē* as more than "just a habit or conditioned reflex"). That remains true no matter what sort of fate (τύχη τις) such a person encounters.

(d) Not expressly stated here, though clearly underlying P.'s train of thought is his view of what constituted such rationally grounded *aretē*: "A soul of perfect constancy and strength is one which can neither by good fortune be corrupted and weakened through *hybris*, nor degraded by adversity" (*Tim.*

Synkr. 2[41].10). To be possessed of excellent character entails the willpower to control one's emotions, in good times and bad; Aemilius Paullus is a prime example (ibid. 2[41].10–11).

(e) Nevertheless persons of sound principle and good natural disposition (προαιρέσεις καὶ φύσεις χρησταί) may lack such a perfect soul because their goodness is not "fully and rationally integrated into [their] psyche" (Gill 481). They may be unable to bear great changes in fortune with the perfect soul's constancy: their character will change accordingly (e.g., *Alk.* 2.1; *Alex.* 42.3–4; *Sulla* 30.6). Especially in great adversity suffered undeservedly (ὑπὸ συμφορῶν μεγάλων παρ' ἀξίαν κακωθεῖσαι), their character may crack, and mutate along with the circumstances (τῷ δαίμονι συμμεταβαλεῖν τὸ ἦθος).

10.7

ὃ καὶ Σερτώριον οἶμαι παθεῖν: contrast *Eum.* 9.1–2, where Sertorius' Greek counterpart is credited with just the kind of constancy and strength in adversity that ultimately failed the Roman. P. usually defends rather than denies his heroes' faults (cf. Swain, *Hermes* 118 [1990] 198–200); here he goes no further than to offer a psychological explanation (though at 25.4–6, there is a subtle attempt to shift the blame). His revulsion at what had become of Sertorius is evident; yet he refuses, nobly and humanely as always, to judge a man's life solely by its final, sad stage.

ἤδη τῆς τύχης αὐτὸν ἐπιλειπούσης: on the worsening situation after the winter of 76/5 B.C. see 21.7–8, 25.1nn. Again P. takes care to emphasize that the deterioration was true only of Sertorius' last years (cf. περὶ τὸν ἔσχατον αὐτοῦ βίον, 10.5), notwithstanding earlier hints of a ruthless streak in his character (see 3.6–10, 5.6–7, 9.5, 9.11nn.). For the importance of *tychē* see 1.11–12.

ἐκτραχυνόμενον ... πρὸς τοὺς ἀδικοῦντας: The wrongdoers obviously were not the hostages themselves, nor can they be the Hispanian leaders whose defection was punished by killing or enslaving the children: P. is at pains to make it clear (25.4–6) that the Hispanians who defected did so not out of disloyalty or treachery, but as the innocent and unsuspecting victims of the evil schemes devised by Roman malcontents in Sertorius' camp. That latter group is meant. Significantly, the oblique admission that Sertorius visited savage acts of vengeance not only upon Hispanians but also on fellow Romans is made here, in a context that does not readily call to mind those Roman followers of the hero, rather than in chapter 25, where the association would be evident. Blandly calling them ἀδικοῦντες enables the biographer to tell the truth yet hope—justifiably, if much of modern scholarship may serve as an indication—that it will go unnoticed by the casual reader. Far from disproving, or even merely denying, the more specific allegations of other sources that Sertorius toward the end of his life turned from a benevolent, charismatic leader into a brutal and paranoid despot (Diodor. 37.22a; Livy *Per.* 96; Appian 112.520–22, 113.526–28), P. in this chapter confirms them in principle if not in detail. What survives of Livy's obituary is strikingly similar to P.'s assessment: *magnus dux et adversus duos imperatores ... ⟨saepe par⟩ vel frequentius victor, ad ultimum et saevus et prodigus*. The testimony of those other authors might be challenged on grounds of "hostile tradition" (as does, e.g., Spann, 133–34; but see Introduction 3.5.a–c and 8–9). Not so P.'s: his sympathy for Sertorius is beyond question. "In times of civil war and rebellion, charges of cruelty are commonly made and are usually true" (T. W. Africa 533).

11.1–12.1

Except for its opening sentence, this long section effects an odd retardation of the narrative, and as an example of the hero's ἀπάτη the story of the doe at first glance might seem better placed with chapters 16 (parable of the horse tails) and 17 (caves of the Characitani). It is found here for good reason. After the disquisition on Sertorius' character in chapter 10, with its less than flattering revelations toward the end, P. thought it prudent to reinforce the reader's impression of the hero as a man of good qualities such as reported in 10.1–4, before resuming the historical narrative. Hence the stress on πραότης, ἀπάτη, and φιλοφρόνησις in 11.2–4. Sertorius' rule over Spain is not based on force but on voluntary consent (τῶν πλείστων ἑκουσίως προστιθεμένων, 11.2, picked up again in 16.1) and crafty exploitation of native beliefs. Religious intimidation (the doe of Diana) proves more effective than the physical kind, and the hero acquires the status of a divinely inspired leader. This in turn sets the stage for chapter 12: the whirlwind conquest of Spain, the near-miraculous (παρὰ λόγον, 12.1) defeat of four Roman generals disposing of vastly superior forces, the reduction of Metellus (ἄνδρα Ῥωμαίων ἐν τοῖς τότε μέγιστον καὶ δοκιμώτατον, 12.5) to military helplessness and despair (exemplified in full color throughout 13). In chapters 12 through 14 Sertorius is at the height of his glory; once Perperna (ch. 15) and Pompeius (ch. 18) arrive, he will never again so completely dominate the enemy, despite continued instances of success, or enjoy the unwavering following of the Hispanians.

11.1

ἀπῆρεν ἐκ Λιβύης: on the date see below, 12.2n.

11.2

καὶ τούτους ⟨τε⟩ συνέτταττεν εὐθύς: "he immediately organized them as an army." Ziegler adds τε, so as to create a closer connection with ὑπήκοον ἐποιεῖτο ("both actions belong together," *Plutarchstudien* 4) and more contrast with ἀπῆρεν. That is to misunderstand rather than improve: the three verbs form a linear sequence of actions, each depending on the successful completion of the preceding one.

αὐτοκράτωρ στρατηγός: In Greek military parlance the term commonly signifies "supreme commander" (e.g., Thuk. 6.8.2; Plut. *Arist.* 11.1; *Nik.* 12.6; *Eum.* 5.1). When found—rarely enough—in a Roman context, no technical or official appellation is intended. Polybios uses the term to explain how the Dictator differs from a Consul (3.87.8), P. once to denote the Dictator (*Pomp.* 61.1; cf. simply αὐτοκράτωρ: Polyb. 3.87.9; Plut. *Fab.* 8.1), though δικτάτωρ is the norm. Its appearance here is somewhat surprising: it might reflect *imperator* in a Latin source, though it is evident from the sling bullets inscribed *Sertor(ius) pro co(n)s(ule)* (particularly the ones found in Navarra and near Huesca—above, 6.6n.—which must date from the later years of the war) that Sertorius was never so acclaimed. The parallel in *Cor.* 27.1, ἀποδείκνυται μετὰ Τύλλου στρατηγὸς αὐτοκράτωρ, may be instructive: another Roman expatriate leading a foreign people against the City. P. is not concerned here with explaining how Sertorius saw his official position in Spain nor with its legitimacy from a Roman point of view; for that, we must wait until 22.5–8. The emphasis is on the theme first struck in 1.11, and running throughout this life and *Eumenes*: leadership of ἀλλοδαποί. As the Volsci with Coriolanus, so the Lusitani (and other Hispanians) in recognizing Sertorius, without reservations, as their commander, give visible proof of the trust they place in him. It seems doubtful if P. realized that this characterization could easily mislead readers into thinking that Sertorius agreed to be the leader of a native revolt against Rome (see above, 10.1n.).

τὴν ἐγγὺς Ἰβηρίαν: Hispania Citerior, cf. 12.4: τῆς ἑτέρας Ἰβηρίας. P. is anticipating: the conquest of Hither Spain belongs with chapters 12–13.

τῶν πλείστων ἑκουσίως προστιθεμένων: "most" is not "all": some were forced to submit to Sertorius' command. P. later provides two examples (ch. 17, the Characitani; ch. 18, Lauro), and Livy another (91 fr. 22 W-M, Contrebia). As elsewhere in this life, what P. does not expressly say deserves close attention (cf. 5.6, 9.5, 9.11, 10.7nn.).

τὸ πρᾷον: "self-restraint, graciousness, forbearance." For a discussion of πρᾳότης in the *Lives* see H. Martin, *GRBS* 3 (1960) 65–73; cf. also Stadter, *Pericles* xxx–xxxi. Of Sertorius, the concept appears here, 25.6, and *Synkr.* 2(21).1; yet P.'s failure to cite a specific example may be significant.

11.3–4

Cf. Gell. 15.22.1–4: *Sertorius, vir acer egregiusque dux, et utendi regendique exercitus peritus fuit. Is in temporibus difficillimis et mentiebatur apud milites, si mendacium prodesset, et litteras compositas pro veris legebat et somnium simulabat et falsas religiones conferebat, si quid istae res eum apud militum animos adiutabant. Illud adeo Sertorii nobile est: cerva alba eximiae pulchritudinis et vivacissimae celeritatis a Lusitano ei quodam dono data est.* Gellius does not name his source; but he is a frequent user of Sallust (fourteen fragments from the *Histories* preserved, and numerous quotations from the monographs), and his story here and in the following (15.22.5–9; cf. *Sert.* 11.3–8, 20.1–5) agrees with P.'s almost to a word: Sallust is virtually certain as the source of both, even though Gellius is not quoting him here verbatim. P.'s much more intricate account, with all the details of the fawn's capture and its emphasis on Sertorius' gladly and kindly accepting gifts from the barbarians, is surely his own: a splendid example of how he embellishes information found in his sources.

The manipulation of religious beliefs reflected in the story of the doe has close parallels in the *Numa* (8.3–11, 13.2–4, 15.2–10), the life of another ruler of an alien people (*Synkr.* 4[26].15) who claimed to be in communication with the deity. The citizens of archaic Rome come across as no less credulous than the barbarians of Sertorius' Spain; but while censuring superstition, P. in either case cannot quite hide his admiration for the way his hero exploits it. Not that he considers such behavior commendable in itself: it is the leader who employs craft and persuasion rather than brute force that earns the biographer's approval (*Numa Synkr.* 4[26].15, καὶ πάντα πειθοῖ μεταβαλεῖν, καὶ κρατῆσαι πόλεως οὔπω συμπεπνευκυίας μήθ' ὅπλων δεηθέντα μήτε βίας τινός; cf. *Sert.* 11.2).

11.3

λευκὴ γὰρ ἦν πᾶσα: for the oracular quality of white animals among Germanic peoples see Tac. *Germ.* 10.2.

11.6

φάσκων Ἀρτέμιδος δῶρον τὴν ἔλαφον εἶναι: numerous relics attest a Hispanian stag cult of a funerary and oracular nature (cf. 12.1n.). It was widespread throughout the Peninsula but especially popular in Lusitania and western Spain, and apparently was associated with a native deity identified with Graeco-Roman Artemis/Diana. See Blázquez, *Diccionario* 58–61 and "Sincretismo" 187–88.

11.7–8

The story of Sertorius' doe was often told: Val. Max. 1.2.4 (exc. Par.), 1.2.5 (exc. Nep.); Plin. *NH* 8.117; Frontin. *Strat.* 1.11.13; Gell. 15.22; Polyain. *Strat.* 8.22.

11.7

γνοὺς γὰρ ... ἀφιστάντας: Harmand (141 n. 35) takes this as indicative of a well-organized military reconnaissance system.

12.1

οὐχ ὑπ' ἀνδρὸς ... ἀλλ' ὑπὸ θεοῦ στρατηγεῖσθαι πειθομένοις: cf. Frontin. *Strat.* 1.11.13, *ut barbari ad omnia tamquam divinitus imperata oboedirent;*

and Gell. 15.22.5, *universi tamquam si deo libentes parebant*. Throughout Eurasian mythology and religions, though especially among Celtic and Germanic peoples, the stag is considered a psychopomp (Eliade 131–63, esp. 147–50; cf. Moeller 408). Small wonder the Lusitani and, later, the Celtiberians should consider Sertorius a divinely inspired leader. As with the Isles of the Blest (9.1n.), Sertorius made the most of his understanding of Celtic ways and beliefs.

12.2–7

This chapter covers, in strictly chronological fashion as far as can be determined, the military events during the first three years of the Sertorian War, 80–77 B.C. Details are eschewed, except for informing the reader that the battle against Cotta was fought at sea and that Fufidius lost 2,000 men; all the more significance attaches to the list of seven Roman commanders, mentioned *nominatim*, who were pitted against the hero. Five of them suffer personal defeat, a sixth is unable to cope with his opponent's style of warfare: P. is emphasizing Sertorius' invincibility and complete domination of the enemy.

12.2

δισχιλίοις γὰρ ἑξακοσίοις, οὓς ὠνόμαζε 'Ρωμαίους, συμμείκτοις δ' ἑπτακοσίοις Λιβύων . . . συνδιαβᾶσι: For an exhaustive discussion of this troublesome passage see Scardigli, "A proposito" 177–81 (with a survey of earlier literature). The natural meaning would seem to be: "with 2,600 men whom he called Romans, and 700 Africans of various origin"—a "motley band," in Perrin's phrase—"who had followed him to Lusitania," and so it is frequently understood (e.g., by Scardigli; cf. Schulten 54; Spann 57). But οὓς ὠνόμαζε 'Ρωμαίους implies that the 2,600 were in fact not Romans, or not altogether, and such a statement on P.'s part begs an explanation: he is, after all, very much concerned with highlighting the hero's *Romanitas* (see 22.5–24.5). There was no need to comment on the troops' nationality (cf. 7.4, μετὰ τρισχιλίων) unless it entailed an anomaly; since he chose to comment we should expect him to explain in what respect they were not Roman. Instead, the next item in an enumeration of Sertorius' forces is all that follows. Something is amiss.

The prevailing view holds that the 2,600—which number included the remnants of Pacciaecus' force (above, 9.5)—were for the most part Italic expatriates (not covered by the extension of citizenship in 90/89) or *Hispanienses*, i.e., Roman or Italic settlers and their descendants (in many cases by native women lacking the *ius conubii*, hence not *cives Romani*): "Romanized but hardly for the most part citizens" (Brunt, *Manpower* 470; similarly Scardigli 180–81; cf. also above, 6.9: *Hispanienses* and Sertorius). That makes excellent sense—to modern scholars; yet it is hard to believe that P., or for that matter, Sallust, should on this occasion have concerned himself with such legal niceties: earlier, P. referred to the *Hispanienses* simply as 'Ρωμαῖοι αὐτόθι μετοικοῦντες (6.9). The logic of his narrative calls for a different interpretation, as seen long ago by, e.g., Mommsen *RG* 3:20, and Drumann and Groebe 4:365 (cf. also the versions of Ziegler, and Flacelière and Chambry): the 700 Africans were part of the 2,600 "he called Romans." Translate: "... but with 700 Africans intermingled..." (συμμείκτοις to be understood as a true verbal adjective).

Yet problems remain. The construction is awkward, and as Scardigli (180) has shown, σύμμεικτος in historical prose generally means "heterogeneous, of mixed origin, composed of different groups or races" (e.g., Herod. 7.55.2; Thuk. 3.61.2, 4.106.1, 6.4.6), and the three other instances of the word in P. agree with that usage. They do, however, exhibit a subtle difference compared with the passage under discussion. *Alex.* 9.1 (τοὺς μὲν βαρβάρους ἐξήλασε, συμμείκτους δὲ κατοικίσας) characterizes the new settlers of Alexander's first foundation. *Crass.* 28.3 (ἐκπεφευγέναι Κράσσον μετὰ τῶν ἀρίστων, τὸ δ᾿ εἰς Κάρρας συνερρυηκὸς ὄχλον εἶναι σύμμεικτον οὐκ ἀξίων σπουδῆς ἀνθρώπων) contrasts the heterogeneous elements with the elite (as in 12.2, the μὲν is omitted), and its contemptuous ring helps explain why the Surenas decided not to move against Carrhae right away, maintaining instead his position near the camp of Crassus, with fatal consequences for the latter. In *Pomp.* 64.2 (τὴν δὲ πεζὴν σύμμεικτον οὖσαν καὶ μελέτης δεομένην) the infantry is contrasted with Pompey's all-Roman cavalry, and its lack of uniformity underscores the need for training. No comparable significance can be discerned in the *Sertorius* passage as long as it is translated "of mixed origin" *vel sim.* Scardigli (179) wanted to see a contrast between Libyans and Romans, which would be perfectly acceptable had P. written δισχιλίοις γὰρ ἑξακοσίοις Ῥωμαίοις. But his very point is that those "Romans" were in fact not entirely Roman; Sertorius merely called them so. The contrast with "Libyans of various origin" is imaginary. We are left with the conclusion that συμμείκτοις here signifies the Africans' presence among a larger group (the "Romans"), not their mixed tribal provenance, and thus provides the answer to the question, in what way were those troops merely called Romans? If that is the correct interpretation, it might suggest that Sertorius had granted or promised Roman citizenship to the 700 Africans in his service. He apparently made a similar promise later to the leading native families of Spain (14.3n.).

Λιβύων: probably Mauretanian cavalry; cf. 19.8.

εἰς Λυσιτανίαν ... συνδιαβᾶσι: Sertorius' return to Spain is best dated to the summer or fall of 80; cf. above, 7.5–6nn., 9.4n.; and Stahl 43. Sertorius did not burn the bridges behind him, though: he left a small force in Mauretania (Sall. *Hist.* 1.104, *levi praesidio relicto in Mauritania*).

πελταστάς: i.e., *caetrati*, so named after the small round shield (*caetra*) with outward-curved rim typical of Lusitanian warriors. They were lightly armed with an all-iron javelin (*soliferreum*) and a sword, either the straight, short *gladius* or the curved *falcata*. Linen corselets were commonly worn, though metal armor was also known. For a full description see Diodor. 5.34.4–5; Strabo 3.3.6; cf. Schulten 59–60, and Harmand 78–80 (with illustrations).

τετρακισχιλίους ... προσλαβών: The rather modest size of this Lusitanian force, along with the notice (below) that Sertorius was initially supported by only twenty towns, indicates that "the Lusitani" in reality constituted only a fraction of the various Lusitanian tribes and communities at that time.

τέτταρσι Ῥωμαίων στρατηγοῖς: On Cotta, Fufidius, Domitius, and Thorius see below, 12.3–4nn.

πεζῶν μὲν ... δισχίλιοι: Ostensibly these figures refer to the four generals mentioned in 12.3–4 who opposed Sertorius in 80 and 79, and for that the numbers are ridiculously large. They are not, however, simply "sensational and incredible" (so Spann 191 n. 57); rather, they derive from a summary of the total of Roman forces engaged in the Sertorian War between 80 and 72 B.C. The 2,000 archers and slingers are entirely credible. Of the 6,000 cavalry, 2,500 are accounted for specifically (Manlius in 78, Pompeius in 77: Oros. 5.23.4, 9); the remaining 3,500 are easily conjectured for the armies of Fufidius, Domitius, and Metellus, and among further cavalry levies by Pompeius. The 120,000 infantry probably reflect a total of twenty legions, reckoned unrealistically but typically (e.g., *Luc.* 8.2, 24.1; *Cic.* 36.1; *Cat. Min.* 45.3: in all instances the legions were manifestly much smaller; cf. Brunt, *Manpower* 687–89) at 6,000 men apiece. No fewer than seventeen can be identified. Fufidius and Domitius each must have had at least two (12.4n.; cf. Sall. *Hist.* 1.108), Manlius had three (12.5n.). Metellus brought considerable reinforcements: three additional legions seems a safe assumption (cf. Brunt, *Manpower* 471). Pompey's 30,000 infantry at Lauro (Oros. 5.23.9; cf. 18nn.) translates into at least five legions (Brunt, 471); two more arrived in 74 (Appian 111.519). The above are minimum estimates, yet only three legions short of the hypothetical total of twenty; the gap is easily filled by attributing more to Metellus and Pompeius. For a fuller discussion see Konrad, "Plutarch on Roman Forces in the Sertorian War."

τοξόται: "archers." Often from Crete: e.g., Caes. *BG* 2.7.1; *BC* 3.4.2; [Caes.] *BAlex* 1.1; Plut. *C. Grac.* 16(37).4; Appian *BC* 2.49.202.

σφενδονῆται: "slingers." Generally employed together with archers, e.g., Caes. *BG* 2.10.1, 2.19.4; *BC* 1.27.5, 3.44.6, 3.88.6; [Caes.] *BAfr* 78.3. The best came from the Balearic Isles: Strabo 3.5.1; cf. Caes. *BG* 2.7.1.

12.3–4: Chronology of Events

The battles in 12.3–4 are listed in strictly chronological order, to judge from internal logic and what survives of Sallust's *Histories*. Obviously the naval engagement off Mellaria came first. The dates of the defeats of Fufidius and Domitius, along with the temporal relationship of five pertinent pieces of the *Histories,* can now be fixed with a high degree of certainty thanks to the publication and discussion of the Vienna fragment by B. Bischoff and H. Bloch (*WS* 13 [1979]). *Hist.* 1.105, 108, 111, 107, and 136 must be arranged in that order. The battle with Domitius probably falls in the same year as the one against Fufidius, i.e., 80 B.C., since the subject of 1.111 (*Domitium proconsulem ex citeriore Hispania cum omnibus copiis quas paraverat arcessivit*) is not Metellus, as hitherto assumed, but Fufidius; 1.107 comes after Fufidius' defeat, 1.136 (the death of Domitius) yet again some time later. The defeat of Thorius belongs at the end of the sequence: he is specified as a Legate of Metellus, and the latter (*cos.* 80) did not succeed Fufidius as commander in chief in Ulterior until late 80 or early 79. Unfortunately Spann's generally sensible discussion (57–66) of these events is marred by his being unaware of the Vienna fragment.

12.3

ἀντιστρατήγων: "generals sent against him," not "Propraetors," as, e.g., Wilsdorf (118), Schulten (54–55), and Broughton (*MRR* 2:80) think. The ἀντιστράτηγοι are clearly the τέτταρες στρατηγοί of 12.2, listed here in order; all except Cotta are specified by an individual title: Fufidius (ὁ ἄρχων τῆς Βαιτικῆς), Domitius (ἀνθύπατος τῆς ἑτέρας Ἰβηρίας), and Thorius (ἡγεμὼν τῶν ὑπὸ Μετέλλου πεμφθέντων). *Antistratēgos* is not used here in its Roman technical sense of "Propraetor," but in its ordinary Greek meaning of "the enemy's general," as is customary for P.: see *Nik.* 27.6; *Sert.* 19.2; *Eum.* 6.6; *Sulla Synkr.* 4(42).8. ("Propraetor" only at *Cat. Min.* 57.6 and *C. Grac.* 6[27].2, where context demands the Roman title.)

Κότταν: The man's identity remains in doubt. He is usually identified with one of the three brothers Aurelii Cottae: Gaius *pr.* by 78, *cos.* 75 (so *MRR* 2:80; Sumner, *Orators* 110, clearly based on mistaking *antistratēgos* for "Propraetor"; Spann, *CJ* 82 [1986–87] 306–9); Marcus *pr.* by 77, *cos.* 74 (*MRR* 2:80, with doubts); and Lucius *pr.* 70, *cos.* 65 (most earlier scholars, e.g., Drumann 4:365 n. 5; Stahl 44). If an Aurelius Cotta, Lucius is the most likely candidate: Praetor in 70, he must have been born no later than 110, and could readily have held a quaestorship in 80; the lot would have assigned him to Fufidius the governor of Farther Spain (cf. 12.4n.). If he was Quaestor before 80, he might have served as a Legate.

But the cognomen Cotta is found in this period also with another family: note L. Aurunculeius Cotta, Caesar's Legate in Gaul from 58 to 54. The *gentilicium* is rare, and attested in Spain (thrice in New Carthage): [*Au*]*runculeia* | (*mulieris*) *l*(*iberta*); see Koch, *MDAI(M)* 28 (1987) 128–29, with further examples, and cf. *CIL* II 3463, 3483, 6247/1. P.'s usage, if it indicates anything, points against an Aurelius Cotta: when referring to those, he always adds the praenomen or some other specification (*Luc.* 5.1, Μᾶρκος Κόττας; *Cic.* 27.3, Λεύκιος Κ.; *Mar.* 4.2–6, Κ. ὁ ὕπατος = L. *cos.* 119). But Caesar's Legate,

Aurunculeius, is plain Κόττας (*Caes.* 24.2), just as here. He or a relative may have been Sertorius' opponent. For a fuller discussion see Konrad, "Cotta" 120–22.

ἐν τῷ περὶ τὴν Μελλαρίαν πορθμῷ: the western half of the Straits of Gibraltar. Mellaria should be sought along the Ensenada de Valdevaqueros, between the mouth of the Río del Valle and the Punta de la Peña, ca. 9 kilometers northwest of the Peninsula's southernmost point at Tarifa (Cádiz Prov., Andalucía): see Schulten, *FHA* 4:145; *RE* 15.1 (1931) 557; and Tovar, *Landeskunde* 1:68. The town is attested by Strabo 3.1.8; Mela 2.96; Plin. *NH* 3.7; *Itin. Anton.* 407.2; however, the usual point of departure to and arrival from Tingis was Baelo (Bolonia, Cádiz Prov.), another 9 kilometers northwest of Mellaria (Strabo 3.1.8; Plin. *NH* 5.2). Since P. mentions the sound of Mellaria rather than the town itself, Sertorius may have been aiming for Baelo, and the fleets may have met not close to Mellaria but farther south and/or west.

After the crossing Sertorius occupied a mountain in the vicinity of Baelo (Sall. *Hist.* 1.105): perhaps the Sierra de la Plata, as suggested by Spann (189 n. 5). Probably the 4,700 Lusitani (12.2) joined him there.

κατεναυμάχησε: Clearly the Roman authorities in Ulterior had been warned of Sertorius' impending return (cf. Spann 57) and kept a naval patrol along the straits; Cotta's fleet, in view of Sertorius' small force (above, 12.2), cannot have been large either. Cotta certainly was not negligent: by crossing on a moonless night (Sall. *Hist.* 1.104, *nactus obscuram noctem aestu secundo furtim aut celeritate vitare proelium in transgressu conatus est*), Sertorius tried to escape detection but evidently was spotted and forced to give battle.

12.4

L. Fufidius (4): a former centurion (Oros. 5.21.3, *primipilaris*) of obscure though not necessarily humble origin. Apparently a longtime friend of Sulla, he suggested late in 82 that the latter publish the Lists of Proscription (*Sulla* 31.4; Flor. 2.9.25; Oros. 5.21.3). He seems to have entered the Senate through Sulla's favor, probably by becoming Praetor in 81. Proconsul of Hispania Ulterior in 80; about his further career nothing is known. He may be identical with the L. Fufidius to whom M. Aemilius Scaurus *cos.* 115 dedicated three books *De vita sua* (Cic. *Brut.* 112; Plin. *NH* 33.21); see Konrad, "Cotta" 122–28.

τὸν ἄρχοντα: "commander, governor." Though less common than στρατηγός, ἄρχων denotes a provincial governor often enough to assure its meaning here: cf. *Flam.* 18.5; *Ti. Grac.* 5.2, 7.1; *C. Grac.* 2(23).7; *Sulla* 23.6; *Pomp.* 29.2 (συνάρξαντος ἐν Ἰβηρίᾳ τῷ Πομπηίῳ); *Galba* 3.5. (The meaning "commander in chief," without a provincial connotation, is frequent: e.g., *Cat. Min.* 57.7; *Aem.* 30.4; *Sert.* 1.10, 10.1, 14.6; *Marc.* 7.1, 4; *Mar.* 23.5.) Against Spann's ill-advised attempt to make Cotta the governor and Fufidius his Legate (*CJ* 82 [1986–87] 306–9, somewhat recklessly presented as fact in his *Sertorius,* 56–57) see Konrad, "Cotta" 119–25.

τῆς Βαιτικῆς: Hispania Ulterior; cf. 8.1n.

περὶ τὸν Βαῖτιν ἐτρέψατο: on the Baetis (Río Guadalquivir), see 8.1n. Evidently Sertorius was marching toward Lusitania, but the vast swamps surrounding the Baetis estuary forced him to cross the river farther upstream, in the vicinity of Sevilla. Probably the battle was fought somewhere between Coria del Río and Cantillana (Sevilla Prov., Andalucía), as Spann (189 n. 15) suggests. Sall. *Hist.* 1.108 preserves a detail: *et mox Fufidius adveniens cum legionibus, postquam tantas ripas, [unum] haud facilem pugnantibus vadum, cuncta hosti quam suis oportuniora videt* (cf. Maurenbrecher, *Bursians Jahresbericht* 113 [1902] 269, abandoning his earlier *tam ⟨al⟩tas ripas*; and see Garbugino, *StudNon* 5 [1978] 74–77). The news of Fufidius' defeat caused panic throughout Farther Spain, and rumors spread that Sertorius' forces included some fifty thousand cannibals: *Hist.* 1.107, securely placed here by its position in the Vienna fragment (above, 12.3–4: Chronology).

δισχιλίους: on casualty figures see Brunt, *Manpower* 694–97. Some exaggeration must invariably be allowed for, but there is no reason to doubt that Fufidius suffered a crushing defeat with severe losses.

M. Domitius (44) Calvinus: probably Praetor *pro consule* in Hispania Citerior in 80. The name is corrupt in the manuscripts—καλούσιον PQM^b: κλούσιον K: καὶ Λούσιον Λ—and restoration is complicated by the differing praenomina given in the other sources: *M. Domitius*, Liv. *Per.* 90; *L. Domitius*, Eutrop. 6.1.2. Following the latter, Amyot, Xylander, and Sintenis in his second edition wrote Δομίτιον δὲ Λεύκιον, which, in ignoring κ(α), is not convincing palaeographically. Sintenis's suggestion (first ed., app. crit.) Καλουῖνον, adopted by Ziegler and by Flacelière and Chambry, clearly renders the correct name, and the identification of this person with the otherwise unknown father of Cn. Domitius (43) M. f. M. n. Calvinus *cos.* 53 should be retained (cf. Wilsdorf 118; Mommsen *RG* 3:21; Stahl 44). But (as Ernst Badian has alerted me) Καλουῖνον cannot be what P. wrote: the evidence of the mss. unmistakably points to Reiske's and Sintenis's (first ed., text) Καλουίσιον, which should be restored in any future edition of the *Sertorius*. P.'s error (it must be his; scribes would not know Calvisius from Calvinus, hence not corrupt the latter to the former) is not alarming: a wrong recollection while writing from memory, or a misreading of his Latin source under the influence of a name prominent from the Second Civil War to his day—e.g., C. Calvisius Sabinus *cos.* 39 B.C. (*Ant.* 58.9–59.1, where the mss. variously read καλουιος, καλβίσιος, or κολουιβίσιος), C. Calvisius Sabinus *cos. ord.* A.D. 26 (cf. *Galba* 12.2), P. Calvisius Ruso *cos. suff.* A.D. 79, and especially P. Calvisius Tullus Ruso *cos. ord.* A.D. 109, whose (alternate) style may in fact have been "Cn. Domitius P. f. Tullus Calvisius Ruso" (Syme, *ZPE* 56 [1984] 189 = *Roman Papers* 4:414).

The Vienna fragment of Sallust's *Histories* now permits us to date Domitius' governorship with certainty: he was in charge of Hither Spain at the time of Fufidius' defeat, in 80 B.C. His death probably falls in the same year, as he was responding to a call for help from Fufidius: *Hist.* 1.111 (above, 12.3-4: Chronology; similarly already Dronke 501-2; Wilsdorf 118). But 79 as the year of his defeat and death remains possible, as we do not know how quickly Domitius reacted (Mommsen, *RG* 3:21, dated his governorship to 80 and his death to 79). Since there is no room for another Praetor in 81, Domitius must have held that office in 80: a warning against the schematic assumption that Praetors in the post-Sullan period invariably stayed in Rome throughout their year of office (cf. Konrad, "Cotta" 124).

ἀνθύπατον: cf. Sall. *Hist.* 1.111, *Domitium proconsulem ... arcessivit.* Eutrop. 6.1.2 calls him *praetor*—good Republican usage for "provincial governor" (cf. Badian, "Silence" 159) and technically correct, as Domitius almost certainly held the praetorship in that year. (Eutropius may not have meant to be so specific, though.)

τῆς ἑτέρας Ἰβηρίας: Hispania Citerior.

διὰ τοῦ ταμίου: L. Hirtuleius (3, cf. 1) L. f. The date of his quaestorship is not attested: 82 is the last year possible, if Sertorius left for Spain in that spring rather than the previous fall; otherwise, 83 (cf. above, 6.4: Mission to Spain). A Quaestor Hirtuleius, however, had a part in implementing the Valerian Law on Debt Reduction of 86: he must be dated to that year or to 85 (Cic. *Font.* 2; Broughton, *MRR* 2:54). The name is fairly rare (cf. Schulze 458), and Sertorius' lieutenant fits the date. His brother Quintus, the only other Republican official of that name safely on record (Cichorius, "Offizierskorps" 131, 167 no. 34; Taylor, *Voting Districts* 220-21), was a mere *contubernalis* in 89 and probably too young to hold a quaestorship by the mid-80s. Hence Sobeck's identification (31) of the Sertorian with the Quaestor of 86 or 85 remains most plausible. As argued earlier (above, 6.1-4: Praetorship), 85 is the most probable date for Sertorius' praetorship. It used to be held that in pre-Sullan times, a governor setting out for his province regularly took his Quaestor from the year of his own praetorship or consulship even if he left Rome when already a promagistrate, the Quaestor in that instance routinely undergoing *prorogatio* and to be styled *pro quaestore* officially (Mommsen, *StR* 2³: 531-32, calling it "wenigstens factisch Regel"; cf. Gruen, *CP* 61 [1966] 106; Mattingly, *Chiron* 9 [1979] 147 n. 3). That well might apply to Hirtuleius and Sertorius, but Badian, while not denying that Quaestors may have served under one commander for more than a year "perhaps even much of the time," has offered an important corrective to the de facto rule by pointing out how extremely tenuous the evidence for it really is; in fact, what evidence we have seems to point against Quaestors' routinely having their office prorogued ("Silence" 158-67). At the same time, two of the most celebrated cases of extended quaestorships—Sulla under Marius in Numidia, Lucullus under Sulla in the East—furnish a strong parallel to Hirtuleius' situation: a close and preexisting personal bond between Quaestor and commander (to be safely postulated as regards Sertorius and Hirtuleius, given the latter's unusual prominence and independence among Sertorian lieutenants and the likely origin of their relationship in the days of the Social War; see above, 4.3: Sertorius in the Social War) as well as—in Lucullus' instance—unsettled times politically (cf. Badian, "Silence" 159, 166). When Sertorius was first scheduled to go to Spain in the winter of 85/4, he was given Hirtuleius as his Quaestor not accidentally but by design, quite likely upon personal request (as Badian suggested for Sulla's assignment to Marius in 107; see *Lucius Sulla, the Deadly Reformer*, Sydney, 1970, 5–8). As events intervened to delay Sertorius' departure (see 6.1–4: Praetorship), so with Hirtuleius; and the latter was prorogued not so much due to a general rule as to his and his commander's wishes. It may be noted, lastly, that, although P. here and Livy (*Per.* 90–91) call him "Quaestor," after the actual year of his quaestorship—which is to say for most or all of his service in Spain—Hirtuleius technically was *pro quaestore*, a distinction rarely observed by the literary sources (see Balsdon, *JRS* 52 [1962] 134–35; Badian, *JRS* 55 [1965] 110–21 and "Silence" 159).

The most capable of Sertorian generals, Hirtuleius defeated and killed the governor of Citerior, Domitius, at the Anas River in 80 or 79 (the battle mentioned here) and routed the governor of Gallia Transalpina, L. Manlius, near Ilerda in 79 or 78 (below, 12.5n.). When Sertorius established his headquarters in Citerior in 77, Hirtuleius was sent back to the Farther Province and put in charge of operations against Metellus. Possibly disobeying orders (Liv. 91 fr. 22.44–5 M-W, *litteras misit* (sc. *Sertorius*) . . . *ad L. Hirtuleium praecipiens, quem ad modum bellum administrari vellet:* . . . *ne acie cum Metello dimicaret, cui nec auctoritate nec viribus par esset*), he engaged in a pitched battle with Metellus near Italica in 76 and was soundly defeated; he fell in the battle of Segontia later in the same year (cf. Konrad, "Segovia and Segontia," sections I–IV).

Nowhere else does P. mention Hirtuleius, although the man figured prominently in Sallust (*Hist.* 2.31, 59) and the Livian tradition: Liv. *Per.* 90–91 with fr. 22 W-M; Frontin. *Strat.* 1.5.8, 2.1.2, 2.3.5, 2.7.5, 4.5.19; Flor. 2.10.6–7; Eutrop. 6.1.2; Oros. 5.23.3–12; Auct. *De vir. ill.* 63.2). The reason for the biographer's silence is evident: to report at greater length on Hirtuleius' part in the war would be diluting this life's singularly focused concentration on the hero. Thus characters of lesser importance (e.g., M. Marius, below, 24.4; or Mallius and Aufidius, 26.1–3) can be mentioned by name, while Sertorius' ablest lieutenant must hide behind his title.

καταγωνισάμενος: Domitius was not only defeated but killed (Eutrop. 6.1.2, *occisus est*; cf. Livy *Per.* 90; Flor. 2.10.6–7; Oros. 5.23.3). The Vienna fragment adds tantalizing hints: *equis armisque minus aliquanto tamen quam metu concedebatur, nisi quia Domitium adstantem et quos noscitabat orantem, ⟨ne⟩ . . . et se duce⟨m?⟩ . . . ⟨h⟩ostib⟨us⟩ . . . ⟨d?⟩arent . . . interfecer⟨e⟩*. One gains the impression that Domitius' army surrendered (*equis . . . concedebatur*) and that his troops either handed him over to Hirtuleius who had him executed, or killed him themselves in order to placate the victor; but certainty eludes us (see Bischoff and Bloch 122–24). The battle was fought at the Anas (Guadiana) River (Flor. 2.10.7), though probably not in connection with Hirtuleius' siege of Consabura (Consuegra, Toledo Prov., Castilla–La Mancha; cf. Frontin. *Strat.* 4.5.19), as Schulten (64) thought. It seems unlikely that Sertorius' forces could have operated so deep into the Hither Province during the early stages of the campaign.

L. Thorius (4) Balbus: an Epicurean from Lanuvium, known for his luxurious and self-indulgent lifestyle (Cic. *Fin.* 63–64). From Cicero and Flor. 2.10.6 it is clear that *Thorius* is the correct name. Ziegler ("Plutarchstudien" 5–6) thought the form θωράνιον in the mss. not to be P.'s but a later "correction." We cannot be certain, though: P. was quite capable of such lapses.

ἄλλον: This might look as if P. counted Domitius as another "commander of the troops sent by Metellus," and as the former was unquestionably *pro consule* in his own right (above, 12.4n.), Dronke (503) wanted to read πρό instead of ὑπό. More plausibly, Ziegler proposed to seclude ἄλλον ("Plutarchstudien" 5), though he did not adopt this in his edition. There is no real problem here. Ἄλλος in enumerations often means "besides" or "in addition," and does not necessarily continue the same sequence (cf. LSJ s.v. II.8). Translate: "and in addition, Thorius, one of the commanders sent with troops by Metellus."

ἡγεμόνα: here simply "general, commander"; but it seems safe to list Thorius as a *legatus* (Broughton, *MRR* 2:84).

πεμφθέντων, μετὰ δυνάμεως ἀνεῖλεν: Ziegler's punctuation is followed by Flacelière and Chambry. Ziegler ("Plutarchstudien" 6) argued that to write with earlier editors πεμφθέντων μετὰ δυνάμεως, ἀνεῖλεν was redundant. But P. is fond of using μετὰ δυνάμεως with verbs of sending or moving, as in 9.5, Σύλλα δὲ Παχχιακὸν ἐκπέμψαντος βοηθῆσαι τοῖς περὶ τὸν Ἀσκαλιν μετὰ δυνάμεως, where it clearly goes with ἐκπέμψαντος, not βοηθῆσαι. Cf. also 12.5, and, e.g., *Luc.* 8.5, 17.2; *Per.* 22.1; *Aem.* 13.3, 25.6; *Eum.* 1.5; *Pel.* 26.2, 29.1; *Dtr.* 7.2; *Arat.* 31.1; *Sulla* 6.11; *Ages.* 24.3.

12.5

Q. Caecilius (98) Metellus Pius: ca. 129–63 B.C. The son of Q. Metellus Numidicus *cos.* 109, he gained the name Pius from his persistent efforts to secure his father's recall from exile in 99. Praetor in 89, Proconsul in 88 in Apulia, where he captured Venusia and defeated Q. Poppaedius Silo, one of the principal Italian leaders in the Social War. He continued to command *pro consule* in Samnium in 87, but was recalled to Rome to aid the Senate in the Civil War against Marius and Cinna. When negotiations—probably for a joint consulship with Cinna in 86—failed, he left Italy and remained in Africa until 84. He joined Sulla in Italy upon the latter's return in 83 and became one of the chief architects of victory. Pontifex Maximus since 81, he was Sulla's colleague in the consulship of 80. As Proconsul of Hispania Ulterior from 79 to 71, he was unable to cope with Sertorius' guerrilla tactics in the early years of the war, but at Italica (near Sevilla, Andalucía) in 76 he annihilated Hirtuleius' Army of Lusitania (cf. 12.4n.), a victory that effectively ended Sertorian power in Farther Spain and allowed Metellus to join Pompeius in Citerior. Later in that year he prevailed in the triple battle of Segontia over both Perperna and Sertorius (21.1–3nn.), and thus destroyed Sertorius' ability to field an army capable of fighting pitched battles. After campaigning in the Celtiberian highlands, he returned to his province towards the end of 75 (22.2–4) and probably spent the remainder of the war restoring and consolidating Roman control in the Baetica and Lusitania. He left Spain in 71 and celebrated a triumph later in the year. In his remaining years he seems to have withdrawn from politics; he died in 63.

οὐκ ὀλίγοις σφάλμασι ... κατέστησεν: On the setbacks suffered by Metellus at the hands of Sertorius see below, chapter 13.

L. Manlius (30): presumably Praetor in 79, *pro consule* Gallia Transalpina in 78. He intervened in Spain with an army of three legions and 1,500 cavalry, but was routed by Hirtuleius near Ilerda (Lleida [Lérida], Catalunya; see Sall. *Hist.* 1.122; Livy *Per.* 90; Oros. 5.23.4), probably in 78. The *L. Manlius proconsul* of Caes. *BG* 3.20.1 is the same person. Whether he is a Torquatus, and if so, how he fits into that family's stemma, we cannot at present tell. P.'s mss. have λόλλιον or λόλιον, but the other sources make Solanus' emendation Μάλλιον virtually certain.

τῆς περὶ Ναρβῶνα Γαλατίας: Gallia Transalpina, or Gallia Ulterior (a form preferred by Caesar: *BG* 1.7.1–2, 1.10.3, 2.2.1). P. uses the name of the province as it was known in the Imperial period, Gallia Narbonensis (after its capital, Narbo Martius, now Narbonne); cf. above, 8.1n.

μετὰ δυνάμεως: 30,000 infantry and 1,000 horse, according to Orosius (quoting Galba) 5.23.9. These figures reflect at least five legions (cf. Brunt, *Manpower* 689), probably more: see above, 12.2n.

12.6–7

This brief but thorough characterization of Sertorius' and Metellus' contrasting styles of warfare is expertly done; it prepares the reader for the grand portraits in chapter 13. Yet one suspects it is not entirely P.'s own. Diodoros in his account of Lusitanian mountain warfare has a stunning parallel: "since they employ light weapons (κούφοις γὰρ χρώμενοι καθοπλισμοῖς; cf. κουφότητι, 12.6) and generally are quick and of the greatest agility, they cause endless difficulty to others. Altogether they treat the rough and jagged mountainsides as their home, and use such places as a refuge since they are impassable for large and heavy armies" (5.34.6–7 = Poseid. *FGrHist* 87 F 117

= F 89 Th). If Poseidonios—directly or through Sallust—is indeed at the bottom of P.'s summary here, it would explain the precise diction and scientific flavor of the passage; it would not, of course, prove that Poseidonios wrote about the Sertorian War (cf. Introduction 3.1.c and 3.13). His later users could easily adapt a general study comparing Lusitano-Hispanian and Roman warfare.

12.6

πάσης ἐξαναδυομένῳ φανερᾶς μάχης: this does not quite agree with the claim in 10.3, πρὸς ... εὐθυμαχίαν οὐδενὸς ἀτολμότερος τῶν καθ' ἑαυτὸν ἡγεμόνων. Reality corresponded to the present characterization.

12.7

αὐτὸς ... γεγυμνασμένης: the emphasis on Metellus' competence at traditional methods of warfare ensures that the reader will not mistake him for easy prey, and renders the hero's achievement all the more significant.

13

After the introductory summary of 12.6-7, the contrasting portrayal of Sertorius and Metellus continues: first on a personal level (13.1-2), then in general terms of warfare (13.3-6), and finally by means of one specific example elaborately told (13.7-12). Thus the hero's superior ability is presented from four different angles; by the end of the chapter, even skeptical readers will be inclined to agree without further questioning, their resistance worn down by a barrage of skillful character painting and storytelling. Yet for all its apparent richness of detail, this longest coherent segment in the life is virtually useless when it comes to reconstructing the actual war between Metellus and Sertorius in the years 79–77: the biographer's priorities are not those of the historian.

13.1

ἤδη πρεσβύτερος ἦν: Metellus was born ca. 130/129 B.C. (*pr.* 89; and cf. Sall. *Iug.* 64.4, *annos natus circiter viginti*, in 108), and was thus just over fifty at the time of his unsuccessful operations against Sertorius between 79 and 77. There are repeated references to Metellus' advanced age, declining strength, and dying ardor for combat: below, 18.1 (γήρᾳ καὶ φυσικῇ βραδυτῆτι); *Luc.* 6.5 (Μετέλλου δ' ἀπειρηκότος ἤδη διὰ γήρας); even more out of place *Pomp.* 8.6, in 83/2 B.C. (τοῦ Μετέλλου τὸ μάχιμον καὶ θαρραλέον ἤδη σβεννύμενον ὑπὸ γήρως). They may suggest that P. thought him significantly older than he was, but La Penna ("*Historiae*" 243) not implausibly traced the portrayal back to Sallust, who apparently treated Metellus as a prime specimen of aristocratic decadence (obvious in *Hist.* 2.70; cf. below, 22.2-4). Such criticism struck a chord with P.: he found withdrawal from public affairs in favor of a life of pleasure and self-indulgence a disgraceful way to spend old age. His views are set out more fully in *An seni res p. ger.*, esp. 784A; 785E–F; 792B–D; and the large-scale portrait of *Luc.* 38–42 speaks for itself. As regards the real Metellus, in the battle of Segontia in 76 he was in the thick of the fighting (19.2–3; cf. Sall. *Hist.* 2.67).

πνεύματος ἀκμαίου γέμοντι: Sertorius was about four years younger than Metellus, possibly less (born ca. 126/5, above, 2.2: Date of Birth), and now approaching fifty himself. Whether P. realized that the difference in age was so small is not clear; the contrast stressed in this passage anyway is less one of age than of lifestyle and character. Metellus (we are meant to believe) had given himself up to luxury and self-indulgence, and as a result was unable to cope with an enemy that did not fight according to the rules, or to deal with any situation that demanded physical exertion or mental alertness. Sertorius had retained his mental vigor and physical strength, qualities which enabled him to wage the kind of war he wanted, and thus force Metellus to fight on his terms.

13.1–2

Frugality and physical fitness not only contrast Sertorius favorably with Metellus, they are necessary for the successful conduct of his guerrilla war, described in the remainder of the chapter. As in 10.2, one suspects Poseidonios' portrait of Viriatus to have sat model: "From earliest youth he had been a shepherd, and thus was accustomed to a life in the mountains. His physical constitution was of great help: for he far surpassed the rest of the Hispanians in strength, swiftness, and agility of limb. He was used to little food and constant exercise, and to sleep only as much as necessary; in general, he carried arms at all times, and battled wild beasts and brigands" (Diodor. 33.1.1–2 = Poseid. F 96a Th; cf. Malitz, *Historien* 121, and see also Diodor. 33.7.1–2 = Poseid. F 105a Th).

13.2–6: The Guerrilla War Against Metellus

In this passage P. gives a short but vivid summary of the kind of warfare Sertorius conducted between 80/79 and 77, when the arrival of Perperna with about fifty Roman cohorts (15.5), plus his own program of arming and training Hispanians in Roman fashion (14.1–2), enabled him to face the enemy in general engagements. The rest of the chapter (13.7–12) illustrates Sertorius' methods in one striking example: Metellus' abortive attack on Langobriga, with the crowning disaster of Aquinus' force, annihilated in an ambush.

Guerrilla warfare was not a novelty in the Roman experience in Spain. It was the indigenous method of fighting practiced by the peoples of the Peninsula, be they Iberian, Celtiberian, Lusitanian, Cantabrian, or Basque, and it survived well into modern times (Schulten 141–46, with references to the Carlist Wars of the nineteenth century). Hit-and-run tactics, ambushes, the use of terrain impassable for the enemy, night attacks, quick dispersal and scattering of one's own forces when under attack, and equally sudden reassembly for a counterattack: such are its main features. Already Poseidonios thought guerrilla methods characteristic of the Hispanians, especially the Lusitani (*Diodor.* 5.34.5–7 = *FGrHist* 87 F 117 = F 89 Th). Appian's account of the wars in Spain in the second century is replete with guerrilla tactics and activities: on Viriatus, e.g., *Iber.* 62.260–64, 63.266–67 (ambush; cf. below, 13.10–12), 64.269–72, 65.275–76 (attack on foragers and defeat of relief force; cf. below, 18.9–10: Battle of Lauro), 67.286–87, 69.292–93, 70.299–300, 71.301; on Celtiberians/Numantia, e.g., 45.184–85, 47.194–48.202, 51.216, 55.231–32, 76.325–78.337, 88.381–89.391. For other examples of Sertorius' own guerrilla methods see Frontin. *Strat.* 1.5.1, 2.3.10–11, 2.12.2.

What is remarkable, therefore, is not so much the guerrilla war itself than that a Roman was waging it, and proved to be an instant master of the art. Surely Spann (diss. 261 n. 53) was right in saying that "Sertorius' skill as a guerrilla commander was innate rather than learned." It should be remembered, though, that Sertorius had spent several years in Spain as a Military Tribune (3.5–10), which experience with the Hispanian way of fighting may have helped his first steps in 80/79. Philopoimen (*Phil.* 13.9) is credited with a similar ability to adapt his style of warfare to native methods (those of Crete).

13.3: Campaigns of 79–77 B.C.

What little information survives of Metellus' campaigns in the years 79–77 suggests he pursued the war without success, though vigorously. Some fragments from Sallust (*Hist.* 1.113–15, 119) and the evidence of place names indicate that he operated deep within Lusitania, with the major theater located between the Guadiana and Tajo/Tejo rivers, west of the line Mérida–Cáceres–Plasencia (Extremadura). Dipo (*Hist.* 1.113) is located about 40 kilometers west of Mérida (Badajoz Prov.) on the Guadiana. *Hist.* 1.114, *Lusitaniae gravem civitatem*, may refer to Olisipo (Lisboa, Portugal); the station named Caeciliana in the Antonine Itinerary (417.2), near Setúbal, ca. 48 kilometers east of Lisbon, has been thought to derive its name from Metellus. Other place names that may be traced back to Metellus are Metellinum (Medellín, Badajoz Prov.), ca. 30 kilometers east of Mérida; Castra Caecilia (*Itin. Anton.* 433.4; cf. Plin. *NH* 4.117), probably identical with the large legionary camp at Cáceres el Viejo (Cáceres Prov.) destroyed in the early 70s B.C. (Ulbert's is the most comprehensive study of the site; see esp. 197–201, with H. J. Hildebrandt's discussion of the numismatic evidence, ibid. 286, 295–97); and Vicus Caecilius (*Itin. Anton.* 434.1), ca. 130 kilometers north of Cáceres in the vicinity of Baños de Monte Mayor (Cáceres Prov.) and Béjar (Salamanca Prov., Castilla y León). If Spann correctly identified the Langobriga attacked by Metellus (13.7) with a site between Oporto and Aveiro in northern Portugal, the Proconsul penetrated Lusitania as far as the Douro/Duero River. For a cautious reconstruction of events see Spann 67–72.

13.5

μονομαχῆσαι: Meeting the enemy in single combat had a long and lively tradition at Rome: see Oakley, *CQ* 35 (1985). But there appears to be no prior instance of the respective commanders in chief challenging each other to a formal duel outside a general engagement; the great captains known to have fought in single combat—e.g., M. Claudius Marcellus (*Marc.* 2.1–2), C. Marius (*Mar.* 3.3)—did so as younger soldiers. (See also Oakley, 395, on Servilius Geminus, *Aem.* 31.4, and Scipio Aemilianus.) Sertorius' challenge, however, may well be historical: while he could not seriously expect Metellus to accept, he could put him in the embarrassing position of having to decline (cf. following note). The hero's contempt for Metellus ("the old woman") is more openly reported in 19.11. Cf. *Ant.* 62.4, where Antony's challenge to Octavian is part of an exchange of offers expressing mutual contempt; his second challenge (75.1) is different (see Pelling, *Antony* 271, 302).

ἀναδυομένον δὲ χλευάζειν: "It would not have been conducive to morale to refuse a challenge from the enemy" (Oakley 407). The soldiers' reaction is understandable; but had Metellus accepted and been killed, their morale would have suffered a good deal worse.

13.6

στρατηγοῦ γὰρ . . . τυχόντος: Though not an advocate of leading from the rear, P. felt strongly about generals who exposed themselves to bodily harm unnecessarily and merely for the thrill of combat: such behavior was irresponsible. His views are set out at length in *Pel.* 2.1–8 and in his comments on the deaths, not worthy of generals, of Pelopidas, Marcellus (*Marc. Synkr.* 3[33].1–8), and Lysander (*Sulla Synkr.* 4[42].3–5). That attitude explains why in a section designed to compare Metellus unfavorably with Sertorius, Metellus' refusal to accept the challenge is attributed not to cowardice or, again, the infirmity of old age, but to prudence and true generalship. At the same time Sertorius, far from being criticized, is cast in heroic posture. P. could have avoided, of course, the resulting inconsistency—the flash of approval for Metellus, and the indulgence shown to the challenge—by simply omitting the episode. Doing so, however, would have deprived him of the opportunity to present the hero's bravado as the climactic item in an enumeration of the ways in which he reduced Metellus to helplessness. Occasionally P. likes to have it both ways.

13.7–12

The siege of Langobriga occurred between 79 and 77, after which year Sertorius was no longer personally active in Ulterior. It marked Metellus' farthest

Commentary 13.7

penetration into Lusitania; since by 77 Sertorius' military situation had improved to the point that he was able to conquer much of the Hither Province, one is inclined to date the Langobriga incident earlier rather than later in that period.

13.7

Λαγγοβρίγας: Langobriga in Callaecia, between Portus Cale (Oporto) and Aveiro (*Itin. Anton.* 421.7; Tovar, *Landeskunde* 2:257–58). As Spann has shown convincingly (*TAPA* 111 [1981]), identifications of P.'s town with a Lac(c)obriga on the site of modern Lagos in southern Portugal (Schulten 71) or the Lac(c)obriga near Olisipo (Mommsen, *RG* 3:21; Bieńkowski, "Chronologie" 156) are untenable. Ziegler's emendation (λαγγοβρίτας codd.) should be retained; Flacelière and Chambry's Λαχοβρίγας, based on a wrong identification, is more difficult palaeographically.

13.9

Μαυρουσίων: cf. 12.2, 19.8.

13.10

Aquinus: A family of this name operated an extensive lead business at New Carthage (Cartagena) in the late second and throughout the first century B.C.: see Domergue, *AEA* 39 (1966); Broughton, "Some Notes on Trade" 16. Recorded praenomina are Gaius and Marcus; a C. Aquinus Mela is attested on coins as *IIvir quinquennalis* (Gil Farrés 267 no. 1053). A connection between the Aquini of Carthago Nova and Metellus' officer cannot be postulated, but would not be surprising. Roman business interests in Spain had little to gain from Sertorian rule. Aquinus' apparent command of a legion (see following note) suggests he was a senior officer: an *eques R*. if a Military Tribune; if a Legate, probably (though not necessarily) a Senator. Direct relation, if any, to the M. Aquinus of [Caes.] *BAfr* 57 (*homo novus parvusque senator*; cf. Nicolet, *L'ordre équestre* 2:785 no. 31) cannot be shown; but the name is rare among the Roman upper class.

ἑξακισχιλίων: probably one legion; cf. 7.1, and see 12.2n.

13.11

ἔκ τινος συσκίου χαράδρας ἐπανίστησιν: cf. Sall. *Hist.* 1.120, *consedit in valle virgulta nemorosaque*, and 1.121, *neque se recipere aut instruere proelio quivere*.

τοὺς μὲν ... ζῶντας: Since Aquinus himself escaped, his entire force may not have been lost, though the number of those who got away was probably small. The circumstances—a successful ambush in a narrow valley—point to a total rout. Those taken prisoner may well have been incorporated into Sertorius' forces (cf. 9.4).

14–15

Like chapters 12 and 13, illuminating various aspects of Sertorius' military genius, these two chapters form a unit, but with a different emphasis. While the focus of 12–13 was very much on the hero himself, 14 and 15 concentrate on how he was perceived and admired by his followers, and why. The Hispanian angle of the subject is explored in 14, the Roman one in 15, which also introduces Perperna. The next time P. mentions him will be in chapter 25, under precisely the same aspect: the Roman fellow exiles' perception of Sertorius.

14.1

Ῥωμαικοῖς ὁπλισμοῖς καὶ τάξεσι: Roman armament would chiefly consist of the large oval or rectangular shield (*scutum*), javelin (*pilum*), and short sword (*gladius*) used by Roman legionaries. The tactical units (τάξεις) were cohorts, probably still subdivided into three maniples of two *centuriae* each. P.'s statement is borne out in detail by Frontin. *Strat.* 2.5.31 (on the battle of Lauro in 77), *cum decem cohortibus in morem Romanorum armatis et decem Hispanorum levis armaturae*; the former are twice referred to as *scutati* in the same passage and are clearly Hispanian (cf. Harmand 79–81, and see below, 18.9–10: Battle of Lauro).

The decision to equip and train Hispanian units in the Roman fashion should not be understood as a complete abandoning of guerrilla tactics, but it does indicate that Sertorius was now aiming at more than mere survival. To wrench Spain from the hands of the government in Rome would sooner or later require facing Roman legions in a pitched battle. A return to Rome by force of arms would require the invasion of Italy, on Sulla's model; but that could never be accomplished with an army of lightly armed guerrillas. So far Sertorius had prevailed over Metellus by denying him—out of necessity as much as by choice—the kind of battle Roman forces fought best: now he was preparing to beat the enemy at that, too.

The buildup of this Roman-style army probably belongs in the years 78 and 77, when Sertorius was extending his power into the Hither Province (below, 16.1: Extent of Sertorian Power). Similarly, the Roman-style units will have been recruited predominantly from Celtiberian tribes—better suited to a fight in the open field than the Lusitani (Diodor. 5.33.1–5, 5.34.4–5 = Poseid. *FGrHist* 87 F 117 = F 89 Th)—and the Iberian peoples inhabiting the Ebro Valley and the area between Ebro and Pyrenees (cf. Appian 108.506; Spann 77–81; and see above, 6.7: Peoples).

συνθήμασι: "passwords" (*tesserae*), cf. 22.11. On Roman procedure concerning passwords, see Polyb. 6.34.7–12.

14.2

ἀργύρῳ ... διεποίκιλλε: Hispanians loved their arms: Diodor. 33.16; Livy 34.17.6; Iustin. 44.2.5. But here the use of gaudy decorations is deliberately encouraged to make the change from native ways to Roman military habits more attractive; Philopoimen did the same when he transformed the traditional Achaean light infantry into a Macedonian-style phalanx (*Phil.* 9, with an explanation of the psychology behind such measures). The conqueror of Gaul, too, liked to see his men equipped with fancy weapons flashing gold and silver trimmings (Suet. *DJ* 67.2, *simul et ad speciem et quo tenaciores eorum in proelio essent metu damni*); the results speak for themselves.

14.3

τοὺς γὰρ εὐγενεστάτους ... ἐξωμηρεύσατο: The giving and receiving of hostages to ensure adherence to the terms of a treaty or other diplomatic agreement was common practice in antiquity. For children of leading citizens to serve as hostages was by no means unusual (e.g., Thuk. 5.77.1–3; Diodor. 33.15; Plut. *Per.* 25.2), and the Romans seem to have preferred them to adults (e.g., Polyb. 15.18, 36.4; Caes. *BG* 2.5.1, 3.2.5; Livy 27.24.5, 32.26.5; Appian *Illyr.* 23, 28). Note that small children were not normally used as hostages; the age of such παῖδες/*liberi*, insofar as the sources permit us to determine it, usually was twelve or older: see Elbern, *Athenaeum* 78 (1990).

On Sertorius' hostages' fate see 25.6. As 18.4 and Livy 91 fr. 22 W-M show, a good many tribes and towns on the East Coast, in the Ebro Valley, and in northern Celtiberia needed more than friendly persuasion to side or stay with Sertorius. See also Schulten's remarks, 82 n. 408.

Ὄσκαν: Osca (Huesca, Aragón), a major town of the Ilergetes in the Ebro Valley near the foothills of the Pyrenees (Strabo 3.4.10; Ptol. *Geogr.* 2.6.67–68; Plin. *NH* 3.24); cf. Schulten, *RE* 18.2 (1942) 1536; Tovar, *Landeskunde* 3:408–9. The town's Iberian name was *bolśkan* (Untermann, *MLH* 1:245–7), a trace of which may be preserved in Livy's *Volciani* (21.19.8, 11; the suggestion is Tovar's). Since the middle of the second century, the silver coinage of Osca was among the most numerous and widely circulated of Spain (Untermann, "Reitermünzen" 102–3; Villaronga, *Numismática* 168–70; Crawford, *CMRR* 91–95). The Latin name Osca/Oscenses is first attested by Caesar (*BC* 1.60.1), next on coins issued by Cn. Domitius Calvinus (*cos.* 53, 40), Proconsul in Spain 39–36 B.C. (Crawford, *RRC* no. 532). The traditional identification of the *bolśkan* denarii with the *argentum Oscense* repeatedly mentioned by Livy in connection with war booty from Spain in the early second century (34.10.4–7, in 195 B.C.; 46.2, in 194; 40.43.6, in 180) appears now untenable: see Villaronga 114 and Crawford, *CMRR* 91. The derivation of *Osca* from *bolśkan* is linguistically problematic; Untermann tentatively considered popular etymology to have had a hand in the formation of the Latin name ("Reitermünzen" 103, with further literature). A dominant presence of

Oscan-Italic settlers in the area (Menéndez Pidal, *Orígenes* 303–6, 461; cf. above, 6.9: *Hispanienses* and Sertorius) prior to the early first century is virtually ruled out by the continuity of the purely Iberian *bolśkan* coinage throughout the Sertorian period (cf. Crawford, *CMRR* 210, for duration of that coinage). An influx of Oscan-speaking emigrants in the wake of the Social War and Sulla's depredations is, however, conceivable; but their congregation in the upper Ebro Valley and the Huesca region—if such indeed was the case—should then be attributed to Sertorius' control of that area from 78/7 onwards, and to the protection he offered. The Latin name Osca might then likewise date from the Sertorian War or its aftermath. By the time of Augustus the town had risen to the rank of *municipium*: *Urbs Victrix Osca* (Brunt, *Manpower* 603).

There were also two towns named Osca and Osqua in Baetica (Plin. *NH* 3.10; Ptol. *Geogr.* 2.4.11–12; cf. Tovar, *Landeskunde* 1:134); but Sertorius' "capital" was the town in Citerior, as is clear from Strabo's placing his assassination there (3.4.10; cf. Vell. 2.30.1). The establishment of his headquarters and of the School at Osca should be dated to 78 or 77 (Schulten 80; Spann 167).

διδασκάλους ... μαθημάτων: This is the first recorded deliberate attempt at Romanizing a provincial ruling elite (cf. Braund 9–12; Elbern 118–120). A generation later, M. Antonius gathered the sons of Eastern potentates at Alexandria for a similar purpose (Dio 51.16.1–2). Augustus' practice of having numerous children of provincial magnates or client dynasts educated in Rome, some in his own household (Suet. *Aug.* 48), is well known and well studied (e.g., Braund 9–21; A. Kuttner, *The Boscoreale Cups of Augustus*, diss., Univ. of California, Berkeley, 1987, 205–27). In Gaul, Sertorius' example was followed quite closely in the establishment of schools for the sons of the provincial nobility (Tac. *Ann.* 3.43) and perhaps even for German (?) hostages (Suet. *Calig.* 45.2). Agricola later introduced the practice in Britain (Tac. *Agr.* 21.2, with Ogilvie's comments in his and Richmond's edition [Oxford 1967] 32–33; cf. Plut. *Def. orac.* 410A, 434C–D).

ὡς ... πολιτείας τε μεταδώσων καὶ ἀρχῆς: Berve (225) and Spann (80–81) not implausibly take this for a promise of Roman citizenship.

14.4

τοὺς παῖδας ἐν περιπορφύροις: The *toga praetexta* was worn by Roman boys until they were given the *toga virilis*, usually between the ages of fifteen and seventeen, and thus became adults in terms of civic life. The toga was the traditional dress of the Italic peoples, and with the extension of Roman citizenship throughout Italy in and after 90 B.C. it came to be considered the formal wear of Romans par excellence (cf. Blümner 210–14; F. W. Goethert, *RE* 6A.2 [1937] 1651–60). On the basis of Suet. *Claud.* 15.2 it is sometimes thought that there existed legal prohibitions against the wearing of a toga by non-Romans, but clearly the passage suggests no such thing, and Tac. *Agr.* 21.2 implies the contrary: *inde etiam habitus nostri honor et frequens toga*—of noncitizens, as evident from the context. (Cf. the similar situation of *Claud.* 16.2, discussed by Levick, *Historia* 38 [1989] 114–16.) If, as suggested (preceding note), πολιτείας τε μεταδώσων καὶ ἀρχῆς refers to a promise of Roman citizenship, Sertorius' encouraging these young Hispanian nobles to anticipate the external effects of being a Roman makes perfect sense. Which is not to say his Roman contemporaries would have approved.

πολλάκις ἀποδείξεις λαμβάνοντα: "displays (of learning)," presumably in the form of a public examination: cf. Plut. *Quaest. conv.* 736D, Ἀμμώνιος Ἀθήνησι στρατηγῶν ἀπόδειξιν ἔλαβεν ... τῶν γράμματα καὶ γεωμετρίαν καὶ τὰ ῥητορικὰ καὶ μουσικὴν μανθανόντων ἐφήβων.

βούλλας: *Bullae* were apotropaic raindrop-shaped metal capsules (usually of gold) worn around the neck by Roman children—originally only by those of senators, though the custom seems to have spread early throughout the freeborn general population (see A. Mau, *RE* 3.1 [1897] 1048–51; Blümner 305–6, with fig. 51). Together with the *toga praetexta* they constituted the public dress of young Romans.

The School at Osca and Sertorius' Hispanian Policy

Sertorius' humane rule in 82 (6.7–9) had made him a desirable governor; the School at Osca further served to unite the Hispanians behind him by giving them a stake in his fight against the ruling *factio* in Rome (cf. Livy 91 fr. 22.32–33 W-M, *quantum Hispaniae provinciae interesset suas partes superiores esse*). Sertorius' own intentions with regard to his Hispanian allies are less clear. To return to Rome always remained his ultimate goal, whether by force of arms or through a negotiated settlement (below, 22.7n., and Spann 73–75). Total victory, i.e., the invasion of Italy and conquest of Rome (against all odds), would enable him easily enough to carry out his promise of citizenship in a meaningful way, and to give permanence to the Romanization of the Hispanian nobility. In the case of a negotiated return, on the other hand, it might at first seem difficult to envisage the Senate agreeing to grant citizenship to dozens or hundreds of Hispanian princelings. But any negotiated settlement, in order to be acceptable to Sertorius, would *eo ipso* entail concessions by the Senate of a magnitude—such as the restoration of their vast properties to the proscribed and other exiles, and reinstatement in their senatorial rank (cf. Spann 148, and below, 22.7n.)—compared to which a confirmation of his *acta* in Spain, including citizenship for noble youths, would pale into insignificance. There is no reason to doubt the sincerity of Sertorius' promise.

That said, however, caution is called for lest we read too much into his policy of Romanizing Spain. To treat him, along the lines of Ehrenberg (190–92, 198–201) or Schulten (82–83, 156–58), as a visionary who anticipated the universal empire of the Principate, an empire that no longer knew Rome and Italy as separate entities ruling the rest of the world, is an absurd flight of fancy. Certainly his measures as governor, both in Spain (6.7–8) and later in Asia (24.5), show a willingness to forgo the oppressive and exploitative patterns so typical of provincial administration under the Republic. Yet his was a unique situation: unlike ordinary governors, he could not have survived but for the goodwill and support of the natives. Unless he was different from the rest, there was no incentive for the Hispanians to fight for him rather than the Senate's commanders. Even so, support came by no means willingly from every part of Spain. At Osca, the youths' function as hostages was as real as was their Roman education; we should not imagine every one of their fathers to have been an ardent partisan of Sertorius. Spann's skepticism (149, 167–68), though overstated, is not entirely without justification.

14.5

ἔθους ... πεσόντι: cf. Sall. *Hist.* 1.125. This practice is attested to have been widespread among the Celto-Hispanians (Strabo 3.4.18; Val. Max. 2.6.11; Dio 53.20.2–4) as well as Gauls (Polyb. 2.17.12; Caes. *BG* 3.22.1–3, 7.40.7) and Germans (Tac. *Germ.* 14; Ammian. 16.12.60). The warriors thus committed to seek death rather than survive their leader were called *soldurii* (Caes. *BG* 3.22.1–3; Nikol. Damask. *FGrHist* 90 F 80), apparently a Celtic word: H. O. Fiebiger, *RE* 3A.1 (1927) 915; cf. Holder, *Alt-celtischer Sprachschatz* 2:1599–1601); *LEW* 2:554. See also the detailed study of Rodríguez Adrados, *Emerita* 14 (1946), esp. 177–80, 189–96.

14.6

The location of this defeat remains unknown, but since Sall. *Hist.* 1.126, reporting the same incident, is securely assigned to book 1, it must have occurred in the early years of the war, before Pompey's arrival in 77.

τοῖς ὤμοις ... τείχη: see Scardigli, *A&R* 19 (1974); Pecere, *SIFC* 50 (1978) 137–39; and Garbugino, *StudNon* 5 (1978) 83–87, for detailed discussions. The passage causes some puzzlement despite the survival of the Sallustian version of the incident: *Sertorius portis turbam morantibus et nullo, ut in terrore solet, generis aut imperii discrimine per calonum corpora ad medium quasi, deinsuper adstantium* (Nonius XII: *stantium*) *manibus in murum adtollitur* (*Hist.* 1.126 = Nonius IV p. 282 M = XII p. 530 M), and Serv. *In Aeneid.* 9.555, *ut etiam Sallustius ostendit, ubi Sertorium umeris sublatum per muros ascendisse commemorat*. It is clear that Sallust described how Sertorius was lifted up onto the city walls, probably by first climbing on the *calones'* shoulders and then being pulled on top of the wall by people standing there. *Deinsuper* is highly suspect; one should read either *dein super adstantium* (e.g., Maurenbrecher and Garbugino, the latter basing his preference on Nonius' practice of citation) or *dein superstantium* (so Pecere, adducing Sall. *Iug.* 60.7

and *Hist.* 2.87A, where *superstantes* = "those standing on top of the ladder/ walls"). As it stands, P.'s text seems to give a different picture. Τοῖς ὤμοις ἐπαραμένους ἄλλους πρό (thus the mss.) ἄλλων ἀνακουφίσαι πρὸς τὰ τείχη is most naturally translated: "and taking him on their shoulders one after another, carried him to the walls" (Perrin; cf. the translations of Doehner, and Flacelière and Chambry). Instead of being lifted up onto the wall, Sertorius here is carried from a distance across the heads of the throng toward the wall. P. may have misunderstood, but a different interpretation of the passage is possible. Clearly ἀνακουφίζω implies an upward rather than horizontal movement: Sallust's *adtollitur*. If ἄλλους rather than τὸν Σερτώριον is taken as the object of ἐπαραμένους, the sentence translates: "taking one another on their shoulders"—i.e., one climbing onto another's shoulders—"they lifted (Sertorius) up towards the walls" ("dass die Spanier . . . einander auf die Schultern traten, ihn so auf die Mauer hoben," Kaltwasser and Floerke; "einander auf die Schultern tretend, ihn zur Mauer hinaufhoben," Ziegler). If that is what P. meant, Emperius' conjecture of ὑπὲρ ἄλλων for πρὸ ἄλλων (adopted by Ziegler; Stenten, and Flacelière and Chambry, write ὑπὲρ in their texts but, to judge from their translations, did not understand its raison d'être) has much in its favor. P. then would not have mistaken a vertical motion for a horizontal one (ἀνακουφίζω, as mentioned, indeed implies vertical motion), but (mis)interpreted *superstantium* (or *superadstantium*) as referring to a second tier of *calones* standing on their comrades' shoulders rather than on top of the wall.

More significant, however, than such a misunderstanding is the deliberate twist P. gives the story, as pointed out by Pecere (138). In Sallust, Sertorius is saved by his *calones* (his camp servants: possibly Hispanians, but clearly not warriors, i.e., *soldurii*) whose level-headed action stands in contrast to the panic-stricken scene at the gates. No such panic and confusion in P.: his account focuses exclusively on how the *Hispanians* neglect their own safety (ἀμελήσαντας αὑτῶν) in order to rescue the hero; only with that feat accomplished do they turn to flight. Thus the biographer uses the incident to illustrate the Hispanians' devotion to Sertorius—an aspect certainly not emphasized here by Sallust, and probably not even implied. Immediately after P.'s description of κατάσπεισις the reader cannot help but assume that "the Hispanians" here are the myriads who devoted their lives to Sertorius.

15.1

τοῖς ἐξ Ἰταλίας στρατευομένοις: not the remainders of his original force (7.4, 12.2) but the troops of Perperna. Having emphasized in the preceding four chapters the hero's magnificent relations with the Hispanians, P. takes care to remind us that Sertorius had not lost his touch where Romans were concerned. Hence Perperna's arrival is narrated here rather than in its proper chronological place between chapters 17 and 18 (but see below, 16.5n.).

15.2

M. Perperna (6) Veiento: perhaps a son of M. Perperna (5) *cos.* 92, *cens.* 86, but since the cognomen Veiento is not attested for the consular Perpernae, he is better identified as the Consul's nephew: i.e., a grandson of Marcus (4) *cos.* 130, and son or younger brother of Gaius (2) *pr.* by 91 (for caution, see Sumner, *Orators* 117). The cognomen is Veiento, not, as P. writes, Vento: see Cic. *Att.* 4.17.3, 7.3.5; Tac. *Ann.* 14.50 (corrupt in all three passages, but clearly not *Vento*); Plin. *Ep.* 4.22.4, 9.13.13, 9.13.19; cf. also numerous inscriptions, e.g., *CIL* VI 38700: *Optatus | C. Perpernae | Veienton[is]*; with other *gentilicia*, VI 5908, 6222, 7813, 26518, 29417. He was Praetor by 83, governor of Sicily in 82 and probably the year before, as a change of governors seems unlikely in view of the ongoing civil war and Sulla's control of southern Italy since summer 83; Perperna may in fact have succeeded Norbanus as early as 85/4 (see Badian, "Governors" 9 = *Studies* 86; cf. above, 6.1n., and *MRR* 3:155). He refused Sulla's offer to join him, but left the island without a fight when Pompeius landed there (Diodor. 38/39.14; Plut. *Pomp.* 10.1–2; cf. *Pomp.* 20.6). He was proscribed (Vell. 2.30.1) and apparently spent the following years in Liguria (but see Spann, "Perperna"), either in hiding or preparing an insurrection (Oros. 5.24.16). In 78 he joined in the revolt of Lepidus, and withdrew with the latter to Sardinia after their defeat in Italy early in 77. After Lepidus' death he took the remainder of their army to Spain, where he joined Sertorius (Appian 107.504, 108.508, 113.527; Oros. 5.24.16; Exuper. 7.1–3 = 42 Z). His performance as a general was disastrous (19.1, 19.6, 21.2nn.); his relationship with Sertorius, probably not very cordial from the start, by 73 had turned into enmity. He arranged the assassination of Sertorius in the same year and assumed command of the insurrection, the military situation of which was already hopeless. In 72 he was finally defeated by Pompeius, captured, and executed. *Gentis clarioris quam animi* was Velleius' verdict (2.30.1), and it may stand.

ἀπὸ τῆς αὐτῆς Σερτωρίῳ στάσεως: the Cinno-Marian government under which Perperna had been Praetor.

εἰς Ἰβηρίαν παραγενομένου: probably in the summer of 77 (see Konrad, "Chronology," section XII). Spann ("Perperna" 47–62) ingeniously argued that Perperna went from Sardinia to Liguria, blocked the landward route along the coast, and urged Sertorius to join him in an invasion of Italy. Pompeius then opened a new pass across the Alps (Sall. *Hist.* 2.98.4; Appian 109.509; Serv. auct. *In Aeneid.* 10.13) and thus threatened to attack Perperna from the rear, whereupon the latter retreated to Spain. Spann's reconstruction remains open to objections. First, if Perperna and his troops were dislodged from their Ligurian position by Pompeius, they must have known then that he was coming to Spain, hard on their heels; but P. (15.3) asserts that Perperna intended to fight Metellus on his own, and was forced by his troops to join Sertorius only when they learned of Pompey's crossing the Pyrenees—news that apparently was unexpected. Second, one must ask why Pompeius should ever have intended to march his army along the Ligurian coast, across the Maritime Alps: that route lacked proper roads, food, and water while abounding in danger and hardships. Spann ("Perperna" 55) calls it "the most convenient route to Spain," but nothing indicates that the Romans used the coastal route to move entire armies: transportation by sea until Massilia was the normal practice (see DeWitt 63–69). Finally, though *hostisque in cervicibus iam Italiae agentis ab Alpibus in Hispaniam summovi* (Sall. *Hist.* 2.98.4) can be interpreted in Spann's favor, *hostis* remains rather vague in a context where Sallust is not reluctant to mention names: it might equally be understood in connection with Cicero's repeated references to Pompey's *bellum Transalpinum* (*Imp. Cn. Pomp.* 28, 30; *Font.* 14). Undoubtedly Cicero exaggerated, and Spann is right in suggesting ("Perperna" 59) that Pompeius did little fighting in Gaul, but the fact remains that Cicero stresses Pompey's activities against the Gauls without ever hinting at Perperna. Pompey's settlement of certain territorial disputes in Transalpina (Cic. *Font.* 14; Caes. *BC* 1.35.4) must be dated in 77, not—as Spann would have it—at the time of his wintering in Gaul in 75/4: Transalpina had its own governor by then, M. Fonteius (Cic. *Font.* 16), and we have no reason to assume that Pompeius interfered with the administration of another's province.

On the other hand, Spann is quite right in stressing that Perperna would not attempt a direct voyage from Sardinia to Spain across the open sea ("Perperna" 54), but would sail along the coast. Thus Liguria lay on his way, and the idea that it was on this occasion that he caused the unspecified mischief reported by Orosius (5.24.16) is appealing. Some support could be derived from the sequence of items in Pompey's Letter (Sall. *Hist.* 2.98), where paragraphs 4–6 are nothing but a summary, in fairly good order overall, of events narrated by Sallust up to that point: *hostisque . . . summovi . . . iter aliud . . . patefeci*; then: *recepi Galliam, Pyrenaeum, Laeetaniam, Indicetes*. The wording might indicate a distinction between Pompey's warfare in the Alps and in Gaul. The strongest argument, lastly, in favor of Spann's reconstruction is the question, why did Pompeius decide to march his forces to Gaul by land, rather than sail to Massilia? Spann was the first to ask (except that he thought of the coastal route as the alternative) and answer it: an army of some five legions (below, 15.5n.) operating in Liguria could not be left in Pompey's rear, unchallenged, free to invade Italy—particularly if Sertorius might somehow join forces with it. (His pirate friends could provide transportation from Spain, at least in theory; but see below, 21.7n.)

Perperna, however, as a *proscriptus*, must have been hiding somewhere between 82 and 78/7, when we find him collaborating with Lepidus. The latter's province was Transalpina (Appian 107.502)—adjacent to Liguria. Of course, Perperna may have been there twice: from 82 to 78, and again in 77 on his way to Spain.

Perperna left Sardinia in mid-summer (no later than 1 August, according to Spann, "Perperna" 61; probably a month or so earlier). Assuming the longest possible route (Olbia/Sardinia–Sacrum Promontorium/Corsica–Nicaea/ Liguria–Massilia–Narbo/ Transalpina–Tarraco/Citerior), he could cover the distance of ca. 600 nautical miles in twenty days (at a low average speed of thirty miles per day: cf. Casson, *TAPA* 82 [1951] 146–48) or less.

μετὰ ... μεγάλης δυνάμεως: see below, 15.5n.

ἰδίᾳ δὲ ... πολεμεῖν πρὸς τὸν Μέτελλον: Like Sertorius, Perperna undoubtedly still considered himself to be *cum imperio*; unlike Sertorius, he could not claim still to be exercising it in his originally assigned province, Sicily. As the latter was one of the very few provinces that did not rate a Proconsul as governor, Perperna will have held his *imperium pro praetore* rather than *pro consule*. Once in Spain, he would naturally continue in command of his army *suis auspiciis*; but he would be expected to defer to Sertorius, both because the Proconsul's *imperium* and auspices outranked his own and because he was operating within Sertorius' province. Treves' notion (145) that Perperna could reasonably expect Sertorius to cede overall command to him, "because of his (i.e., Perperna's) senatorial rank" and because of his status as "the Consul's (i.e., Lepidus') Legate," is nothing if not bizarre. The self-promotion and self-assignment of a new province implied in Spann's suggestion (86) that Perperna may have considered himself now "the proconsul of Farther Spain" is similarly farfetched: granted that the various *Cinnani, Mariani,* and *Lepidani* in exile may have clung to the constitutional fiction that somehow they continued to represent the legitimate government of Rome, such notions were not formalized—if ever they were—until Sertorius formed his "Senate" (see 22.5n.). At any event, Ulterior had been part of Sertorius' *provincia* from the beginning (above, 6.6n.); even if that is questioned (as by Spann), in anyone's definition by 77 his was the prior and stronger claim.

πολὺς ... ἀνιῶν: From the beginning, Sertorius is the Roman soldiers' hero; and from the beginning, Perperna resents the fact. P. makes no mention here of high-ranking Romans in Perperna's and Sertorius' entourage, but when we next encounter Perperna (25) he acts as the mouthpiece of those elements. The common soldiers disappear from the narrative: presumably by the time of chapter 25, most of them no longer considered Sertorius σῴζεσθαι καὶ σῴζειν δυνάμενος (15.4). P. would not care to call attention to their disillusionment.

εὐγενείᾳ ... τετυφομένον: The Perpernae are first attested as a senatorial family (it seems) in 168 B.C. (Livy 44.27.11, 44.32.1–4); they provided Consuls in 130 and 92, and a Censor in 86. The name is Etruscan and found at Clusium, Saena, Volaterrae, and Volsinii (Schulze 88). P.'s characterization has a distinctively Sallustian ring: cf. La Penna, "*Historiae*" 245, though his attempt to see in Perperna a representative of the Etruscan rather than the Roman nobility (a family of two consular generations!) is quite unwarranted.

Πομπήιος ... τὴν Πυρήνην ὑπερβάλλων: late summer or early fall 77 (see Konrad, "Chronology," sections XI–XII).

15.5

συγχωρήσας . . . αὐτούς: Since the siege of Lauro took place soon afterwards, Sertorius probably was on the East Coast when Perperna joined him, somewhere between Tarraco and Cartagena. Dianium (Dénia, Alacant Prov., Comunitat Valenciana), ca. 85 kilometers southeast of València, is a good possibility: here Sertorius established a naval base—perhaps chiefly for his Kilikian pirate allies—and since Sall. *Hist.* 1.124 certainly refers to Dianium, the establishment of the base must precede Pompey's arrival in Spain (book 2 of the *Histories*; cf. below, 21.7n.). On the other hand, Sertorius did not control the East Coast long before 77. Thus it seems reasonable to assume that Dianium was one of his operational bases in the spring and summer of 77. On Dianium see Cic. 2*Verr.* 1.87, 5.146; Strabo 3.4.6, 10; Plin. *NH* 3.20, 25, 76; Ptol. *Geogr.* 2.6.15; Hübner, *RE* 5.1 (1903) 340–41; Schulten 94.

συνέμειξε τῷ Σερτωρίῳ: His agreeing to serve under the Proconsul does not mean that Perperna now became Sertorius' Legate (so *MRR* 2:91, 3:156): there is no reason to assume that he dismissed his lictors and relinquished his *imperium*. Nor is it certain that he lost operational command of his army; what evidence exists points the other way (see following note).

πεντήκοντα καὶ τρεῖς ἔχων σπείρας: fifty-three cohorts. The figure is not to be doubted: this was the remainder of Lepidus' army (estimated at easily six legions by Brunt, *Manpower* 448–49), and what little is known about his defeats near Rome and in Etruria (Appian 107.504; Exuper. 6.8–13 = 38–39 Z) does not warrant the assumption that he incurred unusually heavy losses. In any case, even severe casualties would not automatically reduce the number of tactical units. To argue that with fifty-three cohorts Lepidus and Perperna could easily have taken Sardinia and—since this did not happen—that consequently many of Perperna's troops must have been levied in Spain after his arrival there (Drumann and Groebe 4:370; Stahl 52; Gabba, "Guerra sociale" 302–3) is fallacious: the governor of Sardinia, C. Valerius Triarius, conducted the defense of the island with unusual skill and determination (Ascon. p. 19 C; Exuper. 6.16–20 = 40–41 Z; cf. Spann, "Perperna" 49 n. 6), and Lepidus' superiority in numbers would be of little help against fortified places.

Schulten (79) plausibly identifies these fifty-three cohorts with the 20,000 troops commanded by Perperna in the spring of 76 (Livy 91 fr. 22.35–36 W-M). The average strength per cohort would thus have been 378 men, which is entirely credible. Assuming that Lepidus' legions were about 5,000 strong at the outset, this would amount to a casualty rate of 25 percent. There are indeed other indications that Perperna retained command of his own troops. In the battle at the Sucro he appears to have been in charge, at least temporarily, of the right wing, and Appian's account suggests that Sertorius and Perperna kept separate camps (110.513; cf. below, 19.6–10: Battle at the Sucro). During the battle of Segontia they were evidently operating together but each with his own army (below, 21.2–3: Battle of Segontia). Unless we are prepared to believe that Sertorius would entrust predominantly Hispanian formations to that man, we must conclude that most of the fifty-three cohorts continued to serve under Perperna's immediate command, as directed by Sertorius.

16

After the "Roman" interlude of chapter 15 the focus returns to matters Hispanian. Like chapter 11, this chapter illuminates Sertorius' mastery of psychological leadership; but while 11 treated that aspect on a more elevated and somewhat mysterious level, 16 looks at it from a practical military angle, as befits the heavy emphasis on warfare in the chapters that follow (18–21). Thus 11 and 16 together serve to frame the long and colorful portrait, in chapters 12–15, of the hero at the height of success.

16.1

τῶν ἐντὸς Ἴβηρος ... προστιθεμένων: strictly, *cis Hiberum* from a Roman point of view, i.e., between the Ebro and the Pyrenees. But such a narrow geographic limitation seems pointless in this context; one suspects P. meant to say Hispania Citerior, mistakenly believing the Ebro to be the provincial boundary. (At 12.4, τῆς ἑτέρας Ἰβηρίας clearly signifies Citerior, but the wording may reflect *alterius provinciae,* vel. sim., in his Latin source.) Possibly, however, P. here adopted a view from within Spain, in which case he overlooked the fact that Osca (14.3) was well beyond the Ebro.

The Extent of Sertorian Power in Spain, 77 B.C.

Sertorian forces appear to have operated in the Hither Province since 78 if not earlier; probably in that year or early in 77, a corps commanded by L. Hirtuleius crossed the Ebro and routed the army of Transalpine Gaul under L. Manlius near Ilerda (above, 12.4–5nn.). Those events may have been connected with the Lepidan uprising in Italy (see Spann's soberly cautious discussion, 75–77), but nothing can be said for certain, given a purely conjectural chronology.

Together with a few other pieces of evidence, a long fragment from Livy book 91 (fr. 22 W-M) permits us to reconstruct, within reasonable limits, the extent of Sertorius' rule over Hispania Citerior as of winter 77/6. Ilercaonia and Contestania are specified as his allies (lines 62–63). Pompey's capture of Valentia in 76 (Sall. *Hist.* 2.98.6) suggests that at least the coastal areas of Edetania, i.e., the central part of the País Valencià, had likewise sided with Sertorius. Also Sertorian was the area between the Ebro and the Pyrenees, with the Ilergetes, as is evident from his headquarters at Osca, and the neighboring Lacetani or Iacetani (Strabo 4.3.9–10; cf. above, 6.7: Peoples of the Peninsula).

The situation in north-central Spain appears rather complex. The Vaccaei and probably the Vettones were allied with Sertorius (Livy, line 76; cf. Appian 112.523), as were the Arevaci (Livy, line 71). On the upper Ebro, on the other hand, Bursao, Cascantum, and Graccurris were hostile towns (now Borja, Zaragoza Prov., Aragón; Cascante, Navarra; and Alfaro, La Rioja; Livy, line 67). A little farther north, Calagurris Nasica (Calahorra, La Rioja; Livy, line 68) was allied. But the principal tribe inhabiting what is now La Rioja, the Berones, remained staunchly loyal to the Roman government; so did the Autricones (Livy, lines 53–59) in the far North.

In southern Celtiberia Sertorius appears to have found little welcome. Sometime between 79 and 77, Hirtuleius had been forced to abandon the siege of Consabura (Consuegra, Toledo Prov., Castilla–La Mancha; cf. 12.4n.). Contrebia Belaisca (Botorrita, Zaragoza Prov., Aragón) was taken only after a lengthy siege (Livy, lines 1–14). Strabo (3.4.13) mentions fighting betwen Sertorius and Metellus at Segobriga (on the Cabeza del Griego, near Saelices, Cuenca Prov., Castilla–La Mancha) and Bilbilis (near Calatayud, Zaragoza Prov.), but does not indicate those cities' allegiance. Livy (lines 55–56) characterizes the winter of 77/6 as witnessing the siege of *Celtiberiae urbes*: since the Arevaci were Sertorius' most loyal followers (see 27.1n.) and his expedition along the upper Ebro Valley against Berones and Autricones only commenced in the spring of 76 (Livy, lines 65–83), the locations of those unnamed towns must be sought farther south, perhaps in Zaragoza and Cuenca Provinces.

In the extreme northeast of the Peninsula, the Vascones for the most part sided with the government armies (Sall. *Hist.* 2.93; cf. Strabo 3.4.10 on Pompey's foundation of Pompaelo, now Pamplona, Navarra). The peoples of the northern coastal areas of Catalonia did the same when Pompeius arrived in the summer or fall of 77 (Sall. *Hist.* 2.98.5, *recepi . . . Laeetaniam, Indicetes*; the mss. have *Lacetaniam,* which was allied with Sertorius—a likely error; cf. Plin. *NH* 3.21). The lower Ebro was probably Sertorian (Ilercaonia: Livy line 62), as apparently was Tarraco (Tarragona, Catalunya: Strabo 3.4.10).

In modern geographical terms, then, by the end of 77 Sertorius appears to have controlled northern and central Portugal, Old Castile and León, most of Aragón and the País Valencià, the north and east of New Castile and La Mancha, and the west and south of Catalonia. Andalusia and Murcia were firmly (it seems) in Metellus' hands. The Basque Country, Navarra, and La Rioja supported Pompeius, as did northern and eastern Catalonia. The allegiance of Extremadura and western New Castile (ancient Carpetania) remains uncertain; Livy (line 60) does not permit us to determine whether Sertorius considered the area friendly or hostile. Likewise unclear is the situation in Algarve and Alentejo (southern Portugal).

16.3–4

Frontinus *Strat.* 1.10.2 adds an important detail: only a single troop (*turma*) of cavalry—some thirty men—was permitted to charge the enemy. P. subtly exaggerates. Both accounts contain a striking verbal parallel: ἐπιβοηθήσας ἀνέλαβέ τε φεύγοντας αὐτοὺς καὶ κατέστησεν ἀσφαλῶς εἰς τὸ στρατόπεδον (16.4); *laborantique* (sc. *turmae*) *submisit alias et sic recepit omnes tuti⟨u⟩sque et sine noxa ostendit quis exitus flagitatam pugnam mansisset.* The common source is surely Sallust, known to both; whether P.'s κατέστησεν ἀσφαλῶς (*recepit . . . tutos et . . .* vel *recepit . . . tutisque sine noxa ostendit*) or Frontinus' *tuti⟨u⟩sque et . . . ostendit* (as emended by Goetz) more correctly renders the original, one cannot say.

16.5–11

The anecdote of the two horses is also found in Valerius Maximus (7.3.6) and Frontinus (*Strat.* 1.10.1 = 4.7.6); it is alluded to by Horace (*Ep.* 2.1.45–46) and Pliny (*Ep.* 3.9.11). Cf. also Viriatus' parable of the husband of two wives (Diodor. 33.7.6 = Poseid. F 105b Th).

16.5

μεθ' ἡμέρας ὀλίγας: Front. *Strat.* 1.10.1 (= 4.7.6) reports the same story, immediately before the incident of 16.3–4 (*Strat.* 1.10.2). Conceivably P. here combined two unconnected events into a narrative sequence, reversing their order for greater dramatic and didactic effect. But when Frontinus lists two related (in terms of their nature, not necessarily in place or time) stratagems of the same commander, he often gives the chronologically later one first (e.g., 1.5.17–18, 1.5.20–21, 2.2.6–7, 2.5.21–23, 2.9.6–7, 3.10.3–4), and even if the incidents described in 16.3–4 and 5–11 were separated by a mere few days, he would have treated them as individual *exempla* without necessarily indicating that the one was prompted by the other. As it stands, P.'s story makes perfect sense; too much suspicion can be dangerous.

The incident is difficult to date; one is inclined to assign it to the period 79–77 B.C., not because P. places it before the hero's first encounter with Pompeius (18) but because Sertorius would have wanted to teach his Hispanian troops that lesson early on. Indeed, Valerius Maximus in his version (7.3.6) speaks specifically of Lusitani, which would suggest the early years of the war if much significance could be attributed to it. On the other hand, Frontinus explains Sertorius' motive in staging the horse show *quod experimento didicerat imparem se universo Romanorum exercitui.* Compare 2.1.3, [*Metellus Pius*] *iunctis cum Pompeio castris . . . hoste, qui imparem se duobus credebat, pugnam detrectante, quodam deinde tempore Sertorianos milites animadvertisset magno impetu instinctos, deposcentes pugnam umerosque exserentes et lanceas vibrantes. . . .* Did Frontinus by *universus Romanorum exercitus* in 1.10.1 mean the combined armies of Metellus and Pompeius? The situation described in 2.1.3 does have an odd resemblance to the former as well as to the one in P. A date later than 77 cannot be ruled out, and chapter 16 may be just as displaced chronologically as 15 (cf. above, 15.1n.), or even more so: Metellus and Pompeius do not begin joint operations until after chapter 19.

16.9

ἄνδρες σύμμαχοι: Sertorius' addressing his Hispanian forces as "allies" (*socii*) agrees with the picture gleaned from Livy fr. 22 W-M, esp. lines 17 (*conventum sociarum civitatium ... agebat*), 38, 44, 63, and 69.

17

This is the hero's third stratagem proper, after 3.8–10 and 13.7–12; it is narrated at greater length than any of the others (cf. 18.7–8). Instead of the usual ambush (chs. 13, 18) or deception (ch. 3), Sertorius here employs a natural phenomenon to his advantage. The chapter concludes the central section of the life and leads back to the historical narrative. For the first time, P. allows that not all of Spain sided willingly with Sertorius.

17.1

τὸ περὶ τοὺς λεγομένους Χαρακιτανούς: presumably the Carac(c)a of Ptol. 2.6.56 and the Anon. Ravennas 313.10. Plausibly identified by Schulten (75, 166) with Taracena near Guadalajara (Castilla–La Mancha); cf. Tovar, *Landeskunde* 3:233. On Spann's doubts, see following note. The attempt by M. Beltrán Lloris, *Arqueología e historia* 384–86, to identify Caraca with the Contrebia besieged by Sertorius (Livy 91 fr. 22.1–14 W-M) is unconvincing.

17.2

ὑπὲρ τὸν Ταγώνιον ποταμόν: Schulten (75) takes the Tagonius as the Río Tajuña, a righthand tributary of the Tagus (Tajo) that originates in the north of Guadalajara Province and empties just below Aranjuez (Comunidad de Madrid). In ancient sources the name occurs only here. Spann (194 n. 31) rejects Schulten's identification of both Tagonius-Tajuña and Caraca-Taracena, claiming it "highly unlikely that Plutarch (or his source) knew of this obscure stream" and pointing to a lack of "north-facing caves" at Taracena. Yet the supposed ignorance of P.'s source is special pleading, and while the biographer never mentions the Tagus (Τάγος), that name in its correct form must have occurred so frequently in his sources that it is gratuitous to assume he mistakenly rendered it Ταγώνιος. Moreover, the modern name Tajuña strongly suggests a Latin form *Tagon-*. As for the caves, they are to be found indeed not precisely at Taracena but in a range of heights extending ca. 5–10 kilometers north of it, between the villages Tórtola de Henares and Ciruelas. The caves face north and west, and the marly soil at the foot of the mountain is prone to create dust (see Schulten's addendum, 166).

ἄντρα καὶ κοιλώματα: "natural rock-caves and artificial dug-outs"; so Hübner, *RE* 3.2 (1899) 1566.

βλέποντα πρὸς βορέαν περιέχων: Northern exposure was also characteristic of the caves of the Ichthyophagi on the Red Sea (Diodor. 3.19). As Schulten observes, those who dwell in hot climates are usually concerned more about finding shelter from the heat than from the cold (76 n. 376).

17.4

τὴν λείαν εἴσω συναγαγόντες: In P., λεία is usually "booty, plunder" (e.g., Cam. 41.1; Luc. 31.9, 36.6; Mar. 11.13), and Doehner, Perrin, and Flacelière and Chambry translate thus. But as Scardigli points out ("Vita"), flocks (βότα) of the Characitani are mentioned in 17.7, and there is no hint of the cave dwellers being a warlike and predatory people. Hence the meaning "flocks, (common) possessions" (so Kaltwasser and Floerke, Ziegler) is preferable here.

τότε διακεκριμένον ἀπὸ τοῦ Μετέλλου: in a military context διακρίνομαι normally means "to disengage": contact with the enemy is broken off, but no withdrawal in defeat is implied (cf. Herod. 8.18; Thuk. 1.105.5, μάχης γενομένης ἰσορρόπου . . . διεκρίθησαν ἀπ' ἀλλήλων; 3.9.2). Yet P. seems to be envisaging just such a retreat in the face of superior force (ὡς κεκρατημένον, below); at the very least, he makes it look as if the Characitani interpreted the situation that way. The mention of only Metellus would suggest that the episode falls before Pompey's arrival but after Sertorius' move of his campaign from Lusitania/Ulterior to the Hither Province, hence in 78 or 77. Spann (p. 77) speculates that Metellus pursued Sertorius into Citerior, though διακεκριμένον rules out Metellus' following close on his heels.

17.6

ὃν Καικίαν ἔνιοι καλοῦσιν: *Kaikias* was usually understood to be a wind from the east-northeast (cf. Arist. *Meteor.* 363A-B; Plin. *NH* 2.120; and see Thompson, "Greek Winds" 50-53). Originally, however, the name seems to have signified simply a vehement squall rising rapidly and high against an oncoming thunderstorm (Arist. *Meteor.* 364B12-14; Plin. *NH* 2.126; Gell. 2.22.24; see R. Böker, *KP* 3 [1969] 46), without any particular direction being implied. In light of P.'s subsequent meteorological explanation, the character of the wind, rather than a northeasterly direction, may have prompted the choice of name here (cf. *Praec. ger. rei p.* 823B-C). A wind ἀπὸ τῆς ἄρκτου would more naturally be called Boreas or Aparktias. Indeed, whether or not Caraca is to be identified with Taracena and the Tagonius with the Tajuña, the site's general location between the Tajo and Henares rivers, east of a line Madrid-Aranjuez, is not in doubt. Hence the snow-covered mountains must be the Sierra de Guadarrama (as noted by Spann, 195 n. 31), whose southwest-northeast extension and prevailing wind patterns make an east-northeast "Kaikias" most unlikely. The wind P. describes here evidently is the *cierzo* of present-day Spain (Schulten 166), powerfully blowing from the north-northwest and still betraying its ancient name *Cercius* or *Circius* (Gell. 2.22.20, *nostri . . . Galli ventum ex sua terra flantem, quem saevissimum patiuntur, "circium" appellant a turbine . . . eius ac vertigine*; 2.22.28-29 = Cato *HRR* F 93, *ventus cercius, cum loquare, buccam implet, armatum hominem, plaustrum oneratum percellit*; cf. Plin. *NH* 2.121, *circius . . . nec ullo omnium violentia inferior, Ostiam plerumque secto Ligustico mari perferens*). Originating among the western Greeks, Κιρκίας/Κίρκιος is a well-attested name for the violent mistral from north-northwest otherwise known as Θρασκίας (see Kaibel 596-97, 606-7, 622). Conceivably the biographer mistook, misread, or misremembered *Cercius*/Κιρκίας/Κίρκιος for *Kaikias*; indeed, καικίας for κίρκιος occurs at [Arist.] *De mundo* 394B31 (cf. A. Rehm, *RE* 10.2 [1919] 1500). No transmission error seems indicated (κεκίαν L¹P¹ is insignificant).

17.7

θέρους ἀκμάζοντος: The specific reference to the season may be taken directly from Sallust: Perl, "Kompositionsprinzip" 322.

17.10

σοβαροῦ . . . πρὸς τὸν ἥλιον ἐκχεομένου: Hot air rises above cold; as the ground is heated by the sun, the air above it, heated likewise, rises and leaves a vacuum into which the cold air of the north wind rushes with great force. The intensity of the exchange grows steadily as the warming process continues during the morning and noontime hours, and the violent updrafts and dust storms resulting are characteristic of the open plateaus in central Spain (cf. Schulten 77 with n. 379).

18.1

τοῖς περὶ Μέτελλον: i.e., Metellus: see above, 4.9.n., and cf. 5.6, 27.1.

γήρᾳ καὶ φυσικῇ βραδυτῆτι: on Metellus' age see above, 13.1n.

18.2

Πομπηΐῳ τὴν Πυρήνην ὑπερβαλόντι: Pompeius crossed the Pyrenees in summer or fall 77 (see above, 15.4n.), having defeated the Salluvii in Transalpine Gaul and settled the affairs of that province while on his way to Spain (Cic. *Font.* 14; *Imp. Cn. Pomp.* 28, 30; Caes. *BC* 1.35.4; Plin. *NH* 3.18).

18.3

ἐκ τῶν περὶ Σύλλαν ἀνδραγαθημάτων: Pompey's military exploits during the Sullan Civil War were chiefly his raising of a private army and securing control of central Italy in 83 and 82, and his conquest of Sicily and Africa in

82 and 81: cf. *Pomp.* 6–12; Appian 80.366–68, 87.395, 88.401, 90.413, 95.440, 96.449.

Μᾶγνος: cf. *Pomp.* 13.7–8. Pompeius himself began to use his cognomen only during the Sertorian War: *Pomp.* 13.9.

τιμῶν τε θριαμβικῶν: Pompeius, still *eques Romanus*, celebrated his first triumph on 12 March (Gran. Lic. 36.2 Cr) of a year that has been the subject of much debate. Badian showed that 79 is to be ruled out and forcefully proposed 81 instead (*Hermes* 83 [1955] 107–18, 89 [1961] 254–56); Keaveney has offered additional arguments in support of that year (*AC* 51 [1982] 131–32). Twyman, "The Date of Pompeius Magnus' First Triumph," has revived the case for 80. The evidence at present is not sufficient to make either year a secure conclusion.

οὔπω γενειῶν: cf. *Crass.* 12.4; *Pomp.* 14.2, 23.2. Pompeius was born on 29 September 106 B.C. (Vell. 2.53.4; Plin. *NH* 37.13; cf. Cic. *Brut.* 239), and hence was twenty-four or twenty-five years old at his first triumph. Octavian's first shaving took place in 39 B.C. (Dio 48.34.3), at the age of twenty-three or twenty-four. But P. also calls Clodius μήπω γενειῶν in 62 (*Cic.* 28.2), when he was about thirty—a bit old for not yet having grown a beard, one should think.

18.4

πολλαὶ τῶν ὑπὸ Σερτωρίῳ πόλεων: see 16.1: Extent of Sertorian Power, for a survey of areas friendly or hostile to Sertorius.

εἶτ' ἐπαύσαντο: The fate of Lauro may have prevented further defections, but it did little to persuade those pro-Roman towns and tribes not yet controlled by Sertorius. Livy 91 fr. 22 W-M preserves evidence of tenacious resistance along the middle and upper Ebro River, clearly in the following winter (see Konrad, "Chronology," section XI).

Lauro

The location of Lauro remains elusive. Puig de Santa Maria (València Prov.) is still the most probable identification, but Llerona del Vallès (Barcelona Prov., Catalunya) has much in its favor. There existed at least two and possibly as many as four towns of that name.

(A1) A Lauro in Baetica near which Cn. Pompeius the younger was killed after the battle of Munda (Flor. 2.13.86). The site remains unknown; Schulten, *RE* 12.1 (1924) 1028, tentatively identified it with the Olauro of *CIL* II 1446–48, perhaps modern Lora de Estepa (Sevilla Prov., Andalucía). It should be noted that the *Bellum Hispaniense* 38–39 simply locates Pompeius' end in a *locus munitus natura* with no hint of any town nearby: Florus may be wrong, as often, and the Lauro in Baetica a phantom.

(A2) *Vina Lauronensia* counted among Spain's finest and were exported to

Italy (Plin. *NH* 14.71; *CIL* XV 4577–78). Pliny mentions them together with wines from Tarraco and the Baleares, and viticultural conditions suggest a location on the East Coast in Catalonia or the País Valencià.

(A3) Iberian coins with legend *lauro* are numerous (Villaronga, *Numismática* 87–90, 211); find and circulation patterns make it practically certain that the issuing city was located in eastern Catalonia (Villaronga ibid.; cf. Untermann, "Reitermünzen" 107, 137). It has been plausibly identified by Estrada and Villaronga (139–52) with Llerona del Vallès (Barcelona Prov., Catalunya), ca. 30 kilometers northeast of Barcelona.

(A4) The Lauro besieged and sacked by Sertorius (*Pomp.* 18.4; Frontin. *Strat.* 2.5.31; Appian 109.510–11; Flor. 2.10.7; Oros. 5.23.6–9). There remains the question of its site and possible identification with one or more of the other towns of that name.

(B) Clearly the Lauro in Baetica (A1) can be ruled out. The events described in chapter 18 marked the first encounter between Pompeius and Sertorius (Frontin. *Strat.* 2.5.31), and nothing warrants the assumption that the former penetrated deep into Spain with his first offensive. Hence Sertorian Lauro must be sought on the East Coast, either in Catalonia or the País Valencià. Indeed, it has been commonly located in the latter (e.g., Tovar, *Landeskunde* 3:462), variously at Llaurí, Llíria, or Puig, on the basis of "the literary evidence."

(C) As a matter of fact, the only literary source giving any hint with regard to the town's location is Orosius 5.23.6, *Pompeius contracto apud Palantiam exercitu Lauronem civitatem eqs*. Palantia "most assume to be the river of Saguntum," Spann wrote hesitantly (200 n. 20); indeed, the Río Palancia presumably is the Παλαντίας ποταμός of Ptolemy *Geogr.* 2.6.15. In conversation, Spann has explained his reluctance to accept that identification by pointing out that Orosius never names a river without adding *flumen, fluvius*, or *amnis* and may have been thinking of the town Palantia (Palencia, Castilla y León), a major center of the Hispano-Celtic Vaccaei. Orosius' one lapse from his uniform practice confirms Spann's suspicion at least in part; at 4.14.8 Hannibal's first encounter with Roman forces in Italy is placed *apud Ticinum*: the Presbyter mistook the Ticinus River for the town Ticinum. (The reverse error occurs at 6.16.7, *apud Mundam flumen*.) When writing *apud Palantiam*, Orosius clearly meant a town, not a river. Unfortunately we do not know which town and why. Four explanations come to mind.

(C1) Orosius mistook the Palantia River at Saguntum for a city, either Palantia of the Vaccaei, or a nonexistent one near Saguntum. In either case Lauro must be sought in the vicinity of Saguntum and Valentia.

(C2) Orosius' source contained no reference to the Palantia River, and his confusion was chronological rather than topographical. In 75 B.C., two years after Lauro, Pompeius in fact was operating in Vaccaean territory and unsuccessfully put siege to Palantia (Appian 112.523). Immediately before the Lauro incident (*apud Palantiam*), Orosius summarizes the activities of Metellus: *multis proeliis fatigatus, per devia oberrans hostem mora fatigabat*, *donec Pompei castris consociaretur* (5.23.5). Pompeius and Metellus did not join forces until after the battle of the Sucro, narrated in 5.23.11; on the other hand, in 75 both were operating separately at the time Pompeius attacked Palantia, and combined their armies again soon afterwards (Appian 112.523–24; cf. *Pomp.* 19.9). The error envisaged here is complex but not beyond Orosius' capabilities (in 5.23.5, for instance, he seems to be ascribing Sertorius' guerrilla methods to Metellus). No conclusions regarding the site of Lauro could be drawn from his account in that case.

(C3) Orosius' Palantia is not the city of the Vaccaei but a homonymous town on the East Coast. At 7.40.8 he mentions the *Pallentini campi* plundered by barbarian mercenaries in the early fifth century A.D. Those fields are usually thought to be in the land of the Vaccaei (Tovar, *Landeskunde* 3:342), though the context of his narrative (7.40.5–9) strongly points to a location near the Pyrenees: i.e., the coastal plains of Catalonia. If so, Sertorian Lauro is to be sought in Catalonia.

(C4) The Lauro sacked by Sertorius was near Palantia of the Vaccaei.

(D) The last explanation (C4) can be discounted, as no conceivable reconstruction of Pompey's first moves could lead him all the way to Palencia. Both (C2) and (C3) permit identification of Sertorian Lauro with the Lauro of the coins (A3), in Catalonia. The evident political and economic importance of the town issuing the coins would explain the bitter fight over its possession. Topographically, Llerona appears suitable: several plains—between the rivers Tenes and Congost to the west of Llerona, between the rivers Congost and Cànoves to the east, and in the triangle formed by the juncture of the Congost and Mogent to the south (at Montornès del Vallès, ca. 6 kilometers south of Granollers)—and an abundance of hills provide sufficient grounds for the maneuvering described by P. and Frontinus. Its location on the principal Roman road along the East Coast in Republican times (Estrada and Villaronga 165) would have lent Llerona strategical significance. Pompey's moves are most easily understood if Lauro was in Catalonia: the siege belongs in the fall of 77, immediately after his arrival in Spain (Konrad, "Chronology," sections XI–XII), not too long after Sertorian forces are known to have operated northeast of the Ebro (at Ilerda; see 12.5n.). Both the temptation to defect from Sertorius and Pompey's ability to aid the defectors would seem greater in that area than far to the south.

(E) Yet caution is indicated. Obviously, explanation (C1)—that Orosius mistook the Palantia River for a city—is the simplest and most economical. The País Valencià was of fundamental importance strategically (cf. Spann 95): Pompeius could not hope to link up with Metellus as long as Sertorius held that area. Not surprisingly, he was to make a determined (and, by and large, successful) attempt to secure it in his first full season in Spain, i.e., 76 B.C. He may have tried the same already in the fall of 77.

(E1) Of the Valencian identifications suggested, Llaurí (ca. 9 kilometers east of Alzira, 38 kilometers south of València) is the least probable one, as Valentia

Commentary 18.5   159

was in Sertorian hands until 76 (see 19: Winter 77) and Pompeius is not likely to have pushed so far beyond it.

(E2) Llíria, ca. 25 kilometers northwest of València and long a favorite, offers a suitable topography and an Iberian settlement on the Cerro de San Miguel that was apparently destroyed in the early first century B.C. (see Martín and Gil-Mascarell 24–26; Fletcher Valls, *Atlantis* 16 [1941] 172–78 and in *The Princeton Encyclopedia of Classical Sites,* Princeton, 1976, 495–96). But Llíria is undoubtedly the ancient Edeta (Plin. *NH* 3.23; cf. *CIL* II 3786), principal city of the Edetani, the alternate name of which survives unchanged (Ptol. *Geogr.* 2.6.63, Ἐδέτα ἡ καὶ Λειρία). Attempts to treat *Liria* as a variant of *Lauro,* or vice versa, are obviously begging the question.

(F) If Lauro is to be sought in the plain of València, the small town of El Puig de Santa Maria, proposed by Schulten (93; cf. *RE* 12.1 [1924] 1028), remains the most attractive candidate. The modern town surrounds the base of a double hill, about 11 kilometers south of Saguntum, and shows evidence of a Roman presence. The Iberian town was sited on a slightly larger hill, variously known as La Pedrera or La Cantera ("the stone quarry"), some 400 to 500 meters east of Puig; unfortunately construction of the new coastal highway (Autopista 7) has resulted in the disappearance of most of that hill. (Spann's objection to Puig = Lauro, 220 n. 20, that "the hills . . . are so close together that the race between Sertorius and Pompeius to seize one of them . . . would make no sense," seems to be based on his misunderstanding Schulten and seeking Iberian Lauro on the eastern height of the Puig double hill rather than on the more distant Cantera.) The plain extends north, west, and south of Puig, but the foothills of the coastal mountains rise about 6 kilometers to the north and 12 kilometers to the west: close enough for the move described toward the end of Frontin. *Strat.* 2.5.31. Several sizable and wooded hills within the plain offer ample opportunity for the ambush tactics carried out by Sertorius' forces (see 18.9–10: Battle of Lauro, and 18.9nn.). The plain itself was more wooded and less flat until leveled to make room for orange plantations, beginning in the eighteenth century. (I am indebted to J. Fernández Nieto for bringing that point to my attention.)

Llerona del Vallès (D) is favored by regional importance, as evidenced by its coins, and by permitting a more conservative estimate of Pompey's speed of operations in 77. Yet El Puig de Santa Maria (F) has the undeniable advantage of fitting the topographical requirements implied by P. and Frontinus to an uncanny degree (see 18.9nn.), besides not demanding a complex interpretation of Orosius' *apud Palantiam*. To insist on one over the other may be unwise, but on balance, Puig–La Cantera appears slightly more probable as the Lauro of Sertorius.

18.5

Σερτωρίου γὰρ πολιορκοῦντος αὐτούς: in late summer or fall of 77, soon after Perperna had joined Sertorius (the incident reported by Appian 109.511

surely involved one of Perperna's cohorts, unfamiliar with Sertorius' policy toward the Hispanians; see below, 18.11n.). It is not clear from P.'s account whether Lauro had been previously allied with Sertorius and now was trying to defect, or whether it had never been under his control. The harsh punishment (18.11) may suggest the former.

πανστρατιᾷ: Oros. 5.23.9, quoting Galba (*HRR* F 2), numbers Pompey's forces at 30,000 infantry and 1,000 cavalry. Those figures reflect an army of at least five legions, probably six to eight: see above, 12.2n.

λόφον ... προληψόμενος: If Lauro = Puig–La Cantera (above, 18.4: Lauro F), Sertorius must have occupied the double hill of modern Puig (not merely its eastern, lower peak, as Schulten, 101, thought) to the west of La Cantera. If Lauro = Llerona (18.4: Lauro D), the heights seized by Sertorius may be identified with a double hill ca. 500 meters to the east, between Llerona and Marata; subsequent events, however, would be more intelligible if the Iberian town were located slightly farther south, at Corró de Vall just north of Granollers (which is not impossible: see Estrada and Villaronga 171–75).

18.6–7

The situation described here is best seen as a standoff. Pompeius could not directly relieve Lauro, while Sertorius on his hilltop position opposite the town could not carry out a full-scale siege, or launch an assault. Presumably Pompeius thought that time was on his side: sooner or later Sertorius would run out of provisions, whereas Pompeius, in control of the plain, would have no such problem. Thus Sertorius would eventually have to come down and give battle, and no doubt Roman superior military skill would carry the day.

18.8

ἐκεῖνος δ' ἀκούσας ἐγέλασε: Unless one hazards to conjecture an eyewitness source here, this anecdote is best taken as an example of Plutarchean embellishment.

ὅτι δεῖ τὸν στρατηγὸν κατόπιν ... βλέπειν: a commonplace of generalship going back to *Iliad* 1.343. P. elsewhere ascribes the same maxim to the Athenian Timotheos (*An seni res p. ger.* 788E).

18.9–10: The Battle of Lauro

What follows is one of P.'s less successful attempts at narrative compression. Having already learned how Sertorius occupied the hill opposite Lauro (18.5) and how Pompeius took up a position "trapping" Sertorius between the Roman forces and the town (18.6), we now are told that (a) Sertorius had left 6,000 men behind in his previous camp; (b) those 6,000 can attack Pompeius from the rear, should he move against Sertorius' force on the hill; (c) too late, Pompeius realizes this situation. (d) Fearing encirclement, he does not dare render assistance but, although ashamed to abandon "men in danger," is forced to watch "them" perish, for (γάρ) (e) the Lauronitai give up and surrender to Sertorius.

Clearly for P. the "men in danger" perishing under Pompey's eyes are the inhabitants of Lauro. Yet something is amiss: if Pompeius feared encirclement should he launch an assault, why could he not guard against it? If Sertorius was able to divide his forces, so was Pompeius; he merely needed to detach a legion or two against the "old camp" in order to secure his rear. His predicament as described by P. is not very convincing. Fortunately, Frontinus has preserved a highly detailed account of what happened at Lauro (*Strat.* 2.5.31): it explains much of what P.'s does not.

When Sertorius succeeded in taking the hill opposite Lauro, Pompeius put his camp close enough (*vicina castra*) to threaten his adversary's position. There were, however, only two areas suitable for foraging, and Sertorius, making good use of his superiority in light-armed infantry, effectively denied the Romans the one area that was near their camp. Yet he did not hinder their venturing to the other foraging area, at a considerable distance from their camp, and soon they became convinced that it was safe to go there. Then, during the night, Sertorius sent to the farther area an ambushing force composed of ten Hispanian cohorts of *scutati* armed *in morem Romanorum,* ten cohorts of Hispanian light infantry, and 2,000 cavalry. The infantry was commanded by Octavius Graecinus (on whom see below, 26.4 n.), the cavalry by C. Tarquitius Priscus (below, 26.6n.). The Roman foraging brigade, including *omnia impedimenta,* was completely taken by surprise and massacred to the last man. The fighting did not go unnoticed at headquarters, though, and Pompeius ordered an entire legion under the Legate D. Laelius to succor the foragers. That legion too was annihilated, and Laelius killed; while the fighting was still going on, Pompeius marched out his entire army to come to Laelius' rescue. At that point, *Sertorius quoque e collibus suos instructos ostendit.* The reference must be both to his main force on the hill near Lauro and to the reserve corps in the old camp, presumably also on a hill. Finding himself caught between three different Sertorian forces—main body, reserve in old camp, and the twenty cohorts plus cavalry already in the plain—Pompeius dared not give battle, and retreated to his camp. Given that the foraging brigade probably had legionary strength, at least (for contemporary practice see, e.g., Caes. *BG* 4.32.1, 5.17.2, 6.36.2; [Caes.] *BAfr* 68.1; and above, 13.10), his total losses must have amounted to the equivalent of nearly two legions, along with all his train and most *calones.*

The nature and degree of narrative compression thus becomes apparent. P. has omitted the fighting in the plain, and not for want of details in his source. (Sallust had the full story, *Hist.* 2.29–32, as did Livy: Frontin. *ad fin.*; Obseq. 58.) But Sertorius took no part in the actual battle, and describing it would have compelled the biographer to give credit to the hero's lieutenants, Octavius and Tarquitius, and perhaps to Hirtuleius (see 12.4n.) as well: the latter's participation is certain though the nature of it is not (see below, 18.9n.). Moreover, both Octavius and Tarquitius eventually were to be major figures in the assassination of Sertorius (26.4, 26.6nn.), and P. would not have wished to associate them with what in this life comes across as Sertorius' most splendid victory, or to probe too deeply into the reasons that led such trusted and competent officers to turn against their leader.

Thus P. skips from Sertorius' initial stratagem—leaving a reserve force in the old camp in P.'s rear—to the conclusion of the entire affair, i.e., the surrender of Lauro, and reduces the military aspects to a simple case of Pompeius' finding himself positioned between two enemy camps. Instead P.'s emphasis is on the political repercussions rather than on Pompey's defeat in battle: failure to save Lauro brought not only personal humiliation but, for the time being, put an end to the defection of Hispanian towns away from Sertorius. The biographer failed, however, to eliminate all traces of the fighting in the plain. Hence the "men in danger, abandoned by Pompey, who was forced to sit and watch them perish": P. makes it refer to the town, while his wording still betrays the original context (cf. below, 18.10n.).

18.9

τοῖς πολιορκουμένοις ἐπεδείκνυεν: The "besieged" are the people of Lauro, as is required by the logic both of the situation—Sertorius' own troops obviously would have known about their former camp and their comrades left behind—and the narrative: this is Sertorius' answer to Pompey's grandiloquent message (18.7), and both address the Lauronitai. P. is fudging the facts; Sertorius revealed his hidden corps not to the Lauronitai but to Pompeius, when the latter was preparing to deploy all his forces: *Pompeio totum educente exercitum Sertorius quoque e collibus suos instructos ostendit* (Frontin. *Strat.* 2.5.31). The verbal parallel *ostendit*–ἐπεδείκνυεν speaks for itself; cf. below, 18.10nn. Perrin's translation, making πολιορκουμένοις refer to Sertorius' own "beleaguered troops," is singularly inept, though implicitly followed by Spann (200 n. 30). The latter does not realize that P.'s account is a compressed version of the events Frontinus describes (above, 18.9–10: Battle of Lauro), and treats the fighting in the plain and the maneuvering from the old camp to the hill near Lauro as two unconnected incidents (96–97).

ἑξακισχιλίους: probably one legion (see 12.2n.), if Roman troops (i.e., those of Perperna), but see the following note. Whether Sallust would use the term *legio* for a Hispanian unit, albeit armed and organized in Roman fashion, is uncertain; he had no compunction about applying it to Catilina's irregulars: *Cat.* 32.1, 56.1–2.

ὁπλίτας: either Roman legionaries from Perperna's force or, more likely, in view of their important and independent assignment, Hispanian *scutati* armed in Roman fashion (cf. 14.1n., and esp. Frontin. *Strat.* 2.5.31).

καταλελειμμένους ἐπὶ τοῦ προτέρου χάρακος: If Lauro = Llerona (18.4: Lauro D), the old camp is best sought on the heights of Montornès del Vallès and Vallromanes, ca. 12 kilometers south of Llerona, and the ambush of the foraging brigade and the ensuing battle would have occurred in the plain between the confluence of the Congost and Mogent rivers, just north of Montornès. Pompeius would have camped on one of the hills near Corró de Vall, between Llerona and the lower Mogent. However, that same sizable range of hills could have acted as a barrier between Sertorius' forces at Llerona and the ambush and reserve units near Montornès, and the precariousness of Pompey's position is far more evident if Lauro was in fact at Puig–La Cantera (18.4: Lauro F). Pompeius in that case would have camped in the plain as close as possible to Sertorius, in the vicinity of Puçol (3 kilometers north of Puig) or Rafelbuñol (2.5 kilometers west); both sites are on the Republican coastal road, though Puçol's location would make for easier communications with Lauro (La Cantera). Sertorius' first camp must be sought on one of the foothills of the coastal mountain range, such as La Costera (5 kilometers north-northwest of Puig), Sierra Larga (6 kilometers northwest of Puig), or Bords (8 kilometers northwest-by-west). The annihilation of Pompey's foragers would best be placed in the woodlands of the western plain, where the double hill known as Els Germanells (6 kilometers west-by-north of Puig) is ideally sited for staging an ambush.

From Schol. Bob. 98.9–11 St = Sall. *Hist.* 2.31, *Laelius . . . ab Hirtuleianis interfectus est, ut ait Sallustius: "receptis plerisque signis cum Laeli corpore,"* it is virtually certain that L. Hirtuleius (above, 12.4n.) was present at Lauro. Sallust would not identify a military formation as *Hirtuleiani* unless it was in fact under Hirtuleius' command at the time, for the latter, despite his important independent missions, never was a commanding general in his own right, *suis auspiciis.* (Only once is he termed *dux* by a Latin author, Sall. *Hist.* 2.59, when he was fighting Metellus on his own at Italica; cf. Flor. 2.10.6–7, with its telling distinction between *duces* and *legati.* Different, of course, is Oros. 5.23.3, *ab Hirtuleio Sertorii duce.*) It is quite out of the question that the Bobbio scholiast could have substituted *Hirtuleiani* for some other appellation when Hirtuleius had no part whatsoever in Sallust's account; no more plausible is the suggestion (McGushin 201) that the reference is to Hirtuleius' brother, Quintus—never mentioned by himself in the literary sources (Flor. ibid.; Oros. 5.23.10; Auct. *De vir. ill.* 63.2).

In view of what is known about the operations at Lauro, it seems best to assume that Hirtuleius was in charge of the force left behind in the old camp, and that the ambush of Pompey's foragers was staged from that location rather than from Sertorius' (new) main camp on the hill opposite Lauro. The old camp was in Pompey's rear and presumably closer to the foraging area; since it either remained unknown to Pompeius or was ignored, there would be no close surveillance, and troop movements from it would be less susceptible to detection than such from the new camp. Clearly the old one was much better suited to the purpose. Hence it may be concluded that Sertorius left in the old camp not only the 6,000 *hoplitai* mentioned by P. (18.9), but also the twenty cohorts and 2,000 horse that carried out the ambush and destroyed

Laelius' legion. If this entire second corps was commanded by Hirtuleius and composed of units that had already in previous years fought under him (see 12.4–5nn.), the ambushing force, although actually led by Graecinus and Tarquitius, could properly be called *Hirtuleiani* (similarly, with confusion, Bieńkowski, "De fontibus" 76).

ἐπὶ σφᾶς τρεπομένῳ: i.e., against Sertorius' main force on the hill near Lauro.

18.10

ἀπολιπεῖν δ' ᾐσχύνετο κινδυνεύοντας ἀνθρώπους, ... ἀπολλυμένους: in passing over the battle in the plain, P. has shifted the identity of the κινδυνεύοντες ἄνθρωποι ἀπολλύμενοι from the foragers and Laelius' legion (Frontin. *Strat.* 2.5.31, *Sertorius ... spectatorem quoque eum cladis suorum continuit*) to the people of Lauro. Cf. above, 18.9–10: Battle of Lauro.

⟨περι⟩ορᾶν: Ziegler's addition appears unnecessary.

ἀπέγνωσαν γὰρ ... παρέδωκαν: hence Lauro was not taken by storm but surrendered. Pompeius had lost the equivalent of nearly two legions and was unable to help: Sertorian partisans in the town would have little difficulty convincing their fellow citizens that the situation was hopeless.

18.11

τῶν μὲν σωμάτων ... κατέπρησεν: cf. Appian 109.510. According to Orosius 5.23.7, Lauro was sacked with considerable loss of life; the survivors were deported to Lusitania. The latter measure is entirely credible, the practice of deporting the inhabitants of a disloyal town being common. No doubt that is what lurks behind P.'s πάντας ἀφῆκε, "he let all of them go." As for indiscriminate slaughter, the story of the Iberian woman told by Appian (below)—himself anything but a pro-Sertorian source—implies that Sertorius' troops had orders not to harm the townspeople. Those leading citizens who had supported the cause of the Roman government may indeed have been executed (so Stahl 17), but the terms of surrender no doubt included Sertorius' promise that he would spare the lives of the rest. Here as everywhere, Orosius' first concern was with the bloodthirsty disposition of the pagan world: his reports of massacres are taken at face value at one's peril.

Appian writes that during the sack of Lauro, Sertorius punished the rape of an Iberian woman by executing not only the soldier guilty of the crime, but the man's entire cohort, καίπερ οὖσαν Ῥωμαϊκήν. This was certainly one of the fifty-three cohorts recently arrived under Perperna (above, 15.5); the Roman troops that had shared Sertorius' adventures from the beginning would know better than to mistreat the native population, and Sertorius is not likely to have used such sweeping methods of enforcing discipline against his oldest and most loyal troops. His severity, and Appian's comment that the cohort was thought to take pride in such behavior (ἀγέρωχον ἐς τὰ τοιαῦτ' εἶναι νομιζομένην), indicate that there had been trouble previously with Perperna's *soldatesca*. Spann's dismissal (200 n. 31) of Appian's account as merely reflecting "the propaganda of Pompey's camp" is too simplistic.

οὐχ ὑπ' ὀργῆς ... ἀνήρ: The naive attempt to excuse Sertorius' severity is surely P.'s own, not Sallust's. But the biographer overlooks that if the burning of Lauro was not an emotional reaction, it was an act of calculated terror, and the next sentence (see following note) implies as much. Unwittingly thus, in defending the hero against charges of uncontrolled rage and irrational action (ὀργὴ and θυμός), P. convicts him of deliberate savagery (ὠμότης). Sertorius was not cruel for pleasure or by inclination, but perfectly capable of acting brutally when it served a purpose: cf. 10.5–7nn.

ἀλλ' ἐπ' αἰσχύνῃ ... Πομπήϊον: Lauro was destroyed "pour encourager les autres." P. has personalized an act of political deterrence.

19

Lauro illustrated Sertorius' mastery of swift maneuver; the fight at the Sucro exemplifies his ability to manage a pitched battle. Both qualities have been named in 10.3.

Winter 77 to Summer 76 B.C.

Although P. follows the chronological order of events in chapters 18–19, he makes no attempt at summarizing the intervening course of the war. After the sack of Lauro, Sertorius spent the rest of fall 77 with the siege and capture of towns in lower Celtiberia (Livy 91 fr. 22 W-M, lines 54–55; cf. above, 16.1: Extent of Sertorian Power); the last to surrender was Contrebia Belaisca (Botorrita, Zaragoza Prov., Aragón; Livy, lines 1–12). He kept winter quarters at Castra Aelia (precise location unknown) on the middle Ebro; Hirtuleius went back to Lusitania to keep an eye on Metellus, with strict orders not to engage in an open battle, his forces being much inferior (Livy, lines 13–35, 41–45). The emphasis on Sertorius' military activity clearly had now shifted to the Nearer Province. Metellus wintered in Ulterior, perhaps in Corduba (Sall. *Hist.* 2.28); Pompeius probably in Catalonia.

In the spring of 76 Perperna was sent with 20,000 men (apparently for the most part the army he had brought from Italy: above, 15.5nn.) to Ilercaonia, i.e., southern Catalonia and the northern País Valencià. Another Sertorian commander, C. Herennius (on whose identity, quite uncertain, see *MRR* 3:101), had been stationed in the same area throughout the winter; both he and Perperna were now to protect the East Coast against Pompeius (Livy, lines 35–53). Apparently, though, Sertorius expected Pompeius to draw out the war rather than make an aggressive move (Livy, lines 46–50). He consequently resumed his campaign along the upper Ebro and prepared to march against the Berones and Autricones in the North (Livy, lines 53–83).

The Livy fragment ends at this point, and further developments are obscure. By summer, Pompeius, far from adopting a strategy of attrition, had pushed down the East Coast all the way to Valentia, where he routed Perperna and Herennius, killing the latter, and captured the city (Sall. *Hist.* 2.98.6; cf. 2.54; Plut. *Pomp.* 18.5). At about the same time Hirtuleius—in an apparent violation of orders—engaged in a battle with Metellus at Italica (near Sevilla), only to have his army wiped out (see above, 12.4n.). That victory enabled Metellus to leave his province and move eastward so as to effect a link-up with Pompeius; to prevent which Sertorius was forced to abandon his northern campaign and march to the East Coast. He encountered Pompeius at the Sucro the day before Metellus arrived.

19.1

ἧτται μὲν οὖν . . . συνέβαινον: Unfortunately neither P. nor the other sources allow us to pinpoint more than three of these defeats: 14.6, 16.3; and 21.3 (on which see the following note). The first two incidents (cf. Sall. *Hist.* 1.126; Frontin. *Strat.* 1.10.1–2 = 4.7.6; Val. Max. 7.3.6) cannot be located. P.'s comment should perhaps be seen in context with Appian 113.527, ἡττᾶτο συνεχῶς. Appian's reference is to Sertorius' last years, 74–73, but P.'s is clearly general in nature and presumably includes the same time period. Hence Appian's statement ought to be taken seriously, and negative information about Sertorius found in Appian cannot be dismissed simply on grounds of "hostile tradition." As in his discussion of the hero's character (10.5–7), in his comments on the purpose of the School at Osca and the children's fate (14.3, 25.6), or his account of the treatment of Lauro (18.11), P. here allows us the merest glimpse of the fact that the hero's leadership in Spain was not without setbacks and blemishes.

αὐτὸν μὲν ἀήττητον ἀεὶ φυλάττοντι: According to P. himself (21.3), Sertorius suffered a personal defeat in the battle of Segontia in 76. But as Appian's (110.515) and Livy's (*Per.* 92) accounts of the same battle show, Sertorius' defeat at the hands of Metellus became possible only through Metellus' prior victory over the army of Perperna (see 21.2–3: Battle of Segontia), while Sertorius himself was victorious over Pompeius. Thus P.'s statement, read in context with the following clause (θραυομένῳ . . . ἡγεμόνας), is not untrue—but he chooses his emphasis carefully.

θραυομένῳ δὲ περὶ τοὺς ἄλλους ἡγεμόνας: Known defeats incurred by Sertorius' generals are Hirtuleius' at Italica, Herennius' and Perperna's at Valentia (above, 19: Winter 77), and Perperna's at Segontia (below, 21.2–3), all in 76 B.C. None of the details are found in the *Sertorius*. With impartial focus on the hero, P. suppresses the lieutenants' successes as well as their failures, but for one oblique mention (12.4), and their deeds remain as anonymous as the commanders themselves.

19.2

ἀντιστρατήγων: "enemy generals"; cf. 12.3n.

Σεγουντίαν: Ziegler's emendation (τουττίαν ΛQ: σουντίαν PZ; see "Plutarchstudien" 7) is undoubtedly correct. The traditional "reading" Τουρίαν lacks support both palaeographically and geographically: the battle was fought at Segontia Lanka (Langa de Duero) on the upper Duero, not in the plain of Saguntum (see below, 21.1–3nn.).

19.3

ἡ ... περὶ Σούκρωνι μάχη: "the battle of the Sucro," in 76 B.C. From *Pomp.* 19.2, περὶ δὲ Σούκρωνι ποταμῷ, it is evident that P. locates the battle by the river (Río Júcar) rather than the town of that name; Appian names it after the town: περὶ πόλιν, ᾗ ὄνομα Σούκρων (110.512). The references of Sallust *Hist.* 1.98.6, *apud Sucronem*, Florus 2.10.7, *apud ... Sucronem*, and Cicero *Balb.* 5, *Sucronensi* (sc. *proelio*), are ambiguous. But as P.'s story about Pompeius losing his horse (19.8; *Pomp.* 19.5) appears to be derived from Sallust (2.62–63), it is probably safe to assume that Sallust also located the battle by the river. The town (at the river, ca. 20 kilometers from the coast, near Alzira, València Prov.: Schulten, *RE* 4A.1 [1931] 561) is mentioned by Strabo 3.4.6 and Pliny *NH* 3.20, *Sucro fluvius et quondam oppidum*. Obviously it no longer existed by the middle of the first century A.D.; as Schulten (93 n. 453) points out, Strabo's reference need not imply that it still existed even in his time. Schulten suggests that the town was destroyed during the fighting in 76. The name occurs as that of a road station in later itineraries: *Itin. Anton.* 400.4; *Vas. Vicarell.* 1–4 (*CIL* XI 3281–84).

λέγεται ... Μέτελλος: cf. *Pomp.* 19.1, ἐπ' αὐτὸν ἔσπευδε Σερτώριον, ὡς μὴ μετάσχοι τῆς νίκης Μέτελλος. Schulten (112) and Spann (111) accept this at face value. As P. narrates in the *Pompeius* (18.5–19.1; cf. Sall. *Hist.* 2.98.6), the latter had just administered a crushing defeat to Perperna and Herennius (cf. above, 19: Winter 77) at Valentia: he might reasonably think he had a good chance against Sertorius. P. stresses Sertorius' own desire to give battle before Metellus arrived (19.4; *Pomp.* 19.2), and as is clear from the sequel he did not dare to fight both Roman generals together (19.11; *Pomp.* 19.6). It follows that it was Sertorius who was pressing for the engagement; there is no discernible reason why Pompeius should have refused battle.

As a rule, though, Roman generals were not paragons of cooperation. Were there any facts known to the biographer that could substantiate his accusation? Not if parallels in his work are any indication. In the *Lucullus*, P. levels the same charge against M. Aurelius Cotta (*cos.* 74) at the battle of Kalchedon (8.1) and against Lucullus' Legate, C. Valerius Triarius, in connection with his defeat between Zela and Gaziura in 67 (35.1). In either case the charge is not only manifestly false but preposterous. Cotta retreated to Kalchedon as soon as Mithradates approached; the battle was actually fought by his lieutenant, P. Rutilius Nudus, with the Consul safely behind the walls (Appian *Mithr.* 71.299–304). Triarius, far from trying to preempt Lucullus, had sent to the latter for help, but was forced by his own troops to lead them to a nearby fort in which their baggage was stored; his force was attacked on the march and largely massacred (Dio 36.12.3–4). Interestingly, Appian here repeats P.'s charge (*Mithr.* 89.402). One wonders if there was a common source taking delight in this kind of slander aimed at Roman generals. Sallust is not above suspicion.

19.4

ἑσπέρας: cf. Sall. *Hist.* 2.60, *vespera*, and Plut. *Pomp.* 19.2, τῆς ἡμέρας ἤδη τελευτώσης.

19.5

L. Afranius (6): ca. 112–46 B.C. Legate under Pompeius in Spain 77–73 (?); Praetor 72 (?); *pro consule* in Hispania Citerior 71–67 (?). His capture and destruction of Calagurris (Oros. 5.23.14; cf. Sall. *Hist.* 3.86; Strabo 3.4.10; Val. Max. 7.6. ext. 3; Flor. 2.10.9; Exuper. 8.25 = 56 Z) was the last military event of the Sertorian War and should probably be dated to 71; if so, it provided him with his triumph (in 67?): Cic. *Pis.* 58; for a discussion see *HAnt* 8 (1978) 67–76. Legate under Pompeius against Mithradates 66–62; Consul in 60. From 55 to 49 *legatus pro praetore* for Pompeius in Hither Spain. Together with M. Petreius he unsuccessfully tried to oppose Caesar at Ilerda in 49, but was forced to surrender. With Pompeius in Greece and at Pharsalos, 49–48; in Africa, 47–46. After the Republican defeat at Thapsus he tried to flee to Spain, but was captured and executed.

τὸ ἀριστερόν: the left wing of Pompey's army. Afranius hence at first was pitted against Sertorius, who commanded his own right wing (ἐπὶ τοῦ δεξιοῦ). Appian 110.512–13 makes *Metellus* command the Roman left; an obvious blunder. From P. (19.11; *Pomp.* 19.6) it follows unquestionably that Metellus did not reach the Sucro until the day after the battle.

19.6–10: The Battle at the Sucro

From P.'s account, four phases of the battle can be distinguished. (a) Sertorius is fighting against Afranius on his own right wing, while Pompeius is being victorious against the Sertorian left (19.5–6). (b) Sertorius puts "other generals" in charge of his right and takes command of his left wing (19.6). (c) Sertorius rallies his troops on the left and defeats Pompeius; at the same time, Afranius routs the Sertorian right wing and captures their camp (19.7–9). (d) Sertorius with his victorious left wing returns to the camp and drives back Afranius (19.10).

Appian's account is similar but less complex. On the right wing, Metellus (sic) defeats Perperna and plunders his camp, while on the other wing Sertorius routs Pompeius (110.513). The *Periochae* simply state: *Cn. Pompeius dubio eventu cum Sertorio pugnavit, ita ut singula ex utraque parte cornua vicerint.* Orosius 5.23.11 adds nothing except inflated casualty figures. P. in the *Pompeius* (19.3) labels the battle indecisive, with one wing victorious on either side; "but Sertorius gained the greater glory, since he beat the wing opposing him." That wing was Pompey's, who otherwise would have won equal glory if not the battle. P. there makes no mention of Sertorius switching wings during the fight.

It is evident that Appian substituted Metellus for Afranius (see preceding note). What of Perperna? After his defeat at Valentia (above, 19: Winter 77) he would naturally have retreated south toward Contestania: his presence at the Sucro appears plausible. Schulten (113–14) and Spann (111) would put him in charge of the left wing originally, to be beaten by Pompey's (right) wing. (Schulten would then have Sertorius place Perperna in command of his own right wing when he himself switched to the left—a touching but utterly improbable reconstruction designed further to blacken the man's reputation by making him responsible for a double defeat, one on each wing, in a single battle.) Yet Appian states that [Afranius]—facing the Sertorian right wing—plundered *Perperna's* camp, while according to P., Pompeius on the other wing escaped only because Sertorius' Libyan (i.e., Mauretanian) cavalry chose to loot his horse's golden trappings rather than capture or kill him (19.8; *Pomp.* 19.5). If it can be inferred from this notice that Sertorius' native (i.e., Hispanian and African) troops were stationed on the left wing, and Perperna's Roman cohorts on the right, but with Sertorius himself in charge there at first, a more plausible reconstruction emerges. Having just suffered a rout at Valentia, Perperna's Roman troops would need encouragement, leadership, and close supervision now that they were facing Pompey's army again: hence Sertorius' presence and personal command on their wing (i.e., the right) at the outset. There is no reason to think he would ever entrust his Hispanian units to Perperna: hence the latter should also be sought with the right wing, as second in command. When Sertorius was forced to take charge of the left, Perperna would automatically have remained in command of the right, to be routed by Afranius.

19.6

τὸ μὲν δεξιὸν . . . στρατηγοῖς: If the reconstruction proposed in the preceding note is correct, the plural probably simply signifies Perperna.

19.8

Πομπήιος . . . τραυματισθείς: There are two somewhat different accounts of Pompey's wound. According to P. (*Pomp.* 19.4), he fought on horseback against a huge infantryman; both were using swords; Pompeius severed his enemy's hand, but himself was "merely wounded." According to Appian 110.513, Pompeius was wounded in the thigh with a spear.

Λίβυες: presumably the Mauretanians that had accompanied him on his return from Africa (12.2). See also García y Bellido, *Numisma* 14 (1964) 14.

ὡς ἔλαβον ... δίωξιν: cf. *Pomp.* 19.5. A similar story is told about Mithradates VI of Pontos, who escaped at Kabeira chiefly because a mule packed with gold from the royal treasury got between the king and his pursuers (*Luc.* 17.6–7).

19.9

εἰς τὸ στρατόπεδον κατήραξε: Perperna's camp, according to Appian. That Sertorius and Perperna kept separate camps may also be inferred from other hints: see below, 21.2–3: Battle of Segontia. Concentrating entirely on the hero, P. naturally makes no such distinction.

μήτε ... δυνάμενος: Thus on both sides soldiers' greed for booty caused victory to slip away. Cf. also Plácido, "Sertorio" 98.

19.10

ἐν τούτῳ δὲ Σερτώριος ἀνέστρεψε: As in taking charge of the left wing (19.7), the hero's personal intervention turns the tide of battle and saves the day.

πολλοὺς διέφθειρε: Orosius 5.23.11 gives the total losses as about 10,000 on either side. Such figures tend to be inflated, though the double rout suffered by each army in the course of the battle might account for higher casualties than under "normal" circumstances. Yet both commanders felt strong enough for another round the next morning (19.11; *Pomp.* 19.6, παρετάξαντο μὲν ἀμφότεροι πάλιν).

19.11

πρωὶ ... ἀνέζευξεν: Sertorius had been eager to fight Pompeius before Metellus' arrival (19.4; *Pomp.* 19.2); clearly he did not feel strong enough to face them both. After his severe casualties of the previous day, what would have been dangerous in any case had become impossible. He now withdrew from the coast to the Celtiberian highlands in central Spain. On *Pomp.* 19.6–7 see below, 21.4n.

ἀλλ' ἔγωγε ... ἀπεστάλκειν: cf. *Pomp.* 18.1, λόγους ὑπερηφάνους ὁ Σερτώριος κατὰ τοῦ Πομπηίου διέσπειρε, καὶ σκώπτων ἔλεγε νάρθηκος ἂν αὐτῷ δεῆσαι καὶ σκύτους ἐπὶ τὸν παῖδα τοῦτον, εἰ μὴ τὴν γραῦν ἐκείνην ἐφοβεῖτο, λέγων τὸν Μέτελλον. In fact, the battle at the Sucro, while a tactical defeat for Pompeius, strategically was a victory for the Senate's commanders. In withdrawing to Celtiberia, Sertorius effectively abandoned the

East Coast to his adversaries, who henceforth would be able to pursue joint operations. While a few individual places (chiefly Dianium and Tarraco: see 27.1n.) remained in his hand, he had lost control of the area as a whole. P. himself goes on to attest that his hero in truth had a healthy respect for Pompeius: ἔργῳ μέντοι φυλαττόμενος σφόδρα καὶ δεδοικὼς τὸν Πομπήιον, ἀσφαλέστερον ἐστρατήγει (*Pomp*. 18.2). Velleius (2.29.5) had already presented the same judgment: *ut a Sertorio Metellus laudaretur magis, Pompeius timeretur validius*. As Spann once remarked (diss. 287 n. 34), Sertorius' "sarcasm may have been somewhat hollow."

20

The victory over Pompeius at Lauro (ch. 18) was Sertorius' last unqualified success. In 19 and 21 he suffers at least partial defeat, and thenceforth P. is silent about the war in Spain: the hero's star is sinking. Like 11 and 16, chapter 20 emphasizes Sertorius' mastery of psychological leadership vis-à-vis his Hispanian allies; as the earlier two served to frame the life's long central section detailing the hero's qualities at the height of his career, so the present chapter acts as a hinge connecting 19 and 21, with their first hints of Sertorius' declining fortunes.

20.1

ἠθύμει δὲ . . . εἶναι: On the white doe see above, 11.2-8. Appian 110.514 mentions her only here, in connection with her disappearance after the Sucro battle; Gellius 15.22 comprises what P. has to say in chapter 11 and here. Conceivably Sallust too first told of the doe on occasion of her getting lost, and P. rearranged the material to suit his purpose: as a major instrument of the hero's leadership, he would wish to introduce the animal early on.

τότε δὴ μάλιστα παραμυθίας δεομένους: P.'s way of saying that Sertorius' military situation after the battle at the Sucro was anything but enviable. Naturally he does not dwell on the matter and would rather have the reader marvel at Sertorius' crafty manipulation of the Hispanians.

20.2

νυκτὸς ἄλλως πλανώμενοί τινες: presumably Romans, or perhaps a Mauretanian cavalry patrol. Hispanians might not so easily have been bribed to collaborate in the staged reappearance of the doe (20.3–4).

ἐπιτυγχάνουσιν αὐτῇ: According to Gellius 15.22.6, the animal was hiding *in palude proxima*. Schulten (113 n. 537) would identify that swamp with the enormous lagoon known as La Albufera, between the Júcar and València.

20.3

τοῖς ἡγεμόσι τῶν Ἰβήρων: to be taken as an important footnote to P.'s claim that Sertorius employed exclusively Romans in positions of command (below,

22.6). At least at the unit level (cohorts and smaller), his Hispanians were led by their native chiefs and nobles.

ἀναβὰς ἐπὶ τὸ βῆμα: i.e., his *tribunal* or *suggestus*. Gellius 15.22.8–9 implausibly posits the scene of the doe's return in Sertorius' *cubiculum*, for the benefit of his "friends" (*amici*)—a term that hardly could apply to the "leaders of the Hispanians" (cf. 10.1, 22.10nn.).

τοῖς ἐντυγχάνουσιν ἐχρημάτιζεν: "transacted official (legal) business with those who were present"; cf. *Brut.* 14.6. Doehner elegantly translates: "conscenso tribunali responsa dedit."

20.5

κρότῳ καὶ βοῇ . . . προπέμψαντες: cf. 12.1, ὑπὸ θεοῦ στρατηγεῖσθαι πειθομένοις. Appian 110.514 improbably portrays Sertorius as believing in the doe's divine character himself, and depressed to the point of military paralysis after her disappearance.

ἐν εὐθυμίαις . . . ἦσαν: Spann (113) plausibly suggests that the doe's public reappearance was staged during Sertorius' retreat from the East Coast to the Celtiberian highlands.

21.1

ἐν δὲ τοῖς τῶν Σεγουντίνων πεδίοις: certainly not Saguntum on the East Coast, as Schulten (115–16) and earlier scholars thought. Gabba (*App BC 1* 305) and Spann ("Saguntum vs. Segontia") have shown conclusively that the battle in question was fought near one of several Celtiberian towns named Segontia: perhaps the modern Sigüenza (Guadalajara Prov., Castilla–La Mancha) on the Henares river—so Gabba and Spann—but more likely Segontia Lanka, now Langa de Duero (Soria Prov., Castilla y León) on the upper Duero. The latter location commands support in the manuscript evidence of Cicero (*Balb.* 5) and Sallust (*Hist.* 2.98.6), which uniformly indicates the Duero River: *proeliis . . . Sucronensi et Duriensi* in Cicero, *proelium apud flumen Durium* according to Sallust. Editors, thinking of a battle on the East Coast and unable to conceive of one 300 kilometers inland, almost without exception have altered the texts to read, respectively, *Turiensi* and *Turiam*, thus creating a reference to the river of Valentia and giving rise, in due course, to a sometimes heated debate over which battle Cicero and Sallust were alluding to: Pompey's defeat of Perperna at Valentia (see above, 19: Winter 77) or the last pitched battle of the war, until recently believed to have been fought at Saguntum. Context and rhetoric in both authors prohibit a reference to Valentia; the second option—Saguntum—having been demolished by Gabba and Spann, there remains no alternative to accepting the evidence of the codices and looking for a suitable site on the Duero. For a fuller discussion see Konrad, "Segovia and Segontia," sections V–X.

P.'s use of πεδία need not imply an extended open plain, such as between Valentia and Saguntum. Often the term simply signifies the flat terrain on the banks of a river (e.g., *Luc.* 15.2; *Fab.* 16.1; *Caes.* 25.4), fields suitable for agriculture (e.g., *Luc.* 31.1; *Fab.* 4.6, 6.1; *Phil.* 4.9), or level ground as opposed to mountains (e.g., *Alex.* 20.2; *Ant.* 46.3, 6) or fortifications (*Mar.* 15.7). Just east of Langa, the Duero Valley widens to form a triangular plain of ca. 7 by 5 by 5 kilometers, large enough to accommodate armies in battle. About 100 meters above the floor of the valley, the mountains on either side offer spacious, open plateaus equally suitable. The most plausible reconstruction of the fight requires two separate but neighboring battle sites (see below, 21.2–3: Battle of Segontia); Langa de Duero offers a choice of three.

εἰς τὰς ἐσχάτας ἀπορίας . . . πολεμίους: In following Sertorius to Celtiberia, Pompeius and Metellus overextended their lines of communication and logistics, which became vulnerable to guerrilla attacks (see Spann 113–14).

ἠναγκάσθη συμβαλεῖν αὐτοῖς . . . σιτολογίαν: Maintaining it to be "unlikely that this wily commander was ever 'compelled' by his opponents to give battle," Spann (114) would interpret ἠναγκάσθη as signifying that either Sertorius "could not pass up" this opportunity to destroy the enemy, or was forced by his own officers to fight against his better judgment. P.'s text supports neither. While ἀναγκάζομαι need not mean "forced" in the sense of having no way of avoiding a battle, it clearly implies some form of pressure inherent in the circumstances—to achieve an objective, prevent a loss—that rendered any other course of action not impossible but highly undesirable. Far from pointing at Sertorius' lieutenants, P. connects the need to fight with the logistical straits of the enemy and their setting out to "pillage and forage." The explanation can be found in Pompey's Letter, written in the winter of the following year: *Hispaniam citeriorem, quae non ab hostibus tenetur, nos aut Sertorius ad internecionem vastavimus praeter maritimas civitates* (Sall. *Hist.* 2.98.9). Cut off from their supply lines to the coast, the Roman armies not only lived off the land but adopted a scorched-earth strategy, taking what food and supplies they needed and destroying the rest. Sertorius' Celtiberian allies would be anxious to put a stop to the devastation of their land (though he eventually resorted to the same practice), and some would begin asking themselves whether they were paying too high a price in support of Sertorius and his promises. Hence the attempt to face and destroy Metellus and Pompeius in a pitched battle, despite the lackluster results of such contests previously at Valentia and the Sucro.

21.2–3: The Battle of Segontia

A reconstruction of the battle may be attempted with the help of the other sources (Sall. *Hist.* 2.66–67; Livy *Per.* 92; Appian 110.515–6; Oros. 5.23. 12). According to P., Sertorius came close to defeating Metellus, the Proconsul even being wounded by a spear (cf. Sall. 2.67, *avidis ita atque promptis du-*

cibus, ut Metellus ictu tragulae sauciaretur); then the Romans rallied and put the Hispanians to flight. In Appian, Sertorius defeats Pompeius while Perperna is routed by Metellus; Pompeius loses 6,000 men, Perperna 5,000, and Sertorius (against Pompeius) 3,000. Livy *Per*. 92 reports: *Q. Metellus Sertorium et Perpernam cum duobus exercitibus proelio fudit, cuius victoriae partem cupiens ferre Pompeius parum prospere pugnavit*. The detail "with two armies" is crucial: it starkly contrasts this battle against that of the Sucro, reported by the epitomizer in the preceding sentence, *Cn. Pompeius dubio eventu cum Sertorio pugnavit, ita ut singula ex utraque parte cornua vicerint*. We are therefore dealing not with a repetition of the battle of the Sucro (as Schulten, 116, thought), with Sertorius being victorious on the one wing, Metellus on the other, but with a triple battle in two phases: first two separate engagements (Sertorius–Pompeius; Perperna–Metellus) on separate battlefields, though not far from each other and in the vicinity of the same town, followed by a battle between the respective victors, Sertorius and Metellus. This is supported by the events of the following day, which show that the Roman generals kept separate camps not too close to each other (Appian 110.516; cf. *Pomp*. 19.9, where this is mentioned as usual practice: τὰ πολλὰ δὲ χωρὶς ἐστρατοπεδεύοντο), and by the fact that the entire battle lasted for a very long time, from noon to nightfall (Appian 110.515). Possibly the fighting began with Metellus' attack on Perperna's army (if Liv. *Per*. 92 can be pressed: Pompeius suffered defeat after Metellus' success, which can only be the victory over Perperna; cf. Schulten 116). Sallust *Hist*. 2.66, *antequam regressus Sertorius instruere pugnae suos quiret*, may imply that Metellus, advancing after his rout of Perperna to the site of the other battle, caught Sertorius' troops still in disarray from the pursuit of Pompey's beaten army: thus Schulten 116 n. 549. (Not improbably, La Penna, "Ricostruzione" 38, would also refer *Hist*. 2.102 to this battle: *neque subsidiis, uti soluerat, compositis*. The reconstruction presented above, first set forth in my dissertation [Chapel Hill, 1985], has now been adopted by McGushin, 222–23.)

At Langa de Duero, i.e., Segontia Lanka (above, 21.1n.), those events may be visualized as follows. Sertorius and Perperna with their armies (on Perperna's being semi-independent rather than merely second in command of a unified force see above, 15.5n.) had been shadowing, respectively, Pompeius and Metellus as they penetrated into northern Celtiberia. Eventually the armies found themselves positioned on the plateaus above the Duero Valley near Langa, either all four on the same heights, or Sertorius and Pompeius on one side of the valley, Perperna and Metellus on the other. Shortage of provisions prompted one of the Roman commanders to descend into the valley. (P.'s καταβαίνουσιν may reflect such a move down from the heights, but that turn of phrase obviously cannot bear much weight.) To protect Segontia, an allied town, the Sertorians were compelled to fight: one army likewise descended into the valley and attacked the Romans there; the other engaged, or was engaged by, the remaining Roman force on the plateau so as to prevent each other from intervening in the events at the river. Which army made what move is impossible to guess. Sertorius' subsequent pursuit of the beaten troops of Pompeius might more easily have taken place on the open plateau, which assumption would put Metellus and Perperna in the valley. On the other hand, the plateau might have enabled Sertorius to avoid giving battle to Metellus before he was able to regroup his forces properly; thus perhaps Sertorius and Pompeius fought in the valley. Metellus, in either case, after routing Perperna descended into (or ascended from) the valley to engage and crush the army of Sertorius.

21.2

C. Memmius (7) (**C. f. L. n. Men.?**): ca. 107–76 B.C. He was Pompey's brother-in-law, left in charge of Sicily when Pompeius invaded Africa in 81 (*Pomp.* 11.2), and apparently served under Metellus in Spain between 80 and 77 (Cic. *Balb.* 5). Quaestor in 76 under Pompeius in Hither Spain (Oros. 5.23.12). Under siege by Sertorian forces in New Carthage, perhaps while attempting a naval attack on Dianium (thus Bieńkowski's reconstruction, "Chronologie" 213). After joining Pompey's army, he participated in the battles of the Sucro and Segontia, but was killed in the latter. For a reconstruction of the stemma of the Memmii see Taylor, *Voting Districts* 233–34, and especially Sumner, *Orators* 85–90.

ὁ τῶν ὑπὸ Πομπηΐῳ στρατηγῶν ἡγεμονικώτατος: "the ablest leader among Pompey's lieutenants." What achievements of Memmius' warranted this characterization is unknown.

ἐκράτει δὲ . . . Μέτελλον: P. does not clearly distinguish the phases of this battle (above, 21.2–3: Battle of Segontia). Sertorius has already defeated Pompey's army and is now battling that of Metellus, who in turn has already routed Perperna. The latter's part is completely suppressed (as elsewhere: cf. 19.1n.); the focus remains exclusively on the hero, whose disastrous defeat is never revealed in its full extent.

παίεται δόρατι: cf. Sall. *Hist.* 2.67, *avidis ita atque promptis ducibus, ut Metellus ictu tragulae sauciaretur.*

21.4

γενομένης οὕτω παλιντρόπου τῆς νίκης: "the euphemism of the sympathetic biographer unwilling to say that Sertorius had suffered a defeat" (Spann 115). Not just any defeat: Segontia may be viewed as the turning point of the war. Sertorius' ability to fight pitched battles against large Roman armies rested on his heavy infantry: the fifty-three cohorts of Perperna (ca. 20,000 men; cf. above 15.5) and an unknown number of Hispanian *scutati* armed and trained in Roman fashion. Sertorius' total forces at Lauro were estimated—surely on the high side—by Galba at 60,000 infantry (Oros. 5.23.9): evidently the 20,000 of Perperna and up to 40,000 Hispanians, perhaps half of them *scutati* (ten cohorts of this arm and ten of light infantry are attested, Frontin. *Strat.* 2.5.31; cf. above, 18.9–10: Battle of Lauro). A small covering force, all Hispanian, will have been in Lusitania, but no fighting is recorded there for 77. It probably included few, if any, *scutati*.

Of the Hispanians, a sizable number must have gone back to Lusitania with Hirtuleius during winter 77/6 after the sack of Lauro, to be wiped out at Italica (20,000 reported casualties, Oros. 5.23.10). At Valentia, Perperna and Herennius supposedly lost 10,000 (*Pomp.* 18.5); the same figure is given for Sertorius (and Perperna) at the Sucro (Oros. 5.23.11). At Segontia, Perperna is said to have lost 5,000, and Sertorius against Pompeius alone, 3,000 (Appian 110.515). Sertorius' casualties in the subsequent engagement against Metellus likewise must have been substantial. No doubt all these figures are inflated, but so, probably, is the total of 60,000 attributed to Sertorius at Lauro. Even if the casualty rates are reduced by one-third or one-half, little more than half of Perperna's troops would have been left by late 76. If Hirtuleius lost 3,000 *scutati* at Italica, and Sertorius about the same number each at the Sucro and Segontia (given that these were all exceedingly bloody battles, those estimates may still be on the low side), there were perhaps 10,000 of them left at the end of 76. That would make for at most 20,000 heavy infantry against two consular armies totalling at least ten, probably thirteen legions (see above, 12.2n.)—some 30,000 to 40,000 troops. Unless Sertorius could at least double his remaining heavy infantry, his ability to fight a pitched battle was gone. While he had no difficulties gathering new forces during the following winter (76/5; see 21.5–7), there is no indication that he ever recouped his losses in heavy infantry. Indeed it would take at least a year or two before freshly levied *scutati* would be fully trained in Roman fashion and able to match legionaries in the field.

ὁ Σερτώριος ... ἡσυχίας: Retreat, however, was not immediate. On the day after the battle Sertorius launched a surprise attack on Metellus' camp, but Pompeius intervened and forced him to abandon the attempt (Appian 110.516). At that point Sertorius decided on a general withdrawal, temporarily disbanding most of his forces though giving them orders as to when and where to regroup (Frontin. *Strat.* 2.13.3). P. reports the same practice (*Pomp.* 19.6–7), but in the aftermath of the Sucro battle. Since Frontinus is quite specific—*Q. Sertorius pulsus acie a Q. Metello Pio*, which can only refer to Segontia—and P. makes no mention of that battle in the *Pompeius*, it is best to assume that the biographer transposed the event, either deliberately so as to be able to include it without alerting the reader to Pompey's defeat at Segontia, or simply from faulty memory.

εἰς πόλιν ὀρεινὴν καὶ καρτερὰν ἀναφυγών: That town was Clunia (near Coruña del Conde, Burgos Prov.), ca. 18 kilometers north of Segontia Lanka. Cf. Livy *Per.* 92, *obsessus deinde Cluniae Sertorius adsiduis eruptionibus non leviora damna obsidentibus intulit*. Schulten's attempt (116–17) to place this siege at Saguntum should never have been made; see Gabba, *App BC 1* 306; Spann 116 and "Saguntum vs. Segontia" 119 n. 16.

21.5

ἐκείνῳ γὰρ ... προσδοκῶντες: Spann's suggestion (116) that Frontin. *Strat.* 2.12.2 may refer to the siege of Clunia is attractive.

21.7

περιέκοπτεν ... ἐπιών: cf. *Pomp.* 19.10–11. The siege of Clunia will have lasted some time, but Sertorius escaped and resumed his guerrilla tactics probably before winter set in. On operations during the following year, 75 B.C., see below, 21.8n. After 75, no details of the war are known until Sertorius' death in 73.

The avoidance of pitched battles after Segontia and the return to guerrilla warfare proved highly effective, at least with regard to the disruption of Roman logistics, as Sall. *Hist.* 2.93–96 demonstrate. Yet the same passages indicate that the Sertorians' food supply, by late 75, was not much better than Pompey's (2.93, *neque propin⟨quae⟩ civitates Mutudurei ⟨et ... [lac.] ...⟩ eores hunc aut illum ⟨com⟩meatibus iuvere: fames ⟨am⟩bos fatigavit*). Both sides seem to have carried out a scorched-earth strategy (above, 21.1n.). While Pompeius received abundant supplies in the next year (74 B.C.) from Rome and Gaul (Sall. *Hist.* 2.98D; Plut. *Luc.* 5.3; Appian 111.519; cf. Cic. *Font.* 8, 13, 16), Sertorius had to continue living off the land. Hispanian support was waning too (*Hist.* 2.92–93; Diodor. 37.22a; and see below, 25.4–5nn.: the beginnings of these developments probably belong in 75). Hence despite his spectacular escape from Clunia and the straits into which he put the Roman armies, and some tactical successes (at Palantia and Calagurris; see 21.8n.) notwithstanding, within a year, by the end of 75, Sertorius' position had become more than precarious. He no longer stood a chance of defeating Pompeius in an open engagement, while Pompeius alone could hope for reinforcements. When those arrived in spring 74, Sertorius had lost the war. From then on, he was left—in Spann's words (diss. 197)—with "a miserable struggle for survival."

λῃστρικοῖς σκάφεσι: On Sertorius' initial dealings with Kilikian pirates see 7.5–9.4. It is unknown when that alliance was reestablished; from Livy 91 fr. 22.47–50 W-M it appears that in 77/6 at least, Sertorius lacked significant naval forces, although his establishment of a naval base at Dianium (Dénia, Alacant Prov., Comunitat Valenciana; see Strabo 3.4.6) is to be dated no later than 77 on the basis of Sall. *Hist.* 1.124, *illum raptis forum [et] ⟨in⟩ castra nautica Sertorius mutaverat* (with Frassinetti's emendation, *Athenaeum* 40 [1962] 94–96). According to Strabo, the place was ideally suited for a pirate stronghold. One is tempted to see in P.'s λῃστρικὰ σκάφη the long arm of the King of Pontos: the forty ships lent to Sertorius in accordance with the treaty (below, 24.3). Memnon (*FGrHist* 434 F 1.33.1) calls those vessels τριήρεις, but neither his nor P.'s terms must be pressed. Mithradates employed the pirates like proper naval forces (above, 7.5n.), and they may well have provided the fleet dispatched to Spain. The conclusion of the treaty, however, cannot be safely dated prior to the events described here; see below, 24.3: Treaty.

21.8

ὥστε ἠναγκάσθησαν . . . διαχειμάσαι: The second half of this chapter (21.5–9) covers, in very general fashion, the last phase of joint operations by Metellus and Pompeius, from winter 76 to fall/winter 75. But as P.'s interest in the military course of the war is waning, temptation to compress the narrative is growing; here at the end of the sequence, he conflates two events almost a year apart. The separate winter quarters of the Roman armies as reported by P.—Metellus in Gaul, Pompeius among the Vaccaei—properly belong to 76/5, fairly soon after the siege of Clunia (cf. Livy *Per.* 92). In the spring of 75 Pompeius without success besieged Palantia (Palencia, Castilla y León), a chief city of the Vaccaei, and captured Cauca (Coca, Segovia Prov., Castilla y León) in the same region (Appian 112.523; Frontin. *Strat.* 2.11.2). From Appian it also follows that Metellus at that time was operating separately (ὁ Πομπήιος καὶ ἐς Μέτελλον ἀνεχώρει), probably along the upper Ebro, for next we find both generals attacking Calagurris (Calahorra, La Rioja), 112.524. After failing there too, they parted ways for good. Metellus returned to his province, Hispania Ulterior; Pompeius spent the fall of 75 campaigning in northern Celtiberia, Cantabria, and among the Vascones. The worsening food supply eventually compelled him to winter in Gaul, although he left fifteen cohorts in Celtiberia to protect his allies there (Sall. *Hist.* 2.94–95; Livy *Per.* 93). It was during this second winter after Segontia and the siege of Clunia that Pompeius wrote his letter to Rome: not from among the Vaccaei, where he had wintered in 76/5, but from Gaul. The biographer was in a hurry to wrap up his narrative of the war with Pompey's letter and its implicit testimony to the success of the hero's strategy, posing a continued—or renewed—threat to the regime in Rome (cf. 21.9n.). P.'s resulting anachronism has bedeviled Sertorian chronology ever since: see Konrad, "Chronology," section X.

περὶ Βακκαίους: On the Vaccaei, allied with Sertorius see 16.1: Extent of Sertorian Power. That this is not a mistake for "Vascones," i.e., Navarra and the southern Basque Country (as some scholars hold), has been shown by Perl, "Sallust." P.'s confusion is one of chronology, not topography.

γράφων πρὸς τὴν σύγκλητον: winter 75/4. Sallust's version of that letter is fully extant (*Hist.* 2.98) and justly famous. From its grandiloquent opening, *quotiens a prima adulescentia ductu meo scelestissimi hostes fusi et vobis salus quaesita est,* the piece was designed to reveal a man in love with his achievements and obsessed with self-advancement. At the same time it is filled with mordant criticism, reflecting Sallust's mind at least as much as Pompey's, of the *nobiles* controlling the Senate: sloth and inertia threaten to ruin the war effort in Spain. There can be no doubt that Sallust meant no exaggeration when he had Pompeius describe his army's situation as perilous and deteriorating: in three years past (2.98.2) no reinforcements, no supplies, no money to pay the troops; and now the worst—no food. Clearly the historian had given great attention to that last item in the preceding narrative (2.93–96), and Pompey's claim to have incurred personal debts in order to pay his soldiers was not an idle one (2.97, *argentum mutuum arcessivit*). Shifting to the strategic aspects, the complaints turn into warnings, fist-in-glove: though the enemy's position is no more enviable, it is no worse; victory hangs in the balance (*victor uterque in Italiam venire potest*, 2.98.7; cf. above, 21.7n.), but without support from Rome, Pompeius may be forced to help himself (*necessitatibus privatim mihi consulere*, 2.98.8). Lest that hint be too subtle for some readers, a concluding eye-opener: the brutal *nisi subvenitis, invito et praedicente me exercitus hinc et cum eo omne bellum Hispaniae in Italiam transgradientur* (2.98.10). (One wonders whether Lepidus' famous dispatch of 30 May 43, preserved as Cic. *Fam.* 10.35.1, served Sallust as a model here: *nam exercitus cunctus . . . me[que] tantae multitudinis civium Romanorum salutis atque incolumitatis causam suscipere, ut vere dicam, coegit.*) All that stands between Sertorius and Italy is Pompey's army. Having reached the limits of its endurance, it will return on its own—to protect Italy from a Sertorian invasion, of course; but surely the *grati patres* still had vivid memories of the events surrounding the most recent return from overseas, seven years past, of a Proconsul who felt insufficiently appreciated and supported by the government in Rome (on these features of the letter cf. most recently McGushin 242, 246–47).

P. makes surprisingly little of all that, especially when compared to his lavish use of *Hist.* 2.70 in 22.2–3 below. He is aiming chiefly at presenting Pompey's distress as yet another—the last—example of the hero's military genius; expounding the threatening nuances of the missive would only be a distraction. But his treatment of the letter elsewhere (*Luc.* 5.3; *Pomp.* 20.1–2) shows not much greater awareness of its potential.

ἀπάξοι . . . αὐτῷ: cf. Sall. *Hist.* 2.98.10, quoted in the preceding note.

καταναλωκέναι γὰρ ἤδη τὰ αὑτοῦ: cf. Sall. *Hist.* 2.98.3, *per deos immortalis, utrum censetis vicem me aerari praestare . . . ?* and 2.98.9, *ego non rem familiarem modo, verum etiam fidem consumpsi.*

21.9

πολὺς . . . Σερτώριος: How widely such rumors were actually believed one may question. Spann (147–48) rightly takes a dim view of Sertorius' chances at a successful march on Italy, though widespread discontent with the Sullan settlement might have provided him with enough support to mount a serious challenge to the regime once he crossed the Alps. As in 83–82, desertion—political as well as military—could sway the contest in his favor. But the opportunity to launch such an invasion of Italy never materialized. In 74 Pompeius received all the supplies he needed, including money and two new legions (Sall. *Hist.* 2.98D; Plut. *Luc.* 5.3; Appian 111.519; cf. Cic. *Font.* 8, 13, 16).

εἰς τοσοῦτον ... κατέστησεν: P.'s narrative of the war in Spain ends on an upbeat note. The rapid collapse of Sertorius' military position and political control during the next two years (74–73; see below, 25.1, 25.4nn.) will go unmentioned, and his assassination—really the removal of a leader who had become a liability—will be all the more surprising.

22

The chapter falls into two closely connected parts. The long excursus on Metellus (22.1–4) marks the transition from the chronological narrative to the life's second (after chs. 10–17) major section studying the hero's character (22.5–24.5), and at the same time serves as a foil to the latter. While 10–17 focused on leadership skills, in 22–24 the emphasis is on Sertorius' *Romanitas*. His formation of a Senate and observance of proper Roman custom and privilege (22.5–6) are narrated in deliberate juxtaposition to Metellus' degenerate celebrations; his desire for peace, his fundamental reluctance to engage in the bitter civil war forced on him in Spain (22.7–12), compare favorably to Metellus' callous and cowardly attempt at having the enemy removed through murder and bribery (22.1; cf. Scardigli, "Considerazioni" 57). In the dealings with Mithradates (23–24) it is Sertorius, not his "Senate," who upholds Roman interests in Asia Minor, even at the risk of losing a potentially valuable ally. When after such preparation P. finally turns to the hero's opponents in his own camp (25), he has no difficulty persuading the reader of their utter worthlessness.

22.1

ἐπεκήρυξε γάρ: Metellus' proclamation is usually dated to 75 or 74 B.C., after his victory at Segontia and return to his province (e.g., Schulten 122; Ooteghem, *Metelli* 206; Scardigli, "Considerazioni" 54 n. 1). Spann, however, has argued (p. 74; cf. diss. 192) that such an action better suits the early years before Pompey's arrival, when Metellus was less than successful in combating Sertorius' guerrilla methods and experienced a high degree of frustration. Indeed, although the "triumphal" festivities detailed in 22.2–3 are evidently related to Metellus' victory at Segontia and hence fall after chapter 21 chronologically, P. deliberately masks that connection (see 22.2n.). We cannot simply assume that the events of 22.1 likewise must belong after Segontia. This entire character sketch of Metellus, like the earlier one in 13.1–

Commentary 22.1 181

6, is designed to create an unfavorable comparison with the accompanying portrait of Sertorius, here developed in the remainder of 22. The chapter as a whole closely parallels 13 and 14 (cf. above, 22n.), and the items reported in it cannot be dated by its position in P.'s narrative but only on the basis of external evidence or intrinsic probability. In view of which, to place the proclamation at some point between 79 and 77 B.C. is more plausible than a later date. (I am no longer convinced by the arguments advanced against Spann's view in *Gerión* 6 [1988] 253–54. Berve, 221, had already suggested a date ca. 79, though with questionable reasoning.)

The public proclamation and the limitation of the reward to Romans (if such was indeed the case: see following note) would have made it difficult for Metellus to go back on his promise: despite the enormity of the reward, his offer probably was sincere. In 139 B.C., Q. Servilius Caepio (*cos.* 140) had the Lusitanian leader Viriatus assassinated by three of his associates; when they demanded their promised reward, he referred them to the Senate in Rome, who rejected the claim (Livy *Per.* 54; *Per. Oxy.* 54 col. 197–98, 55 col. 201–2; Appian *Iber.* 74.311–14; Eutrop. 4.16.2–3; Auct. *De vir. ill.* 71.3–4; Oros. 5.4.14). But Caepio had approached the assassins specifically and in private: there was no public proclamation offering a reward to anyone who killed Viriatus. In 121 B.C. the Consul L. Opimius kept his promise, publicly announced, that to anyone bringing him the head of C. Gracchus he would pay its weight in gold (Cic. *De orat.* 2.269; Val. Max. 9.4.3; Plin. *NH* 33.48; Plut. *C. Grac.* 17[38].4–5). Sulla and later the Triumvirs likewise paid the publicly stated awards for the heads of the proscribed.

εἴ τις αὐτὸν ἀνέλοι Ῥωμαῖος: As it stands, P.'s account is unsatisfactory. He is clearly thinking of assassination (ὡς ἀπογνώσει φανερᾶς ἀμύνης ὠνούμενος τὸν ἄνδρα διὰ προδοσίας), not death in combat, which renders the apparent exclusion of Hispanians and restriction of the reward to Romans—i.e., those in Sertorius' camp—puzzling. Sulla in his proscriptions had imposed no such limitations, and neither had L. Opimius when promising his golden reward for the head of C. Gracchus (see preceding note). Even if Sertorius' Hispanian followers could be considered more faithful or less corruptible than his Roman ones, the fate of Viriatus had shown that traitors could be found if the price was right.

Possibly P. substituted "Romans" when in fact Metellus' proclamation was addressed to anyone. Yet Spann (74) may have shown the way to a better explanation when he implicitly assumed that this part of Metellus' offer was directed at his own soldiers rather than at the Romans in Sertorius' camp. As *hostes publici*, the latter might naturally be considered Romans no longer (see below). If so, the biographer, while correctly rendering the formal terms of the announcement, has misunderstood or misrepresented its tenor as appealing to murder and treachery throughout.

ἑκατὸν ἀργυρίου τάλαντα: an exorbitant prize, equivalent to 600,000 denarii or 2.4 million sesterces, and amounting to fifty times the sum paid for the head of an ordinary *proscriptus* (*Sulla* 31.7). On the question of how Metellus might have raised that sum see *Gerión* 6 (1988) 259–60.

πλέθρα δισμύρια γῆς: i.e., 20,000 *iugera*, equivalent to ca. 50 square kilometers; cf. W. Becher, *RE* 21.1 (1951) 235, and O. Viedebantt, *RE* 9.2 (1916) 2507. For comparison, Marius' veterans settled in Africa received 100 *iugera* each (Auct. *De vir. ill.* 73.1), the settlers on the *ager Campanus* in 59, 10 *iugera* (Cic. *Att.* 2.16.1). The land would have been assigned in Spain—more precisely in Ulterior, where Metellus was governor—not in Italy (Schulten 122).

φυγάς: (The following is condensed from *Gerión* 6 [1988] 255–56.) The word normally means "fugitive" or "exile," but the peculiar legal situation of Sertorius' followers may have required Metellus' proclamation to be more specific. Two groups can be readily distinguished: *proscripti* and "mere" *hostes publici*. Only those whose names had appeared on Sulla's lists were *proscripti*. They could be killed with impunity by anyone, the killer being paid a public reward of 48,000 sesterces; their property was confiscated, and their descendants were excluded from public office in Rome (Sall. *Hist.* 1.55.6; Dion. Hal. *Ant. Rom.* 8.80.2; Livy *Per.* 89; Vell. 2.28.4; Plut. *Sulla* 31.7–8; cf. M. Fuhrmann, *RE* 23.3 [1959] 2440–44). *Hostes populi Romani,* upon being so declared by the Senate, also forfeited their lives and property, but there was no fixed reward, if any, for their heads, and the legal and civic status of their descendants born prior to the *hostis* declaration was not affected. Proscribed and public enemies alike ceased to be considered Roman citizens (Mommsen, *StR* 3:1241–50; see also Bauman, *Athenaeum* 51 [1973], and Grasmück 108).

Besides Sertorius himself (above, 7.1n.), two other *proscripti* are securely attested in Spain: M. Perperna (Vell. 2.30.1) and one L. Fabius Hispaniensis (Sall. *Hist.* 3.83; cf. below, 26.6n.). The lieutenants who had accompanied Sertorius from Italy in 83/2 would have come under Sulla's summary condemnation of all who had served as officers for the Marian regime after the summer of 83 (Appian 94.441; cf. Oros. 5.21.10, and above, 7.1n.). Thus L. Hirtuleius and his brother (cf. 12.4n.), Octavius Graecinus and Tarquitius Priscus (26.6n.), and probably M. Marius (24.4n.) can be safely counted among the proscribed. (Cf. now also Hinard, *Proscriptions* 358–59, 404–6). There would have been others, but their number is impossible to estimate.

Hostes publici in Sertorius' camp were all the participants in the Lepidan uprising who had come to Spain with Perperna (Sall. *Hist.* 1.77.22; Flor. 2.10.1–3; Appian 107; Exuper. 7.1–4 = 42 Z; cf. also above, chapter 15 nn.). From Cicero (2 *Verr.* 5.146–47, 151–55) it may safely be inferred that Sertorians who were neither *proscripti* nor *Lepidani* likewise had been declared *hostes,* probably early in the war.

κάθοδον εἰς Ῥώμην: Neither *hostes* nor *proscripti* were barred as such from returning to Rome: their inability to do so rested on the fact that they had forfeited their citizenship and their lives. Hence Metellus' promise technically must have been in the nature of a pardon rather than a mere permission to return. As regards *hostes p. R.*, offering such a pardon seems to have been unproblematic; those willing to return to the Roman fold ceased, by their very action, to be enemies of the Roman People. Lucullus' "pardon" of L. Magius and L. Fannius in the Third Mithradatic War provides an instructive parallel (Appian *Mithr.* 72.308; Dio 36.8.2; Ps.-Ascon. 244.1–5 St; cf. Cic. 2 *Verr.* 1.87, and below, 23.4n.). It was a different matter with the proscribed. Proscription was a death sentence individually specified by law (Cic. *Dom.* 43, *poenam in cives Romanos nominatim sine iudicio constitutam*), and not conditional upon the victim's remaining an enemy of the State. While the *lex Plotia* of 70 B.C. repealed the *hostis* status of the *Lepidani* (see Taylor, *CP* 36 [1941] 121–22, and Broughton, *MRR* 2:130 n. 4), no *proscriptus* is known ever to have received a pardon until 49 B.C., when Caesar restored the sons of the proscribed (and any survivors) to their property and civic rights (Cic. *Att.* 7.11.1, 10.8.2, 10.13.1; Suet. *DJ* 41; Plut. *Caes.* 37.2; Appian *BC* 2.48.198; Dio 41.18.2, 44.47.4, 45.17.1). After Perperna's final defeat in 72, Pompeius willingly pardoned the survivors of the *partes Sertorianae*—except for the proscribed (Cic. 2 *Verr.* 5.153, and see below, 27.6n.). Hence it may be doubted that Metellus, without at least the backing of the Senate, could in good faith guarantee to a *proscriptus* his safe return to Rome. Either the proclamation applied only to *hostes publici* but not to the proscribed, or Metellus was promising more than he could deliver.

22.2

νικήσας ποτὲ μάχῃ: clearly the battle of Segontia (21.1–3), the only full-scale field engagement fought betwen Metellus and Sertorius. The position of the same festivities in Sallust (*Hist.* 2.70) likewise places them firmly after Segontia. By being vague and making it sound like the occasion was some minor, obscure skirmish, P. creates the impression that Metellus' celebrations were not only extravagant but unmerited.

ὥστ' αὐτοκράτωρ ἀναγορευθῆναι: "so as to be acclaimed *imperator*." Segontia can be regarded as the turning point of the war, and by traditional standards Metellus was entitled to his imperatorial acclamation (apparently the second of his career: *CIL* I² 737 = *ILLRP* 366). P.'s hinting otherwise is part of his careful protection of the hero, though in this instance the influence of Sallust may be recognized; see following note.

22.2–3

This passage follows Sallust's account, fortunately preserved in the long fragment *Hist.* 2.70, almost to a word. (Cf. also Cic. *Arch.* 26.) On Sallust's treatment of Metellus see Cichorius, *RS* 228–33, esp. 230.

22.3

ἐσθῆτα θριαμβικὴν ἔχων: cf. Sall. *Hist.* 2.70.4, *toga picta*. P.'s rendering is not literal but certainly correct.

22.4

δραπέτην Σύλλα ... ἀποκαλῶν τὸν Σερτώριον: Surrounded by his own treachery and decadence (21.1–3) and the proofs of the hero's *Romanitas* (21.5–12), Metellus' contemptuous dismissal of Sertorius sounds hollow and underscores his frustration at being unable to bring him to heel.

22.5

τοὺς φεύγοντας ... σύγκλητον ἀναγορεῦσαι: Only one other source, Appian, mentions this "Sertorian Senate": βουλὴν κατέλεξεν ἐκ τῶν συνόντων οἱ φίλων τριακοσίους καὶ τήνδε ἔλεγεν εἶναι τὴν Ῥωμαίων βουλὴν καὶ ἐς ὕβριν ἐκείνης σύγκλητον ἐκάλει (108.507; cf. *Mithr.* 68.286; *Iber.* 101.439). The accounts differ considerably: in P., Sertorius simply accords those Senators that had fled to him the title "Senate"; in Appian, he creates this Senate out of his own followers as a deliberate counterpiece, or mockery, of the Roman Senate, and many of its members were not genuine Senators. Appian's version has been widely accepted by modern scholars (though not by Wiehn, 46), who see in the Sertorian Senate, together with the supposed appointment of Praetors and Quaestors (more on which in the following note), the creation of an Anti-Rome, of a government in exile (e.g., Schulten 156; Berve 214–15; Treves 139; Ehrenberg 191; Gabba, "Guerra sociale" 310–11; "Senati in esilio" 427–32; Gruen, *Last Generation* 12, 17–18). That view is open to serious doubts.

Contrary to Appian's allegation, it is evident that there was a substantial number of genuine Senators (members of Sertorius' original retinue, survivors of the Marian regime, and *Lepidani* accompanying Perperna) in Spain; Spann 86–89 has estimated their total at perhaps as many as 100. To their ranks Sertorius may have added (following Sulla's example of 81 B.C.) some men of equestrian rank, and probably such young gentlemen of senatorial families as had not yet entered upon the *cursus honorum* at Rome. Appian's figure of 300 members should be treated with some caution.

But in what sense did Sertorius call that body a "Senate?" Appian says the same of the 300 advisors gathered around Cato at Utica in 46 B.C. (οὓς ἀπὸ σφῶν ἐκ πολλοῦ προβούλους ἐπεποίηντο τοῦ πολέμου καὶ σύγκλητον ἐκάλουν, *BC* 2.95.397), whereas P. specifies the 300 as Roman citizens resident in Africa and clearly contrasts them with the Senators and Senators' sons in Cato's camp (τοὺς τριακοσίους, οἷς ἐχρῆτο βουλῇ, ... καὶ ὅσοι παρῆσαν ἀπὸ συγκλήτου καὶ παῖδας αὐτῶν, *Cat. Min.* 59.3; cf. 64.1–2, likewise contrasting Senators with the 300); no hint of Cato calling his council a "Senate." [Caes.] *BAfr* 88.1 and 90.1 bears out P.'s version at least in that respect. As regards the Sertorian body, not only Appian's figure of 300 seems questionable, but also his charge that Sertorius claimed it to be the (true) Roman Senate.

On the other hand, P. on two different occasions comes close to telling a similar story. During the Cinno-Marian regime between 87 and 84, dozens of Senators joined Sulla in the East, with the result that his retinue took on "the appearance of a Senate" (περὶ αὐτὸν ὀλίγου χρόνου σχῆμα βουλῆς ἐγεγόνει, *Sulla* 22.1; cf. Livy *Per.* 85; Appian 77.350, 86.390). In 49 B.C. the Senators with Pompeius in Greece were numerous enough to form "a complete Senate" (τῶν ἀπὸ Ῥώμης ἡγεμονικῶν ἀριθμὸς ἦν ἐντελοῦς βουλῆς περὶ αὐτόν, *Pomp.* 64.4), and P. in that context talks of formal Senate meetings and decrees (ἐπεὶ δὲ βουλῆς γενομένης καὶ γνώμην Κάτωνος εἰπόντος, ἐψηφίσαντο κτλ., 65.1; cf. *Cat. Min.* 53.6). Dio 41.43.1–4 confirms the presence of 200 Senators at Thessalonike in 49/8 and reports to what lengths the Republicans went to create the ritual conditions necessary for the continued operation of the Roman government. He does not specify Senate meetings, but Mommsen has pointed out (*StR* 3:926 n. 3) that the Consuls could hold those until their term of office expired at the end of 49. The need for the Senate to meet *in agro Romano in loco inaugurato* (Mommsen, 926–27) no doubt was the reason for the manoeuver described by Dio; for the Republicans did not dare extend such flexibility to the *comitia:* they rejected attempts to elect Consuls for 48 in Greece (Dio ibid.) and never questioned the legitimacy of Caesar's magistrats created in Rome. The institutional framework of a Republican "government in exile" expired with the terms of its Consuls.

In view of the evidence set out above, it is best not to make too much of Sertorius' "Senate." As Proconsul of Spain (he never claimed to be more: see 10.1n.) he lacked, a priori, the ability to convene and consult the Roman Senate. There is no good reason to depart from Mommsen's judgment here: the Sertorian body was "nicht eigentlich ein Gegensenat, sondern nur ein als Surrogat desselben gehandhabtes feldherrliches Consilium" (926). Not an ordinary *consilium*, however, selected by the commander at (largely) his discretion: hence, we may conclude, the appellation "Senate," to underscore the independence and *dignitas* of its members. That appellation certainly did not come about until after the arrival of Perperna and the *Lepidani* in 77. Even so, there was at first probably little difference between what happened in Spain and what had happened around Sulla in the East during the 80s. Certainly Sertorius' was hardly less impressive a collection of genuine Senators than that group, and a lot more so than the advisory body assembled by another pretender in Spain a century later (*e primoribus prudentia atque aetate praestantibus vel instar senatus, ad quos de maiore re quotiens opus esset referretur, instituit*, Suet. *Galba* 10.2). If Sertorius ever formally constituted his "Senate," it may have been as late as on occasion of Mithradates' offer (probably in 76; see below, 24.3: Treaty) to negotiate about the Roman possessions in Asia.

ταμίας τε καὶ στρατηγοὺς ἐξ ἐκείνων ἀποδεικνύναι: Virtually all modern

scholars take this in the sense of "he appointed Quaestors and Praetors"—
even though elsewhere in this life *stratēgos* clearly means "general," not
"Praetor"—and from that deduce the formation of a Roman government in
exile. (See the preceding note; Gabba, "Senati in esilio" 429, voiced reservations regarding the "Praetors"; on Mommsen's view see below.) Yet such
an interpretation overlooks both ἐξ ἐκείνων and the immediate context: P.'s
point being that Sertorius appointed *stratēgoi* and *tamiai* from among the
Senators who had fled to him, rather than from among Romans of lesser rank,
or even, as the next section states more explicitly, from Hispanians. Clearly
P. saw nothing noteworthy or unusual in the appointment of these *tamiai* and
stratēgoi in itself: the hero's *megalophrosynē* manifests itself in his respectful
treatment of fellow Senators, his upholding of the *dignitas* of Spain's Roman
masters, and his general observance of the *mos maiorum*. Only when viewed
through the prism of modern political practice does the passage suggest the
creation of a "government in exile." The notion of Sertorius' appointing Praetors is, in fact, quite untenable. It has found such ready acceptance, of course,
precisely because a government in exile presumably would need regular magistrates (what for, in Spain?), just as modern arrangements of that sort indulge
in having cabinet ministers and undersecretaries and whatnot. But a Praetor
had to be elected by the People, and though a recourse to archaic practice
might perhaps justify his being appointed by his predecessor, he still needed
the *lex curiata,* to be obtained only from the *curiae* in Rome: a requirement
which, in 48 B.C., made it impossible for the Republicans at Thessalonike to
install new magistrates, despite a very conscious attempt to set up something
akin to a government in exile (Dio 41.43.1–5; cf. preceding note).

Such legalistic obstacles might not have hindered Sertorius, of course. The
point is that Praetors appointed by the Proconsul of Spain could not possibly
have been understood by contemporaries as symbolizing Rome or the Roman
government. The representatives of the *populus Romanus,* first and foremost,
were the Consuls. Praetors, created *iisdem auspiciis* with the Consuls (Cic.
Att. 9.9.3; Livy 3.55.11; Gell. 13.15.4; see Mommsen, StR 2³:193, cf. 80–
81, 125–26), are nothing but clones *minore imperio* of the consulship: Consuls can be made without Praetors, but not Praetors without a Consul. It is
manifest that Sertorius never made himself or anybody else Consul—the first
and essential step to establish an Anti-Rome or government in exile. It was
left to Catilina to act in such a fashion (Sall. *Cat.* 36.1; Dio 37.33.2). Sertorius
had lesser ambitions. As is clear from Livy 91 fr. 22 W-M (see Spann 59–62,
entirely convincing, and cf. above, 10.1n.), Sertorius never presumed to be
anything but the governor *pro consule* of Spain, albeit at war with the Roman
government which had outlawed him and which he was trying to force, or
persuade, to readmit him.

The case of L. Hirtuleius may be instructive. The sources that dignify Sertorius' most important lieutenant with a title simply call him "Quaestor": so
P. 12.4 and Livy *Per.* 90, both with reference to the years 80/79–78, and again

Livy *Per.* 91, with reference to his end in 76 B.C. (Note, however, Frontin. *Strat.* 1.5.8, *legatus*; cf. also Flor. 2.10.6–7.) His actual quaestorship, however, belongs probably in 85 and at any event falls no later than the year of his coming to Spain with Sertorius, 83 or 82: throughout his subsequent time there, he was technically *pro quaestore* (see 12.4n.). Yet Hirtuleius, if any man, would have been an obvious candidate for one of Sertorius' praetorships: his failure to secure such elevation vehemently points against the assumption that anyone did. What, then of P.'s *stratēgoi*? Nothing more than the well-known practice of a magistrate's mandating his *imperium* to someone else, thereby appointing an acting commander in chief, *pro praetore* (Mommsen, StR 1³:680–85; cf. 3:925 n. 5, approximating the solution offered here, though thinking of appointment by the Sertorian "Senate"). One such instance can be safely inferred. In 77/6, when Hirtuleius was Sertorius' commander *in altera provincia* (i.e., Ulterior: Livy 91 fr. 22.42 W-M), his title could hardly have read other than *proquaestor pro praetore*; the same may be true for the time of his operations in Hither Spain during 79 and 78, when Sertorius was still based on Lusitania (cf. above, 12.4–5nn.). C. Herennius, who seems to have been in command on the East Coast in the winter and spring of 77/6 (above, 19: Winter 77), similarly may have been (*legatus*) *pro praetore,* unless like Perperna he had come to Spain holding *imperium suis auspiciis* (cf. 15.2, 15.5nn.). M. Marius, still (Pro-)Quaestor in 76 (Livy fr. 22.71), likewise will have gone to Asia *pro praetore*, under Sertorius' auspices rather than his own; certainly P.'s use of *stratēgos* in 24.3–4 (see notes) makes it clear that he was thinking of a "general," not a "Praetor."

The same explanation will serve for the *tamiai*. The word unquestionably means "Quaestor," but even Latin sources use *quaestor* loosely for *proquaestor* and even *legatus pro quaestore* (see above, 12.4n.), the appointment of the latter being within the power of any Roman governor (Mommsen, StR 1³:686–87). That Sertorius would appoint such officials as need dictated should not surprise; his doing so in no way signifies the creation of a parallel set of magistrates for a Roman government in exile.

P. is likely to have found his information on so technical a matter in a Latin source, i.e., Sallust or Livy. Yet it appears doubtful that either of them contained a general note to the effect that Sertorius appointed officers *pro praetore* and *pro quaestore*—being standard Roman procedure this was hardly noteworthy. Hence P.'s blanket statement seems to be based on (a few) individual instances mentioned in these sources, such as the cases of Hirtuleius and Marius suggested above. In which case, the notion of Sertorius' exile government with its anti-magistrates evaporates without need of further argument. We cannot be certain, however, that the biographer understood the proper nature of such appointments *pro praetore:* ταμίας τε καὶ στρατηγοὺς ... ἀποδεικνύναι does sound as if P. here meant Quaestors and Praetors. That this cannot have been what Sertorius did has been demonstrated above, but P. might well have mistaken it so, not recognizing its intrinsic improbability.

22.6

τῆς ἄκρας ἐξουσίας: an odd expression, found only here in P. Evidently the στρατηγοὶ καὶ ἄρχοντες mentioned next are the ones exercising the ἄκρα ἐξουσία: the phrase may be an attempt to render Latin *summum imperium* or *summa imperii*.

στρατηγοὺς καὶ ἄρχοντας: "generals and officers." Use of Romans in command of Hispanian forces is confirmed by Frontin. *Strat.* 2.5.31 (above, 18.9–10: Battle of Lauro). There was nothing remarkable in such a practice. Sertorius' Roman associates were numerous enough to fill the necessary posts with ease, and important enough not to be alienated by undue promotion of barbarians. Hence larger Hispanian formations would be commanded by Roman Legates, Tribunes, or Prefects; the Italic *alae sociorum* of the pre–Social War era may have served as a model. With smaller units, though, native chiefs would have remained as leaders, at least *de facto* (cf. 20.3n.).

ὡς Ῥωμαίοις ... Ῥωμαίων: the clearest statement in P. of Sertorius' aims and purpose in Spain. It agrees with the picture drawn by Livy (91 fr. 22 W-M): not the leader of an Hispanian war of liberation, nor the founder of a private empire in Spain, but a "Roman imperialist engaged in civil war," as Spann once put it succinctly (diss. 164). See also above, 10.1n.

22.7

ἐν δὲ ταῖς νίκαις ... Πομπήϊον: There could be no question of a negotiated return to Italy while Sulla was alive (thus, rightly, Spann 73). After the dictator's death in 78, it is likely that Sertorius made overtures to the government and its commander in Spain, Metellus: most, perhaps all, of his military successes before the arrival of Pompeius had taken place by that time. Whatever potentially compromising correspondence was found in his possession after his death (below, 27.3n.) will have revolved around such attempts to negotiate—exchanges that never reached the level of a formal debate in the Senate. His contacts with Lepidus (if Sall. *Hist.* 1.77.8, *Hispaniae armis sollicitae*, is to be interpreted thus) may have originated as an offer to return in peace if granted a pardon. Following Pompey's defeat at Lauro, Sertorius may have tried again to negotiate (Spann 97–99); at least πρὸς Μέτελλον καὶ πρὸς Πομπήϊον suggests separate attempts on presumably separate occasions. Lauro was the last time he could negotiate from a position of strength.

That all these offers should be rebuffed need not surprise. Nor is it necessary to locate the main obstacle to a peaceful settlement in the hurt pride of Metellus, as Spann 74–75 suggests. The senatorial government of the Republic had a long tradition of refusing to negotiate with any enemy who was considered a serious threat. Sertorius himself, according to P., refused to negotiate whenever he suffered a reverse: δυσπραγῶν μὲν ἠνδραγάθει, καὶ ταπεινὸν μὲν οὐδὲν ἔπραττε πρὸς τοὺς πολεμίους. There could be little doubt in the

Commentary 22.8

minds of the Senate that time was working in their favor, as it always had in the past.

βιοῦν ἰδιώτης καθόδου τυχών: Modest as such an offer may seem, it was not acceptable to the Senate. Clearly Sertorius was seeking amnesty not merely for himself but for all those with him (22.6). The Senate was hardly in a position to grant amnesty to the proscribed and to public enemies in Spain while withholding it from those in Italy and elsewhere, or their descendants. Demands for the restoration of confiscated property were bound to follow; if they were acceded to, the consequences would be dire for many a Senator whose fortunes had improved marvelously during the proscriptions. In substance, Sertorius' terms were no different from the proposals Lepidus had advanced in 78 (see Laffi, *Athenaeum* 45 [1967] 185–86; Keaveney, *Sulla* 233; Spann 98).

22.8

μᾶλλον γὰρ ... ἀναγορεύεσθαι: an interesting inversion of Caesar's famous statement (*Caes.* 11.4).

22.9

λέγεται ... μητέρα: Sertorius' mother had died in 80 B.C., as follows from 22.10, and to claim her as the reason for his subsequent desire to return is rather anachronistic. P.'s attempt to present the hero's attachment to his mother as another example of his *megalophrosynē*, *Romanitas*, and *philopatria* contrasts oddly with the critical remarks in *Alk. Synkr.* 4(43).4–5: Coriolanus' willingness to spare Rome solely for his mother's sake, after spurning the entreaties of Senate, People, and priests, was an insult to the State (ἀτιμία τῆς πατρίδος). Relating Sertorius' uncontrolled grief here rather than in its chronologically proper context (ch. 10) made it easier for P. to put a favorable interpretation on it. There is no reason to think that Sallust was not the source (Scardigli, "Considerazioni" 54–58), but the "senatorial historian" may have taken a less enthusiastic view.

τραφεὶς ὀρφανὸς ὑπ' αὐτῇ: cf. 2.1.

τὸ σύμπαν ἀνακείμενος ἐκείνῃ: Only a chance notice tells us Sertorius had a wife: *repertus est etiam qui se esse diceret Q. Sertorii filium, quem ut agnosceret uxor eius nulla vi conpelli potuit*, Val. Max. 9.15.3. There is no good reason to doubt the fact; the note suggests she did not follow Sertorius to Spain. P.'s silence may be due to ignorance, but one suspects that to reveal details of the marriage might have tarnished the hero's image. Better to concentrate on his filial devotion.

22.10

καλούντων δὲ ... ἐφ' ἡγεμονίᾳ: in the summer of 80, when he was in Mauretania; cf. 10.1n.

τῶν περὶ τὴν Ἰβηρίαν φίλων: not the Lusitani but Roman and Italian exiles that had found refuge in Lusitania in 81 and had brought about the Lusitanian offer of an alliance with Sertorius (see above, 10.1n.).

22.11

ἑπτὰ γὰρ ἡμέρας . . . ἔκειτο: Excessive grief is not something P. generally condones; see Swain, *Hermes* 118 (1990) 198, and cf. *Tim.* 5.3–7.1.

συστράτηγοι καὶ ἰσότιμοι: "fellow generals and equals in rank"; cf. below, 25.1, τῶν . . . συγκλητικῶν καὶ ἰσοτίμων; also *Luc.* 33.2, τοῖς δυνατοῖς καὶ ἰσοτίμοις, and *Lys.* 19.1, τοῖς πρώτοις καὶ ἰσοτίμοις. Both terms loosely refer to Sertorius' officers—Legates, Tribunes, Hirtuleius his Quaestor—and other senatorial (and equestrian?) members of his staff. Clearly no shared supreme command is implied, and the persons in question are his subordinates, as suggested by the scene itself (τὴν σκηνὴν περιστάντες: colleagues presumably would not have hesitated to enter). One is tempted to take ἰσότιμοι here to mean *praetorii*, though it hardly indicates consulars in the *Lucullus* passage. Still, there may have been men of praetorian rank in Sertorius' entourage prior to the arrival of Perperna. Virtually nothing is known about the careers of Antonius, Mallius, and Aufidius, all of whom were involved in the conspiracy against Sertorius. At least Mallius is attested to have been "one of the leaders" (26.1; cf. 26.3–11 on Aufidius and Antonius).

22.12

ἔδοξεν . . . ἐπιεικῶς: cf. *Cat. Min.* 11.3–4, where the hero's excessive grief is excused as a sign of gentleness in an otherwise severe character. Here P. goes a step further: what began as proof of Sertorius' love of country (22.9) has become proof of his thoroughly nonviolent disposition. Soon the slaughter of the hostages will have to be mentioned (25.6).

23.1

Mithradates: see above, 4.7n.

πολιτεύματα: "policy" (thus Ziegler, and Flacelière and Chambry). "Negotiations" (Kaltwasser, Perrin) is too specific.

μεγαλοφροσύνης: cf. 22.5.

23.2

ἐκ τοῦ κατὰ Σύλλαν σφάλματος: Under the terms of the Treaty of Dardanos (85 B.C.) ending the First War, Mithradates was confirmed in his ancestral possessions, i.e., Pontos, but forced to restore Bithynia and Kappadokia to their respective Kings, Nikomedes IV and Ariobarzanes I, and to give up all his other conquests—chiefly Paphlagonia, Phrygia, and Galatia, and of course the Roman province of Asia (Livy *Per.* 83; Vell. 2.23.6; Plut. *Sulla* 22.9–10; Memnon *FGrHist* 434 F 1.25.2; Appian *Mithr.* 55.222–23, 57.231–58.236; Gran. Lic. 35.74–77 Cr).

δεύτερον: P. (rightly) ignores the Second Mithradatic War (83–81 B.C.), an instance of unprovoked and ill-conceived aggression by L. Licinius Murena, left in charge of Asia upon Sulla's departure (Appian *Mithr.* 64–66; see Glew, "Between the Wars" 113–16, and McGing, *Foreign Policy* 132–35).

τῇ 'Ασίᾳ: not just the Roman province but Asia Minor in general; cf. *Cat. Mai.* 12.2 and *Synkr.* 2(29).3; *Luc.* 4.4, 14.6; *Crass. Synkr.* 4(37).2.

μέγα δ' ἤδη τὸ Σερτωρίου κλέος: By 77, the King would have heard about Sertorius' successful resistance to the Roman generals in Spain. Even so, he first attempted to reach an agreement with Pompeius (Cic. *Imp. Cn. Pomp.* 46; cf. below, 24.3: Treaty).

οἱ πλέοντες ἀπὸ τῆς ἑσπέρας: merchants and pirates, the professions being not always sharply distinguished.

ἐπηρμένος μάλιστα ταῖς τῶν κολάκων ἀλαζονείαις: cf. Sall. *Hist.* 2.78, *ibi Fimbriana e seditione, qui regi per obsequelam orationis et maxime odium Sullae graves carique erant*. The verbal parallel establishes, once again, Sallust as P.'s source (see Garbugino, *StudNon* 11 [1986] 41–45; and cf. Scardigli, "Considerazioni" 54–58). Two leading "flatterers" were L. Magius and L. Fannius: below, 23.4n.

23.4

πέμπει δὲ πρέσβεις: From Cic. 2*Verr.* 1.87 and Ps.-Ascon. 244.1–7 St it is certain that the King's emissaries were L. Magius (6) and L. Fannius (12). Both had come to Asia in 86 in the army of L. Valerius Flaccus (*cos.* 86) and C. Flavius Fimbria (see 23.6n.). After the latter's death in 85 and the surrender of his troops to Sulla they did not return to Rome; in 79 they were living in Myndos in Karia (Cic.). In that year they purchased a small, fast ship (*myoparonem pulcherrimum*) from C. Verres, in which three or four years later they sailed from the King to Sertorius and back (*ad omnis populi Romani hostis usque ab Dianio ad Sinopam*). What they did with that ship during the intervening years can only be surmised. *Myoparones* were vessels especially popular among pirates (e.g., Sall. *Hist.* 3.8; Plut. *Luc.* 13.3; Appian *Mithr.* 92.417; Oros. 6.2.24; cf. F. Lammert, *RE* 16.1 [1933] 1081), and Mithradates' close connection with organized piracy in the Mediterranean is well known (above, 7.5n.). Perhaps that is how Magius and Fannius came to meet the King. (Glew's contention, "Between the Wars" 126 n. 69, that the sole purpose of purchasing the ship conceivable was the journey to Sertorius, very much begs the question.)

In 76 or 75 (on the date see 24.3: Treaty) they traveled to Spain. Apparently they called at ports in Italy, for the Senate learned of their enterprise, declared them *hostes publici*, and ordered their arrest, evidently without success (Ps.-Ascon. 244.1–7 St). The journey to Spain and back was completed, it seems, within three months (Sall. *Hist.* 2.79, *illi tertio mense pervenere in Pontum multo celerius spe Mithridatis*; there is no reason to doubt that the fragment refers to the King's envoys). Both served as officers under the King in the early years of the Third War (Ps.-Ascon. ibid.; cf. Oros. 6.2.15 on Fannius), but Magius was already double-dealing with Lucullus during the siege of Kyzikos in the winter of 74/3 (Appian *Mithr.* 72.308–311; cf. Memnon *FGrHist* 434 F 1.28.2). By 68, both had come back to the Roman fold, Fannius as an officer under Lucullus (Dio 36.8.2; Ps.-Ascon.).

Magius is often thought to be one of the two sons of Minatus Magius of Aeclanum who both reached the praetorship before 80 B.C., after their father's *viritim* grant of citizenship in 89 or 88 in recognition of his resourceful and courageous support of Rome during the Social War (Vell.2.16.2–3; cf. Münzer, *RE* 14.1 [1928] 439; Wiseman, *New Men* 239 no. 242). Against that identification, see Sumner, *HSCP* 74 (1970) 261 n. 22, persuasively.

εἰς Ἰβηρίαν: The King's envoys arrived at and departed from Dianium (Cic. *2Verr.* 1.87; on Dianium, see Strabo 3.4.6; cf. above, 21.7n.). It does not strictly follow that the negotiations were actually conducted there, or anywhere along the East Coast, but Spann's assumption (100) that they were held in that region is appealing, especially since the emissaries seem to have returned to Pontos within three months (see preceding note)—which would exclude a lengthy inland journey.

χρήματα καὶ ναῦς παρέξειν: see below, 24.3.

τὴν ... Ἀσίαν πᾶσαν: all of Asia Minor, including the Roman province, as follows from the next sentence; cf. 23.2n.

ἧς ὑπεχώρησε Ῥωμαίοις κατὰ τὰς ... συνθήκας: Strictly speaking, only the province of Asia had been returned to Rome in the Treaty of Dardanos; the other territories affected—Bithynia, Kappadokia, Paphlagonia, Phrygia, and Galatia—reverted to their native dynasts (above, 23.2n.).

23.5

σύγκλητον: see above, 22.5n.

τῶν ἄλλων ... κελευόντων: La Penna ("*Historiae*" 229) suggests that this ready acceptance of Mithradates' terms by the "Senate" reflects the composition of Sertorius' Romano-Italic following, supposedly for the most part lower-class Etruscans and *Hispanienses* indifferent, if not downright hostile, to Roman imperial interests. That is rather unconvincing; P.'s own explanation in the next sentence is entirely sensible and would quite suffice were one required. Yet the reaction itself of the "Senate" is somewhat suspect. The biographer, at pains to demonstrate Sertorius' *megalophrosynē* and *philopatria*, needed a foil for the hero's stand on the issue: we should not expect

Commentary 23.6

him to write that the "Senate" erupted in shouts of protest, even if such had actually been the case. In addition, P. is keenly aware that Sertorius' murderers came from the same circle. The Sertorian Senators' undignified attitude here prepares the reader for their grievances and treachery in chapters 25 and 26.

ὄνομα γὰρ ... τυγχάνουσιν: a reasonable enough approach, reflecting not so much indifference toward Rome's imperial ambitions as a realistic assessment of the situation and the respective bargaining positions. No doubt the King reasoned along exactly the same lines when he agreed to Sertorius' terms and relinquished all claims to the Roman province (below, 24.3). Eventual possession of any territory in the East would be settled not on parchment or bronze but with iron and blood.

23.6

ἔθνη βασιλευόμενα: Berve (208) accused P. of trying to hide, without actually denying it, the cession of Paphlagonia and Galatia, in addition to Bithynia and Kappadokia (cf. Appian *Mithr.* 68.288): "An sich leugnet auch P. ihre Preisgabe nicht, wie daraus hervorgeht, dass nach ihm Sertorius nur hinsichtlich der Provinz Einspruch gegen Mithradates Forderung von ganz Kleinasien erhob, die dynastischen, d.h. die übrigen Gebiete jedoch zuzugestehen bereit war." To render βασιλευόμενα here as "dynastic" is begging the question; Kappadokia and Bithynia were in fact the only kingdoms among the countries under discussion. P.'s omission of Paphlagonia and Galatia is simply another example of his customary desire to concentrate on the most important items rather than an attempt "das überlassene Gebiet nicht zu gross erscheinen zu lassen." See below, 24.3n., and cf. Bieńkowski, "De fontibus" 83–85; Stahl 71.

μηδὲν προσήκοντα Ῥωμαίοις: Apart from the cession itself, the fact that Bithynia could be characterized in these terms firmly places the treaty prior to the death of King Nikomedes IV of Bithynia: bequeathed to Rome in his testament, the kingdom became a Roman possession, and Sertorius' reasons for not ceding Asia would have applied in like manner (McGing, *Foreign Policy* 138 n. 25).

ἦν δὲ ... ἐπαρχίαν: The province of Asia was established in 133 B.C. upon the death of the last King of Pergamon, Attalos III, who in his testament had left his kingdom to the Roman People (cf. *Ti. Grac.* 14.1–2).

ἀφελόμενος καὶ κατασχών: see 4.7n.

C. Flavius (88) Fimbria: ca. 120–85 B.C. The son of C. (87) *cos.* 104, he joined Cinna and Marius in the Civil War of 87 and after the surrender of Rome proved to be their most violent and bloodthirsty supporter (cf. Cic. *Brut.* 233); he was responsible for the murders of L. Caesar (*cos.* 90), C. Caesar Strabo, and P. Crassus (*cos.* 97) and his son (Livy *Per.* 80; Flor. 2.9.14). Early in 86 he undertook to assassinate Q. Mucius Scaevola Pontifex (*cos*. 95), but succeeded only in wounding him (Cic. *Rosc. Amer.* 33; Val. Max. 9.11.2). Later in the year he served on the staff of the Consul L. Valerius Flaccus in Greece and Asia as *praefectus equitum* (Vell. 2.24.1, probably giving the correct title) or Quaestor (so Lintott, *Historia* 20 [1971] 696–701, following Strabo 13.1.27). After quarreling with Flaccus and his Quaestor at Byzantion, he instigated a mutiny, assumed the fasces, and had the Consul— or perhaps by now Proconsul—murdered in Nikomedeia (Livy *Per.* 82; Memnon *FGrHist* 434 F 1.24.1–3; Appian *Mithr.* 52.207–10; Dio fr. 104.3–5). For much of 85 he successfully waged war against Mithradates in Asia and recaptured most of the province (Livy *Per.* 83; Plut. *Luc.* 3.4–8; Memnon 24.4; Appian *Mithr.* 52.210–53.214; Oros. 6.2.10–11). When Sulla after the Treaty of Dardanos marched against him, Fimbria was quickly deserted by his troops; he committed suicide in the temple of Asklepios at Pergamon (Plut. *Sulla* 25.1–3; Appian *Mithr.* 59.241–60.247).

σπενδόμενος ... ἀφῆκε: in the Treaty of Dardanos; above, 23.2n.

ταύτην οὐκ ... γενομένην: P.'s version of this crucial item in the treaty is apparently contradicted by Appian: συνετίθετο τῷ Μιθριδάτῃ δώσειν Ἀσίαν τε καὶ Βιθυνίαν καὶ Παφλαγονίαν καὶ Καππαδοκίαν καὶ Γαλατίαν, *Mithr.* 68.288. Scholars are nearly (and rightly) unanimous in following P.'s account; however, Berve (199–212; preceded by W. Ihne, *Römische Geschichte* 6 [Leipzig 1886] 18–20, and followed by Magie, 1:322–23, 2:1203) rejected it and argued in favor of Appian's version. Berve was carefully and convincingly refuted by Gelzer ("Vertrag"); it seems worthwhile, however, to set out the principal arguments supporting P.'s account.

The sources for the treaty are rather numerous: ancient writers evidently considered the pact between the civil war leader in the West and the king in the East a significant and noteworthy event. Yet Appian stands virtually alone in charging Sertorius with the cession of Asia. The signing away of a province of the Roman People to an oriental despot would have been more than remarkable, a truly momentous and outrageous deed, as both P. and Berve (213, "[ein] ungeheuerlicher Frevel am Staate") are well aware. In the works of Cicero—our earliest, and sole contemporary, source—references to Sertorius are scarce, but the treaty is mentioned or alluded to four times (2 *Verr.* 1.87; *Imp. Cn. Pomp.* 9, 21; *Mur.* 32). Not a single hint of a cession of Asia, not even in the Verrine passage, where the author desperately tries to hold Verres indirectly responsible for the conclusion of the treaty. The scholiasts have nothing to add, neither Pseudasconius, here informed and concise (244.1–7 St), nor the Gronovian, bumbling and clumsy (317.8–11 St). No fragments of Sallust that deal with the terms of the treaty survive, but his favorable attitude towards Sertorius is well attested, both in his own words (*Hist.* 1.88) and in P.'s picture. There is no *a priori* reason to assume that P.'s account of the treaty is based on a source other than Sallust, though Berve (208–9), not surprisingly, would attribute the Plutarchean report to an apologetic Greek source of the Early Principate. Who this source might have been—more favorable toward Sertorius even than Sallust, and trying to rebut a charge of "high treason" a hundred years or so after the event—Berve was unable to say, and wisely chose not to advance any names or details in speculation.

The entire Livian tradition (*Per.* 93; Flor. 2.10.5; Oros. 6.2.12) contains not a hint of a cession of Asia. The most explicit of its representatives, Orosius (6.2.12), agrees with Cicero, Pseudasconius, and probably Sallust (see 23.3–4nn.) on one significant detail: the idea of an alliance with Sertorius was first broached to the King by Magius and Fannius (*Fannius et Magius de exercitu Fimbriae profugi Mithridati sese adiunxerunt: quorum hortatu Mithridates cum Sertorio per legatos in Hispaniam missos foedus pepigit*). Appian concurs: δύο δ' αὐτοῦ (sc. Σερτωρίου) τῶν στασιωτῶν, Λούκιοι Μάγιός τε καὶ Φάννιος, Μιθριδάτην ἔπειθον συμμαχῆσαι τῷ Σερτωρίῳ . . . ὁ μὲν δὴ πεισθεὶς ἐς Σερτώριον ἔπεμψεν, *Mithr.* 68.287–88. P. in that context does not mention names, but then he is not interested in the identity of the *kolakes* who put the idea in the King's mind. It is less clear whether P., Orosius, and even Sallust realized that Fannius and Magius were identical with the envoys actually sent to Spain. But for the testimony of Cicero and Pseudasconius, their part in the negotiations might never be known. Yet Appian at least is obliquely aware of their involvement: upon completion of the deal, Sertorius sends both of them as advisers to the King (*Mithr.* 68.288; on his monumental blunder of mistaking them for original *Sertoriani* see Konrad, "Chronology," section VIII). As P. follows Sallust (see 23.3n.), Appian's version that Sertorius ceded Asia cannot derive from that source. Nor can it derive from Livy, seeing that nothing indicates that Livy's story of the treaty differed substantially from the version of the other sources, be it in the matter of Asia or otherwise.

Thus if Appian's account is a faithful rendering of his source, that source reporting the cession of Asia would have to be different from and independent of any other attested tradition: a tradition unknown to Sallust and Livy, to Cicero and his scholiasts, preserved only in Appian. The notion does not inspire confidence. (See also Brunt's strictures against too readily attributing contradictory evidence to divergent traditions: CQ 30 [1980] 492.) Stahl (72) long ago saw the simple truth: the King's territorial gains according to Appian are identical with the King's territorial demands according to P. The discrepancy is not due to a different tradition, but to Appian himself. Whether carelessness was at work, or malice, we cannot tell; nor does it matter. P.'s account of the treaty, based on Sallust and not demonstrably different from Cicero's or Livy's, is accurate and reliable. That it makes his hero appear in the best possible light is no argument to the contrary.

24.2

Σερτώριος ἐν Παλατίῳ καθεζόμενος: This obvious anachronism led Berve (209) to claim that P. could not possibly be following Sallust in his account of the alliance and instead was using an apologetic source of the Early Principate (above, 23.6n.). Against this, Gelzer ("Vertrag" 140) invoked the

King's knowledge of Roman history: "Ich sehe nicht ein, warum Mithradates, der bekanntermassen sich eingehend mit der römischen Geschichte befasst hatte (Trogus Pompeius bei Justin. 38,4,5ff.), nicht hätte wissen sollen, dass das Palatium als Kern der Stadt Rom galt (Livy 1,7)." That misses the point. P.'s ἐν Παλατίῳ is a metaphor for the seat of the Roman government, and no such usage of the Palatine is known, indeed possible, in the Republican period (cf. Schur, *Sallust* 242). Despite Berve's innocent assertion that P. would not have invented or rephrased the King's comment ("dazu ist ... die Ehrfurcht vor dem historischen Wort bei ihm zu gross," 209 n. 2), there is no reason why P. should not have put it in his own words, or expanded into a royal statement what in his source was a short note to the effect that the King was amazed at Sertorius' reaction.

24.3: The Treaty with Mithradates

Mithradates did not approach Sertorius until hopes for an agreement with Rome had come to nought. During 83–81, when under attack by Murena, the King had scrupulously refrained from military action, and sent emissaries to Rome instead; only when he became convinced that Murena's war had been sanctioned by the Roman government did he defend himself (Appian *Mithr.* 64.265–65.274; cf. Glew, "Between the Wars" 116; McGing, *Foreign Policy* 133–35). In 78 another embassy was still trying to obtain the ratification of the Treaty of Dardanos guaranteeing his possession of his ancestral kingdom; to no avail (Appian *Mithr.* 67.283–84; Reinach 301; Glew 121–25; McGing 136–37; on the Treaty of Dardanos see 23.2n.).

In (late) 77 or 76, an emissary from Mithradates approached Pompeius in Spain (Cic. *Imp. Cn. Pomp.* 46). Although Cicero is silent about the subject of the King's negotiations with Pompeius, it is easily guessed. The Treaty of Dardanos, if ratified, would have made Mithradates a *socius populi R.* (*Sulla* 22.10). By the end of 77, the Roman position in Spain, though not all hopeless, was not very promising. If the King helped Rome to subdue the Sertorian Revolt, he could prove his good faith and expect Rome's recognition in return. Despite his setback at Lauro, Pompeius clearly was the "rising sun" of Roman politics. He, rather than Metellus, was the commander to approach. The King had at least two things to offer: money and a fleet. He will have asked for Pompey's assurance to see to it that the Treaty of Dardanos be ratified by the Senate and People of Rome, after his return from Spain. The King is likely to have also demanded assurance that Bithynia and Kappadokia should become his in the event of their present rulers' demise without issue, or that at least they should remain independent and not be annexed by Rome. From Cicero it appears that Pompeius treated the King's envoy with respect and did not reject his proposals out of hand; it is also evident that no agreement was ever reached. The King must finally have realized that none of the men currently in power at Rome was willing to confirm the Treaty of Dardanos, and thus at least guarantee his ancestral kingdom. On the contrary, he had reason to fear that once order had been restored in Spain, the Roman government would direct its attention toward the East. Rebuffed by Pompeius, Mithradates decided to deal with Sertorius. The latter's chances of ever invading Italy might be slim; but he could bind, for a long time to come, substantial Roman forces in the Peninsula (about a dozen legions in 76–75, and two more by 74: see 12.2n.) and provide the King with the officers needed to train and organize the royal army along Roman lines (cf. 24.3n.).

The negotiations between Mithradates and Sertorius as well as the resulting treaty should be dated to 76 or 75 B.C., as shown conclusively by Maurenbrecher (*Prolegomena* 54; cf. Bieńkowski, "Chronologie" 158; Stahl 70–72; Schulten 106; Spann 100, and most other scholars). Some (e.g., Reinach 311; Gabba, "Guerra sociale" 323 n. 1 and *App BC* 1 308; Scardigli, "Problemi" 253; Glew, "Between the Wars" 126) would date the first contacts between the King and Sertorius to 79, on the basis of Cic. *2 Verr.* 1.87. But that passage merely tells us that the King's envoys, Fannius and Magius (see 23.4n.), in that year acquired the ship which they used for their journeys to Spain and Pontos. There is no indication that they bought it for that purpose, or that the voyage to Dianium followed immediately upon purchase of the vessel (cf. above, 23.4n.). As they were living in Myndos (Karia) in 79, they were hardly yet on intimate terms with the King of Pontos—who, moreover, was concentrating his diplomatic efforts at that time on persuading the Senate to ratify the Treaty of Dardanos (McGing, *Foreign Policy* 138; cf. above).

As for the exact date of the negotiations, Appian *Mithr.* 69 implies that a summer and a winter passed before the King invaded Bithynia in 74, thus opening the Third Mithradatic War. Hence the treaty cannot be much later than the spring of 75. (McGing, *Foreign Policy* 139, is essentially correct except for his belief that the war started in 73; the year 74, long disputed, is now virtually certain: see Merkelbach, *ZPE* 81 [1990], and Keaveney, *Lucullus* 188–205.) Appian's chronology, however, tends to be slippery when it involves events in different and distant theaters. There are indications that the negotiations took place on the East Coast, where Sertorius' presence is not attested after the fall of 76 (see 23.4n.), and the early months of 75 witnessed a sudden reemergence of naval support lent by Kilikian pirates, conceivably in fulfillment of the King's part under the agreement (cf. 21.7n.). The date of the treaty thus falls in a rather narrow window between summer 76 and spring 75.

γίνονταί γε συνθῆκαι καὶ ὅρκοι: The King's envoys probably had full powers to sign any agreement not obviously detrimental to his interests, and no second voyage to Spain and back will have been necessary (Spann, diss. 271 n. 134, *contra* Schulten 107 n. 516).

Καππαδοκίαν καὶ Βιθυνίαν ἔχειν Μιθριδάτην: cf. 23.6n. Whether Paphlagonia and Galatia were also ceded (Appian *Mithr.* 68.288) remains unclear. Since Appian substituted Mithradates' demands for the actual terms of the treaty (above, 23.6n.), his testimony alone is not decisive. But without either

Paphlagonia or Galatia, the King would have had no access to Bithynia except by sea, and during his invasion of Bithynia in 74 he briefly marched across Paphlagonian and Galatian territory (Memnon *FGrHist* 434 F 1. 27.3). Perhaps he had always retained possession of the coastal areas of Paphlagonia (cf. Ruge, *RE* 28.4 [1949] 2524–25); clearly Sinope remained Pontic throughout his reign. Mithradates had, or thought he had, dynastic claims to Paphlagonia (Iustin. 37.4.5; 38.4.5–6); its cession in the Peace of Dardanos was the only territorial clause to which he raised objections (Plut. *Sulla* 23.6–7).

στρατηγὸν . . . καὶ στρατιώτας: Their principal task undoubtedly was to train Mithradates' army according to Roman practice and to supervise its being equipped and organized in Roman fashion (Plut. *Luc.* 7.5; cf. Scardigli, "Problemi" 254; Spann 101–2). The number of soldiers sent to Asia cannot have been large, since at its peak the total of Roman troops with Sertorius was just about sixty cohorts (the fifty-three of Perperna plus the 2,000 or so Romans Sertorius had brought along from Africa; above, 12.2, 15.5nn.). Apparently, several of the *proscripti* ended up with the King's forces in Asia (Oros. 6.2.21): some may have come from Spain.

αὐτῷ: does not imply that the Sertorian general, M. Marius (below, 24.4n.), was to be the King's subordinate, as Berve (210–11) would have it. While Appian *Mithr.* 76.332, Οὐαρίῳ (on the name see 24.4n.) πεμφθέντι οἱ (sc. Μιθριδάτῃ) στρατηγεῖν ὑπὸ Σερτωρίου, might support Berve's view, 70.298 contradicts it: there Appian has the King call Marius, Magius, and Fannius σύμμαχοι. P. 24.4 and Orosius 6.2.12 (*Marium . . . quem rex apud se retentum brevi ducem fecit in locum Archelai*) leave no doubts about the true situation. Under the terms of the treaty, Marius was to be military adviser to the King and Sertorius' acting governor for the province of Asia; in the course of events the King soon found it expedient to put part of his army under Marius' command, always together with one or more Pontic generals: Eumachos at the operations near Kalchedon and in Phrygia (Oros. 6.2.13; cf. Plut. *Luc.* 8.5; Appian *Mithr.* 75.326), Hermaios during the retreat from Kyzikos (Memnon *FGrHist* 434 F 1.28.3, where Jacoby's commentary, III b 281, is confused; cf. Plut. *Luc.* 11.8; Appian *Mithr.* 76.329), and Alexandros and Dionysios for the naval expedition in the Aegean (Appian *Mithr.* 76.332–77.338; cf. Plut. *Luc.* 12.2–5; Oros. 6.2.21–22). Gelzer's suggestion ("Vertrag" 145), "Erst, als Marius sich gegenüber dem legitimen Proconsul Lucullus in Asia nicht mehr halten konnte, wird er in den Dienst des Königs getreten sein," does not agree with the evidence.

τρισχίλια τάλαντα: The King had provided an identical amount of money, but twice the number of ships, for Sulla in the Treaty of Dardanos (Memnon *FGrHist* 434 F 1. 25.2). 3,000 talents (in silver) = 18 million denarii = 72 million sesterces were a sizable sum. Exactly what Sertorius used (or intended to use) the money for is unclear. Some of his Hispanian volunteers (not necessarily all) might fight without pay. The Roman troops that had come with

Perperna seem to have followed him to Spain willingly, but one must not rashly conclude that every man of them was a confirmed enemy of the post-Sullan oligarchy. Perperna had brought along a well-filled war chest (15.2), out of which they may have received regular payments (cf. also Livy 91 fr. 22.23 W-M, *stipendium datum*). Two years later, in 75, these funds would have been running low, and some of the defections to the senatorial forces (Appian 112.520) may be attributed to soldiers' no longer getting paid. For Sertorius, the 3,000 talents held at least two advantages: in the unlikely event of an invasion of Italy, they could be helpful in persuading senatorial troops to switch sides, whereas in Spain they rendered him financially independent of both Romans and Hispanians. Diodoros (37.22a) has an interesting note: "Having accumulated a large amount of silver and gold, he did not place it in the common war chest but kept it under lock in his private treasury; and he did not issue pay to the troops from those funds, nor would he let the other leaders have a share in them." The context of the fragment clearly places this in the period of beginning discontent with his leadership, i.e. 75/4 B.C. (see 25.1n.). Was the gold and silver hoarded by Sertorius the King's subsidy?

τεσσαράκοντα ναῦς: This fleet was certainly not dispatched until after the arrival of Marius and his troops in Pontos. Possibly these advisers traveled in the ship of Magius and Fannius (Appian *Mithr.* 68.288). If the alliance was concluded in the fall of 76, the Pontic fleet may have arrived in Spain as early as spring/summer 75; in the fall of 75 or spring 74, if the treaty is to be dated to 75. Unfortunately the text of Sall. *Hist.* 2.93, ... *it]emq(ue) Sertorius mo{n}[vit s]e, ne ei perinde Asiae [Galli]aeq(ue) vad⟨eren⟩t e facultate* (Perl's restoration, "Sallust" 269) is in too bad a state to permit with certainty the conclusion that Sertorius was expecting the Pontic fleet in the fall of 75 (Perl, "Codex" 37 n. 1; *contra*, Stahl 72; Schulten 107 n. 516). Some scholars think the fleet was not sent until after the outbreak of hostilities in the East, more precisely after the battle of Kalchedon, i.e., summer/fall 74 or spring 73, and perhaps did not even reach Spain before the death of Sertorius: e.g., Magie 1:326, 2:1207 n. 11; Bennett, "Death" 467–69; Scardigli, "Problemi" 256; Spann 101. (Sherwin-White, *Roman Foreign Policy in the East* 170 n. 40, seems to think the ships were not sent at all, against which see Spann 209 n. 40.) But the King did not commence hostilities until well after the death, in late 75, of Nikomedes IV of Bithynia, an event the date of which was not predictable with precision. Sertorius needed help now, not at some unspecified and indeterminable point in the future. Nor was there any need for Mithradates to establish naval control of the Aegean before he could dispatch the fleet: for most of the 70s, the King and the pirates were already in effective control of the Aegean as well as the Mediterranean.

Once in Spain, the Pontic fleet presumably was based at Dianium (cf. 21.7n.). That it "might have enabled Sertorius to take the offensive against the senatorial oligarchy in Italy" (Bennett, "Death" 469) is doubtful. By 74 such an undertaking would have been little short of desperation. But the ships would give Sertorius considerable naval power along the East Coast, something he seems to have been lacking in 76 (thus, by implication, Livy 91 fr. 22.47–49 W-M, *si traheretur bellum, hosti, cum mare ab tergo provinciasque omnes in potestate haberet, navibus undique commeatus venturos*), though he put it to excellent use in 75 (above, 21.7–8nn.). Indeed, if the treaty was already concluded in 76, the ληστρικὰ σκάφη of 21.7 are perhaps none other than the Pontic ships. Certainly the operations in 74 of the Praetor M. Antonius along the Ligurian and Spanish coasts should be seen in this context (Sall. *Hist.* 3.4–6; cf. Cic. 2*Verr.* 2.8, 3.213–18; Ps.-Ascon. 202, 239, 259 St; and see Maróti, *Altertum* 7 [1961] 32–41 and *AAntHung* 19 [1971] 270). After Sertorius' death, or perhaps only after the end of Perperna (below, 27.3–5), the fleet returned to the East, but was destroyed in the second battle of Tenedos in 72 (Memnon *FGrHist* 434 F 1.33.1; cf. 29.2, 5).

24.4

στρατηγὸς εἰς Ἀσίαν: "as governor to Asia."

τῶν ἀπὸ βουλῆς προφευγότων: on the senatorial status of M. Marius see following note.

M. Marius (23): first attested in 76 while serving as Quaestor under Sertorius in Hither Spain (Livy 91 fr. 22.70 W-M). Sent to the East in 75 as military adviser to Mithradates and Sertorian acting governor of Asia, he commanded part of the King's army during the operations at Kalchedon and Kyzikos (Plut. *Luc.* 8.5; Memnon *FGrHist* 434 F 1.28.3; Appian *Mithr.* 70.298; Oros. 6.2.12–13). After the disaster at Kyzikos, he was one of three commanders who tried to enter the Aegean with a royal force of fifty ships and 10,000 picked men. Defeated by Lucullus in two naval battles near Tenedos and Lemnos, he was taken prisoner and executed (Plut. *Luc.* 12.2–5; Memnon 29.2; Appian *Mithr.* 76.332–77.338; Oros. 6.2.20–22; cf. Cic. *Mur.* 33). Like Sertorius, he was one-eyed (*Luc.* 12.5).

Marius is usually thought to have come to Spain with Perperna in 77 (Spann 172). Since τῶν ἀπὸ βουλῆς προφευγότων (cf. Appian *Mithr.* 77.338) clearly refers to the Senate in Rome, not its Sertorian counterpart, he must have held senatorial rank before joining Sertorius. Some have suggested that he was the Quaestor of the Consul Lepidus in 78 (though Münzer's "perhaps Quaestor-designate"—i.e., for 77—is impossible, as no elections took place in 78; cf. Sall. *Hist.* 1.77.22, *interrex*). Yet it is difficult to believe that Sertorius would entrust the Asiatic command to a follower of Perperna, or that he needed to pick such a one to be his (Pro-)Quaestor in 76. If Marius did come with Perperna, he is better seen as politically independent of the latter. In addition, although Orosius does not explicitly call him one of the proscribed, the context of his death strongly suggests that he was: *multi ibi ex his quos Sulla proscripserat interempti sunt. Marius postera die de spelunca, ubi latebat, extractus meritas hostilis animi poenas luit* (6.2.21–22; see also Hinard, *Pro-*

scriptions 405). If so, he must have become Quaestor and a Senator no later than 82 (cf. above, 22.1n.), and may have been a member of Sertorius' original staff.

The name is *Varius* (Οὐάριος) in Appian, but Marius in all the other sources, including Memnon 28.3 (where Jacoby III b *Kommentar* 281, thinking him identical with L. Magius, mistakenly obelized Μάριον). Recently Hinard (*Proscriptions* 405–6) attempted to vindicate Appian's *Varius* by claiming *Marius* as "banalisation" of the correct name. He is unaware of Memnon's testimony, derived from an independent source tradition (see Introduction 3.7). As regards palaeographical "banalisation," for it to occur universally and identically in the manuscript tradition of four different authors—two Latin, two Greek—would seem a tall order indeed.

ᾧ συνεξελὼν ... ἀνειληφώς: The story has been doubted, chiefly by Berve (210), to whom it seemed "impossible and downright absurd" that the King should have found it necessary to assume the second rank after Marius when entering a town of the very province whose possession had been denied to him by Sertorius. Holmes (1:403–4) and Magie (2:1206 n. 10) doubt it because Marius and Mithradates are not known to have entered any city in Asia together.

Berve's argument is fallacious: if indeed Sertorius had not ceded Asia, then there is no reason why the King should not have observed—for the time being—the terms of the treaty, and made a show of respect for "Roman" rule in Asia. Of course, the army, and hence the real power, was the King's. Had Mithradates won the war, Marius could have exercised little control over his province but by the King's good grace. Yet the question here is one of diplomatic protocol, not of military might, and as long as the King needed his Roman advisers, he could afford to humor them.

Holmes's and Magie's objections are serious. Our knowledge of the campaigns of 74 and 73, however, is far from complete: we simply cannot tell whether the King and Marius never entered any town in the province except Parion (Mithradates) and Lampsakos (Marius; Appian *Mithr.* 76.329, 331). Moreover, while P. reports it as a factual event, the story may merely reflect a specific clause in the treaty. It would have been only consistent of Sertorius to insist that in the case of joint operations within the Roman province the Sertorian commander take precedence when entering a city. Quite possibly the occasion never arose, but such terms of the treaty would likely have been emphasized by Sallust.

μετὰ ῥάβδων καὶ πελέκεων: Since the highest office hitherto held by Marius was the quaestorship, he could not have *imperium suis auspiciis,* unless it was granted to him by special enactment. Yet the Sertorians could not pass the necessary *lex curiata* (cf. above, 22.5n.). Hence his title was either *proquaestor pro praetore* or *legatus pro praetore,* i.e., acting governor/commander in chief (cf. Gelzer, "Vertrag" 143), exercising the *imperium,* delegated to him, of the Proconsul Sertorius. From Cic. *Att.* 10.4.9 it is clear that Legates and

(Pro-)Quaestors *pro praetore* had less than the six lictors of a (Pro-)Praetor (Stenten, 96, erroneously would give Marius twelve); to judge from practice during the Imperial period, probably five (Mommsen, *StR* 1³:385–86).

24.5

ὁ δὲ ... κατήγγελλεν: Sertorius had begun his own governorship in Spain in 82 in the same style, and thus gained the goodwill of the provincial population (6.7–8). Presumably Marius had orders to follow that policy. A number of cities probably were affected by these measures simply through Governor's Edict, without Marius actually setting foot in them. Stenten (96) points out that Lucullus later took very similar steps to relieve the plight of Asia (*Luc.* 7.7, and esp. 20.1–4).

τῶν τελωνῶν: *publicani*, here clearly not general contractors but tax farmers.

βαρυνομένην δὲ ... ἐπισκήνων: The quartering of Roman troops in private homes of the province had been a severe burden for the cities of Asia ever since Sulla's victory in 85 (*Sulla* 25.4–5). Sertorius had ended the same practice in Spain in 82 (6.8; cf. 3.5–10).

ἀναπτερωθῆναι ... ἡγεμονίας: not a hint here of the short duration and inglorious end of Marius' tenure as the Sertorian governor in Asia (cf. 24.4n.); that would spoil the effect. The Mithradatic Treaty was the hero's greatest political success, his insistence on retaining the province ultimate proof of his *Romanitas*. It is fittingly narrated as the last of his achievements, just before his fall.

25–27

The final three chapters form a unit centered on the hero's death. Chapter 25 sets the stage: as 22 and 23 portrayed the character of Sertorius, so it presents a comprehensive study of Perperna and other opponents. They are a sorry sight, jealous, selfish, petty, and cruel. Unworthy of their supreme leader, they decide to do away with him (26). Yet success brings swift retribution at the hands of Pompeius (27); in defeat and the face of death they bear themselves no less contemptibly than before and during Sertorius' assassination. *Tychē* and no fault of his own has brought the hero down (cf. 1.9–12).

25.1

ἐν δ' Ἰβηρίᾳ: From the dream world of a Sertorian-ruled Asia the reader is quickly returned to reality.

τῶν περὶ Σερτώριον συγκλητικῶν καὶ ἰσοτίμων: the Roman Senators in his camp; cf. 22.5, 22.11, 23.5nn. For συγκλητικός = "Senator" see also *Cat. Mai.* 16.4; *Cat. Min.* 62.5–6; *Aem.* 38.9; *Sulla* 30.4.

ὡς πρῶτον ... ἐπανέντος τοῦ φόβου: At what time exactly P. envisages Perperna and others first to have voiced their dissatisfaction is not clear. If he was thinking of the fear Perperna's forces displayed at the news of Pompey's impending arrival (15.3–5), ὡς πρῶτον might refer to the time after the victory at Lauro (ch. 18); but while Perperna apparently was an unwilling and unhappy collaborator at all times, there is no evidence that the far more serious and widespread discontent described here in chapter 25 prevailed as early as 77/6 B.C. The events of 76—Hirtuleius' rout at Italica and Perperna's at Valentia, Sertorius' fight to a draw at the Sucro, and their joint defeat at Segontia (19 and 21.1–3nn.)—surely gave little cause for hope. The following winter and the year 75 witnessed a recovery of their fortunes, albeit limited in scope and duration (21.7–9nn.). That same period corresponds to the other sources' first reports of internal trouble (see following note): it seems best to assume that this is what P. had in mind.

φθόνος ἥπτετο καὶ ζῆλος ἀνόητος: It may be doubted that the malcontents were motivated by envy and jealousy thriving in a carefree environment (ἐπανέντος τοῦ φόβου), i.e., a favorable and substantial change in the military situation. The facts, as far as discernible, suggest otherwise. Dissension in Sertorius' camp began in 75, the year after the three battles at Valentia, the Sucro, and Segontia, or perhaps as early as the winter of 76/5, during or after the siege of Clunia (Livy *Per.* 92; Appian 112.520–22). The defeat at Segontia had put an end to Sertorius' ability to field large armies capable of fighting a pitched battle; from then on, it was guerrilla warfare again. But the spectacular successes of the early years, 80–77, failed to repeat themselves. During 75 the Roman armies penetrated farther inland than ever before during the war, and the logistical straits in which Pompeius found himself toward the end of the year did not outlast the winter: in spring 74 Rome sent the necessary supplies and reinforcements (cf. Sall. *Hist.* 2.88–98).

Thus by late 75 Sertorius' military situation had not improved so much as Pompey's had (temporarily) worsened. Sall. *Hist.* 2.93–98 leave no doubts that Sertorius' forces were as close to starvation as were the Romans. In 74 defection of Spanish towns and tribes—many of them wavering, or siding with Pompeius, already in 75 (Sall. *Hist.* 2.92–93)—became rampant, and Pompeius clearly fought a successful campaign (Livy *Per.* 94; Appian 113.525). By the time of his death in 73, Sertorius had lost control of Celtiberia, except for Clunia, Termes, and Uxama; his rule now was limited to the land between the Ebro and the Pyrenees (Calagurris, Osca, Ilerda, Lacetania) and isolated places on the East Coast (Dianium and Tarraco): Strabo 3.4.10; Florus 2.10.9; Oros. 5.23.14; Exuper. 8.24–25 = 56 Z.

τῆς ἐκείνου δυνάμεως: cf. below, 25.4, δεδοικότες αὐτοῦ τὴν δύναμιν, and 25.3nn. Presumably Sallust wrote *potentia* (cf. *Cat.* 17.7, 19.2, 38.1, 38.4, 48.5, 48.7; *Iug.* 15.4, 86.3). The biographer allows us the merest glimpse of Sertorius' position among his fellow exiles during the final years.

25.2

Perperna: see chapter 15 and notes. P. has been careful to avoid any further mention of the man until now; he omits such spectacular defeats as the ones at Valentia (*Pomp.* 18.5) and Segontia (Appian 110.515–16; cf. also 19 and 21.1–3nn. above). Perperna is to be remembered solely as Sertorius' assassin.

δι' εὐγένειαν ... ἡγεμονίαν: cf. 15.2–5. P. makes much of Perperna's *nobilitas* and his looking down on the *homo novus* Sertorius (Sallustian influence may be plausibly suspected); such feelings of loathing and contempt—probably mutual—may indeed have exacerbated their relationship. But Perperna had more substantial reasons to be displeased, even concerned: see below, 25.3n.

τοῖς ἐπιτηδείοις: "friends" (*necessarii, familiares*).

25.3

Though nominally attributed to Perperna (λόγους ... διεδίδου, 25.2), the grievances summarized in direct discourse reflect a general sentiment developing, and soon prevailing, among the Romans with Sertorius. For this use of *oratio recta* in P., cf. *Luc.* 14.2–3; *Crass.* 15.5; *Caes.* 37.6–7; *Pyr.* 13.8–10; *Mar.* 16.6–10, 39.5–6.

δεῦρο δὲ φθάσαντες: thus Ziegler (φθαρέντες mss.), translating: "die wir ... hierhergekommen sind" ("we who have come here"). Admittedly this corresponds more closely to the actual circumstances of Perperna's move to Spain, and more obviously suits the purpose expressed in ὡς ἐλεύθεροι βιωσόμενοι. Yet φθαρέντες, taken as "stranded, lost" (cf. LSJ s.v. II.4), captures the exiles' frustration and despair, the tenor of the passage: they ended up in Spain to live free, but like shipwrecked sailors on an island they have nowhere else to go. Attractive though it is, Ziegler's emendation appears unnecessary.

δουλεύομεν ... τὴν Σερτωρίου δορυφοροῦντες φυγήν: a polemical charge, though not devoid of genuine concern. The battles of Valentia, the Sucro, and Segontia took a heavy toll on the 20,000 or so troops brought by Perperna; by 75 they had shrunk to a rather small force (cf. 21.4n.). Sertorius' only hope now was guerrilla warfare—something in which the Romans that had come with Perperna lacked experience. Consequently, Hispanians again became the paramount force in his army, as they had been before 77. Sertorius kept extending favors and privileges to them (Appian 112.520) that might have seemed, to Roman Knights and Senators, not only excessive but showing a lack of *Romanitas* on his part. Worse, at about the same time he dismissed his Roman bodyguard and replaced it with an all-Hispanian unit (Appian 112.520–22). The Roman guard probably had not consisted of Perpernian troops, but rather were soldiers that had been under Sertorius' command since 82/1 and had shared his African odyssey (7.4–9.11). Their bitterness is easily understood. For Perperna and others, the incident might have a deeper significance.

They had fled to Spain to continue their fight against the ruling *factio* in Rome. Using Hispanians as auxiliaries or allies in properly subordinate roles was an acceptable policy in this struggle, as was fighting the armies of Metellus and Pompeius in regular engagements—something which, indeed, had become possible only through the large number of heavy infantry Perperna had brought to Spain. "Hispanianization" of the war, as it developed—in their eyes, at least—from late 76 on was an entirely different matter. If Sertorius put Hispanians ahead of Romans, even of his oldest and most trusted followers, they might legitimately ask whether his quarrel was still with the post-Sullan government in Rome—or whether he was about to set himself up as the ruler of Spain, *legibus ac more solutus,* in which case the *res publica* they were trying to preserve, for themselves, here in Spain, was lost.

ὕβρεις δὲ . . . ὑπομένοντες: The Roman gentlemen were no longer given preferential treatment; their resentment of the fact is not surprising. Yet P. has nothing to say on the actual loss of stature and importance Perperna and his Roman contingent suffered in 75. With the loss of half if not more of his troops, and probably most of his money spent, Perperna's independence was gone. Sertorius (at last?) could afford to ignore him, as well as his own "Senate." Diodoros 37.22a reports that Sertorius ceased to consult his *consilium*; the detail agrees well with the grievance expressed in more general terms here. With the return to guerrilla warfare, success and survival rested on the support of the native population, as had been the case before 77. The change was not lost on the Hispanians. The chiefs and noblemen who had fought for and with Sertorius for many years need no longer be deferential to Roman Knights and Senators: without them, everything was lost. That they should develop an attitude of contempt toward their Roman betters (cf. Appian 112.521–22) is entirely credible. Yet Perperna and his friends, proscribed and public enemies, had nowhere else to go. From 75 on, they were effectively at one man's mercy: a situation never to the liking of Roman aristocrats.

25.4

τοὺς βαρβάρους ἐκάκουν . . . ὡς Σερτωρίου κελεύοντος: like all of this chapter, an attempt to attribute responsibility for Sertorius' eventual failure to the Roman malcontents around Perperna, and to blame them for the deterioration of Sertorius' character, the change from *clementia* to *saevitia* (cf. the biographer's remarks in ch. 10), the most brutal example of which is described in 25.6. That some of the Romans in Sertorius' camp mistreated Hispanians, and deliberately so, in order to alienate them from their leader, need not be doubted, foolish and ultimately suicidal as such behavior was. But that it could be done on as large and calculated a scale as implied here, without Sertorius' taking notice, or acting against offenders, is questionable.

25.5

ἐξ ὧν ἀποστάσεις ἐγίνοντο καὶ ταραχαὶ περὶ τὰς πόλεις: Appian first mentions Iberian towns defecting in 74 (113.525), but already during the Celtiberian winter campaign of 75 (Sall. *Hist.* 2.92–94) Sertorius was losing the support of many Hispanian towns that, if not openly siding with the Romans, at least tried to remain neutral. Widespread defection of Hispanian allies is also reported by Diodoros (37.22a). Some of this would have been due to the machinations of the malcontents around Perperna, but on the whole the realization that Sertorius could no longer win the war, and that it would be wiser to make peace now with the eventual victors, was probably the principal reason for changing sides.

What P. does not mention is that Romans also went over to Metellus (and Pompeius, presumably) in large numbers as early as 75 (Appian 112.520). Nor do we learn about the numerous executions that were intended to stop further desertions (Livy *Per.* 92; cf. Appian ibid.). Metellus' proclamation putting a prize on the head of Sertorius (above, 21.1) was a signal to the rank and file that deserters to the cause of the Republic would be welcome and pardoned. There had been deserters from Sertorius' forces (whether Hispanians or Romans is impossible to tell) as early as 77 (Livy 91 fr. 22.10–11 W-M, *transfugas liberos ad se adduci iussit*); after the great battles of 76, and under the conciliatory policy of the Roman generals, there were bound to be more and more of them.

25.6

ὥστε ... μεταβαλόντα: The killing or selling into slavery of the hostages at Osca is the only example of Sertorius' change from benevolent leader to despotic ruler given by P. It is also the most damning. Although the breach of treaty inherent in the defection of Sertorius' Hispanian allies rendered the hostages liable to be put to death as a matter of law, actual execution apparently ran counter to Roman practice (see Elbern 116–17). Only two cases, both from the archaic period, are reported prior to this one (Dion. Hal. 6.30.1; Livy 2.16.8–9); the incident of 212 B.C. (Livy 25.7.11–8.1) is slightly different as the hostages had tried to flee. Regardless, in both instances Livy disapproves in no uncertain terms of the *atrocitas poenae*. Two oblique references to the killing of Germanic hostages under Augustus and Valentinian I (Elbern 116 n. 147, where Ammian. 28 [not 27].2.6–8 is the correct reference) might suggest a less restrained attitude when barbarians were involved, but altogether the evidence for Roman execution of hostages is rather scant. Sertorius, moreover, had gone to great lengths to minimize the hostage character of the Hispanian chiefs' and nobles' sons at Osca, emphasizing instead their cultural *Romanitas* and promising citizenship (above, 14.3–4nn.). Avenging their fathers' breach of faith in this fashion was a means of doubtful efficacy in deterring further defections, and apt seriously to damage Sertorius' reputation with leaders still loyal. P. had good grounds for seeking the cause in the man's character rather than attempting to rationalize the killings as necessity imposed by events.

Diodoros 37.22a supplies further details of Sertorius' worsening ways: execution of leading Hispanians and confiscation of their property; refusal to share control over the sums acquired in this way (and possibly from other sources: above, 24.3n.); judging capital cases without his *consilium* (a grave violation of *mos*), and generally becoming more and more reclusive, isolated, and overbearing. Similar charges were listed in Livy (*Per.* 92, 96). Appian adds debauchery with wine and women (113.526).

These accounts should not be rashly dismissed as hostile tradition resulting from anti-Sertorian, pro-Pompeian propaganda cooked up by Poseidonios or Varro (as Spann, 118, 134, would have it). Only too well do they fit the pattern of the charismatic leader forsaken by good luck: developing paranoia and despotic behavior, suspecting treason everywhere, and lashing out with uncontrolled fury at those who (rightly or wrongly) are judged guilty of disloyalty. One may hesitate to accept Appian's tale of debauchery; but the excerptor of Diodoros (37.22a) thought it significant that Sertorius would not admit his generals to his banquets, and P. (26.7) found it necessary to stress that Sertorius' own *convivia* were always held in a decent and orderly manner. For a guerrilla leader close to ultimate defeat, there seems to have been a goodly amount of banqueting. It should also be noted that at least two of the conspirators, Tarquitius and Octavius Graecinus, had held commands of trust and importance in the battle of Lauro and had acquitted themselves with distinction (above, 18.9–10: Battle of Lauro). Both had probably come to Spain on Sertorius' staff in 82 and shared his African odyssey (below, 26.4, 26.6nn.). It seems unlikely that these officers would trade a benign and inspiring leader for a nincompoop such as Perperna.

P.'s own observations on Sertorius' degeneration of character (10.2–7) support the other sources. The hero's cruelty and sullenness (ὠμότης καὶ βαρυθυμία, 10.5) are frankly admitted. P.'s line of defense is not denial, but the omission of details—save one: the hostages—and an explanation, expert and lucid, of how and why a man's natural good character can change for the worse through adverse fortune.

Yet in chapter 25 P. also effects a major shift of emphasis. To Livy, Appian, and other Rome-oriented authors (including Sallust, perhaps) Sertorius' lording it over fellow citizens and Senators, his change from *dux* to *dominus*, was his principal fault: barbarians and their fate mattered little. (Even so, at least Diodoros—drawing on Poseidonios?—did not ignore the acts of cruelty committed against them.) Thus Perperna's conspiracy, while not greeted with approval by any ancient source (as far as we can tell), became nevertheless understandable, perhaps excusable. Not a word about the legitimate concerns of Sertorius' Roman followers in P. Instead they are held responsible, solely, for the leader's worsening relationship with the Hispanians, culminating in his savagery against their sons. For the biographer, herein lies the true change in the hero's character. The Hispanians had made his survival possible for nearly a decade, worshiped him almost like a god, dedicated their lives to him. Instead of protecting them from the machinations of his fellow Romans, he succumbed to distrust, bitterness, and terror against innocents. To the student of character, the execution of disgruntled exiles, many of whom were probably indeed plotting to make their peace with the government while there still was time, had limited significance. But the betrayal of devoted friends, the savagery against innocents, out of suspicion and despair of success, could not be justified by *raison d'état*. The man had changed, not only his methods and policies.

Thus true to his principles outlined in *Kim.* 2.3–5, the biographer mentions his subject's faults, but without dwelling on them (cf. Pelling, *Hermes* 113 [1985] 324). Better to direct the reader's indignation away from the hero to those whose character was base from the beginning. We read the truth in P. and yet barely notice it, and dismiss Livy and Appian and Diodoros as so much hostile propaganda or literary cliché.

περὶ τοὺς ἐν Ὄσκῃ ... παῖδας: on Osca and the young hostages see 14.3nn.

τοὺς μὲν ἀνελόντα: an act of barbarity in keeping with the worst of Thracian chiefs: cf. Diodor. 33.15.

τοὺς δ' ἀποδόμενον: Some apparently survived and were later released by Perperna (Appian 114.532).

26.1

ὁ δ' οὖν Περπέννας ... ἐπίθεσιν: on the number of conspirators and Appian's alleged first conspiracy see below, 26.4, 26.6nn. All the early sources name Perperna as the instigator and leader of the conspiracy: see Diodor. 37.22a; Livy *Per.* 96; Vell. 2.30.1; Appian 113.527–28; *Iber.* 101. Later sources tend to be vague (*oppresso domestica fraude Sertorio*, Flor. 2.10.9; *a suis ... occisus*, Exuper. 8.24 = 55 Z; *per suos occisus*, Eutrop. 6.1.3; ambiguous also Ammian. 26.9.9), and Orosius (5.23.13–16) mistakenly thought that Sertorius was murdered by Hispanians (see Martino, QS 16 [1990] 77–90, very persuasive).

ἐπίθεσιν: "attempt" (sc. ἐπὶ τὸ Σερτωρίου σῶμα).

Μάλλιον: nothing further is known about the man. The name may be *Mallius* (cf. Cn. Mallius Maximus *cos.* 105, *Mar.* 19.3), quite rare and least likely, *Manilius,* or *Manlius*—the former sometimes (*Pomp.* 30.1), the latter always rendered Μάλλιος by P. (e.g., above, 12.5; *Cam.* 27.4, 36.2–8; *Fab.* 9.2; *Cic.* 14.3). If a Manlius, senatorial descent if not membership in the *ordo* seems likely.

26.2–4

There is a certain limited resemblance between P.'s story and the famous "plot of the pages" against Alexander, as told by Arrian, *Anab.* 4.13–14 (cf. Curt.

Ruf. 8.6–8). Although P. in the *Alexander* mentions the pages' conspiracy only in passing (53.3–5), he clearly knew the full story, and it may have colored his account in the *Sertorius*. Certainly the interplay between the *meirakion* and his various *erastai*—neither of whom seems to have taken part in the actual assassination—held little significance for the success of Perperna's plot.

26.3

Aufidius (1): the only one of the conspirators to survive the war and end his life in penury; see 27.7. The name occurs among a senatorial family, but too little is known to attach this man to it, or to postulate membership in the Senate.

26.4

(C.?) Octavius (55) Graecinus: see Wiseman, CQ 14 (1964) 127–28 and *New Men* 247 no. 288. The name is attested twice at Tibur: *C. Octavius C. f. Graecinus tr. mil.*, CIL XIV 3629, and *C. Octavius C. f. Graechin(us) IIIIvir*, XIV 3664. The second inscription is from a theater constructed probably in the early first century B.C.: the man may be identical with the Sertorian (as well as the Military Tribune). Graecinus was in charge of twenty Hispanian cohorts at Lauro (above, 18.9–10: Battle of Lauro), hence probably on Sertorius' staff already in 82, and one of the proscribed: a newcomer (with Perperna) would not have been given such an important assignment.

φράσας . . . ἐπιχειρεῖν: According to Appian 113.527–28, there had been an earlier plot, hatched by Perperna and ten others; it was discovered, some were punished, some fled. Miraculously (παρὰ δόξαν), Perperna's part in that conspiracy remained undetected, but the incident prompted him to accelerate his plans (ἔτι μᾶλλον ἐπὶ τὸ ἔργον ἠπείγετο). That seems too close to P.'s tale of impending discovery due to Mallius' bragging to be a mere coincidence. It might naturally be suggested that P. suppressed the discovery of the original attempt, so as to streamline the story, give more room to the romantic element in it, and avoid mention of the hero's punishing (capitally, no doubt) the plotters. This time, however, Appian appears the stronger suspect. He claims that the original conspiracy involved ten members besides Perperna, most or all of whom were dead or on the run by the time of the final attempt. Yet as many as nine conspirators can be identified in the latter (below, 26.6n.), for which Appian gives no numbers. It is strange that he should be better informed about an abortive attempt than a successful one. His "first conspiracy" is best regarded as nothing else but Mallius' indiscretion and Aufidius' fear that the the plot was about to be discovered.

26.5

παρασκευάσαντες . . . πολεμίων: A mysterious letter written or delivered by a Celtiberian played a part in Sallust's narrative, though its assignment to book 3 and hence to the conspiracy is rather arbitrary: *ut Sallustius de scripto Celtiberi ait: "hanc igitur redarguit Tarquitius"* (Donat. *Ad Terent. Adelph.* 3.2.14 = Sall. *Hist.* 3.81). Together with *Hist.* 3.82—where the text is really too corrupt to permit sound conclusions (see La Penna, "Ricostruzione" 60–61; Mariotti, *StudUrb* 49.1 [1975] 399–404)—the fragment is usually thought to refer to a written attempt by some Celtiberian to advise Sertorius of the plot against him. Yet if Sertorius had received and, for whatever reason, ignored something as dramatic and direct as a written warning, we should expect P. to mention that; after all, he dwells at length on the scroll of Artemidoros (*Caes.* 65).

It is more tempting to see a connection—if one must be seen—between Sallust's letter and the one reported here. They could not be one and the same, of course, since Tarquitius (one of the conspirators) "refuted" the letter in Sallust, whereas the plotters' forged piece, delivered by P.'s unnamed man, was to give Sertorius a false sense of security. The forgery pretended that a great victory had been achieved by one of his commanders; for it to be credible there must have existed circumstances under which Sertorius could reasonably expect a report. What if the commander's genuine report, not of victory but of defeat, or a like communication from some third party, happened to arrive soon after or before the plotters' forgery? Tarquitius' task then would have been to convince Sertorius that the bad news was false.

26.6

περιχαροῦς ὄντος: Evidently, military success had become very rare by that time—rare enough to make Sertorius accept Perperna's invitation to a celebratory dinner. P. implicitly confirms Appian's ἡττᾶτο συνεχῶς (113.527).

οὗτοι δ' ἦσαν ἐκ τῆς συνωμοσίας: Besides Aufidius, Mallius, Octavius Graecinus (26.2–4), and Perperna himself, the following members of the conspiracy are known:

(a) C. Tarquitius (8) L. f. Priscus. Cf. Cichorius, "Offizierskorps" 267–68 no. 37; Sall. *Hist.* 3.81, 83; Diodor. 37.22a. Served under Cn. Pompeius Strabo (*cos.* 89) during the siege of Asculum in 89, together with two more Sertorians-to-be, Q. Hirtuleius (the brother of Sertorius' Quaestor and chief lieutenant, L. Hirtuleius; above, 12.4n.) and L. Insteius (see Livy 91 fr. 22.14 W-M). Tarquitius commanded 2,000 cavalry at Lauro (above, 18.9–10: Battle of Lauro): hence, like Graecinus, presumably on Sertorius' staff since 82, and a *proscriptus* (cf. 22.1n.). Diodoros calls him and Perperna "the leaders of highest standing" (τῶν ἡγεμόνων οἱ μέγιστον ἔχοντες ἀξίωμα); as a *contubernalis* in 89 (Cichorius 267–68), he might have attained a quaestorship before 82, but hardly more. He is not identical with the C. Tarquitius P. f., Quaestor of C. Annius in 81 (above, 7.2n.; cf. Cichorius; Broughton, *MRR* 2:79 n. 4; Crawford, *RRC* no. 366). Heurgon, *Latomus* 12 (1953) 405 n. 5, is wrong, though followed by Wiseman, *New Men* 264 no. 420, and Spann

173. For a detailed discussion see Konrad, "Friends" 522–24. (Hinard, *Historia* 40 [1991] 115, adds nothing, in addition to misunderstanding the argument in "Friends.") The cognomen *Priscus,* attested only by Frontinus *Strat.* 2.5.31, may be spurious: the mss. have *Tarquinius,* and Priscus would be an unsurprising gloss.

(b) M. Antonius (2). Cf. Sall. *Hist.* 3.83; Diodor. 37.22a; Livy *Per.* 96; and below, 26.10–11. The family is senatorial, possibly consular (e.g., M. Antonius *cos.* 99; but a close relation is unlikely as the consular was killed by Marius in 87; above, 5.6n.). Gabba, "Guerra sociale" 307 n. 302, believes him to be related to Q. Antonius Balbus, Marian governor of Sardinia in 83/2 (Livy *Per.* 86). The praenomen M(arcus), given by two codices and the *editio princeps* of the *Periochae,* is surely preferable to the other mss.' M'(anius). Cf. also Badian, *FC* 311.

(c) L. Fabius (84) Hispaniensis. Quaestor in 82 or 81 under C. Annius (above, 7.2nn.; Crawford, *RRC* no. 366); proscribed apparently while serving in Spain (Sall. *Hist.* 3.83, *senator ex proscriptis*), he escaped and joined Sertorius: see Konrad, "Friends" 519–22, where, however, the possibility was not considered that Fabius may have been Quaestor already in 82 and had joined the winning side before year's end. (Hinard, *Historia* 40 [1990] 117–18, would prefer not to identify Annius' Quaestor with the Sertorian; it is rather risky, however, to postulate two contemporaneous L. Fabii with the distinctive cognomen Hispaniensis.) Though not expressly attested as a member of the conspiracy, his presence at the fatal banquet leaves little room for doubt.

(d–e) Two *scribae* of Sertorius, Versius and Maecenas (Sall. *Hist.* 3.83). The latter may have been related to the family of Augustus' minister (Syme, *The Roman Revolution,* Oxford, 1939, 129 n. 4) but more likely was one of its clients (Badian, *Klio* 71 [1989] 590). It may be assumed that they were part of Sertorius' original staff (cf. Badian, 598). Schulten (135) considers them faithful to Sertorius, noting that they were seated apart from him, each between two conspirators (below, 26.9n.); Spann (131) numbers them among the plotters. A secretary would be in the best position to forge the "victory letter" (above, 26.5) convincingly; certainly Sertorius' *scribae* had had ample practice at composing fake letters and messages (Gell. 15.22.2, quoted above, 11.2–3n.). On the other hand, as *scribae quaestorii* they ranked high enough (equestrian status is not to be ruled out) on the Proconsul's personal staff to warrant an invitation to the banquet (cf. Badian, 598–601). Perperna had to include them even at the cost of heightened risk.

πολλὰ λιπαρήσας ἔπεισεν ἐλθεῖν: In his later years Sertorius did not admit his generals to his own dinners (Diodor. 37.22a), and obviously was not in the habit of accepting invitations. The banquet was held at Osca (see 14.3n.; Strabo 3.4.10; Vell. 2.30.1), in the second half of 73 B.C. (see Konrad, "Chronology," sections III, VIII–IX).

26.7

In contrast, see Appian 113.526, τὰ πολλὰ δ' ἦν ἐπὶ τρυφῆς, γυναιξὶ καὶ κώμοις καὶ πότοις σχολάζων. ὅθεν ἡττᾶτο συνεχῶς. Neither Appian's nor P.'s claims should be made too much of. The biographer's emphasis on the orderliness and decency of Sertorius' banquets is rather superfluous unless a considerable amount of dining and drinking went on in his house during the last years, a suspicion supported by Diodor. 37.22a (see preceding note). Observe how P. in a similar manner seeks to downplay, if not deny, the alcoholic excesses of Cato the Younger and Alexander (*Cat. Min.* 6.2–4, 44.1–2; *Alex.* 23.1–2), on which aspect see Geiger, "Munatius Rufus" 55–56, with the intriguing suggestion that this might be due to P.'s writing under the principate of Trajan, "a heavy drinker himself." Some earlier source, be it Sallust, Poseidonios, or Varro, must have dwelt at length on the subject of Sertorius' feasting and imbibing, though Appian's picture of the leader's completely abandoning himself to wine, women, and wantonness may well be a crass exaggeration. The statement that he suffered constant defeat, however, is not far from the truth: above, 26.6n.

26.8

ἀρχὴν ἀψιμαχίας ζητοῦντες: Why the conspirators should have wanted to provoke an angry outburst—or worse—from Sertorius (cf. below, ἠσέλγαινον ὡς παροξυνοῦντες ἐκεῖνον) is not quite clear. A happy victim is more easily dispatched than a resentful one who may be on edge and, hence, on guard. Perhaps the idea was to elicit a last instance of despotic behavior, to legitimize the slaying then and there; the spectacle of Tillius Cimber repeatedly begging the Dictator to pardon his brother may have served a similar purpose on the Ides of March (*Brut.* 17.3–4; though practical considerations were involved as well: *Caes.* 66.5). Ernst Badian suggests the plan may have been to kill Sertorius in a scuffle, with Perperna's dropping the cup (below, 26.10) merely being a fallback in case the victim failed to respond as expected. Yet one wonders if P. is not simply covering for his hero, who may have enjoyed the party and its attendant beverages more than was good for him; see preceding note, and below, 26.9n.

προσποιούμενοι μεθύειν: The plotters stayed sober, as would be advisable. Note that P. nowhere says the same of Sertorius.

26.9

εἴτε τὴν διάνοιαν ... συμφρονήσας: One should think Sertorius would have called his guards had he actually suspected anything.

μετέβαλε τὸ σχῆμα τῆς κλίσεως: In Greek and Roman dining of that period, male guests would be reclining on couches, propped up on their left elbows and facing the table. Thanks to Sallust, that particular evening's order of seat-

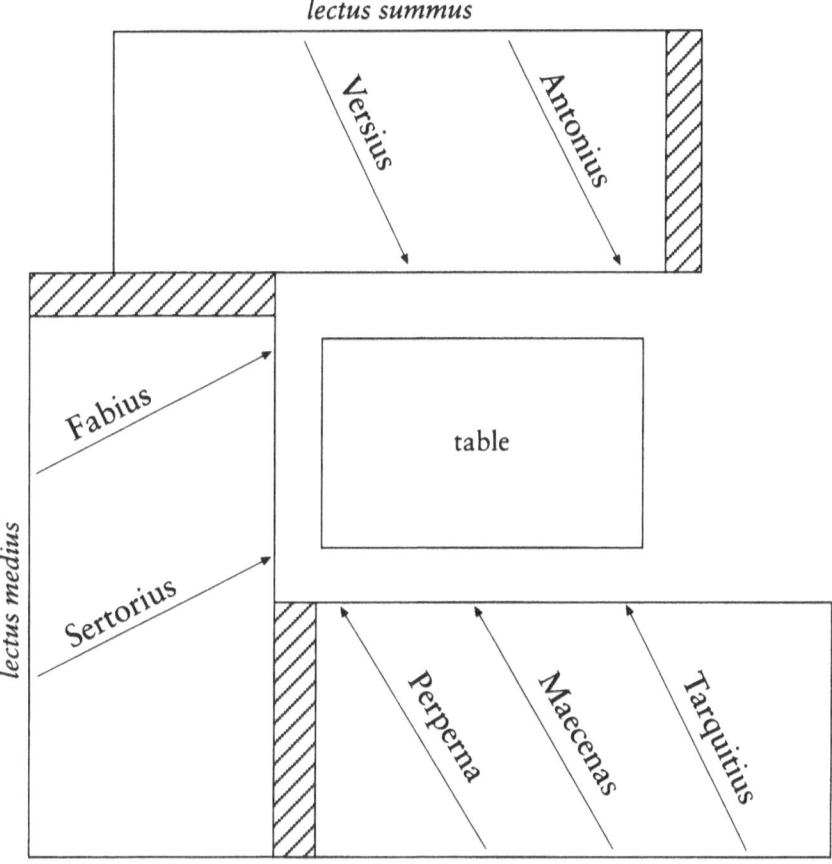

Figure 1. Seating arrangements at Sertorius' assassination
Based on Marquardt, *Privatleben*, 1:304, and Schulten 135

ing is known: *igitur discubuere: Sertorius inferior in medio, super eum L. Fabius Hispaniensis, senator ex proscriptis, in summo Antonius et infra scriba Sertorii Versius, et alter scriba Maecenas in imo medius inter Tarquitium et dominum Perpernam* (Hist. 3.83).

A sketch (figure 1) may help visualize the arrangement. Sertorius occupied the place of honor, the so-called *locus consularis*; as long as he assumed the normal reclining position he would be looking at Perperna, in the traditional place of the host. On Roman dining rooms and customs see Marquardt, *Privatleben* 1:302–6; Blümner, *Privataltertümer* 385–410; cf. also A. Mau, s.v. "Convivium," *RE* 4.1 (1900) 1201–8; A. Hug, s.v. "Triclinium," *RE* 7A.1 (1939) 92–101.

Only seven participants at the banquet are attested, although the *triclinium* could accommodate nine. Aufidius and Graecinus (26.2–4) would be likely candidates to fill the vacant places, but Sallust's arrangement appears to be complete. Their task (and that of any other, unnamed conspirators) may have been to take care of the bodyguard, if indeed Sertorius brought it along (see 26.11n.).

ὕπτιον ἀνεὶς ἑαυτόν: "he threw himself upon his back" (Perrin); cf. *Artax.* 16.3.

ὡς . . . κατακούων: Appian's reason (113.528) for Sertorius' paying no further attention to his surroundings significantly differs from that given by P.: ὁ Περπέννας . . . μεθύσας δ' αὐτόν. Perhaps an exaggeration, yet not to be dismissed out of hand: they were celebrating a rare and unexpected "victory," and the leader had consented—contrary to his habits of late—to feast with his peers. To believe that Sertorius had not been drinking would be absurd. The question is whether he was in (or approaching) a drunken stupor. The serving of unmixed wine (26.10n.) should caution us against expecting much sobriety.

26.10

φιάλην . . . σύμβολον: During a banquet in a state of advanced inebriation, a cup dropped onto the floor would trigger no suspicion, even if Sertorius was still in full control of his senses. This particular sign may have been chosen for yet another reason. Antonius on the upper bed (see 26.9n.) was to deliver the first blow: in order to get at Sertorius on the *lectus medius*, he had to cross the space between the couches, perhaps stepping on the low table in doing so. When Perperna dropped his cup, wine no doubt spilled on the floor, and slaves waiting on the company would immediately busy themselves with cleaning up the mess. The ensuing bustle and commotion would allow Antonius to get up from his place unnoticed and approach his victim. While Sertorius was lying on his back (a circumstance that could not have been foreseen), he was not likely to notice any of this, whereas in a regular position, he would have been resting on his left side, facing Perperna and the lower couch, with Antonius being out of his direct line of vision. If Sertorius was paying any attention at the crucial moment, it was directed towards Perperna, who had caused the commotion. (Spann, 133, adopts a similar reconstruction.)

ἀκράτου: The ancients normally drank their wine diluted with water, usually hot (for details see Marquardt, *Privatleben* 1:331–40). Consumption of wine unmixed, *merum*, was considered advanced, not to say excessive, imbibing.

Ἀντώνιος ὑπερκατακείμενος: inexact or confused; see 26.9n. and figure 1 for the precise seating arrangements. P.'s ὑπερκατακείμενος may be merely a loose way of saying "lying on the upper couch," but if it were not for Sallust one would conclude that Antonius was placed next to Sertorius on the same couch. A mistaken assumption (though understandable, since Antonius was the first to stab Sertorius) or deliberate imprecision for the sake of a more condensed narrative is more likely. The same seems to have happened in Diodoros' account (or, rather, that of his Byzantine excerptor, 37.22a): ὁ Σερτώριος ἀνακλιθεὶς ἀνὰ μέσον Ταρκυτίου καὶ 'Αντωνίου ὑπὸ τούτων ἐσφάγη. On Antonius see 26.6n. at (b).

παίει τῷ ξίφει τὸν Σερτώριον: Marquardt (*Privatleben* 1:306 n. 2) suggested that not Antonius but Fabius Hispaniensis opened the attack on Sertorius, since he was placed next to him. Apart from P., Antonius is attested as the principal assassin by Livy *Per.* 96 and Diodor. 37.22a. There is no reason why the guest next to the victim need have been the first to strike; those farthest from Sertorius could conceal a weapon more easily.

26.11

ἀναστρέψαντος δὲ ... συνεξισταμένου: Sertorius was reclining flat on his back (ὕπτιον, 26.9). With Antonius' dagger or sword bearing down on him he would instinctively, though too late, throw himself on his side to avoid the blow, and attempting to rise he would naturally want to continue the turn so as to be able to push himself up on his arms.

πολλῶν παιόντων ἀποθανεῖν: cf. the purported Sallust fragment no. 31 (Oliver, *TAPA* 78 [1947] 417) from Perotti's *Cornucopiae* (104): *consurrexere omnes simulque in eum impetum fecerunt*. La Penna, "Ricostruzione" 55, is undecided between assigning it to the death of D. Laelius at Lauro (cf. 18.9–10: Battle of Lauro) or to Sertorius' assassination. The latter is preferable by far. *Omnes* need not refer to all in the room, hence not implicate the two *scribae* in the plot; the reference may be merely to *coniurati*.

According to Appian 113.528, Sertorius' Hispanian bodyguard was present, surrounding the *triclinium*; they were made drunk like their master and presumably shared his fate. Neither P. nor Diodoros mentions a bodyguard, but the biographer's silence might be due to dramatic effect: the lonesome hero all surrounded by conspirators.

27

As is customary in the *Lives*, the final chapter looks beyond the hero's end. Where appropriate—as in the *Sertorius*—it wraps up the story with a report on the fate of those responsible for his death (e.g., *Crass.* 32–33; *Cic.* 49; *Dion* 58; *Eum.* 19.2–3; *Caes.* 67–69; *Pomp.* 80.7–9). P. usually also comments on the place and manner of burial; this is one of the few lives in which he gives not even a hint. (The same is true most strikingly of the *Perikles, Dion,* and *Marius*.) Perhaps he lacked information (as probably he did for the *Camillus, Cato Maior,* and *Flamininus*). A notice in Valerius Maximus (7.6.ext.3) may suggest that Sertorius' ashes were taken to Calagurris (cf. 27.2n.), though Spann (212 n. 2) has cautioned against interpreting *quo perseverantius interempti Sertorii cineribus ... fidem praestarent* literally.

27.1

οἱ μὲν οὖν πλεῖστοι ... παρέδωκαν ἑαυτούς: again P. is compressing events. According to Appian 114.529–33, both Roman and Hispanian troops responded with anger and fury to the news of their leader's assassination, especially when it was learned that in his testament he had named Perperna his heir. However, the latter secured some Hispanian support by releasing the surviving hostages (cf. 25.6n.), placated the Roman element by freeing various prisoners, and quickly gained control through a combination of largesse and severity. Yet P. is essentially correct; Hispanian willingness to continue the war waned rapidly after Sertorius' death. Appian stresses the rage of the Lusitani, "on whom Sertorius had relied most of all" (114.530), though in fact they must have accounted for a small part of his army by 73: ever since 77, the war had been fought in the north and east of the Peninsula. Serious Hispanian resistance continued only in Celtiberia and some coastal towns (see notes below, and cf. 25.1n.).

τοῖς περὶ ... Μέτελλον: cf. 4.9, 5.6, 18.1nn. The ones surrendering to Metellus would mostly be Lusitani and Vettones. He had returned to his province in 75 (Konrad, "Chronology," section VI), and probably spent the remaining years safeguarding Ulterior and fighting in Lusitania (Spann 128, 137).

τοὺς δὲ ... πράττειν: Apparently Perperna assumed leadership without rival candidates (Livy *Per.* 96, *imperium partium ad M. Perpernam translatum*; Plut. *Pomp.* 20.3; Appian 114.532–33; Oros. 5.23.13); not surprisingly, if indeed he was the only holder of *imperium suis auspiciis* besides Sertorius (above, 15.2, 15.5, 22.5nn.). But soon he faced opposition and found it expedient to use harsher measures, including the execution of three men of prominence as well as his own nephew (Appian 114.533).

Only a handful of Hispanian towns continued the struggle. In Celtiberia we know of Clunia (Flor. 2.10.9; Exuper. 8.24 = 56 Z; cf. above, 21.4n.), Uxama Argaela (El Burgo de Osma, Soria Prov., Castilla y León: Flor., Exuper. ibid.; Oros. 5.23.14), and Termes (the medieval monastery of Santa María de Tiermes, near Montejo de Liceras, Soria Prov.: Flor. ibid.), all of them towns of the Arevaci. The fanatical resistance of Calagurris Nasica (Calahorra, La Rioja), a city of the Vascones—so we are told, and so the name indicates; but the Vascones supported Pompeius, the town's coins are Celtiberian, and Celtiberians may have occupied it until its demise—became proverbial for cannibalism (Sall. *Hist.* 3.86–87; Val. Max. 7.6.ext.3; Iuven. 15.93–106; cf. Strabo 3.4.10; Flor., Exuper., Oros. ibid.). Between Ebro and Pyrenees, only Osca and Ilerda fought on (Strabo, Flor. ibid.; on the towns, see above, 12.5, 14.3, 16.1nn.). The last holdouts on the East Coast were Tarraco and Dianium (Strabo ibid.; cf. above, 6.9, 16.1, 21.7nn.). Florus' listing Valentia among the cities surrendering at the end of the war has led scholars to believe that it reverted to Sertorius sometime after its capture by Pompeius in 76 (cf. 19: Winter 77). That is rather improbable (Spann, 211

n. 88, expresses justified puzzlement): Florus (as always) was not striving for historical precision, and his inclusion of Valentia in the summary simply reflects the town's original and only capture, in 76.

27.2

The duration of Perperna's final command in Spain is difficult to estimate. The sources (cf. Plut. *Pomp*. 20.3–5; Appian 115.534) give the impression that it was very short. But his end, after the great leader's death, was bound to be anticlimactic: one should allow for some narrative compression. Bennett ("Death" 466) suggested a year and a half, Spann (135) a few months, which is more likely. The desperate struggle of Uxama and Calagurris, the last towns to be taken by the Roman forces (see preceding note), certainly continued for a considerable time after Perperna's end, but at least Uxama (taken by Pompeius) was subdued by the end of 72, when the Senate recalled the commanders in Spain (Appian 119.554). As Sertorius was murdered in the fall of 73 (see above, 26.6n.), Perperna's end is best dated to spring 72.

27.3

ταχὺ συντριβείς: Detailed descriptions of Perperna's last stand can be found in *Pomp*. 20.4–5 and Frontin. *Strat*. 2.5.32; cf. also Appian 115.534–35. Pompeius used ten cohorts as a decoy to draw the enemy; Perperna, apparently having learned nothing from Sertorius' methods, swallowed the bait and pursued them up to a point where he unexpectedly had to face Pompey's entire army. The rout was complete.

γενόμενος αἰχμάλωτος: After the battle, Perperna hid in a thicket, but was found by a troop of cavalry and identified by a muleteer (Sall. *Hist*. 3.85; Appian 115.536; Ammian. 26.9.9).

ὑπισχνεῖτο ... πολιτείαν: Perhaps because of its conspiratorial touch, the story has found general acceptance; but Spann (135–36) voiced serious doubts, and rightly so. Since Pompeius had the letters burned, unread by anyone (27.5), one may ask how anything could possibly be known about their contents and authors. The ultimate source from which all our information about the nature of Sertorius' correspondence derives would seem to be Perperna himself (unless we assume that Pompeius, contrary to the official version, did look at it), and he—as Spann points out (see also Appian's suggestion, 115.536)—would shun no exaggerations in order to be brought into Pompey's presence, and somehow talk the general into sparing his life.

That there were consulars in contact with Sertorius in the manner suggested—urging him to invade Italy and overthrow the government—was already questioned by Gelzer (*APAW 1943* 1:7 n. 1 = *Kleine Schriften* 2:150 n. 18). Spann would limit the possible candidates to M. Perperna (*cos*. 92, *cens*. 86), C. Valerius Flaccus (*cos*. 93), and, if still alive by 73, M. Herennius (*cos*. 93). Flaccus had long since "made his peace with Sulla" (Spann 210 n.

76), and no stretch of the imagination can elevate the aged Perperna to political preeminence in Rome; ditto Herennius, though both he (probably) and Perperna were related to leading Sertorians and thus may have been engaging in some correspondence, probably innocent enough. C. Cassius Longinus (*cos.* 73), put forward by Katz (*RhM* 126 [1983] 359–62), likewise fails to convince. Lepidus in 78, perhaps, had hoped for Sertorius' support (Sall. *Hist.* 1.77.8, *Hispaniae armis sollicitae*). But Lepidus was dead, and no correspondence of his could cause much concern, or surprise. As for the other consulars of the period, they were, in Spann's words, "either dead or ... optimates."

Yet it would be ill advised to reject entirely an exchange of letters between Sertorius and influential figures (cf. ἐπιστολὰς τῶν ἐν Ῥώμῃ δυνατωτάτων ἀνδρῶν, *Pomp.* 20.7—less specific than in the *Sertorius*). Although P. reports Sertorius' repeated offers to negotiate a settlement as directed only at Metellus and Pompeius, it would stand to reason that he also tried to mobilize whatever support and sympathies he could hope for in Rome (see above, 22.7n.). Likely enough he received answers, polite and inoffensive, but hardly of the treasonous character alleged here. Whether the distortion is due to Perperna, Pompeius, P.'s source, or the biographer himself, it is impossible to say. The *Pompey* (20.7–8) tells essentially the same version: which may mean P. did not know better, or fashioned it to show his hero in the best light—there to emphasize Pompey's wisdom, here to illustrate, for a last time, Sertorius' eminence. Oddly, however, it is in the *Sertorius* (27.4) that P. expatiates on Pompey's patriotic judgment. It sounds as if he did believe the story as he tells it.

27.4–5

Destruction of letters and documents incriminating one's vanquished enemies or current rivals was considered a statesmanlike act, and became a favorite topos of Roman historiography (see Kehoe 249 n. 9). Caesar is said to have burned Pompey's letters after Pharsalos and Scipio's after Thapsus without reading them (Plin. *NH* 7.94; Dio 41.63.5, 43.13.2). As a conciliatory move in 35 B.C. Octavian suppressed certain documents after eliminating Lepidus and Sex. Pompeius (Appian *BC* 5.132.548). Again in 29, with his customary mixture of truth and its opposite he let it be known that he had burned all of Antony's correspondence (Dio 52.42.8); Caligula emulated his great-grandfather, no more sincerely though with greater showmanship (Suet. *Calig.* 15.4, 30.2). In A.D. 89 A. Lappius Maximus burned, unread, the correspondence of Antonius Saturninus (Dio 67.11.1–2). The all-powerful minister of Claudius, Narcissus, destroyed the dead emperor's papers containing material that might compromise Agrippina, just before she had him put to death (Dio 60[61].34.5). Similarly, Eumenes destroyed all his correspondence after making his will (*Eum.* 16.4).

27.5

οὔτ' ἀναγνοὺς οὔτ' ἐάσας ἕτερον: Years later, however, Pompeius was to study with great diligence and interest the captured papers and correspondence of Mithradates (*Pomp.* 37.1–4).

τὸν Περπένναν κατὰ τάχος ἀνεῖλε: cf. Livy *Per.* 96; Val. Max. 6.2.8; Plut. *Pomp.* 20.7–8; Appian 115.537; Ammian. 26.9.9; Oros. 5.23.13.

27.6

τῶν δὲ ... συνομοσαμένων ... διεφθάρησαν: In the *Pompey* (20.5) P. has most of the Sertorian leaders—largely identical with the conspirators (26.6n.)—killed in the final battle. The discrepancy is due to different narrative perspectives. The assassination of Sertorius is merely an aside in the *Pompey* (20.3), and the fate of those behind it of no consequence to the story; hence P. simplified. In the *Sertorius* greater precision was called for; moreover, it allowed him to suggest—not outright, but the underlying notion is inescapable—that Pompeius had the plotters executed as punishment for the murder of the hero. Pompeius, of course, was not concerned with avenging Sertorius. At least four of the plotters are known or were very likely to have been proscribed: Perperna, Fabius, Graecinus, and Tarquitius (above, 22.1n.). That, not the assassination, was the reason they were put to death, as were any other *proscripti* whether involved in the plot or not. Lucullus had acted in like manner in the East (24.4n.). On the other hand, Pompeius pardoned all Sertorian soldiers asking for mercy, and seems to have exercised *clementia* in general (Cic. 2*Verr.* 5.153; see also Gelzer, *APAW* 1943 1:5–8 = *Kleine Schriften* 2:149–52). In 70 B.C. the *lex Plotia de reditu Lepidanorum* (for sources see Broughton, *MRR* 2:128; cf. 130 n. 4) granted amnesty and permission to return to Rome to the erstwhile followers of Lepidus, regardless of rank, most of whom had come to Spain with Perperna.

οἱ δὲ φεύγοντες ... κατηκοντίσθησαν: P.'s comments here are all that is known about those who escaped to Africa. Brunt (*Manpower* 164) not implausibly suggests that some may have ended up serving with the *condottiere* P. Sittius. A sizable number of Sertorian troops were settled by Pompeius at Lugdunum Convenarum (St.-Bertrand-de-Comminges) in Gaul, near the Pyrenees (Hieron. *Advers. Vigilant.* 4; Isidor. *Orig.* 9.2.108; cf. Strabo 4.2.1–2; Plin. *NH* 4.108; see also M. Ihm, s.v. "Convenae," *RE* 4.1 [1900] 1172). Others (clearly Hispanians) served as mercenaries for Gallic tribes, in particular in Aquitania, as late as the 50s B.C. (Caes. *BG* 3.23.3–6). The hard core of irreconcilable enemies of the Sullan Restoration, too embittered to ask for pardon, seems to have managed an orderly retreat to Dianium, whence they went by sea to Sicily. Most of them fell into the hands of the island's governor, C. Verres, *homo sanctus et diligens*, and were put to death (Cic. 2*Verr.* 5.72, 146–47, 151–55; cf. Strabo 3.4.10, and, for the epithet, Cic. *Cluent.* 91).

27.7

Aufidius: above, 26.3.

[ὁ τοῦ Μαλλίου ἀντεραστής]: trite and superfluous; Ziegler rightly secludes.

ἔν τινι βαρβάρῳ κώμῳ: apparently in Africa; but P. is concerned more with the squalid nature of Aufidius' existence than with its location, which at any event he may not have known for certain. Spain remains a possibility.

APPENDIX
A Chronology of Sertorius' Life

References to the *Sertorius* are in parentheses.

ca. 126/5	Sertorius born (2.2)
113–101	Cimbrian Wars
106/5	Sertorius *tiro* in Caepio's army
105	Roman defeat at Arausio; Sertorius escapes by swimming across the Rhône (3.1)
104–102	Sertorius serving under Marius in Gaul; his reconnaissance mission (3.2–4)
102	Battle of Aquae Sextiae
101	Battle of Vercellae
98	Sertorius Military Tribune (3.5)
98/7–93	Sertorius under Didius in Spain; he saves his unit at Castulo (3.5–10)
91	Sertorius Quaestor (4.1)
90–88	Social War (4.2–5)
89	Sertorius enrolled in Senate (4.6n.)
89 or 88	Sertorius' failed candidacy for the tribunate of the Plebs (4.6)
89–85	First Mithradatic War
88	Sulla's March on Rome, Marius outlawed and in exile (4.7)
87–83	Sulla in the East (4.7)
87	Civil war between Cinna and Octavius
	Sertorius Tribune of the Plebs (?) (4.6–9n.); fights on Cinna's side during siege of Rome; after victory, massacres Marius' armed slave bands (4.7–5.7)
86	Marius dies (6.1)
86–84	Cinno-Marian *factio* rules in Rome
85	Sertorius Praetor (6.1–4n.)
	Peace of Dardanos
84	Cinna slain by mutinous troops (6.1)
	Sulla in Greece, prepares to invade Italy
83–82	Sulla's civil war (6.1–3)
83/2	Sertorius goes to Spain, *pro consule* (6.4–9)
82	Sulla's final victory in Battle at the Colline Gate (7.1)
	Proscriptions, including Sertorius
81	Sulla Dictator
	Annius forces Sertorius to leave Spain (7.1–4)
	Sertorius, allied with Kilikian pirates, unsuccessfully attacks the Pityussian Islands (7.5–7)
81–80	Sertorius' adventures in Mauretania (8.1–9.11)
80	Sertorius returns to Spain, with Lusitanian help (10.1–12.1); defeats Cotta in Gulf of Mellaria (12.3)
80–71	Sertorian War (12.2)

80/79	Sertorius defeats Fufidius, *pro cos*. Farther Spain (12.4)
	Hirtuleius defeats Domitius, *pro cos*. Hither Spain (12.4)
	Metellus Pius (*cos*. 80) takes charge of the war, *pro consule*, in Farther Spain
79–77	Warfare between Sertorius and Metellus in Farther Spain, i.e., Lusitania and the Baetica (12.5–13.12)
	Sertorius defeats Metellus' officers Thorius and Aquinus (12.4, 13.10–12); relieves Langobriga (13.7–9)
	Sertorian conquest of Hither Spain (11.2); Hirtuleius defeats Manlius, *pro cos*. Transalpine Gaul, at Ilerda (12.5)
	Sertorius establishes "school" at Osca (14.3–4)
78–77	Insurrection of Lepidus (*cos*. 78) in Italy, suppressed by Catulus and Pompeius
77	Summer: Perperna leads remnants of Lepidus' army to Spain, joins Sertorius (15)
	Summer/fall: Pompeius Magnus crosses the Pyrenees and takes command, *pro consule*, in Hither Spain (12.5, 18.2–3)
	Fall: Sertorius defeats Pompeius at Lauro (18.4–11)
	Siege and capture of Contrebia (19n.; Livy 91 fr. 22 W-M)
77/6	Winter: Hirtuleius takes command of Sertorian forces in Farther Spain
76	Summer: Metellus defeats Hirtuleius at Italica
	Pompeius defeats Perperna, captures Valentia (*Pomp*. 18.5)
	Battle at the Sucro (19.2–11)
	Metellus joins forces with Pompeius in Hither Spain (19.11)
	Sertorius' treaty with Mithradates (if not early in 75) (23.2–24.5)
	Fall: Battle of Segontia: Sertorius defeated, Hirtuleius killed (21.1–3)
76/5	Winter: Sertorius under siege at Clunia (21.4–6)
	Metellus winters in Gaul, Pompeius among the Vaccaei (21.8)
75	Sieges of Palantia (Pompeius) and Calagurris (Pompeius and Metellus) (21.8n.)
	Metellus returns to Farther Spain (22.1–4)
	Pompeius campaigns in northern Celtiberia (21.8n.)
75/4	Pompeius winters in Gaul, writes letter to Rome, demanding supplies and reinforcements (21.8–9)
74	Pompeius successfully resumes the offensive (25.1n.)
	Outbreak of Third Mithradatic War
	Dissension in Sertorius' camp (25.1–3)
	Defection of Hispanian allies (25.4–6)
73	Sertorius assassinated (26)
72	Perperna defeated and executed by Pompeius (27)
72–71	Pompeius suppresses remnants of Hispanian resistance

The chronology of the Sertorian War adopted here and throughout the Commentary is set forth at length in "A New Chronology of the Sertorian War," *Athenaeum* 83 (1995), in press. That the supposed battle between Metellus and Hirtuleius at Segovia is merely a mistake (by Florus 2.10.6–7) for Segontia is argued in "Segovia and Segontia," *Historia* 43 (1994), in press.

BIBLIOGRAPHY

Abascal Palazón, J. M. 1983. "Epigrafía romana de la provincia de Guadalajara." *Wad-al-Hayara* 10:49–115.
———. 1986. "En torno a la promoción jurídica de la *Segontia de los Arévacos.*" *Gerión* 4:213–23.
Aebischer, P. 1931. "Toponymie et épigraphie: L'origine du nom de 'Perpignan' et le gentilice 'Perperna.'" *Bul.letí de Dialectologia Catalana* 19:1–18.
Affortunati, M., and B. Scardigli. 1992. "Aspects of Plutarch's *Life of Publicola*." In *Plutarch and the Historical Tradition*, edited by P. A. Stadter, 109–31. London and New York.
Africa, T. W. 1970. "The One-Eyed Man against Rome: An Exercise in Euhemerism." *Historia* 19:528–38.
Aguilar, A., and P. Picón. 1989. "Aproximación a la estructuración territorial en época romano-republicana y alto imperial en la comarca del Vallés occidental (Barcelona)." *Studia Historica: Historia Antigua* 7:29–43.
Albertos Firmat, M. L. 1966. *La onomástica personal primitiva de Hispania: Tarraconense y Bética*. Salamanca.
———. 1983. "Onomastique personelle indigène de la Péninsule Ibérique sous la domination romaine." *ANRW* II.29.2:853–92.
Alföldy, G. 1975. *Die römischen Inschriften von Tarraco*. 2 vols. Berlin and New York.
———. 1981. "Epigraphica Hispanica I: Neue und revidierte Inschriften aus Sagunt." *ZPE* 41:219–43.
———. 1985. "Epigraphica Hispanica VI: Das Diana-Heiligtum von Segobriga." *ZPE* 58:139–59.
———. 1989. "Epigraphische Notizen aus Italien III: Inschriften aus Nursia (Norcia)." *ZPE* 77:155–80.
Alonso-Núñez, J. M. 1979. "Les informations de Posidonius sur la Péninsule Ibérique." *AC* 48:639–46.
———. 1993. "Aspekte der Latinisierung der iberischen Halbinsel." *Latomus* 52:58–64.
Álvarez Delgado, J. 1945. "Las 'Islas Afortunadas' en Plinio." *Revista de Historia Canaria* 11:26–51.
———. 1950. "La navegación entre los Canarios prehispánicos." *AEA* 23:164–74.
Amela Valverde, L. 1989. "El desarollo de la clientela pompeyana en Hispania." *Studia Historica: Historia Antigua* 7:105–17.
Anderson, J. M. 1988. *Ancient Languages of the Hispanic Peninsula*. Lanham, Md.
del Arco, R. 1950. "Sertorio y Huesca." *Argensola* 1:47–52.
Astin, A. E. 1958. *The Lex Annalis before Sulla*. Bruxelles.
Ausbüttel, F. M. 1988. "Die Einrichtung der Provinz *Gallia Cisalpina*." *Hermes* 116:117–22.
Badian, E. 1955. "The Date of Pompey's First Triumph." *Hermes* 83:107–18.
———. 1957. "Caepio and Norbanus. Notes on the Decade 100–90 B.C." *Historia* 6:318–46 = *Studies* 34–70.

———. 1958. *Foreign Clientelae (264–70 B.C.).* Oxford.
———. 1958. "Notes on Provincial Governors from the Social War down to Sulla's Victory." *PACA* 1:1–18 = *Studies* 71–104.
———. 1958. "Appian and Asinius Pollio." Review of E. Gabba, *Appiano e la storia delle guerre civile* (Firenze, 1956). *CR* 8:159–62.
———. 1959. "From the Gracchi to Pompey." Review of E. Gabba, *Appiani Bellorum civilium liber primus* (Firenze, 1958). *CR* 9:272–74.
———. 1959. "Caesar's Cursus and the Interval between Offices." *JRS* 49:81–89.
———. 1959. "The Early Career of A. Gabinius (Consul 58 B.C.)." *Philologus* 103:87–99.
———. 1961. "Servilius and Pompey's Triumph." *Hermes* 89:254–56.
———. 1962. "*Forschungsbericht*: From the Gracchi to Sulla." *Historia* 11:197–245.
———. 1962. "Waiting for Sulla." *JRS* 52:47–61 = *Studies* 206–34.
———. 1963. "Notes on Roman Senators of the Republic." *Historia* 12:129–43.
———. 1963–64. "Marius and the Nobles." *DUJ* 25:141–54.
———. 1964. *Studies in Greek and Roman History.* Oxford.
———. 1965. "M. Porcius Cato and the Annexation and Early Administration of Cyprus." *JRS* 55:110–21.
———. 1966. "The Early Historians." In *Latin Historians,* edited by T. A. Dorey, 1–38. New York.
———. 1966. "Notes on *Provincia Gallia* in the Late Republic." In *Mélanges d'archéologie et d'histoire offerts à André Piganiol,* 2:901–18. Paris.
———. 1969. "Quaestiones Variae." *Historia* 18:447–91.
———. 1970–71. "Roman Politics and the Italians (133–91 B.C.)." *DArch* 4–5:373–409.
———. 1976. "Rome, Athens and Mithridates." *AJAH* 1:105–28.
———. 1983. "The Silence of Norbanus: A Note on Provincial Quaestors under the Republic." *AJP* 104:156–71.
———. 1984. "The Death of Saturninus: Studies in Chronology and Prosopography." *Chiron* 14:101–47.
———. 1984. "Three Non-Trials in Cicero." *Klio* 66:291–309.
———. 1988. "The Clever and the Wise: Two Roman *cognomina* in Context." In *Vir bonus discendi peritus* = *BICS* Suppl. 51:6–12. London.
———. 1989. "The *scribae* of the Roman Republic." *Klio* 71:582–603.
———. 1990. "The Consuls, 179–49 B.C." *Chiron* 20:371–413.
Bailey, D. R. Shackleton. 1965–70. *Cicero's Letters to Atticus.* 7 vols. Cambridge.
———. 1970. "On Cicero, Ad Familiares (II)." *Philologus* 114:88–97.
———. 1982. "Sallustiana." *Mnemosyne* 34:351–56.
Baldwin, B. 1988. "Four Problems with Florus." *Latomus* 47:134–42.
Balil, A. 1956. "Un factor difusor de la romanización: las tropas hispánicas al servicio de Roma (siglos III–I a. de J.C.)." *Emerita* 24:108–34.
Balsdon, J. P. V. D. 1962. "Roman History, 65–50 B.C.: Five Problems." *JRS* 52:134–41.
Barbieri, G. 1943. "Iaccetani, Lacetani e Laeetani." *Athenaeum* 21:113–21.
Barbu, N. 1934. *Les procédés de la peinture des charactères et la vérité historique dans les biographies de Plutarque.* Paris.
Barrow, R. H. 1967. *Plutarch and His Times.* London.
Barti Català, A., and R. Plana Mallart. 1989. "Un modelo de romanización en el litoral gerundense." *Studia Historica: Historia Antigua* 7:11–27.
Bartsch, B. 1908. *Die Legaten der römischen Republik vom Tode Sullas bis zum Ausbruch des zweiten Bürgerkrieges.* Diss. Breslau.
Bauer, W. 1979. *A Greek-English Lexicon of the New Testament and Other Early Christian Literature.* Translated by W. F. Arndt, W. F. Gingrich, and F. W. Danker. 2d ed. Chicago and London.

Bauman, R. A. 1968. "The Abrogation of *Imperium*: Some Cases and a Principle." *RhM* 111:37–50.
———. 1973. "The Hostis-Declarations of 88 and 87 B.C." *Athenaeum* 51:270–93.
Beckers, W. J. 1939. "Die Völkerschaften der Teutonen und Kimbern in der neueren Forschung." *RhM* 88:52–92, 101–22.
Begbie, C. M. 1967. "The Epitome of Livy." *CQ* 17:332–38.
Beltrán Lloris, F. 1980. *Epigrafía latina de Saguntum y su territorium*. Valencia.
———. 1990. "La 'pietas' de Sertorio." *Gerión* 8:211–26.
Beltrán Lloris, M. 1976. *Arqueología e historia de las ciudades antiguas del Cabezo de Alcalá de Azaila (Teruel)*. Zaragoza.
Beltrán Martínez, A. 1964. "Notas sobre cronología del poblado del Cabeza de Alcalá en Azaila." *Caesaraugusta* 23–24:79–86.
———. 1984. "Numismatica antigua del área de Calahorra." In *Calahorra: Bimilenario de su fundación*, 53–67. Madrid.
Benabou, M. 1981. "Rome et la police des mers au 1er siècle avant J.-C.: La répression de la piraterie cilicienne." In *L'homme méditerranéen et la mer*, edited by M. Galley and L. Ladjimi Sebai, 60–69. Tunis.
Bennett, H. 1923. *Cinna and His Times: A Critical and Interpretative Study of Roman History During the Period 87–84 B.C.* Menasha, Wis.
Bennett, W. H. 1961. "The Death of Sertorius and the Coin." *Historia* 10:459–72.
Berve, H. 1929. "Sertorius." *Hermes* 64:199–227.
Bessone, L. 1982. "La tradizione epitomatoria liviana in età imperiale." *ANRW* II.30.2:1230–63.
———. 1984. "Le *Periochae* di Livio." *A&R* 29:42–55.
Biedl, A. 1930. "De Memmiorum familia." *WS* 48:98–107.
———. 1931. "Nochmals zur Familiengeschichte der Memmier." *WS* 49:107–14.
Bieńkowski, P. R. v. 1890. "De fontibus et auctoritate scriptorum historiae Sertorianae." *Pamiętnik akademii umiejętności w Krakowie: Wydział filologiczny i historyczno-filozoficzny* 8:56–109.
———. 1891. "Kritische Studien über Chronologie und Geschichte des sertorianischen Krieges." *WS* 13:129–58, 210–30.
Billows, R. A. 1990. *Antigonos the One-Eyed and the Creation of the Hellenistic State*. Berkeley and Los Angeles.
Bischoff, B., and H. Bloch. 1979. "Das Wiener Fragment der Historiae des Sallust (P. Vindob. L 117)." *WS* 13:116–29.
Blázquez Martínez, J. M. 1965. "Cástulo en las fuentes histórico-literarias anteriores al Imperio." *Oretania* 21:123–28.
———. 1975. *Cástulo, I*. Madrid.
———. 1975. *Diccionario de las religiones prerromanas de Hispania*. Madrid.
———. 1981. "El sincretismo en la Hispania Romana entre las religiones indígenas, griega, romana, fenicia y mistéricas." In *La religión romana en Hispania*, 177–221. Madrid.
———. 1982. "Die Stadt Cástulo (Hispanien) in der römischen Kaiserzeit." In *Romanitas-Christianitas*, 727–48. Berlin and New York.
———. 1983. "Los Astures y Roma." In *Indigenismo y romanización en el conventus Asturum*, 142–63. Madrid.
———. 1985. *Asimilación y resistencia a la romanización entre los pueblos del norte de Hispania*. Vitoria.
Blázquez Martínez, J. M., and J. Valiente. 1981. *Cástulo, III*. Madrid.
Blázquez Martínez, J. M., R. Contreras, and J. J. Urruela. 1984. *Cástulo, IV*. Madrid.
Blázquez Martínez, J. M., M. P. García-Gelabert Pérez, and F. López Pardo. 1985. *Cástulo, V*. Madrid.
Bloch, H. 1961. "The Structure of Sallust's *Historiae*: The Evidence of the Fleury Manuscript." In *Didascaliae: Studies in Honor of Anselm M. Albareda*, 59–76. New York.

Blümner, H. 1911. *Die römischen Privataltertümer*. München.
Boren, H. C. 1989–90. Review of P. O. Spann, *Quintus Sertorius and the Legacy of Sulla* (Fayetteville, Ark., 1987). *CW* 83:239–40.
Bosworth, A. B. 1992. "History and Artifice in Plutarch's *Eumenes*." In *Plutarch and the Historical Tradition*, edited by P. A. Stadter, 56–89. London and New York.
Braun, F. 1909. *Die Entwicklung der spanischen Provinzialgrenzen in römischer Zeit*. Berlin.
Braund, D. 1984. *Rome and the Friendly King: The Character of the Client Kingship*. London and New York.
Breckenridge, J. D. 1989. "A Missing Eye." *AncW* 20:3–4.
Bringmann, K. 1985. "Geschichte und Psychologie bei Poseidonios." In *Aspects de la philosophie hellénistique*, edited by H. Flashar and O. Gigon, 29–66. Genève.
Broughton, T. R. S. 1951–52. *The Magistrates of the Roman Republic*. Vols. 1–2. New York. Vol. 3, *Supplement*. Atlanta, 1986.
―――. 1974. "Some Notes on Trade and Traders in Roman Spain." In *Polis and Imperium: Studies in Honour of E. T. Salmon*, 11–30. Toronto.
―――. 1990. "L. Manlius Torquatus and the Governors of Asia." *AJP* 111:72–74.
Brunt, P. A. 1971. *Italian Manpower (225 B.C.–A.D. 14)*. Oxford.
―――. 1980. "On Historical Fragments and Epitomes." *CQ* 30:477–94.
Büchner, K. 1982. *Sallust*. 2d ed. Heidelberg.
Bulst, C. M. 1964. "'Cinnanum Tempus': A Reassessment of the 'Dominatio Cinnae.'" *Historia* 13:307–37.
Bülz, M. E. 1893. *De provinciarum Romanarum quaestoribus qui fuerunt ab a.u.c. DLXXII ad a.u.c. DCCX*. Diss. Leipzig.
Butrica, J. L. 1983. "Martial's Little Livy." *CB* 59:9–11.
Cagniart, P. F. 1989. "L. Cornelius Sulla's Quarrel with C. Marius at the Time of the Germanic Invasions (104–101 B.C.)." *Athenaeum* 67:139–49.
―――. 1991. "L. Cornelius Sulla in the Nineties: a Reassessment." *Latomus* 50:285–304.
Calahorra: Bimilenario de su fundación. Actas del I Symposium de historia de Calahorra. 1984. Madrid.
Candau Morón, J. M. 1985. "Posidonio y la historia universal." *Habis* 16:107–27.
Canto, A. M. 1991. "*Colonia Patricia Corduba*: nuevas hipótesis sobre su fundación y nombre." *Latomus* 50:846–57.
Carney, T. F. 1958. "The Death of Marius." *AClass* 1:117–22.
―――. 1959. "The Promagistracy at Rome." *AClass* 2:72–77.
―――. 1960. "Plutarch's Style in the Marius." *JHS* 80:24–31.
―――. 1961. "The Flight and Exile of Marius." *G&R* 8:98–121.
―――. 1961. *A Biography of C. Marius*. Proceedings of the African Classical Associations, Supplement, 1. Assen.
―――. 1962. "The Picture of Marius in Valerius Maximus." *RhM* 105:289–337.
Carter, J. M. 1989. Review of C. B. R. Pelling, *Plutarch: Life of Antony* (Cambridge, 1988). *JRS* 79:211–12.
Casson, L. 1951. "Speed under Sail of Ancient Ships." *TAPA* 82:136–48.
―――. 1971. *Ships and Seamanship in the Ancient World*. Princeton.
Castillo, C. 1974. "Hispanos y Romanos en Corduba." *HAnt* 4:191–97.
Cavaignac, E. 1928. "Métellus contre Hirtuléius (à propos du *Sertorius* de M. Schulten)." *REA* 30:98–100.
Caviglia, F. 1966. "Note su alcuni frammenti delle *Historiae* di Sallustio (*Bellum Sertorianum*)." *Maia* 18:156–61.
Chandler, D. C. 1978. "Quaestor Ostiensis." *Historia* 27:328–35.
Chantraine, H. 1959. *Untersuchungen zur römischen Geschichte am Ende des 2. Jahrhunderts v. Chr*. Kallmünz.

Chic García, G. 1980. "Consideraciones sobre las incursiones lusitanas en Andalucía." *Gades* 5:15–25.
———. 1982. "La actuación político-militar de Q. Sertorio durante los años 83 a 80 a.C." In *Actas del I Congreso Andaluz de Estudios Clásicos, Jaén 1981*, 168–71. Jaén.
———. 1986. "Q. Sertorius, procónsul." In *Reunión sobre Epigrafía hispánica de época romano-republicana, Zaragoza, 1–3 de diciembre de 1983: Actas*, 117–76. Zaragoza.
———. 1987. "La campaña de Catón en la Ulterior: el caso de Seguntia." *Gades* 15:23–27.
Chilver, G. E. F. 1941. *Cisalpine Gaul*. Oxford.
Cichorius, C. 1922. "Das Offizierskorps eines römischen Heeres aus dem Bundesgenossenkriege." In *Römische Studien*, 130–85. Leipzig.
———. 1922. "Zu Varros Lebensgeschichte." In *Römische Studien*, 189–207. Leipzig.
———. 1922. "Historisches zu den logistorici." In *Römische Studien*, 226–41. Leipzig.
———. 1922. "Zwei Gegner Caesars." In *Römische Studien*, 253–57. Leipzig.
Commisso, M. G. 1969–70. *Mario il Giovane e i capi dei populares dall'87 all'82*. Diss. Laur. Padua.
Corbellini, C. 1976. "La presunta guerra tra Mario e Cinna e l'episodio dei Bardiei." *Aevum* 50:154–56.
Cordella, R., and N. Criniti. 1982. *Iscrizioni latine di Norcia e dintorni*. Spoleto.
Correa, J. A. 1983. "Ibérico: *Caśt(i)lo, Ibolc(a)*. Latín: *Castulo, Obulco*." *Habis* 14:107–13.
Costa, A. M. de L. 1983. "Meróbriga: Santiago do Cacém (Portugal)." *Caesaraugusta* 57–58:51–109.
Crawford, M. H. 1967. "Coin Hoards and the Pattern of Violence in the Late Republic." *PBSR* 37:76–81.
———. 1969. "The Financial Organization of Republican Spain." *NC*, ser. 7, 9:79–93.
———. 1974. *Roman Republican Coinage*. 2 vols. London and New York.
———. 1985. *Coinage and Money under the Roman Republic: Italy and the Mediterranean Economy*. Berkeley and Los Angeles.
Criniti, N. 1969. "M. Aimilius Q. f. M. n. Lepidus: 'ut ignis in stipula.'" *MIL* 30:319–460.
———. 1970. *L'epigrafe di Asculum di Cn. Pompeo Strabone*. Milano.
———. 1981. *Grani Liciniani reliquiae*. Leipzig.
Curchin, L. A. 1990. *The Local Magistrates of Roman Spain*. Toronto.
———. 1991. *Roman Spain: Conquest and Assimilation*. London and New York.
De Lacey, P. 1952. "Biography and Tragedy in Plutarch." *AJP* 73:159–71.
Delvaux, G. 1988. "Retour aux sources de Plutarque." *LEC* 56:27–48.
Demougeot, E. 1978. "L'invasion des Cimbres-Teutons-Ambrons et les Romains." *Latomus* 37:910–38.
Deonna, W. 1965. *Le symbolisme de l'oeil*. Paris.
Desideri, P. 1973. "Posidonio e la guerra Mitridatica." *Athenaeum* 51:3–29, 237–69.
Detlefsen, D. 1870. "Die Geographie der Provinz Bätica bei Plinius (N.H. III, 6 bis 17)." *Philologus* 30:265–310.
———. 1872. "Die Geographie der tarraconensischen Provinz bei Plinius (N.H. III, 18–30. 76–79. IV, 110–112)." *Philologus* 32:600–68.
Deutsch, M. E. 1918. "The Death of Lepidus, Leader of the Revolution of 78 B.C." *University of California Publications in Classical Philology* 5.3:59–68.
Develin, R. 1977. "*Lex curiata* and the Competence of Magistrates." *Mnemosyne* 30:49–65.
———. 1987. "Sulla and the Senate." *AHB* 1:130–34.
DeWitt, N. J. 1941. "Rome and the 'Road of Hercules.'" *TAPA* 72:59–69.
Diggle, J. 1983. "*Facta dictis aequare*: Sallust, *Hist*. II fr. 98." *PACA* 17:59–60.
Dihle, A. 1956. *Studien zur griechischen Biographie*. 2d ed., 1970. Göttingen.

———. 1987. *Die Entstehung der historischen Biographie*. Heidelberg.
Dionisotti, A. C. 1988. "Nepos and the Generals." *JRS* 78:35–49.
Dodds, E. R. 1933. "The Portrait of a Greek Gentleman." *G&R* 2:97–107.
Doehner, T. 1846/47–77. *Plutarchi Vitae: secundum codices Parisinos recognovit T. D., Graece et Latine*. 2 vols., var. editions. Paris.
Domaszewski, A. v. 1924. "Bellum Marsicum." *SAWW* 201, no. 1:1–31.
Domergue, C. 1966. "Les lingots de plomb romains du Musée Archéologique de Carthagène et du Musée Naval de Madrid." *AEA* 39:41–72.
———. 1970. "Un temoignage sur l'industrie minière et métallurgique du plomb dans la région d'Azuaga (Badajoz) pendant la guerre de Sertorius." In *XI Congreso Nacional de Arqueología, Mérida 1968*, 608–26. Zaragoza.
Domínguez Monedero, A. J. 1986. "La campaña de Anibal contra los Vacceos: sus objectivos y su relación con el inicio de la segunda guerra púnica." *Latomus* 45:241–58.
Donnadieu, A. 1954. "La campagne de Marius dans la Gaule Narbonnaise (104–102 av. J.-C.): La bataille d'Aix-en-Provence (*Aquae Sextiae*) et ses deux épisodes." *REA* 56:281–96.
Drews, R. 1962. "Diodorus and His Sources." *AJP* 83:383–92.
Dronke, G. 1853. "Kritische Studien zur Geschichte der Sertorianische[n] Kämpfe." *Zeitschrift für die Altertumswissenschaft* 11:499–510.
Drumann, W., and P. Groebe. 1899–1929. *Geschichte Roms in seinem Übergange von der republikanischen zur monarchischen Verfassung*. 2d ed. 6 vols. Berlin.
Dunkle, J. R. 1971–72. "The Rhetorical Tyrant in Roman Historiography: Sallust, Livy and Tacitus." *CW* 65:12–20.
Dyson, S. L. 1980–81. "The Distribution of Roman Republican Family Names in the Iberian Peninsula." *AncSoc* 11–12:257–99.
Ebel, C. 1975. "Pompey's Organization of Transalpina." *Phoenix* 29:358–73.
———. 1988. "Southern Gaul in the Triumviral Period: A Critical Stage of Romanization." *AJP* 109:572–90.
Edelstein, L., and I. G. Kidd. 1972. *Posidonius*. Vol. 1, *The Fragments*. 2d ed., 1989. Cambridge.
Edler, O. 1880. *Quaestiones Sertorianae*. Diss. Münster.
Ehrenberg, V. 1935. "Sertorius." In *Ost und West: Studien zur geschichtlichen Problematik der Antike*, 177–201. Praha.
Elbern, S. 1990. "Geiseln in Rome." *Athenaeum* 78:97–140.
Eliade, M. 1972. *Zalmoxis: The Vanishing God*. Chicago.
Engelmann, H., and D. Knibbe. 1989. *Das Zollgesetz der Provinz Asia: Eine neue Inschrift aus Ephesos*. Epigraphica Anatolica, 14. Bonn.
Ensslin, W. 1926. "Appian und die Liviustradition zum ersten Bürgerkrieg." *Klio* 20:415–65.
Erbse, H. 1956. "Die Bedeutung der Synkrisis in den Parallelbiographien Plutarchs." *Hermes* 84:398–424.
Errington, R. M. 1970. "From Babylon to Triparadeisos: 323–320 B.C." *JHS* 90:49–77.
Espinosa Ruiz, U. 1984. "Calagurris y Sertorio." In *Calahorra: Bimilenario de su fundación*, 189–99. Madrid.
Estrada, J., and L. Villaronga. 1967. "La 'Lauro' monetal y el hallazgo de Cànoves (Barcelona)." *Ampurias* 29:135–94.
Evans, R. J., and M. Kleijwegt. 1992. "Did the Romans Like Young Men? A Study of the lex Villia annalis: Causes and Effects." *ZPE* 92:181–95.
Ewins, U. 1955. "The Enfranchisement of Cisalpine Gaul." *PBSR* 23:73–98.
Fantham, E. 1987. "Lucan, His Scholia, and the Victims of Marius." *AHB* 1:89–97.
Fatás Cabeza, G. 1977–78 [1981]. "El nuevo bronce de Contrebia." *Pyrenae* 13–14:193–209.
———. 1980. *Contrebia Belaisca, II: Tabula Contrebiensis*. Zaragoza.
———. 1982. "A quién engañó Sertorio cuando cruzó el Pirineo." In *Estat actual de la*

recerca arqueològica a l'Istme Pirinenc: Homenatge al Dr. Miquel Oliva Prat. 4.rt Col.loqui Internacional d'Arqueologia de Puigcerdà, 23-25 d'octubre de 1980, 235-38. Puigcerdà.
Faust, M. 1975. "Die Kelten auf der iberischen Halbinsel: sprachliche Zeugnisse." *MDAI(M)* 16:195-207.
Feliciani, N. 1905. "I confini della *Hispania citerior* e della *Hispania ulterior.*" *RSA* 10:23-30.
Fernández-Armesto, F. 1982. *The Canary Islands after the Conquest: The Making of a Colonial Society in the Early Sixteenth Century.* Oxford.
―――. 1987. *Before Columbus: Exploration and Colonization from the Mediterranean to the Atlantic, 1229-1492.* Philadelphia.
Fernández-Galiano, D. 1979. "Notas de prehistoria Seguntina." *Wad-al-Hayara* 6:9-48.
Fernández-Galiano, M. 1973. "Sobre el nombre de Sigüenza." *EClás* 17:291-302.
Fernández Nieto, F. J. 1968-69. "Beribraces, Edetanos, e Ilercaones (pueblos pre-romanos en la actual provincia de Castellón)." *Zephyrus* 19-20:115-42.
Fita, F. 1911. "Inscripciones ibéricas y romanas de la diócesis de Sigüenza." *Boletín de la Real Academia de la Historia* 58:325-31.
Flacelière, R., and É. Chambry. 1973. *Plutarque: Vies.* Vol. 8, *Sertorius-Eumène, Agésilas-Pompée.* Paris.
Fletcher Valls, D. 1941. "El poblado ibérico de San Miguel de Liria." *Atlantis* 16:172-78.
Fornara, C. W. 1992. Review of K. S. Sacks, *Diodorus Siculus and the First Century* (Princeton, 1990). *CP* 87:383-88.
Fraccaro, P. 1934. "I 'decem stipendia' e le 'leges annales' repubblicane." In *Per il XIV Centenario delle Pandette e del Codice di Giustiniano,* 475-503. Pavia.
Frassinetti, P. 1962. "Su alcuni frammenti delle 'Historiae' di Sallustio." *Athenaeum* 40:93-102.
―――. 1972. "Sisenna e la guerra sociale." *Athenaeum* 50:78-113.
―――. 1975. "I fatti di Spagna nel libro II delle 'Historiae' di Sallustio." *StudUrb (B)* 49.1:381-98.
Frazier, F. 1987. "A propos de la composition des couples dans les 'Vies parallèles' de Plutarque." *RPh* 61:65-75.
Frier, B. W. 1971. "Sulla's Propaganda and the Collapse of the Cinnan Republic." *AJP* 92:585-604.
Frost, F. J. 1980. *Plutarch's Themistocles: A Historical Commentary.* Princeton.
Foucart, P. 1906. "Les campagnes de M. Antonius Creticus contre les pirates, 74-71." *JS* 4:569-81.
Gabba, E. 1954. "Le origini della guerra sociale e la vita politica romana dopo l'88 a.C." *Athenaeum* 32:41-114, 293-345 = *Esercito e società* 193-345.
―――. 1956. *Appiano e la storia delle guerre civili.* Firenze.
―――. 1958. *Appiani Bellorum civilium liber primus: Introduzione, testo critico e commento con traduzione e indici.* Firenze.
―――. 1960. "Senati in esilio." *BIDR* 32:221-32 = *Esercito e società* 427-41.
―――. 1972. "Mario e Silla." *ANRW* I.1:765-805.
―――. 1973. *Esercito e società nella tarda repubblica romana.* Firenze.
―――. 1979. "Veterani di Metello Pio ad Alba Fucens?" *Revista de la Universidad Complutense de Madrid* 28, no. 118 = *Homenaje a García y Bellido* 4:61-63.
―――. 1981. "True History and False History in Classical Antiquity." *JRS* 71:50-62.
―――. 1990. Review of P. O. Spann, *Quintus Sertorius and the Legacy of Sulla* (Fayetteville, Ark., 1987). *Athenaeum* 78:578-79.
Gaggero, G. 1976. "Sertorio e gli Iberi." In *Contributi di storia antica in onore di Albino Garzetti,* 125-56. Pubblicazioni dell'Istituto di Storia Antica e Scienze Ausiliarie della Università di Genova, 14. Genova.

Galsterer, H. 1971. *Untersuchungen zum römischen Städtewesen auf der Iberischen Halbinsel.* Madrid.
Gamer, G., and T. Ortego y Frías. 1969. "Neue Betrachtungen am römischen Lager bei Almazán (Prov. Soria)." *MDAI(M)* 10:172–84.
Garbugino, G. 1978. "Il I libro delle *Historiae* di Sallustio in Nonio Marcello." *Studi Noniani* 5:39–94.
———. 1986. "Note al II libro delle *Historiae* di Sallustio." *Studi Noniani* 11:31–58.
García y Bellido, A. 1964. "Mercenarios y auxilia africanos en Espana en la antigüedad." *Numisma* 14:9–16.
———. 1972. "Die Latinisierung Hispaniens." *ANRW* I.1:462–500.
García Merino, C. 1976. *Población y poblamiento en la Hispania romana: El Conventus Cluniensis.* Valladolid.
García Mora, F. 1989. "Quintus Sertorius: Propuesta para sus primeros años de actividad." *Studia Historica: Historia Antigua* 7:85–96.
———. 1990. "Quinto Sertorio: 100–98 a.C. *Triennium sine armis?*" *Florentia Iliberritana* 1:137–45.
García Moreno, L. A. 1992. "Paradoxography and Political Ideals in Plutarch's *Sertorius.*" In *Plutarch and the Historical Tradition*, edited by P. A. Stadter, 132–58. London and New York.
———. 1992. "Plutarco, *Sertorius*, 8.2–3 y los orígenes de la geografía paradoxográfica latina." In *Estudios sobre Plutarco: Paisaje y naturaleza*, edited by J. García López and E. Calderón Dorda, 27–35. Madrid.
Geiger, J. 1975. "Zum Bild Julius Caesars in der römischen Kaiserzeit." *Historia* 24:444–53.
———. 1979. "Munatius Rufus and Thrasea Paetus on Cato the Younger." *Athenaeum* 57:48–72.
———. 1981. "Plutarch's Parallel Lives: The Choice of Heroes." *Hermes* 109:85–104.
———. 1985. *Cornelius Nepos and Ancient Political Biography.* Stuttgart.
———. 1988. "Nepos and Plutarch: From Latin to Greek Political Biography." *ICS* 13.2:245–56.
Gelzer, M. 1932. "Hat Sertorius in seinem Vertrag mit Mithradates die Provinz Asia abgetreten?" *Philologische Wochenschrift* 52:185–92 [1129–36] = *Kleine Schriften* 2:139–45.
———. 1941. "Cn. Pompeius Strabo und der Aufstieg seines Sohnes Magnus." *Abhandlungen der Preussischen Akademie der Wissenschaften, philosophisch-historische Klasse*, 1941, no. 14 = *Kleine Schriften* 2:106–38.
———. 1943. "Das erste Consulat des Pompeius und die Übertragung der grossen Imperien." *Abhandlungen der Preussischen Akademie der Wissenschaften, philosophisch-historische Klasse*, 1943, no. 1 = *Kleine Schriften* 2:146–89.
———. 1959. *Pompeius.* 2d ed. München.
———. 1962–64. *Kleine Schriften.* Edited by H. Strasburger and C. Meier. 3 vols. Wiesbaden.
Georgiadou, A. 1988. "The *Lives of the Caesars* and Plutarch's Other *Lives.*" *ICS* 13.2:349–56.
Gianfrotta, P. A. 1982. "Lentulo Augure e le anfore laietane." *Tituli* 4:475–79.
Gil Farrés, O. 1966. *La moneda hispánica en la edad antigua.* Madrid.
Gill, C. 1983. "The Question of Character-Development: Plutarch and Tacitus." *CQ* 33:469–87.
Gillis, D. 1969. "Sertorius." *RIL* 103:711–27.
Glew, D. G. 1977. "Mithridates Eupator and Rome: A Study of the Background of the First Mithridatic War." *Athenaeum* 55:380–405.
———. 1981. "Between the Wars: Mithridates Eupator and Rome, 85–73 B.C." *Chiron* 11:109–30.

Gómez-Moreno, M. 1949. *Misceláneas: Historia, arte, arqueología*. Vol. 1, *La antigüedad*. Madrid.
———. 1962. *La escritura bástulo-turdetana (primitiva hispánica)*. Madrid.
Gomme, A. W. 1956. *A Historical Commentary on Thucydides*. Vol. 1. Oxford.
González Blanco, A. 1984. "El hambre de Calahorra de año 72 a.C." In *Calahorra: Bimilenario de su fundación*, 207–15. Madrid.
Gozalbes, E. 1991. "La imagen de los *mauri* en Roma (siglos III–II a. de C.)." *Latomus* 50:38–55.
Grasmück, E. L. 1978. *Exilium: Untersuchungen zur Verbannung in der Antike*. Paderborn.
Greenhalgh, P. A. L. 1980. *Pompey: The Roman Alexander*. London.
Grispo, R. 1952. "Dalla Mellaria a Calagurra." *NRS* 36:189–225.
Grueber, H. A. 1910. *Coins of the Roman Republic in the British Museum*. 3 vols. London.
Gruen, E. S. 1966. "The Dolabellae and Sulla." *AJP* 87:385–99.
———. 1966. "The Quaestorship of Norbanus." *CP* 61:105–7.
———. 1966. "Political Prosecutions in the 90's B.C." *Historia* 15:32–64.
———. 1968. *Roman Politics and the Criminal Courts, 149–78 B.C.* Cambridge, Mass.
———. 1971. "Pompey, Metellus Pius, and the Trials of 70–69 B.C.: The Perils of Schematism." *AJP* 92:1–16.
———. 1974. *The Last Generation of the Roman Republic*. Berkeley.
Hackl, U. 1988. "Die Gründung der Provinz Gallia Narbonensis im Spiegel von Ciceros Rede für Fonteius." *Historia* 37:253–56.
Hahn, I. 1964. "Appien et le cercle de Sénèque." *AAntHung* 12:169–206.
———. 1970. "Appianus Tacticus." *AAntHung* 18:293–306.
———. 1972. "Appian und Hannibal." *AAntHung* 20:95–121.
———. 1974–75. "Appians Darstellung der sullanischen Diktatur." *ACD* 10–11:111–20.
———. 1982. "Appian und seine Quellen." In *Romanitas-Christianitas*, 251–76. Berlin and New York.
Hall, U. 1972. "Appian, Plutarch, and the Tribunician Elections of 123 B.C." *Athenaeum* 50:3–35.
Hamilton, J. R. 1969. *Plutarch, Alexander: A Commentary*. Oxford.
Hansen, G. C. 1985. "Das Datum der Schlacht bei Vercellae." *Klio* 67:588.
Harmand, J. 1967. *L'armée et le soldat à Rome, de 107 à 50 avant notre ère*. Paris.
Harris, W. V. 1976. "The Development of the Quaestorship, 267–81 B.C." *CQ* 26:92–106.
Hauler, E. 1886. "Ein neues Palimpsestfragment zu Sallusts Historien." *WS* 8:315–30.
———. 1887. "Die Orleaner Palimpsestfragmente zu Sallusts Historien." *WS* 9:25–50.
———. 1924–25. "Zu den Orleaner Bruchstücken des III. Buches von Sallusts Historien." *WS* 44:188–210.
Havas, L. 1968. "Mithridate et son plan d'attaque contre l'Italie." *ACD* 4:13–25.
———. 1974. "Catilina en Hispania ulterieur?" *WZRostock* 23:229–32.
———. 1985. "Geschichtsphilosophische Interpretationsmöglichkeiten bei Cornelius Nepos." *Klio* 67:502–6.
Hayne, L. 1972. "M. Lepidus (cos. 78): A Reappraisal." *Historia* 21:661–68.
———. 1990. "Livy and Pompey." *Latomus* 49:435–42.
Helmbold, W. C., and E. N. O'Neill. 1959. *Plutarch's Quotations*. N.p.
Heurgon, J. 1953. "Tarquitius Priscus et l'organisation de l'ordre des haruspices sous l'empereur Claude." *Latomus* 12:403–17.
Hill, H. 1932. "Sulla's New Senators in 81 B.C." *CQ* 26:170–77.
Hillard, T. W. 1987. "Plutarch's Late-Republican Lives: Between the Lines." *Antichthon* 21:19–48.
Hillman, T. P. 1990. "Pompeius and the Senate: 77–71." *Hermes* 118:444–54.

———. 1992. "Plutarch and the First Consulship of Pompeius and Crassus." *Phoenix* 46:124–37.
Hinard, F. 1985. *Les proscriptions de la Rome républicaine*. Paris and Rome.
———. 1990. Review of P. O. Spann, *Quintus Sertorius and the Legacy of Sulla* (Fayetteville, Ark., 1987). *Latomus* 49:213–15.
———. 1991. "Philologie, prosopographie et histoire à propos de Lucius Fabius Hispaniensis." *Historia* 40:113–19.
Hine, H. M. 1978. "Livy's Judgement on Marius (Seneca, *Natural Questions* 5.18.4; Livy, *Periocha* 80)." *LCM* 3:83–88.
Hirzel, R. 1912. *Plutarch*. Leipzig.
Historia de Castilla y León. Vol. 1, *La prehistoria del valle del Duero*. 1985. Valladolid.
Holder, A. 1896–1922. *Alt-celtischer Sprachschatz*. 3 vols. Leipzig.
Holmes, T. R. 1923. *The Roman Republic and the Founder of the Empire*. Vol. 1. Oxford.
Hose, M. 1992. "C. Sulpicius Galba als griechischer Historiker: zu FGrHist 92." *ZPE* 92:151–52.
de Hoz, J. 1986. "La epigrafía celtibérica." In *Reunión sobre Epigrafía hispánica de época romano-republicana, Zaragoza, 1–3 de diciembre de 1983: Actas*, 43–102. Zaragoza.
Hübner, E. 1893. *Monumenta linguae Ibericae*. Berlin.
Huss, W. 1985. *Geschichte der Karthager*. München.
Jacob, P. 1988. "L'Ebre de Jérôme Carcopino." *Gerión* 6:187–222.
Jal, P. 1962. "La rôle des Barbares dans les guerres civiles de Rome, de Sylla à Vespasien." *Latomus* 21:8–48.
———. 1967. *Florus: Oeuvres*. 2 vols. Paris.
Jimeno, A. 1980. *Epigrafía romana de la provincia de Soria*. [Soria.]
Jones, C. P. 1966. "The Teacher of Plutarch." *HSCP* 71:205–13.
———. 1966. "Towards a Chronology of Plutarch's Works." *JRS* 56:61–74.
———. 1971. *Plutarch and Rome*. Oxford.
Júdice Gamito, T. 1986. "The *Oppidum* of Segóvia (Elvas, Portugal) and the Decisive Battle between Metellus and Hirtuleius, Sertorius' Quaestor in Hispania Ulterior." *BIAL* 23:17–27.
Kaibel, G. 1885. "Antike Windrosen." *Hermes* 20:579–624.
Kaltwasser, J. F. 1799–1806. *Plutarch: Lebensbeschreibungen*. Revised by H. Floerke, 1913. Vol. 4, *Nikias–Crassus, Sertorius–Eumenes, Agesilaos–Pompeius, Alexandros–Caesar*. Reprinted München, 1964.
Katz, B. R. 1975. "The First Fruits of Sulla's March." *AC* 44:100–125.
———. 1976. "Studies on the Period of Cinna and Sulla." *AC* 45:497–549.
———. 1976. "The Siege of Rome in 87 B.C." *CP* 71:328–36.
———. 1977. "Caesar Strabo's Struggle for the Consulship—and More." *RhM* 120:45–63.
———. 1979. "The Selection of L. Cornelius Merula." *RhM* 122:162–66.
———. 1981 [1984]. "Sertorius, Caesar, and Sallust." *AAntHung* 29:285–313 = *Helios* 11 (1984) 9–46.
———. 1981. "Sallust and Varro." *Maia* 33:111–22.
———. 1982. "Sallust and Pompey." *RSA* 12:75–83.
———. 1983. "Notes on Sertorius." *RhM* 126:44–68.
———. 1983. "Sertorius' Overlooked Correspondent?" *RhM* 126:359–62.
———. 1985. "Varro, Sallust, and the *Pius aut de pace*." *C&M* 36:127–58.
Keaveney, A. 1978. "Pompeius Strabo's Second Consulship." *CQ* 28:240–41.
———. 1979. "Sulla, Sulpicius and Caesar Strabo." *Latomus* 38:451–60.
———. 1980. "Young Sulla and the *Decem Stipendia*." *RFIC* 108:165–73.
———. 1981. "Four Puzzling Passages in Appian." *GIF* 33:247–50.
———. 1982. "Young Pompey: 106–79 B.C." *AC* 51:111–39.

———. 1982. "Sulla and Italy." *CS* 19:499–544.
———. 1982. *Sulla: The Last Republican*. London and Canberra.
———. 1983. "What Happened in 88?" *Eirene* 20:53–86.
———. 1984. "Who Were the Sullani?" *Klio* 66:114–50.
———. 1984. "A Note on Servius, *Ad Aeneid.* 7, 637." *Philologus* 128:138–39.
———. 1992. *Lucullus: A Life*. London and New York.
Keaveney, A., and J. Madden. 1983. "Metellus Pius: The Evidence of Livy, *Epitome* 76." *Eranos* 81:87–51.
Keay, S. J. 1988. *Roman Spain*. Berkeley and London.
Kehoe, D. 1984–85. "Tacitus and Sallustius Crispus." *CJ* 80:247–54.
Keyser, P. T. 1991. *Geography and Ethnography in Sallust*. Diss. Univ. of Colorado, Boulder.
Kidd, I. G. 1988. *Posidonius*. Vol. 2 (in two volumes), *The Commentary*. Cambridge.
Kiene, A. 1845. *Der römische Bundesgenossenkrieg*. Leipzig.
Klotz, A. 1909. "Zur Litteratur der Exempla und zur Epitoma Livii." *Hermes* 44:198–214.
———. 1910. *Cäsarstudien, nebst einer Analyse der Strabonischen Beschreibung von Gallien und Britannien*. Leipzig and Berlin.
———. 1913. "Die Epitoma des Livius." *Hermes* 48:542–57.
———. 1936. "Zu den Periochae des Livius." *Philologus* 91:67–88.
———. 1938. "De Plutarchi vitae Caesarianae fontibus (Tanusius)." *Mnemosyne*, ser. 3, 6:313–19.
Knapp, R. C. 1977. *Aspects of the Roman Experience in Spain, 201–100 B.C.* Valladolid.
———. 1983. *Roman Córdoba*. Berkeley and Los Angeles.
Koch, M. 1987. "Neue römische Inschriften aus Carthago Nova III." *MDAI(M)* 28:127–34.
———. 1989. "Ein neuer Beamtenname aus dem republikanischen Hispanien." *Chiron* 19:27–35.
Konrad, C. F. 1978 [1982]. "Afranius Imperator." *HAnt* 8:67–76.
———. 1987. "Some Friends of Sertorius." *AJP* 108:519–27.
———. 1988. "Why Not Sallust on the Eighties?" *AHB* 2:12–15.
———. 1988. "Metellus and the Head of Sertorius." *Gerión* 6:253–61.
———. 1989. "Cotta off Mellaria and the Identities of Fufidius." *CP* 84:119–29.
———. 1990–91. Review of P. O. Spann, *Quintus Sertorius and the Legacy of Sulla* (Fayetteville, Ark., 1987). *CJ* 86:83–85.
———. 1994. "Segovia and Segontia." *Historia* 43, in press.
———. 1995. "A New Chronology of the Sertorian War." *Athenaeum* 83, in press.
———. In press. "Plutarch on Roman Forces in the Sertorian War." In *Homenaje al Profesor Blázquez*, vol. 5. Madrid.
Kornemann, E. 1896. "Die historische Schriftstellerei des C. Asinius Pollio, zugleich ein Beitrag zur Quellenforschung über Appian und Plutarch." *Jahrbücher für classische Philologie*, Suppl. 22:557–691.
Kromayer, J., and G. Veith. 1928. *Heerwesen und Kriegführung der Griechen und Römer*. München.
Kühne, H. 1962. "Zur Teilnahme von Sklaven und Freigelassenen an den Bürgerkriegen der Freien im 1. Jahrhundert v.u.Z. in Rom." *StudClas* 4:189–209.
Laffi, U. 1967. "Il mito di Silla." *Athenaeum* 45:177–213, 255–77.
———. 1992. "La provincia della Gallia Cisalpina." *Athenaeum* 80:5–23.
Laffranque, M. 1962 [1964]. "Poseidonios historien: Un épisode significatif de la première guerre de Mithridate." *Pallas* 11:103–13.
Lange, L. 1863–71. *Römische Alterthümer*. 2d ed. 3 vols. Berlin.
La Penna, A. 1963. "Le *Historiae* di Sallustio e l'interpretazione della crisi repubblicana." *Athenaeum* 41:201–74.

———. 1963. "Per la ricostruzione delle 'Historiae' di Sallustio." *SIFC* 35:5–68.
———. 1969. *Sallustio e la rivoluzione romana*. 2d ed. Milano.
———. 1987. "Cesare secondo Plutarco." In *Plutarco, Vite parallele: Alessandro–Cesare*, edited by D. Magnino, 217–306. Milano.
Lara Peinado, F. 1970. "La 'Ilerda' romana: Crítica histórica y relación de materiales romanos de Lérida." In *XI Congreso Nacional de Arqueología, Mérida 1968*, 627–62. Zaragoza.
Lendle, O. 1967. "Ciceros ὑπόμνημα περὶ τῆς ὑπατείας." *Hermes* 95:90–109.
Lengle, J. 1931. "Die Verurteilung der römischen Feldherrn von Arausio." *Hermes* 66:302–16.
Leo, F. 1901. *Die griechisch-römische Biographie nach ihrer litterarischen Form*. Leipzig.
Leopold, E. H. G. 1795. *Plutarchi Marius, Sulla, Lucullus et Sertorius*. Leipzig.
Lepore, E. 1950. "I due frammenti Rylands delle Storie di Sallustio." *Athenaeum* 28:280–91.
Levick, B. M. 1989. "Claudius Speaks: Two Imperial Contretemps." *Historia* 38:112–16.
Lewis, R. G. 1974. "Catulus and the Cimbri, 102 B.C." *Hermes* 102:90–109.
———. 1991. "Sulla's Autobiography: Scope and Economy." *Athenaeum* 79:509–19.
Linden, E. 1896. *De bello civili Sullano*. Diss. Freiburg.
Linderski, J. 1975. "Two Quaestorships." *CP* 70:35–38.
Lintott, A. W. 1968. "*Nundinae* and the Chronology of the Late Roman Republic." *CQ* 18:189–94.
———. 1971. "The Offices of C. Flavius Fimbria in 86/85 B.C." *Historia* 20:696–701.
Luce, T. J. 1961. "Appian's Magisterial Terminology." *CP* 56:21–28.
———. 1968. "Political Propaganda on Roman Republican Coins, circa 92–82 B.C." *AJA* 72:25–39.
———. 1989. "Ancient Views on the Causes of Bias in Historical Writing." *CP* 84:16–31.
Magie, D. 1950. *Roman Rule in Asia Minor, to the End of the Third Century after Christ*. 2 vols. Princeton.
Magnino, D. 1987. *Plutarco, Vite parallele: Alessandro–Cesare*. Milano.
Malavolta, M. 1977. "La carriera di L. Afranio (cos. 60 a.C.)." *MGR* 5:251–303.
Malitz, J. 1972. "C. Aurelius Cotta cos. 75 und seine Rede in Sallusts Historien." *Hermes* 100:359–86.
———. 1983. *Die Historien des Poseidonios*. München.
Mangas Manjarrés, J. 1970. "El papel de la diplomacía romana en la conquista de la península ibérica (226–19 a.C.)." *Hispania* 30:485–513.
Mariner Bigorra, S. 1983. "Hispanische Latinität und sprachliche Kontakte im römischen Hispanien." *ANRW* II.29.2:819–52.
Mariotti, S. 1975. "Sall. 'Hist.' III 82 M." *StudUrb* (B) 49.1:399–404.
Maróti, E. 1961. "Die Rolle der Seeräuberei zur Zeit der römischen Bürgerkriege." *Altertum* 7:32–41.
———. 1971. "On the Problem of M. Antonius Creticus' *imperium infinitum*." *AAntHung* 19:252–72.
———. 1971. "Die Rolle der Seeräuber in der Zeit der Mithridatischen Kriege." In *Ricerche storiche ed economiche in memoria di Corrado Barbagallo*, 481–93. Napoli.
Marquardt, J. 1886. *Das Privatleben der Römer*. 2d ed. Leipzig.
Marshall, B. A. 1977. "Two Court Cases in the Late Second Century B.C." *AJP* 98:417–23.
———. 1977. "Another Rigged Voting Tablet? The Case of Cn. Domitius Ahenobarbus against D. Iunius Silanus in 104 B.C." *LCM* 2:11–12.
Martín, G., and M. Gil-Mascarell. 1969. *La romanización en el campo de Liria*. Valencia.

Martin, H., Jr. 1960. "The Concept of *Prāotēs* in Plutarch's *Lives*." *GRBS* 3:65–73.
Martín Bueno, M. A. 1970. "Yacimiento ibero-romano, en Botorrita (Zaragoza)." In *XI Congreso Nacional de Arqueología, Mérida 1968*, 685–92. Zaragoza.
Martín Bueno, M. A., and M. L. Cancela Ramírez de Arellano. 1984. "Arqueología clásica de Calahorra y su entorno." In *Calahorra: Bimilenario de su fundación*, 77–91. Madrid.
Martín Valls, R. 1966. "La circulación monetaria ibérica." *BSEAA* 32:207–366.
———. 1985. "Segunda edad de hierro." In *Historia de Castilla y León*, 1:104–31. Valladolid.
Martínez Gázquez, J. 1974. *La campaña de Catón en Hispania*. Barcelona.
Martino, P. 1986. *Plutarco: Sertorio*. Palermo.
———. 1990. "La morte di Sertorio: Orosio e la tradizione liviana." *QS* 16:77–101.
Mason, H. J. 1974. *Greek Terms for Roman Institutions: A Lexicon and Analysis*. Toronto.
Mateu y Llopis, F. 1947. "Identificación de cecas ibéricas pirenáicas: Ensayo de localización de topónimos monetarios altoaragoneses." *Pirineos* 3.5:39–77.
———. 1951. "Sobre la localización de Lauro." *Ampurias* 13:218–19.
Mattingly, H. B. 1975. "The Consilium of Cn. Pompeius Strabo in 89 B.C." *Athenaeum* 53:262–66.
———. 1979. "L. Julius Caesar, Governor of Macedonia." *Chiron* 9:147–67.
Mauny, R. 1955. "La navigation sur les côtes du Sahara pendant l'antiquité." *REA* 57:92–101.
Maurenbrecher, B. 1891–93. *C. Sallusti Crispi Historiarum reliquiae*. Fasciculus 1, *Prolegomena*. Fasciculus 2, *Fragmenta*. Leipzig.
———. 1902. "Bericht über die Litteratur zu C. Sallustius Crispus 1878–1898 (Fortsetzung). VII: Die Historiae Sallusts." *Bursians Jahresbericht* 113:228–72.
Mayer, M. 1910. *Vexillum und Vexillarius: Ein Beitrag zur Geschichte des römischen Heerwesens*. Diss. Freiburg.
McDonald, A. H. 1953. Review of T. R. S. Broughton, *The Magistrates of the Roman Republic*, vols. 1–2 (New York, 1951–52). *JRS* 43:142–45.
———. 1960. "On Emending Livy's Fourth Decade." *PCPS* 6:43–48.
McGing, B. C. 1984. "The Date of the Outbreak of the Third Mithridatic War." *Phoenix* 38:12–18.
———. 1986. *The Foreign Policy of Mithridates VI Eupator, King of Pontus*. Leiden.
McGushin, P. 1992. *Sallust: The Histories*. Vol. 1. Oxford.
Menéndez Pidal, R. 1926. *Orígenes del español: Estado lingüístico de la Península Ibérica hasta el siglo XI*. 3d ed., 1950. Madrid.
———. 1952. *Toponimia prerrománica hispana*. Madrid.
Merkelbach, R. 1990. "Hat der Bithynische Erbfolgekrieg im Jahre 74 oder 73 begonnen?" *ZPE* 81:97–100.
Mewaldt, J. 1907. "Selbstzitate in den Biographieen Plutarchs." *Hermes* 42:564–78.
Meyer, Ed. 1879. *Geschichte des Königreichs Pontos*. Leipzig.
Miltner, F. 1940. "Der Germanenangriff auf Italien in den Jahren 102/1 v. Chr." *Klio* 33:289–307.
Moeller, W. O. 1975. "Once More the One-Eyed Man against Rome." *Historia* 24:402–10.
Momigliano, A. 1971. *The Development of Greek Biography*. Cambridge, Mass.
———. 1972. "Tradition and the Classical Historian." *H&T* 11:279–93.
———. 1978. "Greek Historiography." *H&T* 17:1–28.
Mommsen, Th. 1860. *Geschichte des römischen Münzwesens*. Berlin.
———. 1861. "Zu den Scholien der virgilischen Georgica." *RhM* 16:442–53 = *Gesammelte Schriften* 7 (Berlin, 1909) 505–8.
———. 1887–88. *Römisches Staatsrecht*. 3 vols. (vols. 1–2: 3d ed.). Leipzig.
———. 1912–17. *Römische Geschichte*. 11th ed. 5 vols. Berlin.

Montenegro Duque, A. 1960. "Toponimia latina de España." In *Enciclopedia lingüística hispánica*, 1:501–30. Madrid.
Monteverde, J. L. 1939. "Un denario ibérico de 'Segotius' (Sigüenza)." *Boletín de la Comisión Provincial de Monumentos Históricos y Artísticos de Burgos, Institución Fernán González* 5.67:225–27.
Morgan, M. G. 1969. "The Roman Conquest of the Balearic Isles." *CSCA* 2:217–31.
Morr, J. 1926. *Die Quellen von Strabons drittem Buch*. Philologus Suppl. 18.3. Leipzig.
Müller, C., and T. Müller. 1841–51. *Fragmenta Historicorum Graecorum*. 4 vols. Paris.
Müller, C. 1902. *Studien zur Geschichte der Erdkunde im Altertum*. Diss. Breslau.
Münzer, F. 1932. "Norbanus." *Hermes* 67:220–36.
Neira Jiménez, M. L. 1986. "Aportaciones al estudio de las fuentes literarias antiguas de Sertorio." *Gerión* 4:189–211.
Neuhausen, K. A. 1979. "Ciceros Vater, der Augur Scävola und der junge Cicero." *WS* 13:76–87.
Nicolet, C. 1966–74. *L'ordre équestre à l'époque républicaine (312–43 av. J.-C.)*. 2 vols. Paris.
———. 1967. "Tribuni militum a populo." *MEFR* 79:29–76.
———. 1967. "Arpinum, Aemilius Scaurus et les Tullii Cicerones." *REL* 45:276–304.
———. 1969. "Armée et societé à Rome sous la république: à propos de l'ordre équestre." In *Problèmes de la guerre à Rome*, edited by J. P. Brisson, 117–56. Paris and Den Haag.
Nissen, H. 1883–1902. *Italische Landeskunde*. 2 vols. Berlin.
Oakley, S. P. 1985. "Single Combat in the Roman Republic." *CQ* 35:392–410.
Ogilvie, R. M. 1984. "Titi Livi Lib. XCI." *PCPS* n.s. 30:116–25.
Oikonomides, A. N. 1982. *Hanno the Carthaginian: Periplus*. Chicago.
———. 1989. "The Portrait of King Philip II of Macedonia." *AncW* 20:5–16.
———. 1989. "The Elusive Portrait of Antigonos I, the 'One-Eyed' King of Macedonia." *AncW* 20:17–20.
Oliver, R. P. 1947. "'New Fragments' of Latin Authors in Perotti's *Cornucopiae*." *TAPA* 78:376–424.
Olmos, R. 1979. *Cástulo, II*. Madrid.
Olshausen, E. 1972. "Mithradates VI. und Rom." *ANRW* I.1:806–15.
van Ooteghem, J. 1954. *Pompée le Grand, bâtisseur d'Empire*. Bruxelles.
———. 1964. *Caius Marius*. Namur.
———. 1967. *Les Caecilii Metelli de la République*. Namur.
Ormerod, H. 1924. *Piracy in the Ancient World: An Essay in Mediterranean History*. Liverpool and London.
d'Ors, A. 1978. "Un episodio jurídico de la guerra sertoriana." *AHDE* 48:269–76.
do Paço, A., and L. J. Baçao. 1966. "Castelo da Lousa, Mourão (Portugal): Una fortificación romana de la margen izquierda del Guadiana." *AEA* 39:167–83.
Padró, J., and C. Piedrafita. 1987. "Les étapes du contrôle des Pyrénées par Rome." *Latomus* 46:356–62.
Pais, E. 1916. "I dodici Romani fatti dichiarare pubblici nemici da Silla nell'88 a.C." *Atti della Reale Accademia di Archeologia, Lettere e Belle Arti di Napoli* 4.1:67–72.
Pareti, L. 1952–61. *Storia di Roma e del mondo romano*. 6 vols. Torino.
Passerini, A. 1934. "Caio Mario come uomo politico." *Athenaeum* 12:109–43, 257–97, 348–80 = *Studi su Caio Mario* 13–194.
———. 1941. *Caio Mario*. Roma.
———. 1971. *Studi su Caio Mario*. Milano.
Pastor Muñoz, M. 1989. "Société, religion et épigraphie dans le *municipium* de Cástulo." *Latomus* 48:632–41.
Paul, G. M. 1984. *A Historical Commentary on Sallust's Bellum Jugurthinum*. Liverpool.

Pecere, O. 1976. "Un frammento di Sallustio tra propaganda politica e polemica storiografica." *RFIC* 10:399–417.
———. 1978. "Note sui frammenti di Sallustio." *SIFC* 50:131–60.
Pelling, C. B. R. 1979. "Plutarch's Method of Work in the Roman Lives." *JHS* 99:74–96.
———. 1980. "Plutarch's Adaptation of His Source-Material." *JHS* 100:127–40.
———. 1984. "Plutarch on the Gallic Wars." *CB* 60:88–103.
———. 1985. "Plutarch and Catiline." *Hermes* 113:311–29.
———. 1986. "Plutarch and Roman Politics." In *Past Perspectives: Studies in Greek and Roman Historical Writing*, edited by I. S. Moxon, J. D. Smart, and A. J. Woodman, 159–87. Cambridge.
———. 1986. "'Synkrisis' in Plutarch's Lives." In *Miscellanea Plutarchea: Atti del I Convegno di Studi su Plutarco, Roma, 23 novembre 1985*, edited by F. E. Brenk and I. Gallo, 83–96. Ferrara.
———. 1988. "Aspects of Plutarch's Characterization." *ICS* 13.2:257–74.
———. 1988. *Plutarch: Life of Antony*. Cambridge.
———. 1992. "Plutarch and Thucydides." In *Plutarch and the Historical Tradition*, edited by P. A. Stadter, 10–40. London and New York.
Pena, M. J. 1981. "Contribución al estudio del culto de Diana en Hispania, I: Templos y fuentes epigráficas." In *La religión romana en Hispania*, 47–57. Madrid.
Pereira Menaut, G. 1979. *Inscripciones romanas de Valentia*. Valencia.
Perl, G. 1963. "Zu Sallust Hist. II 93." *WZRostock* 12:269–73.
———. 1965. "Die Rede Cottas in Sallusts Historien." *Philologus* 109:75–82.
———. 1967. "Sallusts Todesjahr." *Klio* 48:97–105.
———. 1967. "Die Rede Cottas in Sallusts Historien (Fortsetzung)." *Philologus* 111:137–41.
———. 1967. "Die Zuverlässigkeit der Buchangaben in den Zitaten Priscians." *Philologus* 111:283–88.
———. 1968. "Zur Chronologie der Königreiche Bithynia, Pontos und Bosporos." In *Studien zur Geschichte und Philosophie des Altertums: Kongress für klassische Philologie, Budapest 1965*, 299–330. Amsterdam.
———. 1969. "Der alte Codex der 'Historiae' Sallusts." *BIRT* 15:29–38.
———. 1970. "Die römischen Provinzbeamten in Cyrenae und Kreta zur Zeit der Republik." *Klio* 52:319–54.
———. 1971. "Die römischen Provinzbeamten in Cyrenae und Kreta zur Zeit der Republik: Nachträge zum Beitrag Klio 52, 1970, 319–354." *Klio* 53:369–79.
———. 1973. "Das Kompositionsprinzip der Historiae des Sallust (zu Hist. fr. 2., 42)." In *Actes de la XIIe Conference Internationale d'Études Classiques Eirene, Bucuresti 1972*, 317–37. Amsterdam.
Perrin, B. 1919. *Plutarch's Lives*. Vol. 8, *Sertorius and Eumenes, Phocion and Cato the Younger*. London and New York.
Peter, H. 1865. *Die Quellen Plutarchs in den Biographieen der Römer*. Halle.
———. 1906–14. *Historicorum Romanorum reliquiae*. 2 vols. (vol.1, 2d ed.). Leipzig.
Pfefferkorn, [K.?] 1851. "Der Kampf des Sertorius und der Spanier gegen Rom." *Programm des kgl. Paedagogiums zu Putbus*. Putbus.
Picard, C. 1920. "Fouilles de Délos (1910): Observations sur la société des Poseidoniastes de Bérytos et sur son histoire." *BCH* 44:263–311.
Plácido Suárez, D. 1989. "Sertorio." *Studia Historica: Historia Antiqua* 7:97–104.
Polman, G. H. 1974. "Chronological Biography and *Akmē* in Plutarch." *CP* 69:169–77.
Powell, J. G. F. 1990. "The Tribune Sulpicius." *Historia* 39:446–60.
Pozzi, E. 1913–14. "Studi sulla Guerra Civile Sillana." *AAT* 49:641–79.
Prieto Arciniega, A. 1987–88. "Un punto oscuro en la invasión romana de las Baleares: La piratería." *Habis* 18–19:271–75.

Radnitzky, H. 1908/9. "Plutarch's Quellen in der vita des Sertorius." *Jahresbericht über das K. K. Akademische Gymnasium in Wien 1908/9*, 3–19.
Radt, S. L. 1980. "Noch einmal Aischylos, Niobe Fr. 162 N² (278 M.)." *ZPE* 38:47–57.
———. 1988. "Οἱ (αἱ etc.) περὶ + acc. nominis proprii bei Strabon." *ZPE* 71:35–41.
Ramage, E. S. 1973. *Urbanitas: Ancient Sophistication and Refinement*. Norman.
Ramírez Sádaba, J. L. 1985. "Limitaciones inherentes a las fuentes literarias: Consequencias de la guerra sertoriana para Calagurris." *Gerión* 3:231–43.
Rawson, E. 1979. "L. Cornelius Sisenna and the Early First Century B.C." *CQ* 29:327–46.
———. 1987. "Sallust on the Eighties?" *CQ* 37:163–80.
Rebuffat, R. 1976. "Arva beata petamus arva divites et insulas." In *L'Italie préromaine et la Rome républicaine: Mélanges offerts à Jacques Heurgon*, 877–902. Paris.
Reeve, M. D. 1988. "The Transmission of Florus, *Epitoma de Tito Livio* and the *Periochae*." *CQ* 38:477–91.
———. 1991. "The Transmission of Florus and the *Periochae* Again." *CQ* 41:453–83.
Reinach, Th. 1895. *Mithradates Eupator, König von Pontos*. Rev. ed., translated by A. Goetz. Leipzig.
La religión romana en Hispania: Symposio organizado por el Instituto de Arqueología "Rodrigo Caro" del C.S.I.C. de 17 al 19 de diciembre de 1979. 1981. Madrid.
Richards, H. 1903. "Critical Notes on Plutarch's *Lives*." *CR* 17:333–39.
———. 1910. "Adversaria on Plutarch's *Lives*." *CQ* 4:11–22.
Richardson, J. S. 1986. *Hispaniae: Spain and the Development of Roman Imperialism, 218–82 B.C.* Cambridge.
———. 1989. Review of P. O. Spann, *Quintus Sertorius and the Legacy of Sulla* (Fayetteville, Ark., 1987). *JRS* 79:197.
Rijkhoek, K. G. 1992. *Studien zu Sertorius, 123–83 v. Chr.* Bonn.
Roberts, C. H. 1938. *Catalogue of Greek and Latin Papyri in the John Rylands Library at Manchester*. Vol. 3. Manchester.
Roddaz, J.-M. 1986. "Guerres civiles et romanisation dans la vallée de l'Ebre." *REA* 88:317–38.
Rodríguez Adrados, F. 1946. "La 'Fides' ibérica." *Emerita* 14:128–209.
Roldán Hervás, J. M. 1974. *Hispania y el ejército romano: Contribución a la historia social de la España antigua*. Salamanca.
———. 1975. *Itineraria hispana: Fuentes antiguas para el estudio de las vías romanas en la Península Ibérica*. Valladolid.
———. 1978. "La guerra civil entre Sertorio, Metelo y Pompeyo (82–72 a.C.)." In *Historia de España Antigua*, vol. 2, *Hispania Romana*, edited by J. M. Blázquez et al., 113–39. Madrid.
Romanitas-Christianitas: Untersuchungen zur Geschichte und Literatur der römischen Kaiserzeit, Johannes Straub zum 70. Geburtstag, edited by G. Wirth. 1982. Berlin and New York.
de Romilly, J. 1988. "Plutarch and Thucydides, or the Free Use of Quotations." *Phoenix* 42:22–34.
Rowland, R. J. 1966. "Numismatic Propaganda under Cinna." *TAPA* 97:407–19.
Rubinsohn, Z. 1981. "The Viriathic War and Its Roman Repercussions." *RSA* 11:161–204.
Ruiz de Arbulo Bayona, J. 1991. "Los inicios de la romanización en occidente: Los casos de Emporion y Tarraco." *Athenaeum* 79:459–93.
Ruschenbusch, E. 1993. "Der Endpunkt der Historien des Poseidonios." *Hermes* 121:70–76.
Russell, D. A. 1963. "Plutarch's Life of Coriolanus." *JRS* 53:21–28.
———. 1966. "On Reading Plutarch's *Lives*." *G&R* 13:139–54.
———. 1966. "Plutarch, 'Alcibiades' 1–16." *PCPS* 12:37–47.

———. 1975. *Plutarch*. London.
Sadée, E. 1939. "Sulla im Kimbernkrieg." *RhM* 88:43–52.
———. 1940. "Die strategischen Zusammenhänge des Kimbernkriegs 101 v. Chr. vom Einbruch in Venetien bis zur Schlacht bei Vercellae." *Klio* 33:225–34.
Salinas de Frías, M. 1986. *Conquista y romanización de Celtiberia*. Salamanca.
Sallmann, K. 1979. "De Pomponio Mela et Plinio maiore in Africa describenda discrepantibus." In *Africa et Roma. Acta omnium gentium ac nationum conventus Latinis litteris linguaeque fovendis, Dakar 13–16 April 1977, Leopold Sedar Senghor dicatum*, 164–73. Roma.
Salmon, E. T. 1958. Review of J. Zennari, *I Vercelli dei Celti nella Valle Padana* (Cremona, 1956). *Phoenix* 12:85–87.
———. 1964. "Sulla Redux." *Athenaeum* 42:60–79.
———. 1967. *Samnium and the Samnites*. Cambridge.
Sansone, D. 1981. "Totus Livius: Martial XIV, 190." *CB* 57:86–87.
———. 1988. "Notes on Plutarch: *Pericles* and *Fabius*." *ICS* 13.2:311–18.
———. 1990. Review of C. B. R. Pelling, *Plutarch: Life of Antony* (Cambridge, 1988). *CP* 85:329–32.
———. 1991. Review of P. A. Stadter, *A Commentary on Plutarch's Pericles* (Chapel Hill and London, 1989). *CP* 86:347–51.
Sartori, F. 1972. "Cinna e gli schiavi." In *Actes du Colloque 1971 sur l'Esclavage, Besançon*, 151–69. Paris.
Scardigli, B. 1970. "A proposito di due passi su Sertorio." *A&R* 15:174–81.
———. 1971. "Sertorio: Problemi cronologici." *Athenaeum* 49:229–70.
———. 1971. "Considerazioni sulle fonti della biografia plutarchea di Sertorio." *SIFC* 43:33–64.
———. 1974. "Sallustio, *Hist*. I 126 M. e Plutarco, *Sert*. 14, 6." *A&R* 19:48–55.
———. 1979. *Die Römerbiographien Plutarchs: Ein Forschungsbericht*. München.
———. 1983. *Grani Liciniani reliquiae*. Introduzione, commento storico e traduzione, in collaborazione con A. R. Berardi. Firenze.
———. 1990. Review of P. O. Spann, *Quintus Sertorius and the Legacy of Sulla* (Fayetteville, Ark., 1987). *Gnomon* 62:428–32.
Schmidt, P. L. 1968. *Iulius Obsequens und das Problem der Livius-Epitome: Ein Beitrag zur Geschichte der lateinischen Prodigienliteratur*. AAWW 1968, no. 5. Wiesbaden.
Schmoll, U. 1956. "Turma Salluitana: Einige Bemerkungen zur lateinischen Umschreibung hispanischer Eigennamen." *Glotta* 35:304–11.
———. 1959. *Die Sprachen der vorkeltischen Indogermanen Hispaniens und das Keltiberische*. Wiesbaden.
———. 1961. *Die südlusitanischen Inschriften*. Wiesbaden.
Scholz, U. W. 1989. "Catos Rede *de Indigetibus*." *RhM* 132:148–54.
Schovánek, J. G. 1972. "The Date of M. Octavius and His Lex Frumentaria." *Historia* 21:238–43.
Schüle, G. 1970. "Navegación primitiva y visibilidad de la tierra en el Mediterráneo." In *XI Congreso Nacional de Arqueología, Mérida 1968*, 449–62. Zaragoza.
Schulten, A. 1902–03. "Italische Namen und Stämme." *Klio* 2:167–93, 440–65, 3:235–67.
———. 1911. "Polybius und Posidonius über Iberien und die iberischen Kriege." *Hermes* 46:568–607.
———. 1926. *Sertorius*. Leipzig.
———. 1940. "Die Tyrsener in Spanien." *Klio* 33:73–102.
———. 1959–63. *Geografía y etnografía antiguas de la Península Ibérica*. 2 vols. Madrid.
Schulten, A., and P. Bosch Gimpera, eds. 1922–40. *Fontes Hispaniae Antiquae*. 5 vols. Barcelona.
Schulze, W. 1904. *Zur Geschichte lateinischer Eigennamen*. Berlin.

Schur, W. 1942. *Das Zeitalter des Marius und Sulla*. Klio Beiheft 46, N.F. 33. Leipzig.
———. 1943. *Sallust als Historiker*. Stuttgart.
Schwartz, Ed. 1931. "Einiges über Assyrien, Syrien, Koilesyrien." *Philologus* 86:373–99.
Scuderi, R. 1990. Review of C. B. R. Pelling, *Plutarch: Life of Antony* (Cambridge, 1988). *Athenaeum* 78:567–68.
Segre, M. 1927. "Le cognizioni di Giuba Mauritano sulle Isole Fortunate." *Rivista Geografica Italiana* 34:72–80.
Serra Ráfols, J. de C. 1941. "El poblado ibérico del Castellet de Banyoles." *Ampurias* 3:15–34.
Sherk, R. K. 1969. *Roman Documents from the Greek East: Senatus Consulta and Epistulae to the Age of Augustus*. Baltimore.
Sherwin-White, A. N. 1939. *The Roman Citizenship*. 2d ed., 1973. Oxford.
———. 1984. *Roman Foreign Policy in the East 168 B.C. to A.D. 1*. London.
Siles, J. 1986. "Sobre la epigrafía ibérica." In *Reunión sobre Epigrafía hispánica de época romano-republicana, Zaragoza, 1–3 de diciembre de 1983: Actas*, 17–42. Zaragoza.
Simon, H. 1962. *Roms Kriege in Spanien, 154–133 v. Chr.* Frankfurt.
Sintenis, C. 1881. *Plutarchi Vitae parallelae*. Vol. 3, *Nikias–Crassus, Sertorius–Eumenes, Agesilaos–Pompeius, Alexandros–Caesar*. 2d ed. Leipzig.
Smith, R. E. 1940. "Plutarch's Biographical Sources in the Roman Lives." *CQ* 34:1–10.
———. 1957. "The *Lex Plotia Agraria* and Pompey's Spanish Veterans." *CQ* 7:82–85.
———. 1958. *Service in the Post-Marian Roman Army*. Manchester.
———. 1960. "Pompey's Conduct in 80 and 77 B.C." *Phoenix* 14:1–13.
Smits, A. H. G. J. 1867. *De Quinto Sertorio*. Diss. Utrecht.
Sobeck, F. 1909. *Die Quaestoren der römischen Republik*. Diss. Breslau.
Soltau, W. 1899. "Appians Bürgerkriege." *Philologus* Suppl. 7:595–634.
Spann, P. O. 1976. *Quintus Sertorius: Citizen, Soldier, Exile*. Diss. Univ. of Texas, Austin.
———. 1977. "M. Perperna and Pompey's Spanish Expedition." *HAnt* 7:45–62.
———. 1977. "Sallust, Plutarch, and the 'Isles of the Blest.'" *Terrae Incognitae* 9:75–80.
———. 1981. "Lacobriga Expunged: Renaissance Forgeries and the Sertorian War." *TAPA* 111:229–35.
———. 1984. "Saguntum vs. Segontia." *Historia* 33:116–19.
———. 1986–87. "C., L. or M. Cotta and the 'Unspeakable' Fufidius: A Note on Sulla's *Res Publica Restituta*." *CJ* 82:306–9.
———. 1987. *Quintus Sertorius and the Legacy of Sulla*. Fayetteville, Ark.
Speidel, M. 1965. *Die equites singulares Augusti*. Bonn.
Spranger, P. 1958. "Zur Lokalisierung der Stadt Castulo und des Saltus Castulonensis." *Historia* 7:95–112.
Stadter, P. A. 1965. *Plutarch's Historical Methods: An Analysis of the Mulierum Virtutes*. Cambridge, Mass.
———. 1972. "The Structure of Livy's History." *Historia* 21:287–307.
———. 1975. "Plutarch's Comparison of Pericles and Fabius Maximus." *GRBS* 16:77–85.
———. 1983–84. "Searching for Themistocles." Review of F. J. Frost, *Plutarch's Themistocles: A Historical Commentary* (Princeton, 1980). *CJ* 79:356–63.
———. 1987. "The Rhetoric of Plutarch's *Pericles*." *AncSoc* 18:251–69.
———. 1988. "The Proems of Plutarch's *Lives*." *ICS* 13.2:275–95.
———. 1989. *A Commentary on Plutarch's Pericles*. Chapel Hill and London.
———. 1992. "Paradoxical Paradigms: Lysander and Sulla." In *Plutarch and the Historical Tradition*, edited by P. A. Stadter, 41–55. London and New York.
———, ed. 1992. *Plutarch and the Historical Tradition*. London and New York.
Stahl, W. 1907. *De bello Sertoriano*. Diss. Erlangen.

Starr, R. J. 1981. "The Scope and Genre of Velleius' History." *CQ* 31:162–74.
Stenten, F. L. G. 1969. *Ploutarchos' Leven van Sertorius*. Tekst, Nederlandsche Vertaling, Historisch Kommentaar. Diss. Nijmegen.
Stewart, R. L. 1987. *Sors et Provincia: Praetors and Quaestors in Republican Rome*. Diss. Duke Univ., Durham.
Stiefenhofer, M. A. 1915. *Die Echtheitsfrage der biographischen Synkriseis Plutarchs*. Diss. Giessen.
Stolle, F. 1912. *Das Lager und Heer der Römer*. Strasbourg.
Stoltz, C. 1929. *Zur relativen Chronologie der Parallelbiographien Plutarchs*. Lund.
Strasburger, H. 1965. "Poseidonios on Problems of the Roman Empire." *JRS* 55:40–53.
Suchet, L. G. 1828. *Mémoires du maréchal Suchet, Duc d'Albufera, sur ses campagnes en Espagne, depuis 1808 jusqu'en 1814, écrit par lui-même*. 2 vols., maps. Paris.
Sumner, G. V. 1964. "Manius or Mamercus?" *JRS* 54:41–48.
———. 1970. "Proconsuls and Provinciae in Spain, 218/7–196/5 B.C." *Arethusa* 3:85–102.
———. 1970. "The Truth about Velleius Paterculus: Prolegomena." *HSCP* 74:257–97.
———. 1973. *The Orators in Cicero's Brutus: Prosopography and Chronology*. Toronto.
———. 1977. "Notes on Provinciae in Spain (197–133 B.C.)." *CP* 72:126–30.
———. 1978. "Sulla's Career in the Nineties." *Athenaeum* 56:395–96.
Suolahti, J. 1955. *The Junior Officers of the Roman Army in the Republican Period: A Study in Social Structure*. Helsinki.
———. 1958. "The Council of L. Cornelius Lentulus Crus in the Year 49 B.C. (Ios. ant. 14.229; 238–239)." *Arctos* 2:152–63.
Sutherland, C. H. V. 1939. *The Romans in Spain, 217 B.C.–A.D. 117*. London.
Swain, S. C. R. 1988. "Plutarch's *Philopoimen and Flamininus*." *ICS* 13.2:335–48.
———. 1989. "Plutarch: Chance, Providence, and History." *AJP* 110:272–302.
———. 1989. "Plutarch's *de Fortuna Romanorum*." *CQ* 39:504–16.
———. 1989. "Plutarch's Aemilius and Timoleon." *Historia* 38:314–34.
———. 1989. "Character Change in Plutarch." *Phoenix* 43:62–68.
———. 1990. "Plutarch's Lives of Cicero, Cato, and Brutus." *Hermes* 118:192–203.
———. 1990. "Hellenic Culture and the Roman Heroes of Plutarch." *JHS* 110:126–45.
———. 1991. "Plutarch, Hadrian and Delphi." *Historia* 40:318–30.
———. 1992. "Novel and Pantomime in Plutarch's 'Antony.'" *Hermes* 120:76–82.
———. 1992. "Plutarch's Characterization of Lucullus." *RhM* 135:307–16.
Syme, R. 1955. "Missing Senators." *Historia* 4:52–71 = *Roman Papers* 1:271–91.
———. 1957. "A Fragment of Sallust?" *Eranos* 55:171–74 = *Roman Papers* 1:336–38.
———. 1963. "Ten Tribunes." *JRS* 53:55–60 = *Roman Papers* 2:557–65.
———. 1964. *Sallust*. Berkeley and Los Angeles.
———. 1979–91. *Roman Papers*. Edited by E. Badian (vols. 1–2) and A. R. Birley (vols. 3–7). Oxford.
———. 1980. "Biographers of the Caesars." *MH* 37:104–28 = *Roman Papers* 3:1251–75.
———. 1984. "P. Calvisius Ruso, One Person or Two?" *ZPE* 56:173–92 = *Roman Papers* 4:397–417.
———. 1988. "Military Geography at Rome." *ClAnt* 7:227–51 = *Roman Papers* 6:372–97.
Taracena Aguirre, B. 1928 [1929]. "Excavaciones en las provincias de Soria y Logroño: Memoria de las excavaciones practicadas en 1928." *JSEAM* 103, no. 5. Madrid.
———. 1931 [1932]. "Excavaciones en la provincia de Soria." *JSEAM* 119, no. 3. Madrid.
———. 1941. *Carta arqueológica de España: Soria*. Madrid.
Taradell, M. 1965. "Nuevos datos para la localización de la ceca de Lauro." *Numisma* 73:9–13.

Taylor, L. R. 1941. "Caesar's Early Career." *CP* 36:113–32.
———. 1960. *The Voting Districts of the Roman Republic.* Rome.
———. 1966. "Appian and Plutarch on Tiberius Gracchus' Last Assembly." *Athenaeum* 44:238–50.
———. 1966. *Roman Voting Assemblies from the Hannibalic War to the Dictatorship of Caesar.* Ann Arbor.
———. 1968. "The Dating of Major Legislation and Elections in Caesar's First Consulship." *Historia* 17:173–93.
Theander, C. 1950–51. "Plutarch und die Geschichte." *Bulletin de la Société Royale des Lettres de Lund 1950–51,* no. 1. Lund.
———. 1958. "Zur Zeitfolge der Biographien Plutarchs." *Eranos* 56:12–20.
———. 1959. "Plutarchs Forschungen in Rom: Zur mündlichen Überlieferung als Quelle der Biographien." *Eranos* 57:99–131.
Theiler, W. 1982. *Poseidonios: Die Fragmente.* 2 vols. Berlin.
Thompson, D. W. 1918. "The Greek Winds." *CR* 32:49–56.
Thompson, L. A. 1962. "The Appointment of Quaestors *extra sortem.*" *PACA* 5:17–25.
Thomsen, R. 1942. "Das Jahr 91 v. Chr. und seine Voraussetzungen." *C&M* 5:13–47.
Torelli, M. 1969. "Senatori etruschi della tarda repubblica e dell' impero." *DArch* 3:285–363.
Torres, C. 1951. "La fundación de Valencia." *Ampurias* 13:113–21.
Tovar, A. 1949. *Estudios sobre las primitivas lenguas hispánicas.* Buenos Aires.
———. 1957. *The Basque Language.* Translated by H. P. Houghton. Philadelphia.
———. 1958. "Toponimos con *-nt-* en Hispania, y el nombre de Salamanca." *Acta Salmanticensia* 11.2:95–116.
———. 1959. *El euskera y sus parientes.* Madrid.
———. 1961. *The Ancient Languages of Spain and Portugal.* New York.
———. 1974–89. *Iberische Landeskunde.* Teil 2, *Die Völker und die Städte des antiken Hispanien.* 3 vols. Baden-Baden.
Tovar, A., and J. M. Blázquez. 1975. *Historia de la Hispania Romana: La Península Ibérica desde 218 a.C. hasta el siglo V.* Madrid.
Treves, P. 1932. "Sertorio." *Athenaeum* 10:127–47.
Tullio, R. 1942. "Cohors praetoria e cohors amicorum." *RFIC* 20:54–61.
Tuplin, C. 1979. "Coelius or Cloelius? The Third General in Plutarch, Pompey 7." *Chiron* 9:137–45.
Twyman, B. L. 1976. "The Date of Sulla's Abdication and the Chronology of the First Book of Appian's *Civil Wars.*" *Athenaeum* 54:77–97, 271–95.
———. 1979. "The Date of Pompeius Magnus' First Triumph." In *Studies in Latin Literature and Roman History,* edited by C. Deroux, 174–208. Bruxelles.
Ulbert, G. 1984. *Cáceres el Viejo: Ein spätrepublikanisches Legionslager in Spanisch-Extremadura.* Mainz.
Ungern-Sternberg v. Pürkel, J. 1970. *Untersuchungen zum spätrepublikanischen Notstandsrecht: Senatus consultum ultimum und hostis-Erklärung.* München.
Untermann, J. 1961. *Sprachräume und Sprachbewegungen im vorrömischen Hispanien.* Wiesbaden.
———. 1964. "Zur Gruppierung der hispanischen 'Reitermünzen' mit Legenden in iberischer Schrift." *MDAI(M)* 5:91–155.
———. 1965. *Elementos de un atlas antroponímico de la Hispania antigua.* Madrid.
———. 1975–. *Monumenta linguarum Hispanicarum.* Wiesbaden.
———. 1983. "Die althispanischen Sprachen." *ANRW* II.29.2:791–818.
Valgiglio, E. 1975. "L'autobiografia di Silla nelle biografie di Plutarco." *StudUrb (B)* 49.1:245–81.
———. 1982. "Alcuni aspetti di Cicerone come fonte di Plutarco." In *Studi in onore di Aristide Colonna,* 283–99. Perugia.

vanderLeest, J. 1988. *Appian and the Writing of the Roman History*. Diss. Univ. of Toronto. Toronto.
———. 1989. "Appian's References to His Own Time." *AHB* 3:131–33.
van der Valk, M. 1982. "Notes on the Composition and Arrangement of the Biographies of Plutarch." In *Studi in onore di Aristide Colonna*, 301–37. Perugia.
Vedaldi Iasbez, V. 1981. "I figli dei proscritti sillani." *Labeo* 27:163–213.
Veith, G., and J. Kromayer. 1928. *Heerwesen und Kriegführung der Griechen und Römer*. München.
Vidal de la Blache, P. 1903. "Les Purpurariae du roi Juba." In *Mélanges Georges Perrot*, 325–29. Paris.
Vilaret i Monfort, J. 1976. "Una troballa numismàtica de l'època sertoriana a l'Empordà." *Acta Numismatica* 6:47–60.
Villacampa Rubio, M. A. 1984. "Calahorra y su entorno a traves de las fuentes escritas desde sus orígenes hasta el siglo IV d.C." In *Calahorra: Bimilenario de su fundación*, 173–87. Madrid.
Villaronga, L. 1960. "Las monedas ibéricas con leyenda Lauro." *Nummus* 20–21:59–66.
———. 1968. "En torno a un hallazgo de denarios de Beligio." *Ampurias* 30:225–36.
———. 1977. *Los tesoros de Azaila y la circulación monetaria en el valle del Ebro*. Barcelona.
———. 1979. *Numismática Antigua de Hispania: Iniciación a su estudio*. Barcelona.
Wagenvoort, H. 1971. "The Journey of the Souls of the Dead to the Isles of the Blessed." *Mnemosyne* 24:113–61.
———. 1971. "Nehalennia and the Souls of the Dead." *Mnemosyne* 24:239–92.
———. 1971. "A Noteworthy Inscription." *Mnemosyne* 24:395–96.
———. 1972. "Once More Nehalennia." *Mnemosyne* 25:82–83.
Walsh, J. J. 1992. "Syzygy, Theme and History: A Study in Plutarch's *Philopoemen* and *Flamininus*." *Philologus* 136:208–33.
Wardman, A. E. 1971. "Plutarch's Methods in the *Lives*." *CQ* 21:254–61.
———. 1974. *Plutarch's Lives*. London.
Watkins, O. D. 1988. "The Death of Cn. Pompeius Strabo." *RhM* 131:143–50.
Wehrmann, P. 1875. *Fasti praetorii ab u.c. DLXXXVIII ad u.c. DCCX*. Diss. Berlin.
Weizsäcker, A. 1931. *Untersuchungen über Plutarchs biographische Technik*. Berlin.
de Wet, B. X. 1990. "Contemporary Sources in Plutarch's Life of Antony." *Hermes* 118:80–90.
White, D. Churchill. 1980. "The Method of Composition and Sources of Nonius Marcellus." *Studi Noniani* 8:111–211.
Wickert, L. 1954. "Sertorius." In *Rastloses Schaffen: Festschrift für Friedrich Lammert*, 97–106. Stuttgart.
Wiegels, R. 1974. "Liv. per. 55 und die Gründung von Valentia." *Chiron* 4:153–76.
———. 1982. "Iliturgi und der 'deductor' Ti. Sempronius Gracchus." *MDAI(M)* 23:152–221.
———. 1985. *Die Tribusinschriften des römischen Hispanien: Ein Katalog*. Berlin.
Wiehn, E. 1926. *Die illegalen Heereskommanden in Rom bis auf Caesar*. Diss. Marburg.
Willems, P. 1878–83. *Le sénat de la république romaine: Sa composition et ses attributions*. 2 vols. Louvain and Paris.
Wilsdorf, D. 1878. "Fasti Hispaniarum provinciarum." *Leipziger Studien zur classischen Philologie* 1:63–140.
Wilson, A. J. N. 1966. *Emigration from Italy in the Republican Age of Rome*. Manchester.
Wimmel, W. 1967. "Die zeitlichen Vorwegnahmen in Sallusts 'Catilina.'" *Hermes* 95:192–221.
Wiseman, F. J. 1956. *Roman Spain: An Introduction to the Roman Antiquities of Spain and Portugal*. London.

Wiseman, T. P. 1964. "Some Republican Senators and Their Tribes." *CQ* 14:122–33.
———. 1965. "Mallius." *CR* 15:263.
———. 1967. "L. Memmius and His Family." *CQ* 17:164–67.
———. 1971. *New Men in the Roman Senate, 139 B.C.–A.D. 14*. Oxford.
Wölfflin, E. 1861. "Sallustius (Jahresbericht)." *Philologus* 17:519–48.
Zennari, J. 1956. *I Vercelli dei Celti nella Valle Padana e l'invasione Cimbrica della Venezia*. Cremona.
———. 1958. *La battaglia dei Vercelli o dei Campi raudii (101 a.C.)*. Cremona.
Ziegler, K. 1907. *Die Überlieferungsgeschichte der vergleichenden Lebensbeschreibungen Plutarchs*. Leipzig.
———. 1934. "Plutarchstudien." *RhM* 83:1–20, 211–50.
———. 1949. *Plutarchos von Chaironeia*. 2d ed., 1965. Separatum of *RE* 21.1 (1951) 636–962. Stuttgart.
———. 1960. *Plutarch: Grosse Griechen und Römer*. Vol. 5. Zürich.
Ziegler, K., and C. Lindskog. 1964. *Plutarchi Vitae parallelae*. Vol. 2.1, *Phokion–Cato Minor, Dion–Brutus, Aemilius–Timoleon, Sertorius–Eumenes*. 2d ed. Leipzig.

INDEX

All ancient dates are B.C. unless indicated otherwise. Most Roman authors and emperors are listed under their conventional English names; otherwise, Roman names are arranged by *gentilicium*.

Actium, battle of, 109
Adige River, 44–45, 46
Aemilius Lepidus, M. (*cos.* 78), xlix, 146, 147–49, 150, 188, 189, 200, 218
Aemilius Lepidus, M. (*IIIvir r.p.c.*), 179, 218
Aemilius Paullus, L. (*cos. II* 168), 121
Afranius, L. (*pr.* 72?), li, 168–69
Africa, 62, 67, 78, 99, 106–7, 111–12, 133, 155, 168, 182, 184, 219–20. *See also* Sertorius, Q.—Sertorian War: Africa
Africans, 125–26, 169, 170
Agis IV of Sparta (King, 244–241), xxviii–xxix
Albinovanus, P. (Sullan officer), 79
Aleksandr Nevskii (film, 1938), 110
Alentejo, 90, 151
Alexander III of Macedon (King, 336–323), xxviii, xxxi, xxxiii, 32, 33, 109, 126, 208, 212
Alexander of Pherai (tyrant, 370–358), 119
Alexander Polyhistor, 114
Alexandros (Pontic general, ca. 73), 198
Algarve, 90, 91, 151
Alkibiades (ca. 450–404, Athenian statesman), xxix, 35
Alps, 40, 44–45, 87, 109, 146–47
Alt Urgell, 87, 93
Ambrones, 40, 44–45, 46
Ammianus Marcellinus, 43, 44
Ampelius, xlvii, xlviii(n)
Anas River. *See* Guadiana River
Andalusia, 90, 91, 94, 105, 151

Annius, C. (*pr.* by 82?), 89, 97, 99–103, 105, 210, 211; improbability of Luscus as cognomen, 100
Annius, T. (*cos.* 153), 100
Annius, T. (*cos.* 128), 100
Annius, T. (*tr. mil.* 89), 100
Antaios, 113–15
Antigenes (Macedonian officer), 32
Antigonos Monophthalmos (King, 307/6–301), xxxi, xxxii, 31, 32, 33, 47
antistratēgos, 128, 167
Antonine period, l(n), lii
Antonius, M. (*cos.* 99), 70, 78, 85, 211
Antonius, M. (Sertorian officer), 190, 211, 213–15
Antonius, M. (*IIIvir r.p.c.*), xli, 62, 109, 115, 138, 142, 218
Antonius Balbus, Q. (*pr.* by 83), 211
Antonius Creticus, M. (*pr.* 74), 200
Antonius Saturninus, L. (*suff.* ca. A.D. 83), 218
Appian of Alexandria, xlii, xliii, li, 79, 99, 184, 201; Sertorian narrative of, li–lii, 74–76, 81, 82, 102, 118, 164–66, 168–70, 184–85, 194–95, 197, 207–8, 209, 212
Appuleius Saturninus, L. (*tr. pl. II* 100), 78
Aquae Sextiae, battle of, 45, 46, 47
Aquinus (officer of Metellus), 136, 139
Aquinus, M. (Senator, ca. 46), 139
Aquinus Mela, C. (*IIvir qq.*), 139
Aquitania, 92, 219
Aragón, 90, 92, 151
Aranjuez, 153
Arausio, battle of, 38, 39, 40–44
Archers, 127

aretē, lv, 12–21
Arevaci, 93, 151, 216
Argyraspides, xxxii
Ariobarzanes I of Kappadokia (King, ca. 95–64), 190
Aristeides (ca. 525–467, Athenian statesman), 59
Aristion of Athens (tyrant, 87–86), 119
Armor, 43, 44, 126–27
Arno River, 32
Asculum, 54, 56, 210
Asia, 32, 33, 180, 192, 194; Roman province, 62, 185, 191, 192, 193–95, 198, 200–202
Askalis (Mauretanian dynast, ca. 81/80), 110–12, 115
Assemblies, Roman, 64
Astures, 94
Athens, xxv–xxvi, xlii, 32, 36, 119
Atlantic Islands, 106–8, 110, 111
Atlantic Ocean, 106, 108, 109
Attalos III of Pergamon (King, 138–133), 193
Aufidius (Sertorian officer), 132, 190, 209, 210, 213–14, 220
Augusta Praetoria, 87
Augustus (Imp. Caesar Divi f. Aug., *cos.* XIII 2), l, 34, 37, 115, 138, 142, 156, 206, 218
Aurelius Cotta, C. (*cos.* 75), 128
Aurelius Cotta, L. (*cos.* 119), 128
Aurelius Cotta, L. (*tr. pl.* 103), 37
Aurelius Cotta, L. (*cos.* 65), 125, 127, 128–29
Aurelius Cotta, M. (*cos.* 74), 128, 167–68
Aurelius Scaurus, M. (*suff.* 108), 42
Aurunculeia (mulieris) l., 128
Aurunculeius Cotta, L. (d. 54), 128–29
Ausci, 92
Ausetani, 93
Autricones, 93, 151, 165
Auxiliaries, 46, 55, 73, 116, 205
Avalon, Isle of, 108
Aveiro, 137, 139
Avidius Nigrinus, C. (Senator under Domitian), xxv
Avidius Nigrinus, C. (*suff.* A.D. 110), xxv–xxvi
Avidius Quietus, T. (*suff.* A.D. 93), xxv
Avidius Quietus, T. (*suff.* A.D. 111), xxv

Badajoz, 105
Baelo, 129

Baetica, 95, 96, 97, 134, 142, 156, 157; name and geographical extent, 105. *See also* Hispania Ulterior
Baetis River, 49, 105, 130
Balearic Isles, 96, 103, 127, 157
Barcelona. *See* Barcino
Barcino, 102, 157
Bardyaei. *See* Slave bands
Basque Country, 90, 91, 94, 136, 151, 178; language, 91–92
Bastetani, 92
Batavians, 43
Belgae, 41
Berones, 93, 151, 165
Bilbilis, 93, 151
Billeting of troops, 50–51, 95, 202
Bissagos Islands, 106
Bithynia, 62, 85, 190, 192–93, 196, 197–98; as Roman province, 193
Blessed Isles. *See* Isles of the Blest
Bocchus I of Mauretania (King, ca. 110–80), 111
Bogud I of Mauretania (King, ca. 80–50), 111
Boii, 40
Bona Dea, 37
Bracara Augusta, xlviii
Britain, 142
Bruttians, 119
bullae, 143
Bursao, 151

Caeciliana, 137
Caecilius Cornutus, M. (*pr.* by 90), 85
Caecilius Metellus Numidicus, Q. (*cos.* 109), 39, 133
Caecilius Metellus Pius, Q. (*cos.* 80), xlix, l–lii, 89, 127, 132, 133–34, 146, 151, 152, 154, 157–58, 188, 196, 218; contrasted with Sertorius, xxxvii–xxxviii, 88, 134, 135–36, 138, 180–84; celebrates victory, lii, liv, 180, 183–84; age of, 39, 135, 138, 155; in Civil War, 69–70, 79, 83, 98, 100; in Farther Spain/Lusitania, 97, 128, 134, 137–39, 166, 178, 216; inability to defeat Sertorius, 117, 122, 140; winter quarters of, 165, 178; places prize on Sertorius' head, 180–82, 206. *See also* Italica: battle of; Segontia, battle of; Sucro: battle of
Caecilius Metellus Pius Scipio Nasica, Q. (*cos.* 52), 47, 119, 218
Caesarea Mauretaniae, 113

Index

caetrati, 126–27, 161, 176
Calagurris Nasica, 151, 168, 177, 178, 203, 215, 216–17
Cales, 80, 83
Caligula (C. Caesar Germanicus Aug., *cos. IV* A.D. 41), 218
Callaeci, 94
Calpurnius Lanarius, P. (?) (Sertorian officer), 100–101
Calvisius Ruso, P. (*suff.* A.D. 79), 130
Calvisius Sabinus, C. (*cos.* 39), 130
Calvisius Sabinus, C. (*cos.* A.D. 26), 130
Calvisius Tullus Ruso, P. (*cos.* A.D. 109), 130
Campania, 65, 78, 79, 80, 84, 182
Canary Islands, 106–8
Cannae, battle of, 42
Cannibalism, 130, 216
Cantabria, 94, 136, 178
Capua, 78, 80, 81, 82–84
Caraca, 153–54
Carlist Wars, 136
Carpetania, 94, 151
Carrhae, battle of, 126
Cartagena. *See* Carthago Nova
Carteia, 95, 97
Carthage, xlii
Carthago Nova, 95, 97, 102, 139, 149, 175
Cascantum, 151
Cassiodorus, xlvii
Cassius Longinus, C. (*cos.* 73), 218
Cassius Longinus, L. (*cos.* 107), 41
Cassius Longinus, Q. (*tr. pl.* 49), xli
Castilla–La Mancha. *See* La Mancha; New Castile
Castilla y León. *See* Old Castile
Castra Aelia, 165
Castra Caecilia, 137
Castulo, xxx, xxxviii, liv, 40, 49–51, 52, 88, 95, 113
Catalonia, 87, 90, 91, 92, 151, 157–58, 165
Catilinarian conspiracy, l; debates concerning, xl
Cauca, 178
Cavalry. *See* Sertorius, Q.—Sertorian War: Forces, Roman; Sertorius, Q.—Sertorian War: Forces, Sertorian
Cave dwellers, 153–54
Celtiberia, 116, 141, 151, 165, 170, 173, 174, 178, 203, 216; geographical extent, 93; Celtiberian highlands, 134, 170, 172

Celtiberians, 33, 44, 50, 72, 96, 102, 109, 116, 125, 136–37, 140, 172, 173, 209–10, 216; ethnography, 92, 93–94; coinage, 93, 94, 216; language, 93–94, 116
Celto-Hispanians, 33, 93–94, 108–10, 144, 157
Celts, 46–47, 90, 93–94, 108–10; language, 93, 94, 115–16
Cerdanya, 87, 93
Cerne Island, 106
Cerretani, 87, 93
Cessetani, 92
Chaironeia, xxv–xxvi, 36
Christian view of history, xlviii
Cierzo, 154–55
Cilicia, 78, 102
Cimbri, 40–42, 44–45, 46
Cimbrian Wars, xxxiii, xlii, 40–42, 44–45
Cinnani. See Cinno-Marians
Cinno-Marians, 60, 63–65, 68, 71, 73, 74, 75–76, 78–80, 85, 86, 146; as refugees, 73, 87, 97, 116–17, 148, 184
Citizens, new, 63–65, 142
Civil War: First (83–82), xxxiii, xxxvi, xlii, 65, 75–76, 78, 80–82, 96, 98, 117, 146; Second (49–45), xli, 130; of 87 (*see* Rome: siege of)
Claudius Caesar Aug. Germanicus, Ti. (*cos. V* A.D. 51), 218
Claudius Marcellus, M. (*cos. V* 208), xliii(n), 138
Claudius Marcellus, M. (*cos. III* 152), 95
Claudius Narcissus, Ti. (d. A.D. 54), 218
Claudius Pulcher, Ap. (*cos.* 79), 65, 100
Clodius Pulcher, P. (*aed. cur.* 56), 37, 38, 156
Clodius Thrasea Paetus, T. (*suff.* A.D. 56), xxv
Clunia, 93, 203, 216; siege of, xl, 176–77, 178, 203
Clusium, battle of, 79, 98
Coelius Caldus, C. (*cos.* 94), 53
cohors amicorum, 42
Col de la Perche, 87
Col du Perthus, 87
Conii, 91
Consabura, 133, 151
Consul, 62, 64, 70, 77–78, 81, 84, 88, 185, 186; *stratēgos* for "Consul," 48; distinguished from Dictator, 123
Consulars, correspondence with Sertorius, 217–18
Contestania, 92, 150, 169

Index

Contrebia Belaisca, xlvi, 151, 153, 165
contubernales, 42, 43, 49, 56, 210
Corduba, liv, 95, 165
Cornelia, *mater Gracchorum*, xxviii–xxix, 36
Cornelius Cethegus, P. (Senator by 90), 79
Cornelius Cinna, L. (*cos. IV* 84), xxxvi, xli, 56, 59–61, 63–72 passim, 75–77, 85, 133, 193
Cornelius Merula, L. (*flam. Dial.* ?–87), 64, 70
Cornelius Nepos, xlv–xlvi, xlix, lv–lvi, 34
Cornelius Scipio Africanus, P. (*cos. II* 194), 31, 95, 102
Cornelius Scipio Africanus Aemilianus, P. (*cos. II* 134), 31, 39, 50, 138
Cornelius Scipio Asiaticus, L. (*cos.* 83), xlix, 76, 78, 79, 80–84
Cornelius Scipio Nasica, P. (*pr.* by 93), 88–89
Cornelius Sisenna, L. (*pr.* 78), xlii, xliv, liv
Cornelius Sulla, L. (*dict.* 81), xxviii, xxxvi, xlix, l, 48, 49, 63, 85–86, 89, 96, 99–100, 101, 110, 111, 116, 129, 131–32, 133–34, 184–85, 188, 191; march on Rome, xxxiii, 58, 61; opposes Sertorius' candidacy, xxxvi, 58–59; memoirs, xli–xlii, liv, 81–82, 84; in Civil War, 75–84 passim, 98, 146, 179
Courts, criminal, 76
Cúchulainn, 33
Cyprus, 32

Dardanos, treaty of, 190, 192, 194, 196–98
Dayan, Moshe (1915–81), 33
Demetrios Poliorketes of Macedon (King, 293–287), xxix, 32
Deserters, 113, 206
Diana, 122, 124
Dianium, 92, 171, 175, 192, 197, 203, 216, 219; as Sertorian naval base, 149, 177, 199
Dictator, 123
Didius, T. (*cos.* 98), 48–50, 52, 53, 55–56, 58, 72, 94
dikaiosynē, xxviii
Diodoros of Sicily, xlv, liii, 81, 207–8, 215
Diodoros son of Herakles, 114
Dionysios (Pontic general, ca. 73), 198
Dipo, 137
Domitius Ahenobarbus, Cn. (d. 81), xlix

Domitius Calvinus, Cn. (*cos. II* 40), 130, 141
Domitius Calvinus, M. (*pr.* 80?), 127–28, 130–31, 132–33
Douro River. *See* Duero River
Duero River, 93, 94, 105, 116, 138, 172–73, 174
Durius River. *See* Duero River

Ebro River, 90, 92, 93, 102, 150–51, 156, 158, 165, 216
Ebro Valley, 92, 96, 97, 140, 141–42, 151
Ebusus (Eivissa), 103–5
Edetania, 92, 150, 159
Elephants, 47
Elysium. *See* Isles of the Blest
Emporion, 91, 95–96
equites Romani, 39, 42, 184, 190, 204–5, 211
Etruria, 67, 72, 84, 85, 98
Etruscans, 97, 192
Eumachos (Pontic general, ca. 74), 198
Eumenes of Kardia (362–316), xxix, xxxi–xxxii, 33, 47, 121, 218
Eutropius, xlvii–xlviii, li
Executions, 70–71, 112–13, 206–8
Exploitation of provinces, 94, 95, 116, 144
Extremadura, 90, 105, 151
Exuperantius, xliv, 74–75, 77–78, 82, 84–85

Fabius Hispaniensis, L. (*q.* 82 or 81), 182, 211, 213, 215, 219
Fabius Maximus, Q. (*dict.* 217), xxviii, 47, 119
factio: Metellan, 56, 58–59; ruling, 143, 205; Cinno-Marian (*see* Cinno-Marians)
Fannius, L. (Senator by 86), 183, 191–92, 195, 197–99
Faventia, battle of, 79, 98
Fidentia, battle of, 98
Flavius Fimbria, C. (*cos.* 104), 193
Flavius Fimbria, C. (*q.?* 86), 85, 86, 191, 193–94
Florus, xlvii, xlviii(n), xlix–l, lii, 156, 163
Fonteius, M. (*pr.* 76?), 147
Fufidius, L. (*pr.* 81?), 117, 125, 127–28, 129–31
Furius Camillus, M. (*dict. V* 367), xxviii

Gades, 91, 106, 107
Galatia, 190, 192, 193, 197–98

Galba (Ser. Galba Imp. Caes. Aug., *cos. II* A.D. 69), xlv, 185
Gallia Cisalpina, 52–53, 54, 55, 65, 78, 87, 98
Gallia Transalpina, 41, 54, 85–87, 89, 132, 134, 147, 150, 155
Gaul, 40–42, 44, 46, 54, 85–86, 88, 108, 128, 142, 177, 178, 219. *See also* Gallia Cisalpina; Gallia Transalpina
Gauls, 33, 46–47, 55, 73, 109, 144; Gallic auxiliaries, 46, 55, 73; Gaulish language, 46–47, 110. *See also* Celts; Religion: Celtic
Gellius, A., lii, 123–24
Germans, 33, 46–47. *See also* Religion: Germanic
Gibraltar, Straits of, 105, 129
Gorgades Islands, 106
Graccurris, 96, 151
Granius Licinianus, lii
Greeks in Spain, 90; script, 90, 91
Guadalén River, 51
Guadalimar River, 49
Guadalquivir River. *See* Baetis River
Guadiana River, 94, 105, 116, 132, 133, 137
Guerrilla. *See* Sertorius, Q.—Sertorian War: Guerrilla
Guiribaile, 51

Hadrian (Imp. Caes. Traianus Hadrianus Aug., *cos. III* A.D. 119), xxvi, xlix
Hamilqar Barqa (d. 229/8, Carthaginian leader), 32
Hannibal (ca. 247–183, Carthaginian leader), 31–33, 47, 88, 108, 109, 157
Hasdrubal (d. 221, Carthaginian leader), 102
hēgemōn, 55, 133
Helvetii, 41
Henares River, 154
Heraklean Way, 108
Herakles, 108–10, 113, 114–15
Herennius, C. (Sertorian officer), 165–66, 167, 176, 187
Herennius, M. (*cos.* 93), 217–18
Hermaios (Pontic general, ca. 73), 198
Hermes, 110
Herne Island. *See* Cerne Island
Hesiod, 108
Hirtuleius, L. (*q.* by 82), xl, l, 56, 99, 131–33, 134, 150, 161, 163–64, 165–66, 176, 182, 186–87, 203, 210

Hirtuleius, Q. (Sertorian officer), 56, 131, 163, 182, 210
Hispalis, 106, 130
Hispania Citerior, lii, 48, 49, 54, 85, 88–89, 95, 97, 100, 116, 123, 132, 134, 139, 142, 150, 154, 165, 168, 187
Hispanians, xvii, xxxv, xxxvii, xxxviii, 32, 95, 98, 110, 117, 121, 122–23, 137, 143, 150, 181, 205, 206–8; ethnography, 90–94; use of Latin alphabet, 92, 94; manner of warfare, 136–37. *See also* Celtiberians; Celto-Hispanians; Iberians; Lusitani; Sertorius, Q.—Sertorian War: Forces, Sertorian; Sertorius, Q.—Sertorian War: Hispanians
Hispania Ulterior, lii, 41, 49, 85, 88–89, 116, 129–30, 138, 154, 165, 182, 187. *See also* Baetica; Lusitania
Hispanienses, 95–98, 125–26, 192
Hispano-Celtic. *See* Celto-Hispanians
Hitler, Adolf (1889–1945), 110
Homer, 108, 160
Horatius Cocles, 43
Hortensius, Q. (*cos.* 69), 35
Hostages, 141, 206; of Eumenes, xxxiii; of Sertorius, xxxiii, xxxvii, 50, 119, 121, 141, 144, 206–8; of Scipio, 80–81
hostes publici, xlv, 62, 67, 181–83, 189, 192, 205
Huesca. *See* Osca
Hyginus, xlix

Iacetani. *See* Lacetania
Ianiculum, 69, 70
Iaphras son of Abraham, 114
Iberian Peninsula. *See* Spain
Iberians, 50, 90–93, 95, 96, 97, 136, 140, 159; language, 90, 141; script, 90–91, 93; coinage, 91, 157, 158, 159. *See also* Hispanians
Ichthyophagi, 154
Ilercaonia, 92, 150, 151, 165
Ilerda, 92, 93, 203, 216; battle of (ca. 78), 132, 150
Ilergetes, 92, 97, 150
Illyrians, 73, 79, 116
Illyricum, 77
imperator, 48, 123, 183
Indicetes, 92, 151
Indo-European, 90, 108, 115–16; non-Indo-European, 90, 94, 115–16
Infantry, 127, 134, 160. *See also* Sertorius, Q.—Sertorian War: Forces,

Infantry (*continued*)
  Roman; Sertorius, Q.—Sertorian War: Forces, Sertorian
Insteius, C. (Sertorian officer), 56
Insteius, L. (Sertorian officer), 56, 210
Iphinoë (wife of Antaios), 114
Ipsos, battle of, 32
Isère River, 44–46
Islands of the Gods, 108
Isles of the Blest, 108–10. *See also* Sertorius, Q.—Image, propaganda, religious manipulation: Isles of the Blest, intended visit to
Isthmos brigands, 119
Isturgi, 51
Italians, 62, 95–97, 142, 188, 192; and siege of Rome, 65; in Civil War, 77; in Social War, 78, 133; in Spain, 125, 141–42, 190. *See also Hispanienses*
Italica, 95, 97; battle of, lii, 132, 134, 166, 176, 203
Italy, 43, 44–45, 53, 62, 80, 85–86, 97, 99–100, 108, 114, 133, 142, 144, 146, 150, 157, 165, 179, 182, 189, 191; in Social War, 55, 56, 61; siege of Rome, 64, 67, 70; in Civil War, 75–79, 87, 98, 101, 155
Iuba I of Numidia (King, ca. 55–46), 115, 119
Iuba II of Mauretania (King, ca. 25 B.C.–A.D. 23/4), lv, 106–7, 113, 115
Iulia Agrippina (A.D. 15–59), 218
Iulius (*mag. mil.* A.D. 378), 72
Iulius Agricola, Cn. (*suff.* A.D. 76 or 77), 142
Iulius Caesar, C. (*dict. perp.*), xxviii, xl, xli, xlv, l, lii, 37, 38, 43, 47, 59, 94, 95, 109, 111, 115, 128, 141, 168, 183, 189, 218; assassination, xxxviii, 212
Iulius Caesar, L. (*cos.* 90), 48, 70, 193
Iulius Caesar Strabo, C. (*aed. cur.* 90), 58–59, 70, 193
Iulius Civilis, C. (?) (Batavian leader), 32, 33
Iulius Frontinus, Sex. (*cos. III* A.D. 100), lii, 151–52, 161–62, 176
Iunius Brutus, M. (*pr.* 88), 60
Iunius Brutus, M. (*tr. pl.* 83), xlix
Iunius Brutus, M. (*pr.* 44), xxx, 37
Iunius Brutus Callaicus, D. (*cos.* 138), 116
Iunius Silanus, M. (*cos.* 109), 41

Jalón River, 90, 93

Júcar River. *See* Sucro River
Jugurthine War, l
Julian (Imp. Caes. Fl. Claudius Iulianus Aug., *cos. IV* A.D. 363), 43

Kaikias, 154–55
Kalchedon, battle of, 167–68, 198, 199, 200
Kappadokia, 33, 190, 192–93, 196, 197
Kassandros of Macedon (King, 305–297), 32
Kilikia. *See* Cilicia
Kilikians. *See* Pirates
Kimon (ca. 510–450, Athenian statesman), 38
Kleodemos Malchos, 114–15
Kleomenes III of Sparta (King, 235–222), 38
Kleopatra VII Philopator of Egypt (Queen, 51–30), xlix, 109, 115
Kleopatra Selene, 115
Krateros (d. 321, Macedonian leader), 33
Kutuzov, Mikhail Illarionovich (1745–1813, Field Marshal), 33
Kyzikos, siege of, 192, 200

La Albufera, 171
Lacetania, 93, 150, 151, 203
Laelius, D. (*leg.* 77), 161, 163–64, 215
Laietania, 92, 147, 151
La Mancha, 90, 151
Langa de Duero. *See* Segontia Lanka
Langobriga, xxx, 136, 137, 138–39
Languedoc, 90
Lappius Maximus, A. Buccius (*suff. III* A.D. 100), 218
La Rioja, 92, 93, 151
Lauro, battle of, xxx, xxxvii, xl–xli, lii, 56, 127, 140, 149, 171, 188, 196, 203, 207, 209, 210; sack of Lauro, xxxviii, xlix, 164–65, 166, 176; maneuvers, 160–64
Lauro, location of, 156–58; Puig, 156, 157, 159, 160, 163; Llerona, 156, 157–58, 160, 162–63; Llíria, 157, 159
leges Sulpiciae, 67
Legions, 99, 101–3, 127, 134, 139, 140, 147, 149, 160–64, 176, 180, 197
León, 151
Lepidani, 148–49, 182–83, 184, 185, 219
Levantine script. *See* Iberians: script
lex curiata, 186, 201
lex Iulia de civitate sociis danda, 63

lex Plautia Papiria, 63
lex Plotia de reditu Lepidanorum, 219
Libyans. *See* Africans
Libyo-Phoenician script, 91
Licinius Crassus, L. (*cos.* 95), 35, 36, 54
Licinius Crassus, M. (*cos. II* 55), li, 47, 85, 112, 126
Licinius Crassus, P. (*cos.* 97), 70, 193
Licinius Lucullus, L. (*cos.* 151), 50, 94
Licinius Lucullus, L. (*cos.* 74), 37, 38, 59, 109, 131–32, 167–68, 183, 192, 200, 202
Licinius Murena, L. (*cos.* 62), 100, 191, 196
Lictors, 67, 88, 149, 202
Liguria, 44, 116, 146–47, 200
Limia River, 108–9
Livius Drusus, M. (*tr. pl.* 91), 54
Livius Salinator, L. (?) (Sertorian officer), 97, 99, 101
Livy, xlvi–xlvii, xlix, li, lii, lvi, 80–82, 161, 187; view of Sertorius, xlvi–xlvii, l, 44, 122, 188, 207–8; Livian tradition, xlvii–xlix, 44, 195; Epitome and *Periochae*, xlvii–xlviii, li, lii, 80
Lix, 113
Llaurí, 157, 158
Lleida. *See* Ilerda
Llerona del Vallès. *See* Lauro, location of: Llerona
Llíria. *See* Lauro, location of: Llíria
Lucan, 1
Lucretius Afella, Q. (Sullan officer), 79
Lug, 33, 110
Lugdunum Convenarum, 219
Lusitani, 41, 108, 109, 110, 117, 118, 125, 127, 190, 216; Southern Lusitanian script, 91; use of Latin alphabet, 94; ethnography, 94, 115–16; leadership of, assumed by Sertorius, 110, 116–17, 123; manner of warfare, 116, 134–35, 136–37, 140
Lusitania, lii, 108–9, 117, 124, 130, 134, 137–38, 139, 154, 164, 165, 176, 187; geographical extent, 94, 105, 116
Lutatius Catulus, Q. (*cos.* 102), 44–45, 46, 70
Lysander (d. 395, Spartan leader), xxviii, 138
Lysimachos (King of Thrace and Macedon, 305–281), 32

MacArthur, Douglas (1880–1964, General of the Army), 110

Macedonia, 48, 75, 79
Macedonians, xxxi–xxxii, 33, 141
Madeira Archipelago, 107
Maecenas (Sertorian *scriba*), 211, 213
Magius, L. (Senator by 86), 183, 191–92, 195, 197–99, 201
Magius, Minatus, 192
Mag Mell, 108
Malaca, 91, 102
Mallius (Sertorian officer), 132, 190, 208–10
Mallius Maximus, Cn. (*cos.* 105), 41, 42
Mallorca, 96
Manlius, L. (*pr.* 79?), 127, 132, 134, 150
Manlius Torquatus, A. (*pr.* ca. 70), 49
Marcius Coriolanus, Cn., xxix, 123, 189
Marcius Philippus, L. (*cos.* 91), 79, 100
Marians. *See* Cinno-Marians
Marius, C. (*cos. VII* 86), xliii, xlix, 36, 37, 39, 43, 49, 74, 76, 80, 95, 119, 131–32, 138, 182; and Sertorius, xxxvi, 47–48, 58–59, 60, 63–64, 66–68, 74; in Cimbrian Wars, 44–45, 46; exile of, 62, 66–67, 77; and siege of Rome, 62–73 passim, 133, 193; massacres his enemies, 70, 85, 211
Marius, C. (*cos.* 82), 63, 73, 74, 77–78, 80, 85, 88, 98, 119
Marius, M. (*q.* by 82?), xli, 99, 132, 182, 187, 198, 199, 200–202
Marius Gratidianus, M. (*pr. II* 82), 60
Massilia, 79, 147
Mauretania. *See* Sertorius, Q.—Sertorian War: Mauretania
megalophrosynē, xxviii, 186, 189, 192
meirakion, 37–38, 209
Mellaria, battle of, 127, 129
Memmius, C. (*q.* 76), 175
Memnon of Herakleia, xlix, 201
Mestrius Florus, L. (*suff.* ca. A.D. 75), xxv
Metellinum, 137
Milonius, C. (*tr. pl.?* 87), 60
Minturnae, 82
Mistral, 103–4
Mithradates VI Eupator of Pontos (King, ca. 120–63), xl, xli, 62, 103, 168, 170, 177–78, 185, 198, 200, 219; negotiates with Sertorius, 190–202 passim; negotiates with Pompeius, 191, 196–97. *See also* Sertorius, Q.—Sertorian War: Mithradates, treaty with
Mithradatic Wars: First, 62, 67, 103, 190; Second, 191, 196; Third, xxxiv, 183, 192, 197, 199

Mucius Scaevola Augur, Q. (*cos.* 117), 36
Mucius Scaevola Pontifex, Q. (*cos.* 95), 193–94
Muluccha River, 102
Munda, 156–57
Murcia, 90, 151
Mussolini, Benito (1883–1945), 110
Myndos, 191, 197

Navarra, 91–92, 151, 178
Nelson, Horatio, 1st Viscount (1758–1805, Vice Admiral), 33
New Carthage. *See* Carthago Nova
New Castile, 90, 151
Nikomedeia, 85, 194
Nikomedes IV Philopator of Bithynia (King, 94–75), 190, 193, 199
nobiles, 39, 49, 52, 55, 79, 148, 179, 204, 205
Norbanus, C. (*cos.* 83), 78–79, 80–81, 83, 98, 146
Noreia, battle of, 41
novi homines, 36, 49, 53, 58, 74, 204
Numantia, 37, 39, 93
Numidia, 102, 131
Nursia, 34, 35–37

Obsequens, xlvii
Octavian. *See* Augustus
Octavius, Cn. (*cos.* 128), 62
Octavius, Cn. (*cos.* 87), xxxvi, 60, 62–63, 64–65, 69–70
Octavius, L. (*cos.* 75), 62
Octavius, M. (*tr. pl.* 133), 62
Octavius, M. (*tr. pl.* by 87), 62
Octavius Graecinus, C. (?) (Sertorian officer), 161–62, 182, 207, 209, 210, 213–14, 219
Octavius Ruso, Cn. (*q.* 105), 63
Odin. *See* Wotan
Odysseus, 109
Old Castile, 93, 105, 151
Olisipo, 137, 139
One-eyedness, 31–33, 43, 109, 200
Onuba, 105, 109
Ophiussa, 103
Opimius, L. (*cos.* 121), 181
Oporto, 137, 139
Optimates, 63, 218
Orators, Roman, 35–37
Oretani, 50, 92
Orosius, xlvii, xlviii–xlix, li, lii, 44, 157–58, 159, 163, 164, 195, 208

Osca, 50, 92, 93, 97, 119, 141–42, 150, 203, 216; Sertorian School at, xxxvii, 142, 143–44, 166, 206; coinage, 141–42; site of Sertorius' assassination, 211
Oscans, 96–97, 141–42

Pacciaecus (Paccianus). *See* Vibius Pacciaecus
Paciaeci *fratres*, 112
País Valencià, 90, 150, 151, 157, 158–59, 165
País Vasco. *See* Basque Country
Palaimon son of Herakles, 114
Palantia, 94, 157–58; siege of, 177, 178
Palantia River, 157–58, 159
Palatine, 195–96
Palencia. *See* Palantia
Palma, 96
Paphlagonia, 33, 190, 192, 193, 197–98
Papirius Carbo, C. (*cos.* 120), 35
Papirius Carbo, Cn. (*cos.* 113), 41
Papirius Carbo, Cn. (*cos. III* 84), xlix, 60, 68, 69, 74–76, 77, 78, 85, 87, 88, 98, 99
Parthians, 119
Pelopidas (d. 364, Theban leader), 138
Peninsula, Iberian. *See* Spain
Perdikkas (d. 321/20, Macedonian leader), 33
Perikles (ca. 490–429, Athenian statesman), xxviii
Perperna, C. (*pr.* by 91), 146
Perperna, M. (*cos.* 130), 146
Perperna, M. (*cos.* 92), 146, 217–18
Perperna, M. (*pr.* by 83), xxxvii–xxxix, xli, xliv, 96, 122, 134, 136, 140, 145–48, 184, 185, 187, 190, 199, 200, 206, 207; submits to Sertorius, xxxvii, 146, 148–49, 159; denigrated by Plutarch, xxxviii–xxxix, 117, 180, 202, 204; forces of, 145, 149–50, 159–60, 165, 169, 174, 203–4; proscribed, 146, 147, 182, 219; Propraetor, 148; grievances of, 203, 204–5; plots assassination, 207, 208–10, 212, 213–14; assumes leadership, 216; death of, 217–19. *See also* Segontia, battle of; Sucro: battle of; Valentia: battle of
Petreius, M. (*pr.* 64?), 168
Pharsalos, battle of, 168, 218
Pherekydes, 114
Philip II of Macedon (King, 360/59[356]–336), xxxi, 31, 32, 33, 47

Philip V of Macedon (King, 221–179), 37, 119, 120
Philopoimen (253–183, Achaean statesman), 37, 137, 141
Phoenicians in Spain, 90, 107; script, 90, 91
Phokion (401–318, Athenian statesman), 38
Phrygia, 32, 190, 192, 198
Picenum, 65, 79
Pirates, xliii, 102–3, 104, 106, 111, 147, 177–78, 191, 197, 199–200
Pityussian Islands, 103, 111
Plancius, Cn. (*aed. cur.* 55 or 54), 49
Plautus, 108
Pliny the Elder, lii
Plutarch
—Biography, personal qualities
  Amphiktyonic Council, member of, xxvi
  Athenian citizen, xxvi
  Life, xxv–xxvi
  Roman citizenship (L. Mestrius Plutarchus), xxv
  Roman friends, xxv–xxvi
  Travel, xxv
—Intellectual, authorial qualities
  Ambition, views on, xxviii
  Cross-references, xxvii, xxix(n)
  Drinking, views on, 212
  Escapism, views on, xxviii, xxxvi–xxxvii, 109
  Ethical perspective, xxvi, xxx–xxxi, xxxv, liv–lv, 120–21, 207–8
  Exploitation of provinces, views on, xxxvi, liv, 50, 94–95, 202
  Failure, views on, xxviii
  Generalship, views on, 33, 138, 167–68
  Heroes, choice of, xxvii–xxix, xxxi–xxxiii, lv–lvi
  Latin, knowledge of, liii, 101, 184, 188
  Platonic philosophy, interest in, xxv
  Rhetoric, knowledge of, xxv, xxxv–xxxvi
—*Lives of the Caesars*, xxvi
—Methods
  Age of subjects, 37–38, 135–36
  Chronology, xxxix, 58, 77, 80, 125, 127, 178, 180
  Composition of *Lives* in pairs, xxvi–xxvii, xxxi
  Compression, xl, 48, 62, 73, 77, 84, 125, 160–62, 178, 214–15, 219
  Conflation, xl, 178
  Displacement, xl, 117–18, 121, 145, 152, 176, 180–81, 183, 189
  Embellishment, expansion, xli, 47, 55, 66–67, 124, 160, 196, 201
  Errors, 57, 101, 135, 136, 162, 187, 214
  Exaggeration, 65, 79, 118, 127, 151–52, 166
  Generalization, 187, 201
  Heroes: protection of, xxxv–xxxix, 65, 68, 71, 79, 82, 112–13, 115, 117–18, 121, 122, 135, 162, 165, 175, 206, 207–8, 212; emphasis on, xl–xli, 48, 62, 63, 65, 73, 77, 125, 132, 161–62, 166, 175, 215
  Historical method, xxxix–xli
  Identity, shift of, 162, 164
  Memory, xxxix, liv, 176
  Note taking, xxxix
  Omissions, xxxvi, 61, 62, 77, 161–62, 180, 193, 206, 207
  Personal element emphasized, 59, 87, 165, 170, 189, 207–9
  Proems, 31
  Quaestors and their commanders, 53–54
  Responsibility, shift of, xxxviii, 111, 167–68, 205, 207–8
  Selectiveness, xxx, 81–82
  Substitution of "Perperna" for "Roman exiles," 204
  Suppression, xl–xli, 132, 161, 166, 175, 204, 209
  Transfer, xli
  Vagueness, 46, 62, 63, 65, 183
—*Parallel Lives*
  Alexander, 209
  Caesar, xxxviii
  Cato Minor, 49, 184–85
  Lucullus, xxxiv, liii(n), 135, 167–68
  Marius, 66, 67, 71–72
  Pompey, xxxiv, 135, 167–68, 169–71, 176, 185, 218, 219
  Purpose, xxvi–xxvii, xxx
  Structure and order, xxvii–xxix
  Sulla, xxxiv, 80, 81, 185
—*Sertorius*
  and *Eumenes,* xxxi–xxxiii
  Purpose, xxx–xxxi
  Structure, xxxiii–xxxv
  Textual problems, 51, 98, 99, 112, 117, 122, 130, 133, 134, 139, 145, 155, 164, 167, 204, 220

Plutarch (*continued*)
—Sources, xli–lvi
  Biographies, supposed use of, lv–lvi, 33–34
  Choice of, 81–82
  Contemporary sources, xli–xliv, liv
  Oral tradition, liii
  Poseidonios, familiarity with, liv–lv. *See also* Poseidonios of Apameia
  Reading, xxxix, liii–liv
  Sallust: chief source for *Sertorius*, liii; verbal parallels with, 57, 100–101, 104–5, 108, 183–84, 191. *See also* Sallustius Crispus, C.
Pollentia, 96
Polyainos, lii
Polybios of Megalopolis, xlii, 43, 44, 93, 109, 123
Polyperchon (regent of Macedon, 319–317), 33
Pompaelo, 151
Pompeius Magnus, Cn. (*cos. III* 52), xxxvii, xl–xli, xliii, xliv, xlix, l, li, 55, 56, 59, 88, 126, 191, 196–97; in First Civil War, 78, 79, 98, 99–100, 155–56; arrival in Spain, 89, 117, 122, 146–48, 154, 155, 188, 203; and war in Hither Spain, 96, 127, 134, 151, 152, 156–59, 177, 206, 218, 219; sojourn in Gaul, 147, 155, 178; first triumph, 156; winter quarters, 165, 178; letter to Senate, 178–79; supply problems, 178–79, 203; burns Sertorius' correspondence, 217–18. *See also* Lauro, battle of; Segontia, battle of; Sucro: battle of; Valentia: battle of
Pompeius Magnus, Cn. (d. 45), 112, 156
Pompeius Magnus Pius, Sex. (*cos. des.* 35), 218
Pompeius Strabo, Cn. (*cos.* 89), 56, 63, 65, 69, 83, 210
Poppaedius Silo, Q. (d. 88, Italian leader in Social War), 133
Porcius Cato, L. (*cos.* 89), 56, 63
Porcius Cato, M. (*cos.* 195), l, 36, 37, 38
Porcius Cato, M. (*pr.* 54), xxx, 39, 184, 212
Poros (d. 317, King in India), 47
Porta Collina, 56, 65, 69; battle of, 77, 81, 89, 98, 99
Portugal, 90, 91, 94, 105, 151
Poseidonios of Apameia, xlii–xliii, xliv, xlv, 137, 207; on Sertorius, liv–lvi, 33–34, 43, 46, 50, 106–7, 108, 110, 118, 135, 136, 212
Praeneste, 77
praetextati: as orators, 38; Hispanians, 142–43
Praetors, 60, 75, 76, 131; Sertorian, 184–87
princeps senatus, 85–86
privatus cum imperio, 67, 74, 100
Proca, xlix
Promagistrates, titles of, 88, 128, 131–32
pro praetore (acting commander in chief), 53–54, 61, 86, 187, 201–2
proscripti, 146, 147, 182–83, 198, 200–201, 205, 209–11, 219
Proscriptions, 70, 79, 98–99, 111, 129, 143, 181–83, 189
Psychopomps, 110, 125
Ptolemaios I Soter of Egypt (King, 305–282), 32
Public enemies. *See hostes publici*
Puig de Santa Maria. *See* Lauro, location of: Puig
Pyrenees, 44, 87, 88, 92, 93, 97, 99, 101, 102, 140, 141, 146, 150, 158, 216, 219

Quaestors, 53–54, 99, 131–32; Sertorian, 184–87

Raia. *See* Sertorius, Q.—Biography, personal qualities: Mother
Reconnaissance, 45–46, 124
Religion: Celtic, 33, 93, 108–10, 116, 125; Germanic, 32–33, 108–10, 124, 125
Rhône River, 42, 43, 44, 45, 88
Romanization, 142–44, 206
Romans. *See* Sertorius, Q.—Sertorian War: Roman exiles
Rome, xxviii, 35–37, 76, 114, 124, 217–18; siege of, xlviii, 56, 60, 65, 68–70, 71, 73, 133, 193; Marian liquidations in, 70–71
Rommel, Erwin (1891–1944, Field Marshal), 110
Romulus Martis f., xlix
Rutilius Nudus, P. (*pr.* by 74?), 168
Rutilius Rufus, P. (*cos.* 105), 85

Sabines, 34–35
Sacrifice, human, 116, 120
Sacriportus, battle of, 77, 98
Saguntum, 92, 157, 159, 167, 172–73, 176

Salamis on Cyprus, battle of, 32
Salassi, 87
Salduba. *See* Salluia
Salluia, 92
Sallustius Crispus, C. (*pr.* 46), xxxi(n), xliv–xlv, xlix, l, li, lii, lvi; as source for Sertorius, liii–liv, 34, 44, 65, 67, 79, 82, 83, 123–24, 151, 168, 187, 189, 194–95, 201, 203, 204, 207; on Blessed Isles, 106–7, 109–10; Vienna fragment, 127–28, 130, 132; on Metellus, 135, 183–84; Pompey's Letter, 147, 173, 178–79; on Perperna, 148, 204; on battle of Lauro, 161–63, 165; on battle of Segontia, 174; on Sertorius' assassination, 209–10, 212–14, 215
Salluvii, 155
Samos, 119
Sardinia, 100, 146, 149
Scordisci, 40, 48
Scribonius Curio, C. (*cos.* 76), 37
scutati, 136, 140–41, 161, 162, 175–76
Sedetania, 92
Segobriga, 93, 151
Segontia (Sigüenza), 93, 172
Segontia, battle of, xxxvii, xli, 118, 132, 134, 136, 149, 166, 167, 176, 177, 178, 203; location of, 172–73; maneuvers, 173–75
Segontia Lanka, 93, 167, 172–73, 174, 176
Segovia, 93, 222
Seleukos I Nikator (King, 305–281), 32
Sempronius Gracchus, C. (*tr. pl. II* 122), xxviii–xxix, 35, 38, 62, 181
Sempronius Gracchus, Ti. (*cos. II* 163), 96
Sempronius Gracchus, Ti. (*tr. pl.* 133), xxviii–xxix, li, 35, 62
Senate: Roman, 62, 64, 67, 70, 129, 143, 179, 181, 182, 184–85, 188–89, 191, 196; Sertorian (*see* Sertorius, Q.—Sertorian War: "Senate")
Senators, 34, 36, 49, 62–64, 184–85, 190, 200, 202, 204–5, 208–9
Sergius Catilina, L. (*pr.* 68), 162, 186
Sertoriani, 56, 96, 182–83, 201, 212, 219
Sertoria Q. l. Antiopa, 34
Sertorius, Q. (*pr.* 85?)
—Biography, personal qualities
  Assassination, liii, 146, 180, 212–15; compared to Caesar's, xxxviii, 212; date, 211; at Osca, 211; drunkenness, 212, 214–15; banquet seating at, 212–13
  Birth, 38–39
  Education, 35
  eques Romanus, 34, 36, 42
  Eye, loss of, 57
  Family, 34
  Mother, 35, 36, 189
  Name, 34
  Physical strength, 40, 43–44; endurance, 118, 136
  Wife, lii, 189
—Career, political and military
  Arausio, battle of, 42–44
  Castulo, saves unit at, 49–51, 52, 88, 95
  Civil War, 77, 79–80, 81–82; captures Suessa, xxxvi, 74, 76, 81–84; recruitment, 84–85; criticizes war effort, 85
  Connections, political, 42, 55–56, 58–59, 60, 61, 63–64, 74
  Consulship, desire for, 77–78
  Decorations, 57; by Marius, 47–48
  Forum massacre, 64
  Marius: relations with, xxxvi, 47–48, 58–59, 63–64; disagreements with, 60, 71, 74; opposes recall of from exile, 66–68; criticizes son of, 77–78, 80, 85
  Military service, early, 38, 41, 42–44, 45–48
  Praetor, 74–76, 131
  Proconsul, 87–88, 116, 123, 185, 186; of both Spains, 88–89
  Proscribed, 98–99, 182
  Quaestor, 52–54
  Reconnaissance mission, xxxvi, 45, 46–47
  Rhetorical career, 35–38
  Rhône, swim across, xxxiii, xxxvi, 43–44
  Rome, siege of, xlviii, 56–57, 60, 68–70; support for Marian liquidations, 71
  Senator, 58
  Slave bands, massacre of, xxxvi, 71–73, 74
  Social War, 52–57, 59, 132; recruitment for, 55, 73, 88
  Suessa, capture of, xxxvi, 74, 76, 81–84
  Sulla, enmity with, xxxvi, 58–59
  Tribune, Military, 48–49, 52–53, 56, 110, 137

Sertorius, Q. *(continued)*
  Tribune of the Plebs, 59–62; failed candidacy, xxxvi, 52, 58–59, 61
—Character
  aretē, lv, 120–21
  Change to worse (*metabolē*), xxxv–xxxvi, xxxviii, xliv, liv–lv, 118, 120–22, 205, 206–8
  Cleverness, guile (*apatē*), xxx, xxxiv, 46, 119, 122, 150, 153, 171
  Courage, 46
  Cruelty (*ōmotēs*), xxxv, xxxvii, xxxviii, 50, 119–20, 121–22, 164–65, 205, 206–8
  Debauchery, 207, 212
  Deception, 51, 72, 153
  Disguises, 46, 109
  ēthos, lv, 117–18, 120–21
  Foresight, 67, 68, 80
  Grief, excessive, 189–90
  Jealousy, 68
  Leadership, 50, 52, 95, 117–19, 123–25, 141, 152, 153, 171–72
  megalophrosynē, xxxv, 186, 189, 192
  Moderation, lv, 117, 119; in Civil War, xxxiv, xxxvi, 65, 68, 71; as governor, 94–95, 144, 202; in Africa, 115; in drinking, 117, 207, 212; at Lauro, 164–65
  Overbearing, 207
  Paranoia, 207
  Peace, desire for, xxxii, xxxvii, 109, 180, 188–89, 190
  Persuasiveness, 67
  philopatria, 188–89, 190, 192
  physis, lv, 120–21
  Reclusiveness, 211
  Romanitas, xxxv, xl, 114, 125, 180, 184, 202, 204
  Ruthlessness. *See* Sertorius, Q.—Character: Cruelty
  Self-restraint (*praotēs*), xxviii, xxxii, xxxiv, 117–18, 122, 123
  Swiftness (*tachos*), 88, 119, 136
  synesis, 46, 47
  tychē, victim of, xxx–xxxi, xxxvii, lv, 120–21, 202, 207
—Comparison: with Eumenes, xxxi–xxxiii, 31, 47, 88, 121, 123; with Viriatus, 118, 119, 136, 152, 181
—Historiographical tradition, xxxv–xxxvi, xlii–lvi, 43–44, 65, 82, 117–18, 123–24, 151–52, 161, 164–65, 184, 194–95, 206, 207, 212

  Cynic-Stoic ruler-sage, xxx, 109
  Unknown to Greek audience, 31
—Image, propaganda, religious manipulation
  Antaios, tomb of, 113–14
  Hannibal, reincarnation of, 32, 109
  Heraklean associations, 109–10, 113–14
  Isles of the Blest, intended visit to, xxxvi, liv, 106, 109–10, 111, 114, 125
  Shamanic elements, 33, 109–10
  White Doe, xxx–xxxi, lii, 109–10, 122, 123–25, 171–72
—Sertorian War, xlv, xlvi, xlviii, l, liii, liv, 96, 127, 156, 168
  Africa: sojourn in, xlv, 89, 111, 112–14, 204, 207; return from, 89, 97, 122, 126
  Ambushes, 101, 118, 139, 153, 159, 161, 163–64
  Asia, government of, 144, 202
  Battles, pitched, 118, 134, 136, 140, 172, 173–76, 177, 203, 205. *See also* Italica: battle of; Segontia, battle of; Sucro: battle of; Valentia: battle of
  Bodyguard, 204, 212, 214–15
  Campaigns: of 79–77 B.C., 137–38; of 77–76 B.C., 165–66; of 76–74 B.C., 177–78, 206; of 74–73 B.C., 203
  Casualties, 104, 112, 130, 139–40, 161, 164, 170, 174, 175–76, 204
  Celtiberia, campaigns in, 165, 170, 172–73, 178, 203
  Characitani, xxx, liii, liv, 122, 153–54
  Chronology, 127–28, 131, 152, 178, 180–81, 221–22
  Clunia, siege of, xl, 176–77, 178, 203
  Conspiracy: participants, 208–9, 210–11; fate of conspirators, 219
  Correspondence, 188, 217–18
  Defeats, 166, 210, 212
  Defection: of Hispanians, 121, 156, 158, 162, 177, 203, 206, 216; of Romans, 199, 206
  Deportations, 164
  Executions, 112–13, 206–8
  Finances, 198–99
  Forces, Roman, 101, 103, 112, 127, 133, 134, 139, 160, 161, 164, 175–76, 197, 203; cavalry, 127, 134, 160
  Forces, Sertorian: Romans, 99, 102, 112, 139–40, 145, 149–50, 162, 164, 165, 169, 175, 181, 198–99,

204, 216; so-called Romans, 125–26; Mauretanian cavalry, 126, 139, 169–71; Hispanians, 127, 145, 150, 153, 169, 171, 181, 188, 198, 204, 209, 216, 219; Hispanian light infantry, 127, 161, 176; Hispanians armed in Roman fashion, 136, 140–41, 161–63, 175–76; Hispanian cavalry, 151–52, 161, 163, 210
Generalship, 167, 168–69, 170
Government in exile, 184, 185–87
Guerrilla, 118, 134, 136–37, 140, 158, 173, 177, 180, 203, 204, 205
Hispania Citerior, conquest of, 132, 133, 139, 140
Hispanians: allies, 116–17, 150–51, 153, 173, 205, 206; forced to submit, 123, 153; promised citizenship, 142–43, 206; devoted to Sertorius, 144–45; officers, 171–72, 186, 188; final resistance, 216–17. *See also* Celtiberia; Celtiberians; Celto-Hispanians; Iberians; Lusitani; Lusitania
Italy: departure from, 73, 74, 79, 80, 85–87, 102, 132, 182; invasion of, 140, 143, 146–47, 179–80, 197, 199, 217
Lusitani, leader of, 110, 116–17, 123
Mauretania, 102, 110–11, 113–15, 126; intervention in, 110–14, 115
Mithradates, treaty with, xl, xli, 177–78, 180, 190, 191–202; date, 178, 197
Naval forces: Sertorian, 97, 103–5, 111, 129, 147, 149, 177–78, 197, 199–200; Roman, 103, 129, 175. *See also* Dianium; Pirates
Pityussian Islands, 103–5, 111
Power, extent of, 150–51, 156, 203
Roman exiles, xxxvii–xxxviii, 146, 181–83, 184, 186, 188, 190, 192, 219; grievances of, 202–5; mistreatment of Hispanians, 205–6
Rome, desire to return to, xxxv, 140, 143, 186, 188–89, 218
School at Osca, xxxvii, 142, 143–44, 166, 206
Scorched-earth strategy, 173, 177, 203
"Senate," xl, lii, 148, 180, 187, 200, 205; character and composition of, 184–85, 192–93
Sertoriani, 56, 96, 182–83, 201, 212, 219

Sling bullets, 87–88, 116, 123
Spain: assigned as province, 74–76; departure for, 85–87; previous governors, 88–89; governorship, 94–95, 97–98, 116, 117, 143–44; expulsion, 102, 116; return, 117, 126
Sertorius Q. l. Eutichus, Q., 34
Servilia, 37
Servilius Caepio, Q. (*cos.* 140), 181
Servilius Caepio, Q. (*cos.* 106), 39, 40–43, 48, 78
Servilius Caepio, Q. (*pr.* by 91), 56, 58
Servilius Caepio, Q. (*tr. mil.* 72), 39
Servilius Pulex Geminus, M. (*cos.* 202), 138
Settlers, Roman, in Spain. *See Hispanienses*
Sevilla. *See* Hispalis
Shamanism, 109–10
Sherbro Island, 106
Sicily, 78, 97, 99, 146, 148, 155, 219
Sierra de Guadarrama, 154
Sikyon, 36
Single combat, 138
Sittius, P. (Caesarian leader), 219
Slave bands, 71–73
Slingers, 127
Social War, xxxiii, xlii, 48, 52–53, 54–55, 57, 59, 63, 73, 78, 133, 142, 192
soldurii, 144
Sophron (grandson of Herakles), 114
Sora, 37
Sosius Senecio, Q. (*cos. II* A.D. 107), xxvi, xxvii
Souls of the dead, 108, 110
Spain, xvii, xxxvi, 44, 52, 53, 88, 94–95, 98, 99–100, 102, 105, 108, 110, 112, 116, 117, 122, 124, 150, 192, 199, 217, 220; Roman wars in, xlii, 48, 93, 94, 116, 136–37; ethnography, 89–94; East Coast, 90, 91, 92, 95, 96, 97, 141, 149, 157–58, 165–66, 170–71, 172, 187, 192, 203, 216. *See also* Baetica; Hispania Citerior; Hispania Ulterior; Sertorius, Q.—Sertorian War: Spain
Spain, Farther. *See* Hispania Ulterior
Spain, Hither. *See* Hispania Citerior
Sparta, xxviii, 36
Spartacus (d. 71, leader in Slave War), 39, 47
Spoletium, battle of, 98
Stalin (Iosif Vissarionovich Dzhugashvili, 1879–1953), 110

Strabon of Amaseia, xliii, xlvi, lv, 93, 107, 113
stratēgos, 32, 33, 79, 186–87; not "Praetor," 48, 94
Successor Wars, xxxi, 32, 33
Sucro, 167; battle of, xxxvii, li, 118, 149, 166, 167–71, 176, 203
Sucro River, 90, 92, 93, 167, 171
Suessa Aurunca, xxxvi, 81, 82–84
Sullani, 79–80, 85–86, 87, 97, 98, 101
Sulpicius, P. (*tr. pl.* 88), 37, 59, 62, 63, 78
Sulpicius Galba, C. (*pr.*, first century B.C.), xlv, liii, lv, 134, 160, 175
Sulpicius Galba, Ser. (*cos.* 144), 50, 94
Surenas (i.e., Vizier of Parthia), 47, 126
synkrisis, xxxi–xxxii
Syrakuse, 36

Tagonius River, 153–54
Tagus River. *See* Tajo River
Tajo River, 93, 94, 116, 137, 153, 154
Tajuña River. *See* Tagonius River
tamias, 186–87
Tanusius Geminus, xlv, liii, lv
Taracena, 153–54
Tarentum, 119
Tarquitius L. f. Priscus, C. (Sertorian officer), 56, 161–62, 182, 207, 210–11, 213, 215, 219
Tarquitius P. f., C. (*q.* 81), 210
Tarraco, 95, 96, 97, 102, 149, 151, 171, 203, 216
Tarraconensis, 105
Tartessians, 91
Tauroggen, convention of, 83
Teanum Sidicinum, 79, 80, 82–83
Tectosages (Volcae T.), 41
Tejo River. *See* Tajo River
Terentius, L. (*contubernalis* 89), 56
Terentius Varro, M. (*pr.* by 67), xliii, xliv, li, liii, liv, 207, 212
Terentius Varro Lucullus, M. (*cos.* 73), 98
Termes, 93, 203, 216
Teutoni, 40–42, 44–45, 46
Thapsus, battle of, 115, 168, 218
Themistokles (ca. 525–460, Athenian statesman), xxviii, 47, 59
Theseus, 38
Thessalonike, 185, 186
Thorius Balbus, L. (officer of Metellus), 127, 128, 133
Tiberius (Ti. Caesar Aug., *cos.* V A.D. 31), xlvii
Tiber River, 69

Ticinum, 157
Tigris River, 43
Tigurini, 41, 44, 46
Timagenes of Alexandria, li
Tinge (wife of Antaios), 114
Tingis, 111, 113, 114, 115
Tirnan Oc, 108
Toga, 142–43, 184
Toletum, 105
Tolosa, 41
Toygeni, 41, 44, 46
Trajan (Imp. Caes. Nerva Traianus Optimus Aug., *cos.* VI A.D. 112), xxv, xxvi, 212
Trasumenian Lake, battle of, 43
Tremellius Scrofa, Cn. (*q.* 71), 49
Tribunes, Military, 48–49
Triparadeisos, conference of, 32, 33
Tritium Magallum, 93
Triumviral period, 34, 87
Tullius Cicero, M. (*cos.* 63), xliii–xliv, liii(n), 35, 36, 37, 64, 80, 83, 147, 194–96
Turdetania, 90
Turia River, 92, 172
tychē, xxviii, xxx, lv, 31. *See also* Sertorius, Q.—Character: *tychē*, victim of

Umbria, 98
Uxama Argaela, 93, 216–17

Vaccaei, 94, 151, 157–58, 178
Valentia, 96, 97, 102, 149, 150, 157–59, 171, 172–73, 216–17; battle of, 166, 176
Valentinian I (Imp. Caes. Fl. Valentinianus Aug., *cos.* IV A.D. 373), 206
Valerius Flaccus, C. (*cos.* 93), 52, 85–87, 89, 94, 217
Valerius Flaccus, L. (*cos.* 100), 85–86
Valerius Flaccus, L. (*suff.* 86), 85–86, 191, 194
Valerius Flaccus, L. (*pr.* 63), 85–86
Valerius Maximus, xlvii, lii, 44, 152, 189
Valerius Soranus, Q. (orator), 37
Valerius Triarius, C. (*pr.* by 78), 149, 167–68
Varduli, 72, 94
Vareia, 93
Vascones, 92, 151, 178, 216
Velleius Paterculus (*pr.* A.D. 15), xlix, 66, 81
Vercellae, battle of, 45, 47, 48
Vergilius (Verginius?), M. (*tr. pl.* 87), 61

Verres, C. (*pr.* 74), 80, 191, 219
Versius (Sertorian *scriba*), 211, 213
Vespasian (Imp. Caes. Vespasianus Aug., *cos. IX* A.D. 79), xxv, 34
Vespasia Polla, 34
Vespasius Pollio, 34
Vettius Scato, P. (d. 83, Italian leader in Social War), 83
Vettones, 94, 151, 216
Via Appia, 80, 82
Via Latina, 80, 82–83
Vibius (?) Pacciaecus (Sullan officer), 112–13, 125

Vibius Paciaecus (protector of Crassus, ca. 87), 112
Vibius Paciaecus, L. (Caesarian partisan), 112
Vicus Caecilius, 137
Viriatus (ca. 180–139, Lusitanian leader), 118, 119, 136, 152, 181
Visigoths, xlviii

Winds, 154–55
Wine, 92, 156–57, 212; unmixed, 214
Wotan, 32–33, 110

Yorck von Wartenburg, Johann David (1759–1830, Field Marshal), 83